State–Religion Relationships and Human Rights Law

Studies in Religion, Secular Beliefs and Human Rights

VOLUME 8

State–Religion Relationships and Human Rights Law

Towards a Right to Religiously Neutral Governance

By

Jeroen Temperman

MARTINUS
NIJHOFF
PUBLISHERS

LEIDEN • BOSTON
2010

This book is printed on acid-free paper.

Library of Congress Cataloging-in-Publication-Data

Temperman, Jeroen.
State-religion relationships and human rights law : towards a right to religiously neutral governance / by Jeroen Temperman.
p. cm.—(Studies in religion, secular beliefs, and human rights ; v. 8)
Includes bibliographical references and index.
ISBN 978-90-04-18148-9 (hardback : alk. paper) 1. Religion and state. 2. Freedom of religion. I. Title. II. Series.

K3280.T46 2010
342.08'52–dc22

2010001513

ISSN 1871-7829
ISBN 978 90 04 18148 9

PRINTED IN THE NETHERLANDS

For Irene

CONTENTS – SUMMARY

CONTENTS

PART II STATE–RELIGION IDENTIFICATION: A HUMAN RIGHTS ANALYSIS

ACKNOWLEDGEMENTS

This work is greatly indebted to the stimulating guidance of Professor Joshua Castellino. For his advice and friendship over the years I am very grateful.

Special thanks to Dr. Nazila Ghanea, for thoroughly commenting on an earlier draft of this book, for her support, and for being a great friend and colleague in the fascinating world of religion & human rights.

Enormous thanks goes to Joseph Powderly, for providing precious comments on the entire work.

Particular thanks to Professor Malcolm D. Evans, Dr. Dennis de Jong, Professor W.A. Schabas, Dr. Stéphanie Lagoutte, Dr. Caroline Suransky-Dekker, Professor Harry Kunneman, to my former colleagues at the Irish Centre for Human Rights, my former colleagues at the Department of International Law of the University of Amsterdam, and, finally, to my colleagues at the Department of International Law of the Erasmus University of Rotterdam.

JT
November 2009, Amsterdam

TABLE OF INTERNATIONAL INSTRUMENTS

Treaties & Declarations

Concordats with the Holy See

TABLE OF DOMESTIC LEGISLATION

TABLE OF INTERNATIONAL CASES

Views of the Human Rights Committee

Views of the Committee on the Elimination of Discrimination Against Women

Decisions of the European Court of Human Rights and Former European Commission

TABLE OF DOMESTIC CASES

ABBREVIATIONS

BiH	Bosnia and Herzegovina
CAT	Convention against Torture and Other Cruel, Inhuman or Degrading Treatment or Punishment
CEDAW	Convention on the Elimination of All Forms of Discrimination against Women
CERD	Convention on the Elimination of All Forms of Racial Discrimination
CRC	Convention on the Rights of the Child
DPRK	Democratic People's Republic of Korea
ECHR	[European] Convention for the Protection of Human Rights and Fundamental Freedoms
ECommHR	European Commission of Human Rights
ECtHR	European Court of Human Rights
FGM	female genital mutilation
FoRB	freedom of religion or belief
GA	UN General Assembly
HRC	Human Rights Committee
ICCPR	International Covenant on Civil and Political Rights
ICESCR	International Covenant on Economic, Social and Cultural Rights
ILO	International Labour Organization
MP	Member of Parliament
ODIHR	Office for Democratic Institutions and Human Rights
OIC	Organization of the Islamic Conference
OSCE	Organization for Security and Co-operation in Europe
SR on FoRB	Special Rapporteur on freedom of religion or belief
SAARC	South Asian Association for Regional Cooperation
UAE	United Arab Emirates
U.N.T.S.	United Nations Treaties Series
UDHR	Universal Declaration of Human Rights
UNESCO	United Nations Educational, Scientific and Cultural Organization
UNICEF	United Nations International Children's Economic Foundation

PREFACE

It is trite to say that a newly published work is 'timely' – yet it is difficult to avoid saying so with regard to this impressive and provocative new study of the relationship between, on the one hand, the state and religion and, on the other, the relationship which those forms of relationship may take with human rights law. As this book demonstrates through the various case studies which make up its latter chapters, there is increasing interest – and concern – at the manner in which questions concerning the enjoyment of the right to the freedom of religion or belief bear upon key questions concerning the governance of democratic society. Issues raised involve matters concerning employment, education, expression, association and, more generally, the interface between religion and political life. The existing literature often traces these concerns back to the need to consider the place of religion in contemporary society – but leaves matters there. Another body of academic literature explores the theoretical dimensions of that relationship but fails to connect it to the practice of states in order to test out the propositions which are the product of these reflections.

The great virtue of this work is that is seeks to unite these various enterprises and engages head on with the challenges which this produces. Its opening chapters chart various forms of relationships between religion and governance, and through the drawing of careful distinctions seek to illuminate the breadth of the spectrum of possibilities involved. The second part of the work then explores the manner in which a number of key issues are addressed within states adopting the various configurations identified. The aim is to demonstrate and illustrate the key contention made in Chapter 7, which stands as the fulcrum to the book, and the logic of which is further developed in the final concluding section: this is that there is an emergent right to religiously neutral governance, and that this is incompatible with the continuation of systems which offer preference to particular forms of belief system – religious or otherwise. A chief virtue of this book is that it works through the consequences of this claim in a fearless fashion, posing challenges for those states which continue to use their legal frameworks to offer support (directly or indirectly) for historical, dominant or favoured forms of religion or belief. It challenges received assumptions and, by driving the logic of contemporary human rights thinking to the foundations of state-religion relationships, performs a valuable service for those engaging with this most difficult – and timely – of questions.

The author is to be congratulated on offering a powerful and penetrating critique of current state practice and this is surely destined to become an important point of reference for, as well as an important contribution to, these pressing debates.

Malcolm D. Evans
Professor of Public International Law, University of Bristol

CHAPTER ONE

INTRODUCTION

1.1 The Relevance of State–Religion Identification under International Human Rights Law

Worldwide state practice shows an enormous variety of perceptions of the appropriate relationship between the state and religion. Some states are explicitly secular, other countries are clear examples of 'religious states', while still others exhibit the many conceivable alternatives in between or indeed 'beyond' these two extremes—one could readily claim that there are as many different systems in this respect as there are states.[1]

On the face of it, international human rights law appears indifferent as to the parameters of 'state–religion identification', i.e. the type and degree of interrelation between the state and religion.[2] Human rights law does not prescribe a specific relationship between the state and religion. That is to say, human rights law does not *explicitly* identify a specific form of state–religion identification as a prerequisite for compliance with human rights norms. Human rights law does not, as such, *explicitly* condemn certain modes of state–religion identification.

Arguably, the global framework of universal human rights protection suffers from this lack of consensus in relation to the appropriate domestic political framework best suited to actually taking these fundamental rights adequately into account. The underlying rationale is nonetheless very

---

[1] If not more than that, given the fact that some states reflect multiple regimes of state–religion identification within one and the same jurisdiction; *e.g.* states which are partly secular and partly not, or states which provide for a separation of state and religion that only applies to a certain part of the country, or states which provide for a 'partial establishment of religion'. In Switzerland, as state–religion relationships are considered a 'cantonal matter', different cantons have taken a different approach to state–religion identification. One might in this context of course also think of the different constituent states of the United Kingdom: England and Scotland both have established churches, whereas Northern Ireland and Wales disestablished their state churches a long time ago. Another good example is the Republic of the Sudan, where we can discern a separation of state and religion which is applicable to the Southern States of the Sudan only (etc., these and other examples will be elaborated upon in more detail).

[2] This definition is cf. George R. Ryskamp, *The Spanish Experience in Church-State Relations: A Comparative Study of the Interrelationship between Church-State Identification and Religious Liberty*, 3 Brigham Young University Law Review 616 (1980), discussing Church–State identification (p. 617); and W. Cole Durham, *Perspectives on Religious Liberty: A Comparative Framework, in* Religious Human Rights in Global Perspective: Legal Perspectives 1 (J.D. van der Vyver & J. Witte, eds., The Hague/Boston/London: Martinus Nijhoff Publishers, 1996), see pp. 15–36 for his state–religion identification model.

clear: states show their commitment to human rights by signing and ratifying international conventions. These human rights treaties, however, do not seek to prescribe the kind of political framework that is necessary for the effective implementation and protection of human rights norms. Thus, whilst the High Contracting States have to comply with international human rights which are codified within established international forums, these forums have no clear competence on the question of how to organize the state internally. On the contrary, a vital condition for the ultimate impact and preservation of these international norm-setting institutions is a great deal of subsidiarity.[3] States that ratify human rights conventions have a fairly free hand in selecting the means by which they seek to achieve the set standards. An intrusive human rights convention, that is, one that clearly prescribes the limitations of state power and that creates clear state obligations towards the protection and promotion of human rights, is more likely to result in a relatively low rate of state consent (and, possibly, in more reservations or opt-out clauses[4]). This naturally affects the universal applicability of the human rights standards in question. Any prescription regarding the domestic form of political organization is destined to be considered exceptionally intrusive since internal political organization is typically considered to belong to the untouchable sphere of state sovereignty. Conversely, a 'worse'—or less intrusive or demanding—convention will plausibly result in a higher rate of state consent and may therefore be more universal. The question is what is the worth of a universal yet half-hearted human rights treaty? And conversely, what is the worth of a generous treaty which results in but a few ratifications? Drafting human rights conventions involves balancing on this fine line between drafting provisions with teeth and aiming at a maximum degree of universality in terms of worldwide applicability.

An important premise underlying this study is as follows: the fact that international human rights conventions do not, *prima facie*, adopt a position in relation to the different conceivable relations between the state and religion does not mean—as one might be inclined to deduce—that international human rights law does not provide convincing legal arguments in favour of, or against certain types of state–religion relationships. The fact that human rights law does not explicitly condemn certain forms of state–religion identification

[3] I.e., "the importance of reasoned decision-making at the lowest level of social and political structures in which decisions are implemented"; definition by: Robert John Araujo, *International Law Clients: the Wisdom of Natural Law*, 28 Fordham Urban Law Journal 1751 (2001), para. IV; see also Paolo G. Carozza, *Subsidiarity as a Structural Principle of International Human Rights Law*, 97:1 American Journal of International Law 38 (2003), on subsidiarity as a principle of international human rights law specifically.

[4] Sec. II of the Vienna Convention on the Law of Treaties, 1155 U.N.T.S. 331, 8 I.L.M. 679, of 23 May 1969 (entered into force: 27 January 1980; hereinafter: Vienna Convention on the Law of Treaties). The issue of reservations and particularly of so-called 'religious reservations' will be discussed in more detail (see Part II, Chapter 8, section 8.4).

does not demonstrate that 'anything goes', but should rather be considered exemplary of the above outlined realities of international law and international relations.[5] In other words, from the perspective of state sovereignty in relation to the politics of international treaty negotiation, it is quite understandable that human rights conventions avoid any direct endorsement or condemnation of concrete state practice, that is, of concrete forms of state–religion identification. It is postulated here that this does not mean that no convincing legal arguments can be derived from international human rights law on which basis certain systems may be considered advisable or, on the contrary, untenable. International human rights monitoring bodies may not be in a position to dictate in detail how states ought to organize their political system internally; however, they are most definitively in a position to interpret internationally codified standards of human rights law that states have, on their own volition, subscribed to. These official interpretations and applications of internationally adopted fundamental norms could very well, in themselves, have a bearing on the legitimacy and, ultimately, the tenability of certain forms of political organization.

It is stressed from the outset that whilst there are indeed no universal legal standards that directly deal with the issue of state–religion relationships, some benchmarks can be extrapolated from the workings of international human rights bodies. Most importantly, the Human Rights Committee, in its *General*

---

[5] De Jong argues something similar with respect to the drafting process of the principal international human rights law provisions regarding freedom of religion or belief and the right not to be discriminated against on the basis of one's religion or belief: "Denying [the discriminatory] effect [of forms of positive state–religion identification], as happened almost continuously during the codification process as well as in some of the relevant literature, is somewhat hypocritical and can only be explained by the need for consensus, taking into account that any form of criticism of an established or recognized Church would have been unacceptable for a number of States." Cornelis D. de Jong, The Freedom of Thought, Conscience and Religion or Belief in the United Nations (1946-1992) (Antwerp/Groningen/Oxford: Hart/Intersentia, 2000), p. 287. Evans and Thomas make a similar observation in the European context with respect to the European Convention on Human Rights ([European] Convention for the Protection of Human Rights and Fundamental Freedoms, ETS No. 5, 213 U.N.T.S. 222, of 4 November 1950; entered into force: 3 September 1953; hereinafter European Convention on Human Rights or ECHR): "At the time that the ECHR was drafted, a number of member states had established churches, including the United Kingdom, Sweden, and Norway. If the ECHR had prohibited establishment, then it is quite possible that significant states would not have ratified the ECHR or would have included substantial reservations to their acceptance. These states included important supporters of the ECHR, such as the United Kingdom, which maintains its established church to this day and would likely oppose any attempts to include establishment as a rights violation." Carolyn Evans & Christopher A. Thomas, *Church-State Relations in the European Court of Human Rights*, 3 Brigham Young University Law Review 699 (2006), P. 706. As this study has a global outlook, it will predominantly focus on universal (UN) human rights instruments, policies and practice. Occasionally reference will be made to parallel issues within the regional human rights organizations (predominantly the Council of Europe), yet only to the extent that a regional system has dealt with relevant issues that, as yet, have not been dealt with by the UN or to the extent that a regional system has explicitly derogated from UN norms or practices.

Comment No. 22 on the right to freedom of thought, conscience and religion (as enumerated in article 18 of the UN *International Covenant on Civil and Political Rights*),[6] has stated that:

> The fact that a religion is recognized as a state religion or that it is established as official or traditional or that its followers comprise the majority of the population, shall not result in any impairment of the enjoyment of any of the rights under the Covenant, including [the right to freedom of thought, conscience, and religion and the rights of members of ethnic, religious and linguistic minorities], nor in any discrimination against adherents to other religions or non-believers.[7]

Whilst short of a condemnation in absolute terms, it is clear that a state of non-secularity does raise concerns with respect to questions of human rights compliance in the eyes of the UN Human Rights Committee.[8] Putting these very criteria into practice, the Human Rights Committee has certainly not shied away from closely scrutinizing state practice in the field of state–religion relationships.[9] These guidelines will be at the heart of the human rights analysis (Part II) of this study. In the second part of this study it will be endeavoured to further elaborate on these and other available legal benchmarks.

1.2 Objectives, Methodology & Outline

The principal research question motivating this study is: how does the mode of state–religion identification affect the state's scope for compliance with human rights? The contribution to the existing literature on religion–state relations this study intends to make is the presentation of a human rights-based assessment of the various modes of state–religion identification and of the various measures and forms of state practice that surround these different state–religion relationships. Thus, state–religion relationships are scrutinized with a particular view towards understanding their impact and effects on the implementation of norms of international human rights law. This study is divided into two main parts (followed by a concluding section). Part I provides

[6] International Covenant on Civil and Political Rights, G.A. Res. 2200A (XXI), 21 U.N. GAOR Supp. (No. 16) at 52, U.N. Doc. A/6316 (1966), 999 U.N.T.S. 171, of 16 December 1966 (entered into force: 23 March 1976) [hereinafter International Covenant on Civil and Political Rights or ICCPR].

[7] Human Rights Committee, *General Comment No. 22: The Right to Freedom of Thought, Conscience and Religion (Art. 18)*, CCPR/C/21/Rev./Add.4 (1993), para. 9 [hereinafter: General Comment 22]. General Comments are authoritative statements issued by the Human Rights Committee; they are intended to clarify the provisions of the Covenant.

[8] The Human Rights Committee was established to monitor member states' compliance with the UN Covenant on Civil and Political Rights, the principal universal (UN) human rights convention dealing with civil and political rights, including the right to freedom of religion or belief and fundamental non-discrimination norms and principles.

[9] See Bahiyyih G. Tahzib, Freedom of Religion or Belief: Ensuring Effective International Legal Protection (The Hague/Boston/London: Martinus Nijhoff Publishers, 1996), pp. 260–262. See Part II of this study for a comprehensive analysis.

a comprehensive comparative legal analysis of religion–state relationships. In Part II those state–religion relationships are analysed from a human rights perspective.

Part I of this study aims at providing a comprehensive comparative legal analysis of the different ways in which states relate to religion. The comparative legal framework that is proposed is intended to do justice to the large spectrum of state–religion identification. The level of detail here is of particular importance to the human rights analysis in the second part of the study. The data represents a breakdown of a global comparative constitutional survey and a complementary comparative legal analysis of relevant statutory laws and relevant state practice.

Forms of unequivocal positive state identification with religion will be analysed in Chapter 2. The historical background of and contemporary conceptions and practices surrounding the notions of 'religious states', 'state religions' and 'state churches' are examined in detail. Besides making a global inventory of relevant state practice under these headings, this Chapter aims at providing a comprehensive overview of the main legal ramifications that delineate the different religious states and other regimes of positive state–religion identification. The principal indicator that will be used in determining the place of religion in a state will be the extent to which the legislative, executive and judicial branches of the state are subjected to the normative framework of a religion. In that regard, a comparative constitutional analysis will be made of all such measures that give a further indication of the exact degree of positive state–religion identification, including constitutional provisions that ensure a religion–law nexus, measures that cluster together secular and religious institutions, measures that reserve political seats for members of the state religion, royal protection of the state religion and measures that seek to perpetually preserve the status of a religion as state religion.

In Chapter 3 forms of state support and state acknowledgement of religion will be distinguished from the more stringent forms of positive state–religion identification discussed in the previous Chapter. It is the objective of this Chapter to chart the different legal ramifications of different types of state support. Some states constitutionally acknowledge certain religious phenomena whilst others simply acknowledge the historical role of a religion or the position of a religion as predominant religion (numerically). It will be outlined that some forms of 'state acknowledgement' are preferential while other forms are purely non-preferential in nature.

Chapter 4 focuses on more neutral forms of religious accommodation. It will illustrate how states may cooperate or interrelate with religions, or accommodate religions, without treating one religion preferentially. It is also pointed out that some states are constitutionally indifferent to the question of religion: these states have not established a religion as state religion, they do not distinctly support one religion over other religions or accommodate more than one religion simultaneously; yet, they do not expressly or proactively seek to internalize the ideal of secularism or separationism (a policy of strict separation of state and religion) either. State practice is scrutinized closely in order to assess whether such states are *de facto* secular or non-secular.

Chapter 5 focuses on the more secular end of the state–religion identification spectrum. This Chapter deals with outspoken forms of secularism and separationism. It will become apparent that many states constitutionally establish themselves as secular states, many states constitutionally separate religion from the state, whilst some states, in fact, do both. The ideals of secularism and separationism are scrutinized in light of existing state practice so as to chart the main trends and differences that can be discerned among the different 'secular' and 'separationist states'. In addition, the history of so-called (American) 'non-establishmentarianism' will be discussed in connection with contemporary forms of state practice based on the principle of non-establishment of religion.

Chapter 6 deals with states that officially identify with secular ideologies and with the rare situation of 'negative state–religion identification' or official hostility towards all forms of religious belief and religious activity. Among other things, it is outlined that states which officially identify with secular worldviews should not be confused with states that act on the legal-political notion of secularism.

Part II provides a human rights-based assessment of the various modes of state–religion identification and, more specifically, of the various laws, policies, measures and other forms of state practice that surround the different state–religion relationships. It is precisely the described lacuna, or grey area, within international human rights law that has fostered such imposing scholarship in the field of domestic state–religion relationships as manifested by the vast amount of literature on the (il)legitimacy of specific forms of state–religion relationships. This account is premised on the notion that the issue of state–religion identification does not only bear upon the state's scope for compliance with the right to freedom of religion or belief. Consequently, fundamental religious rights are not the only rights in light of which state–religion relationships should be analysed. Part II attempts to offer a wider analysis of the large variety of (often interwoven) human rights-related issues that emerge under the different discernible parts of that spectrum. A range of thematic case studies are intended to shed light on the question as to how the issue of state–religion identification impacts on such fundamental rights as freedom of expression, freedom of association, fundamental civil and political rights, educational rights and the equality or non-discrimination principle.

However, before delving deeper into the various concrete human rights related issues that emerge under the different relationships between the state and religion, the preliminary question as to whether there are forms of state–religion identification that are *per se* unacceptable will be addressed in Chapter 7.

This Chapter further explores the question whether it is possible to identify forms of relationships between the state and religion that amount to, so-called, '*ipso facto* violations' of international human rights law.

Chapter 8 deals with what arguably characterizes the most stringent type of 'religious states': state enforcement of 'religious laws' and religious principles. Although the issue of 'religious laws' is a well explored territory within the human rights discipline, this study aims to contribute new elements to the debate by identifying a series of what might be considered more fundamental or systemic human rights problems surrounding those systems of domestic political organization that are premised on state enforcement of religious laws. These systemic objections amount to a dismissal of state interference with the observance of religious laws in terms of a pro-active role as enforcer and guardian. These fundamental concerns are based on the notions of: (i) freedom *from* religion; (ii) equality before the law; and (iii) transparency, legal certainty and checks and balances.

Chapter 9 is intended to further demonstrate that most, if not all of the states that are officially entangled with a single religion fail to *fully* comply with the principle that no one should be treated differently because of one's religion or belief. The large majority of existing regimes of positive state identification with a religion are not devoid of forms of institutionalised discrimination and *de facto* practices of discrimination on grounds of religion or belief (or lack thereof). This claim will be substantiated by carrying out a range of thematic case studies on, among other issues, Establishment of Religion & the 'Equal Religious Rights of Others', Religion & Freedom of Expression, Religion & Freedom of Association and Religion & Equal Employment Opportunities. At the same time it must be observed that in some secular or separationist states, the ideals of state secularism and separationism have come to be considered ends in themselves. This has given rise to situations where the principles of secularism and separationism are construed so as to impose special limits on the activities of religions, principally in the field of organizational freedom of religious organizations, or special limits on the manifestation of certain beliefs, principally in the field of the freedom to manifest a religion, including the issue of conscientious objections.

The issues of 'Religion & Education' and 'Religion & Politics' will be particularly underscored in this study as the keys to preventing and redressing most of the human rights violations and concerns. Chapter 10 is premised on the acknowledgment that there is a tension between the liberty of parents to ensure the religious and moral education of their children in conformity with their own convictions on the one hand, and children's autonomous right to freedom of religion or belief on the other. This Chapter examines the state's role in guaranteeing children's rights (to education, freedom of religion or belief and equality) as well as parental rights, in the context of its overall obligation to provide education. As soon as it is clear what an educational system that takes sufficient account of these rights looks like, it will be possible to further scrutinize the position and role of teachers within such a system. Chapter 11, finally, identifies a range of pitfalls which are to be avoided in the area of Religion & Politics. This Chapter also proposes a set of safeguards that specifically deal with the issue of religion–state relationships which are intended to prevent or remedy human rights abuses in this field.

Part I

State–Religion Identification: A Comparative Legal Analysis

CHAPTER TWO

RELIGIOUS STATES, STATE RELIGIONS & STATE CHURCHES

2.1 Introduction

The notion of 'state-religion identification' as used throughout this study refers to the type and degree of interrelation between the state and religion. This first Part of this study aims at providing a comprehensive comparative legal analysis of the different ways in which states relate to religion. The data represents a breakdown of a global comparative constitutional research and a complementary comparative legal analysis of the relevant statutory laws and of other relevant official documents that shed light on a state's relation to religion.[1] In order to do justice to important nuances, a comprehensive spectrum of state-religion relationships should focus on the different discernible forms of state identification with religion, as well as the different secular forms of identification.[2]

---

[1] I.e. the 192 UN Member States and the State of the Vatican City. For alternative approaches and alternative global inventories of state-religion relationships, see, *e.g.*: Robert J. Barro & Rachel M. McCleary, *Which Countries Have State Religions?*, 120 Quarterly Journal of Economics 1331 (2005); Paul Marshall (ed.), Religious Freedom in the World (Nashville: Broadman & Holman, 2000); Jonathan Fox & Shmuel Sandler, World Separation of Religion and State in the Twenty First Century, (Montreal, 2004); Johan D. van der Vyver, *Legal Dimensions of Religious Human Rights: Constitutional Texts, in* Religious Human Rights in Global Perspective: Legal Perspectives (J.D. van der Vyver & J. Witte, eds., The Hague/Boston/London: Martinus Nijhoff Publishers, 1996), particularly pp. xi–xlvii. See also Kevin Boyle & Juliet Sheen, Freedom of Religion and Belief: A World Report (London: Routledge, 1997). The comparative constitutional research of this study is indebted to the translations of the world's constitutions provided by the following sources: Albert P. Blaustein & Gisbert H. Flanz (eds.), Constitutions of the Countries of the World: A Series of Updated Texts, Constitutional Chronologies and Annotated Bibliographies (New York: Oceana Publications, Inc., 1971 plus subsequent supplements); the comparative constitutional law projects and databases hosted by: OSCE/ODIHR documentation centre; University of Richmond; A. Tschentscher's International Constitutional Law (ICL) Project; Georgetown University (Political Database of the Americas); Centre for Human Rights, University of Pretoria (Database for Africa); Pacific Islands Legal Information Institute, University of the South Pacific School of Law (Pacific Law Database). The comparative legal analysis of statutory laws on religious association and domestic laws on freedom of religion or belief is indebted to the database maintained by the International Center for Law and Religion Studies in association with OSCE/ODIHR (ICLRS database).

[2] It must also seek to include those forms of identification that would appear to go 'beyond' secularism or religious establishment. For a critical discussion of oversimplifying bipartite models (i.e. secular vs. religious) or tri-partite models (i.e. secular, religious and an 'in-between' category), see, *e.g.*, W. Cole Durham, *Perspectives on Religious Liberty: A Comparative*

As a first step in drawing up such a spectrum of state–religion identification, this Chapter will enquire into the unequivocal forms of 'positive identification' of the state with religion: the focus will be on so-called 'religious states' (paragraph 2.2), 'state religions' (paragraph 2.3.1) and 'state churches' (paragraph 2.3.2).[3] These terms are, strictly speaking, not interchangeable.[4] Focusing on the exact degree of interrelation between the state and religion, a comprehensive overview of the main legal ramifications that delineate the different religious states and other regimes of 'positive state–religion identification' will be provided in a separate section (paragraph 2.4).

2.2 Religious States

For the purposes of this study, a fairly legal-positivistic definition of religious states will be used: a state will be identified as a 'religious state' if it has explicitly established itself as or if it explicitly positions itself as a confessional state. However, in order to do justice to the precise characteristics of the different state–religion regimes, it is acknowledged that it is often crucial to go beyond a strictly legal-positivistic approach and to assess actual state practice.[5] Naturally, a state cannot 'be religious' in the strict sense of the word, it rather is established as such by either its founders or by the powers that be. It should also be borne in mind that it is hard to identify a univocal reading of a religion. Thus, whenever a regime pinpoints the religious nature of the state down to the state-sanctioned or promoted version of a religion, it—deliberately—ignores the numerous doctrinal nuances and differences of opinion that often

Framework, *in* Religious Human Rights in Global Perspective: Legal Perspectives 1 (J.D. van der Vyver & J. Witte, eds., The Hague/Boston/London: Martinus Nijhoff Publishers, 1996); and Jeroen Temperman, *The Neutral State: Optional or Necessary? – A Triangular Analysis of State–Religion Identification, Democratisation & Human Rights Compliance*, 1(3) Religion and Human Rights: An International Journal 269 (2006), particularly pp. 273–274. See Arcot Krishnaswami, *Study of Discrimination in the Matter of Religious Rights and Practices* (U.N. Doc. E/CN.4/Sub.2/200/Rev.1, 1960), for a good example of a juridical classification of state–religion relationships into three broad categories (Ch. IV); Philip Halpern, *Study on Discrimination in the Matter of Religious Rights and Practices* (E/CN.4/Sub.2/162, 1954), pp. 8–9, distinguishes between four main categories.

[3] Terminology (the distinction between forms of "positive identification" and "negative identification") is cf. Durham, *ibid.*, see particularly pp. 15–36; and George R. Ryskamp, *The Spanish Experience in Church-State Relations: A Comparative Study of the Interrelationship between Church-State Identification and Religious Liberty*, 3 Brigham Young University Law Review 616 (1980), discussing forms of Church–State identification (p. 617).

[4] Though in certain cases the overlap is so great that the distinctions nearly lost their meaning (see discussion *infra*).

[5] Evidence of 'state practice' can be discerned in governmental declarations and in any state act or state-instigated act with or without a concrete basis in state law. As demonstrated in this Chapter, in exceptional cases actual state practice provides sufficient reason for considering a state 'religious'.

surround a religion. In that respect, establishing a religion is, besides a religiously motivated act, always a political act.

The religious identity of the state is as a rule enshrined in the state's constitution (and occasionally included in the official name of the country). As a country's constitution can be regarded the legal-political backbone of the state, that is, the foremost legal document underpinning the state's fundamental characteristics and its ethos, the legal-political significance of such a religious reference can hardly be overstated. The constitution of a state is also the principal document outlining the main functions, powers, procedures, principles, structures and duties of the different branches of the state (typically the legislative, executive and the judicial branches). The comparative constitutional analysis in this section shows that the constitutional ethos of many a religious state is essentially a religious ethos. This implies that religion in these states occupies an important place within the functions, powers and duties of the principal state bodies.

By declaring itself religious the state reserves a determinative role for religion within the overall functioning of the state. This Chapter is intended to show the main trends and practices in that regard. The precise role that religion plays in religious states, it must be acknowledged from the outset, varies from state to state and can only be determined by unveiling the extent to which the state apparatus, most importantly the legislative, executive and judicial branches of the state, identifies with and is subjected to religion.[6] The category of contemporary religious states includes: Christian states, Islamic states, 'monotheist states' (unspecified) and—disputably—a Jewish state. There are of course many states that identify strongly with a religion in a way that does not amount to the category at hand ('religious states'); these forms of state practice will be discussed in subsequent sections of this Chapter and in the following Chapters.

2.2.1 *Christian States*

In this section the phenomenon of the 'Christian state' will be analysed. It commences with a few remarks on the history of such a state; subsequently, contemporary forms of Christian states will be analysed in more detail.

(i) *History: the Imperium Christianum*

The *Imperium Christianum* arguably goes back as far as, or was at least substantially instigated by, the notorious conversion in 312 of Emperor Constantine I the Great (ca. 288–337):[7]

---

[6] Such will be the objective of paragraph 2.4 of this Chapter.

[7] Christianity as a state religion goes back even further: Armenia declared Christianity the state religion at the very beginning of the 4th century (ca. 301 CE).

> On the eve of the battle of the Milvian Bridge, in 312, he saw in a dream, according to Eusebius, a cross bearing the inscription, 'In hoc signo vinces': 'In this sign you will conquer'. Following his victory, he gave favoured status to the Church...[8]

The first three centuries of the Common Era had seen many waves of hostility towards Christianity. St. Augustine of Hippo (354–430) suggested ten highlights of state-instigated hostility vis-à-vis early Christianity, namely: under Nero (37–68),[9] Domitian (51–96), Trajan (53–117), Antonius (86–161), Septimius Severus (146–211), Maximinus (ca. 270–313), Decius (ca. 201–251), Valerian (ca. 200–260), Aurelian (214–275) and Diocletian (ca. 245–312).[10] Schaff, one of the foremost experts on the history of the Christian Church, argued in this respect:

> This number was suggested by the ten plagues of Egypt taken as types (which, however, befell the enemies of Israel, and present a contrast rather than a parallel), and by the ten horns of the Roman beast making war with the Lamb, taken for so many emperors. But the number is too great for the general persecutions, and too small for the provincial and local. Only two imperial persecutions—those, of Decius and Diocletian—extended over the empire; but Christianity was always an illegal religion from Trajan to Constantine, and subject to annoyance and violence everywhere. Some persecuting emperors—Nero, Domitian, Galerius, were monstrous tyrants, but others—Trajan, Marcus Aurelius, Decius, Diocletian—were among the best and most energetic emperors, and were prompted not so much by hatred of Christianity as by zeal for the maintenance of the laws and the power of the government. On the other hand, some of the most worthless emperors—Commodus, Caracalla, and Heliogabalus—were rather favorable to the Christians from sheer caprice.[11]

It is debatable whether, following his conversion, Constantine's treatment of Christianity as per the *Edict of Milan* of 313 immediately 'established' Christianity in the legal sense of the word,[12] since the Edict of Milan dealt chiefly with the broader issue of religious tolerance.[13] What cannot be contested is the fact that Constantine the Great broke with a trend of official

---

[8] Oxford Dictionary of World Religions (John Bowker, ed., 1st ed. 1997) (hereinafter: Oxford Dictionary of World Religions), p. 235.

[9] The years mentioned refer to these emperors' lives, not to their reign or specifically to the era of religious persecution.

[10] Augustine, De Civitate Dei, vol. 18.

[11] Philip Schaff, History of the Christian Church (1882), Vol. II, Ch. II, para. 13.

[12] *E.g.* P.R. Coleman-Norton, Roman State & Christian Church: A Collection of Legal Documents to A.D. 535 (Vol. I) (London: S.P.C.K., 1966), p. 33; Bill Leadbetter, *From Constantine to Theodosius (and beyond), in* The Early Christian World (Vol. I) (Ph.F. Esler, ed., London/New York: Routledge, 2000), pp. 267, 275 and 288; Oxford Dictionary of World Religions, p. 235.

[13] *Letter of Constantine I and Licinius on Restoration of the Church of 313* [Edict of Milan of 313 (Constantine I)] (included in: Coleman-Norton, *ibid.*, pp. 30–32).

hostility towards the Christian religion.[14] His Edict formed the basis for the transition from three centuries of persecution of Christians to state protection of Christianity, and ultimately indeed to the legal establishment thereof.[15] As to the question of what the precise legal-political consequences were of Constantine's conversion, and particularly of the edicts on religious tolerance, Schaff contends that the Milan Edict:

> ...was a decisive step from hostile neutrality to friendly neutrality and protection, and prepared the way for the legal recognition of Christianity, as the religion of the empire. It ordered the full restoration of all confiscated church property to the *Corpus Christianorum*, at the expense of the imperial treasury, and directed the provincial magistrates to execute this order at once with all energy, so that peace may be fully established and the continuance of the Divine favor secured to the emperors and their subjects.[16]

He concludes that Constantine I:

> ...openly protected and favored the church, without forbidding idolatry, and upon the whole remained true to his policy of protective toleration till his death (337)...With Constantine, therefore, the last of the heathen, the first of the Christian emperors, a new period begins. The church ascends the throne of the Caesars under the banner of the once despised, now honored and triumphant cross, and gives new vigor and lustre to the hoary empire of Rome...What a contrast between Nero, the first imperial persecutor...and Constantine...![17]

Constantine also had an important hand in the early development of Christian doctrine. He summoned the first Ecumenical Council (i.e. an assembly of bishops and Church representatives)[18] which came to be known as the Council of Nicaea of 325. Among other issues, it adopted the *Homoousion* formula ("of one substance") as a tenet, thus settling long-standing conflicts over the issue of the Father and the Son as being part of a single God-notion. The conflict was significantly sparked by the Arian controversy: Arianism held that the Son was not simultaneously God.[19]

---

[14] See for a detailed account: Charles M. Odahl, Constantine and the Christian Empire (London/New York: Routledge, 2004).

[15] The decriminalization of Christianity two years earlier (311) by Emperor Galerius (ca. 250–311) –being until this final act just before his death a fervent religious persecutor himself– should also be acknowledged as an important step in this development. See the *Edict of Galerius on Toleration of Christians* of April 311 (included in: Coleman-Norton, *supra* note 12, pp. 19–20).

[16] Schaff, *supra* note 11, Vol II, Ch. II, para. 25.

[17] *Ibid.*, Vol. II, Ch. II, para. 25.

[18] This first Council is traditionally held to have consisted of 318 Church representatives; though the number was probably less (220–250, with very few western representatives) (Oxford Dictionary of World Religions, p. 696).

[19] The Alexandrian priest Arius (ca. 250–336) led the movement which was considered heretical by the Council and of which the slogan was: "There was [a time] when he was not", referring to the perceived non-eternity of the Son. See Ninian Smart, The World's Religions (Victoria: Cambridge University Press, 1992), pp. 248–253, for a more detailed historical description.

Since then, Roman Emperors were all 'Christian Emperors'—with the clear exception of Julian the Apostate (332–363)[20]—in that they in one way or another maintained and advanced the Christian nature of their empire. Yet it was not until the rule of Theodosius (347–395; r. 379–395) that Christianity can be considered truly *de jure* established as the state religion and that Roman paganism was officially abolished.[21] The *Edict of Theodosius* of 380 provided as follows:

> Edict to the people of the Constantinopolitan city: All peoples, whom the moderation of our Clemency rules, we wish to be engaged in that religion, which the divine Peter, the apostle, is declared—by the religion which has descended even to the present from him—to have transmitted to the Romans...according to apostolic discipline and evangelical doctrine we should believe the sole Deity of the Father and the Son and the Holy Spirit under an equal Majesty and under a pious Trinity. We order those following this law to assume the name of Catholic Christians, but the rest, since we judge them demented and insane, to sustain the infamy of heretical dogma and their conventicles not to take the name of churches, to be smitten first by divine vengeance, then also by the punishment of our authority, which we have claimed in accordance with the celestial will...[22]

It is clear from this Edict that it was not only Theodosius' intention to establish Christianity as the Church of the Roman Empire— 'heretical sects' were to be outlawed for once and for all. Coleman-Norton argues: "Henceforward revolt against the Church, which regulates the relation between God and man, caused heretics and schismatics to be considered both as a menace to the Empire and as rebels against the state. Subsequently such sectaries saw themselves increasingly subject to civil disabilities in respect to status and rights..."[23]

Following the above described events, Christianity was to become firmly legally and politically linked with empires and states in Europe, notably during: (i) the later stages of the Roman Empire until its fall (476); (ii) the Byzantine Empire until its fall (1453); and (iii) the Holy Roman Empire/Holy Roman Empire of the German Nation until its fall (1806).[24] It is beyond the

[20] Flavius Claudius Iulianus, or Julian 'the Apostate' as he was called by Christians, who ruled the Roman Empire only briefly (361–363), was hostile towards Christianity and favoured traditional paganism. He introduced educational reforms to that effect and wrote the (lost) treatise *Against the Christians*: Oxford Dictionary of World Religions, pp. 515–516. See also Leadbetter, *supra* note 12, pp. 275–278; and Michael Bland Simmons, *Julian the Apostate, in* The Early Christian World (Vol. I) (Ph.F. Esler, ed., London/New York: Routledge, 2000), pp. 1251–1272, for a detailed biography.

[21] See Schaff, *supra* note 11, Vol. III, Ch. I, para. 6. It was also Theodosius who convened the important second Ecumenical Council, now known as the Council of Constantinople I of 381.

[22] *Edict of Gratian, Valentinian II and Theodosius I on Establishment of the Catholic Religion* of 380 (included in: Coleman-Norton, *supra* note 12, p. 354).

[23] Coleman-Norton, *supra* note 12, p. 353.

[24] See for a comprehensive account on the rise and spread of early Christianity: Philip F. Esler (ed.), The Early Christian World (London/New York: Routledge, 2000); for a comprehensive account on the 200–1000 CE period: Peter Brown, The Rise of Western Christendom: Triumph and Diversity (Cambridge, USA: Blackwell Publ., 1996); and for an

scope of this study to further explore the rise of early and medieval Christianity and its relation to empires and states. Suffice it to say that history has of course shown that neither Theodosius nor subsequent leaders were able to conserve the universal character of the Christian church. That being said, the conversion of the Roman Empire under Constantine, Theodosius and subsequent emperors, facilitated the steady spread of Christianity throughout the continent and Christianity indeed never left the legal-political scene of the greater Europe since. We will now turn to contemporary state practices of Christian nation-building. During the early modern period, many independent European nation states established different Christian denominations as their official religion. Since the (post-)colonial era we can indeed add to that list many non-European countries.

(ii) *Present*

Whilst the length of the (later to be discussed) list of contemporary states that have either established a Christian denomination as the state religion or as the established church can be considered quite impressive, there are at present few states that constitute or position themselves explicitly as a 'Christian State'.

The Roman Catholic State of the Vatican City is, of course, the best contemporary example of a Christian state.[25] The State of the Vatican City, originally established by the *Lateran Pacts* of 1929,[26] approximates most faithfully the ideal-typical conception of a theocratic Roman Catholic state. The Pope is *ex officio* simultaneously leader of the Roman Catholic Church as well as Head of State and Head of the Government of the State of the Vatican City;[27] he also possesses (*de jure*) absolute authority over the legislative, executive and judicial branches.[28] Practically all acts and policies of the Vatican City revolve

authoritative account on the Holy Roman Empire: James Bryce, The Holy Roman Empire (Macmillian, 1919; originally published in 1862).

[25] See the New Fundamental Law of the State of Vatican City (2000) and the Lateran Pacts of 1929.

[26] Lateran Pacts of 1929: a set of treaties between Italy and the Vatican City consisting of 3 main parts: (i) an Agreement by which Italy acknowledges the sovereignty of the State of the Vatican City; (ii) a Financial Convention on matters of compensation; and (iii) a Concordat between Italy and the Vatican City. The Agreement between the Italian Republic and the Holy See (1984), which entered into force in 1985, amended the Lateran Pacts and loosened the ties between Italy and the Holy See, most importantly by disestablishing the Roman Catholic Church from the Republic of Italy (art. 1 of the Lateran Treaty had hitherto declared – along with art. 1 of the Italian Constitution of 1848 – that the Catholic Apostolic Roman religion is the state religion of Italy).

[27] The primacy of the Roman Pontiff (Pope) as supreme religious authority is firmly enshrined in Canon Law. See, *e.g.*, sec. 1 ("Supreme Authority of the Church"; Cann. 330–367) of Part II of Book II of the Code of Canon Law (see Cann. 330–335 on the authority of the Roman Pontiff specifically and Cann. 360–361 on the Roman Curia, i.e. the administration of the Holy See, and on how the Roman Pontiff conducts business through this institution).

[28] Art. 1 of the New Fundamental Law of the State of the Vatican City (2000). Art. 1, para. (1), reads: "The Pope, Sovereign of the State of the Vatican City, has full legislative, executive and judicial powers" (transl. author).

around the interests of the Holy See and, apart from the members of the Pontifical Swiss Guard, virtually all inhabitants of the Vatican City are members of the clergy.[29]

Zambia is officially a Christian state as well,[30] though the legal ramifications clearly do not compare to the latter state. The Preamble of the Constitution of Zambia establishes Zambia as a Christian state without specifying "Christian" denominationally.[31] It simply proclaims: "WE, THE PEOPLE OF ZAMBIA… DECLARE the Republic a Christian nation…"[32] As far as state practice is concerned, it may be pointed out that the Government maintains relations with the Zambian Council of Churches and requires Christianity to be taught in the public school curriculum.[33] It will be clear, however, that the cited constitutional provision does not quite translate into an ecclesiastical system as exhibited by the Vatican City.

Some Pacific states undoubtedly officially identify strongly with Christianity. The Constitution of Samoa, for instance, proclaims in the Preamble:

> IN THE HOLY NAME OF GOD, THE ALMIGHTY, THE EVER LOVING WHEREAS sovereignty over the Universe belongs to the Omnipresent God alone, and the authority to be exercised by the people of Samoa within the limits prescribed by His commandments is a sacred heritage; WHEREAS the Leaders of Samoa have declared that *Samoa should be an Independent State based on Christian principles* and Samoan custom and tradition…[34]

This phrase, "a state based on Christian principles", certainly approximates (*de jure*) the notion of a religious state (particularly when used in combination with such extensive religious references). On the other hand, the Preamble makes clear that Samoa is not exclusively founded upon Christian principles yet also on "Samoan custom and tradition". The Constitution of Tuvalu in a similar vein constitutes Tuvalu as "an independent State based on Christian principles…and Tuvaluan custom and tradition";[35] and also the Constitution of Vanuatu proclaims in its Preamble: "[we] HEREBY proclaim the establishment of the united and free Republic of Vanuatu founded on traditional

---

[29] Holy See Press Office, *Vatican Citizenship* (2005).

[30] Preamble of the CONSTITUTION OF THE REPUBLIC OF ZAMBIA (of 1991; amended 1996) (hereinafter: CONST. OF ZAMBIA of 1991).

[31] An estimated 87 percent of the population of Zambia is Christian; the wide denominational variety could explain the non-specified "Christian" (large numbers of Roman Catholics as well as many different Protestant denominations are present in Zambia).

[32] Preamble of the CONST. OF ZAMBIA (1991).

[33] The Council was founded in 1945 as the Christian Council of Northern Rhodesia. It became the Christian Council of Zambia in 1964 and the Council of Churches in Zambia in 2003. It functions as a forum in which Christian organizations can cooperate so as to further Christian tasks and objectives.

[34] Preamble of the CONSTITUTION OF THE INDEPENDENT STATE OF SAMOA (1960), emphasis added.

[35] Preamble and art. 29 of the CONSTITUTION OF TUVALU (1986).

Melanesian values, faith in God, and Christian principles..."[36] Christianity is undeniably officially supported in all three states, yet the religious constitutional references have not translated into a degree of state–religion identification that would amount to a clear-cut confessional regime.[37]

2.2.2 *Islamic States*

In this section the notion of an 'Islamic state' will be analysed from a historical and contemporary legal perspective. In the first sub-section the history of the 'first Islamic state' will be briefly outlined; subsequently, contemporary forms of Islamic states will be analysed in more detail.

(i) *History of Pre-modern Islamic Imperialism*

The very first 'Islamic state' *avant la lettre* was founded in Medina (then Yathrib) by Muhammad ibn Abdallah ('son of Abdallah') himself. Medina, after the *Hijra* of 622,[38] was the place were the religion, the laws and indeed the empire of Islam first saw the light of day. This 'move' or 'emigration' from Mecca (the place where he was born in 570) had become necessary as Muhammad and his followers faced increasing opposition. The presence of a small group of early converts in Medina accommodated Muhammad's religious–political cause perfectly.[39] With the arrival of Muhammad in Medina the traditional legal–political landscape of the region was swiftly to become radically altered. As Karsh remarks: "At one fell swoop Muhammad was transformed from a private preacher into a political and military leader and head of a rapidly expanding community, and Islam from a persecuted cult into a major religious and political force in the Arabian Peninsula."[40] Endress elaborates on this crucial period by indicating four key factors:

> [i] With the revelation of God the Creator judge as the benevolent almighty, a revelation given in the Arabic language, he founded Arab monotheism—a world view, a code of values and a social order—and the Arab nation. [ii] Above the solidarity of individual tribes he placed the solidarity of the community (*Umma*) which was sanctioned by the duty of every individual towards God, and thus gave new direction to a society in transition. [iii] It was the revelation of the Medinan period above all...that laid the foundation of the legal and governmental system of the empire which was to come. [iv] With the subjugation of the Arab tribes in the last years of his life Muhammad created the military and—by

---

[36] Preamble of the CONSTITUTION OF THE REPUBLIC OF VANUATU (1980).

[37] See also section 2.4, *infra*, on the differing degrees of positive state–religion identification between states that identify with a religion.

[38] Which year was to become (after Muhammad's death) the start of the Islamic calendar.

[39] For a more detailed account, see EFRAIM KARSH, ISLAMIC IMPERIALISM: A HISTORY (New Haven/London: Yale University Press, 2006), particularly pp. 11–12.

[40] *Ibid.*, p. 12.

> converting the community to faith in Islam—the spiritual basis of an expansion which was to begin after his death.[41]

Thus the first Islamic state can be considered to be Medina and beyond, i.e. 'Islamic Arabia', as formed between 622 and 632 (the year of Muhammad's death).[42] At the time of Muhammad's death—a decade after his arrival in Medina—a substantial part of the Arabian Peninsula (present-day Saudi-Arabia, Yemen, Oman and the United Arab Emirates) was already under the realm of Islamic Arabia.[43] The initial relations between the different tribes, including adherents of other religions (e.g. Jews and pagans), in and around Medina were settled and organized by Mohammed as per the Constitution of Medina,[44] a social contract consisting most likely of various agreements.[45] Khan argues in this context that:

> ...the Medina Constitution lit the torch of freedom by establishing a Free State for a pluralistic community composed of Muslims, Jews, and pagans...The Medina Constitution offered social contract in real time, in real space, to real people through a real agreement, hundreds of years before the theory of fictional social contract [e.g. Hobbes, Rousseau and, much later, Rawls] gained wide-spread approval, mostly in the West.[46]

Muhammad's original Islamic state was succeeded by the Caliphates[47] (the very issue of succession to Muhammad and the question whether appointed or rather hereditary leadership would be most appropriate would in fact become a crucial factor in the split between Sunni and Shi'a Muslims[48]). Under his successors, in three decades' time, Islam and the Islamic empire spread towards the West (North Africa: a northern stroke of Egypt and slightly beyond), the North (as far as the Black Sea) and the East (roughly incorporating

---

[41] Gerhard Endress, An Introduction to Islam (Edinburgh: Edinburgh University Press, 1994), p. 118.

[42] *Ibid.*, pp. 117–118.

[43] *Ibid.*, see map on p. 119.

[44] Constitution of Medina of 622.

[45] Cf. Ali Khan, *Commentary on the Constitution of Medina, in* Understanding Islamic Law: From Classic to Contemporary (H.M. Ramadan, ed., Lanham: AltaMira Press, 2006), pp. 205–206.

[46] Khan, *ibid.*, pp. 205–206. Karch is of a rather different opinion, suggesting that "the formation of the umma [Muslim community] created a sharp dichotomy between Muslims and 'infidels' and presupposed a permanent state of war between them. This vision was already expressed in the Constitution of Medina, which declared the believers 'friends one to the other to the exclusion of outsiders'..." (Karch, *supra* note 39, pp. 18–19).

[47] *Khalīfa* means 'successor' in Arabic.

[48] Muhammad had left no son to succeed him. The closest blood relative was Ali, cousin and son in law of Muhammad. However, the Muslim community chose Abu Bakr as the first Caliph (Muhammad had during his lifetime appointed him as future leader of the *salāt*, prayer). Ali, much later, was to become the fourth Caliph. Shi'a Muslims are of the view that Ali should have been the first Caliph which would have had important consequences for subsequent succession. Shi'ites would later develop their own system of Imāms which revolves around Ali and his descendents. Oxford Dictionary of World Religions, p. 543.

present-day Iran).[49] The first four Caliphates were run by the so-called 'rightly guided' or orthodox Caliphs: Abu Bakr (from 632 until 634), Umar (from 634 until 644), Uthman (from 644 until 656) and Ali (from 656 until 661). Islam would, in the next centuries under the subsequent Caliphates, spread even more extensively over Central Asia, Western Asia (the Anatolian peninsula), Northern Africa and as far as Southern Europe (the Iberian Peninsula). Such happened under the Caliphates of the Umayyad Dynasty (661–750), the Caliphate of the 'Abbasids (750–1258) and finally the Ottoman Caliphate (1517–1924).[50] Atatürk (1881–1938), founder of the secular Republic of Turkey and its first President, ultimately abolished the Caliphate in 1924.[51] Thirteen centuries of Islamic imperialism have left firm traces in the legal–political systems of contemporary states in this region.[52] Though the *modus operandi* and religio-political structure of Muhammad's *umma* (Muslim community) and the religio-political tenets disclosed by him have remained the proto-type for Islamic state organization and nation-building,[53] many important differences between the original Islamic state and contemporary Islamic states can be discerned.

(ii) *Present*

Contemporary 'Islamic states' include: Afghanistan, Bahrain, Brunei Darussalam, Iran, Mauritania, Morocco, Oman, Pakistan, Saudi Arabia and Yemen.[54] Naturally, if one considers the *khalīfa* a necessary aspect of an Islamic state then one must indeed conclude that there are no 'Islamic states' presently. However, even short of the ideal-typical concept, all contemporary Islamic states reflect many features indicative of a strong positive identification with Islam. In these states several constitutional safeguards are in place to

---

[49] Endress, *supra* note 41, map p. 119.

[50] *Ibid.*, pp. 120–135, for a more detailed historical account.

[51] Abolishment of the Caliphate Law of 3 March 1924. See for a detailed account: Andrew Mango, Atatürk (London: John Murray Publ., 1999), particularly Ch. 20: "The End of the Caliphate", pp. 396–414.

[52] For an analysis of parallels and differences between Christian and Islamic Imperialism, see Karsh, *supra* note 39, p. 5.

[53] Cf. Karsh, *supra* note 39, p. 18.

[54] Art. 1 of the Constitution of the Islamic Republic of Afghanistan (2004); art. 1 of the Constitution of the Kingdom of Bahrain (2002); artt. 3–4 of the Constitution of Brunei Darussalam (1959); preamble and artt. 1–2 of the Constitution of the Islamic Republic of Iran (of 1979; amended 1989; hereinafter: Const. of Iran of 1979); art. 1 of the Constitution of Mauritania (1991); preamble of the Constitution of the Kingdom of Morocco (of 1972; amended 1992 and 1996; hereinafter: Const. of Morocco of 1972); art. 1 of the Basic Statute of the State of Oman (Royal Decree No. 101/96; hereinafter: Basic Statute of Oman of 1996); art. 1 of the Constitution of the Islamic Republic of Pakistan (of 1973; as amended through 2003: Seventeenth Amendment Act; hereinafter: Const. of Pakistan of 1973); art. 1 of the Basic Law of Saudi Arabia (Royal Decree A/90 of 1 March 1992; hereinafter: Basic Law of Saudi Arabia of 1992); and art. 1 of the Constitution of the Republic of Yemen (of 1990; amended 1994; hereinafter: Const. of Yemen of 1990).

ensure that legislative, executive and judicial activity is informed by Islamic principles. That being said, many differences can be discerned between contemporary Islamic states—some of them follow Muhammad's example closer than others.[55]

States which reflect the Islamic nature of the state in the official (constitutional) name of the state are: the Islamic Republic of Afghanistan, the Islamic Republic of Iran, the Islamic Republic of Mauritania and the Islamic Republic of Pakistan (the Constitutions of these states contain further references to the Islamic nature of the state).[56] The Islamic nature of a state alternatively follows solely from a constitutional declaration to that effect. Such is the case with respect to the following states: the Kingdom of Bahrain (the Constitution of the Kingdom of Bahrain speaks of an "Islamic Arab State"),[57] the Kingdom of Morocco (the Constitution of the Kingdom of Morocco speaks of an "Islamic State"),[58] the Kingdom of Saudi Arabia (the Basic Law of Government of Saudi Arabia speaks of an "Arab Islamic State")[59] and the Republic of Yemen (the Constitution of the Republic of Yemen speaks of an "Arab Islamic State").[60] Finally, a state can also be deemed Islamic if it is constituted as a sultanate.[61]

In all the above cases, the Islamic nature of the state is firmly enshrined in the opening articles of the Constitution, which is indicative of the fundamental character of this aspect of political organization (the first chapter of a Constitution typically outlines the political and ideological foundations of the state). The following excerpt strikingly illustrates the Islamic nature of Iran:

> The form of government of Iran is that of an Islamic Republic, endorsed by the people of Iran on the basis of their longstanding belief in the sovereignty of truth and Koranic justice, in the referendum of 29 and 30 March 1979...held after the victorious Islamic Revolution led by Imam Khomeini...The Islamic Republic is a system based on belief in: (1) the One God (as stated in the phrase "There is no god except Allah"), His exclusive sovereignty and right to legislate, and the necessity of submission to His commands; (2) Divine revelation and its fundamental role in setting forth the laws; (3) the return to God in the Hereafter, and the constructive role of this belief in the course of man's ascent towards God; (4) the justice of God in creation and legislation; (5) continuous leadership and perpetual guidance, and its fundamental role in ensuring the uninterrupted process of the revolution of Islam; (6) the exalted dignity and value of man, and his freedom coupled with responsibility before God...[62]

---

[55] See section 2.4, *infra*.
[56] See art. 1 of the Const. of Afghanistan (2004); preamble and artt. 1–2 of the Const. of Iran (1979); art. 1 of the Const. of Mauritania (1991); and art. 1 of the Const. of Pakistan (1973).
[57] Art. 1 of the Const. of Bahrain (2002).
[58] Preamble of the Const. of Morocco (1972).
[59] Art. 1 of the Basic Law of Saudi Arabia (1992).
[60] Art. 1 of the Const. of Yemen (1990).
[61] See *infra*.
[62] Artt. 1–2 of the Const. of Iran (1979).

The lengthy Preamble of the Constitution dedicates numerous paragraphs to the Islamic nature of Iran. The following excerpt discusses the nature of 'Islamic Governance':

> The plan of the Islamic government as proposed by Imam Khomeini…at the height of the period of repression and strangulation practiced by the despotic regime, produced a new…motive for the Muslim people, opening up before them the true path of Islamic ideological struggle, and giving greater intensity to the struggle of militant and committed Muslims both within the country and abroad…In the view of Islam, government does not derive from the interests of a class, nor does it serve the domination of an individual or a group. Rather, it represents the fulfilment of the political ideal of a people who bear a common faith and common outlook, taking an organized form in order to initiate the process of intellectual and ideological evolution towards the final goal, i.e., movement towards Allah…The mission of the Constitution is to realize the ideological objectives of the movement and to create conditions conducive to the development of man in accordance with the noble and universal values of Islam…[63]

The Iranian Constitution stands out in the present context as practically the entire text is dedicated to outlining the determinative role of Islam within the political organization of Iran.

The first article of the Constitutional law of Saudi Arabia fairly extensively describes the Islamic nature of the state as follows: "The Kingdom of Saudi Arabia is a sovereign Arab Islamic State with Islam as its religion; God's Book and the Sunnah of His Prophet, God's prayers and peace be upon him, are its constitution …"[64] By contrast, the first article of the Afghan Constitution mentions the Islamic nature of the state as part of a list of fundamental characteristics of the state: "Afghanistan is an Islamic Republic, independent, unitary and indivisible state."[65] The Constitutions of Bahrain, Mauritania, Morocco, Pakistan and Yemen similarly mention the Islamic identity of the state as part of a list of fundamental state characteristics.[66]

Brunei Darussalam and Oman are somewhat unique Islamic states as these countries are the last remaining well-defined sultanates.[67] The title of Sultan is an Islamic hereditary title. The holder of this title was commonly bestowed, in pursuance of Quranic interpretations, with both spiritual as well as political authority, though in time the latter (profane, governmental powers) came to

---

[63] Preamble of the CONST. OF IRAN (1979).

[64] Art. 1 of the BASIC LAW OF SAUDI ARABIA (1992).

[65] Art. 1 of the CONST. OF AFGHANISTAN (2004).

[66] Art. 1 of the CONST. OF BAHRAIN (2002); art. 1 of the CONST. OF MAURITANIA (1991); preamble of the CONST. OF MOROCCO (1972); art. 1 of the CONST. OF PAKISTAN (1973); and art. 1 of the CONST. OF YEMEN (1990).

[67] Art. 4 of the CONST. OF BRUNEI DARUSSALAM (1959); in a treatise entitled *National Philosophy*, the Government of Brunei Darussalam has further outlined the official interpretation of the so-called MIB concept (*Melayu Islam Beraja*: Malay Islamic Monarchy); artt. 1 and 5 of the BASIC STATUTE OF OMAN (1996) establish Oman as sultanate (art. 1 also lists the Islamic nature of the state as one of the fundamental characteristics of the state).

have the upper hand. The Sultan of Brunei, however, remains constitutionally *ex officio* both Head of Religion and Head of State.[68] Sultanates may be established regionally as well. The best example in this context is Malaysia, which, as a federal state, is not a declared religious state. However, nine out of the 13 states that compose the Federation of Malaysia are either sultanates (Johor, Kedah, Kelantan, Pahang, Perak, Selangor and Terengganu) or clearly styled after a sultanate (Negeri Sembilan and Perlis). The Sultan of Kelantan, Sultan of Terengganu, Sultan of Pahang, Sultan of Kedah, Sultan of Perak, Sultan of Selangor, Sultan of Johor, the Raja of Perlis and the *Yang di-Pertuan Besar* of Negeri Sembilan are Head of Religion of their state and are vested with profound (worldly) executive powers over their state. The remaining four states (Malacca, Penang, Sabah and Sarawak) do not have a Sultan exercising authority over religious affairs. For these states the King, or *Yang di-Pertuan Agong*, is Head of the Religion of Islam.[69] These latter states are thus by no means secular states, yet they do not qualify as clear-cut religious states either, thereby making the Federal State of Malaysia a 'partly religious state'. Finally, the Special Region of Yogyakarta (Indonesia) is formally a sultanate. It has to be acknowledged that the manner in which the Yogyakarta Sultanate has traditionally administered its 'Muslim monarchy', has been seriously excavated by the central Indonesian Government, which requires that the governor of this special region to be a popularly elected official (which Sri Sultan Hamengkubuwono X, has succeeded in becoming for the time being).

The Maldives, though not a genuine Islamic state (*de jure*), is certainly inclined towards a strong positive identification with Islam (the Republic of Maldives is occasionally considered an Islamic state, despite the fact that there is no express constitutional provision to that effect).[70] The second article of the Constitution of the Republic of Maldives proclaims though that the Maldives shall be "based on the principles of Islam".[71] In that respect one could draw a parallel between the Maldives and the predominantly Christian states Samoa,[72] Tuvalu and Vanuatu which are proclaimed as states "based" (Samoa and Tuvalu) or "founded" (Vanuatu) on Christian principles (yet not explicitly

---

[68] Artt. 3–4 of the CONST. OF BRUNEI DARUSSALAM (1959).

[69] Art. 3, para. (3), of the CONSTITUTION OF MALAYSIA (1957). The *Yang di-Pertuan Agong* is also Head of the Religion of Islam in the federal territories of Kuala Lumpur and Labuan (art. 3, para. 4).

[70] *E.g.* United States Commission on International Religious Freedom, *The Religion-State Relationship and the Right to Freedom of Religion or Belief: A Comparative Textual Analysis of the Constitutions of Predominantly Muslim Countries* (Washington D.C.: USCIRF, 2005), p. 7; Maldives is listed under "Declared Islamic States".

[71] Art. 2 of the CONSTITUTION OF THE REPUBLIC OF MALDIVES (2008).

[72] 'Predominantly Muslim country', 'predominantly Christian country', etc., will be used to refer to a country in which 50 per cent or more of the population adheres to the same religion (*i.e.* it will have a demographical rather than a legal or political meaning).

established as 'Christian states').[73] An important difference, however, is that in the case of the Maldives the religion in question, Islam, is expressly declared the official religion of the state and one can find numerous constitutional references to Islam and Islamic law (*Shari'a*).

Algeria, finally, cannot be considered an Islamic state for the same reasons (a lack of an unequivocal constitutional statement to that effect). However, the Preamble of its Constitution does describe Algeria as "a land of Islam".[74]

2.2.3 *A Jewish State?*

Israel is established as a "Jewish state" according to the *Declaration of the Establishment of the State of Israel* (1948) and the Basic Laws of Israel.[75] The Declaration elaborates on a "natural right of the Jewish people to be masters of their own fate, like all other nations, in their own sovereign State" as follows:

> ...we, members of the People's Council, representatives of the Jewish Community of Eretz-Israel and of the Zionist Movement, are here assembled on the day of the termination of the British Mandate over Eretz-Israel and, by virtue of our natural and historic right and on the strength of the resolution of the United Nations General Assembly, hereby declare the *establishment of a Jewish state* in Eretz-Israel, to be known as the State of Israel...[76]

The polysemic adjective "Jewish", as used here and in several of the Basic Laws,[77] can refer both to the people adhering to the Jewish faith as well as to Jews as a people.[78] Since the establishment of the State of Israel, this issue of

[73] Discussed in section 2.2.1, *supra*; see the preamble of the CONST. OF SAMOA (1960); preamble and art. 29 of the CONST. OF TUVALU (1986); and the preamble of the CONSTITUTION OF THE REPUBLIC OF VANUATU (1980).

[74] Preamble of the CONSTITUTION OF THE PEOPLE'S DEMOCRATIC REPUBLIC OF ALGERIA (1976) (amended through 1996; hereinafter: CONST. OF ALGERIA of 1976). The preamble of the CONSTITUTION OF THE UNITED ARAB EMIRATES (of 1971; which was subsequently made permanent by Constitutional Amendment No. 1 of 1996; hereinafter: CONST. OF THE UNITED ARAB EMIRATES of 1971), it might be added, speaks of taking steps towards a democratic "Islamic society".

[75] It should be noted that, in focusing on present-day Israel, one might easily overlook the fact that other states once, albeit for relatively brief periods, officially identified with Judaism. Eight/ninth-century Khazaria (the Khazars were an Eastern European nation from the seventh until the 11th century) is a good example in this respect. Smart, *supra* note 19, p. 262, names pre-Islamic Yemen as a state which briefly established Judaism.

[76] Declaration of the Establishment of the State of Israel (1948) (emphasis added).

[77] *E.g.* art. 1a of the Basic Law: Human Dignity and Liberty (1992): "The purpose of this Basic Law is to protect human dignity and liberty, in order to establish in a Basic Law the values of the State of Israel as a Jewish and democratic state"; art. 2 of the Basic Law: Freedom of Occupation (1994): "The purpose of this Basic Law if to protect freedom of occupation, in order to establish in a Basic Law the values of the State of Israel as a Jewish and democratic state".

[78] Ruth Gavison, *Jewish and Democratic? A Rejoinder to the "Ethnic Democracy" Debate*, 4.1 ISRAEL STUDIES (1999), p. 52, gives a third possible meaning: "At least three different meanings may be identified: a state with a large Jewish majority, *a nation-state in which the Jewish people exercises political self-determination*, and a state inspired by Jewish religious law" (emphasis added).

the difference between a 'Jewish state' and a 'state of the Jews', has been the subject of ongoing debate between Jews and non-Jews and, of course, amongst Jews themselves (spanning the spectrum of 'Orthodox Judaism' as well as 'Conservative', 'Reform' or 'Progressive', 'Traditional' and 'Secular Judaism'). The Declaration of Independence does refer to the "eternal Book of Books"[79] (the Tanakh) which undeniably is an important first indication as to the religious nature of the state. Some would argue that the state's identification with Judaism, at least as far as the moment of the initial establishment of the Sate of Israel is concerned, was quite evident. Edelman, for instance, argues that "Israeli independence was accompanied by the establishment of Orthodox Judaism as the sole, official, state-recognized and supported religion for the nation's Jewish citizens".[80] He further contends that:

> There is no denying...that Orthodox Judaism has functioned in the Israeli polity as if it were the state religion. Through the Ministry of Religious Affairs, all recognized religions were supposed to receive state funding on a proportional basis. Since Jews constitute 79 percent of the population, Jewish institutions receive the lion's share of the state appropriations.[81]

However, as Edelman argues, that situation may have changed over time:

> ...the original dominant collectivist ethos that supported that arrangement has been replaced by an increasingly pervasive individualism. The emergent political culture has fuelled a major culture clash...over the role of Orthodox Judaism in the polity. Israel's Orthodox communities seek to preserve the status quo, while its non-Orthodox Jewish citizens increasingly seek to promote religious pluralism.[82]

Others, on the other hand, would argue that Israel is not established as a religious, Jewish state. Maoz, for instance, holds that "[i]t is obvious...that when declaring Israel to be a Jewish state, the Knesset certainly did not have in mind a Halakhic state [i.e. a state based on Jewish laws]".[83] However, also Maoz concludes, at the same time, that "[n]ational and religious components of Judaism are inseparable. A Jewish state divorced of religion is an impossibility".[84]

The constitutional laws of Israel—the Declaration of Independence, strictly speaking, lacks constitutional status[85]—do not give a straightforward answer

---

[79] First paragraph of the Declaration of the Establishment of the State of Israel (1948).

[80] Martin Edelman, *A Portion of Animosity: The Politics of the Disestablishment of Religion in Israel*, 5 Israel Studies (2000), p. 204.

[81] *Ibid.*, p. 206–207.

[82] *Ibid.*, p. 204.

[83] Asher Maoz, *Religious Human Rights in the State of Israel, in* Religious Human Rights in Global Perspective: Legal Perspectives (J.D. van der Vyver & J. Witte, eds., The Hague/Boston/London: Martinus Nijhoff Publishers, 1996), p. 358.

[84] *Idem.*

[85] Elyakim Rubinstein, *The Declaration of Independence as a Basic Document of the State of Israel*, 3 Israel Studies 199 (1998), acknowledges this yet argues that this document ought to

as to the religious question. This omission in itself could be seized upon to argue that the drafters must have had a secular Jewish state in mind or at least must not have intended to establish a clear-cut religious state. This could *a fortiori* be contended since Judaism is not (*de jure*) declared the official religion of Israel in the constitutional regulations (again, some might argue that *de facto* this is different). Rendering official status to the religion in question is, strictly speaking, not necessary for a country to qualify as a religious state (e.g. Zambia); yet the absence of a state religion can most definitely be employed as an argument in favour of a more secular interpretation of the "Jewish" State of Israel.

On the other hand, the existence of religious courts and the state-controlled or state-sanctioned application of religious laws are in the main exemplary of religious states, and it may be argued that the presence of these courts, at the very least, pose questions as to the clear-cut secular nature of the state. Then again, in the particular case of the Israeli judicial system the presence of religious courts is not evidently a clear expression of the Jewish nature of the state, as besides rabbinic courts (which have exclusive jurisdiction over such issues as marriage and divorce) there are also Shari'a courts, Christian courts and Druze courts operating in Israel (clearly an exponent of the so-called *millet* system, as inherited from the Ottoman Empire). Edelman argues in this context:

> While Israel is not a theocracy, the State does more than simply recognize the existence of certain religions...The Government maintains formal links with the institutional organs of the 14 religious denominations, and legally subjects individuals to religious rules by vesting the religious courts of those religions with the authority to resolve certain matters. The Courts of each community have exclusive jurisdiction over specific matters of personal status, particularly marriage and divorce; there is no secular marriage and divorce in Israel... Legally, then, Israel does not have *an* established religion; it has a multiple establishment.[86]

More answers can be found in the state practice of Israel as certain adopted laws and state policies have been considered exemplary of the Jewish (religious) nature of the State of Israel. The Law of Return is a most striking example in this respect. The Law of Return defines the noun 'Jew' as "a person who was born of a Jewish mother or has become converted to Judaism and who is

---

be upgraded. See also David Kretzmer, *Constitutional Law, in* INTRODUCTION TO THE LAW OF ISRAEL (A. Shapira, ed., Amsterdam: Kluwer, 1995) on the constitutional laws of Israel.

[86] Edelman, *supra* note 80, p. 206; see also Ruth Gavison, *supra* note 78, on the achieved status quo. Interestingly, it may be added at this point, Israel is among the few non-predominantly Christian states that have entered into agreements with the Holy See. See the Fundamental Agreement between the State of Israel and the Holy See of 30 December 1993 and the Agreement between the State of Israel and the Holy See of 10 November 1997 (Legal Personality Agreement).

not a member of another religion".[87] "Hence", Ottolenghi remarks, "a religious basis for nationality has determined a situation where it is both impossible to disentangle religion from politics, or ground citizenship on purely secular criteria..."[88] In the *Rufeisen* (or 'Brother Daniel') case, the Israeli Supreme Court endorsed the decision of the Israeli authorities to deny a person the right to citizenship under the Law of Return because of a conversion into another religion (Catholicism, in this particular case).[89] The Israeli Supreme Court argued as follows:

> Need it be remembered that the declaration for establishing the State of Israel opens with a description of "the historical and traditional ties" of the Jewish People to Eretz Israel "where the spiritual, religious, and political character [of the nation] was formed"...and in this spirit, the Law of Return has been legislated...whose significance is not to be severed from past sources where nationalism and religion are bound together without differentiation.[90]

In view of this interpretation, Edelman's final conclusion with respect to the Law of Return is: "The secular law of the Jewish State is thus partly based on *Halakhah* [Jewish religious law] – a Jew is a person born of a Jewish mother – and partly departs from the *halakhic* definition in that it does not specify Orthodox *halakhic* criteria for conversion and insofar as it automatically excludes all members of other religions."[91]

Another example is the Foundations of Law Act, which orders courts, when faced with a hiatus or ambiguity in the law, to make a decision "in light of the principles of freedom, justice and peace of the Jewish heritage".[92] Maoz adds to these examples the fact that the "Jewish character of the State is... reflected in its national days of rest and festivals and in State education. The national flag, the State emblem, and the anthem are all packed with Jewish symbols."[93]

---

[87] Art. 4B of the Law of Return 5710–1950 (1950) (as amended in 1970).

[88] Emanuele Ottolenghi, *Religion and Democracy in Israel, in* Religion and Democracy (D. Marquand & R.L. Nettler, eds., Oxford: Blackwell Publishers, 2000), p. 45.

[89] *Rufeisen v. Minister of the Interior*, [1962] 16 P.D. 2428.

[90] *Idem*. See Rubinstein, *supra* note 85, p. 207, for an analysis of this case.

[91] Edelman, *supra* note 86, p. 218. It should be borne in mind, as Ottolenghi argues, that the "wording of the Law of Return [including the 1970 amendments] is such that many individuals who are not Jews from a strictly religious point of view can still enjoy a right of return as Jews" (Ottolenghi, *supra* note 88, p. 45); He goes on arguing (p. 45): "But the existence of religious courts, and their virtual monopoly on personal matters, suggests that individuals considered as Jews by the state might not necessarily be so in a religious court".

[92] Foundations of Law Act (1980). See also Anat Scolnicov, *Religious Law, Religious Courts and Human Rights within Israeli Constitutional Structure*, 4 International Journal of Constitutional Law (2006), p. 732, on this point.

[93] Maoz, *supra* note 83, p. 358. See also Chapter 3, section 3.3.3(iii), *infra*, on state symbolism.

2.2.4 *The Secularization of the Last Hindu State*

In this section the notion of a 'Hindu state' will be analysed. It commences with a few remarks on the history of this concept; subsequently, the ongoing process of 'disestablishing' Hinduism in what was the last Hindu state will be outlined.

(i) *History*

Hinduism dates back as far as the Indus Valley civilizations of Mohenjo-Daro (on the Indus) and Harappa (on the Ravi) of the third millennium before the Common Era (BCE), followed by the Aryan invasion (early second millennium BCE) and the subsequent spread of the Vedic religious traditions.[94] The Vedas—the most important and earliest sacred Indian texts composed of the Rigveda, Samaveda, Yajurveda and the much later added Atharvaveda[95]—and the later texts of the Brahmanas (books on ritual and prayer)[96] show a clear nexus between kingship and the religious rituals of ancient India. One might think of, for instance, the kingship rituals of *Vajapeya* ("the drink of victory"), *Rajasuya* ("the royal consecration") or *Asvamedha* ("the horse sacrifice").[97] It is not uncommon to consider the Maurya Dynasty (ca. 321–180 BCE) under Bindusara's reign (r. 298–ca. 272 BCE) the first Hindu Empire.[98] It has to be acknowledged that the different Mauryan Emperors had diverse personal religious preferences and some were supporters of Buddhism or Jainism rather than Hinduism (though not necessarily at the expense of the latter).[99] The first Mauryan ruler, Chandragupta Maurya (r. 322–298 BCE), for instance, personally embraced Jainism while Emperor Aśoka the Great (r. 272–232 BCE) famously promoted and spread Buddhism.

It is beyond the scope of this study to further explore the entanglement of pre-modern empires with Hinduism. Suffice it to say that the history of state–religion identification on the Indian sub-continent in the post-Maurya period reflects many notable periods of state promotion of Hinduism, including:[100]

---

[94] Smart, *supra* note 19, pp. 50–52.

[95] See Smart, *supra* note 19, pp. 53–55 for a description of the early Vedic Period; see Ninian Smart & Richard D. Hecht (eds.), SACRED TEXTS OF THE WORLD: A UNIVERSAL ANTHOLOGY (London: Quercus, 2007), p. 195 for a description of the four Vedas.

[96] Smart & Hecht, *ibid.*, p. 195, for a brief description and excerpts.

[97] Included in English translation in the anthology by Smart & Hecht, *ibid.*, pp. 224–230.

[98] *E.g.* Benoy Kumar Sarkar, *Hindu Political Philosophy*, 33 POLITICAL SCIENCE QUARTERLY (1918), p 485; Benoy Kumar Sarkar, *Public Finance in Ancient India*, 97 ANNALS OF THE AMERICAN ACADEMY OF POLITICAL AND SOCIAL SCIENCE (1921), p. 153.

[99] *E.g.* KLAUS K. KLOSTERMAIER, A CONCISE ENCYCLOPEDIA OF HINDUISM (Oxford: Oneworld Publ., 1998), p. 5.

[100] This overview is a synthesis of: Klostermaier, *ibid.*, pp. 5–6 and Sarkar, *supra* note 98, pp. 485–486.

the Empire of the Kushans under certain rulers (parts of the first and parts of the second century CE); the major renaissance of Hinduism under the Gupta Empire (320–600 CE); the Chalukya Dynasty and the Rastrakuta Hindu Dynasty (ruling the Deccan from the sixth until the 13th century); the Hindu affiliation of the Chola Dynasty in Southern India (900–1300); the Hindu Kingdoms of Kashmir in the North (14th century); the Hindu Empire of Vijayanagara in the Deccan (1336–1565); and the Maratha Hindu Empire (1674–1818).

(ii) *Present*

India (and thus a large part of the Indian subcontinent) has, particularly due to Mahatma Gandhi (1869–1948) and Jawaharlal Nehru (1889–1964), since its independence (1947) been organized along secular lines.[101] For Nepal, this was quite different until very recently. The Constitution of the Kingdom of Nepal of 1990 expressly established Nepal as a Hindu Kingdom.[102] However, in May 2006, the newly resumed Parliament unanimously passed a proclamation declaring Nepal a secular state.[103] The 2007 Interim Constitution of the *State* of Nepal confirmed both earlier attempts to curtail the monarch's powers (the Monarchy was abolished altogether in May 2008) as well as the move towards secularity: it establishes Nepal as a secular state.[104] The future permanent Constitution is likely to uphold this.

2.2.5 *(Mono)theist States*

The Republic of Indonesia could be considered a religious state as the Constitution of Indonesia proclaims that the "State shall be based upon the belief in the One and Only God" (a repetition of a similar proclamation contained in the Preamble).[105] Indonesia can therefore be considered a 'monotheist state' (without further specification as to the exact nature of this monotheism). The Indonesian Constitution does not establish a specific religion as the state religion. Indonesia's religious pluralism in itself could account for this unspecified religious affiliation of the state: Indonesia is predominantly Sunni Muslim, but significant Shi'a Muslim, Catholic and Protestant communities are present as well. The constitutional phrase in fact has its origin in the political philosophy of *Pancasila* (Sanskrit for 'five

---

[101] An explicit provision on the principle of secularism was incorporated into the Constitution of India as late as 1976; see the preamble and art. 2 of the Constitution (Forty-second Amendment) Act, Bill No. 91/1976, of 18 December 1976. The unique form of Indian secularism will be discussed at a later stage; see Chapter 5, section 5.5.4, *infra*.

[102] Art. 4 of the Constitution of the Kingdom of Nepal (1990; abrogated).

[103] Sec. 5, para. (8), House of Representatives Proclamation (18 may 2006).

[104] Art. 4 of the Interim Constitution of Nepal (2007).

[105] Preamble and art. 29 of the Constitution of the Republic of Indonesia (1945).

principles').[106] The constitutional references clearly echo the first of the five political principles: *Ketuhanan yang Maha Esa*, or the belief in the one and only God. In the Annotations to the Constitution this is further elaborated upon:

> The...basic idea in the preamble is that the state shall be based on the belief in the One and Only God and on just and civilized humanity [the second *Pancasila* principle]. It follows that the constitution must make it the duty of the state and all its institutions to foster high human ethical norms and to live up to the noble moral aspirations of the people.[107]

Some predominantly Christian states in the Americas can be considered (*de jure*) 'theist states', meaning states that are constitutionally established "on the belief in God" (e.g. Saint Kitts and Nevis)[108] or states that are constitutionally "founded upon principles that acknowledge the supremacy of God" (e.g. Antigua and Barbuda, Barbados, Belize, Canada, Dominica, Grenada and Trinidad and Tobago).[109] Numerous Constitutions make references to God;[110] the just mentioned constitutional references stand out in that they postulate that the very foundation of the state is directly premised on the belief in God.

2.3 State Religions & State Churches

Though it clearly depends on the specific arrangement, typically the rationale behind establishment of religion is one of mutual interest: to foster a religio-ethical legitimization of state authority in return for financial, ethical, pragmatic and other forms of support for the religion in question.[111] In this section

---

[106] See Smart, *supra* note 19, p. 483, for a description of Pancasila.

[107] Part 5 (Annotations to the Constitution), para. II, of the Const. of Indonesia (1945).

[108] Preamble of the Federation of Saint Kitts and Nevis Constitutional Order (1983) (hereinafter: Const. of Saint Kitts and Nevis of 1983).

[109] Preamble of the Antigua and Barbuda Constitutional Order (1981; hereinafter: Const. of Antigua and Barbuda of 1981); preamble of the Constitution of Barbados (1996); preamble of the Constitution of Belize (1981); preamble of the [Canadian] Constitution Act (1982; Schedule to the Canada Act); preamble of the Constitution of the Commonwealth of Dominica (1978; hereinafter: Const. of Dominica of 1978); preamble of the Grenada Constitution Order (1973; hereinafter: Const. of Grenada of 1973); preamble of the Constitution of the Republic of Trinidad and Tobago (Schedule to the 1976 Constitution of the Republic of Trinidad and Tobago Act; hereinafter: Const. of Trinidad and Tobago of 1976).

[110] See Chapter 3, section 3.3.3, *infra*.

[111] An interesting legal-sociological issue is whether a religion, when established, is ultimately truly better off in terms of its religious objectives: gaining adherents and fostering religious devotion. Adam Smith answered this question in the negative: Adam Smith, An Inquiry into the Nature and Causes of the Wealth of Nations (London: Strahan, 1791), Book V, Article III. More recent research by Barro & McCleary suggests the affirmative: "The presence of an official state religion tends to increase religiosity, probably because of the subsidies that flow to organized religion". See Robert J. Barro & Rachel M. McClearly, *Religion and Political Economy in an International Panel*, 45.2 Journal for the Scientific Study of Religion

we will see that many states establish a specific religion or church as the official religion or official church of the state. Such constitutional declarations establishing a state religion or state church are as a rule to be found in either a constitutional chapter pinpointing the fundamental characteristics of the state, or in a separate chapter solely dedicated to state–religion relationships. Both arrangements give evidence of the importance attached to the religious affiliation in question.

Virtually all religious states declare the religion in question the state religion. Though it can consequently be considered typical for religious states to do so, the establishment of a state religion is not a prerequisite to qualify as a religious state as the few exceptional arrangements in this context prove. For instance, the Zambian Constitution declares Zambia a Christian state, however, neither Christianity nor a specific Christian denomination is expressly established as the official religion of the nation.[112] With respect to Nepal it has just been pointed out that it is consolidating its transition towards secularity. In this context it is interesting to note that when Nepal was still a Hindu Kingdom, Hinduism was not explicitly established as the state religion of Nepal. Indonesia is constitutionally established as a monotheist state; however, the state refrains from declaring a monotheist religion the official religion. And finally, if one is of the opinion that Israel is a religious state, then Israel too can be seen as an exception for Judaism is not (*de jure*) established as the religion of the State of Israel.

In what follows presently the different contemporary *state religions* will be analysed (2.3.1). Following a few remarks on historical forms of establishment of religion, contemporary *state churches* will be scrutinized (2.3.2). It will, finally, be explained that in some states the issue of state–religion identification is not a national or federal matter but is left at the discretion of the constituent states or provinces (2.3.3).

2.3.1 *State Religions*

A religion in its entirety or a specific religious denomination can be established as the official religion of the state. State practice shows that occasionally

(2006), pp. 149–175. Questions as to the other side of the coin are equally interesting: are states better off if they link up to religion, for instance economically? See Robert J. Barro & Rachel M. Mclearly, *Religion and Economic Growth across Countries*, 68 AMERICAN SOCIOLOGY REVIEW (2003), on this correlation.

[112] An alternative reading would be that those states that are *de jure* religious states but that do not also establish the religion in question as state religion are not truly religious states. In this study, following the definition stated above, a state will be considered a religious state if it positions itself as such. The lack of an establishment clause, however, may in specific cases tone down the degree of religious affiliation of the state. Still another alternative reading would be that in these states the religion in question is *de facto* the state religion (that is, simply by virtue of the official religious nature of the state).

a religion in its entirety is *de jure* established whilst a specific denomination is *de facto* preferentially treated. The exact legal and pragmatic ramifications of establishing a religion as state religion vary from state to state.[113] In this section we will see that Islam and Buddhism are established as state religions by certain states and that the specific religious denominations that are constitutionally granted official status include: the Shafi'i school of Sunni Islam, the Twelver Ja'fari school of the Shi'a branch of Islam, Lamaistic—Tibetan Mahayana—Buddhism (or *Drukpa Kargyupa*); Roman Catholicism (commonly established as the 'Roman Catholic Apostolic Religion'), Evangelical Lutheranism and Eastern Orthodoxy.

(i) *Christian State Religions*

States no longer declare Christianity in its entirety as the state religion. History has seen the establishment of Christianity as the state religion, for instance in Armenia in ca. 301 under Tiridates III (commonly considered the very first establishment of Christianity)[114] and in Georgia (then Georgian Kingdom of Kartli or Caucasian Iberia) in 337. An early draft of the Constitution of Swaziland provided "[t]he official religion of Swaziland is Christianity" but this provision was ultimately dropped.[115] Presently, all Constitutions of states with ties with Christianity point out a specific Christian denomination as the state religion or as the *state church*.[116]

In this study the constitutional references to the state's religious affiliation are closely followed. It is possible to legally distinguish between a state religion and a state church. In practice, however, the legal significance of this distinction is often belied by reality: in the event that a Christian denomination is appointed the state religion, the Church in question (i.e. the national Church of this specific denomination) will almost automatically have a privileged position and special ties with the state. Some differences can nonetheless be discerned. Historically, under state church systems states had more far-reaching powers to interfere with internal church affairs.[117]

Roman Catholicism

Roman Catholicism is established as the state religion in Costa Rica, Malta, Monaco and the State of the Vatican City.[118] In the latter state this follows from

[113] See section 2.4, *infra*.

[114] Smart, *supra* note 19, p. 260 dates this event to 314 CE.

[115] Compare the Constitution of Swaziland (2005) and art. 4 of the Draft-Constitution of Swaziland (2003).

[116] See section 2.3.2, *infra*.

[117] This will be further elaborated upon in the section on state churches (section 2.3.2, *infra*) and in section 2.4. Note, once more, that the precise role of the Christian state religion or church in question varies from state to state (see section 2.4, *infra*).

[118] Art. 75 of the Constitution of the Republic of Costa Rica (1949); art. 2 of the Constitution of Malta (1964); art. 9 of the Constitution of the Principality of

the very construction of this ecclesiastical state: it is the sovereign territory of the Vatican City which engenders the Holy See in its function as the administrative and spiritual capital of the Roman Catholic Church.[119] In other words, in this exceptional case the state virtually coincides with a religion/church. The case of Malta perfectly illustrates that whenever a religious denomination is officially established as the state religion, the related Church in question as a rule has a privileged position (and is thus *de facto* a state church).[120] The fact that Roman Catholicism is the state religion implies, according to the Maltese Constitution, that the "authorities of the Roman Catholic Apostolic Church have the duty and the right to teach which principles are right and which are wrong".[121]

Roman Catholicism arrived and became firmly rooted in Latin America in the late 15th century. Daudelin and Hewitt argue in this context that:

> ...both the discovery itself [of the New World in 1492] and the subsequent exploration and development of the region were undertaken as a joint effort of church and state...For the state, the goal was territorial and material acquisition. For the Church, Latin America represented virgin territory for the conquest of souls... the colonial and later the national governments counted on the moral support of the Church to maintain a status quo favouring the political and economic elite. The Church freely offered this support in return for state assistance in maintaining Catholic religious hegemony.[122]

Thus, it does not come as a surprise that many of the Constitutions of states in this region grant a special position to and acknowledge the role of the Roman Catholic Church.[123] In Costa Rica, despite a fairly large Protestant minority, the Roman Catholic Apostolic Religion is granted the status of state religion: "The Roman Catholic and Apostolic Religion is the religion of the State, which contributes to its maintenance, without preventing the free exercise in the Republic of other forms of worship that are not opposed to universal morality or good customs".[124] This phrase "Catholic and Apostolic" is a reference to the Nicene Creed, which reads:

Monaco (1962); and (by implication) the New Fundamental Law of the State of Vatican City (2000).

[119] See the New Fundamental Law of the State of Vatican City (2000). Nonetheless, the state of the Vatican City and the Holy See – the Episcopal See, in this particular case assumed by the Pope – are commonly distinguished from each other. Interestingly, it is the Holy See and not the State of the Vatican City that maintains diplomatic relations with other states or which negotiates concordats, treaties, agreements and the like.

[120] See also the Concordat between Malta and the Holy See of 3 February 1993.

[121] See art. 2, paras. (1) and (2), of the Const. of Malta (1964).

[122] Jean Daudelin & W.E. Hewitt, *Churches and Politics in Latin America: Catholicism at the Crossroads*, 16 Third World Quarterly (1995), p. 221.

[123] See also *infra*, under State Churches and the next Chapter, under state-supported churches.

[124] Art. 75 of the Const. of Costa Rica (1949).

> We believe in one God, the Father, the almighty, maker of heaven and earth, and of all things seen and unseen. We believe in one Lord, Jesus Christ, the only Son of God, eternally begotten of the Father, God from God, Light from Light, true God from true God, begotten not made, of one Being with the Father. Through him all things were made. For us men, and for our salvation he came down from heaven; by the power of the Holy Spirit he became incarnate of the Virgin Mary, and was made man. For our sake he was crucified under Pontius Pilate; he suffered death and was buried. On the third day he rose again in accordance with the Scriptures; he ascended into heaven and is seated at the right hand of the Father. He will come again in glory to judge the living and the dead, and his kingdom will have no end. We believe in the Holy Spirit, the Lord, the giver of life, who proceeds from the Father (and the Son). With the Father and the Son together is worshipped and glorified. He has spoken through the prophets. *We believe in one holy catholic and apostolic Church.* We acknowledge one baptism for the forgiveness of sins. We look for the resurrection of the dead, and the life of the world to come. Amen.[125]

Notwithstanding profound denominational conflicts as to the exact interpretation, the phrase "One, Holy, Catholic and Apostolic Church" (emphasizing the unity, holiness, universality and apostolicism of the Christian Church) is of course a commonly used formula in the various Christian denominations. In the present constitutional context (Costa Rica), however, this phrase is clearly used to endorse the Catholic Church as reference is made to Roman Catholicism and to the Holy See. Until very recently, the Constitution of Bolivia stated: "The State recognizes and upholds the Roman Catholic Apostolic Religion…Relations with the Catholic Church shall be governed by concordats and agreements between the Bolivian State and the Holy See".[126] In early 2009, however, Bolivia disestablished this church and provided for a separation of state and religion.[127]

It must be acknowledged that in order to identify the religious affiliation of the state, it is often necessary to go beyond the constitutional formulations and take into account statutory law and actual state practice. Haiti, for instance, would appear to have disestablished its state religion—Roman Catholicism—with the adoption of the 1987 Constitution.[128] However, the government has never officially renounced the 1860 Concordat between Haiti and the Holy See which formed the basis of the role of the Catholic Church in Haiti and in which Haiti guaranteed to protect the Roman Catholic Church. In fact, the relations between the Republic of Haiti and the Church are still by and large

---

[125] Oxford Dictionary of World Religions, p. 696 (emphasis added).

[126] Art. 3 of the Constitution of Bolivia of 1967 (replaced).

[127] The Political Constitution of Bolivia (2009), which drops the establishment clause and which states in art. 4: "The state is independent from religion". The new Constitution is effective from 7 February 2009, after having been approved by the Bolivarian people in a public referendum on 25 January 2009.

[128] See the Constitution of the Republic of Haiti (1987).

managed in conformance with this Concordat.[129] The Constitution of the Dominican Republic,[130] similarly, appears *prima facie* secular (compared with an earlier version of the Constitution which contained references to the Apostolic Roman Catholic Religion being the dominant religion). It does not establish a state religion and it does not give any indication as to a possible religious identification of the state with religion. Be that as it may, a Concordat between the Dominican Republic and the Holy See endorses Roman Catholicism as the official religion and grants the Roman Catholic Church important privileges.[131]

Lutheranism

Evangelical Lutheranism is the state religion of Norway. The Constitution of Norway proclaims: "The Evangelical-Lutheran religion shall remain the official religion of the State. The inhabitants professing it are bound to bring up their children in the same".[132] The King of Norway is the official protector of the Lutheran religion.[133] Moreover, the "King ordains all public church services and public worship, all meetings and assemblies dealing with religious matters, and ensures that public teachers of religion follow the norms prescribed for them".[134] In various other countries the Lutheran Church is established as state church.[135]

Eastern Orthodoxy

The manner of endorsement of Eastern Orthodoxy by Greece can be considered rather unique. The Constitution of Greece establishes the Eastern Orthodox Church of Christ as its "prevailing religion" rather than as its state or official religion. The constitutional provision in question reads:

1. The prevailing religion in Greece is that of the Eastern Orthodox Church of Christ. The Orthodox Church of Greece, acknowledging our Lord Jesus Christ as its head, is inseparably united in doctrine with the Great Church of Christ in Constantinople and with every other Church of Christ of the same doctrine, observing unwaveringly, as they do, the holy apostolic and synodal canons and sacred traditions. It is autocephalous and is administered by the Holy Synod of serving Bishops and the Permanent Holy Synod originating thereof and assembled as specified by the Statutory Charter of the Church in compliance with the provisions of the Patriarchal Tome of June 29, 1850 and the Synodal Act of September 4, 1928.

---

[129] Concordat between Haiti and the Holy See of 28 March 1860.

[130] See the CONSTITUTION OF THE DOMINICAN REPUBLIC (1966).

[131] Concordat between the Dominican Republic and the Holy See of 16 June 1954 (entered into force: 6 August 1954).

[132] Art. 2, para. (2), of the CONSTITUTION OF THE KINGDOM OF NORWAY (1814).

[133] Art. 4 of the CONST. OF NORWAY (1814).

[134] Art. 16 of the CONST. OF NORWAY (1814).

[135] See section 2.3.2, *infra*.

2. The ecclesiastical regime existing in certain districts of the State shall not be deemed contrary to the provisions of the preceding paragraph.
3. The text of the Holy Scripture shall be maintained unaltered. Official translation of the text into any other form of language, without prior sanction by the Autocephalous Church of Greece and the Great Church of Christ in Constantinople, is prohibited.[136]

The term "prevailing religion" is fairly indeterminate. Generally speaking, it could (i) be a special way to denote a state religion; (ii) it could be used to emphasize the fact that the overwhelming majority of the Greeks are adherents of the Orthodox Church;[137] (iii) it could be used as a historically and culturally motivated honorary distinction (the Orthodox Church as *primus inter pares*); or (iv) it could be a *sui generis* constitutional reference (and thus imply something different altogether).[138] The protective and preferential attitude towards Christian Orthodoxy, manifested by the state, goes beyond factual recognition of a predominant religion and arguably even beyond state support.[139] Besides the state's involvement in religious affairs as sanctioned by the Constitution itself, it has to be pointed out that the Greek Orthodox Church exercises important political powers (it plays a prominent role in state ceremonies; it has a significant influence on the educational system; it has a say in the conferring of building permits for religious buildings, etc.) and that the salaries of the clergy are paid by the state.[140]

(ii) *Islam as State Religion*

All Islamic states—Afghanistan, Bahrain, Brunei Darussalam, Iran, Mauritania, Morocco, Oman, Pakistan, Saudi Arabia and Yemen—expressly declare Islam the state religion.[141]

The constitutional provisions regarding Islam as the state religion of the constitutions of Iran and Brunei are unique in that they establish a specific

---

[136] Art. 3 of Constitution of Greece (2001).

[137] This would come down to 'state acknowledgement of religion', something that in itself would not necessarily come down to preferential treatment (see also section 3.3, *infra*, on State Acknowledgment).

[138] Cf. Kyriakos N. Kyriazopoulos, *The "Prevailing Religion" in Greece: Its Meaning and Implications*, 43 Journal of State and Church 511 (2001), p. 525–529.

[139] Cf., *e.g.*, Kyriazopoulos, *ibid.*, p. 525.

[140] Winfried Brugger, *On the Relationship between Structural Norms and Constitutional Rights in Church-State-Relations, in* Religion in the Public Sphere: A Comparative Analysis of German, Israeli, American and International Law (Brugger & Karayanni, eds., Berlin: Springer, 2007), p. 43, speaks for these reasons of a "state church".

[141] Art. 2 of the Const. of Afghanistan (2004); art. 2 of the Const. of Bahrain (2002); art. 3 of the Const. of Brunei Darussalam (1959); art. 12 of the Const. of Iran (1979); art. 5 of the Const. of Mauritania (1991); art. 6 of the Const. of Morocco (1972); art. 2 of the Basic Law of the Sultanate of Oman (1996); art. 2 of the Const. of Pakistan (1973); art. 1 of the Basic Law of Saudi Arabia (1992); and art. 2 of the Const. of Yemen (1990).

branch of Islam as the state religion. Iran is the only state establishing the Shi'a branch of Islam as the official religion and even more specifically: the Twelver sect. Shah Ismail I (1487–1524; r. 1501–1524), founder and first ruler of the Persian Safavid Dynasty, first established Shi'a Islam as the state religion. Presently, the Iranian Constitution declares:

> The official religion of Iran is Islam and the Twelver Ja'fari school, and this principle will remain eternally immutable. Other Islamic schools are to be accorded full respect, and their followers are free to act in accordance with their own jurisprudence in performing their religious rites. These schools enjoy official status in matters pertaining to religious education, affairs of personal status (marriage, divorce, inheritance, and wills) and related litigation in courts of law. In regions of the country where Muslims following any one of these schools constitute the majority, local regulations, within the bounds of the jurisdiction of local councils, are to be in accordance with the respective school, without infringing upon the rights of the followers of other schools.[142]

The Twelvers, adhering to the cult of the 12 Imams descending from Ali,[143] form the largest Shi'a sect. These twelve Imams (not to be confused with the general Islamic notion of 'Imam' as leader of the congregational prayer) are considered "the chosen of God, who direct the destiny of humanity, and preserve and guide the world. Through them lies salvation, and without them is perdition. Those who die without knowing their Imām, die as unbelievers".[144] The differences with other Shi'a schools, the Ismaili and the Zaidi Muslims, pertain predominantly to diverging opinions as to the number and the exact course of succession of the Imams. The Ja'fari school stems from Ja'far al-Sadiq (702–765), the sixth Imam in Twelvers' doctrine (the term Ja'fari is in fact often used in reference to the Twelvers as such or to Shi'a Islam with the exclusion of the Ismaili and the Zaidi sects). The 12th Imam was Muhammad al-Mahdi who disappeared at a very young age. Shi'a doctrine holds that the 'Hidden Imam' will return one day. For the time being, Ayatollahs are to rule on religious matters.[145]

Brunei Darussalam is the only state establishing a specific sect of the Sunni branch as state religion, namely, Shafi'i Islam.[146] Though its constitution points out "Islam" as the state religion, arguably, the same Sunni sect—Shafi'i Islam—is *de facto* specifically endorsed by Malaysia.

---

[142] Art. 12 of the CONST. OF IRAN (1979).

[143] The twelve Imams in Shi'a Islam are: Ali, al-Hasan, al-Husain, Ali Zayn, al-Abidin, Muhammad al-Baqir, Ja'far al-Sadiq, Musa al-Kazim Ali al-Rida, Muhammad al-Taqi, Ali al-Naqi, al-Hasan al-Askari and Muhammad al-Mahdi.

[144] OXFORD DICTIONARY OF WORLD RELIGIONS, p. 483.

[145] Irshad Abdal-Haqq, *Islamic Law: An Overview of Its Origin and Elements, in* UNDERSTANDING ISLAMIC LAW: FROM CLASSIC TO CONTEMPORARY (H.M. Ramadan, ed., Lanham: AltaMira Press, 2006), p. 41.

[146] Art. 3, para. (1), of the CONST. OF BRUNEI DARUSSALAM (1959). The four Sunni *Madhhabs*, schools of Islamic jurisprudence, are Hanafi, Hanbali, Maliki and Shafi'i. The Shafi'i school is

In addition to the 'Islamic states', states that have constitutionally established Islam as the state religion include: Algeria, Bangladesh, Djibouti, Egypt, Iraq, Jordan, Kuwait, Libya, Malaysia, Maldives, Qatar, Tunisia and the United Arab Emirates.[147] Also Somalia can be considered to have established Islam as the state religion. The Constitution for the Somali Democratic Republic (1979) declared Islam the state religion of Somalia;[148] however, this Constitution is without effect as Somalia has not had a stable central government since 1991. The Transitional Federal Charter of the Somali Republic (2004), which is only partially and sluggishly being implemented, reiterates: "Islam shall be the religion of the Somali Republic".[149]

Finally, it must be borne in mind that certain states that have not been discussed yet offer either *de jure* or *de facto* exclusive state support to Islam. Such does not necessarily amount to establishing Islam as the state religion; however, occasionally the form of exclusive state support appears in practice not to differ significantly from states with an established state religion.[150]

(iii) *Buddhism as State Religion*

This section focuses on the notion of Buddhism as a state religion. It will commence with a few remarks on the history of Buddhist empires;[151] subsequently, contemporary examples of states which have established Buddhism will be analysed.

History

Presently there are no 'Buddhist states' but only states that have established Buddhism as a state protected religion. History has seen Buddhist empires and states, starting with the Maurya Empire under Emperor Aśoka the Great

named after Imam al-Shafi'i (Abu Abdullah Muhammad ibn Idrīs al-Shafi'i, 769–820). The Ja'fari school of thought is the recognized Shi'a school of jurisprudence.

[147] Art. 2 of the CONST. OF ALGERIA (1976); art. 2 of the CONSTITUTION OF THE PEOPLE'S REPUBLIC OF BANGLADESH (1972); preamble of the CONSTITUTION OF DJIBOUTI (1992); art. 2 of the CONSTITUTION OF THE ARABIC REPUBLIC OF EGYPT (1971); art. 2 of the CONSTITUTION OF THE REPUBLIC OF IRAQ (2005); art. 2 of the CONSTITUTION OF THE HASHEMITE KINGDOM OF JORDAN (1952); art. 2 of the CONSTITUTION OF THE STATE OF KUWAIT (1962); art. 2 of the CONSTITUTIONAL PROCLAMATION OF LIBYA (1969); art. 3 of the CONST. OF MALAYSIA (1957); art. 10 of the CONST. OF MALDIVES (2008); art. 1 of the PERMANENT CONSTITUTION OF THE STATE OF QATAR (2003); art. 1 of the AMENDED CONSTITUTION OF THE TUNISIAN REPUBLIC (1959; hereinafter: CONST. OF TUNISIA of 1959); and art. 7 of the CONST. OF THE UNITED ARAB EMIRATES (1971).

[148] Art. 3 of the Constitution for the Somali Democratic Republic (1979; without effect).

[149] Art. 8 of the TRANSITIONAL FEDERAL CHARTER OF THE SOMALI REPUBLIC (2004; largely without effect).

[150] This will be discussed in the following Chapter.

[151] The notion of a 'Buddhist state' has not been discussed previously in this study as there are no contemporary Buddhist states but only states with Buddhism as its official religion.

(Emperor from 272–232 BCE), who transformed the religious nature of the Empire of his father, Bindusara (a Hindu and Emperor from 297–272 BCE). Aśoka famously converted, as legend holds,[152] after his victory in the devastating war against Kalinga, an ancient Eastern Kingdom (he gave up warfare afterwards). Buddhism spread rapidly over the Indian subcontinent including Sri Lanka, and later even beyond the subcontinent. It can be contended that "[a] major reason for the rapid spread of Buddhism in [South East] Asia was its acceptance by monarchs who modelled their role on that of the Indian emperor, Aśoka Maurya."[153] Smart argues with special regard to Theravada Buddhism in Sri Lanka:

> It became a civilizational religion, both forming and being formed by the culture of the island. A solid bond related monarchy to the Sangha [i.e. the order of monks]. The king was to keep an eye on the monastic community, in case moral and spiritual abuses became too widespread. The Sangha ensured the prosperity and order of the kingdom. Monarchy contributed in a worldly way to the spiritual health of religion, and religion in a spiritual way to the worldly health of monarchy. Such a pattern was to be followed in Thailand and other Buddhist societies of South and Southeast Asia.[154]

In the centuries after Aśoka's conversion, Buddhism was indeed to become embraced (often fused with elements from Hinduism) by Kings and rulers in Thailand, Burma, Laos and Cambodia.[155] Buddhism subsequently emerged in China at the beginning of the Common Era due to travelling Buddhist monks. Here it took several centuries before this religion became intermingled with the state, rulers and politics. Such happened chiefly during the first centuries of the Tang Dynasty:

> By the time China was unified again in 589, followers of the religion included members of Chinese society at all levels, rulers to the common people. Buddhism was now ready to enter its golden age under the T'ang dynasty (618-907). During its heyday, it provided spiritual protection to the ruling families, economic benefits to the rich and noble, social welfare for needy commoners, and a bewildering array of deities for every believer.[156]

This was all ended by the period of anti-Buddhist persecution (also targeting other foreign religions) instigated by Emperor Tang Wuzong (814–846; r. 840–846). By that time (Chinese) Buddhism, coming from the Chinese

---

[152] Smart, *supra* note 19, p. 75; Oxford Dictionary of World Religions, p. 99.

[153] Oxford Dictionary of World Religions, p. 176; see also Smart, *supra* note 19, p. 75: "Aśoka gave an example of the virtuous king, which was to remain an important ideal both in Hindu and Buddhist tradition".

[154] Smart, *supra* note 19, p. 76

[155] Oxford Dictionary of World Religions, p. 176.

[156] *Ibid.*, p. 173.

mainland, was already introduced and firmly rooted in Korea and Japan. In Korea this happened during the so-called Three Kingdom period (ca. 350–668), though the real zenith of Korean Buddhism arguably took place under the later Goryeo Dynasty (935–1392).[157] The Choson Dynasty (1392–1910), under which Neo-Confucianism was to become the state protected ideology,[158] eventually broke with the Buddhist tradition and introduced anti-Buddhist policies. Buddhism arrived in Japan in the fifth century CE and was to become dominant after Emperor Shōtoku Taishi (574–622) embraced this religion at the end of the sixth century.[159] Also the Malay Archipelago has seen Buddhist Empires, such as the ancient Kingdom of Sri Vijaya on Sumatra, Indonesia (7th–12th century CE).

Present

Presently, Cambodia and Bhutan have proclaimed Buddhism the state religion. The Constitution of the Kingdom of Cambodia declares that Buddhism "shall be the religion of the state." Though the overwhelming majority of Cambodians adhere specifically to the Hinayana branch, the religion in its entirety is officially established.[160] Bhutan, on the other hand, traditionally considered the *Drukpa Kargyupa* school of Tibetan Buddhism (a Lamaistic form of Mahayana Buddhism) the official religion.[161] The recently ratified Constitution (2008) refers, more modestly, to Buddhism as the "spiritual heritage of Bhutan",[162] but retains the influence of the *Druk Gyalpo* (the Dragon King) in matters of religion.[163]

It is debatable whether or not Buddhism is the state religion of Thailand. Constitutionally, Buddhism is identified as a so-called state-supported religion; however, it can be argued that the position of Buddhism in Thailand in effect goes beyond that status and approximates a state religion.[164]

(iv) *Historical State Religions*

Focusing on contemporary constitutional law, there is of course the risk that one overlooks important historical forms of positive state–religion identification. It is beyond the scope of this study and probably impossible to take account of the numerous different historical regimes of state–religion

---

[157] *Ibid.*, p. 175.

[158] Smart, *supra* note 19, p. 431.

[159] Oxford Dictionary of World Religions, p. 174.

[160] Art. 43 of the Constitution of the Kingdom of Cambodia (1993).

[161] Para. II, sec. (a), point (i), of 'Document Four', included in the Royal Decree on the Constitution of the National Assembly of Bhutan (1953).

[162] Art. 3, para. (1), of the Constitution of the Kingdom of Bhutan (2008).

[163] Art. 3, paras. (2) and (4), of the Const. of Bhutan (2008). Para. (3) of the same article stipulates that religious institutions and personalities shall remain *above* politics.

[164] See the following Chapter on state-supported religions.

identification. History has seen many forms of establishment of religion which cannot be traced in present-day constitutional law for the simple reason that the states concerned no longer officially identify with those religions. Solely to give somewhat of an idea of what types of positive state–religion identification have existed in past times, some of these historical regimes are highlighted in what follows.

Eastern religio-philosophical systems of belief such as Confucianism and Taoism serve as good examples in the present context. Though we cannot, presently, discern a 'Confucian state' or a state with Confucianism as its official belief,[165] history has definitely seen those forms of state–religion identification. Emperor Ming (28–75) of the Han Dynasty turned Confucianism into the state-protected cult of China in 59 CE. Smart explains that "[o]fferings were to be made to K'ung [i.e. Confucius], and these were linked to state ceremonies in which the emperor made sacrifices to Heaven."[166] The basic Confucian writings, which perfectly lend themselves to that purpose because of the important emphasis in these works on good conduct and good governance,[167] formed the main substance of the civil service examinations.[168] It has been noted that the Confucian Classics "were by far the most important moral and intellectual influence in Chinese society, memorized by every student, tested in the imperial examinations that led to civil office, extensively quoted as a matter of course in government documents as well as private literary writings."[169] An examination system strongly centred upon Confucian ideology was to be officially abandoned as late as 1905.[170] Taoism has, at intervals, been the state protected belief of the Chinese empire, for instance (together with Buddhism) under Kao-tsung (or Gaozong; r. 649–683) of the Tang Dynasty.[171]

Following the Meiji Restoration of the Japanese imperial government in 1868, Shintoism was established as the official religion of the empire of Japan. 'State Shinto', which lasted until the end of the Second World War, sought to separate Shintoism from Buddhism so as to weaken the influence of the latter and to subsequently position Shintoism as a compulsory aspect of the Japanese ethos and identity.[172] On 1 January 1946, after having lost the war, Emperor

[165] Singapore endorses Confucian-ethical teachings through its state school system.

[166] Smart, *supra* note 19, p. 115.

[167] See Confucius, Analects, particularly Book II: "K'ung said: 'The ruler who governs the state through virtue is like the pole star, which stays put while other stars revolve round it'… K'ung said, 'If you control the people by government acts and keep them in line with law and order, they will refrain from doing wrong, but they will not have a sense of honour or shame. But if you lead them through virtue and regulate them by the laws of propriety, then they will have a sense of shame and will attain goodness'" (transl. A. Waley, The Analects of Confucius, London, 1964).

[168] Smart & Hecht, *supra* note 95, p. 331.

[169] Oxford Dictionary of World Religions, p. 231.

[170] Smart & Hecht, *supra* note 95, p. 344.

[171] Smart, *supra* note 19, p. 120.

[172] *Ibid.* pp. 452–455.

Hirohito (Shōwa), under the influence of the American military authorities,[173] separated Shinto and state and officially denounced some of the metaphysical claims made under the Meiji rule,[174] stating:

> The ties between Us and Our people have always stood upon mutual trust and affection. They do not depend upon mere legends and myths. They are not predicated on the false conception that the Emperor is divine, and that the Japanese people are superior to other races and fated to rule the world.[175]

Zoroastrianism was the (*de facto*) state religion under the Persian Achaemenid Dynasty (6th–4th century BCE) and much later it was to become the official religion of the Persian Sassanid Dynasty (226–651). A Sikh empire, to give another example, ruled the Punjab under Maharaja Ranjit Singh (r. 1799–1839). This empire—though *de facto* secular—was built on the foundations of the Sikh Confederation and came to an end in 1849 after the British triumphed in the Anglo–Sikh Wars.

Finally, many of the ancient religions show a profound nexus between kingship and sacred rituals which render official status to the religions involved. The Inca emperors of Peru, for instance, were considered mediators between the Gods and their subjects. Smart argues:

> The imperial ideology represented the emperor (the Inca) as responsible for the welfare of the empire, and so he was the chief point of intersection of his subjects and the great gods. He had to preside over earthly affairs during the present cosmic cycle; so he was himself a god, the offspring of the Sun, which was the great deity at the heart of the ritual complex at the temple of Cuzco.[176]

The Aztec emperors of Mexico, similarly, presided over the most important rites of the empire.[177] Notions of divine kingship can be traced in ancient Mesopotamian, Egyptian and Canaanite religions.[178] Of course, many of the traditional African religions embraced notions of divine kingship too (e.g. the Ashanti in Ghana). Smart argues in this context: "kingship is typically regarded as a sacred institution, and in societies which are united under the rule of a king he will himself have priestly functions in representing the divine order in the world over which he rules..."[179]

---

173 Smart & Hecht, *supra* note 95, pp. 345.

174 See *Kokutai ni Hongi* (or the Cardinal Principles of the National Entity of Japan), as redefined under the Meiji era, summing up the religio-ideological principles of the regime (Smart & Hecht, *supra* note 95, pp. 345 and 350).

175 Imperial Rescript (part of the *Ningen-sengen* or Humanity Declaration) of 1 January 1946, issued by Emperor Hirohito (Shōwa).

176 Smart, *supra* note 19, p. 179.

177 *Ibid.*, 185.

178 *Ibid.*, pp. 197 and 202.

179 *Ibid.*, p. 303.

2.3.2 *State Churches and National Churches*

The notion of a 'state church' is exclusively associated with the relationships between states and Christianity.[180] All current state churches are forms of national endorsement of a specific Christian denomination rather than of a general, non-affiliated 'Christian Church'. The concept of a 'state church' is largely a European phenomenon and is inextricably linked with the history of Europe's royal houses. Historically, it may be argued that under a state church regime the state had significant influence over religious affairs compared with a state religion regime, under which the religion in question may enjoy a significant degree of autonomy. One might think in this context of those states that established Catholicism as state religion and entered into detailed Concordats with the Holy See so as to ensure that the Catholic Churches in these countries remain answerable to the Vatican rather than to the state in question.

Nowadays, the monarch's connections to the established church are of course often far more symbolic. It should also be reiterated that in states in which a specific Christian denomination is *de jure* established as the state *religion*, the related Christian church has, as a rule, an official, national character and enjoys certain privileges. The latter naturally further blurs the distinction.

Constitutionally recognized 'state churches' and so-called 'national churches' include: the Roman Catholic Church, the Evangelical Lutheran Church, the Armenian Apostolic Holy Church, the (Anglican) Church of England and the (Presbyterian) Church of Scotland.

(i) *Roman Catholic Church*

From the above discussion on state religions it follows that Roman Catholicism, in predominantly Catholic states with a constitutional establishment clause, is as a rule established as the state religion and not, strictly speaking, as a state church. This finds it explanation in the fact that the Holy See is vested with the central government of (the whole of) this church. The Constitution of Liechtenstein deviates—*de jure*—from this pattern as it explicitly proclaims that the Roman Catholic Church "is the *State Church* and as such shall enjoy the full protection of the State".[181] The Constitution, furthermore, lists the

---

[180] The notion 'Church' (from the Greek: *kuriakon*, i.e. 'Lord's [house]'), as such, is of course commonly though not exclusively associated with Christianity. "Church" is used 129 times in the New Testament of the Christian Bible, most famously in Matthew 16:18 (Holy Bible, English Standard Version): "And I tell you, you are Peter, and on this rock I will build my church, and the gates of hell shall not prevail against it."

[181] Art. 37, para. (2), of the Constitution of the Principality of Liechtenstein (1921), emphasis added.

protection of the "religious interests of the people" among the highest responsibilities of the state.[182]

(ii) *Evangelical Lutheran Church*

The Evangelical Lutheran Church is established as the state church in Denmark, Finland and Iceland. The Constitution of Denmark speaks of the Evangelical Lutheran Church as the "established church". The provision reads in full: "The Evangelical Lutheran Church shall be the Established Church of Denmark, and, as such, it shall be supported by the State".[183] The Danish Constitution provides furthermore that the "constitution of the Established Church shall be laid down by Statute" (the same applies to those religious bodies dissenting from the Established Church).[184] The Minister for Ecclesiastical Affairs is the highest administrative authority of the state church. State support comes down to providing funds towards clergy salaries and pensions and the collection of so-called church taxes.

Finland's endorsement of two churches is unique, especially since one of the two churches is a minority church (which finds its explanation in Finland's history of being part of the Russian empire until the end of the First World War). The Constitution of Finland and the Church Acts endorse the Evangelical Lutheran Church of Finland (with, nominally, over 80 per cent of the Finns adhering to this church) and the Orthodox Church of Finland (with just over 1 per cent of the Finns belonging to this church), not as clear-cut state churches (as the Evangelical Lutheran Church had been prior to independence),[185] but rather as 'national churches'.[186] A 'national church' is a church that claims national pastoral jurisdiction, whose claim may or may not be endorsed by the state (the endorsement of a national church can thus be distinguished from the more far-reaching establishment of a state church or official religion). Finland undoubtedly endorses these two churches as national churches: it collects church income taxes on their behalf (payment can only be evaded by officially leaving the church), grants other financial privileges (for instance, the two churches are granted a share of the corporate tax revenues, and the

---

[182] Art. 14 of the CONST. OF LIECHTENSTEIN (1921).

[183] Art. 4 of the CONSTITUTION OF THE KINGDOM OF DENMARK ACT (1953; hereinafter: CONST. OF DENMARK of 1953).

[184] Artt. 66 and 69 of the CONST. OF DENMARK (1953).

[185] The Church of Sweden (until 1809) and the Evangelical Lutheran Church of Finland (until 1919; the first signs of disestablishment can already be perceived in the Church Act of 1870) have been state churches in Finland in the past.

[186] Sec. 76 of the CONSTITUTION OF FINLAND (1999) refers to the Church Act: "(1) Provisions on the organization and administration of the Evangelic Lutheran Church are laid down in the Church Act. (2) The legislative procedure for enactment of the Church Act and the right to submit legislative proposals relating to the Church Act are governed by the specific provisions in that Code".

wages of military and prison chaplains are paid by the state) and engages in a form of cooperation under which the two churches provide such public services as the registration of deaths, births and marriages of church members.

Finally, also the Constitution of the Republic of Iceland provides that the Evangelical Lutheran Church is the state church and that it consequently shall support and protect this church.[187] Interestingly, leaving the church in Iceland will not suffice if one wishes to avoid paying church contributions as non-believers are to pay their dues to the University of Iceland.[188] Ministers of religion are civil servants and, consequently, paid by the state.

(iii) *Armenian Apostolic Holy Church*

The public role of Christianity in Armenia has a long history as Armenia was the first state to establish Christianity as the state religion at the very beginning of the fourth century (ca. 301), after King Tiridates III was converted by St. Gregory 'the Illuminator'[189] (a full decade before Roman Emperor Constantine's notorious conversion to Christianity and eight decades before Theodosius' establishment of Roman Catholicism as the state religion of the Roman Empire). Armenia's Constitution presently formally separates the church from the state.[190] However, constitutional and statutory law simultaneously—and indeed rather contradictorily—grant the Armenian Apostolic Holy Church a special status as "national church". The Constitution provides:

> The Republic of Armenia recognises the exclusive historical mission of the Armenian Apostolic Holy Church as a national church, in the spiritual life, development of the national culture and preservation of the national identity of the people of Armenia...The relations of the Republic of Armenia and the Armenian Apostolic Holy Church may be regulated by the law.[191]

The Law on Freedom of Conscience reaffirms the special status of the Armenian Apostolic Holy Church: "Being cognizant of the Armenian Apostolic Church as the national Church of the Armenian people and as an important bulwark for the edification of its spiritual life and national preservation...".[192] Moreover, while the law seeks to ensure that the activities of other religious organizations can be scrutinized by the state (by subjecting them to a regime of registration), the Armenian Apostolic Holy Church is exclusively granted a range of special privileges and exemptions:

---

187 Art. 62 of the Constitution of the Republic of Iceland (1944).

188 Art. 64, para. (3), of the Const. of Iceland (1944).

189 Oxford Dictionary of World Religions, p. 89, dates the event of the conversion to ca. 294 CE.

190 Art. 8.1, para. (1), of the Constitution of the Republic of Armenia (2005); see also art. 17 of the Law on the Freedom of Conscience and Religious Organizations of 17 June 1991 (amended 1997 and 2001; hereinafter: "1991 Armenian Law").

191 Art. 8.1, para. (2) and (4), of the Const. of Armenia (2005).

192 Preamble of the 1991 Armenian Law (*supra* note 190).

The State shall not obstruct the following efforts which are the monopoly of the Armenian Church:

- To freely preach and proselyte on the whole territory of the Republic of Armenia. The teachings of the Armenian Apostolic Church can be officially covered in mass media outlets or during mass-scale events only with approval of the Armenian Apostolic Church.
- To preach and disseminate her faith freely throughout the Republic of Armenia.
- To re-create her historical traditions, structures, organization, dioceses, and communities.
- To construct new churches, make historical churches belonging to it to function, whether at the request of the faithful or on its own initiative.
- To contribute to the spiritual edification of the Armenian people and to carry out the same in the state educational institutes within the law.
- To take practical measures which enhance the moral standards of the Armenian people.
  To expend benevolent and charitable activities.
- To have permanent religious representatives in hospitals, shelters for senior citizens and invalids, military units, detention facilities, including isolators.[193]

It follows that the Armenian Church may freely disseminate its faith throughout the state, whereas proselytism is forbidden to other religions.[194] It is difficult to reconcile such privileges and such a degree of state protection and endorsement of a single church with a separation of state and religion.

2.3.3 *Regional Establishment*

In some states the issue of state–religion identification is not a national or federal matter but is left at the discretion of the constituent states or provinces. This, when it leads to the situation that some constituent parts have an established religion while others have not, could be referred to as 'regional establishment'.

(i) *The Anglican Church of England and the Presbyterian Church of Scotland*

The United Kingdom in its entirety does not have a state religion. The United Kingdom of Great Britain and Northern Ireland is amongst the states that reflect a 'multiple regime of state–religion identification'. Each of the constituent countries has defined its own approach: England and Scotland have an established and national church respectively; whereas in Northern Ireland and Wales the (Anglican) Church of Ireland and the (Anglican) Church in Wales have been disestablished since 1871 and 1920 respectively.[195]

---

193 Art. 17 of the 1991 Armenian Law (*supra* note 190).

194 Moreover, art. 8 of the 1991 Armenian Law (*supra* note 190) leaves no doubt about this.

195 Irish Church Disestablishment Act 1869 (entry into effect: 1 January 1871); and the Welsh Church Act 1914 (entry into effect 1920). The Church in Wales was the Church of England until the moment of disestablishment. Taylor argues that the Church in Wales maintains some of the

(ii) *Regional Endorsement: the Swiss Approach*

Switzerland similarly reflects a multiple regime of state–religion identification. The Constitution of Switzerland does not identify a state religion for the entire federation. It rather declares the regulation of the relationship between the state and religion a "cantonal matter".[196] The Swiss Constitution, however, stipulates a degree of 'shared' involvement from the federal state in religious affairs as it added: "The Federation and the Cantons may, within the framework of their powers, take measures to maintain public peace between the members of the various religious communities".[197]

As a result of the decentralisation of the regulation of state–religion relationships, different Christian churches—Roman Catholic, Old Catholic, or Protestant (Swiss Reformed Church)—are established or preferentially treated by different cantons (occasionally more than one simultaneously). Two out of the 26 cantons have opted for a separation of state and religion (Geneva and Neuchatel). Religious identification and tensions were also at the heart of the actual formation or subdivision of the different cantons as the former canton of Appenzell shows strikingly. Catholic Appenzell Innerrhoden and Protestant Appenzell Ausserrhoden split up into two separate cantons at the end of the 16th century.

(iii) *Other Examples*

Sudan, it may be added at this point, is divided up in terms of state–religion identification into a northern part which officially identifies with Islam and a more secular southern part. It has been outlined already that in Indonesia the Special Region of Yogyakarta is formally a sultanate, whilst Indonesia in its entirety is an unspecified monotheist state. These instances of *de facto* bifurcation are to be distinguished, however, from the 'Swiss approach' in which the federal state expressly delegates, as a matter of policy, the issue of state–religion identification to the different provinces. In the latter instances it is rather a result of religious strife.

2.4 Implications

The objective of this section is to give a more comprehensive overview of the main legal ramifications that delineate the different religious states and other

---

essential characteristics of an established church: Simon J. Taylor, *Disestablished Establishment: High and Earthed Establishment in the Church in Wales*, 18 Journal of Contemporary Religion 227 (2003).

[196] Art. 72, para. (1), of the New Constitution of the Swiss Federation (1999; hereinafter: Const. of Switzerland of 1999).

[197] Art. 72, para. (2), of the Const. of Switzerland (1999).

regimes of positive state–religion identification. A distinction has been made between 'religious states' and states which constitutionally declare a specific religion the state religion. Virtually all religious states declare the religion in question the official religion. Not all states with a state religion expressly position themselves as religious states. It would be tempting to identify religious states with the far positive end of the state–religion identification spectrum. A religious state expressly propagates the fact that the religion in question should play a determinative role within all fields of public authority—perhaps, *prima facie*, more so than states which 'solely' establish a religion as state religion. However, taking into consideration actual state practice in this respect, the issue appears to be far more complicated. The exact position and role of religion in a state can be determined by unveiling the extent to which the state apparatus identifies itself with a single religious doctrine—to what extent is the state, as it were, in service of religion? A crucial indicator in any attempt at determining the place of religion in a state should be the extent to which the legislative, executive and judicial branches of the state are subjected to the normative framework of a single religion. It is when we take these parameters fully into account that we can appreciate the full complexity of the issue of state–religion identification. Some states with a state religion that do not position themselves explicitly as religious states appear to be far more 'religious'—that means, with a perceivably higher degree of interrelation between the state and religion—than some of the religious states. The different arrangements which ensure a strong identification of the state with religion will be discussed in the following paragraphs.[198] These measures include constitutional provisions that ensure a religion–law nexus, measures that cluster together secular and religious institutions, measures that reserve political seats for members of the state religion, royal protection of the state religion and measures that seek to perpetually preserve the status of a religion as state religion.

2.4.1 *Constitutional Religion–Law Nexus*

A constitutional provision declaring that no law may be contrary to the tenets of the state religion is one of the most far-reaching measures of ensuring a positive identification with a single religion. Such a measure seeks to ensure that the state shall be strictly governed by regulations that spring from or are in line with the religion in question. There are various constitutional formulations perceivable to that effect, including the standard phrases 'no law may be contrary to religion *x*' or 'no law may be contrary to the laws of religion *x*'. Other formulations put it positively: 'all laws shall derive from religion *x*' or 'religious laws of religion *x* shall be the principal source for all

[198] The different measures are not mutually exclusive (some states will be discussed more than once under the different headings).

legislation', etc. All these alternatives have in common that they have profound implications for the legislative, the executive and the judicial branches of the state. Put differently, any of these formulations blurs the divisions of state vs. religion, state institutions vs. religious institutions, profane laws vs. religious laws and state courts vs. religious institutions. It is noteworthy that these constitutional arrangements ensuring such a far-reaching identification of the state with the normative principles of a single religion are presently chiefly to be found in states that identify exclusively with Islam. The Islamic adage *al-Islam din wa dawla* (Islam is religion and the state), often used to describe the ideal-typical implications of 'the Islamic state' (namely, a unity of religion and state), sheds some light on this historical nexus.[199]

(i) *No Law Contrary to Islam*

The Islamic Republic of Iran is a regime based on the belief of "[d]ivine revelation and its fundamental role in setting forth the laws".[200] The Constitution of Iran elaborates on this cornerstone of the Islamic state by stipulating that:

> All civil, penal, financial, economic, administrative, cultural, military, political, and other laws and regulations must be based on Islamic criteria. This principle applies absolutely and generally to all articles of the Constitution as well as to all other laws and regulations, and the wise persons of the Guardian Council are judges in this matter.[201]

The functions of the legislature are exercised through the Islamic Consultative Assembly while a Guardian Council is established to safeguard Islamic ordinances by means of examining the compatibility of adopted legislation with Islam.[202] As an additional safeguard, judges of courts are obliged to refrain from executing statutes and regulations of the government that are in conflict with the laws or the norms of Islam.[203] Anyone can at all times demand the annulment of a regulation on the basis of its incompatibility with Islam from the Court of Administrative Justice.[204] The Iranian Constitution provides for numerous additional checks and safeguards ensuring strict compliance with the ordinances of Islam. For instance, the Ministry of Islamic Culture and Guidance, and the Ministry of Intelligence and Security are to monitor religious activity, while an Islamic Revolution Guards Corps safeguards the

---

[199] *E.g.* Ann Elizabeth Mayer, *Law and Religion in the Muslim Middle East*, 35 American Journal of Comparative Law (1987), pp. 127–130, on this notion. For a critical discussion of this concept, see Bassam Tibi, *Post-Bipolar Order in Crisis: The Challenge of Politicised Islam, in* Islam: Critical Concepts in Sociology (Bryan S. Turner, ed., London: Routledge, 2003), pp. 153–157; and Bassam Tibi, The Challenge of Fundamentalism: Political Islam and the New World Disorder (Berkeley: University of California Press, 1998), pp. 159 *et seq.*

[200] Art. 2, para. (2), of the Const. of Iran (1979).

[201] Art. 4 of the Const. of Iran (1979).

[202] Artt. 58, 64, and 91 of the Const. of Iran (1979).

[203] Art. 170 of the Const. of Iran (1979).

[204] Art. 170, 2nd sentence, of the Const. of Iran (1979).

Islamic Revolution and its achievements.[205] The army of the Islamic Republic of Iran is established as an "Islamic Army", which is defined as an army that is "committed to Islamic ideology and the people"; it must "recruit into its service individuals who have faith in the objectives of the Islamic Revolution and are devoted to the cause of realizing its goals".[206]

The Government of Saudi Arabia claims to derive its power from the Holy Quran and the Prophet's tradition. Governance is based on and must at all times remain in accordance with Shari'a law.[207] The Constitution identifies the Quran and the *Sunnah* (Muhammad's sayings and the religious examples he set) as Saudi Arabia's true Constitution.[208] The Constitution provides, furthermore, that "Saudi society will be based on the principle of adherence to God's command" and that the "state protects Islam; it implements its Shari'ah; it orders people to do right and shun evil; it fulfils the duty regarding God's call".[209] In terms of legislative action this means the following: the Council of Ministers proposes regulations in accordance with Shari'a law; the King ensures that the Prime Minister and Ministers indeed implement Shari'a law as he ultimately needs to give his consent to the proposed legislation by royal decree.[210] Also the courts are commissioned to apply the rules of the Islamic Shari'a in all cases that are brought before them.[211] The armed forces are under a direct duty to defend the Islamic religion.[212] Compliance with, and the defence of, Islam is ultimately a duty of each and every citizen.[213]

Pakistani laws, similarly, must be in conformance with Islam. The Constitution of Pakistan provides: "All existing laws shall be brought in conformity with the Injunctions of Islam as laid down in the Holy Quran and Sunnah…and no law shall be enacted which is repugnant to such Injunctions".[214] The Federal Shari'a Court may, either on its own accord or after a petition of a citizen of Pakistan, the Federal Government or a Provincial Government, examine and decide the question whether or not any law or provision of law is indeed repugnant to the 'Injunctions of Islam'. The latter injunctions are laid down, according to the Constitution, in the Holy Quran and Sunnah of the Holy Prophet.[215] If a repugnancy is observed, the law has to be brought into conformity with Islam or ceases to have effect.[216] A Council of Islamic Ideology

[205] Art. 150 of the Const. of Iran (1979).
[206] Art. 144 of the Const. of Iran (1979).
[207] Artt. 7–8 of the Basic Law of Saudi Arabia (1992).
[208] Art. 1 of the Basic Law of Saudi Arabia (1992).
[209] Artt. 11 and 23 of the Basic Law of Saudi Arabia (1992).
[210] Artt. 55, 57 and 67 of the Basic Law of Saudi Arabia (1992).
[211] Art. 48 of the Basic Law of Saudi Arabia (1992).
[212] Art. 33 of the Basic Law of Saudi Arabia (1992).
[213] Art. 34 of the Basic Law of Saudi Arabia (1992). People are, moreover, to be raised and educated in the Islamic faith (artt. 9 and 13 of the Basic Law of Saudi Arabia of 1992).
[214] Art. 227, para. (1), of the Const. of Pakistan (1973).
[215] Art. 203D, para. (1), of the Const. of Pakistan (1973).
[216] Art. 203D, para. (3), of the Const. of Pakistan (1973).

(or the 'Islamic Council') is established to advise on the conformity of laws with Islam. It makes recommendations "as to the ways and means of enabling and encouraging the Muslims of Pakistan to order their lives individually and collectively in all respects in accordance with the principles and concepts of Islam as enunciated in the Holy Quran and Sunnah".[217] State laws, including the penal code, reflect Shari'a law and are enforced by the Shari'a Courts.

Similar measures are in place in the Republic of Maldives. The Constitution of Maldives provides that "[n]o law contrary to any tenet of Islam shall be enacted in the Maldives".[218] The Legislature, Executive and Judiciary are all instructed to ensure that Islamic tenets are respected at all times.[219] Only Muslims can become citizens of Republic of Maldives and all citizens are obliged to "preserve and protect the State religion of Islam".[220]

Iraq and Afghanistan are governed by Islamic principles as well. The Iraqi Constitution identifies Islam as a fundamental source of legislation and stipulates, moreover, that no law that contradicts the established provisions of Islam may be adopted (a combination, in other words, of the positive and negative alternative of anchoring a state in Islamic principles).[221] The judges of the Federal Supreme Court should consist of, besides other judges, a number of experts in Islamic jurisprudence.[222] The Constitution of Afghanistan provides that "no law can be contrary to the beliefs and provisions of the sacred religion of Islam".[223] Courts, moreover, are explicitly instructed to apply Shi'a law to (certain) cases between members of the Shi'a sect.[224]

Perhaps a weaker provision than 'no law shall be contrary to Islam/Islamic law', is the Algerian constitutional provision that forbids state institutions to initiate or engage in practices that are contrary to Islamic morality.[225] A High Islamic Council, affiliated to the office of the President, is established to promote legal interpretations of Islamic law and to provide its opinion on religious laws.[226]

(ii) *Religion as Sole or Principal Source for Legislation*

Some Constitutions demand that all laws derive from, or are based on, Islam or Islamic law. The Constitution of Mauritania, for instance, considers the precepts

---

[217] Art. 230, para. (1), sec. (a), in conjunction with artt. 228–229 of the CONST. OF PAKISTAN (1973).

[218] Art. 10 of the CONST. OF MALDIVES (2008); in the article listing the powers and authority of the President it is reiterated that nothing shall be done contrary to Shari'a law (art. 100).

[219] Artt. 70, 100, and 142 of the CONST. OF MALDIVES (2008).

[220] Artt. 9 and 67, para. (g), of the CONST. OF MALDIVES (2008).

[221] Art. 2, para. (1), of the CONST. OF IRAQ (2005).

[222] Art. 89 of the CONST. OF IRAQ (2005).

[223] Art. 3 of the CONST. OF AFGHANISTAN (2004).

[224] Art. 131 of the CONST. OF AFGHANISTAN (2004).

[225] Art. 9 of the CONST. OF ALGERIA (1976).

[226] Art. 171 of the CONST. OF ALGERIA (1976).

of Islam “the sole source of law”.[227] A High Islamic Council, whose members are appointed by and who are to cooperate with the President of the Republic, is established to advise on the issue of conformity of the laws and regulations with Islamic law.[228] The Constitution of Yemen similarly proclaims that Islamic Shari’a is the source of all legislation.[229] Yemen’s policy as to its domestic economy should be founded on the principle of “Islamic social justice”.[230] The issue of inheritance, the “rights and duties” of women and the issue of “crime and punishment” are directly governed by Shari’a law according to the Constitution.[231] Defending the Muslim religion is considered a “sacred duty” for everyone.[232]

The Constitution of Bahrain provides that the Islamic Shari’a is “a principal source for legislation”.[233] The Constitution indicates that the issues of inheritance and the “duties of women towards the family” are directly governed by Shari’a law[234] and that the state is to safeguard the “Islamic heritage”.[235] The Bahraini Ministry of Islamic Affairs has an important role in fulfilling these matters while a High Council for Islamic Affairs is concerned with the appointment of clerics. The Constitution of Egypt similarly holds that Islamic jurisprudence is “the principal source of legislation”.[236] It provides, again similar to the Bahraini Constitution, more particularly that the “proper coordination between the duties of women towards the family and her work in the society, considering her equal with man in the fields of political, social, cultural and economic life” is not to violate the rules of Islamic jurisprudence.[237] The courts are instructed to apply Shari’a as interpreted by the Egyptian Government. Shari’a is also the “principal” source of legislation in the United Arab Emirates.[238] Moreover, the foreign policy of the United Arab Emirates is expressly directed towards support for Islamic causes.[239] Shari’a law is applicable to family affairs and criminal offences and enforced by Shari’a Courts.

Finally, Oman and Somalia render Shari’a the “basis” and “basic source” for legislation respectively.[240] Oman lists compliance with Shari’a law also under

---

227 Preamble of the Const. of Mauritania (1991).
228 Art. 94 of the Const. of Mauritania (1991).
229 Art. 3 of the Const. of Yemen (1990).
230 Art. 7 of the Const. of Yemen (1990).
231 Art. 23, 31 and 46 of the Const. of Yemen (1990).
232 Art. 59 of the Const. of Yemen (1990).
233 Art. 2 of the Const. of Bahrain (2002).
234 Art. 5, paras. (b) and (d), of the Const. of Bahrain (2002).
235 Art. 6 of the Const. of Bahrain (2002).
236 Art. 2 of the Const. of Egypt (1971). Prior to 1980, Shari’a had more modestly been “a source” of legislation.
237 Art. 11 of the Const. of Egypt (1971).
238 Art. 7 of the Const. of the United Arab Emirates (1971).
239 Art. 12 of the Const. of the United Arab Emirates (1971).
240 Art. 2 of the Basic Law of the Sultanate of Oman (1996); and art. 8, para. (2), of the Transitional Federal Charter of the Somali Republic (2004). Caveat: Somalia is without a stable central government since 1991; the 1979 Constitution for the Somali Democratic

the political principles of the state;[241] while the issue of inheritance is directly governed by Shari'a.[242]

(iii) *Religion as a Source for Legislation*

An analytical distinction can be made between those regimes that render Islam and/or Islamic Shari'a the only/principal source for legislation and those that consider Islam simply *a* source for legislative action, as under the latter regime there is, in theory, a wider scope for legislative action, including legislative acts not strictly based on the normative framework provided by the official religion.

Kuwait is among those states with Islam as the state religion that provide that Islamic Shari'a shall be "a main source" of legislation, thereby indicating that there are other sources that could be drawn upon in principle.[243] That being said, a 'Higher Advisory Committee on Completion of the Application of Islamic Shari'a Provisions' is established to advise on how to fully implement Shari'a law and how to bring all regulations in conformity with Shari'a law. Inheritance issues are directly governed by Shari'a.[244] Qatar similarly considers Islam and Shari'a law main sources of legislation.[245] Inheritance issues are directly governed by Shari'a and Shari'a is also applicable to other matters of personal status such as marriage and divorce.[246] Syria, though not an Islamic state or a state with Islam as the state religion, considers Islamic jurisprudence "a main source of legislation" as well.[247]

It must be acknowledged that many measures can be discerned that fall short of the above categories—constitutional provisions that require that laws have a sound basis in Islam—but that are nonetheless quite comparable. The Constitution of Bangladesh, for instance, provides that the principle of "absolute trust and faith in the Almighty Allah" is to constitute the fundamental principle of state policy and shall be the basis of all state actions.[248] The Ministry of Religious Affairs, contrary to some of the examples mentioned before, is not exclusively concerned with Islamic affairs. The constitutional laws of Libya also do not explicitly require that all laws be based on Islam or

Republic is without effect. The TRANSITIONAL FEDERAL CHARTER OF THE SOMALI REPUBLIC (2004) is sluggishly being implemented. In the absence of a well-established federal system of judiciary, Shari'a law is -often in conjunction with other traditional laws- partly applicable and enforced by the courts.

241 Art. 10 of the BASIC LAW OF THE SULTANATE OF OMAN (1996).

242 Art. 11 of the BASIC LAW OF THE SULTANATE OF OMAN (1996).

243 Art. 2 of the CONST. OF KUWAIT (1962).

244 Art. 18, para. (2), of the CONST. OF KUWAIT (1962).

245 Art. 1 of the CONST. OF QATAR (2003).

246 Art. 51 of the CONST. OF QATAR (2003).

247 Art. 3, para. (2), of the CONSTITUTION OF THE SYRIAN ARAB REPUBLIC (1973; hereinafter: CONST. OF SYRIA of 1973).

248 Art. 8, paras. (1) and (1A), of the CONST. OF BANGLADESH (1972).

Islamic law.[249] However, the 1977 *Declaration on the Establishment of the Authority of the People* provides that the Holy Quran is "the Constitution of the Socialist People's Libyan Arab Jamahiriya".[250] In another Proclamation it is provided that:

> ...judgements of the members of the Jamahiriyan society are *based on sacred law*, religion or custom, the terms of which are stable, unchangeable and for which there can be no substitute. They declare that religion is an absolute belief in the divinity and a sacred spiritual value. It is personal to each person and common to everyone. It is a direct relationship with the Creator, without intermediary.[251]

The Constitution of Jordan does not explicitly require that laws be based on Islam either. That said, it should be noted that the Constitution identifies certain matters which are to be governed directly by Shari'a law: (i) matters of personal status of Muslims (matters of religion, marriage and inheritance);[252] (ii) cases concerning blood money (*Diyya*) where the two parties are Muslims or where one of the parties is not a Muslim and the two parties consent to the jurisdiction of the Shari'a Courts; and (iii) matters pertaining to Islamic *Waqfs* (religious endowments or trusts, dealing with the designation and administration of religious premises).[253] Shari'a Courts rule exclusively on these cases and are commissioned to apply the provisions of Shari'a law in the exercise of their jurisdiction.[254]

2.4.2 *Clustering Profane and Sacred Authority*

In the above, measures have been discussed that seek to ensure a direct nexus between state law and religion. Alternatively, or in combination with the above measures, a fairly far-reaching degree of positive state identification with religion can be ensured by merging state bodies or public offices with religious institutions.

A perfect example is the State of the Vatican City. The Pope, leader of the Roman Catholic Church, is *ex officio* simultaneously Head of State of the Vatican City, Head of the Government of the State of the Vatican City and exercises (*de jure*) a form of absolute authority over the legislative, executive

---

[249] Libya does not have a genuine constitution; Libya's constitutional law is composed of different proclamations, resolutions and charters.

[250] Art. 2 of the Declaration on the Establishment of the Authority of the People of 2 March 1977.

[251] Art. 10 of the Great Green Charter of Human Rights of the Jamahiriyan Era (1988), emphasis added.

[252] Art. 103 in conjunction with art. 105, para. (i), of the CONST. OF JORDAN (1952).

[253] Art. 105, paras. (ii) and (iii) in conjunction with art. 107 of the CONST. OF JORDAN (1952).

[254] Art. 106 of the CONST. OF JORDAN (1952). The Hanafi School of Islamic jurisprudence is the state-sanctioned interpretation of religious laws and is to be followed in relation to matters of personal status.

and judicial branches of state power.[255] Indeed, practically all state acts revolve around the interests of the Holy See.

The Iranian Constitution reserves a position of supreme political authority for the "Religious Leader" (presently Grand Ayatollah Ali Khamenei),[256] the highest religio-political position in Iran. Among the powers and task directly attributed by the Constitution to the Supreme Religious Leader are the following:

> 1. Delineation of the general policies of the Islamic Republic of Iran after consultation with the Nation's Exigency Council.
> 2. Supervision over the proper execution of the general policies of the system.
> 3. Issuing decrees for national referenda.
> 4. Assuming supreme command of the Armed Forces.
> 5. Declaration of war and peace and the mobilization of the Armed Forces.
> 6. Appointment, dismissal, and resignation of:
>   a. the religious men on the Guardian Council,
>   b. the supreme judicial authority of the country,
>   c. the head of the radio and television network of the Islamic Republic of Iran,
>   d. the chief of the joint staff,
>   e. the chief commander of the Islamic Revolution Guards Corps, and
>   f. the supreme commanders of the Armed Forces.
> 7. Resolving differences between the three wings of the Armed Forces and regulation of their relations.
> 8. Resolving the problems which cannot be solved by conventional methods, through the Nation's Exigency Council.
> 9. Signing the decree formalizing the election of the President of the Republic by the people. The suitability of candidates for the Presidency of the Republic, with respect to the qualifications specified in the Constitution, must be confirmed before elections take place by the Guardian Council, and, in the case of the first term of a President, by the Leadership.
> 10. Dismissal of the President of the Republic, with due regard for the interests of the country, after the Supreme Court holds him guilty of the violation of his constitutional duties, or after a vote of the Islamic Consultative Assembly testifying to his incompetence…
> 11. Pardoning or reducing the sentences of convicts, within the framework of Islamic criteria, on a recommendation from the Head of judicial power.[257]

In the Malay Islamic Monarchy (*Melayu Islam Beraja*) of Brunei Darussalam, the Sultan is both "Head of Religion" as well as "Supreme Executive Authority" and as such is bestowed with virtually absolute authority over state affairs.[258] Though the Constitution of Brunei Darussalam calls into being the office of

---

[255] Art. 1 of the New Fundamental Law of the State of the Vatican City (2000).
[256] Art. 5 and 107 of the Const. of Iran (1979).
[257] Art. 110 of the Const. of Iran (1979).
[258] Artt. 3–4 of Const. of Brunei Darussalam (1959).

Prime Minister, the Constitution stipulates that he shall be directly answerable to the Sultan "for the exercise of executive authority".[259] Besides a Prime Minister there "shall be such other Ministers as His Majesty the Sultan and Yang Di-Pertuan may appoint".[260] The *National Philosophy* of Brunei Darussalam, as proclaimed by the Government of Brunei, further defines and outlines this regime of *Melayu Islam Beraja*. The legal-political implications of this regime and the crucial role of Islam within it are extensively elaborated upon in this proclamation:

> Islam is tolerant of all religions so the MIB philosophy cannot be viewed as a force which stifles the practice of other religions. Rather it is a vehicle by which other religions can carry on as usual their religious practices and rites with the respects and peace they deserve. Brunei Darussalam as an Islamic nation honours everything which embodies Islam in a moderate way. It observes special days in the Islamic calendar such as Hari Raya Aidil Fitri and Hari Raya Puasa and important events in the Islamic history such as the birth of Prophet Muhammad (peace be upon him), Hijrah, Nuzul Al-Quran (The Revelation of The Quran) and Isra' Mikraj. The Brunei government also shows its respect during the fasting month of Ramadan when all government officers and staff work only six hours daily (as opposed to the seven an half hours daily of normal working hours outside Ramadan) while all entertainment and sport activities are temporarily suspended. Doa, a very important link to God's blessing, is incorporated in every government function and project. His Majesty also encourages the recital of the Holy Quran every morning prior to the start of work in order to obtain blessing and guidance from God. The nation hopes that through the true adoption and practice of the MIB philosophy, the purity of Islam, the purity of the Malay race and the institution Monarchy can be maintained and preserved as a lasting legacy for future generations.[261]

The Ministry of Islamic Affairs deals with the issue of Islamic law in Brunei. Laws and state practice reflect a clear inclination to implement Islamic principles according to the Shafi'i school of Islam specifically.

Oman's political organization is quite comparable. The Basic Law of the Sultanate of Oman provides: "The system of government is [a] hereditary Sultanate in which succession passes to a male descendant of Sayyid Turki bin Said bin Sultan".[262] The Sultan is Head of State and has, similar to the Sultan of Brunei Darussalam, far-reaching political power. Among his functions are:

- preserving the country's independence and territorial integrity and assuring its internal and external security, maintaining the rights and freedoms of its citizens, guaranteeing the rule of law, and guiding the general policy of the State;

---

[259] Art. 4, para. (3), of the CONST. OF BRUNEI DARUSSALAM (1959).

[260] Art. 4, para. (4), of the CONST. OF BRUNEI DARUSSALAM (1959).

[261] Brunei Government, *National Philosophy: MIB Concept* (excerpt; original date of publication unknown).

[262] Art. 5 of the BASIC LAW OF THE SULTANATE OF OMAN (1996).

- taking prompt measures to counter any threat to the safety of the State or its territorial integrity, the security and interests of its people, or the smooth running of its institutions;
- representing the State both internally and externally in all international relations;
- presiding over the Council of Ministers or appointing a person to serve in that position;
- presiding over the Specialised Councils or appointing chairmen for them;
- appointing and dismissing Deputy Prime Ministers, Ministers and those of their rank;
- appointing and dismissing Under-Secretaries, General Secretaries and those of their rank;
- appointing and dismissing senior judges;
- declaring a state of emergency, general mobilisation, or war, and making peace in accordance with the provisions of the Law;
- issuing and ratifying laws;
- signing international treaties and agreements in accordance with the provisions of the Law (or authorising a signatory to sign them) and issuing decrees ratifying them;
- appointing and dismissing political representatives to other States and international organisations according to the limits and circumstances laid down by the Law;
- accepting accreditation of representatives of States and international organisations;
- waiving or commuting punishments;
- conferring honours, decorations and military ranks.[263]

It has been described before that the Yang di-Pertuan Agong (Supreme Ruler or King) of Malaysia is Head of the Federation. In the present context it is worth reiterating that most of the constituent states of Malaysia are constituted as regional sultanates with a Sultan as Head of the constituent state and as Head of Religion.[264]

---

[263] Art. 42 of the Basic Law of the Sultanate of Oman (1996). He is, moreover, Supreme Commander of the Armed Forces. It is furthermore provided that his person "is inviolable and must be respected and his orders must be obeyed. The Sultan is the symbol of national unity as well as its guardian and defender" (art. 41 of the Basic Law of the Sultanate of Oman (1996).

[264] It may be added at this point that Shari'a Courts are established to implement Shari'a law which is applicable to a wide range of issues. The Constitution of Malaysia describes the scope of Islamic law and the jurisdiction of Shari'a Courts as follows: "Except with respect to the Federal Territories of Kuala Lumpur and Labuan, Islamic law and personal and family law of persons professing the religion of Islam, including the Islamic law relating to succession, testate and intestate, betrothal, marriage, divorce, dowry, maintenance, adoption, legitimacy guardianship, gifts, partitions and non-charitable trusts, Wakafs and the definition and regulation of charitable and religious endowments, institutions, trusts, charities and charitable institutions, [applies] wholly within the State…Syariah courts…shall have jurisdiction only over persons professing the religion of Islam and in respect only of any of the matters included in this paragraph…". See Ninth Schedule (Legislative Lists: List II – State List) to the Const. of Malaysia (1957).

Bhutan, finally, serves as a useful example. The newly adopted Constitution of the Kingdom of Bhutan (2008) sheds some light on the exact role Buddhism plays in Bhutan:

1. Buddhism is the spiritual heritage of Bhutan, which promotes the principles and values of peace, non-violence, compassion and tolerance.
2. The Druk Gyalpo is the protector of all religions in Bhutan…
3. The Druk Gyalpo shall, on the recommendation of the Five Lopons, appoint a learned and respected monk ordained in accordance with the Druk-lu, with the nine qualities of a spiritual master and accomplished in ked-dzog, as the Je Khenpo.
4. His Holiness the Je Khenpo shall, on the recommendation of the Dratshang Lhentshog, appoint monks with the nine qualities of a spiritual master and accomplished in ked-dzog as the Five Lopons…
5. The Zhung Dratshang and Rabdeys shall continue to receive adequate funds and other facilities from the State.[265]

It follows that the *Druk Gyalpo* (the Dragon King) has an important say in religious matters as he is to appoint the *Je Khenpo*: the religious leader who presides over the Central Monk Body and functions as personal advisor to the King. The Buddhist Monk Body, in turn, decides on religious affairs.

2.4.3 *Reserving Political Seats for Members of the State Religion*

Some states with a state religion reserve a percentage of seats within state bodies for members of the state religion. The Norwegian Constitution, for instance, stipulates that more than 50 per cent of the members of the Government must profess the state religion (Evangelical Lutheranism).[266] The Church of England exercises a limited degree of influence in British politics as 26 (of the 731) seats of the House of Lords—the upper house of the UK Parliament—are reserved for representatives of the Church. The so-called 'Lords Spiritual', who in fact formed the majority of the House in the 16th century, include the Archbishop of Canterbury, the Archbishop of York, the Bishop of London, the Bishop of Durham, the Bishop of Winchester and other diocesan bishops (in accordance with the seniority of their ecclesiastical appointment).[267] Some influence of Buddhism within the domestic politics of Bhutan is ensured as ten out of the 150 seats in the National Assembly are reserved for Buddhist monks.[268]

---

[265] Art. 3 of the Const. of Bhutan (2008).

[266] Art. 12, para. (2), of the Const. of Norway (1814).

[267] Companion to the Standing Orders and Guide to the Proceedings of the House of Lords (UK Parliament, 2007); Clergy Act of 1661 and the Bishopric of Manchester Act of 1847.

[268] It may be added at this point that in Bolivia, previously, the state church exercised a limited degree of political influence through the Catholic Bishops' Conference. It is as yet unclear if this mechanism will survive, since the Catholic Church was disestablished in early 2009 and a separation of religion and state was introduced.

2.4.4 *Royal Protection of the State Religion*

In many states the established religion is historically interwoven with the royal house. Europe's Christian state churches were of old, inextricably linked with the different European royal houses (thus, reflecting the adage *cuius regio, eius religio*: whose realm, his religion). Some Constitutions still give evidence thereof and reiterate the present Monarch's commitment to the dominant or traditional religion. The Norwegian Constitution, for instance, proclaims the King upholder of the Evangelical-Lutheran religion.[269] It is added that the King "ordains all public church services and public worship, all meetings and assemblies dealing with religious matters, and ensures that public teachers of religion follow the norms prescribed for them".[270] The Danish Constitution similarly requires the Monarch to be a member of the Evangelical Lutheran Church.[271] The British Monarch upholds, protects and promotes the Anglican religion in the capacity of "Supreme Governor of the Church of England".[272] Article XXXVII ("Of the Civil Magistrates") of the 39 Articles on Religion of 1562 outlines the Monarch's supreme role as both secular leader and defender of the faith:

> The Queen's Majesty hath the chief power in this Realm of England, and other her Dominions, unto whom the chief Government of all Estates of this Realm, whether they be Ecclesiastical or Civil, in all causes doth appertain, and is not, nor ought to be, subject to any foreign Jurisdiction. Where we attribute to the Queen's Majesty the chief government, by which Titles we understand the minds of some slanderous folks to be offended; we give not to our Princes the ministering either of God's Word, or of the Sacraments, the which thing the Injunctions also lately set forth by Elizabeth our Queen doth most plainly testify; but only that prerogative, which we see to have been given always to all godly Princes in holy Scriptures by God himself; that is, that they should rule all estates and degrees committed to their charge by God, whether they be Ecclesiastical or Temporal, and restrain with the civil sword the stubborn and evildoers. The Bishop of Rome hath no jurisdiction in this Realm of England. The Laws of the Realm may punish Christian men with death, for heinous and grievous offences. It is lawful for Christian men, at the commandment of the Magistrate, to wear weapons, and serve in the wars.[273]

The British Monarch vows, as Supreme Governor of the Church of England, to uphold the Anglican Church at all times.[274] The Coronation Oath Act describes the protocol as follows:

---

[269] Art. 4 of the Const. of Norway (1814).

[270] Art. 16 of the Const. of Norway (1814).

[271] Art. 6 of the Const. of Denmark (1953).

[272] Second Act of Supremacy 1559 (which replaced supreme "head" with supreme "governor").

[273] The Anglican Church League, *The Thirty-Nine Articles* (Articles of Religion, agreed upon by the Archbishops, Bishops, and the whole clergy of the Provinces of Canterbury and York, London, 1562).

[274] First Act of Supremacy of 1534 and Second Act of Supremacy of 1559.

Archbishop/Bishop:

Will You to the utmost of Your power Maintaine the Laws of God the true Profession of the Gospell and the Protestant Reformed Religion Established by Law? And will You Preserve unto the Bishops and Clergy of this Realme and to the Churches committed to their Charge all such Rights and Priviledges as by Law doe or shall appertaine unto them or any of them.

King/Queen:

All this I Promise to doe.[275]

The Monarch's connection to the established church is fairly symbolic nowadays, considering the fact that her most important prerogative, appointing church leaders, is presently preponderantly assumed by the Prime Minister. The role of the Prime Minister in appointing church officials is currently the main characteristic of England's involvement with church affairs. The Prime Minister, in turn, acts by and large in accordance with church nominations and recommendations made by the so-called Crown Appointments Commission.[276]

In the Muslim world, very similar ties between ruling families and religion were and still are perceivable. One may think of, for instance, the Al Khalifa Dynasty of Bahrain, the House of Hashim of Jordan, the Alaouite Dynasty of Morocco, the Al Bu Sa'id Dynasty of Oman, the House of Thani of Qatar and the House of Saud of Saudi Arabia. This is in some cases enshrined in the Constitution. The Constitution of Qatar, for instance, explicitly stipulates that the Heir Apparent must be a Muslim.[277] The King of Morocco is constitutionally proclaimed the "defender of the Faith".[278]

2.4.5 *Religious Nature of the State as an Irrevocable Status*

Any form of state–religion identification is in principle a changeable status as the numerous historical shifts and alterations in this respect prove. In Europe alone, since the late 18th century, dozens of churches and religions have been disestablished, the disestablishment of the Church of Sweden in January 2000 being the most recent example.[279] Disestablishmentarianism should not be considered an exclusively Western or European tendency or possibility. The Union of Comoros was, according to the Constitution of the Federal Islamic

---

[275] Act for Establishing the Coronation Oath, c.6 of 1688.

[276] For a detailed outline of the procedure of appointing an Archbishop of Canterbury, see Church of England, *Outline of Procedures for the Appointment of an Archbishop of Canterbury*, 2002.

[277] Art. 9 of the CONST. OF QATAR (2003).

[278] Art. 19 of the CONST. OF MOROCCO (1972).

[279] Madagascar is a good example of the opposite development: in April 2007 constitutional reforms including the removal of the term "secular state" (*état laïque*) were adopted in a referendum and subsequently entered into effect. *De facto*, however, Madagascar remains thus far fairly secular.

Republic of the Comoros of 1996, an Islamic state with Islam as the state religion. The newly adopted Constitution of the Union of Comoros of 2001 has dropped these provisions.[280] Bolivia disestablished its Catholic Church in early 2009.[281] The recent transition towards secularity in Nepal is another striking example.[282] That being said, one way of emphasizing the importance attached to the religious nature of the state is by expressly declaring the establishment of a religion an irrevocable state characteristic.

(i) *State Religion as an Irrevocable Status*

In theory both the religious nature of the state as such (e.g. 'Islamic Republic', 'Hindu Kingdom', 'Jewish State') and the state religion can be constitutionally protected against any future amendments. The religious nature of the state is, for instance, expressly declared unalterable in Iran. The Iranian Constitution states: "The contents of the articles of the Constitution related to the Islamic character of the political system; the basis of all the rules and regulations according to Islamic criteria; the religious footing; the objectives of the Islamic Republic of Iran…are unalterable".[283] The Afghan Constitution similarly states: "The provisions of adherence to the provisions of the sacred religion of Islam… cannot be amended" (which would appear to apply to both the religious nature of the state as well as the state religion).[284] The Moroccan Constitution in a similar vein decrees: "Neither the state system of monarchy nor the prescriptions related to the religion of Islam may be subject to a constitutional revision".[285] The Constitutions of Afghanistan, Algeria, Bahrain, Iran and Morocco stipulate that the constitutional provisions pertaining to the state religion are not subject to revision.[286] The Malaysian Constitution introduces a certain threshold for amendments with regard to the official religion of some of the states within the federation.[287] All these measures give evidence of the importance the regime attaches to a strong, positive identification of the state with Islam.

---

[280] Compare the preamble of the Constitution of the Federal Islamic Republic of the Comoros (1996; replaced) and the CONSTITUTION OF THE UNION OF COMOROS (2001). It must be acknowledged though that the preamble still refers to Islam as a source of inspiration and that despite these constitutional changes the endorsement of Islam is in practice still very much perceivable.

[281] Compare art. 3 of the Constitution of Bolivia of 1967 (replaced) and art. 4 of the POLITICAL CONST. OF BOLIVIA (2009).

[282] Compare art. 4 Constitution of the Kingdom of Nepal (1990; abrogated) and art. 4 of the INTERIM CONST. OF NEPAL (2007).

[283] Art. 177, para. (5), of the CONST. OF IRAN (1989).

[284] Art. 149 of the CONST. OF AFGHANISTAN (2004).

[285] Art. 106 of the CONST. OF MOROCCO (1972).

[286] Art. 149 of the CONST. OF AFGHANISTAN (2004); art. 178 of the CONST. OF ALGERIA (1976); art. 120 in conjunction with art. 2 of the CONST. OF BAHRAIN (2002); artt. 12 and 177 CONST. OF IRAN (1979); and art. 106 of the CONST. OF MOROCCO (1972).

[287] Art. 161E, para. (2), of the CONST. OF MALAYSIA (1959), pertaining to the states of Sabah and Sarawak.

(ii) *Exception: State Religion as Explicitly Changeable Status*

If a Constitution is completely silent on the issue of the alterability of the state religion, one would assume—in a democratic state—that the political act of disestablishment is a viable one. The Constitution of Iceland is unique in that it does not leave any doubt as to this issue. It expressly codifies an 'opt-out clause': a provision indicating that the Evangelical Lutheran religion can be disestablished from the state if popular vote decides it.[288]

2.5 Concluding Remarks

From the above discussion it follows that the precise role that religion plays in religious states or in states with a state religion or a state church varies from state to state, ranging from the extreme situation in which the state apparatus acts, as it were, in service of the dominant religion, to instances in which the state allows the traditional religion to retain but some of its historical political prerogatives or privileges. We have seen that in some states the legislative, executive and judicial branches of the state are for an important part subjected to the normative framework of the dominant religion. In other cases this is less so. That being said, in all religious states or states with a state religion or a state church there is some degree of interrelation between the state and religion. Also, in all these instances such may give rise to questions of human rights compliance. Those questions will be explored in the second part of this book. Now we will turn to the other parts of the state–religion identification spectrum. First up are those religion–state relationships that fall short of the above described categories, but that nonetheless may still be considered forms of 'positive identification'.

[288] Art. 79 of the Const. of Iceland (1944). The provision which establishes the Evangelical Lutheran Church as state church already makes unmistakably clear that this is not necessarily a permanent status (art. 62): "The Evangelical Lutheran Church shall be the State Church in Iceland and, as such, it shall be supported and protected by the State. *This may be amended by law*" (emphasis added).

CHAPTER THREE

STATE SUPPORT & STATE ACKNOWLEDGEMENT OF RELIGION

3.1 Introduction

It is common state practice to legally or *de facto* support a specific religion, religious denomination or church. With respect to many states, in different parts of the world, it can be observed that one particular religion has played a determinative role in the country's history. Such is often still reflected—albeit perhaps somewhat toned down over the years—in the way the state and this traditional, dominant religion interact today. What we then see is that some of the historical prerogatives or privileges which the religion in question has acquired over the centuries may, with the state's consent, be retained. This modus of state–religion identification, 'state support', can—at least analytically—be distinguished from the practices discussed in the previous Chapter in as far as they do not amount to constitutionally establishing the religion or church in question as state religion or church. Different forms of state support have different legal, political, financial and pragmatic implications. It is the objective of this Chapter to chart these precise ramifications. It will be outlined that some forms of constitutional state support can and indeed should be distinguished from the far-reaching implications of systems of positive state–religion identification that were discussed in the previous Chapter, whilst other forms, though *de jure* presented as 'state support', approximate to the establishment of religion. In the latter case the choice to avoid the terminology of 'state' or 'official' religion would appear to be a political one. Some states constitutionally acknowledge certain religious phenomena, or simply acknowledge the historical role of a religion or the position of a religion as predominant religion (numerically). It will be contended that some forms of 'state acknowledgement' are preferential while other forms are purely non-preferential in nature. It will often be necessary to go beyond constitutional terminology and take into account statutory law and state practice as well.

3.2 State Support

State support is offered to a religion in its entirety or to specific denominations or churches. Present constitutional arrangements and state practice show different forms of state support for Buddhism, Islam and Christianity (within

Christianity, for the Roman Catholic Church and the Greek-Orthodox Church of Cyprus specifically).

3.2.1 *State-Supported Buddhism*

The Constitutions of Sri Lanka and Thailand express an intention to support Buddhism. Particularly in the case of Thailand practices surrounding the endorsement are inclined towards an establishment of Buddhism proper, yet the constitutional provisions avoid such terminology.

The Sri Lankan Constitution provides: "The Republic of Sri Lanka shall give to Buddhism the foremost place and accordingly it shall be the duty of the state to protect and foster the Buddha Sasana".[1] An attempt to introduce a constitutional amendment which would establish Buddhism as the state religion (proposed in 2004 by the Jathika Hela Urumaya Party, a political party led by Buddhist Monks) has been unsuccessful. The proposed constitutional amendment was considered unconstitutional by the Sri Lankan Supreme Court.[2]

The Constitution of Thailand states: "The State shall patronise and protect Buddhism and other religions, promote good understanding and harmony among followers of all religions as well as encourage the application of religious principles to promote virtues and develop the quality of life".[3] The King of Thailand—who "shall be enthroned in a position of revered worship"[4]—must be a Buddhist and is described as the "Upholder of religions".[5] Theravada Buddhism is regarded, although it is not constitutionally identified as such, as Thailand's *de facto* or unofficial state religion.[6] The Constitution of the Kingdom of Thailand of 1997 was officially abrogated by the military junta which seized power on 19 September 2006. The Interim Constitution of 2006 issued by the junta did not deal with the issue of religion,[7] but it paved the way towards the 2007 Constitution. Thai Buddhists strongly urged the Constitution Drafting Committee to include a provision in the new permanent constitution establishing Buddhism as the state religion.[8] However, the Constitution

[1] Art. 9 of the Constitution of the Democratic Socialist Republic of Sri Lanka (1978).
[2] Supreme Court of Sri Lanka, Case concerning the *Draft-19th-Amendment* to the Constitution, Judgement of January 2005.
[3] Sec. 78 of the Constitution of the Kingdom of Thailand (2007).
[4] Sec. 8 of the Const. of Thailand (2007).
[5] Sec. 9 of the Const. of Thailand (2007).
[6] *E.g.* US Department of State, *Annual Report on International Religious Freedom: 2006* (Bureau of Democracy, Human Rights and Labor, 2006), Chapter on Thailand.
[7] Constitution of the Kingdom of Thailand (Interim Edition) of B.E. 2549 [Buddhist Era].
[8] The Nation, *Monks, Supporters urge Charter Drafters to name Buddhism National Religion*, 14 February 2007.

Drafting Committee appears to have resisted the pressure as the constitutional provisions regarding religion remain by and large the same.[9]

Laos, despite its socialist polity and its self-proclaimed secular government, endorses Buddhism to some extent as well. The Constitution of Laos reflects Laos' support for Buddhism in moderate terms:

> The state respects and protects all lawful activities of the Buddhists and of other religious followers [and] mobilises and encourages the Buddhist monks and novices as well as the priests of other religions to participate in the activities which are beneficial to the country and people.[10]

The phrasing is relatively neutral as the mentioned privileges are extended to members of other religions; however, a decree which regulates religious practice privileges and promotes (Theravada) Buddhism by means of exempting Buddhism from the restrictions that are imposed on other religious organizations.[11]

3.2.2 *State-Supported Christianity (Unspecified)*

The (Anglican) Church of Ireland, which was numerically inferior, was formally disestablished in Ireland in 1871. However, Ireland cannot be considered a clear-cut secular state. The Constitution of Ireland expresses itself favourably towards Christianity (not specifically towards Roman Catholicism, though, the predominant Christian denomination in Ireland).[12] The Preamble to the Constitution commences with the following words:

> In the name of the Most Holy Trinity, from Whom is all authority and to Whom, as our final end, all actions both of men and States must be referred, We, the people of Ireland, humbly acknowledging all our obligations to our Divine Lord, Jesus Christ, Who sustained our fathers through centuries of trial.[13]

It is furthermore provided that the "State acknowledges that the homage of public worship is due to Almighty God. It shall hold His Name in reverence,

---

[9] Compare sections 9, 37, 69, 78 and 94 of the CONST. OF THAILAND (2007) with sections 9, 38, 66, 73 and 106 of the Constitution of the Kingdom of Thailand (1997) (abrogated).

[10] Art. 9 of the CONSTITUTION OF THE LAO PEOPLE'S DEMOCRATIC REPUBLIC (1991; hereinafter: CONST. OF LAOS of 1991).

[11] Prime Ministerial Decree No. 92 of 5 July 2002 on the Administration and Protection of Religious Activities in Lao PDR.

[12] The latter was different before 1972. The Fifth Amendment of the Constitution Act of 1972 deleted the following words from the Irish Constitution: "The State recognizes the special position of the Holy Catholic Apostolic and Roman Church as the guardian of the Faith professed by the great majority of the citizens"; i.e. ex-article 44, para. (1), point (ii). To this is was added that the State "also recognizes the Church of Ireland, the Presbyterian Church in Ireland, the Methodist Church in Ireland, the Religious Society of Friends in Ireland, as well as the Jewish Congregations and the other religious denominations existing in Ireland at the date of the coming into operation of this Constitution"; i.e. ex-article 44, para. (1), point (iii).

[13] Preamble of the CONSTITUTION OF IRELAND (1937).

and shall respect and honour religion".[14] This goes beyond a form of historical acknowledgement of the role of Christianity in the country. This endorsement translates most clearly into state support for Christianity in the field of education.[15]

Similar constitutional endorsements of Christianity can be seen in the Constitutions of the Bahamas, Papua New Guinea and Tonga.[16] The Constitution of the Bahamas compels the Government of the Bahamas to respect and ensure respect for Christian values.[17] This endorsement, however, does not translate into evident financial or other privileges for Christian churches. The Constitution of Papua New Guinea provides: "WE, THE PEOPLE OF PAPUA NEW GUINEA…pledge ourselves to guard and pass on to those who come after us our noble traditions and the Christian principles that are ours now".[18] The Constitution of Tonga endorses Christianity, again without establishing this religion expressly as state religion, in a fairly unique fashion, namely by paraphrasing and consequently endorsing one of the Ten Commandments, namely, to respect the Sabbath as a holy day of rest. The Constitution provides: "The Sabbath Day shall be kept holy in Tonga and no person shall practise his trade or profession or conduct any commercial undertaking on the Sabbath Day except according to law; and any agreement made or witnessed on that day shall be null and void and of no legal effect".[19] This formulation clearly echoes Deuteronomy:

> Observe the Sabbath day, to keep it holy, as the LORD your God commanded you. Six days you shall labour and do all your work, but the seventh day is a Sabbath to the LORD your God. On it you shall not do any work, you or your son or your daughter or your male servant or your female servant, or your ox or your donkey or any of your livestock, or the sojourner who is within your gates, that your male servant and your female servant may rest as well as you. You shall remember that you were a slave in the land of Egypt, and the LORD your God brought you out from there with a mighty hand and an outstretched arm. Therefore the LORD your God commanded you to keep the Sabbath day.[20]

---

[14] Art. 44, para. (1), of the CONST. OF IRELAND (1937).

[15] See Chapter 10, section 10.2.3, *infra*.

[16] It has been discussed already (see *supra*, Chapter 2.2.1) that Samoa, Tuvalu and Vanuatu approximate Christian states as their Constitutions establish these states as states "based on"/"founded on" Christian principles. These forms of endorsement could alternatively be perceived as forms of state support for Christianity.

[17] Preamble of the CONSTITUTION OF THE COMMONWEALTH OF THE BAHAMAS (1973).

[18] Preamble of the CONSTITUTION OF THE INDEPENDENT STATE OF PAPUA NEW GUINEA (1975).

[19] Art. 6 of the CONSTITUTION OF TONGA (1875).

[20] HOLY BIBLE (English Standard Version), Deuteronomy 5:12–15. The Sabbath is referred to as religious duty in numerous other passages; *e.g.* Exodus 20:8–11; 31:12–17; Leviticus 19:3, 19:30, 23:3; Numbers 28:9–10; Isaiah 56: 4, 6; Nehemiah 9:14.

3.2.3 *State-Supported Roman Catholicism*

Argentina "supports" (morally and financially) the Roman Catholic Church.[21] Constitutional state support to Roman Catholicism has translated into several agreements with the Holy See.[22] Several other states support the Roman Catholic Church by means of granting it a special legal position with exclusive rights and prerogatives. For instance, the Constitution of Andorra:

> …guarantees the Roman Catholic Church free and public exercise of its activities and the preservation of the relations of special co-operation with the state in accordance with the Andorran tradition. The Constitution recognizes the full legal capacity of the bodies of the Roman Catholic Church which have legal status in accordance with their own rules.[23]

The Constitutions of El Salvador and Guatemala single out the Catholic Church in a similar fashion.[24] In Equatorial Guinea, the Roman Catholic Church enjoys special privileges (exemption from the regime of registration and from certain taxes); however, it has to be acknowledged that the Reform Church of Equatorial Guinea is granted much of the same treatment.[25] Although the Constitution of Poland formally separates the state from religious organizations, it nevertheless provides for the special treatment of the Roman Catholic Church.[26] A Concordat between Poland and the Holy See, ratified by the Polish Parliament in 1998, reiterates the special position of the Catholic Church in Poland.[27] The Constitution of Peru describes the Catholic Church as an important element in the historical, cultural, and moral development of Peru and therefore "lends the Church its cooperation".[28] A separate

---

[21] Sec. 2 of the CONSTITUTION OF THE ARGENTINE NATION (1853; hereinafter: CONST. OF ARGENTINA of 1853).

[22] Agreement between the Republic of Argentina and the Holy See of 10 October 1966; and the Agreement between the Republic of Argentina and the Holy See of 28 June 1957. The latter deals with pastoral care to the Armed Forces; the former includes, among other things, a prohibition for the state to interfere in ecclesiastical affairs. See MICHAEL A. BURDICK, FOR GOD AND THE FATHERLAND: RELIGION AND POLITICS IN ARGENTINA (Albany: State University of New York Press, 1995), p. 216. It was updated in 1992 by a new agreement; see the Exchange of Diplomatic Notes Constituting an Agreement between the Republic of Argentina and the Holy See on Military Jurisdiction and Pastoral Care to the Armed Forces of 21 April 1992.

[23] Art. 11, para. (3), of the CONSTITUTION OF THE PRINCIPALITY OF ANDORRA (1993).

[24] Art. 26 of the CONSTITUTION OF THE REPUBLIC OF EL SALVADOR (1983). It provides: "The judicial personality of the Catholic Church is recognized". "The other churches", on the other hand, "may obtain recognition of their personality in conformity with the law". Art. 37, para. (1), of the POLITICAL CONSTITUTION OF THE REPUBLIC OF GUATEMALA (1985) contains a similar provision. Moreover, the Constitution exclusively guarantees the property rights of the Catholic Church; art. 37, para. (2), of the CONST. OF GUATEMALA (1985).

[25] As per a 1992 Presidential Decree on Freedom of Religion.

[26] Compare paras. (3) and (4) of art. 25 of the CONSTITUTION OF THE REPUBLIC OF POLAND (1997).

[27] Concordat between Poland and the Holy See of 28 July 1993 (ratified and entered into force: 25 March 1998).

[28] Art. 50 of the CONSTITUTION OF PERU (1993).

agreement between the State of Peru and the Holy See lays down many privileges (e.g. immigration benefits for Catholic Church officials) and financial benefits that are not granted to other religious organizations.[29] The Constitution of Spain also singles out the Catholic Church as it provides that "the public powers shall take into account the religious beliefs of Spanish society and maintain the appropriate relations of cooperation, with the Catholic Church and other denominations".[30] Though the offer of cooperation is expressly extended to the "other denominations",[31] Concordats between Spain and the Holy See give the Catholic Church a special position and forms the basis for (predominantly financial) benefits.[32] The Constitution of Venezuela appears *prima facie* secular. The state, however, subsidizes the Roman Catholic Church in pursuance of a Concordat with the Holy See.[33] Finally, it should be noted that Concordats between the Holy See and Croatia,[34] Hungary,[35] Italy[36] and Poland[37] have not been repealed despite the establishment of a separation between the state and religion in each of these states. In these countries the Catholic Church maintains a position in which it is able to exercise political influence.

3.2.4 *State Support for the Greek Orthodox Church of Cyprus and Vakf*

The Constitution of Cyprus recognizes the exclusive rights of both the Autocephalous Greek-Orthodox Church of Cyprus as well as the *Vakf*, the institution dealing with Muslim affairs in Cyprus. The Greek Orthodox Church of

[29] Legislative Decree No. 23211 endorsing the Concordat between the Holy See and the Republic of Peru. Such expressions of preferential treatment seem indeed difficult to reconcile with Peru's separation of state and religion enshrined in art. 50 of the Constitution of Peru (1993).

[30] Art. 16, para. (3), of the Constitution of Spain (1987).

[31] Which resulted in the 1992 Agreements with representatives from the Jewish, Muslim and Protestant communities: Agreement between Spain and FCI [Federation of Israelite Communities of Spain], 25/1992, of 10 November 1992; Agreement between Spain and CIE [Union of Islamic Communities in Spain], 26/1992, of 10 November 1992; and the Agreement between Spain and FEREDE [Federation of Protestant Entities in Spain], 24/1992, of 10 November 1992.

[32] Concordats between Spain and the Holy See of 3 January 1979 (ratified 4 December 1979); consisting of the Agreement on legal affairs; the Agreement on education and cultural affairs; the Agreement on the armed forces; and the Agreement on economic affairs.

[33] Concordat between Venezuela and the Holy See of 6 March 1964.

[34] Concordats between the Holy See and Croatia of 19 December 1996 and 9 October 1998.

[35] Concordat between Hungary and the Holy See establishing diplomatic relations and stating that issues related to the Church are to be settled by Canon law and the new Hungarian law on religious freedom of 9 February 1990; Concordat between Hungary and the Holy See establishing a military chaplaincy of 10 January 1994; and Concordat between Hungary and the Holy See on finances of 20 June 1997.

[36] Concordat between the Italian Republic and the Holy See of 18 February 1984.

[37] Concordat between Poland and the Holy See of 28 July 1993 (ratified and entered into force: 25 March 1998).

Cyprus which is autocephalous, in other words independent from the Greek Orthodox Church, is constitutionally granted the right of regulating and administering its own internal affairs and property in accordance with the Holy Canons.[38] The Cypriot Constitution guarantees similar rights and freedoms to the *Vakf*:

> The institution of Vakf and the Principles and Laws of, and relating to, Vakfs are recognised by this Constitution. All matters relating to or in any way affecting the institution or foundation of Vakf or the Vakfs or any Vakf properties, including properties belonging to Mosques and any other Moslem religious institution, shall be governed solely by and under the Laws and Principles of Vakfs (*ahkamul evkaf*) and the laws and regulations enacted or made by the Turkish Communal Chamber, and no legislative, executive or other act whatsoever shall contravene or override or interfere with such Laws or Principles of Vakfs and with such laws and regulations of the Turkish Communal Chamber.[39]

The Church of Cyprus and the *Vakf* are exempt from taxes.[40] It may be added at this point that the—not internationally recognized—Turkish Republic of Northern Cyprus has constitutionally established itself as a secular state.[41]

3.2.5 *State-Supported Orthodox Church*

The State of Bosnia and Herzegovina reflects multiple regimes of state–religion identification as the two political entities composing the state, namely, the Federation of Bosnia and Herzegovina and Republika Šrpska, each take their own approach to managing state–religion affairs. Whereas the Federation of Bosnia and Herzegovina does not adopt religiously preferential terminology in its Constitution, the Republic of Šrpska constitutionally extends financial and moral support to the Serbian Orthodox Church.[42] Though Belarus' position *vis-à-vis* religion may generally be characterized as 'state control' over religion,[43] in recent times it has started to grant forms of (exclusive) state support to the Orthodox Church.[44]

---

[38] Art. 110, para. (1), of the CONSTITUTION OF THE REPUBLIC OF CYPRUS (1960).

[39] Art. 110, para. (2), of the CONST. OF CYPRUS (1960).

[40] Other recognized religious groups – Armenian Apostolic Christians, Maronite Christians and Roman Catholics – are eligible to similar benefits under Cypriot law.

[41] See the preamble and art. 1 of the Constitution of the Turkish Republic of Northern Cyprus (1983).

[42] Art. 28 of the Constitution of the Republic of Šrpska (1992) states: "The Serbian Orthodox Church shall be the church of the Serb people and other people of Orthodox religion. The State shall materially support the Orthodox church and it shall co-operate with it in all fields and, in particular, in preserving, cherishing and developing cultural, traditional and other spiritual values".

[43] See the restrictive Law of the Republic of Belarus on Religious Freedom and Religious Organizations, Law No. 137-3, of 31 October 2002 (hereinafter: "2002 Belarusian Law").

[44] See, *e.g.*, the Agreement on Cooperation between the Republic of Belarus and the Belarusian Orthodox Church of 12 June 2003.

3.2.6 *State-Supported Islam*

In 2001, the Union of Comoros adopted an entirely new Constitution which removed Islam from its position as the expressly established religion of Comoros.[45] The present Constitution of the Union of Comoros (2001) still refers to Islam, but does so far more moderately: "The Comorian People solemnly affirm their will to…draw from Islam the permanent inspiration for the principles and rules that shall govern the Union".[46] State practice shows that Islam is still strongly supported by the Union, if not tightly interwoven with the state apparatus. For instance, a Ministry of Islamic Affairs oversees religious affairs and religious activity in the Union and a Grand Mufti—a person qualified under Islamic law to give legal opinions on Islamic law—advises the Government on the enforcement of Islamic laws. The Constitution furthermore provides that the Council of the *Ulemas*—a group of renowned Islamic legal scholars—shall assist the government of the Union in formulating decisions that affect the religious, economic and social life of the country.[47] It is, moreover, not permitted for non-Muslims to proselytise amongst Muslims. In light of these considerations, dropping the establishment clause thus far proves to have been a symbolic gesture only.

Syria is not a declared Islamic state nor has it established Islam as its state religion. However, the Constitution of Syria exclusively favours Islam simply by declaring Islamic jurisprudence the main source for legislation,[48] which, as we have seen in the previous Chapter, is a common feature of an Islamic state. The same holds true with regard to the Northern states of the Sudan in which Shari'a is expressly considered a source of legislation.[49]

3.3 State Acknowledgement

It is possible for a state to acknowledge certain aspects, characteristics or elements of a religion without treating this religion preferentially. Such acknowledgment may relate to the determinative role this religion has played in the country's history. A state can also simply acknowledge the presence of a

---

45 Before 2001, Comoros was, moreover, constituted as a "Federal Islamic Republic". Compare the preamble of the Constitution of the Federal Islamic Republic of the Comoros (1996) (replaced) and the Const. of Comoros (2001).

46 Preamble of the Const. of Comoros (2001).

47 Art. 36 of the Const. of Comoros (2001).

48 Art. 3, para. (2), of the Const. of Syria (1973).

49 Art. 5 of the Interim National Constitution of the Republic of the Sudan (2005; hereinafter: Interim Const. of the Sudan of 2005). Southern Sudan is far more secular and in fact stipulated a separation of State and religion in its own constitution. See art. 8 of the Interim Constitution of Southern Sudan (2005). The former Constitution of the Republic of the Sudan of 1998 used to exclusively refer to Islam; see the Constitution of the Republic of the Sudan (1998; replaced), which considered Islam "the religion of the majority" (art. 10)

certain Church or religion in a country, or point out the fact that a certain religion is the country's predominant religion numerically. These forms of state acknowledgement are in principle perfectly compatible with a secular state. Some types of acknowledgment, on the other hand, could be intended as a form of exclusive endorsement. The designation of the Eastern Orthodox Church as "the prevailing religion" by Greece, as described in the previous Chapter, serves as a useful example. Though semantically this designation might mean nothing more than the fact that Eastern Orthodoxy is the predominant religion (an overwhelming majority of the Greek population identifies itself as Greek Orthodox: around 98 per cent); taking account of the constitutional context and looking at state practice one could argue that the provision amounts to establishment of religion. Besides providing an overview of different preferential and non-preferential forms of state acknowledgment, it will in this section be argued that the constitutional acknowledgment of a God-notion or of other metaphysical phenomena can be considered an indication of a religious preference on the part of the state and as such rules out characterization as a clear-cut secular state.

3.3.1 *Historical Acknowledgment*

'Historical acknowledgment' refers to any form of constitutional recognition of the special role played by a certain religion in the country's history and development. This religion would normally be the state's predominant religion.

(i) *Acknowledgement of Christianity (Unspecified)*

Fiji and Poland constitutionally acknowledge their Christian heritage. The Constitution of Fiji, whilst recalling the events "in our history that have made us what we are", emphasizes "the conversion of the indigenous inhabitants of these islands from heathenism to Christianity through the power of the name of Jesus Christ; the enduring influence of Christianity in these islands and its contribution, along with that of other faiths, to the spiritual life of Fiji".[50] This constitutional acknowledgment of the historical position and role of Christianity in Fiji could *in abstracto* be reconciled with a provision separating the state and religion,[51] although one might sense a degree of marginalization of Hindus and Muslims.[52]

Poland acknowledges its Christian heritage by dint of a constitutional reference in the Preamble of the Constitution: "Beholden to our ancestors for their

[50] Preamble of the Constitution of the Republic of the Fiji Islands (1998).

[51] Art. 5 of the Const. of the Fiji Islands (1998).

[52] Religion is one of the main factors dividing indigenous Fijians (predominantly Christian) and Indo-Fijians. Roughly 52 per cent of the population is Christian (predominantly adhering to the Methodist Church of Fiji), 30 per cent is Hindu and seven per cent is Muslim.

labours, their struggle for independence achieved at great sacrifice, for our culture rooted in the Christian heritage of the Nation and in universal human values".[53] The acknowledgement of a Christian heritage can in principle be considered compatible with Poland's separation of state and religion (however, we have previously seen that Poland has granted the Roman Catholic Church special recognition as per Concordat with the Holy See).[54]

(ii) *Acknowledgement of Eastern Orthodoxy*

Several states constitutionally acknowledge either a specific Eastern Orthodox Church or Eastern Orthodoxy as such. The Constitution of Georgia, for instance, recognizes "the special role of the Apostle Autocephalous Orthodox Church of Georgia in the history of Georgia" and separates the church from the state in the same provision,[55] a clear indication that the historical acknowledgement was intended to be purely non-preferential. The Georgian Orthodox Church is in fact one of the oldest Christian Churches and the relationship of Georgia with this Church was already initiated during the ancient Georgian Kingdom of Kartli (or Caucasian Iberia). It would become also the first state after Armenia to declare Christianity the state religion in 337. A second paragraph was added to the cited provision by constitutional amendment, stipulating:

> The relations between the state of Georgia and the Apostle Autocephalous Orthodox Church of Georgia shall be determined by the Constitutional Agreement. The Constitutional Agreement shall correspond completely to universally recognised principles and norms of international law, in particular, in the field of human rights and fundamental freedoms.[56]

This provision paved the way for a Concordat between the State of Georgia and the Georgian Orthodox Church, which reiterates the special role of this church in Georgia's history and which is, arguably, a bit more preferential in that it expressly and exclusively designates authority over religious affairs to the Georgian Orthodox Church.[57] Though this could *prima facie* be perceived as simply an elaboration on the separation principle, the fact remains that no such agreements are made with other religious organizations.

The Constitution of Bulgaria characterizes Eastern Orthodox Christianity as the "traditional religion".[58] It is clear from the context of the provision that it

---

[53] Preamble of the Const. of Poland (1997).

[54] See section 3.2.3, *supra*. Art. 25 of the Const. of Poland (1997) codifies Poland's special interpretation of the separation principle.

[55] Art. 9, para. (1), of the Constitution of Georgia (1995).

[56] Constitutional Law of Georgia of 30 March 2001.

[57] Concordat between Georgia and the Georgian Orthodox Church of 14 October 2002.

[58] Art. 13, para. (3), of the Constitution of the Republic of Bulgaria (1991). The designation of Eastern Orthodox Christianity as the "traditional religion" in the Bulgarian Constitution could alternatively be interpreted as an indication of the predominant religion of Bulgaria (i.e. numerically). An estimated 82–83 per cent of Bulgarians adhere – nominally – to

was not intended to establish Eastern Orthodox Christianity as a state religion (the same article explicitly separates religion from the state).[59] This legal analysis, however, is belied by state practice as the state grants the Bulgarian Orthodox Church some financial support.[60]

A 1997 Russian Law on freedom of conscience recognizes "a special role" of the Orthodox Church in the history of Russia, the formation and development of its spirituality and culture.[61] This form of recognition as such does not prejudice Russia's secularity.[62] A 2002 Belarusian Law similarly acknowledges "the defining role of the Orthodox Church in the historical formation and development of spiritual, cultural and state traditions of the Belarusian people".[63]

(iii) *Catholic Church in Timor-Leste and Paraguay*

The Constitution of East Timor acknowledges and values the participation of the Catholic Church in the process of national liberation of Timor-Leste (an estimated 98 per cent of the population adheres to Catholicism).[64] This acknowledgment of the role that the Catholic Church played in the history and establishment of Timor-Leste as an independent state can be reconciled with Timor-Leste's separation of the state and religion.[65] In that respect it is of particular importance that secular liberation movements are recognized by the Constitution as well.[66]

---

this religion. The Bulgarian Orthodox Church has traditionally had and still has a dominant position in Bulgarian society.

[59] Art. 13, para. (2), of the CONST. OF BULGARIA (1991). The *de jure* secular character of the state has been affirmed by the Constitutional Court as well in Decision No. 2 of 18 February 1998; cf. Jenja Peteva, *Church and State in Bulgaria, in* LAW AND RELIGION IN POST-COMMUNIST EUROPE (Ferrari & Durham, eds., Leuven: Peeters, 2003), p. 42.

[60] It must be acknowledged, however, that other religions which have a historic nexus – namely, Jewish, Muslim and Roman Catholic communities – with the Bulgarian society are eligible for state support as well.

[61] Preamble of the Law on the Freedom of Conscience and Religious Associations, No. 125-FZ, of 1997 (amended by Law No. 45-FZ of 26 March 2000 and by Law No. 112-FZ of 25 July 2002; hereinafter: "1997 Russian Law").

[62] Particularly so since the secular nature of Russia is underscored by the same sentence in the preamble of this law ("proceeding from the fact that the Russian Federation is a secular state").

[63] Preamble of the 2002 Belarusian Law (*supra* note 43). This acknowledgement leans towards (exclusive) state support. The Agreement on Cooperation between the Republic of Belarus and the Belarusian Orthodox Church of 12 June 2003 leaves little doubt about that.

[64] Art. 11, para. (2), of the CONSTITUTION OF THE DEMOCRATIC REPUBLIC OF EAST TIMOR (2002).

[65] Art. 45, para. (1), and art. 12 of the CONST. OF EAST TIMOR (2002). It is debatable, though, to what extent the neutral form of support for religion as a whole—art. 12, para. (2)—can be reconciled with the separation principle (see also next Chapter).

[66] Art. 11, para. (1), of the CONST. OF EAST TIMOR (2002): "The state acknowledges and values the secular resistance of the Maubere People against foreign domination and the contribution of all those who fought for national independence".

Paraguay constitutionally recognizes the role played by the Catholic Church in the historical and cultural formation of the state in a manner that does not, in itself, manifestly run counter to its separation of state and religion.[67] This cannot so easily be argued with respect to the exact way the relationships between the state and the different religions are defined by the Paraguayan Constitution as it guarantees the *independence* and *autonomy* of all churches and religious denominations, without restrictions other than those imposed by the Constitution and the law; yet the relations between the state and the Catholic Church specifically are based on "independence, *cooperation*, and autonomy".[68] In short, the Catholic Church is made an exclusive offer to cooperate with the state, which in fact has resulted in some forms of preferential treatment (notably, Catholicism's exclusive ceremonial role in the public realm).

3.3.2 *Acknowledgement of a Predominant Religion*

The Constitution of Panama acknowledges that "the Catholic religion is practiced by the majority of Panamanians" (an estimated 80–85 per cent of the Panamanian population identifies itself as Catholic).[69] This type of constitutional acknowledgment of demographical data does not amount to an establishment of religion.[70]

Mongolia has declared by law that it "shall accept the predominant status of Buddhism in Mongolia in order to respect the historical traditions of harmony and civilization of the people of Mongolia" (roughly 94 per cent of the population adheres to Tibetan Lamaistic Buddhism).[71] It would appear that this acknowledgement does not prejudice the separationist nature of the state.[72] The recently adopted Burmese Constitution similarly acknowledges the fact that Buddhism is the predominant religion. Although Burmese state practice reveals strong ties with Theravada Buddhism, all attempts to establish Buddhism as the state religion have failed. The military junta of the Union of Myanmar suspended the Constitution of the Socialist Republic of the Union of Burma (1974) and recently replaced it with a new Constitution in May 2008 (which should not be seen as a move towards democracy as the new law

[67] Artt. 24 and 82 of the Constitution of the Republic of Paraguay (1992).

[68] Compare the difference in phrasing in art. 24, paras. (2) and (3), of the Const. of Paraguay (1992), emphasis added. The constitutional reference to God ("Pleading to God") in the preamble, moreover, is undeniably incompatible with the separation principle.

[69] Art. 35, 2nd sentence, of the Constitution of the Republic of Panama (1972).

[70] In the case of Panama, the neutrality of the state may however be questioned on other grounds; one can particularly think of the fact that it considers "respect for Christian morality" a legitimate ground for limiting the right to freedom of religion or belief (art. 35 of the Const. of Panama of 1972). This will be discussed further in the human rights analysis (Part II).

[71] Art. 4, para. (1), of the Law of Mongolia on the Relationship between the State and Religious Institutions of 11 November 1993.

[72] Art. 9 of the Constitution of Mongolia (1992).

reserves many political seats for the military). The new Constitution states that "[t]he State recognizes the special position of Buddhism as the faith professed by the great majority of the citizens of the State."[73] Although this provision is strictly speaking of a non-preferential nature, the fact remains that the regime maintains close ties with Buddhist organizations (through the Department for the Perpetuation and Propagation of the Sasana) and, moreover, Buddhism plays an important ceremonial role in the public realm and forms a mandatory part of the primary school curriculum.

3.3.3 *Acknowledgement of Religious Phenomena*

The constitutional acknowledgment of a God-notion or of other metaphysical phenomena can be considered an indication of religious preference on the part of the state. It may be useful to distinguish between states that constitutionally endorse a specific theistic religion *and* refer one or more times to God in their constitution on the one hand, and states that 'solely' acknowledge the existence of God or of other religious phenomena. In the first case the reference to God in the constitution is simply another expression of the concrete religious nature and preference of the state (be it for Christianity, Islam, etc). If not accompanied by a clear-cut establishment of religion, state acknowledgement of God comes down to the state taking a general religious stance without necessarily treating a specific theistic religion preferentially. These constitutional acknowledgments do undeniably give evidence of a general religious preference for *theism*, thereby deliberately excluding non-theistic, atheistic, agnostic beliefs and possibly also polytheistic belief systems (because of the singular "God").

(i) *Constitutional Acknowledgement of God*

Nearly half of the world's states refer in one way or another to God in their Constitution. Doing so does not, *ipso facto*, make a state a 'religious state' on an equal footing with the religious states as described in the previous Chapter. However, as it is by no means compulsory to speak of God in the Constitution, the incorporation of references to God gives evidence of a religious stance (theism). Besides "God", many other notions are employed, for instance, "Almighty",[74] "Creator",[75] "Father"[76], "Lord"[77] (the latter, it must be noted, may

---

[73] Art. VIII, para. (19), of the CONSTITUTION OF MYANMAR (2008).

[74] See *infra*, for a detailed inventory.

[75] Preamble of the CONST. OF BELIZE (1981); preamble of the CONST. OF DOMINICA (1978); art. 10 of the Great Green Charter of Human Rights of the Jamahiriyan Era of 1988 (Libya); and the preamble of the CONSTITUTION OF THE REPUBLIC OF MADAGASCAR (1992).

[76] Preamble of the CONSTITUTION OF KIRIBATI (Schedule to the Kiribati Independence Order of 1979).

[77] Preamble of CONST. OF BRUNEI DARUSSALAM (1959): "Lord of the Universe"; art. 11 of the CONST. OF IRAN (1979); preamble of the CONSTITUTION OF NAURU (1968); and the preamble of the CONST. OF TUVALU (1986): "everlasting Lord".

also be used in combination with Jesus Christ: "our Lord Jesus Christ")[78] and "Most High".[79] Mentions of God in Constitutions are as a rule made in an affirmative fashion. An exception that comes to mind is a constitutional provision speaking of "those who believe in God".[80] Another non-confessional usage of the word God is the codification of an oath of office in which swearing to God is strictly optional.[81]

Unsurprisingly, the frequency of constitutional references to God correlates neatly with the state–religion spectrum: at the religious side of the spectrum these references abound whilst at the more secular end they appear to be much rarer. Nearly all the religious states and states with a state religion refer one or more times to God in their Constitution.[82] The Iranian Constitution clearly

---

[78] Art. 3 of the Const. of Greece (2001); and the preamble of the Const. of Ireland (1937): "our divine Lord, Jesus Christ".

[79] Art. 9 of the Lebanese Constitution (1926).

[80] Preamble of the Const. of Poland (1997). Note that the same preamble refers to God in more confessional terms as well: "Recognizing our responsibility before God or our own consciences".

[81] This refers to public office oaths that contain religious elements but which allow for a secular alternative (i.e. a solemn affirmation) to be taken or allow omission of the religious aspects of the standard oath. See Chapter 11, section 11.2.1(v), *infra*, for an overview of compulsory and optional religious oaths of office.

[82] Preamble of the Const. of Afghanistan (2004); preamble of the Const. of Algeria (1976); preamble and art. 78 (oath) of the Const. of Bahrain (2002); preamble and art. 8 of the Const. of Bangladesh (1972) ("Allah" in the official version by the Prime Minister's Office); preamble of the Const. of Brunei Darussalam (1959); preamble of the Royal Decree on the Constitution of the National Assembly of Bhutan (1953); preamble of the Const. of Costa Rica (1949); art. 67 of the Const. of Denmark (1953); preamble of the Const. of Djibouti (1992); art. 54 (oath) and art. 96 of the Const. of the Dominican Republic (1966); preamble, art. 79 (oath) and art. 90 (oath) of the Const. of Egypt (1971); artt. 131 and 187 (oaths) of the Const. of Haiti (1987); preamble, art. 9 (oath), art. 29 and Annotation 5 and 6 of the Const. of Indonesia (1945); preamble (five times), artt. 2 (six times), 5, 14, 17, 56, 67 (oath; two times), 121 (oath; three times) and 151 (two times) of the Const. of Iran (1979); preamble of the Const. of Iraq (2005); artt. 43 and 80 (oaths) of the Const. of Jordan (1952); preamble and artt. 60 and 91 (oaths) of the Const. of Kuwait (1962); preamble of the Great Green Charter of Human Rights of the Jamahiriyan Era of 1988 (Libya); preamble, artt. 54 and 108 (oaths) and several times in the Annex to Const. of Liechtenstein (1921); Schedule (oaths) to the Const. of Maldives (2008) ("Allah" in the official version by the President's office); preamble of the Const. of Mauritania (1991); art. 7 of the Const. of Morocco (1972); art. 9 (oath) of the Const. of Norway (1814); artt. 7 and 50 (oaths) of the Basic Statute of Oman (1996); preamble of the Const. of Pakistan (1973) ("Allah" in the official version by the Government of Pakistan); artt. 10, 74, 92 and 119 (oaths) of the Const. of Qatar (2003); preamble and Third Schedule (oaths) of the Const. of Samoa (1960); artt. 1, 3, 9, 11, 14, 23 and 45 of the Basic Law of Saudi Arabia (1992); preamble and Schedule 4 (oaths) to the Const. of Saint Kitts and Nevis (1983); preamble of the Const. of Switzerland (1999); preamble and art. 42 of the Const. of Tunisia (1959); preamble and artt. 52, 57 and 73 of the Const. of the United Arab Emirates (1971); the United Kingdom does not have a written, unified constitution; constitutional references to God can be found in the different constitutional laws, *e.g.* art. 17 (oath) of the Constitutional Reform Act (2005); preamble, Principles of the Constitution and Schedule 4 (oaths) of the Const. of Tuvalu (1986); preamble of the Const. of Vanuatu (1980); art. 159 (oath) of the Const. of Yemen (1990). As to the other states that were mentioned in Chapter 2 (not being clear-cut religious states), constitutional references to God can be found in: preamble of the Const. of Antigua and Barbuda (1981); preamble and

excels in this regard with over 20 references to God. Furthermore, the majority of states with a state-supported religion refer to God.[83] Most states that acknowledge the historical role or the numerical predominance of certain religions or churches similarly acknowledge God in their Constitution (Bulgaria is an exception in this regard).[84] This adds weight to the point made above that although state acknowledgment of religion (historically or numerically) as such does not rule out a secular nature of the state, most of these states appear in practice inclined to offer some degree of state support for the religion in question. Some of the states that reflect a non-preferential form of state–religion identification or a form of moderate interaction between the state and religion (see the following Chapter), refer to God in their Constitution.[85] One would assume that at the secular end of the spectrum, references to God in official documents are taboo. However, some states which have explicitly declared themselves secular or which have codified a

---

First Schedule (oaths) to the Const. of Barbados (1996); preamble and Schedule 3 (oaths) to the Const. of Belize (1981); preamble of the [Canadian] Constitution Act (1982; Schedule to the Canada Act); preamble of the Const. of Dominica (1978); preamble and Schedule 3 to the Const. of Grenada (1973); and the preamble of the Const. of Trinidad and Tobago (1976).

[83] Preamble of the Const. of Argentina (1853); preamble of the Const. of the Bahamas (1973); preamble of the Const. of El Salvador (1983); preamble of the Fundamental Law of Equatorial Guinea (1991); preamble of the Const. of Guatemala (1985); art. 6, artt. 12, 31, 34 (oaths) and art. 44 of the Const. of Ireland (1937); preamble and art. 7 (oath) of the Const. of Papua New Guinea (1975); preamble of the Const. of Peru (1993); preamble and artt. 85, 104, 130, 151 (oaths) of the Const. of Poland (1997); preamble and art. 42 (oath) of the Transitional Federal Charter of the Somali Republic (2004) (it must be noted that the more secular Interim Const. of Southern Sudan of 2005, which is applicable to the Southern States of the Sudan only, refers to God in its preamble as well); art. 7 (oath) of the Const. of Syria (1973); preamble, art. 5 and artt. 34, 83 and 95 (oaths) of the Const. of Tonga (1875); and preamble of the Constitution of the Bolivarian Republic of Venezuela (1999).

[84] Preamble and art. 77 (oath) of the Const. of East Timor (2002); preamble and art. 5 of the Const. of the Fiji Islands (1998); art. 71 (oath) of the Const. of Georgia (1995); preamble and art. 176 (oath) of the Const. of Panama (1972); preamble of the Const. of Paraguay (1992); and the preamble and artt. 104, 130 and 151 of the Const. of Poland (1997).

[85] Art. 81 (oath) of the Constitution of the Republic of Malawi (1994); preamble of the Constitution of the Republic of South Africa (1996); preamble of the Constitution of the Republic of the Marshall Islands (1979); art. 9 (the "Most High") and art. 50 (oath) of the Lebanese Const. (1926); preamble of the Constitution of Saint Lucia (Schedule to the 1978 Saint Lucia Constitution Order); and the Third Schedule (oaths) of the Constitution of Mauritius (1968). States which are constitutionally non-preferential with respect to religion in each respect *apart from* reference(s) to God include: Ecuador, Honduras, Jamaica, Kiribati, Lesotho, Madagascar, Nauru, Solomon Islands, St. Vincent and the Grenadines, Suriname, Zimbabwe and Swaziland. See the preamble of the Political Constitution of Colombia (1991); preamble of the Constitution of the Republic of Ecuador (1998); preamble of the Constitution of the Republic of Honduras (1982); First Schedule (oaths) to Constitution of Jamaica (1962); preamble and Schedule 1 (oaths) to the Const. of Kiribati (1979); Schedule 1 and 3 (oaths) to the Constitution of Lesotho (1993); preamble of the Const. of Madagascar (1992; in April 2007 constitutional reforms including the removal of the term "secular state" (*état laïque*) were adopted in a referendum and subsequently entered

non-establishment clause or a separation between state and religion (see Chapter 5) do refer to God in their Constitution.[86]

(ii) *Constitutional Acknowledgement of Other Religious Notions*

Numerous other references that give evidence of a state's stance on religion can be discerned, including the attribution of particular characteristics to God, references to founders of religions or founding religious documents and (metaphysical) notions of sacredness and holiness.

Specific Characteristics of God

Some Constitutions attribute special characteristics to God which give evidence of the state's stance on theological and dogmatic questions of faith. The following overview is intended to shed some more light on this phenomenon:

- *Creationism*

Some Constitutions (e.g. Belize, Dominica, Libya and Madagascar)[87] explicitly consider God a creationist God by referring to God as "the Creator", which presumably denotes God as the creator of humanity, life, Earth, the Universe, etc. The Constitution of Tonga more specifically states that God created mankind; it claims: "Since it appears to be the will of God that man should be free as He has made all men of one blood therefore shall the people of Tonga and all who sojourn or may sojourn in this Kingdom be free for ever".[88]

---

into effect); preamble and Schedules (oaths) to the Const. of Nauru (1968); preamble and Schedule 1 (oaths) to the Constitution of Solomon Islands (Schedule to the 1978 Solomon Islands Independence Order); preamble of the Constitution of Saint Vincent and the Grenadines (Schedule to the 1979 Saint Vincent Constitution Order); artt. 65, 93, 114 and 125 (oaths) of the Constitution of the Republic of Suriname (1987); Schedule One (oaths) to the Constitution of Zimbabwe (1979); and the preamble and Second Schedule (oaths) to the Const. of Swaziland (2005).

[86] Preamble and Second Schedule (oaths) to Constitution of the Republic of Ghana (1992); preamble of the Constitution of the Republic of Liberia (1986); art. 37 (oath) of Decree No. 92-073 Concerning Promulgation of the Constitution [of Mali] (1992; hereinafter: Const. of Mali of 1992); art. 30 (oath) of the Constitution of the Republic of Namibia (1990); artt. 61 and 104 (oaths) of the Constitution of the Republic of Rwanda (2003); preamble of the Const. of Seychelles (1993); preamble of the Constitution of the Fourth Republic of Togo (1992); preamble of the Constitution of the Republic of Uganda (1995); preamble of the Constitution of the Republic of Palau (1979); preamble of the Constitution of the Republic of the Philippines (1987); preamble and art. 56 (oath) of the Basic Law for the Federal Republic of Germany (1949); art. 5 (oath) of the Law on the Enforcement of the Constitution of Lithuania (1992); art. 82 (oath) of the Constitution of Romania (1991); preamble of the Constitution of Ukraine (1996); artt. 60, 69 and 159 (oaths) of the Constitution of India (1950); preamble of the Constitution of the Federative Republic of Brazil (1988); and the preamble of the Political Constitution of the Republic of Chile (1980).

[87] As indicated before: see *supra*, note 75.

[88] Art. 1 of the Const. of Tonga (1875).

- *Omnipotence*

Many Constitutions depict God as an omnipotent entity. The Constitution of Mauritania literally declares its trust in "the omnipotence of Allah".[89] Depicting God as "almighty" of course boils down to the same thing: faith in an omnipotent God (the different constitutional descriptions to that effect include: "God the Almighty," "God Almighty" and "the almighty God").[90]

- *Omniscience*

The Norwegian Constitution, indirectly, stands by a conception of God as an omniscient God. The King of Norway is constitutionally compelled to swear before the Parliament, upon inauguration, to an (almighty and) omniscient God.[91]

- *Omnipresence*

As indicated before, Samoa is established as a state based on Christian principles. Samoa also constitutionally acknowledges the omnipresence of God.[92]

- *Supremacy*

Some Constitutions argue that God has exclusive sovereignty when it comes to ruling the Universe. The Constitution of Pakistan, for instance, provides that "sovereignty over the entire Universe belongs to Almighty Allah alone"; authority can nonetheless "be exercised by the people of Pakistan within the

89 Preamble of the Const. of Mauritania (1991).

90 Preamble of the Constitution of the Gambia (1996); preamble of the Const. of Djibouti (1992); preamble and Schedule 2 (oaths) to the Const. of Ghana (1992); Schedule 1 (oaths) to the Const. of Lesotho (1993); preamble of the Const. of Seychelles (1993); preamble of the Interim Const. of the Sudan (2005); preamble of the Const. of Swaziland (2005); preamble and art. 9 (oath) of the Const. of Indonesia (1945); preamble and Schedule 1 (oaths) to the Const. of Kiribati (1979); preamble of the Const. of Nauru (1968); preamble of the Const. of Palau (1979); preamble of the Const. of the Philippines (1987); preamble and Schedules (oaths) of the Const. of Samoa (1960); art. 34 (oath) of the Const. of Tonga (1875); preamble of the Const. of Tuvalu (1986); artt. 12 (oath) and 44 of the Const. of Ireland (1937); art. 9 (oath) of the Const. of Norway (1814); preamble of the Const. of Switzerland (1999); art. 78 (oath) of the Const. of Bahrain (2002); artt. 79 and 90 (oaths) of the Const. of Egypt (1971); art. 67 (oath) of the Const. of Iran (1979); art. 43 (oath) of the Const. of Jordan (1952); artt. 60 and 91 (oaths) of the Const. of Kuwait (1962); art. 50 (oath) of the Lebanese Const. (1926); artt. 7 and 50 (oaths) of the Basic Law of the Sultanate of Oman (1996); artt. 10, 74, 92 and 119 (oaths) of the Const. of Qatar (2003); art. 7 (oath) Const. of Syria (1973); art. 42 (oath) of the Const. of Tunisia (1959); art. 52 (oath) of the Const. of the United Arab Emirates (1971); art. 159 (oath) of the Const. of Yemen (1990); preamble of the Const. of Afghanistan (2004); preamble and art. 8 of the Const. of Bangladesh (1972); Schedule (oaths) to the Const. of Maldives (2008); preamble of the Const. of Pakistan (1973); preamble of the Const. of Peru (1993); preamble of the Const. of Saint Kitts and Nevis (1983); preamble of the Const. of Saint Lucia (1978); and the preamble of the Const. of Suriname (1987).

91 Art. 9 (and art. 44: oath of the temporary executor) of the Const. of Norway (1814).

92 Preamble of Const. of Samoa (1960).

limits prescribed by Him".[93] The Constitution of Samoa similarly holds that whilst sovereignty over the Universe in principle belongs to the omnipresent God alone, authority over Samoa is "to be exercised by the people of Samoa within the limits prescribed by His commandments".[94] The Constitution of Brunei Darussalam depicts God as "Lord of the Universe".[95]

- *Immortality*

An everlasting God seems *prima facie* somewhat tautological as 'God' as a metaphysical notion is necessarily an impalpable concept not susceptible to death[96] (although it must be noted that in Greek religious mythology immortals occasionally fell whilst mortals occasionally acquired immortality).[97] Some Constitutions nonetheless seem determined to categorically exclude the possibility of God as a mortal God and explicitly attribute perpetuity to this notion.[98]

- *Interventionism*

The Sudanese Constitution depicts God as an interventionist God and notes the 2005 Sudan Peace Agreement as evidence of this fact.[99]

- *Trinitarianism*

Greece and Ireland constitutionally subscribe to the Holy Trinity doctrine,[100] the metaphysical notion within Christianity[101] which holds that God simultaneously manifests itself, whilst being one and the same being, as the Father, the Son and the Holy Spirit.[102]

---

[93] Preamble of the Const. of Pakistan (1973).

[94] Preamble of the Const. of Samoa (1960).

[95] Preamble of the Const. of Brunei Darussalam (1959).

[96] Then again, a truly *omni*potent God is in theory able to terminate its own existence.

[97] *E.g.* Ganymedes, born mortal, acquired immortality and became the Gods' cupbearer (and Zeus' lover); later he was further immortalized as Zeus turned him into a star (the constellation Aquarius); on the other hand, Pterelaus, who was thought immortal, died after his golden hair was pulled.

[98] Preamble of the Const. of Nauru (1968); preamble of the Const. of Tuvalu (1986).

[99] Preamble of the Interim Const. of the Sudan (2005).

[100] Preamble ("In the name of the Holy and Consubstantial and Indivisible Trinity…") and artt. 33 and 59 (oaths) of the Const. of Greece (2001); preamble of the Const. of Ireland (1937): "In the name of the Most Holy Trinity, from Whom is all authority and to Whom, as our final end, all actions both of men and States must be referred, We, the people of Ireland, humbly acknowledging all our obligations to our Divine Lord, Jesus Christ, Who sustained our fathers through centuries of trial…"

[101] Note that the notion of trinity is not unique to Christianity (*e.g. Trimurti*, Hindu trinity; Ayyavazhi trinity; the Shinto trinity; Triple Goddess notions in neo-pagan religions and Wicca; Zoroastrian trinity, etc.).

[102] The Holy Trinity, though not explicitly mentioned in the New Testament of the Christian Bible, is based on various passages in it, *e.g.* Matthew 28:19 ("Go therefore and make disciples of all nations, baptizing them in the name of the Father and of the Son and of the Holy Spirit"); 2 Corinthians 13:14 ("The grace of the Lord Jesus Christ and the love of God and the fellowship of the Holy Spirit be with you all"); and John 10:30 ("I and the Father are one"; Holy Bible, English Standard Version).

- *Positive Characteristics*

Notable (other) positive characteristics that are attributed to God in Constitutions include: God as the Ever Loving,[103] God the Exalted,[104] God the Compassionate,[105] God the Merciful,[106] God the Beneficent,[107] God as Protector and Defender,[108] and God as the Giver of all Good Things.[109] Some of these names in Constitutions of Islamic states are references to the so-called 'Ninety-nine Most Beautiful Names of God', i.e. names given to Allah in the Quran.[110]

- *Monotheism*

Finally, it could be argued that all the above constitutional references to a singular 'God' are equivalent of state endorsement of monotheism. It has to be acknowledged, though, that a reference to the "one and only God" (as codified by the Indonesian Constitution)[111] does so in a much more outspoken fashion.

Religious Founders

Unlike, for instance, constitutional God-notions or constitutional references to the Holy Trinity, constitutional references to such historical persons as Jesus Christ or Muhammad could in theory be made in a neutral manner, or at least in a manner that does not amount to a confession of faith. In practice, however, these references are rarely devoid of some confessional connotation.

Constitutions that speak in praiseworthy terms of Jesus Christ include the Constitution of Fiji, Greece and Ireland. The most neutral reference is perhaps the one in the Fijian Constitution: "RECALLING the events in our history

---

[103] Preamble of the CONST. OF SAMOA (1960).

[104] Art. 67 (oath) of the CONST. OF IRAN (1979).

[105] Preamble of the CONST. OF ALGERIA (1976); preamble of the CONST. OF BRUNEI DARUSSALAM (1959); art. 67 (oath) CONST. OF IRAN (1979); preamble of the CONST. OF IRAQ (2005) ("the most compassionate"); and the preamble of the CONST. OF TUNISIA (1959).

[106] Preamble of the CONST. OF ALGERIA (1976); preamble of the CONST. OF BANGLADESH (1972); preamble of the CONST. OF BRUNEI DARUSSALAM (1959); art. 67 (oath) of the CONST. OF IRAN (1979) ("the most Merciful"); preamble of the CONST. OF IRAQ (2005) ("the most Merciful"); preamble of the CONST. OF KUWAIT (1962); preamble of the TRANSITIONAL FEDERAL CHARTER OF THE SOMALI REPUBLIC (2004); and the preamble of the CONST. OF TUNISIA (1959).

[107] Preamble of the CONST. OF BANGLADESH (1972); preamble of the CONST. OF KUWAIT (1962); and the preamble of the TRANSITIONAL FEDERAL CHARTER OF THE SOMALI REPUBLIC (2004).

[108] Preamble of the CONST. OF THE UNITED ARAB EMIRATES (1971).

[109] Preamble of the CONST. OF NAURU (1968); and the preamble of the CONST. OF TUVALU (1986).

[110] Based on Quran 7:180: "The most beautiful names belong to Allah" (THE HOLY QUR'AN, transl. Abdullah Yusuf Ali). The Quran in fact contains more than 99 names for Allah; the 'Ninety-nine' are supposed to be the most beautiful. There have been different attempts to list them; *e.g.* MUHAMMAD AL-MADANĪ, TASBIH ASMĀ ALLĀH AL-HUSNĀ.

[111] Preamble and art. 29 of the CONST. OF INDONESIA (1945).

that have made us what we are, especially...the conversion of the indigenous inhabitants of these islands from heathenism to Christianity through the power of the name of Jesus Christ".[112] The reference in the Greek Constitution is of a more confessional nature as it speaks of "our Lord Jesus Christ".[113] The same holds true, *a fortiori*, for the Irish Constitution as it provides that the people of Ireland "humbly [acknowledge] all our obligations to our Divine Lord, Jesus Christ, Who sustained our fathers through centuries of trial".[114]

Several states that identify with Islam refer to Muhammad in the Constitution. It goes without saying that these references are not devoid of confessional connotations. His name is as a rule preceded by the epithet "Prophet" (for instance, in the Constitutions of Afghanistan, Iraq, Maldives, Pakistan, Saudi Arabia and Yemen).[115] The Constitution of Brunei Darussalam refers to "our leader Muhammad".[116]

Founding Sources

Constitutional references to religious sources, similar in that respect to references to historical religious leaders or founders, could in theory be made in a non-confessional fashion. As is to be expected, in practice these references function as a further exemplification of the state's form of state–religion identification. The Greek Constitution refers to the Bible ("the Holy Scripture") and constitutionally protects it against alteration or unauthorized translations (prior consent to translate is to be obtained form the Church).[117] The Declaration of the Establishment of the State of Israel of 1948 refers to the "eternal Book of Books",[118] a reference to the Hebrew Bible of course. Bahrain, Brunei Darussalam, Iran, Maldives, Pakistan, Saudi Arabia and Yemen refer one or more times to the Quran in their Constitution.[119] The Constitution of

---

[112] Preamble of the CONST. OF THE FIJI ISLANDS (1998). Though this is perhaps not a religious reference in itself, it should be read in conjunction with and in light of other statements made in the preamble (such as: "seeking the blessing of God who has always watched over these islands") to fully appreciate the nature of this reference.

[113] Preamble of the CONST. OF GREECE (2001).

[114] Preamble of the CONST. OF IRELAND (1937).

[115] Art. 19 of the CONST. OF AFGHANISTAN (2004); preamble of the CONST. OF IRAQ (2005); art. 274 of the CONST. OF MALDIVES (2008); art. 203D of the CONST. OF PAKISTAN (1973); preamble and artt. 3, 6 and 7 of the BASIC LAW OF SAUDI ARABIA (1992); and art. 159 (oath) of the CONST. OF YEMEN (1990).

[116] Preamble of THE CONST. OF BRUNEI DARUSSALAM (1959).

[117] Art. 3, para. (3), of the CONST. OF GREECE (2001). The CONST. OF CYPRUS (1960) refers to the "Holy Canons" (art. 110).

[118] As mentioned before; see first para. of the Declaration of the Establishment of the State of Israel (1948).

[119] Preamble of the CONST. OF BAHRAIN (2002); in Brunei's case, the references are contained in: Governmental Proclamation: *National Philosophy* [of Brunei Darussalam]; preamble (nine times), and artt. 1, 2, 7, 8, 11, 16, 67 (oath: "the Glorious Quran") and 151 of the CONST. OF IRAN (1979); art. 274 of the CONST. OF MALDIVES (2008); preamble and artt. 31, 203D, 227, 228 and 230 of the CONST. OF PAKISTAN (1973); artt. 6 and 7 of the BASIC LAW OF SAUDI ARABIA (1992); and art. 159 (oath) CONST. OF YEMEN (1990).

Iran mentions the Quran (including the adjective Quranic) more than 15 times and quotes quite extensively from it.[120] Some of these states also refer explicitly to the *Sunna*, Muhammad's traditions (literally translated as 'path') in terms of the sayings and acts he is credited with.[121]

Notions of Sanctity

Constitutional declarations as to the "holy"[122] or "sacred"[123] nature of things/places/people are fairly common. "Sacred" means "connected with God and treated as holy",[124] whilst "holy" means "dedicated to God or a religious purpose".[125] Declaring or considering something or someone "holy" or "sacred" is thus arguably a confessional act in itself. There are some exceptions in this regard. A few states in the western hemisphere have opted for a constitutional definition of a minister of religion as a "person in holy orders".[126] Such use of the word 'holy' is arguably purely procedural as a person in holy orders simply denotes a person who is appointed by the Church to function as a deacon,

---

[120] To be precise: Quran, verses 2:143, 3:28, 3:159, 4:58, 7:157, 8:60 (two times), 9:71, 21:92 (two times), 21:105, 28:5 and 42:38.

[121] Art. 2 of the Const. of Iran (1979); preamble and artt. 31, 203D, 227, 228 and 230 of the Const. of Pakistan (1973); artt. 1, 45 and 48 of the Basic Law of Saudi Arabia (1992); and art. 159 (oath) of the Const. of Yemen (1990).

[122] Preamble of the Const. of Samoa (1960); *National Philosophy* of Brunei Darussalam as proclaimed by the Government ("Holy Quran"); art. 6 of the Const. of Tonga (1875); art 110 ("Holy Canons") of the Const. of Cyprus (1960); preamble, art 3 ("Holy Scripture", among other references) and art. 33 (oath) of the Const. of Greece (2001); preamble of the Const. of Ireland (1937); artt. 2 and 177 of the Const. of Iran (1979); art. 10 ("holy shrines") of the Const. of Iraq (2005) (in the preamble a reference to "saints" is made as well); Declaration of the Establishment of the State of Israel of 1948 ("Holy Places"); artt. 6 ("holy Quran"), 7, 24 ("Holy Places", *i.e.* Mecca and Medina) and 33 of the Basic Law of Saudi Arabia (1992); art. 31 ("Holy Quran"), art. 203D ("Holy Quran" and "Holy Prophet") and artt. 227, 228 and 230 ("Holy Quran") of the Const. of Pakistan (1973). The Constitution of the Kingdom of Bhutan (2008), finally, uses "holiness".

[123] Preamble of the Const. of Samoa (1960); art. 3 of the Const. of Greece (2001); artt. 11 and 14 ("sacred verse of the Quran") of the Const. of Iran (1979); art. 10 ("sacred law" and "sacred spiritual value") of the Great Green Charter of Human Rights of the Jamahiriyan Era of 1988 (Libya); art. 59 ("sacred duty") of the Const. of Yemen (1990); artt. 2, 3, 19 and 149 of the Const. of Afghanistan (2004); and the preamble of the Const. of Pakistan (1973); the Const. of Iraq (2005) uses "sanctity" (art. 10).

[124] Oxford English Dictionary (compact 3rd ed., 2005), p. 907; another meaning is: "religious rather than secular". Caveat: such terminology could in theory be used in a procedural way, i.e. something is referred to as sacred/holy because the relevant religious institutions or religious people present in the state consider it to be so. Particularly referring to a founding religious document as a sacred text is not necessarily a confessional act as 'sacred' in this context can simply refer to a text considered holy by a religious community (the same dictionary indeed lists as another possible meaning of 'sacred': "containing the doctrines of a religion"). In practice, however, these notions appear to be employed rather so as to further substantiate the state's positive form of state–religion identification.

[125] Oxford English Dictionary (compact 3rd ed., 2005), p. 483.

[126] Art. 32 of the Const. of Dominica (1978); art. 28 of the Const. of Saint Kitts and Nevis (1983); artt. 28 and 32 of the Const. of Saint Lucia (1978); and art. 26 of the Const. of Saint Vincent and the Grenadines.

priest of bishop (in other words, it could be argued that the states in question do not endorse the holiness of such orders here, but simply follow the Church's terminology as to the ordination of Church officials).[127] Obviously, the expression "things held sacred by religion" (Turkish Constitution) is perfectly neutral.[128]

Other Metaphysical Notions

A few Constitutions endorse notions of "divinity" or "divine" (mostly in conjunction with other God-notions).[129] The Egyptian Constitution is unique in using the adjective "heavenly".[130] The Declaration of the Establishment of the State of Israel refers to the "prophets of Israel".[131] The Iraqi Constitution refers to Adam,[132] who is in Islam considered the first prophet (and, as in all Abrahamic religions, the first person to be created by God).[133] The term *jihad* (literally meaning struggle) in the Constitutions of Afghanistan and Iran is not devoid of a religious connotation either.[134]

(iii) *State Symbolism & Religion*

God or other religious notions can be acknowledged in many other more or less official ways. One might think of the design of bank notes or coins (for example, the infamous "In God We Trust" on the US currency).

[127] Holy orders may be described as "…the sacrament through which the mission entrusted by Christ to his apostles continues to be exercised in the Church until the end of time: thus it is the sacrament of apostolic ministry. It includes three degrees: episcopate, presbyterate, and diaconate [i.e. bishop, priest and deacon]…The word *order* in Roman antiquity designated an established civil body, especially a governing body. *Ordinatio* means incorporation into an *ordo*. In the Church there are established bodies which Tradition, not without a basis in Sacred Scripture, has since ancient times called *taxeis* (Greek) or *ordines*. And so the liturgy speaks of the *ordo episcoporum*, the *ordo presbyterorum*, the *ordo diaconorum*". See art. 6 (1536 and 1537; part II, Ch. II, sec. II) of the *Catechism of the Catholic Church* (2003).

[128] Art. 24, para. (5), of the Constitution of the Republic of Turkey (1982).

[129] Art. 10 ("divinity") Great Green Charter of Human Rights of the Jamahiriyan Era of 1988 (Libya); for "divine", see preamble of the Const. of Liberia (1986); preamble of the Const. of Palau (1979); preamble of the Const. of Ireland (1937); and artt. 2 and 61 of the Const. of Iran (1979).

[130] Preamble of the Const. of Egypt (1971).

[131] See the Declaration of the Establishment of the State of Israel (1948). Which presumably are those persons identified as prophets by the Hebrew Bible, *e.g.*: Ahijah, Amos, Azariah, Eliezer, Elijah, Elisha, Ezekiel, Gad, Habakkuk, Haggai, Hanani, Hosea, Huldah, Iddo, Isaiah, Jahaziel, Jehu, Jeremiah, Joel, Jonah, Malachi, Micah, Micaiah, Nahum, Nathan, Obadiah, Oded, Samuel, Shemaiah, Uriah, Zechariah and Zephaniah.

[132] Preamble of the Const. of Iraq (2005).

[133] Adam is frequently mentioned in the Quran, *e.g.* verses 2:31, 2:33-35, 2:37, 3:33, 3:59, 5:22, 7:11, 7:19, 7:26-27, 7:31, 7:35 and 7:172.

[134] Preamble and art. 147 of Const. of Iran (1979); and the preamble of the Const. of Afghanistan (2004). Ninian Smart, The World's Religions (Victoria: Cambridge University Press, 1992), p. 288, considers *jihad* the "Sixth Pillar" of Islam. Jihad, as a struggle for God, is also one of the ten so-called 'Practices of the Religion' (duties) of the Twelver school of Shi'a Islam, *i.e.* the official religion of Iran.

Also the official coat of arms of a state may contain religious connotations (for instance, the coat of arms of the Dominican Republic shows the words "Dios, Patria, Libertad", or "God, Fatherland, Liberty", an opened bible and a cross).[135] In the following, the focus will be on official state mottos and national flags, as these may be considered the fields—outside the realm of state laws—most commonly used by states to (semi-)officially propagate a religious message.

State Mottos

A state motto is a national slogan that expresses in one short phrase some of the main characteristics of a nation. State mottos that endorse religious notions include the mottos of: Brunei Darussalam ("Always Render Service by God's Guidance"); Dominica ("After the Good Lord, We Love the Earth"); Ecuador ("God, Homeland and Liberty"); El Salvador ("God, Union, Liberty"); Fiji ("Fear God and Honour the Queen"); Granada ("Ever Conscious of God We Aspire, and Advance as One People"); Iraq ("God is Great");[136] Jordan ("God, Country, Sovereign"); Liechtenstein ("For God, Prince and Fatherland"); Monaco ("With God's Help"); Nauru ("God's Will First"); Philippines ("God, People, Nature and Country");[137] Samoa ("God be the Foundation of Samoa"); Tonga ("God and Tonga are My Inheritance"); Tuvalu ("Tuvalu for the Almighty"); Uganda ("For God and My Country"); United Kingdom ("Dieu Et Mon Droit");[138] United States of America ("In God We Trust");[139] and Vanuatu ("In God we Stand").

Some religious state mottos have a basis in the Constitution. Morocco's Constitution, for instance, lays down that the official motto is: "God, The Country, the King".[140] The official motto of Iran is the *Takbir* ("God is the Greatest", or "God is Great").[141] The motto of Saudi Arabia is the *Shahadah* ("There is But One God and Mohammed is his Prophet"),[142] that is, the Islamic profession of faith (being one of the five

---

[135] As per art. 96 of the Const. of the Dominican Republic (1966).

[136] *I.e.* the *Takbir*: "*Alahu Akbar*".

[137] As per sec. 40 of the Republic Act No. 8491 – An Act Prescribing the Code of the National Flag, Anthem, Motto, Coat-of-Arms and other Heraldic Items and Devices of the Philippines.

[138] Adopted by Henry V in the 15th century (meaning: "God and my Right" and presumably denoting the monarch's right to govern – under divine guidance – the state). Also used on the royal coat of arms.

[139] As per Act of Congress P.L. 84-140, Law 36 U.S.C. 186, approved by the President on 30 July 1956.

[140] Art. 7 of the Const. of Morocco (1972); transliteration: "*Allāh, al Waṭan, al Malik*".

[141] Transliteration: *Alahu Akbar*. As referred to in art. 18 of the Const. of Iran (1979). The *de facto* motto however is: "Independence, freedom, the Islamic Republic".

[142] Art. 3 of the Basic Law of Saudi Arabia (1992); transliteration: "*Lā ilāhā illā-llāhu; muhammadun rasūlu-llāhi*".

pillars of Islam).[143] The official motto of the Kingdom of Cambodia is: "NATION, RELIGION, KING".[144] The Constitution of the Dominican Republic provides that its motto is "GOD, FATHERLAND, LIBERTY".[145]

Flags

The design of the national flag may or may not have a basis in the Constitution.[146] Many predominantly Christian states show a cross, symbolising Christianity, on their national flag. The Union flag of the United Kingdom of Great Britain and Northern-Ireland makes reference to three Christian patron saints: the patron saint of England, represented by the red cross of Saint George, the patron saint of Ireland, represented by the red saltire of Saint Patrick, and the patron saint of Scotland, represented by the saltire of Saint Andrew.[147] The so-called Scandinavian crosses or Nordic crosses on the flags of the Nordic countries—Denmark, Finland, Iceland, Norway and Sweden—also represent Christianity. The Swiss flag, depicting a white cross on a red background (very similar to a 13th century banner of the Holy Roman Empire), presumably has a Christian connotation as well. The same holds true for the flag of Tonga, which shows a red cross on a white background. The cross on the flag of Dominica represents Christianity while the three colours of which the cross consists stand for the Trinity. The coat of arms depicted on the flag of Slovakia shows a double cross. The flag of the Dominican Republic shows the words "God, Fatherland, Liberty", an opened bible and a cross (depicted in the coat of arms which is represented in the centre).[148] The 'five-cross-flag' of Georgia shows four small crosses and a large St. George's Cross, referring to the patron saint of Georgia (the national flag of England shows the St. George's Cross as well). The white cross on the flag of Greece symbolizes Greek Orthodoxy. The flag of Moldova shows its coat of arms in the centre: an eagle with a Christian Orthodox cross in its beak. The coat of arms of Serbia, as depicted on the national flag, also shows an Orthodox cross. The flag of the Vatican City shows the keys to the kingdom of heaven, given to Peter by Jesus Christ according to the bible (popes are considered

---

[143] *Viz.*, *Shahadah* (profession of faith, affirming that one believes that there is no God but Allah, and that Muhammad is His messenger), *Salah* (ritual prayer five times each day), *Sawm* (fasting during Ramadan), *Zakat* (charity given to the poor) and the *Hajj* (pilgrimage to Mecca).

[144] Art. 4 of the CONST. OF CAMBODIA (1993).

[145] As per art. 96 of the CONST. OF THE DOMINICAN REPUBLIC (1966) ("*Dios, Patria, Libertad*").

[146] This exercise in vexillology is indebted to the excellent FOTW database.

[147] Thus, the same holds true, indirectly, for some Commonwealth states such as Australia, Fiji, New Zealand, and Tuvalu, as their flags (among other things) represent the Union flag (in the top left-hand corner).

[148] As per art. 95 of the CONST. OF THE DOMINICAN REPUBLIC (1966). The civil flag omits the coat of arms.

successors of Peter in Catholic doctrine).[149] Also depicted is the Papal Tiara, the papal crown.

Turning to the flags of predominantly Muslim states, religious symbols can be found in equal measure. The green colour on flags usually (though not necessarily)[150] symbolizes Islam (see, for instance, the flags of Algeria, Azerbaijan, Libya,[151] Mauritania, Morocco and Pakistan). The crescent symbol, although the use of the symbol has a long pre-Islamic past,[152] on the flags of predominantly Muslim states also symbolizes Islam (e.g. Comoros, Malaysia, Maldives, Mauritania and Tunisia), as does a five-pointed star (Tunisia).[153] On the national flag of the Kingdom of Saudi Arabia the *Shahadah* ("There is but one God and Mohammed is His Prophet") is inscribed in the centre with a sword placed underneath it.[154] The flag of the Islamic Republic of Afghanistan also cites the *Shahadah*, together with the *Takbir* ("God is the greatest", *Alahu Akbar*).[155] The Iraqi and the Iranian flags, too, cite the *Takbir*.[156] The five white points on the Bahraini flag represent the five pillars or duties of Islam.[157] The seven-pointed star on the flag of Jordan stands for the first seven verses (together composing the first *Sura*, chapter) of the Quran.[158]

The *Ashoka Chakra* (the Wheel of Dharma) on the Indian flag—a wheel with 24 spokes—dates back to Aśoka the Great and could be considered a reference to the wisdom of the Indian Dharmic religions. The *Soyombo* symbol depicted on the flag of Mongolia is closely connected with Tibetan (Lamaistic)

---

[149] Holy Bible (English Standard Version), Mathew 16:19: "I will give you the keys of the kingdom of heaven, and whatever you bind on earth shall be bound in heaven, and whatever you loose on earth shall be loosed in heaven."

[150] *E.g.* Bangladesh, Kuwait, Oman, Sudan, Tajikistan and United Arab Emirates; in which cases it rather appears to symbolize the greenery or fertility of the landscape, prosperity and occasionally agriculture.

[151] Libya's flag is entirely green, which is arguably also a reference to Gaddafi's Green Revolution. See Muammar Abu Minyar al-Gaddafi, The Green Book (1975), for Gaddafi's revolutionary agenda.

[152] *E.g.* Whitney Smith, Flags through the Ages and Across the World, (New York: McGraw-Hill Book Co., 1975), on the crescent and star in the Ottoman context.

[153] Presumably denoting the five pillars or duties in Islam.

[154] In accordance with art. 3 (c) of the Basic Law of Saudi Arabia (1992).

[155] As per art. 19 of the Const. of Afghanistan (2004). The flag of the not internationally recognized state of Somaliland also contains the Islamic creed (adopted by the National Conference on 14 October 1996).

[156] Flag of Iran: designed by Hamid Nadimi and officially approved by Ayatollah Khomeini in 1980; the coat of arms, made of four crescents and a sword and positioned in the middle, forms the word Allah. Flag of Iraq: in 2008 the handwriting of Saddam Hussein was replaced by a neutral font.

[157] See *supra*, footnote 143.

[158] The Holy Qur'an (transl. Abdullah Yusuf Ali), 1:1–1:7: "In the name of Allah, Most Gracious, Most Merciful. Praise be to Allah, the Cherisher and Sustainer of the worlds; Most Gracious, Most Merciful; Master of the Day of Judgment. Thee do we worship and Thine aid we seek. Show us the straight way, The way of those on whom Thou hast bestowed Thy Grace, those whose (portion) is not wrath, and who go not astray."

Buddhism.[159] The Sacred Fig (*Ficus religiosa*) leaves depicted on the flag of Sri Lanka are references to Buddhism (Siddhartha Gautama attained enlightenment sitting under a Bodhi tree). The orange colour on the flag of Bhutan presumably stands for Buddhism as well.

The Israeli flag, which was adopted in October 1948 shortly after its establishment, depicts a blue *Magen David*. The precise origin of associations of the Star of David (a hexagram) with Jewry is still subject of scholarly debates.[160] The symbol is by no means a symbol designed by Judaism. This does of course not mean that the flag of Israel is devoid of a religious connotation. Art historian Alec Mishory contends:

> Unlike the *menora* (candelabrum), the Lion of Judah, the *shofar* (ram's horn) and the *lulav* (palm frond), the Star of David was never a uniquely Jewish symbol… According to Sholem, the motive for the widespread use of the Star of David was a wish to imitate Christianity. During the Emancipation, Jews needed a symbol of Judaism parallel to the cross, the universal symbol of Christianity. In particular, they wanted something to adorn the walls of the modern Jewish house of worship that would be symbolic like the cross. This is why the Star of David became prominent in the nineteenth century and why it was later used on ritual objects and in synagogues and eventually reached Poland and Russia. The pursuit of imitation, in Sholem's opinion, led to the dissemination of an emblem that was not really Jewish and conveyed no Jewish message. In his opinion, it was also the reason why the Star of David satisfied Zionism: it was a symbol which had already attained wide circulation among the Jewish communities but at the same time evoked no clear-cut religious associations. The Star of David became the emblem of Zionist Jews everywhere. Non-Jews regarded it as representing not only the Zionist current in Judaism, but Jewry as a whole.[161]

The blue lines on the flag are intended as reference to the *tallit*, the Jewish prayer shawl.[162]

3.4 Concluding Remarks

In this chapter it has been outlined that there are more subtle ways than outright establishment for the state to identify with a religion. In most cases the difference is not but a matter of terminology: many of the most far-reaching measures (a constitutional religion–law nexus, etc.) employed to ensure a strong identification of the state with the dominant religion practised by

---

[159] John S. Major, The Land and People of Mongolia 183 (New York: Lippincott, Williams & Wilkins, 1990).

[160] *E.g.* Gerbern S. Oegema, The History of the Shield of David: the Birth of a Symbol (Frankfurt am Main/New York: Peter Lang Publ., 1996).

[161] Alec Mishory, *The Flag and the Anthem* (published by the Israeli Ministry of Foreign Affairs as part of the Israel at 50 series, 2003).

[162] *Idem.*

religious states we do not see in regimes of state support. Mutual moral and political support and (one-way) financial support is what seems mostly at stake in the context of state support. Having said that, we have also seen examples where the choice of state support over legal establishment would seem to be a political one (establishment 'disguised' as support, as it were). Also, concluding that some forms of state support are less far-reaching than some of the instances described in the previous Chapter does not necessarily mean that human rights law does not come into play here (see Part II of this book). As far as the phenomenon of state acknowledgement is concerned, we have seen that there are ways of recognizing a certain religious heritage or certain demographical data which are perfectly non-preferential. However, we have also seen that there is a very fine line in that regard and that terminology that seems *prima facie* impartial, may—upon closer inspection—very well be used at the exclusion of certain beliefs or groups of people. We will presently turn to the more intermediate part of the state–religion identification spectrum: slowly but surely we are moving away from the part of the spectrum which is characterized by an evident, clear-cut identification of the state with one religion. The following Chapter will discuss the phenomenon of accommodation of religion*s* and regimes of non-identification.

CHAPTER FOUR

ACCOMMODATION OF RELIGIONS & NON-IDENTIFICATION

4.1 Introduction

In the previous Chapter the focus was on those states that, without an explicit intention of establishing a religion as the state religion, support a single religion or constitutionally acknowledge the role or position of the traditional religion within the state. States may cooperate or interrelate with religions, or accommodate religions, without treating a specific religion preferentially. Such forms of state practice would certainly not come down to establishing or endorsing a religion for it is 'Religion' *in abstracto* that is being accommodated. This (potentially) non-preferential form of interaction between the state and religion would, strictly speaking, also rule out a clear-cut separationist state (see Chapter 5) as under such regimes all forms of state interference with religious affairs or religious interference with state affairs are in principle taboo. Different regimes of accommodation have emerged in different states for different reasons; moreover, they all have different legal consequences. This also means that the precise degree of 'non-preferentiality' varies. The objective of this Chapter is to chart the precise legal ramifications of the phenomenon of accommodation of religion. States that are constitutionally 'indifferent' to the question of religion can and must be distinguished from states that actively accommodate religion. These states have not established a religion as state religion, they do not distinctly support one religion over other religions nor expressly accommodate more than one religion simultaneously; yet, they do not explicitly or proactively seek to internalize the ideal of secularism or separationism (a policy of strict separation of state and religion) either. In these instances of ostensible 'non-identification', state practice must be scrutinized closely in order to assess whether such states are *de facto* secular or non-secular.

4.2 Accommodation of Religion: Unspecified Support vs. Support for Various Religions

Most states at some point in time have actively supported the country's traditional or dominant religion. Accommodation of different religions is a relatively recently emerging modus of state–religion identification. This phenomenon begs the question what could be the rationale behind this policy. Looking at state practice, 'accommodation of religion' as an arrangement has come to the fore as a political solution to recent religious strife; in other cases it seems that the state in question considers this arrangement to flow logically from—also relatively recently emerging—norms of international law.

It is postulated at the outset that in most cases of apparent 'accommodation of religion', the arrangement is not, upon closer inspection, as non-preferential as the term suggests. A distinction must be made between states that seek to accommodate and render support to religion (unspecified) and states that support the officially recognized religions.[1] The two systems are comparable in that neither institute a preference for a single religion on the part of the state. The difference is that under the former system all religions are in principle eligible for state support whilst under the latter regime there may be religions that are devoid of official recognition and consequently of state support. The discussion of state practice below demonstrates that the number of states which genuinely accommodate and support religion *in abstracto* is fairly small. Constitutional accommodation of religion in practice, more often than not, translates into practices of cooperation and support from which some (but not all) religions and beliefs benefit.

Within the category of accommodation of religion it is possible to further distinguish between arrangements that allow for direct political representation of religions; systems that provide for an advisory role of religions; financial support; and, finally, a few *sui generis* arrangements.

4.2.1 *Direct Political Representation of Religions*

Direct political representation of the various religious groups present in a country is the measure *par excellence* in seeking to accommodate differing religious interests. For instance, up to eight of the 70 seats of the National Assembly of Mauritius are taken by members belonging to one of the four recognized ethnic/religious communities,[2] namely, the Hindu community, the Muslim community, the Sino-Mauritian (Chinese Mauritanians) community and 'others' (i.e. Creole).[3] Another good example is the Constitution of Malawi which provides that the—as yet to be established—Senate of Malawi shall partly consists of representatives of the "major religious faiths" in Malawi.[4] The major religious faiths are Protestantism (55 per cent), Roman Catholicism (20 per cent) and Islam (20 per cent).[5]

---

[1] It will come as no surprise that this is also very relevant indeed from a human rights perspective; see Part II of this study, particularly Chapter 9.

[2] Art. 31, para. (2), in conjunction with First Schedule of the Const. of Mauritius (1968).

[3] William F.S. Miles, *The Mauritius Enigma*, 10(2) Journal of Democracy 101 (1999).

[4] Art. 68 of the Const. of Malawi (1994).

[5] This means that several beliefs do not benefit from this arrangement; *e.g.* indigenous beliefs; Hinduism, the Bahá'í faith, Rastafarianism and non-religious beliefs.

The Constitution of Lebanon takes political representation of religions to a different level as it provides for a complete confessional distribution of seats for the Parliament[6] and the Senate,[7] as well as other public offices and positions (e.g. senior public service positions, the judiciary, but also the security institutions and so-called public and mixed agencies).[8] The system of equal representation[9] with respect to Muslims and Christians (both religions occupy 64 out of the 128 seats in Parliament) does not come down to proportional representation as there are more Muslims than Christians in Lebanon.[10] The system in fact used to be less proportional. The sectarian division of seats was slightly straightened as a consequence of the Taif Agreement which was concluded at the end of the Lebanese Civil War (1975–1990), by virtue of which a six-to-five ratio was brought back to a 50:50 ratio.[11] Within each of the two religions seats are allocated proportionally to every specific denomination: Maronite Christian, Greek Orthodox, Greek Catholic, Armenian Apostolic, Armenian Catholic and Protestant on the one hand; and Sunni, Shi'a, Druze and Alawite on the other. The National Pact of 1943 had already divided up the most senior public offices:[12] the President of the Republic is to be a Maronite Christian, the Prime Minister (President of the Council of Ministers) a Sunni Muslim, the speaker of Parliament a Shi'a Muslim and the deputy speaker of the Parliament a Greek Orthodox. It must be acknowledged that the Taif Agreement clearly contained short-term and longer-term objectives. The first revolved around an immediate rebalancing of the sectarian division of power, which predominantly came down to curtailing the privileges Christians had gained under French rule and which were further consolidated within the framework of the National Pact of 1943. Besides the already mentioned rebalancing of the sectarian representation in Parliament, the fact that the (Sunni) Prime Minister would henceforth no longer be answerable to the (Maronite) President but to the Parliament may be mentioned as another striking example. The long-term objective of the Agreement was the eventual abolition of political sectarianism. However, even though the end of "political confessionalism"[13] is also constitutionally anticipated, it is as yet far from being replaced by "the principle of expertise and competence".[14]

---

[6] Art. 24 (Chamber of Deputies or National Assembly) of the Lebanese Const. (1926).

[7] Art. 22 of the Lebanese Const. (1926).

[8] Art. 95 of the Lebanese Const. (1926).

[9] Art. 24, para. (1), sec. (a), of the Lebanese Const. (1926).

[10] To which it may be added that no seats are allocated to minorities which are both non-Muslim *and* non-Christian; *e.g.* Bahá'ís, Buddhists, Hindus, Jews and non-believers.

[11] Taif Agreement of 22 October 1989. Prior to the Taif Agreement the situation was as follows: Christians: 54 out of 99 seats; Muslims: 45 out of 99 seats (as per the National Pact of 1943).

[12] National Pact of 1943: unwritten agreement concluded in the summer of 1943.

[13] Art. 95 of the Lebanese Const. (1926).

[14] Art. 95, para. (3), sec. (b), of the Lebanese Const. (1926). With the main exception perhaps being the Lebanese Armed Forces.

4.2.2 *Advisory Role of Religions*

To be distinguished from systems of direct religious representation within the political realm are those systems which ensure that the religious communities are consulted with respect to certain political decisions. The Constitution of East Timor, for instance, promotes "the cooperation with the different religious denominations that contribute to the well-being of the people of Timor Leste",[15] which in practice translates into such a form of consultation. The body that has been established for this purpose functions as an inter-religious consultative body and consists of Catholics (the predominant religion with approximately 98 per cent of the population adhering to this denomination), as well as Protestant and Muslim representatives (the remaining two per cent with roughly one per cent each). It is asked for its advice whenever the state deals with matters that potentially touch upon religious interests. In St. Lucia, to give another example, "religious associations" (unspecified) have a limited role in the appointment of new members of the Senate.[16]

4.2.3 *Financial State Support for Religions*

Religious states or states with a state religion as a rule provide the protected religion in question with funding (in some instances this arrangement may be partially extended to other religions by means of additional agreements).[17] Many state church regimes were historically characterized by so-called 'tithing schemes' by virtue of which the official church would benefit from certain tax revenues. Thus, the state helps or urges Church members to fulfil certain duties that are derived from ancient Canon law.[18] Remnants thereof can still be seen within some predominantly Catholic states, but also for instance within the Scandinavian state church systems. Some currently secular states, rather than doing away with this system altogether, have extended the benefits to non-traditional or non-dominant religions. The Constitution of Germany, for instance, has created a form of permanent partnership between the state and religion which manifests itself chiefly in the management of financial affairs on behalf of religious organizations.[19] The state collects, on behalf of these

---

15 Art. 12 of the CONST. OF EAST TIMOR (2002).

16 Art. 24 of the CONST. OF SAINT LUCIA (1978) provides that two (out of 11) members shall be appointed "by the Governor-General, acting in his own deliberate judgment after he has consulted those religious, economic or social bodies or associations from which he considers that such Senators should be selected".

17 A clear exception in this context is the United Kingdom which does not provide direct financial support to its established church.

18 *E.g.*, Book II, Pt. I, Title I of the Code of Canon Law; Cann. 222:1: "The Christian faithful are obliged to assist with the needs of the Church so that the Church has what is necessary for divine worship, for the works of the apostolate and of charity, and for the decent support of ministers."

19 Another notable expression of this partnership: registered religious organizations are granted tax-exemptions (as non-profit organizations).

organizations, a tax (a levy or tithe which equates to roughly 9 per cent of income tax) from the members of those religious organizations which are granted a "corporation under public law" status.[20] Such religious organizations also have "the right of entry for religious purposes" into the army, hospitals, prisons or other public institutions (i.e. a right to run chaplaincies).[21] Non-religious organizations ("associations adopting as their work the common encouragement of a world-philosophy") are placed on an equal footing.[22] Around 180 religious organizations have acquired corporation-under-public-law status.[23] The Austrian system is similar in that the various recognized religions that have acquired the status of corporation under public law are granted significant benefits and privileges, including tax advantages and benefits flowing from a similar tithing scheme.[24] Also the system in San Marino is characterized by the levy of a form of church tax,[25] from which presently the Catholic Church, the Waldesian Church and the communities of Bahá'ís and Jehovah's Witnesses profit.

Some states explicitly provide funding to several religious organizations on an equal basis. The Republic of the Marshall Islands, for instance, offers financial support for religious institutions (unspecified). The provision in question states:

> Nothing in this Section [Sec. 1: on Freedom of Thought, Speech, Press, Religion, Assembly, Association, and Petition] shall be construed to prevent government from extending financial aid to religiously supported institutions insofar as they furnish educational, medical or other services at no profit, provided such aid does not discriminate among religious groups or beliefs on the basis of a governmental preference for some religions over others...[26]

This provision does not privilege any particular religion. The Constitution of Luxembourg, to give another example, provides that the salaries and pensions

---

[20] Art. 137, para. (5) in conjunction with para. (6), of the Weimar Constitution of 1919 (incorporated, pursuant art. 140, into the BASIC LAW FOR THE FEDERAL REPUBLIC OF GERMANY of 1949).

[21] Art. 141 of the Weimar Constitution (1919).

[22] Art. 137, para. (7), of the Weimar Constitution (1919).

[23] Including: the Jewish community and many Christian denominations; notably excluding: the Muslim community.

[24] Law on the Recognition of Churches, RGBl. 68/1874, of 1874; and the Law on the Status of Religious Confessional Communities, BGBl. 19/1998, of 1998 (hereinafter: "1998 Austrian Law"). The Catholic, the Protestant, the Eastern Orthodox and the Islamic Community meet the new law's requirements for recognition. The previously recognized religious groups (previously, a total of 13 religious groups were recognized), however, retain their status and privileges. Other religious groups can apply for a (lower) status as "confessional community", which is granted fewer privileges. The FEDERAL CONSTITUTIONAL LAW OF THE REPUBLIC OF AUSTRIA (1920) (hereinafter: Const. of Austria) authorizes the federal legislature to adopt legislation in the field of "religious matters" (art. 10, para. (1), point 13). See also the Concordat between the Republic of Austria and the Holy See ('Dollfuss Concordat') of 5 July 1933 (amended in the 1960s).

[25] As per Law No. 9 of 1993.

[26] Art. 2, para (3), of the CONST. OF THE MARSHALL ISLANDS (1979).

of ministers of religion (unspecified) shall be borne by the State and regulated by the law.[27] Catholic, Greek and Russian Orthodox, Jewish and various Protestant denominations have successfully reached agreements with the state to that effect. The Belgian system can be considered a degree more non-preferential as it takes non-religious, or secular-humanist, organizations explicitly into account.[28] Belgian religious leaders of recognized religions as well as non-religious leaders ("representatives of organisations recognized by the law as providing moral assistance according to a non-religious philosophical concept")[29] are granted remuneration and pensions. Both religious education as well as "non-denominational moral teaching"[30] is financed by the state and the state contributes to the premises of faith organizations. The recognized beliefs at present are Anglicanism, Islam, Judaism, Orthodox Christianity, Protestantism, Roman Catholicism and Secular Humanism. Another good example in the present context is Chile. Roman Catholicism was the state religion in Chile from 1818 until 1925.[31] The 1925 Constitution broke with that tradition by disestablishing the church from the state and granting equal religious freedom to adherents of different religions.[32] The current 1980 Constitution, in conjunction with the 1999 Law on Religions,[33] installs a regime that is characterised by its support of different religions.[34] Churches and other recognized religious organizations which are assigned exclusively for religious activities are exempt from all types of taxes.[35] The 1999 law stipulates how religious organizations can acquire legal personality (which may not be denied by the state)[36] and which other rights and benefits are to be granted to these organizations.[37] The Constitution of the Netherlands, finally, explicitly provides that both public as well as religious primary schools are equally eligible for state

---

[27] Art. 106 of the Constitution of the Grand Duchy of Luxembourg (1868).

[28] Art. 181, para. (1) and (2), of the Constitution of Belgium (1994).

[29] Art. 181, para. (2), of the Const. of Belgium (1994).

[30] Art. 24, para. (1.4), of the Const. of Belgium (1994).

[31] Patrick J. Thurston, *The Development of Religious Liberty in Chile, 1973–2000*, 3 Brigham Young University Law Review (2000), p. 1190.

[32] *Ibid.*, p. 1195.

[33] Law on Religions, No. 19.638, of 1 October 1999 (hereinafter: 1999 Chile Law).

[34] Art. 17 of the 1999 Chile Law states: "The juridical persons of religious entities governed by this law will have the same rights, exemptions, and tax benefits that the Political Constitution of the Republic, the laws, and existing regulations grant and recognize to other churches, confessions, and religious institutions existing in the country" (transl. Thurston). This article, in the words of Isaacson, "can only be an indirect way of saying that all tax exemptions and other benefits enjoyed by the Catholic Church under prior law and practice can be enjoyed by all religious entities that register under the new law". Scot E. Isaacson, *A Practical Comparison of the Laws of religion of Colombia and Chile*, 1 International Journal of Not-for-Profit Law (2003), para. IIIB.

[35] Art. 19, para (6), of the Const. of Chile (1980) in conjunction with Chapter IV of the 1999 Chile Law (*supra* note 33).

[36] Art. 11 of the 1999 Chile Law (*supra* note 33).

[37] See Chapter III and IV of the 1999 Chile Law (*supra* note 33).

funding if they satisfy the general quality conditions which are set by law.[38] Also non-confessional special schools (schools based on a special didactical or secular philosophy; for instance, so-called 'Freinet-style' education, 'Iederwijs' education, 'Jenaplan' education, 'Montessori-style' education or 'Free-school' education) are eligible for state funding. There are clear parallels between the Belgian educational system and the Dutch system in this respect.[39] In both countries religious and secular-humanist organizations are also eligible for allocation of broadcasting time on radio and television.[40]

4.2.4 *Other Types of Cooperation between the State and Various Religions*

Various Constitutions or so-called religious association laws (laws that contain provisions pertaining to the founding and functioning of religious organizations) extend offers of cooperation to organized religion. A Moldovan law on religious activity provides, for instance, that the state "may conclude, as required, agreements or conventions on collaboration with any recognized denomination".[41] Romania constitutionally determines that religious cults shall enjoy support from the state, "including the facilitation of religious assistance in the army, in hospitals, prisons, homes, and orphanages".[42] Unlike the 1923 Constitution,[43] this provision is not intended to single out a particular religion. At the same time it must be noted that in practice the Orthodox Church is a dominant political voice in Romania and the Orthodox denomination is granted a range of financial and pragmatic privileges.[44] Portugal

---

[38] Art. 23 of the CONSTITUTION OF THE KINGDOM OF THE NETHERLANDS (1983) in conjunction with Title II ("Public Schools and Special Schools Financed by the State") of the Law on Primary Education (1981); see particularly art. 8 on the objectives of education; art. 9 on the required contents of education; and art. 10 on the quality of education.

[39] Art. 24 of the CONST. OF BELGIUM (1994) in conjunction with the School-Pact Law of 29 May 1959.

[40] See Flemish Community Council Decree of 15 October 1999 [on the allocation of broadcasting time to religious and non-religious organizations] and French [Walloon] Community Council Decree of 31 May 2000, on the allocation of broadcasting time to religious and non-religious organizations.

[41] Art. 13 of the Law of the Republic of Moldova on Denominations, No. 979-XII, of 24 March 1992 (amended in 1998 and 2002; hereinafter: "1992 Moldovan Law"). In practice, however, the Government privileges the Moldovan Orthodox Church (see also the first paragraph of art. 13 of the 1992 Moldovan Law) and is rather selective in granting recognition to religious groups.

[42] Art. 29, para. (5), of the CONST. OF ROMANIA (1991).

[43] The Constitution of 1923 (replaced) designated the Romanian Orthodox Church as the dominant church.

[44] Lavina Stan & Lucian Turescu, *The Romanian Orthodox Church and Post-communist Democratisation*, 52 EUROPE-ASIA STUDIES (2000); see also Romanita E. Iordache, *Church and State in Romania, in* LAW AND RELIGION IN POST-COMMUNIST EUROPE (Ferrari & Durham, eds., Leuven: Peeters, 2003), pp. 252–253, on the fact that the Romanian Orthodox Church receives special financial treatment. It must be observed, at the same time, that certain regulations on religion that stem from the communist-era and which are still intact are indicative of a form of state control over religion (see, *e.g.*, Decree no. 177/1948 and Law on Cults of 1948).

(though *de jure* a secular and clear-cut separationist state) is another example of a state that explicitly contemplates cooperation with different religions in its Law on Religious Freedom.[45] The Constitution of Brazil expressly sanctions cooperation between the state and religions, though only in so far as this is in the "public's interest".[46] One such field of collaboration is that of the armed forces (in the form of pastoral care).[47] The scope for any form of cooperation is clearly circumscribed by constitutional provisions that declare that no particular religion may be established, subsidized or otherwise supported by Brazil and that no relationships of dependency or alliance between the state and religion are permitted.[48] This system of cooperation is on paper non-preferential (no religion or church is singled out to cooperate with), contrary to for instance the Constitution of Paraguay.[49] South Africa constitutionally accepts that "religious observances" may be conducted at state or state-aided institutions.[50] This could be considered as the exact opposite of a ban on religious manifestations in the public realm such as is practised by some strictly separationist states. Thus, it could be seen as a measure to ensure or at least permit a limited link between the state and the various religions (unlike the 1983 Constitution,[51] the present Constitution does not single out Christianity).[52]

---

[45] Art. 5 of the Law on Religious Freedom, No. 16/2001, of 21 June 2001 (hereinafter: "2001 Portuguese Law").

[46] Art. 19 Const. of Brazil (1988).

[47] See also art. 5, para. VII, of the Const. of Brazil (1988). It has to be acknowledged that Brazil has entered with the Holy See into an agreement that further outlines the special role of the Catholic Church within the field of pastoral care: Concordat between the Federal Republic of Brazil and the Holy See of 23 October 1989.

[48] Art. 19 of the Const. of Brazil (1988).

[49] The Constitution of Paraguay guarantees the independence and autonomy of all churches and religious denominations; it offers the Catholic Church independence, autonomy *and cooperation*. Compare the difference in phrasing in paras. (2) and (3) of art. 24 of the Const. of Paraguay (1992).

[50] Art. 15, para. (2), of the Const. of South Africa (1996). Art. 15, para. (3), sec. (a), moreover, sanctions legislation that recognizes marriages concluded under any tradition, or a system of religious, personal or family law. See Denise Meyerson, Rights Limited: Freedom of Expression, Religion and the South African Constitution (Cape Town: Juta & Co, 1997), pp. 32–36 for a more detailed analysis of these clauses.

[51] The preamble of the Constitution of South Africa (1983) (replaced) read: "In humble submission to Almighty God…we declare that we are conscious of our responsibility to God and man; are convinced of standing united and of pursuing the following national goals: to uphold Christian values and civilized norms…" See Lourens M. du Plessis, *Religious Human Rights in South Africa, in* Religious Human Rights in Global Perspective: Legal Perspectives (J.D. van der Vyver & J. Witte. eds., The Hague/Boston/London: Martinus Nijhoff Publishers, 1996), pp. 443–446 on the pre-1994 situation. See Cornel W. du Toit, *Religious Freedom and Human Rights in South Africa after 1996: Responses and Challenges*, 3 Brigham Young University Law Review (2006), pp. 678–680 on the historical ties between law and religion in South Africa.

[52] The present preamble of the Const. of South Africa (1996) still refers to God ("May God protect our people…God bless South Africa") and thereby promotes theism; however it omits explicit references to Christianity.

Most of the Constitutions which envisage a form of cooperation between the state and religion*s* in practice translate into preferential treatment of the predominant religion or of the dominant, traditional religions (some of the following examples were therefore already mentioned under state support in the previous Chapter). The relationship between the Polish state and its "churches and other religious organizations" is, according to the Constitution, to be based on the principle of respect for their autonomy and mutual independence.[53] Nevertheless, the Constitution explicitly sanctions, in similar vein to the Brazilian Constitution, "cooperation for the individual and the common good".[54] The plural, "churches and other religious organizations", would seem to suggest that cooperation between the state and various religious groups is envisaged; however, it must be acknowledged that a significant level of cooperation is realised with regard to the Catholic Church in particular.[55] The Constitution of Spain also singles out the Catholic Church as it provides that "the public powers shall ... maintain the appropriate relations of cooperation with the Catholic Church and other denominations".[56] Though the offer of cooperation is expressly extended to the "other denominations",[57] it must be observed that Concordats between Spain and the Holy See exists since 1979 which affirm the special legal position of the Catholic Church and which form the basis for certain benefits (predominantly financial and in the field of education).[58] The Jewish, Muslim and Protestant communities, meanwhile, have entered into agreements with the state as well and are granted some of the same benefits;[59] however, they are not placed on an exact equal footing,

[53] Art. 25, para (3), of the CONST. OF POLAND (1997).

[54] *Idem.*

[55] Art. 25, para (4), of the CONST. OF POLAND (1997) points out that the relations between Poland and the Roman Catholic Church shall be determined by international treaty concluded with the Holy See, which resulted in: Concordat between Poland and the Holy See of 28 July 1993 (ratified and entered into force: 25 March 1998). The relations between the Republic of Poland and other churches and religious organizations can in principle be determined by Concordat-style agreements as well, see art. 25, para (5), of the CONST. OF POLAND (1997) and artt. 16-16a of the Law Regarding the Guarantees of Freedom of Religion and Belief [of Poland] of 1989 (hereinafter: "1989 Polish Law").

[56] Art. 16, para. (3), of the CONST. OF SPAIN (1987).

[57] This possibility was reiterated and further developed by art. 7 of the General Act on Religious Liberty of 1980 (hereinafter: "1980 Spanish Law"): "The State, taking account of the religious beliefs existing in Spanish society, shall establish, as appropriate, Co-operation Agreements or Conventions with the Churches, Faiths or Religious Communities enrolled in the Registry where warranted by their notorious influence in Spanish society, due to their domain or number of followers".

[58] Concordats between Spain and the Holy See of 3 January 1979 (consisting of separate Agreements on legal questions, economic questions, teaching and cultural issues and the issue of pastoral care).

[59] As per the 1992 Agreements with representatives from the Jewish, Muslim and Protestant communities: Agreement between Spain and FCI [Federation of Israelite Communities of Spain], 25/1992, of 10 November 1992; Agreement between Spain and CIE [Union of Islamic Communities in Spain], 26/1992, of 10 November 1992; and the Agreement between Spain and FEREDE [Federation of Protestant Entities in Spain], 24/1992, of 10 November 1992.

especially as far as economic cooperation is concerned.[60] This construction of 'neutralizing', to some extent,[61] historically rooted state support for a single religion or church by means of extending it to other religions is fairly common state practice. Portugal's 1976 Constitution positions Portugal as a secular state and explicitly demands a separation between the state and religion.[62] Rather than completely revoking the 1940 Concordat with the Holy See, it was replaced by a new agreement between Portugal and the Holy See which creates the possibility of granting some of the benefits that the Catholic Church enjoys to other religious organizations (e.g. tax-exemption and legal recognition of marriages performed by non-Catholics, etc.).[63] Concordats between the Holy See and Croatia,[64] Hungary,[65] and Italy[66]—which have not been

---

[60] See Javier Martínez-Torrón, *Religious Freedom and Democratic Change in Spain*, 3 Brigham Young University Law Review (2006), particularly pp. 803–806. Moreover, religious groups that are not recognized in this way do not benefit at all from this system.

[61] Such neutralization would of course only be complete, strictly speaking, if other religions are granted the exact same benefits and if the support is extended to all and not just to the traditional or larger religions (something that is, more often than not, not the case as can be seen in the present examples).

[62] Art. 41, para. (4), of the Constitution of the Portuguese Republic (1976).

[63] This is also in line with the 2001 Portuguese Law (*supra* note 45). See Concordat between Portugal and the Holy See of 18 May 2004; and the Concordat between Portugal and the Holy See of 7 May 1940 (abrogated). The 2004 Concordat, however, does not completely neutralize the original state support to the Catholic Church: see particularly the clauses (art. 19) on the role of Catholicism in the public school curriculum and the dominance if not monopoly of the Catholic ecclesiastical authorities in the field of teaching of religious subjects.

[64] Concordats between the Holy See and Croatia of 19 December 1996 and 9 October 1998. Pursuant art. 9 of the Law on Legal Position of Religious Communities of 4 July 2002 (hereinafter: "2002 Croatian Law"), other agreements have been concluded. *E.g.* Agreement between Croatia and the Serbian Orthodox Church (2002); Agreement between Croatia and the Islamic Community (2002); Agreements between Croatia and the Evangelical Church, Reformed Christian Church, Pentecostal Church, Union of Pentecostal Churches of Christ, Christian Adventist Church, Union of Baptist Churches, Church of God, Church of Christ and the Reformed Movement of Seventh-day Adventists (2003); and the Agreement between Croatia and the Bulgarian Orthodox Church, Macedonian Orthodox Church and Croatian Old Catholic Church (2003). The revised (extended) state support principles are based on the 2002 Croatian Law and art. 41, para. (2), of the Constitution of the Republic of Croatia (1990), which provides that religious communities shall in their activity enjoy the protection and assistance of the State.

[65] Concordat between Hungary and the Holy See establishing diplomatic relations and stating that issues related to the Church are to be settled by Canon law and the new Hungarian law on religious freedom of 9 February 1990; Concordat between Hungary and the Holy See establishing a military chaplaincy of 10 January 1994; and Concordat between Hungary and the Holy See on finances of 20 June 1997. Contractual relations between the state and other religions are possible; see Baláza Schanda, *Church and State in Hungary, in* Law and Religion in Post-Communist Europe (Ferrari & Durham, eds., Leuven: Peeters, 2003), p. 125.

[66] Concordat between the Italian Republic and the Holy See of 18 February 1984; see, *e.g.*, Agreement between Italy and the Waldesian Church (1984); Agreement between Italy and Adventists and Assembly of God (1988); Agreement between Italy and the Jewish religion (1989); and the Agreement between Italy and Baptists and Lutherans (1995). The revised (extended) state support principles are based on the 1984 Concordat.

repealed despite the establishment of a separation between the state and religion in these countries—are similarly neutralized to a certain extent.

4.3 Non-Identification

If a state does not establish or support one specific religion (or accommodate various religions simultaneously in a manner as outlined above), yet neither does it position itself as a clear-cut secular or separationist state (to be discussed in the next Chapter), we may speak of a regime of 'non-identification'. Thus, non-identification is characterised by the avoidance of all language that would give evidence of religious preferences on the part of the state (including the 'mere' reference to God).[67] This may or may not be a deliberate state of affairs. Under such systems it is by no means out of the question that the state (*de facto*) interferes with religious affairs or that religion (*de facto*) interferes with public affairs. Conversely, even though the state is not explicitly (constitutionally) secular, the powers that be may have a secularist agenda. Though no religion is established, there is no provision prohibiting the future establishment of a state religion either (a so-called non-establishment clause). This is a clear contrast with states that are outspokenly secular or separationist. At the secular end of the state–religion identification spectrum such precautions against establishment can be found in abundance.[68]

Part I of this study demonstrates that nearly all state constitutions do give (either comprehensive or more concise) indications as to the state's desired relation to religion. The Constitutions of Bosnia-Herzegovina, Botswana, Central African Republic, Eritrea and New Zealand are among the ones that avoid the question of religion;[69] whilst the Constitutions of Kenya, Tanzania and Sierra Leone, it may be added at this point, contain very limited information. In these cases, it is thus merely state practice that informs us as to the *de facto* nature of state–religion identification. Those forms of state practice are discussed in what follows in this section.

Following the Dayton Peace Agreement of 1995,[70] the Constitution of Bosnia and Herzegovina divides executive and legislative powers along ethnic lines: Bosniaks, Croats and Serbs are to be represented in the state institutions

---

[67] It is worth repeating that states which are constitutionally non-preferential with respect to religion in every respect except the codification of a God-notion include: Ecuador, Honduras, Jamaica, Kiribati, Lesotho, Nauru, Solomon Islands, St. Vincent and the Grenadines, Suriname, Zimbabwe and Swaziland (see Chapter 3, section 3.3.3, *supra*).

[68] See Chapter 5, section 5.3, *infra*.

[69] Apart from standard provisions on freedom of religion or belief and non-discrimination that follow the international standards (which commitment may, of course, be seen as somewhat of an indication in its own right with respect to a government's position on Religion).

[70] General Framework Agreement for Peace in Bosnia and Herzegovina of 14 December 1995.

of the State of Bosnia and Herzegovina.[71] The Presidency of Bosnia and Herzegovina (BiH), for instance, consists of three members: one Bosniak and one Croat, each directly elected from the territory of the Federation (i.e. the Federation of Bosnia and Herzegovina, being one of the two entities composing the State of Bosnia and Herzegovina), and one Serb directly elected from the territory of the Republika Šrpska (being the other political entity of the State of Bosnia and Herzegovina).[72] The Parliamentary Assembly consists of two chambers, the House of Peoples and the House of Representatives. The House of Peoples comprises 15 Delegates, two-thirds from the Federation (five Croats and five Bosniaks) and one-third from the Republika Šrpska (five Serbs).[73] The House of Representatives follows the same tripartite model: it comprises 42 Members, two-thirds to be elected from the territory of the Federation (Croats and Bosniaks from Bosnia and Herzegovina), one-third from the territory of the Republika Šrpska (Serbs).[74] The word religion is carefully avoided in the Dayton accords. Though ethnic representation is not to be equated with religious representation, it will be clear that this system has important ramifications for the three major religions (Islam, Roman Catholicism and Serbian Orthodoxy) in terms of political inclusion.[75] BiH's religious association law largely accommodates the different religions and grants them equal rights.[76] It must be observed that BiH's Presidency recently entered into agreements with the Catholic Church and with the Serbian Orthodox Church, affirming their legal personality.[77] It may be worth reiterating at this point that the Constitution of Šrpska (being predominantly Serbian Orthodox since the end of the Bosnian war) does not avoid religiously preferential terminology. Šrpska explicitly supports the Serbian Orthodox Church.[78]

The Constitution of Botswana does not, contrary to neighbouring state Zambia, give evidence of a preference for Christianity (the predominant religion of the nation) on the part of the state. On the other hand, Botswana has not explicitly positioned itself as a secular state either, contrary to neighbouring state Namibia. State practice provides enough reason to refrain from depicting Botswana as a *de facto* secular state (for instance, Christianity plays an important ceremonial role in the public realm and religious instruction in

---

[71] See Samuel Issacharoff, *Constitutionalizing Democracy in Fractured Societies*, 58 Journal of International Affairs (2004), pp. 77–79 for a detailed account.

[72] Art. V of the Constitution of Bosnia and Herzegovina (1995).

[73] Art. IV, para. (1), of the Const. of Bosnia and Herzegovina (1995).

[74] Art. IV, para (2), of the Const. of Bosnia and Herzegovina (1995).

[75] Bosniaks are largely associated with Islam, Bosnian Croats with Roman Catholicism and Bosnian Serbs with Orthodoxy. It is clear at the same time that this system excludes those who do not belong to any of these groups, *e.g.* Jewish and Roma communities.

[76] Law on Religious Freedom [BiH] of 2004 (hereinafter: 2004 BiH law).

[77] Concordat between Bosnia and Herzegovina and the Holy See of 20 August 2007; Agreement between Bosnia and Herzegovina and the Serbian Orthodox Church of 7 May 2008.

[78] Art. 28 of the Const. of Šrpska (1992).

public schools emphasizes Christianity). It must also be observed that, though Botswana does not constitutionally acknowledge its belief in the existence of God, statutory laws do contain references to God.[79]

The predominantly Christian Central African Republic by no means establishes a religion constitutionally. It does, unlike many African states, not constitutionally acknowledge God. Neither does it, unlike neighbouring states Cameroon, Chad, Democratic Republic of the Congo (Kinshasa) or Republic of the Congo (Brazzaville), position itself explicitly as a secular state. The Republic does constitutionally stipulate one reservation with respect to the free exercise of religion: "Any form of religious fundamentalism and intolerance is forbidden".[80] Regulations on religious association largely accommodate the larger religious communities (Protestantism, Catholicism and Islam). The Unification Church (founded by Korean religious leader Sun Myung Moon and drawing on both biblical and Asian religious traditions) was banned in the 1980s and 1990s but is presently tolerated again.

Eritrea's Constitution (which has officially entered into effect but which is not being implemented) is largely silent on the issue of religion (roughly 50 per cent of the population is Christian, 48 per cent Muslim, whilst the remainder of the population belongs to indigenous beliefs).[81] The Government officially recognizes four religions, namely, Eritrean Orthodoxy, Evangelical Lutheranism, Catholicism and Islam, as per special decree of 2002.[82] This clearly puts the minor faiths at a disadvantage as they need to obtain prior permission from the Government to carry out their religious activities.

New Zealand's Constitution, similar in that respect to the United Kingdom, Israel and Canada, does not consist of a single supreme document but rather of a collection of statutes and unwritten constitutional norms. The Constitution Act of 1986 does not touch upon the issue of state–religion identification.[83] It should be observed that New Zealand, although it is a so-called Commonwealth

---

[79] The Constitution of Botswana (1966), although it does not incorporate a God-notion itself, refers several times to oaths which are to be prescribed by Parliament; *e.g.* art. 37 (President's oath), art. 45 (oaths to be taken by Ministers and Assistant Ministers), art. 71 (oaths to be taken by Speaker and Members), art. 80 (oath of allegiance), art. 98 (oaths to be taken by judges of the High Court) and art. 102 (oaths to be taken by judges of the Court of Appeal). A series of laws on this issue has indeed codified these oaths, *e.g.*: Law 36 of 1966; Act 39 of 1968; Act 41 of 1972; Act 20 of 1977; S.I. 66 of 1988; and Act 14 of 2005. It must be observed that the religious affirmation ("So help me God") is considered non-obligatory both by the Constitution (see art. 11, para. 4) as well as the Act on oaths itself (art. 5).

[80] The freedom of religion provision of art. 8 of the Constitution of the Central African Republic (1994) is followed by this sentence.

[81] Art. 19 of the Constitution of Eritrea (1997) lists freedom of religion or belief. This provision, too, is, as evidenced by ongoing religious strife and the limitations that are put on religious practice by the government, largely unimplemented.

[82] Decree on registration, issued by Minister of Information, of May 2002.

[83] Constitution Act of 1 January 1987. Neither do the other constitutional statutes, *e.g.*: Judicature Act of 1908; Legislative Council Abolition Act of 1950; Imperial Laws Application Act of 1988; Electoral Act of 1993; or the Supreme Court Act of 2003. The New Zealand Bill of Rights Act of 1990 codifies the right to freedom of religion in sections 13 and 15.

realm (that is, a Commonwealth country that recognizes the British Monarch as its Monarch), did not follow England's example and establish the Anglican Church.[84] The Supreme Court of New Zealand acknowledged in 1910:

> There is no State Church here. The Anglican Church in New Zealand is in no sense a State Church...and, although no doubt it has a very large membership, it stands legally on no higher ground than any of the religious denominations in New Zealand.[85]

This was reiterated by the Supreme Court in 1998: "Unlike England and Scotland, New Zealand does not have a national established church".[86] However, at official occasions Elizabeth the Second is to be referred to by her official royal titles: "by the Grace of God Queen of New Zealand and Her Other Realms and Territories, Head of the Commonwealth, *Defender of the Faith*".[87] Christianity is also, undeniably, to some extent part of political life in New Zealand. For instance, oaths of office are normally taken on the Old or New Testament.[88] Furthermore, parliamentary custom is that the Speaker of the House of Representatives opens proceedings with a prayer:

> Almighty God, humbly acknowledging our need for Thy guidance in all things, and laying aside all private and personal interests, we beseech Thee to grant that we may conduct the affairs of this House and of our country to the glory of Thy holy name, the maintenance of true religion and justice, the honour of the Queen, and the public welfare, peace, and tranquillity of New Zealand, through Jesus Christ our Lord. Amen.[89]

Other examples include official ceremonial practices[90] and anti-blasphemy regulations.[91] Ahdar contends that such examples stand "in stark contrast to New Zealand's official non-establishment and are found in various forms throughout the country's history. They reflect an unofficial, yet firm establishment of Christianity in official State affairs".[92] One clear exception in this context is educational law which gives evidence of more secular inclinations.

---

[84] Rex J. Ahdar, *Reflections on the Path of Religion-State Relations in New Zealand*, 3 Brigham Young University Law Review (2006), p. 622. See also Sir James Hight & Harry D. Bamford, The Constitutional History and Law of New Zealand (Christchurch: Whitcombe & Tombs, 1914), p. 378 (referenced by Ahdar).

[85] *Carrigan v. Renwood*, [1910] 30 N.Z.L.R. 244, 252.

[86] *Mabon v. Conference of the Methodist Church of New Zealand*, [1998] 3 N.Z.L.R. 513, 523 (referenced by Ahdar).

[87] Art. 2 of the Royal Titles Act of 1974 (emphasis added).

[88] Secular affirmations are permitted though. Artt. 3–4 of the Oaths and Declarations Act of 1957.

[89] Adopted by Resolution of the House in 1962; practised since 1854.

[90] *E.g.* the national flag or the national anthem ("God Defend New Zealand").

[91] Article 123 of the Crimes Act of 1961.

[92] Ahdar, *supra* note 84, p. 632. Ahdar argues that the *de facto* Christian establishment is presently being eroded, in which process human rights might become a powerful force (pp. 633–657).

The notorious 'secular clause' states that teaching at state primary schools "shall be entirely of a secular character".[93]

The Constitutions of Kenya, Tanzania and Sierra Leone contain some provisions which refer to the state's relation to religion. Thus, strictly speaking, we cannot speak of 'non-identification' in these cases. However, the constitutional provisions in question do not give unequivocal evidence of a secular or non-secular form of state–religion identification. With regard to these three states, it is again largely actual state practice that informs us about the Government's relation to religion.

Tanzania does not explicitly support Christianity or Islam (the Muslim and Christian communities are roughly equal in size).[94] On the issue of organized religion the Constitution only provides that the affairs and management of religious bodies shall not be part of the activities over which the state has authority.[95] Tanzania forbids religious organizations to engage in politics.[96] Banning religious political parties is a form of state practice that can be found in abundance at the secular end of the state–religion identification spectrum.[97] It must be observed, however, that state practice provides sufficient ground for not considering Tanzania a *de facto* secular state. Most importantly in that respect, state courts occasionally apply Islamic law to Muslims in cases concerning personal status or family affairs (e.g. marriage, divorce, child custody and inheritance).[98] Semi-autonomous Zanzibar, which was a sultanate until 1964,[99] has a much more homogeneous demography as roughly 99 per cent of the archipelago is Muslim. This explains the much stronger ties between Islam and this part of the state. For instance, (Islamic) Kadhi Courts form part of the judicial system of Zanzibar.[100] Furthermore, Zanzibar has adopted a law which authorizes a Mufti (a person qualified to give legal opinions on Islamic law)[101] to oversee religious affairs and inform the Government about Islamic principles.[102] The Mufti works

[93] Art. 77, para. (b), of the Education Act of 1964. Religious instruction and religious schools are also permitted.

[94] Each group consists of an estimated 30-40 per cent of the population, whilst the remainder of the population adheres to indigenous beliefs.

[95] Art. 19, para (2), of the CONSTITUTION OF THE UNITED REPUBLIC OF TANZANIA (1977).

[96] Political Parties Act of 1992 and art. 20, para (2), sec. (i), of the CONST. OF TANZANIA (1977).

[97] See Chapter 11, section 11.2.2, *infra*.

[98] See also Rita Alice Mwaipopo, *Gender and the Law in Tanzania: Aspects of the Position of Women on Land and Property, in* HUMAN RIGHTS, CONSTITUTIONALISM AND THE JUDICIARY: TANZANIAN AND IRISH PERSPECTIVES (W. Binchy & C. Finnegan, eds., Dublin: Clarus Press, 2006), pp. 93–109 on the role of Islamic law in Tanzania.

[99] Sultanate from 1806–1964. The first Sultan was Said bin Sultan and the 12th and last was Jamshid bin Abdullah Al-Busaidi who ruled until 12 January 1964

[100] Artt. 93–99 of the CONSTITUTION OF ZANZIBAR (1984). It must be observed that a debate about the introduction of Kadhi Courts in mainland Tanzania is ongoing.

[101] Zanzibar Mufti Law of 2001.

[102] See Joseph Oloka-Onyango & Maria Nassali, *Constitutionalism and Political Stability in Zanzibar: the Search for a New Vision* (Report of the Fact Finding Mission Organised under the

formally under the Ministry of Constitutional Affairs of Zanzibar. Oloka-Onyango and Nassali argue that the re-introduction of the Mufti's office "undermines the position of Zanzibar as a secular state".[103]

Christianity (the predominant religion) is not established as the state religion in Kenya.[104] Though Kenya's Constitution is largely silent on the issue of religion–state relations, it does explicitly sanction Kadhi Courts to adjudicate marriage, divorce or inheritance cases between Muslims.[105] The Constitution in that respect confirmed a prerogative that had already been established.[106] Interestingly, a 2005 draft for a new Constitution[107] intended to adopt a similar system with respect to other religious communities (e.g. Christian Courts, Hindu Courts).[108] These religious courts are to have jurisdiction in matters relating to personal status, marriage, divorce, inheritance and succession. Other novelties announced by the draft-Constitution include: a reference to God;[109] an Advisory Committee on the Presidential Power of Clemency which is to include, among other persons, a Christian, a Muslim and a Hindu;[110] and a ban on religious political parties.[111] Somewhat paradoxically, the draft-Constitution, unlike the present Constitution, explicitly requires religion to be separated from the state.[112] The draft-Constitution was voted down by the Kenyans, thus it remains to be seen which of these proposals will be implemented and which will be abandoned.[113]

Auspices of Kitua Cha Katiba; Tanzania: Friedrich Ebert Stiftung, 2003), pp. 64–65; and Bruce E. Heilman & Paul J. Kaiser, *Religion, Identity and Politics in Tanzania*, 23 THIRD WORLD QUARTERLY (2002), pp. 704–705 on the historical position and authority of Muftis in Tanzania in general.

[103] OLOKA-ONYANGO & NASSALI, *ibid.*, pp. 65 and 71.

[104] See Galia Sabar-Friedman, *Church and State in Kenya, 1986–1992: The Churches' Involvement in the 'Game of Change'*, 96 AFRICAN AFFAIRS (1997), pp. 25–52 on the role of Kenya's churches in processes of political reform.

[105] Art. 66 of the CONSTITUTION OF KENYA (1969).

[106] See Kadhis' Courts Act, no.14/67, of 1967.

[107] Proposed New Constitution of Kenya, Kenya Gazette Supp. No. 63, of 22 August 2005.

[108] Art. 195 of the Proposed New Constitution of Kenya (2005). All such religious courts are envisaged to function as "subordinate courts", *i.e.* under the superior Supreme Court, Court of Appeal and High Court (art. 179).

[109] The present Constitution lacks a preamble; the preamble of the draft-Constitution refers to God several times. The preamble of the Proposed New Constitution of Kenya (2005) states: "ACKNOWLEDGING the supremacy of the Almighty God of all creation" and "GOD BLESS KENYA". Other references to God can be found in the First and Second Schedule to the draft-Constitution.

[110] Art. 157, para (3), sec. (f), of the Proposed New Constitution of Kenya (2005).

[111] Art. 112, para (2), sec. (a), of the Proposed New Constitution of Kenya (2005). See Lindsey Gustafson, *Kenya: the Struggle to Create a Democracy*, 2 BRIGHAM YOUNG UNIVERSITY LAW REVIEW (1995), pp. 647–671 on some of the present regulations that limit the freedom to associate for religious purposes.

[112] Art. 10 of the Proposed New Constitution of Kenya (2005) provides: "(1) State and religion shall be separate. (2) There shall be no state religion. (3) The State shall treat all religions equally".

[113] The draft was voted down by the Kenyan electorate in a referendum on 21 November 2005 (58 per cent voted against the constitutional reforms).

The Constitution of Sierra Leone does not elaborate much on the relation of the state to religion either.[114] However, it does, by implication, sanction the application of religious laws by state courts.[115] As a consequence, a rather pluralistic legal system is perceivable, consisting of a mixture of constitutional, statutory, common and religious customary law. Tully observes that, though Islam is the predominant religion,[116] the role of Islamic law remains in practice fairly limited.[117] Its role is mainly limited to marriage cases before local courts.[118]

4.4 Concluding Remarks

Most states at some point in time have actively supported one particular religion: the traditional and predominant belief. Accommodation of religion*s* could be regarded as a relatively recent form of state–religion identification. In theory, states could opt for this arrangement out of a genuine intention to ensure that all religions can flourish. However, the answer to the question what the rationale behind supporting religion *in abstracto*, or supporting the different religion*s* present in a country, may be, can only be answered on a case-by-case basis. Looking at state practice, it appears that in some instances 'accommodation of religion' as an arrangement has come to the fore as a political solution to recent religious strife; while in other cases it seems that the state in question considers this arrangement to flow logically from—also relatively recently emerging—norms of international law. Thus, in both cases it would seem that the arrangement is not perceived as an end in itself but is rather considered to be instrumental to achieving other norms: maintaining the domestic peace by means of a political status quo, or ensuring compliance with international obligations. Looking at state practice and concrete examples,

---

[114] The Constitution does mention "God" but it must be observed that all constitutional references to God are made in the sections that deal with oaths of office (the Constitution indicates that the religious aspects of the oaths may be omitted). See Second and Third Schedule of the Constitution of Sierra Leone (1991). The state, moreover, bans political parties which associate with a particular religious faith; art. 35, para (5), of the Const. of Sierra Leone (1991).

[115] Art. 27, para. (1), of the Const. of Sierra Leone (1991) states that "no law shall make provision which is discriminatory either of itself or in its effect". This rule, according to para. (4) (d) of the same article, "shall not apply to any law so far as that law makes provision:…with respect to adoption, marriage, divorce, burial, devolution of property on death or other interests of personal law". This provision should be read in light of art. 170 which lists customary law among the laws applicable in Sierra Leone and which defines customary law as "the rules of law which by custom are applicable to particular communities in Sierra Leone".

[116] An estimated 60 per cent of the population is Muslim.

[117] James J. Tully, *The Place of Islamic Law in Sierra Leone*, 84 The Muslim World (1994), pp. 300–316; see also Joko Smart, *The Place of Islamic Law with the Framework of the Sierra Leone Legal System*, 18 African Law Studies (1980).

[118] Tully, *ibid.*, pp. 303–307. See Mohammedan Marriage Ordinance of 1905; and Courts Act of 1965.

non-identification, too, seems—somewhat paradoxically—as much of an 'active' state policy as the other, more outspoken regimes of state–religion identification. However, whatever the precise historical or political reasons may be to avoid a clear-cut official stance on religion, it is clear that under such systems it is by no means ruled out that the state may interfere with religious affairs or that religion may interfere with public affairs. This is in clear contrast with those states that wish to ascertain that such interaction between religion and state is out of the question.

CHAPTER FIVE

SECULARISM & SEPARATION OF STATE AND RELIGION

5.1 Introduction

The previous Chapter dealt with a number of states which lack a firm positive identification with a religion and some of the Governments of these states, it was concluded, can largely be considered *de facto* secular. This Chapter deals with more outspoken forms of secularism and separationism (a policy of strict separation of state and religion). Though there are important overlaps, and although, moreover, domestic jurisprudence drawing on these concepts has in practice often largely erased the differences in implications, 'secularism' and 'separation of state and religion' can be analytically distinguished from each other. In this Chapter it will become apparent that many states constitutionally establish themselves as secular states, many states constitutionally separate religion from the state, whilst some states, in fact, do both. A secular state declares that it will not be bound by religious laws or principles. In establishing itself as a non-religious and non-denominational state, the state denies any form of positive identification with religion. Historically, such proclamations of secularity were of course particularly intended as a means of cutting the ties with the dominant religion or church. A constitutional secular state deliberately and outspokenly positions itself as impartial with regard to doctrinal questions of religion. Separation of state and religion can be considered a legal-political endeavour aimed at internalizing and consistently preserving a regime in which the state apparatus and religious institutions do not interfere with each other's activities. Notwithstanding these preliminary theoretical observations, it will be clear that maintaining a secular status necessitates a significant degree of separation; whilst upholding the separation between the state and religion presupposes a fairly secularist Government.

Firstly, 'secular states' will be identified and discussed (section 5.2). Subsequently, the principles of 'separation of state and religion' (section 5.3) and so-called 'non-establishment clauses' (section 5.4) will be analysed. Section 5.5 endeavours to further chart the legal ramifications of these principles on the basis of existing state practice.

5.2 Secular States

In this study, states which expressly (i.e. constitutionally) position themselves as non-religious or non-denominational will be considered "secular states".

A constitutional declaration of secularity means, first and foremost, that the state does not wish to invoke religion as a justification for its authority, actions and decisions. It must be emphasized that proclamations of secularity, both historically as well as presently, in the majority of cases denote official impartiality in matters of religion rather than official 'irreligiosity'.[1] Secular states in that respect should certainly not to be confused with declared atheist or anti-religious states.[2] Having said that, the official secularity of the state (that is, secularism as impartiality) may in practice translate into instances of religious scepticism or ideological secularism. The precise legal and practical ramifications of declarations of state secularism vary from state to state (these ramifications will be charted in section 5.5).

Official state secularism as the innovative endeavour to legitimize state authority precisely by *not* anchoring it in the dominant religious doctrine stems from the late 18th century and was instigated by American and French Revolutionary ideology. It must be observed that secularism as a *de facto* standard has been practised for much longer. One can think, for instance, of the Punjab under the secular rule of Maharaja Ranjit Singh (1780–1839; r. 1801–1839).[3] The United States of America and France compete for the distinction of being the first officially secular state.[4] The influence of American revolutionary discourse on secularism ultimately resulted in the infamous 'non-establishment clause' (which will be further discussed below). With respect to France, it may be noted that the Revolution of 1789 largely secularized the state in a

---

[1] It is important to distinguish between secularism simply as a condition or quality (i.e. secularity) and secularism as a principled notion or an ideology. See also, *e.g.*, DAVID MARTIN, ON SECULARIZATION: TOWARDS A REVISED GENERAL THEORY (Aldershot: Ashgate, 2005), p. 81 and p. 85. In the context of comparative constitutional analysis, "secularity" (i.e. of a non-religious nature, or: not overtly or expressly religious) would perhaps be a more appropriate label than "secularism" (i.e. a more ideologically motivated secular position). For the simple reason that such has become common usage, here "secularism" will be used in the meaning of secularity unless explicitly indicated otherwise ("ideological secularism"). Also, an official state of secularity does not, as a rule, in itself foster secularization of society; cf. Martin, *ibid*, p. 47 *et seq.*

[2] See next Chapter on state atheism. Some states make this important distinction explicit in their laws. Colombia, for instance, has codified a non-establishment clause to which it has explicitly added: "Nevertheless, the State is not atheistic, agnostic, or indifferent to the religious feelings of the Colombians" (art. 2 of Law 133 of 23 May 1994 on Religion; hereinafter: "1994 Colombian Law").

[3] See KARTAR S. DUGGAL, RANJIT SINGH: A SECULAR SIKH SOVEREIGN, (Dehli: Abhinav Publications, 1989).

[4] *E.g.* BRYAN R. WILSON, THE SOCIAL DIMENSIONS OF SECTARIANISM AND NEW RELIGIOUS MOVEMENTS IN CONTEMPORARY SOCIETY, (Oxford: Clarendon Press, 1990), p. 25, who describes the US as the first secular state in the sense of "the first state which does not embrace specific religious principles as part of its legitimation"; vs., *e.g.* Jean Baubérot, *The Secular Principle* (discussion paper reproduced by the Embassy of France in the United States and the Embassy of France in the United Kingdom, 2001): "While secularity is in no way exclusive to France –other countries have more or less adopted it, each in its own fashion, and there are schools of thought on the subject in several– it may nevertheless be said that, overall, we are here dealing with a 'French invention' ".

legal-political sense, with immediate consequences for the position of the Catholic Church. It is clear at the same time that the French system of *laïcité* (literally, governance by laymen)[5] was not developed and consolidated overnight or without conflict.[6] With respect to the direct post-revolutionary period, Baubérot argues:

> ...the French Revolution very soon found itself in conflict with the Catholic religion. In that conflict, it tried first to control Catholicism (1790), then to turn itself into a religion (the revolutionary cults of 1793, accompanied by politico-religious persecution), before establishing a short-lived separation of Church and State (1795) which, coexisting with the maintenance of quasi-religious revolutionary fervour, did not in the end resolve the conflict. In all, then, the Revolution proclaimed secular principles but did not succeed in applying them. Understandably, therefore, the heritage of the revolution would long continue to appear ambivalent.[7]

After another century of strife, the matter was finally settled in favour of state secularism in 1905 (as per the Law Regarding the Separation of the Churches and the State).[8] It must be noted that secularism became a constitutional principle as late as 1946.[9] It has since maintained a prominent position in the French Constitution.[10]

5.2.1 *Declared Secular States*

States that have explicitly declared themselves secular include: Angola, Azerbaijan, Benin, Burkina Faso, Burundi, Cameroon, Chad, Democratic Republic of the Congo, Republic of the Congo, Côte d'Ivoire, France, Gabon,

---

[5] For a comprehensive historical discussion of this principle, see *e.g.*: MAURICE BARBIER, LA LAÏCITÉ (Paris: L'Harmattan, 1995); Jean Baubérot (ed.), LA LAÏCITÉ: EVOLUTION ET ENJEUX (Paris: La Documentation Française, 1996); JEAN BAUBÉROT, HISTOIRE DE LA LAÏCITÉ FRANÇAISE (Paris: PUF, 2000); JEAN BOUSSINESCQ, LA LAÏCITÉ FRANÇAISE (Paris: Le Seuil, 1994); JACQUELINE COSTA-LASCOUX, LES TROIS ÂGES DE LA LAÏCITÉ (Paris: Hachette, 1996); CLAUDE DURAND-PRINBORGNE, LA LAÏCITÉ (Paris: Dalloz, 1996); GUY HAARSCHER, LA LAÏCITÉ (Paris: PUF, 1996); and PIERRE KAHN, LA LAÏCITÉ (Paris: Le Cavalier Bleu, 2005).

[6] Recently adopted laws, such as *Loi en application du principe de laïcité, le port de signes ou de tenues manifestant une appartenance religieuse dans les écoles, collèges et lycées publics*, Law No. 2004–228 of 15 March 2004, or the in 2001 adopted 'About-Picard Law' (Law Intended to Reinforce the Prevention and Repression of Sectarian Movements that Infringe on Human Rights and Fundamental Freedoms of 2001), show that the French ideal of *laïcité* still gives rise to new debates and a need for further clarification.

[7] Baubérot, *supra* note 4.

[8] *Loi Concernant la Séparation des Eglises et de l'Etat*, of 9 December 1905.

[9] See the Constitution of the Fourth Republic of France (1946; replaced).

[10] Art. 1 of the CONSTITUTION OF THE FRENCH REPUBLIC (1958). The Concordat between France and the Holy See of 15 July 1801 (entered into force 10 September 1801) has been abrogated. A caveat concerning the secularity of France must be made: the now French Departments of Upper Rhine, Lower Rhine and Moselle formally are still subjected to the terms of the Concordat since these regions were at the time of the abrogation of the Concordat under German rule and thus not affected by its annulment.

Guinea, Guinea-Bissau, Guyana, India, Kazakhstan, Kyrgyzstan, Latvia, Mali, Mozambique, Namibia, Nepal, Poland, Portugal, Russia, Rwanda, Sao Tome and Principe, Senegal, Serbia, Slovak Republic, Tajikistan, Togo, Turkey and Turkmenistan.[11] In the next section (5.3) it will be outlined that so-called 'non-establishmentarian states' can be considered secular as well.

The secular nature of the state is as a rule established in one of the opening articles (outlining the principal political characteristics of the state) of the Constitution.

5.2.2 *State Neutrality*

Some states have adopted a more descriptive approach; these states can be considered secular even though their Constitutions do not explicitly mention the word "secular". The first article of the Constitution of Slovakia, for instance, reads: "The Slovak Republic is a sovereign, democratic, and law-governed state. *It is not linked to any ideology or religious belief*".[12] This phase largely corresponds with the definition of "secularity".[13] Another example is the Albanian Constitution, which stipulates that there is no official religion and that the

---

[11] Article 10 of the Albanian Constitution (1998); article 8 of the Constitutional Law of the Republic of Angola (1992); art. 2 of the Constitution of the Republic of Benin (1990); art. 31 of the Constitution of Burkina Faso (1991); article 1 of the Post-transition Constitution of the Republic of Burundi (2005); art. 1 of the Constitution of the Republic of Cameroon (1972); art. 1 of the Constitution of the Republic of Chad (1996); art. 1 of the Constitution of the Democratic Republic of the Congo (2006); art. 1 of the New Constitution of the Republic of the Congo (2002); art. 30 of the Constitution of the Republic of Côte d'Ivoire (2000); art. 1 of the Const. of France (1958); art. 2 of the Constitution of the Republic of Gabon (1991); art. 1 of the Fundamental Law of the Second Republic of Guinea (1990; hereinafter: Fundamental Law of Guinea of 1990); art. 1 of the Constitution of the Republic of Guinea-Bissau (1991); art. 25 of Const. of Mali (1992); preamble and art. 1 of the Const. of Namibia (1990); art. 1 of the Const. of Rwanda (2003); art. 1 of the Constitution of the Republic of Senegal (2001); art. 7 of the Constitution of the Azerbaijan Republic (1995); art. 1 of the Constitution of the Slovak Republic (1992); preamble of the Const. of India (1950); art. 1 of the Constitution of the Republic of Kazakhstan (1995); art. 1 of the Constitution of the Kyrgyz Republic (1993); art. 1 of the Constitution of the Republic of Tajikistan (1994); art. 1 of the Const. of Togo (1992); art. 1 of the Constitutional Law of Turkmenistan (1992); art. 1 of the Constitution of the Co-operative Republic of Guyana (1980); article 12 of the Constitution of the Republic of Mozambique (1990); art. 10, para. (1), of the Law Regarding the Guarantees of Freedom of Religion and Belief [of Poland] of 1989 (hereinafter: "1989 Polish Law"); article 14 of the Constitution of the Russian Federation (1993; hereinafter: Const. of Russia of 1993); art. 8 of the Constitution of the Democratic Republic of Sao Tome and Principe (1975); art. 11 of the Constitution of the Republic of Serbia (2006); article 2 and the preamble of the Const. of Turkey (1982); art. 4 of the Interim Const. of Nepal (2007); and art. 5, para. (1), of the Law on Religious Organizations [of Latvia] of 7 September 1995 (amended by Laws of 17 June 1996; 27 February 1997; 19 February 1998 and 19 July 2000; hereinafter: "1995 Latvian Law").

[12] Art. 1, para. (1), of the Const. of Slovakia (1992), emphasis added. Caveat: this constitutional provision is hard to reconcile with the Concordat between the Slovak Republic and the Holy See about Catholic upbringing and education of March 2004.

[13] See *supra*, note 1.

state shall remain "neutral in questions of belief and conscience".[14] The Constitution of Cameroon appears to use the term "neutrality" to define or elaborate on what is meant by the Constitution's provision for secularism.[15] Czech law similarly provides for a sense of state neutrality as it declares that the state "may not be bound either by an exclusive ideology or by a particular religious faith."[16] Portugal describes itself as a "non-denominational state".[17]

In Chapter 3 it was outlined that the state's identification with religion is often accompanied with official forms of ceremonial celebration and recognition of the religion in question (for instance, in state mottos, national flags, the national coat of arms, the national anthem, etc.).[18] It is clear that state-instigated secular symbolism does not compare to religious state symbolism, presumably also because too ardent a celebration of the secular nature of the state would defeat its own purpose. An interesting historical example of ceremonial use of the principle of state secularism is given by the flag of the People's Party of Turkey of 1935 (the political party of Atatürk and at the time the only sanctioned political party). It depicts six arrows on a red background; each arrow symbolizes one of the principles of Kemalism: republicanism, nationalism, populism, statism, revolutionism and indeed secularism. This does not come as a surprise as Kemalist secularism is essentially of an ideological nature.[19]

5.3 Non-establishment Clause

Several states have codified a so-called 'non-establishment clause'. Such a clause boils down to a self-addressed prohibition of treating a specific religion as the state, official or otherwise privileged religion. Thus, 'non-establishmentarian states' can be considered secular in so far as they promise to remain impartial with respect to the different religious communities. State practice shows that non-establishmentarianism leads to differing degrees of separationism. Whilst American non-establishmentarianism, as we will see presently, has ultimately translated into a fairly strict 'wall of separation'; the German or Estonian non-establishment clauses, for instance, do in practice not prevent relatively far-reaching forms of interaction and cooperation between the state and

---

[14] Art. 10 of the Albanian Const. (1998).

[15] Preamble of the Const. of Cameroon (1972): "...the State shall be secular. The neutrality and independence of the State in respect of all religions shall be guaranteed".

[16] Art. 2, para. (2), of the Charter of Fundamental Rights and Basic Freedoms of 16 December 1992. One could interpret this provision as a 'non-establishment clause' (to be discussed *infra*, section 5.4).

[17] See the official title above art. 4 of the Law on Religious Freedom [of Portugal], No. 16/2001, of 21 June 2001 (hereinafter: "2001 Portuguese Law").

[18] See section 3.3.3 on State Symbolism & Religion, *supra*.

[19] For the different meanings of secularism, see *supra*, note 1.

religion.[20] Notwithstanding American state practice, the principles of non-establishmentarianism and separation can analytically be distinguished from each other. The separation principle is (ideal-typically)[21] broader: it endeavours to maintain the autonomy of the state by freeing it from religious interferences whilst it denotes a promise to respect the internal autonomy of religions. States that more explicitly provide for a separation are identified in the next section (5.4).

5.3.1 *American Non-establishmentarianism*

Most constitutional non-establishment clauses echo, in one way or another, the classic provision in this respect: the infamous First Amendment (1789) to the Constitution of the United States of America (1787) which provides that:

> "Congress shall make no law respecting an establishment of religion, or prohibiting the free exercise thereof".[22]

Clearly distinguishable are the non-establishment clause and the so-called free-exercise clause (the right to freedom of religion). Notwithstanding earlier remarks on the analytical differences between a separation clause and a non-establishment clause, the American non-establishment clause, according to some of the jurisprudence this principle has generated, equates to an unabbreviated separation of state and religion.

The novelty of the non-establishment clause is generally attributed to American Founding Fathers Thomas Jefferson (1743–1826) and James Madison (1751–1836).[23] Jefferson, who in turn was influenced by European Enlightenment thinkers such as John Locke (1632–1704), was himself in the 1770s responsible for the creation of the pioneering Virginia Bill on Religious Freedom.[24] Barron & Dienes argue in this regard:

> Jefferson was a child of the eighteenth century Enlightenment. He emphasized reason and was sceptical of religious dogmas. While he championed personal freedom of conscience and religious belief, Jefferson was suspicious

[20] Germany collects on behalf of those religious organizations that are granted a "corporation under public law" status a church tax from the religious adherents (see section 4.2.3, *supra*). Estonia's non-establishment clause has not prevented a degree of cooperation between the state and religious communities either; cf. Merilin Kiviorg, *Church and State in Estonia, in* Law and Religion in Post-Communist Europe (Ferrari & Durham, eds., Leuven: Peeters, 2003), pp. 105–106 and p. 119.

[21] In section 5.5, *infra*, it will be outlined that separation principles are occasionally in fact interpreted in a rather one-sided manner, solely as 'governmental autonomy' or solely as 'church autonomy' (or religious autonomy).

[22] Amendment I (1789) to the Constitution of the United States of America (1787).

[23] *E.g.* Jerome A. Barron & C. Thomas Dienes, First Amendment Law (St Paul, Minn.: West Group, 2000), p. 426, who name theologian Roger William (1603–1683) as third important advocate.

[24] Virginia Statute on Religious Freedom (entry into force: 1786).

> of institutional religion and was fearful that it might have a corrupting influence on the body politic.[25]

Madison is thought to have had a rather different motivation for supporting this revolutionary principle:

> [he] accepted the importance and value of institutional religion in public life. Religion bolstered the public morality and public morality was an essential part of fostering civic virtue. This did not mean, however, that government should actively support and involve itself in religious life. For Madison, religious freedom was best safeguarded by preserving and encouraging a multiplicity of religious sects. In this way, no one denomination would become dominant.[26]

The non-establishment clause was not seriously tested until the 1947 case of *Everson v. Board of Education*,[27] in which for the first time the principle was used to scrutinize a state law.[28] Notwithstanding the fact that the Court ultimately upheld the challenged New Jersey law, the Supreme Court (Justice Black) gave a first clear separationist signal:

> The 'establishment of religion' clause of the First Amendment means at least this: Neither a state nor the Federal Government can set up a church. Neither can pass laws which aid one religion, aid all religions or prefer one religion over another. Neither can force nor influence a person to go to or to remain away from church against his will or force him to profess a belief or disbelief in any religion. No person can be punished for entertaining or professing religious beliefs or disbeliefs, for church attendance or non-attendance. No tax in any amount, large or small, can be levied to support any religious activities or institutions, whatever they may be called, or whatever form they may adopt to teach or practice religion. Neither a state nor the Federal Government can, openly or secretly, participate in the affairs of any religious organizations or groups and vice versa. In the words of Jefferson, the clause against establishment of religion by law was intended to erect 'a wall of separation between Church and State.'[29]

Thus, it is interesting to note, the Supreme Court largely acted in accordance with the instructions of Thomas Jefferson written down nearly 150 years earlier:

---

[25] Barron & Dienes, *supra* note 23, p. 426.

[26] *Ibid.*, pp. 426–427.

[27] *Everson v. Board of Education*, 330 U.S. 1 (1947), which revolved around a New Jersey state law which authorised the reimbursement of travel expenses pertaining to bus services to schools, including religious educational institutions. This is not to say that there are no earlier cases that indirectly touched upon the matter, *e.g.*: *Bradfield v. Roberts*, 175 U.S. 291 (1899), on financial support to a hospital run by the Catholic Church (sanctioned); and *Quick Bear v. Leupp*, 210 U.S. 50 (1908), on indirect funding of Catholic schools (sanctioned). See Steven H. Shiffrin & Jesse H. Choper, The First Amendment: Cases – Comments – Questions (St Paul, Minn.: West Publishing Co., 2000), p. 616

[28] Cf. John H. Garvey & Frederick Schauer, The First Amendment: a Reader (St Paul, Minn.: West Publishing Co., 2000), p. 429.

[29] *Everson v. Board of Education*, 330 U.S. 1 (1947), 15–16.

> Believing with you that religion is a matter which lies solely between Man & his God, that he owes account to none other for his faith or his worship, that the legitimate powers of government reach actions only, & not opinions, I contemplate with sovereign reverence that act of the whole American people which declared that their legislature should "make no law respecting an establishment of religion, or prohibiting the free exercise thereof," thus building a wall of separation between Church & State. Adhering to this expression of the supreme will of the nation in behalf of the rights of conscience, I shall see with sincere satisfaction the progress of those sentiments which tend to restore to man all his natural rights, convinced he has no natural right in opposition to his social duties.[30]

The US Supreme Court has since 1947 at times acted as strictly 'seperationist', thus raising Jefferson's 'wall of separation'. It must be observed, however, that the Supreme Court at other times adopted a much more accommodationist approach, presumably on account of a lack of precise definitions or formulas as to what qualifies as 'religion' and as to what amounts to an 'establishment' thereof.[31] It is beyond all dispute, though, that the clause prohibits installing a state religion as well as all direct forms of preferential treatment of a religion.[32]

5.3.2 *Other Non-establishment Clauses*

Several states have followed America's example. Presently, non-establishment clauses can be found in the Constitutions (or laws)[33] of: Albania, Australia, Brazil, Colombia, Czech Republic, Estonia, Ethiopia, the Gambia, Germany, Ghana, Republic of Korea, Liberia, Lithuania, Micronesia, Moldova, Nicaragua, Nigeria, Palau, Paraguay, Philippines, Portugal, Russia, Serbia, Seychelles, Spain, Tajikistan, Uganda and Ukraine.[34] There exists some state practice that resembles America's interpretation of non-establishment as a fairly strict

---

[30] Jefferson's Letter to the Danbury Baptists of 1 January 1802; in: Albert E. Bergh (ed.), THE WRITINGS OF JEFFERSON (Washington, D. C.: The Thomas Jefferson Memorial Association of the United States, 1907), pp. 281–282.

[31] Cf. Barron & Dienes, *supra* note 23, p. 427–435; see also Shiffrin & Choper, *supra* note 27, pp. 620–694; Garvey & Schauer, *supra* note 28, pp. 430–577; and Donald E. Lively, Dorothy E. Robert & Russell L. Weaver (eds.), FIRST AMENDMENT ANTHOLOGY (Cincinnati: Anderson Publishing Company, 1994), pp. 419–470.

[32] Cf. Barron & Dienes, *supra* note 23, p. 436.

[33] Colombia's non-establishment clause is not codified by its Constitution but by the 1994 Colombian Law (*supra* note 2); Portugal's non-establishment clause can be found in art. 4, para. (1), of the 2001 Portuguese Law (*supra* note 17).

[34] Art. 116 of the CONSTITUTION OF AUSTRALIA (1900); art. 11, para. (2), of the CONSTITUTION OF THE FEDERAL DEMOCRATIC REPUBLIC OF ETHIOPIA (1995); art. 100, para. (2), of the CONST. OF THE GAMBIA (1996); art. 56 of the CONST. OF GHANA (1992); art. 14 of the CONST. OF LIBERIA (1986); art. 10 of the CONSTITUTION OF THE FEDERAL REPUBLIC OF NIGERIA (1999); art. 21, para. (6), of the CONSTITUTION OF THE REPUBLIC OF SEYCHELLES (1993); art. 7 of the CONST. OF UGANDA (1995); art. 20 of the CONSTITUTION OF THE REPUBLIC OF KOREA (1948); art. IV, sec. (2), of the CONSTITUTION OF THE FEDERATED STATES OF MICRONESIA (1978); art. IV, sec. (1), of the CONST. OF PALAU (1979); art. 3, sec. (5), of the CONST. OF THE PHILIPPINES

separation principle.[35] In other states, however, a strict separation between state and religion appears not to be required by the constitutional non-establishment clause.[36] In what follows in this sub-section, the different constitutional provisions will be analysed.

Some non-establishment clauses are clearly crafted after the American example. The Gambian clause, for instance, provides that the National Assembly of Gambia shall not pass a Bill "to establish any religion as a state religion".[37] The Constitution of Ghana similarly stipulates that "Parliament shall have no power to enact a law to establish or authorise the establishment of a body or movement with the right or power to impose on the people of Ghana a common programme or a set of objectives of a religious [nature]".[38] The Constitution of Seychelles provides that a "law shall not make provision for the establishment of any religion or the imposition of any religious observance".[39] The Constitution of Micronesia holds that "[n]o law may be passed respecting an establishment of religion or impairing the free exercise of religion".[40] The Constitution of the Philippines provides that no law "shall be made respecting an establishment of religion, or prohibiting the free exercise thereof. The free exercise and enjoyment of religious profession and worship, without discrimination or preference, shall forever be allowed".[41] The Constitution of Australia, finally, also echoes the American non-establishment clause: "The Commonwealth shall not make any law for establishing any religion, or for imposing any religious observance, or for prohibiting the free exercise of any religion, and no religious test shall be required as a qualification for any office or public trust under the Commonwealth."[42]

(1987); art. 10, para. (1), of the ALBANIAN CONST. (1998); art. 40, para. (2), 2nd sentence, of the CONSTITUTION OF THE REPUBLIC OF ESTONIA (1992); article 137, para. (1), of the Weimar Constitution of 1919 as incorporated by the BASIC LAW FOR THE FEDERAL REPUBLIC OF GERMANY (1949); art. 43, final sentence, of the CONSTITUTION OF THE REPUBLIC OF LITHUANIA (1992); art. 5, para. (2), of the CONSTITUTION OF THE REPUBLIC OF MOLDOVA (1994); art. 14, para. (1), 2nd sentence, of the CONST. OF RUSSIA (1993); art. 11, 3rd sentence, of the CONST. OF SERBIA (2006); art. 16, para. (3), of the CONST. OF SPAIN (1978) (see also art. 1, para. (3) of the General Act on Religious Liberty [of Spain] of 1980; hereinafter: "1980 Spanish Law"); art. 35, para. (3), 2nd sentence, of the CONST. OF UKRAINE (1996); art. 19 of the CONST. OF BRAZIL (1988); art. 14 of the POLITICAL CONSTITUTION OF THE REPUBLIC OF NICARAGUA (1986); art. 8 of the CONST. OF TAJIKISTAN (1994); and art. 24, para. (1), 2nd sentence, of the CONST. OF PARAGUAY (1992).

35 Most explicitly so by the Constitutional Court of Lithuania; cf. Jolanta Kuznecoviene, *Church and State in Lithuania, in* LAW AND RELIGION IN POST-COMMUNIST EUROPE 177 (Ferrari & Durham, eds., Leuven: Peeters, 2003), p. 181.

36 *E.g.* Germany and Estonia; see *supra*, note 20.

37 Art. 100, para. (2), of the CONST. OF THE GAMBIA (1996).

38 Art. 56 of the CONST. OF GHANA (1992).

39 Art. 21, para. (6), of the CONST. OF SEYCHELLES (1993).

40 Art. IV, sec. (3), of the CONST. OF MICRONESIA (1978).

41 Art. 3, sec. (5), of the CONST. OF THE PHILIPPINES (1987).

42 Art. 116 of the CONST. OF AUSTRALIA (1900).

Many alternative provisions are perceivable, including clauses providing that: there shall be "no state religion" (Albania, Ethiopia and Lithuania);[43] there shall be "no official religion" (Nicaragua and Paraguay);[44] or that there shall be "no state church" (Germany and Estonia).[45] Constitutions may also provide that: the state "does not adopt any religion whatsoever" (Portugal);[46] the state "shall not adopt a state religion" (Uganda);[47] the state "shall establish no state religion" (Liberia);[48] the state "shall not adopt any religion as state religion" (Nigeria);[49] "no state religion may be recognized" (Republic of Korea);[50] "no religion shall have a state character" (Spain);[51] no religion may be instituted as state-sponsored or "mandatory" religion (Russia, Serbia and Ukraine);[52] the state "shall not recognize or establish a national religion" (Palau);[53] or the state may not "establish religious cults or churches" (Brazil).[54]

The Colombian version of the non-establishment clause provides that no church or religious confession will be deemed official. To this it is added: "Nevertheless, the State is not atheistic, agnostic, or indifferent to the religious feelings of the Colombians".[55] It has been argued before that state secularism or non-establishmentarianism should indeed not be equated with official atheism or state hostility vis-à-vis religion. In this particular case, the Government's admission that it is not indifferent to the religious feelings of its subjects is perhaps further explained by the fact that the Roman Catholic Church (to which an estimated 90–95 per cent of the population adheres) was the state church of Colombia until the adoption of the 1991 Constitution.[56] The state, presumably, felt the need to additionally

---

43 Art. 11, para. (2), of the Const. of Ethiopia (1995); art. 10, para. (1), of the Albanian Const. (1998); and art. 43, final sentence, of the Const. of Lithuania (1992).

44 Art. 14 of the Const. of Nicaragua (1986); and art. 24, para. (1), 2nd sentence, of the Const. of Paraguay (1992).

45 Art. 40, para. (2), 2nd sentence, of the Const. of Estonia (1992).

46 Art. 4, para. (1), of the 2001 Portuguese Law (*supra* note 17).

47 Art. 7 of the Const. of Uganda (1995).

48 Art. 14 of the Const. of Liberia (1986).

49 Art. 10 of the Const of Nigeria (1999).

50 Art. 20 of the Const. of the Republic of Korea (1948).

51 Art. 16, para. (3), of the Const. of Spain (1978).

52 Art. 14, para. (1), 2nd sentence, of the Const. of Russia (1993); art. 11, 3rd sentence, of the Const. of Serbia (2006); and art. 35, para. (3), 2nd sentence, of the Const. of Ukraine (1996).

53 Art. IV, sec. (1), of the Const. of Palau (1979).

54 Art. 19 of the Const. of Brazil (1988).

55 Art. 2 of the 1995 Colombian Law (*supra* note 2).

56 As per the Concordat between Colombia and the Holy See of 12 June 1973 (which, in fact, has never been annulled). Preferential treatment has been declared unconstitutional by the Constitutional Court since 1993: Constitutional Court of Colombia Decision no. C-027 [1993]; Constitutional Court of Colombia Decision no. C-088 [1994]; Constitutional Court of Colombia Decision no. C-350 [1994]. See Viviane A. Morales Hoyos, *Religious Liberty and Cultural and Ethnic Pluralism in the Colombian Constitution of 1991*, 2 Brigham Young University Law Review (1999), pp. 566–567. Hoyos (p. 564) depicts Colombia, on the basis of these constitutional developments and subsequent Law 133 on religious liberty, as a secular state.

underscore the fact that the disestablishment of the official church and the move towards secularism, by no means implies hostility vis-à-vis religion on the part of the state.

The Constitution of Moldova proclaims that no ideology may be instituted as an official state ideology.[57] Arguably, the scope of this non-establishment clause is broader than the previous examples as it also intends to prohibit the establishment of secular ideologies as the official *esprit de corps* of the state (one can think of, for instance, an establishment as 'Communist state' or 'Atheistic state'). The Constitutions of Russia and Tajikistan codify this principle as well (alongside a regular non-establishment clause)[58] as does the Constitution of Belarus.[59] The Constitution of Kazakhstan identifies a similar principle as it emphasizes the need for "ideological diversity".[60] A Czech law, in a similar vein, declares that the introduction of democracy is intended to ensure that the state will "not be bound either by an exclusive ideology or by a particular religious faith".[61]

5.4 Separation of State and Religion

A significant number of states have established the separation of the state and religion. This principle can be defined as the legal-political endeavour which aims at internalizing and consistently preserving a regime in which the state apparatus and religious institutions function independently from each other. In these states, in short, state bodies are not to interfere with religious affairs, whilst religious institutions are not to get involved in state affairs. Consistently upholding such a state of affairs, naturally, presupposes a fairly secular Government. States that have established the separation of state and religion include: Albania, Angola, Armenia, Azerbaijan, Belarus, Benin, Bolivia, Brazil, Bulgaria, Cameroon, Cape Verde, Chad, Croatia, Cuba, Czech Republic, Ethiopia, Fiji, France, Gabon, Georgia, Germany, Guinea, Guinea-Bissau, Hungary, Italy, Japan, Kazakhstan, Republic of Korea, Kyrgyzstan, Latvia, Liberia, Lithuania, Macedonia, Mexico, Moldova, Mongolia, Montenegro, Mozambique, Nepal, Niger, Paraguay, Peru, Philippines, Poland, Portugal, Romania, Russia, Sao Tome and Principe, Senegal, Serbia, Singapore, Slovak Republic, Slovenia, Tajikistan, Timor-Leste, Turkey,

---

[57] Art. 5, para. (2), of the Const. of Moldova (1994).

[58] Art. 13, paras. (1–2), Const. of Russia (1993); and art. 8 of the Const. of Tajikistan (1994).

[59] Art. 4 of the Const. of Belarus (1996) reads (partly): "The ideology of political parties, religious or other public associations, social groups may not be made mandatory for citizens."

[60] Art. 5 of the Const. of Kazakhstan (1995).

[61] Art. 2, para. (2), of the Charter of Fundamental Rights and Basic Freedoms of 16 December 1992.

Turkmenistan, Ukraine, Uruguay, Uzbekistan and Venezuela.[62] It must be observed that some of these states have in fact been discussed before under the different headings of state support for a specific religion.[63] This shows that there may in practice be a discrepancy between constitutional separationism

[62] Art. 8, para. (1), of the CONST. OF ANGOLA (1992); art. 23 of the CONST. OF BENIN (1990); preamble of the CONST. OF CAMEROON (1972); art. 2 of the CONSTITUTION OF THE REPUBLIC OF CAPE VERDE (1992); art. 1 of the CONST. OF CHAD (1996); art. 11 of the CONST. OF ETHIOPIA (1995); art. 2 of the CONST. OF GABON (1991); art. 14 of the FUNDAMENTAL LAW OF GUINEA (1990); art. 6 of the CONST. OF GUINEA-BISSAU (1991); art. 14 of the CONST. OF LIBERIA (1986); art. 12 of the CONST. OF MOZAMBIQUE (1990); artt. 4 and 8 of the CONSTITUTION OF NIGER (1999); art. 8 of the CONST. OF SAO TOME AND PRINCIPE (1975); art. 45, para. (1), of the CONST. OF EAST TIMOR (2002); art. 5 of the CONST. OF THE FIJI ISLANDS (1998); art. 20 of the CONSTITUTION OF JAPAN (1946); art. 20, para. (2), of the CONST. OF THE REPUBLIC OF KOREA (1948); art. 9 of the CONST. OF MONGOLIA (1992); art. 2, sec. (6), of the CONST. OF THE PHILIPPINES (1987); art. 15, para. (3), of the CONSTITUTION OF THE REPUBLIC OF SINGAPORE (1963); art. 10, paras. (3–6), of the ALBANIAN CONST. (1998); art. 8.1 of the CONST. OF ARMENIA (2005); art. 18, para. (1), of the CONST. OF AZERBAIJAN (1995); art. 16 of the CONSTITUTION OF THE REPUBLIC OF BELARUS (1996) in conjunction with art. 8 of the Law of the Republic of Belarus on Religious Freedom and Religious Organizations, Law No. 137–3, of 31 October 2002 (hereinafter: "2002 Belarusian Law"); art. 13, para. (2), of the CONST. OF BULGARIA (1991); art. 41 of the CONST. OF CROATIA (1990); art. 16, para. (2), of the Charter of Fundamental Rights and Basic Freedoms (1992) in conjunction with art. 3 of the CONSTITUTION OF THE CZECH REPUBLIC (1992); art. 1 of the CONST. OF FRANCE (1958) in conjunction with the Law Concerning the Separation of the Churches and the State (1905); art. 9 of the CONST. OF GEORGIA (1995); art. 137, of the Weimar Constitution (1919) as reiterated by the BASIC LAW FOR THE FEDERAL REPUBLIC OF GERMANY (1949); art. 60, para. (3), of the CONSTITUTION OF THE REPUBLIC OF HUNGARY (1949); art. 7 of the CONST. OF THE ITALIAN REPUBLIC (1947); art. 99 of the CONSTITUTION OF THE REPUBLIC OF LATVIA (1922); art. 43 (which has been interpreted as a separation clause by the Constitutional Court) of the CONST. OF LITHUANIA (1992); art. 19 (as amended by Amendment VII) of the CONSTITUTION OF THE REPUBLIC OF MACEDONIA (1991); art. 31, paras. (2) and (4), of the CONST. OF MOLDOVA (1994); art. 14 of the CONSTITUTION OF THE REPUBLIC OF MONTENEGRO (2007); art. 25, paras. (1–3), of the CONST. OF POLAND (1997); art. 41, para. (4), of the CONST. OF PORTUGAL (1976); art. 29, paras. (3) and (5), of the CONST. OF ROMANIA (1991); art. 14, para. (2), of the CONST. OF RUSSIA (1993); art. 24 of the CONST. OF SENEGAL (2001); art. 11, para. (2), in conjunction with art. 44, of the CONST. OF SERBIA (2006); art. 24, para. (3), of the CONST. OF SLOVAKIA (1992); art. 7 of the CONSTITUTION OF THE REPUBLIC OF SLOVENIA (1991); preamble of the CONST. OF TURKEY (1982); art. 35, para. (3), of the CONST. OF UKRAINE (1996); art. 26 of the CONST. OF INDIA (1950); art. 23, para. (2), INTERIM CONST. OF NEPAL (2007); art. 4 of the Law on Freedom of Religion and Religious Associations [of Kazakhstan] of 5 May 1992 (amended 2005) (hereinafter: "1992 Kazakh Law"); art. 8, para. (3), of the CONST. OF THE KYRGYZ REPUBLIC (1993); art. 8 of the CONST. OF TAJIKISTAN (1994); art. 11, para. (1), of the CONST. OF TURKMENISTAN (1992); art. 61 of the CONSTITUTION OF THE REPUBLIC OF UZBEKISTAN (1992); art. 4 of the POLITICAL CONST. OF BOLIVIA (2009); art. 19 of the CONST. OF BRAZIL (1988); art. 8 of the CONSTITUTION OF THE REPUBLIC OF CUBA (1976); art. 130 of the POLITICAL CONSTITUTION OF THE UNITED MEXICAN STATES (1917; hereinafter: CONST. OF MEXICO of 1917); art. 24, paras. (2–3), of the CONST. OF PARAGUAY (1992); art. 50 of the CONST. OF PERU (1993); art. 5 of the CONSTITUTION OF THE ORIENTAL REPUBLIC OF URUGUAY (1966); and art. 59 of the CONST. OF VENEZUELA (1999).

[63] See sections 3.2.3 and 4.2.4, *supra*. *E.g.* Armenia: Armenian state practice is rather ambivalent as the Armenian Apostolic Holy Church is, simultaneously, established as 'national church' and expressly supported by the State (see section 2.3.2, *supra*). Croatia, Italy, Peru, Poland and Venezuela have been identified before as states that have entered into special agreements with the Vatican so as to confirm a special legal status for the Catholic Church. These types of contradictions will be further analyzed in the next section (see sub-section 5.5.4, *infra*).

and actual state practice. It must be acknowledged, secondly, that this inventory also includes states with rather weak forms of separation. The main trends and differences that can be discerned on the basis of existing state practice will be charted in the next section of this Chapter (5.5). In what follows in this section, the different constitutional formulations that are used will be analysed in more detail.

5.4.1 *Separation of State and Church*

A 'separation between state and church' clearly has a profound Christian[64] connotation and this formulation indeed mainly appears in the Constitutions of states with a predominantly Christian background (for instance, Latvia, Cape Verde, Philippines and Armenia).[65] There are exceptions though: the official English version of the Constitution of the Republic of Korea also separates church and state.[66]

The Constitution of Italy, more narrowly, separates the state explicitly from the *Catholic* Church.[67] This type of formulation should be interpreted within the relevant historical context. Some states, however, wish not to leave any doubt as to this issue and explicitly separate the church *and the other religious communities* from the state (for instance, Portugal, Serbia and Ukraine).[68] Some states separate the state from the churche*s* (for instance, Angola, France and Mexico).[69] It must be noted that all these formulations are construed so as to separate the state from religion proper.

5.4.2 *Separation of State and Religion*

A 'separation of state and religion' (or derivatives) appears to be increasingly employed by the drafters of contemporary constitutions, obviously by states with non-Christian backgrounds, but in fact also by states with predominantly Christian populations. It may indeed be argued that this terminology does more justice to what is actually intended. It is true that historically separation principles were often introduced to raise a wall of separation between the state and the dominant church or religion specifically. This construction, however, was normally not intended to insulate non-dominant or non-traditional

---

64 See also Chapter 2, text in and around footnote 180.

65 Art. 99 of the CONST. OF LATVIA (1922); art. 2 of the CONST. OF CAPE VERDE (1992); art. 2, sec. (6), of the CONST. OF THE PHILIPPINES (1987); art. 8.1 of the CONST. OF ARMENIA (2005).

66 Art. 20, para. (2), of the CONST. OF THE REPUBLIC OF KOREA (1948; official transl. as published by the Constitutional Court).

67 Art. 7 of the CONSTITUTION OF THE ITALIAN REPUBLIC (1947).

68 Art. 41, para. (4), of the CONST. OF PORTUGAL (1976); art. 11, para. (2), of the CONST. OF SERBIA (2006); and art. 35, para. (3), of the CONST. OF UKRAINE (1996).

69 Art. 8, para. (1), of the CONST. OF ANGOLA (1992); art. 1 of the CONST. OF FRANCE (1958) in conjunction with the Law Concerning the Separation of the Churches and the State (1905); and art. 130 of the CONST. OF MEXICO (1917).

religions from the ramifications of the principle of separation. In short, a neutral phrasing of the separation principle would appear to be preferable in terms of legal clarity.

Azerbaijan, Chad, Ethiopia, Fiji, Gabon, Liberia and Niger, constitutionally affirm the principle in this standard form (a separation of/between the state and religion).[70] Many alternatives can be found that have the same effect (establishing a separation between the state and all the different religions communities): a separation of the state and "religious institutions" (Guinea-Bissau, Sao Tome and Principe, Bulgaria and Cuba);[71] a separation of the state and "religious denominations" (Mozambique);[72] a separation of the state and "religious communities" (Croatia and Slovenia);[73] a separation of the state and "religious cults" (Moldova, Romania and Kyrgyzstan);[74] a separation of the state and "religious associations" (Russia, Kazakhstan and Uzbekistan);[75] and a separation of the state and "religious organizations" (Tajikistan and Turkmenistan).[76] The Constitution of Macedonia lists all the officially recognized "religious communities"—the Macedonian Orthodox Church, the Islamic Religious Community in Macedonia, the Catholic Church, the Evangelic Methodist Church and the Jewish Community—to subsequently declare them separate from the state.[77]

5.4.3 *Regional Separation of State and Religion*

The Republic of the Sudan can certainly not be considered a secular state. The fact that Shari'a law is considered a source of legislation applicable to the states of the Northern Sudan denotes a profound affiliation of this part of the state with Islam.[78] The Southern States of the Sudan are excluded from the scope of

---

[70] Art. 18, para. (1), of the Const. of Azerbaijan (1995); art. 1 of the Const. of Chad (1996); art. 11, para. (1), of the Const. of Ethiopia (1995); art. 5 of the Const. of the Fiji Islands (1998); art. 2 of the Const. of Gabon (1991); art. 14 of the Const. of Liberia (1986); and art. 4 of the Const. of Niger (1990).

[71] Art. 6, para. (1), of the Const. of Guinea-Bissau (1991); art. 8 of the Const. of Sao Tome and Principe (1975); art. 13, para. (2), of the Const. of Bulgaria (1991); and art. 8 of the Const. of Cuba (1976). A caveat in this context is that as far as the translated Constitutions are concerned, naturally much comes down to the discretion of the translator.

[72] Art. 12 of the Const. of Mozambique (1990).

[73] Art. 41, para. (1), of the Const. of Croatia (1990); and art. 7, para. (1), of the Const. of Slovenia (1991).

[74] Art. 31, paras. (2) and (4), of the Const. of Moldova (1994); art. 29, para. (5), of the Const. of Romania (1991); and art. 8, para. (3), of the Const. of the Kyrgyz Republic (1993), which speaks of a separation of the state and religions and all religious cults.

[75] Art. 14, para. (2), of the Const. of Russia (1993); art. 4 of the 1992 Kazakh Law (*supra* note 62); art. 61 of the Const. of Uzbekistan (1992), separates the state from religious organizations as well as religious associations.

[76] Art. 8 of the Const. of Tajikistan (1994); art. 11, para. (1), of the Const. of Turkmenistan (1992).

[77] Art. 19 (as amended by Amendment VII) of the Const. of Macedonia (1991).

[78] Art. 5, para. (1), of the Interim Const. of the Sudan (2005). Also the constitutional references to God, strictly speaking, rule out a secular character of the state. See the preamble

these regulations based on Shari'a law and, moreover, the Southern States have expressly stipulated a separation of state and religion.[79] Switzerland is another example of a state which shows regional preferences for separation: whilst most Swiss cantons identify with different Christian denominations, some cantons indeed practice a separation between canton and religion.[80]

5.5 Implications

The objective of this section is to further examine the ideals of secularism and separationism on the basis of existing state practice so as to concisely chart the main trends and differences. In particular, account is to be taken of the differing extent to which the legislative, executive and judicial branches of the state are influenced by the regimes of state secularism and separationism.[81] Some Constitutions outline in some detail the specific legal-political ramifications of the separation clause and/or secularism clause. Arguably the most far-reaching provision in this respect is a ban on religious political parties. The following parameters need to be taken into account as well. Different separation clauses have different structural implications, in terms of the political organization of the state. Separation clauses, typically, safeguard the autonomy of the state apparatus and religious institutions. In practice, however, often an emphasis on separationism as governmental autonomy or separationism as religious or church autonomy can be discerned. Some secular and separationist states additionally underscore the importance that is attached to the concepts of secularism and separation by means of constitutionally declaring these principles irreversible. It will be pointed out, finally, that some secular and separationist states show evidence of state practice that cannot, strictly speaking, be reconciled with the principles of secularism or separationism. The latter shows that there may in practice be a discrepancy between constitutional secularism/separationism and actual state practice.

5.5.1 *Political Implications of Secularism/Separationism*

Some states construe the principles of secularism and separationism so as to imply that political parties may not be based on religion. It goes without saying that such an interpretation has an important bearing on the legislative branch of the state. Religious political parties are banned by the following

of the Interim Const. of the Sudan (2005) as well as the several official oaths which include references to God (artt. 56 and 71).

[79] Art. 8 of the Interim Const. of Southern Sudan (2005): and art. 5, paras. (1) and (2), of the Interim Const. of the Sudan (2005).

[80] See Chapter 2 (section 2.3.3), *supra*.

[81] In this way it is demonstrated that the states discussed presently and the states discussed in Chapter 2 (see section 2.4) in many respects adopt opposite measures.

secular and separationist states: Belarus, Bulgaria, Burkina Faso, Cape Verde, Republic of the Congo, Guinea, Guinea-Bissau, Kyrgyz Republic, Liberia, Mexico, Moldova, Mozambique, Nigeria, Portugal, Rwanda, Senegal, Tanzania, Togo, Turkmenistan and Uzbekistan.[82] Different types or degrees of prohibitions of religious political parties can be found, ranging from absolute, blanket prohibitions of such parties, to bans that forbid political parties to associate with a particular religion by name or emblem.[83]

A range of other concrete political ramifications of the principles of secularism and separationism follow from the differing interpretations of states that practice these principles. The Turkish Constitution, for instance, mainstreams the principle of secularism into all areas of the Constitution. For instance, Turkish Members of Parliament, upon assuming office, have to take the following oath: "I swear upon my honour and integrity…to remain loyal to the… democratic and secular Republic, and to Atatürk's principles and reforms".[84] The President of Turkey must take a similar oath to affirm that he or she will abide by the principles of the secular Republic of Turkey.[85] The Constitution dictates that the Department of Religious Affairs shall exercise its duties "in accordance with the principles of secularism".[86] Also the role of the judiciary and its relation to state secularism is addressed. It is provided that all reform laws that have been adopted to safeguard the secular nature of the state may not be rendered unconstitutional.[87] Besides individual MPs, also political parties have to respect the secular status of Turkey at all times.[88]

Benin and Mali similarly codify a requirement that political parties have to respect the secular nature of the state.[89] Other states, short of demanding that political parties are bound to respect the secularity of the state, raise some

---

[82] Art. 11 of the CONST. OF BULGARIA (1991); art. 13 of the CONST. OF BURKINA FASO (1991); art. 125 of the CONST. OF CAPE VERDE (1992); art. 52 of the NEW CONST. OF THE REPUBLIC OF THE CONGO (2002); art. 3 of the FUNDAMENTAL LAW OF GUINEA (1990); art. 4 of the CONST. OF GUINEA-BISSAU (1991); art. 8 of the CONST. OF THE KYRGYZ REPUBLIC (1993); art. 79 of the CONST. OF LIBERIA (1986); art. 130 of the CONST. OF MEXICO (1917); art. 20 of the Law of the Republic of Moldova on Denominations, No. 979-XII, of 24 March 1992 (amended in 1998 and 2002; hereinafter: "1992 Moldovan Law"); art. 76 of the CONST. OF MOZAMBIQUE (1990); art. 222 of the CONST. OF NIGERIA (1999); art. 51 of the CONST. OF PORTUGAL (1976); art. 54 of the CONST. OF RWANDA (2003); art. 4 of the CONST. OF SENEGAL (2001); art. 20 of the CONST. OF TANZANIA (1977); art. 7 of the CONST. OF TOGO (1992); art. 28 of the CONST. OF TURKMENISTAN (1992); and art. 57 of the CONST. OF UZBEKISTAN (1992).

[83] See Chapter 11, section 11.2.2, *infra*, for a comprehensive discussion. In that Chapter it will also be outlined that such bans may be adopted so as to deal with historical or emerging politicized religious strife or, as the case may be, rather from a desire to outlaw a specific extremist organization. This also explains why several *non*-secular states have adopted similar prohibitions.

[84] Art. 81 of the CONST. OF TURKEY (1982).

[85] Art. 103 of the CONST. OF TURKEY (1982).

[86] Art. 136 of the CONST. OF TURKEY (1982).

[87] Art. 174 of the CONST. OF TURKEY (1982).

[88] Art. 68 of the CONST. OF TURKEY (1982).

[89] Art. 5 of the CONST. OF BENIN (1990); art. 28 of the CONST. OF MALI (1992).

concerns about the issue of political affiliation with religion in their Constitutions. The Constitution of Burundi, for instance, states: "In their organisation and functioning the political parties must respond to the democratic principles…They may not foment violence, exclusion, and hatred in any of their forms…in particular those based on…religious…affiliation".[90] Russia prohibits public associations that incite religious strife whilst Serbia forbids political parties that incite religious hatred.[91] The latter type of prohibitions can, strictly speaking, be distinguished from an absolute ban on religious political parties. The requirement to respect the secularity of the state forbids political parties from proposing laws or policies that would contravene the secular nature of the state or to propose amendments to the Constitution that would have the same effect. This requirement, however, does not rule out political parties being affiliated with a religion per se.[92]

5.5.2 *Structural Implications of Separation*

Separation of state and religion is generally implemented with a view to ensuring that the state apparatus and religion function independently from each other. Thus, the underlying rationale is that both authorities—the profane and the religious—benefit from being guarded against possible, undesired interferences. Having said that, history has seen many forms of so-called 'hostile separation' where religion is not separated from the state so as to establish and protect two autonomous spheres for respectively state and religious powers, but rather so as to subject religion to the will of the state. Occasionally this amounted to practices of official hostility or even state-instigated practices of elimination of religion, for instance, under (certain periods of) former Soviet rule.[93] These forms of state practice that are characterized by anti-religious sentiments on the part of the state will be dealt with in the next Chapter. Strictly speaking, it cannot be maintained that we are dealing with 'separation' in these (largely historical) instances as religion is not separated but rather fully controlled by the state.

---

[90] Art. 78 of the Post-transition Const. of Burundi (2005).

[91] Art. 13, para. (5), of the Const. of Russia (1993); art. 5 of the Const. of Serbia (2006). Also Šrpska forbids political parties inciting religious hatred (art. 31 of the Const. of the Republic of Šrpska of 1992).

[92] This will be discussed in more detail in the second part if this study, focusing on the human rights questions surrounding this issue (see particularly Chapter 11).

[93] *E.g.* Michael Bordeaux, *The Former Soviet Union: Trends in Religious Liberty, in* Religious Freedom in the World. A Global Report on Freedom and Persecution (P. Marshall, ed., Nashville: Broadman & Holman Publishers, 2000). Bordeaux argues (pp. 35–42) that all Soviet leaders put their "personal stamp" on state policies of hostility vis-à-vis religion: Lenin confiscated churches; Stalin destroyed religious buildings and eliminated church leaders; and Khrushchev and Brezhnev persecuted religious dissidents.

In short, separationism is normally characterised by *mutual* non-interference.[94] Most constitutional provisions for separation emphasize the two different sides of the principle.[95] It must be observed that some constitutions one-sidedly underscore either state autonomy from religion or religion's autonomy from the state.

(i) *Separation as Mutual Independence*

The ideal of *mutual* non-interference can be discerned in most of the more descriptive constitutional separation clauses. The Constitution of Poland, for instance, elaborates on the principle of separation in the following way:

> The relationship between the State and churches and other religious organizations shall be based on the principle of respect for their autonomy and the mutual independence of each in its own sphere...[96]

Also officially "neutral" Albania has declared that the "state and the religious communities mutually respect the independence of one another".[97] The Constitution of Peru similarly recognizes and elaborates on such a "framework of independence and autonomy".[98] The formulation in the Constitution of Brazil approximates the ideal of mutual independence in so far as it is forbidden for the state to hamper the activities of religions, whilst relations of "dependency or alliance" with representatives of religion are equally prohibited.[99] Benin clearly recognizes the two angles of the separation principle as well. The Constitution on the one hand affirms that "[t]he institutions and the religious or philosophical communities shall have the right to develop without hindrances. They shall not be subject to the guardianship of the state. They shall regulate and administer their affairs in an autonomous manner."[100] On the other hand it is stipulated that "[t]he exercise of a creed and the expression of beliefs shall take place with respect for the secularity of the state."[101] The Constitution of Cameroon provides that the state is to be "independent" from

---

[94] Cf. Norman Redlich, John Attanasio & Joel K. Goldstein, Understanding Constitutional Law (New York: Matthew Bender, 1999), p. 505; see also Brett G. Scharffs, *The Autonomy of Church and State*, 4 Brigham Young University Law Review (2004), pp. 1217–1348.

[95] See also the generic separation clauses outlined in sections 5.4.1–5.4.2, *supra*.

[96] Art. 25, para. (3), of the Const. of Poland (1997). It must be observed that this principle in Poland has not resulted in the removal of religious symbols or artefacts from governmental buildings.

[97] Art. 10 of the Albanian Const. (1998). This provision is fairly flexible as it is added in the same article that this does not rule out working together "for the good of each of them and for all". See also Evis Karandrea, *Church and State in Albania, in* Law and Religion in Post-Communist Europe (Ferrari & Durham, eds., Leuven: Peeters, 2003), pp. 29–30, on Albania's separation principle.

[98] Art. 50 of the Const. of Peru (1993).

[99] Art. 18 of the Const. of Brazil (1988).

[100] Art. 23, final sentences, of the Const. of Benin (1990).

[101] Art. 23 of the Const. of Benin (1990).

religion; the state also guarantees not to interfere with religious affairs by proclaiming the neutrality of the state in respect of all religions.[102]

Some state laws, elaborating on the separation principles applicable in these countries, dictate that state bodies and religious institutions should not assume each other's powers or prerogatives. A Lithuanian Law, for instance, provides that "[r]eligious communities and associations shall not fulfil state functions, while the state shall not fulfil the functions of religious communities and associations."[103] A Kazakh law on religious associations similarly determines that "[r]eligious associations do not perform any state functions and the state does not interfere in the activities of religious organisations".[104] The Ethiopian Constitution concisely provides that "[t]he state shall not interfere in religious matters and religion shall not interfere in state affairs".[105] The Constitution of Mongolia does the same: "State institutions may not engage in religious activities and the Church may not pursue political activities".[106]

The question as to whether the political act of disestablishment, when it is not explicitly accompanied by the creation of a wall of separation, may, in itself, be equated to *de facto* separationism is not as straightforward as it would appear. The answer very much depends on the incentives behind the disestablishment. The act of disestablishment would normally be a first decisive step towards (secularism and/or) separationism. For instance, the disestablishment of the Dutch Reformed Church from the then Batavian Republic (Netherlands) ultimately led to a fairly separationist state (though such has never been explicitly acknowledged by a constitutional provision to that effect).[107] In Ireland the disestablishment of the (Anglican) Church of Ireland in 1871 formally ended the ties between the state and this numerically inferior Church, which was made possible under British Prime Minister William Gladstone. The act of disestablishment never translated into clear-cut state separationism. It rather fostered a nexus between the state and the majority religion, Catholicism.[108]

---

[102] Preamble of the CONST. OF CAMEROON (1972).

[103] Art. 7 of the Law on Religious Communities and Associations, Law No. 89-1985, of 1995 (amended by Law No. VIII-394 of 2 July 1997 and by Law No. VIII-1677 of 11 May 2000; hereinafter: "1995 Lithuanian Law").

[104] Art. 4 of the 1992 Kazakh Law (*supra* note 62).

[105] Art. 11, para. (3), of the CONST. OF ETHIOPIA (1995). It has already been mentioned that a clear-cut separation clause is codified by art. 11, para. (1).

[106] Art. 9, para. (2), of the CONST. OF MONGOLIA (1992). The first paragraph of the same article adds that the State "shall respect the Church" and that the Church "shall honour the State".

[107] It must be observed that, although no religion has an official or privileged position, certain practices which contravene, strictly speaking, the principles of secularism and separationism have not yet come to a halt; *e.g.* the Monarch is officially considered Head of State "by the grace of God", the Monarch tends to refer to a God in official speeches, etc.

[108] It must be acknowledged that the Constitution does not single out Catholicism since the adoption of the Fifth Amendment of the Constitution Act in 1972. The state's *de facto* entanglement with Catholicism can mainly be discerned within Ireland's educational system. For constitutional religious references, see preamble and art. 44 of the CONST. OF IRELAND (1937).

The example of Sweden holds the middle between the latter two cases. The disestablishment of the Church of Sweden in 2000 took place after decades of political and public debate on the matter. Though the underlying incentives can be considered to be of a separationist nature,[109] the final outcome does not equate to a clear-cut separation of state and religion as the state continues to have a say in church affairs. Gustafsson argues in this regard: "although the Church of Sweden has gained greater liberty from the state, it has not gained any greater independence from the political system".[110] This mainly expresses itself, in the words of the same author, as follows: "political parties can still, through the Church Assembly and its other elected bodies, retain a certain amount of influence in the church."[111]

(ii) *Separation as Governmental Independence*

Some formulations are not based on reciprocity, but instead one-sidedly emphasize the need for Government to be independent and free from religious interference. A constitutional emphasis on the need for governmental affairs to be free from religious intrusion can be perceived in the Constitutions of Belarus, Bolivia, France, Japan, Niger, Tajikistan, Turkey and Turkmenistan.[112] It must be observed that in some cases this has a historical explanation: the establishment of a wall of separation may have been specifically instigated by the will of those who came to power to free the state from (real or supposed) religious control, manipulation or other negative interferences. This may hold true, for instance, for France and Turkey. It must be acknowledged at the same time that there are regimes that do in fact simply take a greater interest in the ideal of governmental autonomy than in religious autonomy (e.g., most distinctly, Belarus).[113]

---

[109] See for a detailed account on the deconstruction of Sweden as a confessional state: Göran Gustafsson, *Church–State Separation Swedish-Style, in* CHURCH AND STATE IN CONTEMPORARY EUROPE: THE CHIMERA OF NEUTRALITY (J.T.S. Madeley & Z. Enyedi, eds., London: Frank Cass Publ., 2003), pp. 53–71.

[110] *Ibid.*, p. 69.

[111] *Ibid.*, p. 70. He continues arguing that: "The Swedish people seem hardly to have noticed the change of church–state relations since the work of the church has not changed at all."

[112] See the 2002 Belarusian Law (*supra* note 62) in conjunction with art. 16 of the CONST. OF BELARUS (1996); art. 4 of the POLITICAL CONST. OF BOLIVIA (2009); art. 1 of the CONST. OF FRANCE (1958) in conjunction with the 1905 Law Regarding the Separation of the Churches and the State (1905); art. 20 of the CONST. OF JAPAN (1946): "No religious organization shall receive any privileges from the State, nor exercise any political authority"; art. 8 of the CONST. OF NIGER (1999); art. 8 of the CONST. OF TAJIKISTAN (1994): "Religious organizations are separate from the state and may not interfere in governmental affairs"; preamble of the CONST. OF TURKEY (1982): "there shall be no interference whatsoever of the sacred religious feelings in State affairs and politics"; art. 11, para. (1), of the CONST. OF TURKMENISTAN (1992): "Religious organizations are separate from the government, and may not perform governmental functions".

[113] Belarusian state practice is based on regulations on religion–state relations (most importantly, the 2002 Belarusian Law, *supra* note 62) which are largely characterized by restraint of

(iii) *Separation as Church or Religious Autonomy*

By contrast, the Constitutions of the Czech Republic, Germany, Georgia, Guinea, Nepal, Paraguay, Senegal, Serbia, Singapore, Slovakia, Timor-Leste, Uruguay, Uzbekistan and Venezuela underscore the independence of religious organizations from the state.[114] Thus, religious organizations are considered autonomous and must remain free from state intervention or interference.

Again it must be acknowledged that the choices behind some of these constitutional formulations have a historical explanation. A particular stress on religious autonomy may historically have been motivated by a desire to mark the end of an era of persecution of religions or of a particular Church or religion (for instance, former Soviet states). At the same time it must be observed that some of these less stringent and one-sided formulations of the separation principle are indeed motivated by a desire to leave open the option of some

---

religious practice. The objectives of these regulations seem to be to fully preserve the state against 'unwelcome' religious interventions. Particularly non-traditional or non-dominant religious groups (i.e. religious groups other than Belarusian Orthodoxy) are affected as they need prior governmental permission for practicing many basic religious freedoms. In that respect, Belarus is leaning towards the more negative types of state–religion identification that are discussed in the next Chapter (an important difference is that Belarus appears more selective in applying its restrictions on the manifestation of religions). See also Alexander Vashkevich, *The Relationship of Church and State in Belarus: Legal Regulation and Practice*, 2 Brigham Young University Law Review 681 (2003), pp. 703–708, on the stringent registration criteria for religious associations.

[114] Art. 16, para. (2), of the Charter of Fundamental Rights and Basic Freedoms [Czech Republic] (1992): "Churches and religious societies govern their own affairs; in particular, they establish their own bodies and appoint their clergy, as well as found religious orders and other church institutions, independent of state authorities"; art. 12, para. (1), of the Const. of East Timor (2002): "The State shall recognise and respect the different religious denominations, which are free in their organisation and in the exercise of their own activities…"; art. 9 of the Const. of Georgia (1995); art. 137, para. (3), of the Weimar Constitution of 1919 as expressly sanctioned by the Basic Law for the Federal Republic of Germany (1949): "Each religious body regulates and administers its affairs independently…It appoints its officials without the cooperation of the Land, or of the civil community"; art. 14 of the Fundamental Law of Guinea (1990): "Religious institutions and communities freely create and administer themselves. They shall not be subject to the tutelage of the state"; art. 23, para. (2), of the Interim Const. of Nepal (2007); art. 24, para. (3), of the Const. of Paraguay (1992): "The independence and autonomy of all churches and religious denominations…are hereby guaranteed"; art. 24 of the Const. of Senegal (2001): "Religious institutions and communities shall have the right to develop without hindrance. They shall not be subject to direct supervision by the state. They shall regulate and administer their affairs autonomously"; art. 44 of the Const. of Serbia (2006): "Churches and religious communities shall be equal and free to organize independently their internal structure"; art. 15, para. (3)(a), of the Const. of Singapore (1963): "Every religious group has the right…to manage its own religious affairs"; art. 24, para. (3), of the Const. of Slovakia (1992): "Churches and religious communities administer their own affairs. In particular, they constitute their own bodies, inaugurate their clergymen, organize the teaching of religion, and establish religious orders and other church institutions independently of state bodies"; art. 5 of the Const. of Uruguay (1966); art. 61 of the Const. of Uzbekistan (1992): "The state shall not interfere with the activity of religious associations"; and art. 59 of the Const. of Venezuela (1999): "The autonomy and independence of religious confessions and churches is…guaranteed".

(limited) forms of interaction or even cooperation between religions and the state. Germany's separation of state and religion, for instance, has not prevented Germany form entering into a rather sophisticated partnership with religions.[115] Paraguay's separation does not in practice rule out a degree of interaction between the state and religion (Catholicism, in particular, plays an important ceremonial role).[116] Venezuela's separation does not forestall the state from subsidizing religious organizations, particularly the Roman Catholic Church. Arguably, some of these practices would be incompatible with French *laïcité* or American-style separation.

5.5.3 *Secularity/Separation as an Irrevocable Characteristic*

It has been outlined above that some religious states underscore the importance attached to the religious nature of the state by declaring this characteristic of the state inviolable and irrevocable.[117] Some secular states do precisely the same: the secular nature is regarded as such an eminent quality of the state that this trait is not to be questioned and may not be subject to constitutional revision. This is the case in: Benin, Côte d'Ivoire, Gabon, Guinea, Guinea-Bissau, Mali, Tajikistan, Togo and Turkey.[118] It may be added at this point that in principle all so-called non-establishmentarian states (states that have codified a non-establishment clause) could be added to this list in so far as a non-establishment clause equally forbids any future revision of the Constitution which would come down to an establishment of a state religion or church.[119]

Other constitutional indications as to the irreversible nature of the principle of secularism can be discerned. The Constitution of Mali, rather uniquely, refers to the obligation to safeguard the secularity of the state as a civic duty of the people in its Preamble.[120] The Constitution of Chad forbids all religious or other propaganda that is meant to affect the secularity of the state.[121]

---

[115] Germany collects on behalf of those religious organizations that are granted a "corporation under public law" status a church tax from the religious adherents (see section 4.2.3, *supra*).

[116] Moreover, in art. 24, para. (2), of the CONST. OF PARAGUAY (1992), the Catholic Church is made an exclusive offer to cooperate with the state (as discussed *supra* in sections 3.3.1 and 4.2.4).

[117] See Chapter 2, section 2.4.5, *supra*.

[118] Art. 156 of the CONS. OF BENIN (1990); art. 127 of the CONST. OF CÔTE D'IVOIRE (2000); art. 7 of the CONST. OF GABON (1991); art. 91 of the FUNDAMENTAL LAW OF GUINEA (1990); art. 102 of the CONST. OF GUINEA-BISSAU (1991); art. 118 of the CONST. OF MALI (1992); art. 100 of the CONST. OF TAJIKISTAN (1994); art. 144 of the CONST. OF TOGO (1992); and art. 4 (in conjunction with art. 2) of the CONST. OF TURKEY (1982).

[119] See section 5.3, *supra*.

[120] Preamble of the CONST. OF MALI (1992): "The Sovereign People of Mali...solemnly engage to defend the republican form and the secularity of the State".

[121] Art. 5 of the CONST. OF CHAD (1996).

In a similar vein, Mozambique, Niger and Portugal underscore the importance attached to the separation principle by means of declaring the establishment of the separation between the state and religion irreversible.[122]

5.5.4 *Contradictory State Practice*

It must be observed that some secular and separationist states show evidence of state practice that cannot, strictly speaking, be reconciled with the principles of secularism or separationism. The latter shows that there may in practice be a discrepancy between constitutional secularism/separationism and actual state practice.

(i) *Secularism & Religious Affirmations*

Numerous non-secular states acknowledge "God" or other metaphysical phenomena by way of referring to such notions in their Constitution or by means of state symbolism.[123] Secular states do not disapprove of people believing in a religion. But because secular states for themselves deny any form of positive identification with religion, one would assume that any active confession of faith on the part of the state would be taboo. This consideration largely holds true as far as state practice is concerned; however, some states can be discerned that reflect contradictory messages. The Constitution of Togo, for instance, defines Togo as a secular state but puts at the same time the Togolese people "under the protection of God".[124] A number of other secular states refer to "God" in their Constitutions or laws by way of including God-notions in the official oaths of office (e.g. India, Mali, Namibia and Rwanda).[125] This should not be considered a clear-cut profession of faith on the part of the state, in particular since the religious aspects of these oaths in some cases are expressly considered optional and thus may be omitted by the person who is taking one.[126] Having

---

[122] Art. 292 of the CONST. OF MOZAMBIQUE (1990), art. 136 of the CONST. OF NIGER (1999) and art. 288 of the CONST. OF PORTUGAL (1976).

[123] See Chapter 3, section 3.3.3, *supra*.

[124] Preamble of the CONST. OF TOGO (1992).

[125] Art. 37 of CONST. OF MALI (1992); art. 30 of the CONST. OF NAMIBIA (1990); artt. 61 and 103 of the CONST. OF RWANDA (2003); artt. 60, 69 and 159 in the CONST. OF INDIA (1950). In addition, several non-establishmentarian states refer to God in their Constitution, including Gambia, Ghana, Nigeria, Palau, Seychelles and Uganda. See the preamble of the CONST. OF THE GAMBIA (1996); preamble and the second schedule (on oaths) to the CONST. OF GHANA (1992); preamble of the CONST. OF NIGERIA (1999); preamble of the CONST. OF PALAU (1979); preamble of the CONST. OF SEYCHELLES (1993); and the preamble of the CONST. OF UGANDA (1995). The Gambian and Nigerian Constitutions, moreover, despite the non-establishment clause, expressly endorse Shari'a Courts to oversee implementation of Shari'a law; see artt. 7, para. (f), and art. 137 of the CONST. OF THE GAMBIA (1996); and artt. 260 and 275–279 of the CONST. OF NIGERIA (1999). The latter combination (non-establishment clause & sanctioning the implementation of religious laws), it goes without saying, is equally contradictory.

[126] See Chapter 11 on the important difference (from a human rights perspective) between compulsory and optional religious oaths.

said that, including religious elements in oaths of office reflects a deliberate choice, considering the fact that they could alternatively be formulated as secular, solemn affirmations. In particular with respect to Mali this begs the question why the Constitution on the one side asks the People of Mali to "solemnly engage to defend the secularity of the State",[127] whilst the state, on the other side, does not shy away from using non-secular terminology.

It may be pointed out at this point that India's conception of secularism is unique in many ways.[128] India is in fact the only declared secular state within the South Asian Association for Regional Cooperation (SAARC). Although India, since its independence (1947), has been organized along fairly secular lines (for which the way was largely paved by Gandhi and Nehru), an explicit provision on the principle of secularism was incorporated into the Constitution as late as 1976. The rationale behind an express reference to the "high ideal of secularism" was described as follows: "there could be no denial that these [democratic state] institutions have been subjected to considerable stresses and strains and that vested interests have been trying to promote their selfish ends to the great detriment of public good".[129] It must be observed that Indian secularism by no means prevents forms of interaction between the state and religions and certainly has not translated into a strict wall of separation. Most importantly, in that regard, the state upholds the existing system of parallel jurisdictions whereby the religious communities (particularly, Christians, Parsis, Muslim, Hindus, Buddhists, Jains and Sikhs) are accommodated to enforce their differing sets of (religious) personal laws.[130]

(ii) *Separationism & Religious Affirmations*

A number of states that are explicitly separationist, nevertheless, refer to God in their Constitution (Brazil, Fiji, Germany, Liberia, Poland, Paraguay, Peru, Romania, Ukraine and Venezuela).[131] Non-interference with religious affairs

---

[127] Preamble of the Const. of Mali (1992).

[128] See Gary Jeffrey Jacobsohn, The Wheel of Law: India's Secularism in Comparative Constitutional Context (Princeton University Press, 2003).

[129] See the preamble and art. 2 of the Constitution (Forty-second Amendment) Act, Bill No. 91/1976, of 18 December 1976.

[130] Tahir Mahmood, *Religion, Law, and Judiciary in Modern India*, 3 Brigham Young University Law Review 755 (2006). See for instance the Indian Christian Marriage Act of 1872, the Parsi Marriage and Divorce Act of 1936, the Hindu Marriage Act of 1955, the Hindu Succession Act of 1956, the Hindu Adoption and Maintenance Act of 1956, the Hindu Minority and Guardianship Act of 1956 and the Muslim Personal Law Application Act of 1937. Art. 26 of the Const. of India (1950) grants religious communities the freedom to manage their own affairs.

[131] Preamble of the Const. of Brazil (1988); preamble of the Const. of the Fiji Islands (1998); preamble of the Basic Law for the Federal Republic of Germany (1949); preamble of the Const. of Liberia (1986); preamble of the Const. of Poland (1997); preamble of the Const. of Paraguay (1992); preamble of the Const. of Peru (1993); art. 82 (presidential oath) of the Const. of Romania (1991); preamble of the Const. of Ukraine (1996); and the preamble of the Const. of Venezuela (1999).

would, arguably, also rule out confessions of fate on the part of the state, in particular in so far as these references can be considered preferential towards theistic religions.

A number of other contradictory forms of state practice can be discerned. The Constitution of Fiji, for instance, uniquely establishes a separation between state and religion whilst it, at the same time, tones down, if not questions, the importance of the clause: "Although religion and the State are separate, the people of the Fiji Islands acknowledge that worship and reverence of God are the source of good government and leadership".[132] It may indeed be concluded that the latter part of the acknowledgement runs counter to the rationale of the separation principle. The establishment of a separation of state and religion by Ethiopia and Singapore is not easily reconcilable with the constitutional recognition of religious courts in these countries.[133]

Finally, in the Chapter on state support (Chapter 3) it has already been outlined that several states, including Croatia, Hungary, Italy, Peru, Poland, Spain, Uruguay and Venezuela, support the Roman Catholic Church by means of granting it a special legal position (by virtue of special constitutional recognition and/or Concordats endorsing agreements with the Holy See).[134] These forms of endorsement are often difficult to reconcile with the separation clause.[135] It must be observed, though, that some of these states extend some of the forms of cooperation to other religions or explicitly leave open the option of entering into similar agreements with the non-dominant or non-traditional religions.[136] However, such 'neutralization' of historical privileges

---

[132] Art. 5 of the CONST. OF THE FIJI ISLANDS (1998).

[133] Compare artt. 11 and 78, para. (5), of the CONST. OF ETHIOPIA (1995); compare art. 15 of the CONST. OF SINGAPORE (1963) and art. 153 of the Constitution in conjunction with the Administration of Muslim Law Act (1968). Art. 35 of this Act outlines the jurisdiction of Shari'a Courts and the applicability of Shari'a Law.

[134] Paras. (3) and (4) of art. 25 of the CONST. OF POLAND (1997) in conjunction with the Concordat between Poland and the Holy See of 28 July 1993 (ratified and entered into force in 1998); art. 50 of the CONST. OF PERU (1993) in conjunction with Legislative Decree No. 23211 endorsing the Concordat between the Holy See and the Republic of Peru; art. 16, para. (3), of the CONST. OF SPAIN (1978) in conjunction with the Concordats between Spain and the Holy See of 4 December 1979; art. 5 of the CONST. OF URUGUAY (1966); and the Concordat between Venezuela and the Holy See of 6 March 1964.

[135] In one account this is attempted by considering that the founders of the Constitution in that particular state (Poland) understood the separation notion to be a "flexible principle". See Michael Pietrzak, *Church and State in Poland, in* LAW AND RELIGION IN POST-COMMUNIST EUROPE (Ferrari & Durham, eds., Leuven: Peeters, 2003), p. 223.

[136] *E.g.* Agreement between Croatia and the Serbian Orthodox Church (2002); Agreement between Croatia and the Islamic Community (2002); Agreements between Croatia and the Evangelical Church, Reformed Christian Church, Pentecostal Church, Union of Pentecostal Churches of Christ, Christian Adventist Church, Union of Baptist Churches, Church of God, Church of Christ and the Reformed Movement of Seventh-day Adventists (2003); Agreement between Croatia and the Bulgarian Orthodox Church, Macedonian Orthodox Church and Croatian Old Catholic Church (2003); Agreement between Italy and the Waldesian Church (1984); Agreement between Italy and Adventists and Assembly of God (1988); Agreement between Italy and the Jewish religion (1989); Agreement between Italy and Baptists and

and prerogatives can hardly be considered complete as, for that to happen, other religions must strictly speaking be granted the exact same benefits and support must be extended to all and not just to the more traditional or larger religions.[137]

5.6 Concluding Remarks

In modern times, many states have cut the official ties with the traditional religion practised by the majority of inhabitants. Thus, states officially declared that they no longer wish to be in competition with forms of 'sacred authority', or to be bound by religious principles. In establishing itself as a non-denominational state, the state denies any form of positive identification with religion. Accordingly, it will not have an official preference for any particular religion; it also does not wish to justify the exercise of its power by reference to (a) religion. In a significant number of states this act of disconnecting itself from the state religion was accompanied by or was complimented by a proactive policy of *keeping* state and religion, profane spheres and sacred spheres, separated from each other henceforward. This legal-political endeavour that is aimed at internalizing and consistently preserving a regime in which the state apparatus and religious institutions do not interfere with each other's activities has, arguably, been realized by a number of states, albeit in very differing degrees. In most instances, secularism or separationism seem to be adopted as legal-political maxims for instrumental reasons. The underlying rationale seems to be that both the state and religion will be better off when they act independently from each other, in their own (semi-)autonomous spheres. It is true, though, that some states take a particular interest in ensuring that government shall be free from religious intrusion, whilst there are also examples in which we can see a particular emphasis on religious autonomy. Clear-cut ideological secularism or ideological separationism is the exception rather than the rule. Secularism and separationism, as manifested by the forms of state practice discussed in this Chapter, should not be interpreted as official steps towards the eradication of religion or as preferences on the part of the state for atheism. In none of the examples thus far is religion separated from the state so as to force inhabitants to become atheists or so as to eradicate religion from life altogether. Religion is separated from the state, or the state is declared non-religious, not because the state takes a negative view of religion per se, but because the state takes a negative view of a situation in which religion is entangled with the state. Religion's entanglement with the state is seen

Lutherans (1995); Agreements between Poland and other religions are possible pursuant artt. 16-16a of 1989 Polish Law (*supra* note 11).

[137] See Chapter 4, section 4.2.4, *supra*.

as unhealthy; which is not saying that religion per se is unhealthy. In short, looking at contemporary state practice, state secularism and state separationism have, as a rule, no explicit anti-religious agenda. It could in fact be argued that express hostility towards religion on the part of the state would, strictly speaking, be at odds with the very principles of secularism and separationism: hostile separation defeats its own purpose. Two important caveats are in order: none of this means that some manifestations of state secularism or separationism may not in actual practice lead to unacceptable limitations on religious freedoms (see Part II of this study); secondly, a limited number of contemporary forms of state practice and a number of notorious historical examples show that separation may take 'hostile' forms. The antagonistic attitude of the state vis-à-vis religion may be such that one may indeed wonder whether we are in fact dealing with 'separation' or rather with 'state control' and/or 'state atheism'. Such negative forms of state–religion identification will be discussed in the next Chapter.

CHAPTER SIX

SECULAR STATE IDEOLOGIES & NEGATIVE IDENTIFICATION

6.1 Introduction

Some states officially identify with secular ideologies.[1] Ninian Smart has dealt extensively with the interesting question of the extent to which we should consider the nature of secular world-views 'religious'.[2] He argues that religions have seven different dimensions: the practical or ritual dimension, the experiential or emotional dimension, the narrative or mythic dimension, the doctrinal or philosophical dimension, the ethical or legal dimension, the social or institutional dimension, and the material dimension.[3] Applying this model to some secular ideologies he ultimately concludes:

> Though to a greater or lesser extent our seven-dimensional model may apply to secular worldviews, it is not really appropriate to try to call them religions, or even "quasi-religions" (which by implication demotes them below the status of "real" religions). For the adherents of Marxism and humanism wish to be demarcated strictly from those who espouse religions – they conceive themselves, on the whole, as antireligious. However, we have seen enough of the seven-dimensional character of the secular worldviews (especially nationalism and state Marxism) to emphasize that the various systems of ideas and practices, whether religious or not, are competitors and mutual blenders, and can thus be said to play in the same league. They all help to express the various ways in which human beings conceive of themselves, and act in the world.[4]

Thus, secular worldviews are not profoundly of a religious (or metaphysical) nature and yet as a rule they are, for the most part, composed of meta-religious ideas: that is, critical ideas *about* religion, religious doctrine and religious practices.

---

[1] Terminology (the distinction between forms of "positive identification" and "negative identification") is cf. W. Cole Durham, *Perspectives on Religious Liberty: A Comparative Framework, in* Religious Human Rights in Global Perspective: Legal Perspectives 1 (J.D. van der Vyver & J. Witte, eds., The Hague/Boston/London: Martinus Nijhoff Publishers, 1996), see particularly pp. 15–36; and George R. Ryskamp, *The Spanish Experience in Church-State Relations: A Comparative Study of the Interrelationship between Church-State Identification and Religious Liberty*, 3 Brigham Young University Law Review 616 (1980), discussing forms of Church-State identification (p. 617).

[2] Ninian Smart, The World's Religions (Victoria: Cambridge University Press, 1992), pp. 21–28.

[3] *Ibid*, pp. 10–21.

[4] *Ibid*, p. 25.

From this it follows that secular worldviews should not be confused with the legal-political notion of secularism as discussed in the previous Chapter. Although the historical underlying incentives that accompanied the establishment of a secular state may have been characterized by criticism of certain religious doctrines or practices, presently a state of secularity in itself does not necessarily reflect value judgements about religion. In other words, state secularism does not come down to an official rejection of religion. State secularism denotes an intention on the part of the state to not affiliate itself with religion, to not consider itself *a priori* bound by religious principles (unless they are reformulated into secular state laws) and to not seek to justify its actions by invoking religion. Such a state of secularity denotes official impartiality in matters of religion rather than official irreligiosity. By contrast, secularism as a philosophical notion can indeed be construed as an ideological defence of the secular cause, which might include criticism of or scepticism towards religion. Thus, states that are 'ideologically secular' and that declare secular worldviews the official state doctrine give evidence, explicitly or by implication, of judgements about the value of religion within society. Most versions of state communism, for instance, embrace Marxist criticism of religion. These states must still be distinguished, as will be done in what follows, from an outright negative identification of the state with religion as could be perceived in, for instance, atheist Albania after the Albanian Cultural Revolution of the 1960s and as can to some extent still be perceived in the Democratic People's Republic of Korea, under the rule of the so-called *Juche* doctrine.

6.2 Secular State Ideologies

Before the end of the Cold War, many Communist States did not shy away from being openly hostile to religion. In most instances, communist ideology translated unperturbedly into state atheism, which, in turn, triggered measures aimed at the eradication of religion. As much was acknowledged by some Communist Constitutions. The 1976 Constitution of the People's Socialist Republic of Albania, for instance, was firmly based on a Marxist dismissal of religion as the opiate of the masses. It provided: "The state recognizes no religion of any kind and supports and develops the atheist view so as to ingrain in to the people the scientific and materialistic world-view."[5]

---

[5] Art. 37 of the Constitution of the People's Socialist Republic of Albania (1976; replaced); see Winfried Brugger, *On the Relationship between Structural Norms and Constitutional Rights in Church-State-Relations, in* Religion in the Public Sphere: A Comparative Analysis of German, Israeli, American and International Law (Brugger & Karayanni, eds., Berlin: Springer, 2007), p. 31. See Evis Karandrea, *Church and State in Albania, in* Law and Religion in Post-Communist Europe (Ferrari & Durham, eds., Leuven: Peeters, 2003), pp. 26–27, for a historical account of militant atheism in Albania.

Militant state atheism is, at least *de jure*, largely a thing of the past. Those 'socialist states' that have retained their socialist status after the collapse of the communist block mostly have removed direct references to state atheism from their constitutions and policies. However, it goes without saying that an official identification of the state with Marxism–Leninism still reflects a critical stance on religion. From the discussion of Chinese, Cuban and Vietnamese state practice it will follow that this official stance on religion generally translates into a strong degree of state control over religion.[6]

China is a "socialist state" with Marxism-Leninism as its official ideology.[7] The basic task of the nation, according to the Constitution of the People's Republic of China, is:

> …to concentrate its efforts on socialist modernization along the road of Chinese-style socialism. Under the guidance of Marxism-Leninism, Mao Zedong Thought, Deng Xiaoping Theory and the important thought of 'Three Represents', the Chinese people of all nationalities will continue to adhere to the people's democratic dictatorship…[8]

Although the Constitution does not explicitly position China as an atheistic state, China's *de facto* or governmental atheistic status flows from China's political organization. The Constitution safeguards the position of the Communist Party of China as the ruling political party and Communist Party members have to adhere to the Party's code of atheism.[9] The official governmental position is that religion will ultimately die out. Until such time, however, religions are to be tightly controlled: "Religion will eventually disappear from human history. But it will disappear naturally only through the long-term development of Socialism and Communism, when all objective requirements are met".[10] Though Communist Party members are expected to be atheists, the state or any of its organs are not allowed to actively compel citizens to become atheists.[11] China constitutionally protects "normal" religious activities.[12] The Government has recognized Buddhism, Catholicism, Islam, Protestantism and Taoism as religions. The Religious Affairs Bureau (RAB) strictly monitors these religions. The actions of the sanctioned religions are

---

[6] It has been argued before that Belarus' treatment of religious organizations could be considered a form of state supervision of religion (see Chapter 5, *supra*, text around note 113).

[7] Preamble and art. 1 of the CONSTITUTION OF THE PEOPLE'S REPUBLIC OF CHINA (1982).

[8] Preamble of the CONST. OF CHINA (1982).

[9] Notice on Further Strengthening Marxist Atheism Research, Propaganda and Education of 27 May 2004; see Eric R. Carlson, *China's New Regulations on Religion: A Small Step, Not a Great Leap, Forward*, 3 BRIGHAM YOUNG UNIVERSITY LAW REVIEW (2005), pp. 749–750.

[10] Document 19: The Basic Viewpoint and Policy on the Religious Question during our Country's Socialist Period, March 1982, sec. 1.

[11] Art. 36, para. (2), of the CONST. OF CHINA (1982).

[12] Art. 36, para. (3), of the CONST. OF CHINA (1982).

governed by the 2005 Regulations on Religious Affairs.[13] These Regulations show that religions in China are by no means granted autonomy. They state that "[t]he religious affairs department of People's Governments at the county level or higher shall, according to law, exercise administrative control over religious affairs that involve state interests...".[14] Though the 2005 Regulations are in some respects less stringent than earlier laws and regulations on religion,[15] it can be concluded that:

> The stated purposes and intent of the regulations as evidenced by the registration requirements for religious bodies and sites, the supervision of religious personnel and practice, and the discrimination against religious groups indicate that the new regulations intend to continue strong state control over religion.[16]

Vietnam, similarly, is a Communist Party-led state guided by Marxism-Leninism. The Constitution provides:

> The Communist Party of Vietnam, the vanguard of the Vietnamese working class, the faithful representative of the rights and interests of the working class, the toiling people, and the whole nation, acting upon the Marxist-Leninist doctrine and Ho Chi Minh's thought, is the force leading the State and society.[17]

State control over religion in Vietnam is chiefly realized through the 2004 Ordinance on Religious Belief,[18] an Act which regulates in detail all religious activity in Vietnam. State supervision of religion is explicitly sanctioned by the Constitution.[19]

Marxism-Leninism has played, since the Cuban Revolution and the overthrow of the Batista regime (1959), an important role within the political organization of Cuba. A (replaced) provision in the 1976 Constitution stated that the "socialist state...bases its activity on, and educates the people in, the scientific materialist concept of the universe" (i.e. atheism).[20] Also the following post-revolutionary principles leave little doubt as to what the new regime intended to do with religious belief:

> The Party considers the main task for the communist education of our people and the internal and external ideological confrontation to be:

---

[13] Religious Affairs Regulations of 30 November 2004; entry into effect: 1 March 2005 (hereinafter also: 1994 Chinese Religious Affairs Regulations).

[14] Art. 5 of the 1994 Chinese Religious Affairs Regulations.

[15] *E.g.* Regulations Governing Places of Religious Activity of 31 March 1994 (replaced).

[16] Carlson, *supra* note 9, p. 766.

[17] Art. 4 of the Constitution of the Socialist Republic of Vietnam (1992). See also the preamble on the role of Marxism-Leninism in Vietnam.

[18] Ordinance of the Standing Committee of the National Assembly regarding Religious Belief and Religious Organisations, No. 21/2004/PL-UBTVQH11, of 18 June 2004 (entry into effect: 15 November 2004). See also Governmental Decree 22/2005/ND-CP of 1 March 2005, further outlining the implementation of the Ordinance.

[19] Art. 112, para (9), of the Const. of Vietnam (1992).

[20] Art. 54 (replaced/amended); see current art. 55 of the Const. of Cuba (1976).

> -the widest propagation of Marxism-Leninism and of the works of Marx, Engels and Lenin…
> -the defence of the purity of Marxism-Leninism…
> -the gradual overcoming of religious beliefs by materialistic scientific propaganda and the cultural advancement of the workers.[21]

The 1992 constitutional amendments, however, abandoned the state's official atheistic policy. The Communist Party of Cuba, the only allowed political party, is constitutionally considered:

> …a follower of Martí's ideas and of Marxism-Leninism, and the organized vanguard of the Cuban nation, [it] is the highest leading force of society and of the state, which organizes and guides the common effort toward the goals of the construction of socialism and the progress toward a communist society.[22]

In contrast to China, the Cuban Communist Party presently accepts the membership of religious persons. The activities of religions are overseen by a special Office of Religious Affairs (of the Cuban Communist Party).

6.3 Negative Identification

The regime of the Democratic People's Republic of Korea (DPRK or North Korea) has, on the basis of radical interpretations of secular ideologies, attempted (at intervals) to eradicate religion. Presently, the *Juche* doctrine and the cults of personality of Kim Il-sung (1912–1994) and his son Kim Jung-il compose the official ideology of the DPRK.[23] The Constitution of DPRK elaborates extensively on these principles:

> The Democratic People's Republic of Korea is a socialist fatherland of Juche which embodies the idea of and guidance by the great leader Comrade Kim Il Sung. The great leader Comrade Kim Il Sung is the founder of the DPRK and the socialist Korea. Comrade Kim Il Sung founded the immortal Juche idea… Comrade Kim Il Sung put forward an independent revolutionary line, wisely guided the social revolution and construction at various levels, strengthened and developed the Republic into a people-centered socialist country and a socialist state of independence, self-sustenance, and self-defense…The great leader Comrade Kim Il Sung is the sun of the nation and the lodestar of the reunification of the fatherland. …Comrade Kim Il Sung was a genius ideological theoretician and a genius art leader, an ever-victorious, iron-willed brilliant commander,

---

[21] Department of Revolutionary Orientation, *Programmatic Platform of the Communist Party of Cuba* (1976), section "Tasks of the Ideological Struggle", pp. 111-114; see Margaret I. Short, Law and Religion in Marxist Cuba: A Human Rights Inquiry (New Brunswick: Transaction Publishers, 1993), p. 19.

[22] Art. 4 of the Const. of Cuba (1976).

[23] It is also, officially, a socialist/communist state; see art. 1 (and the preamble) of the Constitution of the Democratic People's Republic of Korea (1972; hereinafter: Const. of DPRK of 1972). Artt. 29 and 40 refer to both "Socialism" and "Communism".

> a great revolutionary and politician, and a great human being. Comrade Kim Il Sung's great idea and achievements in leadership are the eternal treasures of the nation and a fundamental guarantee for the prosperity and efflorescence of the DPRK. The DPRK and the entire Korean people will uphold the great leader Comrade Kim Il Sung as the eternal President of the Republic, defend and carry forward his ideas and exploits and complete the Juche revolution under the leadership of the Workers' Party of Korea. The DPRK Socialist Constitution is a Kim Il Sung constitution which legally embodies Comrade Kim Il Sung's Juche state construction ideology and achievements.[24]

The guiding principle of *Juche* (self-reliance) "calls on the people to be masters of their destiny, while accepting central leadership, and to avoid spiritual deference to outside influences."[25] The Constitution calls for the elimination of "the way of life inherited from the outmoded society" and aims at establishing "a new socialist way of life in every sphere."[26] Up until 1992, the *Juche* principles were construed so as to mean that all religious activity be prohibited.[27] The Workers' Party of Korea, led by Kim Jung-il and the *Juche* ideology, seeks to guide all aspects of life. There have been reported campaigns of state-instigated indoctrination.[28] Reflecting on its closed and isolationist position, Macdonald observed:

> How much religion exists in private is as yet unknown; it must struggle against the officially promoted Marxist-Leninist and *juche* philosophies, which in north Korea are supposed to respond to all people's spiritual as well as physical and social problems.[29]

Juche is not just a variant of Marxism-Leninism, but can be considered an ideology in its own right, unique to the DPRK.[30] According to French, besides creative applications of Marxism-Leninism, *Juche* consists primarily of: Confucianism, Maoism and a "hyper-traditionalist reading of traditional Korean culture".[31] This begs the question (that was already briefly touched upon in the introduction to this chapter): to what extent can North Korea be

---

[24] Preamble of the Const. of DPRK (1972).

[25] J.E. Hoare & Susan Pares, North Korea in the 21st Century. An Interpretative Guide (Kent: Global Oriental, 2005), p. 6.

[26] Art. 42 of the Const. of DPRK (1972).

[27] The 1992 Amendments to the Constitution of the Democratic People's Republic of Korea removed these measures and introduced (*de jure*, that is) a limited degree of religious freedom (art. 68).

[28] *E.g.* J.E. Hoare & Susan Pares, *supra* note 25, particularly pp. 6–9; Paul Marshall (ed.), Religious Freedom in the World (Nashville: Broadman & Holman, 2000), p. 189.

[29] Donald Stone Macdonald (revised and edited by D.N. Clark), The Koreans: Contemporary Politics and Society (Oxford: Westview Press, 1996), pp. 98–99.

[30] Cf. Paul French, North Korea: The Paranoid Peninsula. A Modern History (London: Zed Books, 2005), p. 30; and Dae-Sook Suh, Kim Il Sung: The North Korean Leader (New York: Columbia University Press, 1988), p. 302.

[31] Cf. French, *ibid.*, pp. 32–42.

said to have a state religion? Cho Tae-hoon does not hesitate to answer in the affirmative:

> …Juche Ideology…has been a political tool to justify the so-called "monolithic leadership of Kim Il-sung." Juche Ideology has contributed greatly to the beautification of all instructions given by Kim Il-sung. It has taught the people to be faithful to Kim Il-sungs [sic] instructions like Christians or Buddhists are to the Bible or the Sutra. Juche Ideology has reigned over the North Korean people as a religious doctrine already since the late 1950s, but noteworthy is that those who have failed to abide by the ideology, or religion, have faced severe punishment… It has played the role of indoctrinating the people with the belief that the working masses are the masters of revolution, while all others are targets to be expelled in the course of carrying out the revolution…[I]n North Korea the principle of the class struggle has been designed to indoctrinate the people to harbor a spirit of blind obedience to the Great Leader, and Juche Ideology has developed into a religion designed to worship Kim Il-sung and Kim Jong-il as virtual demigods.[32]

The present situation perhaps does not compare to the initial wave of state-instigated repression of all religious belief that was launched after the Korean War (1950–1953). Be that as it may, in spite of the announcement of Kim Il-sung's "benevolent politics",[33] the level of state control over religious activity in DPRK remains exceptionally high.

6.4 Concluding Remarks

It will be clear that in this Chapter we have entered a part of the state–religion identification spectrum that is 'beyond' secularism. In particular as far as the latter state is concerned (DPRK), no intention on the part of the state to not affiliate itself with a belief can be discerned, albeit that the belief in question (*Juche*) is largely of a non-religious nature and, at the same time, of an anti-religious nature, namely, as far as all competing claims about the truth are concerned. This phenomenon has urged some scholars to portray the state–religion identification spectrum as a continuum, ranging from totalitarian forms of positive religion–state identification to totalitarian forms of state identification with non or anti-religious ideologies.[34] Now that the state–religion identification spectrum is sketched, it will be possible to make a human rights-based assessment of those different state–religion regimes and of the different forms of state practice that characterize those state–religion models.

---

[32] Cho Tae-hoon, *Juche Ideology*, 12 East Asian Review (1997), paras. 1–2.

[33] The 1992 constitutional revisions erased, among other things, the state's "freedom of antireligious activity". See for an elaboration on his concept of "benevolent politics": Kim Jong-il, *Socialism is Science*, Juche 83 (1994).

[34] See Durham, *supra* note 1, particularly pp. 15–36 for a description of the continuum.

Part II

State–Religion Identification: A Human Rights Analysis

CHAPTER SEVEN

PRELIMINARY LEGAL QUESTIONS CONCERNING ESTABLISHMENT OF RELIGION AND STATE ATHEISM

7.1 Introduction

The objective of the second part of this study is to provide a comprehensive human rights-based assessment of the various laws, policies, measures and other forms of state practice that surround and characterize the different state–religion relationships. Chapters 8–11 are intended to present the data generated by different thematic case studies which are focused on, among other issues, Religious Laws and the State, Religion & Politics, Religion & Education, Religion & Employment, Religion & Civil Association, Free Speech & Religion, and State Entanglement with Religion & the Equal Religious Rights of Others. However, before delving deeper into the various concrete human rights-related issues that emerge under the different relationships between the state and religion, the preliminary legal question as to whether there are forms of state–religion identification that are, *per se*, unacceptable must be addressed. In other words: is it possible to identify specific relationships between the state and religion that would amount to so-called '*ipso facto* violations' of international human rights law? In this Chapter it will be argued that a close assessment of human rights law substantiates that, notwithstanding the fact that human rights law on the face of it appears fairly indifferent as to the issue of state–religion identification, legal principles can in fact be extrapolated that have a profound and direct bearing on state–religion relationships in terms of their (il)legitimacy. It will be clear that these observations aim at the more extreme ends of the spectrum of state–religion identification, namely clear-cut establishment of religion on the one hand (as discussed in Chapter 2) and clear-cut state atheism on the other (as discussed in Chapter 6).

7.2 Establishment of Religion under International Human Rights Law

The Introduction to this study pointed out that international human rights law does not contain any explicit condemnations (or endorsements, for that matter) of specific forms of state–religion identification. Thus, based on the principles of subsidiarity and state sovereignty, human rights law would appear to largely leave it up to the individual states to design a political system that is capable of adequate human rights protection. These considerations do not imply, however, that there are no human rights guidelines whatsoever on the issue of state–religion identification. Also, these preliminary observations do not, strictly speaking, mean that no principles could be deduced from human rights law reflecting a fundamental incompatibility with certain types of state–religion identification. Having said that, the fact that human rights law does not contain any *explicit* condemnations of specific forms of state–religion identification, in combination with the principles of subsidiarity and state sovereignty, does mean that human rights monitoring bodies may be reluctant to point out such structural shortcomings within the very system of political organization of a state.

The work of the UN Human Rights Committee, which oversees the domestic implementation of the *International Covenant on Civil and Political Rights*, is illustrative of these observations. The UN Human Rights Committee has argued as follows on the issue of establishment of religion:

> The fact that a religion is recognized as a state religion or that it is established as official or traditional or that its followers comprise the majority of the population, shall not result in any impairment of the enjoyment of any of the rights under the Covenant, including…[the right to freedom of thought, conscience, and religion and the rights of members of ethnic, religious and linguistic minorities], nor in any discrimination against adherents to other religions or non-believers. In particular, certain measures discriminating against the latter, such as measures restricting eligibility for government service to members of the predominant religion or giving economic privileges to them or imposing special restrictions on the practice of other faiths, are not in accordance with the prohibition of discrimination based on religion or belief and the guarantee of equal protection…[of the law without any discrimination].[1]

Although it is clear that the Human Rights Committee in this General Comment does not condemn establishment of religion per se, it certainly provides some legal benchmarks concerning forms of state practice that surround and characterize forms of establishment of religion (these guidelines form the basis of the human rights analysis in subsequent Chapters). The very fact that the Committee raises the point of establishment of religion reveals a concern on the part of the Committee Members about systems of establishment. It must be observed, moreover, that the Human Rights Committee has in fact dealt with state–religion relationships in a more direct fashion. Within the framework of the state reporting procedure under the ICCPR it has repeatedly pointed out the difficulty of reconciling the very existence of an established

---

[1] Human Rights Committee, General Comment 22, para. 9 (pertaining to art. 18 of the ICCPR).

religion with the state's human rights obligations.[2] Other UN treaty monitoring bodies have observed similar fundamental problems surrounding regimes of establishment.[3]

Nevertheless, a significant number of scholars argue that establishment of religion is not per se in conflict with human rights law.[4] The gist of their

---

[2] *E.g.* A/56/40 vol. I (2001) 49 at para. 77(25) (Venezuela): "The privileged status of the Roman Catholic Church...is of concern"; A/54/40 vol. I (1999) 44 at para. 220 (Chile): "The State party should amend the law so as to give equal status to all religious communities that exist in Chile"; A/46/40 (1996), para. 402 (UK); A/50/40 vol. I (1995) 42 at para. 212 (Paraguay); A/49/40 vol. I (1994) 31 at para. 158 (Costa Rica): "With respect to article 18 of the Covenant, the pre-eminent position accorded to the Roman Catholic Church is of concern"; CCPR/C/SR.1128 (1992), para. 38 (Algeria); A/46/40 (1991), para. 341 (Sweden); A/41/40 (1986), para. 69 (Luxembourg); A/41/40 (1986), para. 146 (Sweden); A/36/40 (1981), para. 366 (Norway); A/36/40 (1981), para. 82 (Denmark); CCPR/C/SR.327 (1981), para. 63 (Morocco); CCPR/C/SR.301 (1981) (Norway), para. 36 (the question was asked by Committee Members whether "the predominance of the Evangelical Lutheran Church might not be tantamount to discrimination against other religions"); CCPR/C/SR.236 (1980), para. 12 (Costa Rica: a Member reasoned that "Article 75 of the Constitution made the Catholic religion the State religion and *thus* seemed to confer a privilege on the Catholic Church...that was perhaps not strictly in conformity with the Covenant"; emphasis added); CCPR/C/SR.251 (1980), paras. 17, 20 and 57 (Denmark); CCPR/C/SR.222 (1980) (Colombia), para. 7; and CCPR/C/SR.170 (1979), para. 6 (Finland).

[3] *E.g.* Committee on Economic, Social and Cultural Rights, *e.g.*: E/1999/22 (1998) 43 at para. 236 (Israel): "It is of concern that excessive emphasis upon the State as a "Jewish State" encourages discrimination and accords a second-class status to its non-Jewish citizens. It is noted with concern that the Government of Israel does not accord equal rights to its Arab citizens, although they comprise over 19 per cent of the total population"; Committee on the Elimination of Discrimination against Women, *e.g.*: A/53/38/Rev.1 part I (1998) 28 at para. 351 (Dominican Republic): "Steps should be taken to ensure the de facto separation of the secular and religious spheres, with a view to ensuring the full implementation of the Convention"; and Committee on the Elimination of Racial Discrimination, *e.g.*: A/57/18 (2002) 50 at para. 282 (Armenia): concerns were expressed about the privileged position of the Armenian Apostolic Church.

[4] One of the most recent and, arguably, the most comprehensive contemporary establishmentarian account is: REX AHDAR & IAN LEIGH, RELIGIOUS FREEDOM IN THE LIBERAL STATE (Oxford: Oxford University Press, 2005), particularly Ch. 5 ("Is Establishment Consistent with Religious Freedom"), in which chapter they argue that mild or weak forms of establishment are not at odds with freedom of religion or belief; furthermore specifically on this issue: Stephen C. Neff, *An Evolving International Legal Norm of Religious Freedom: Problems and Prospects*, 7 CALIFORNIA WESTERN INTERNATIONAL LAW JOURNAL 543 (1977), p. 571; Theodore S. Orlin, *Religious Pluralism and Freedom of Religion: Its Protection in Light of Church/State Relationships, in* THE STRENGTH OF DIVERSITY: HUMAN RIGHTS AND PLURALIST DEMOCRACY (A. Rosas and J. Helgesen, eds., Dordrecht: Martinus Nijhoff Publishers, 1992), pp. 92–93. More generally, *e.g.*: MANFRED NOWAK, U.N. COVENANT ON CIVIL AND POLITICAL RIGHTS: CCPR COMMENTARY (Kehl am Rhein: N.P. Engel Publ., 2005, 2nd rev. ed.), p. 415; MALCOLM D. EVANS, RELIGIOUS LIBERTY AND INTERNATIONAL LAW IN EUROPE (Cambridge: Cambridge University Press, 1997); or, with respect to the European context particularly: CAROLYN EVANS, FREEDOM OF RELIGION UNDER THE EUROPEAN CONVENTION ON HUMAN RIGHTS (Oxford: Oxford University Press, 2001), pp. 19–22 (see also p. 50 and pp. 80–87), commenting (seemingly, though not explicitly, approvingly) on the non-disestablishmentarian approach taken by the European Court of Human Rights. See also the early UN religious freedom reports/guidelines, *e.g.*: Philip Halpern, *Study on Discrimination in the Matter of Religious Rights and Practices* (E/CN.4/Sub.2/162, 1954); Arcot Krishnaswami, *Study of Discrimination in the Matter of Religious Rights and Practices* (U.N. Doc. E/CN.4/Sub.2/200/Rev.1, 1960), Ch. 5; Francesco Capotorti, *Study on the Rights of Persons Belonging to Ethnic, Religious and Linguistic Minorities* (U.N. Doc. E/CN.4/Sub.2/384/Rev.1, 1979), para. 389 (none of these report condemn establishment per se).

arguments is twofold: (i) the drafters of the relevant human rights treaties never intended to outlaw forms of establishment of religion (sometimes in combination with the observation that human rights conventions do in fact not explicitly object to establishment); and (ii) establishment of religion does not per se prejudice the religious rights of people who do not adhere to the state religion. It is also claimed, or implied, that there is in fact a consensus in the legal doctrine to that effect.[5]

First of all, whether or not the original drafters of international human rights treaties intended to outlaw forms of establishment of religion, and whether or not an express non-establishment clause can presently be found in international human rights conventions, is only of limited legal relevance. If both questions would be answered in the negative, it still may not be assumed that human rights monitoring bodies will not be able or will not be allowed to extrapolate principles from human rights law on the basis of which different relations between the state and religion may be scrutinized.[6] The most important consideration in that regard is the fact that human rights law is a constantly evolving body of law: human rights treaties are commonly considered 'living instruments'.[7] In fact, such is precisely what human rights monitoring

---

[5] *E.g.*, explicitly, Nowak, *ibid.*, p. 415: "a system of *State religion* or a *State church* does not conflict with passive freedom of religion as long as the state permits other religions alongside the official one and does not exercise direct or indirect coercion to join the latter. This is made clear by the *travaux préparatoires* and is basically recognized in the literature as well".

[6] The interpretative value of the recorded drafting history is fairly minimal according to the 1969 Vienna Convention on the Law of Treaties: see artt. 31 and 32. The *travaux* are listed as a last resort, i.e. they may only be referred to in case all other techniques of interpretation have failed to bring about anything conclusive. First in the hierarchy of treaty interpretation is the "ordinary meaning" that must be given to the terms of the treaty in their context and in the light of the object and purpose of the treaty in question (art. 31).

[7] For a practical account on the 'living instrument approach/doctrine', see PHILIP PLOWDEN & KEVIN KERRIGAN, ADVOCACY AND HUMAN RIGHTS: USING THE CONVENTION IN COURTS AND TRIBUNALS (London: Cavendish Publ., 2004), particularly pp. 26–27. Particularly the European Court of Human Rights has consistently argued in its case law that the European Convention on Human Rights must be seen as "a living instrument" which "must be interpreted in the light of present-day conditions" (*e.g.* ECtHR, *Soering v. the United Kingdom*, Application No. 14038/88, Judgement of 7 July 1989, para. 102; ECtHR, *Leyla Şahin v. Turkey*, Application No. 44774/98, Judgement of 10 November 2005, para. 136; ECtHR, *Loizidou v. Turkey* (Preliminary Objections), Application No. 15318/89, Judgement of 23 March 1995, para. 71). For an analysis of the dynamic treaty interpretation doctrine at the European level, see, *e.g.*, Rudolf Bernhardt, *Evolutive Treaty Interpretation, Especially of the European Convention on Human Rights*, 42 GERMAN YEARBOOK OF INTERNATIONAL LAW (1999), pp. 11-25. The Human Rights Committee, too, has considered "that the [ICCPR] should be interpreted as a living instrument and the rights protected under it should be applied in context and in the light of present–day conditions" (Human Rights Committee, *Roger Judge v. Canada*, Communication No. 829/1998, U.N. Doc. CCPR/C/78/D/829/1998 (2003), Views of 5 August 2002). The observation about human rights conventions as evolving, living instruments, consequently, is often extended to the international human rights discourse; *e.g.*: Tom Campbell, Jeffrey Goldsworthy & Adrienne Stone (eds.), PROTECTING HUMAN RIGHTS: INSTRUMENTS AND INSTITUTIONS (Oxford: Oxford University Press, 2003), p. 139; and Michael P. Van Alstine, *Dynamic Treaty Interpretation*, 146 UNIVERSITY OF PENNSYLVANIA LAW REVIEW (1998), pp. 687–793.

bodies constantly do: interpreting fairly abstract legal notions and applying them to concrete cases. True, there is no explicit non-establishment clause to be found in international human rights conventions. Does this mean that the ordinary meaning that must be given to the terms of international human rights treaties is that establishment is allowed? In other words, should we conclude that whenever there is no (utterly) concrete point of departure in a human rights treaty to be found regarding a certain subject matter, that the legislative act in question is automatically permissible? That would clearly be an absurd conclusion.[8] Fortunately, this is also not what we see in practice. Half a century ago, nobody could have conjectured the way in which abstract notions of human rights law are currently applied to numerous and diverse concrete situations (think of the equal rights of postoperative transsexuals; think of the important positive state obligations that have been formulated in the field of physical integrity; think of the right to life and the due diligence obligations that have come to the fore in that context, or the gradual expansion of private and family life and the numerous positive obligations states must, according to present legal doctrine, fulfil in that regard, etc).

Nowhere in human rights covenants is there an express provision prohibiting the state from establishing itself as a White State, though everyone—or at least many—would agree that the ordinary meaning that must be given to the non-discrimination principle would stand in the way of doing precisely that. In other words, the traditional state sovereignty argument (states are and should be utterly free as far as shaping their internal framework of political organization is concerned) is no longer sacred in the era of human rights law.

Which precise legislative acts are prohibited, and which are not, is not (always) neatly listed in international human rights treaties. It is often only when we scrutinize certain acts in the light of the ordinary meaning of specific treaty provisions that we may decide on questions of legitimacy. Following this train of thought, establishment of religion, although one will not find anything explicitly written on this notion in human rights conventions, may be assessed on the basis of concrete, relevant human rights provisions. Such a concrete examination may establish whether a certain legislative act is acceptable or not. This is precisely what will be done in what follows (see section 7.2.3). Particularly an assessment of establishment of religion on the basis of the autonomous 'equality before the law' principle shows most conclusively that legal establishment of religion is very problematic indeed from the perspective of human rights law.

First, however, two further misconceptions will be addressed. The point has already been made that the intentions of the original drafters of human rights

---

[8] There is also no explicit provision to be found that explicitly tolerates forms of establishment; such a fact *in itself*, similarly, does not mean that establishment would automatically not be allowed under international law.

treaties are only of limited legal relevance.[9] Notwithstanding, it may still be interesting to chart what those intentions actually were: it will be outlined that these intentions were far more ambiguous than commonly assumed and that we cannot speak of a clear-cut consensus (section 7.2.1). Secondly, it will be contended that there is in fact no (longer) a clear-cut consensus in the literature as to whether establishment of religion in itself does or does not prejudice the religious rights of people who do not adhere to the state religion. An increasing body of literature, including some of the leading academic authorities on the issue of religious freedom, can be discerned that raise fundamental concerns regarding establishment based on the right to freedom of religion or belief (section 7.2.2). As announced, a legal assessment of establishment of religion on the basis of the equality principle will follow subsequently (section 7.2.3).

7.2.1 *Travaux Préparatoires on Establishment of Religion*

The *travaux préparatoires* (recorded drafting history) are much more ambiguous on the issue of religion–state identification than commonly assumed. It must be observed that, contrary to what is sometimes assumed,[10] the *travaux* do in fact not unequivocally support the view that the issue of state–religion identification should be considered immaterial in the light of the (then yet to be adopted) provisions on freedom of religion or belief. The different positions will be identified in what follows in this section.

The 'anything goes' position does indeed occasionally show up in the *travaux*. The Argentine representative to the Third Committee, for instance, argued that:

> Article 18 laid down the general principle of freedom of religion, but its application must vary with the customs of the different countries and was therefore a matter for domestic legislation. As long as the principle of freedom of religion was respected, it was immaterial whether, in a given country, there was or was not a separation between Church and State.[11]

It is not hard to see that this statement is very much in the interest of the state on whose behalf it is made.[12] Also Bolivia was eager to point out that it could not find fault with its own endorsement of Roman Catholicism as the official

[9] Cf. Jan Klabbers, *International Legal Histories: The Declining Importance of Travaux Préparatoires in Treaty Interpretation?*, 50(3) NETHERLANDS INTERNATIONAL LAW REVIEW (2003), pp. 267-288.

[10] See footnote 5, *supra*.

[11] Third Committee, 1025th Meeting (1960), A/C.3/SR.1025, para. 28.

[12] The Government of Argentina has traditionally strongly supported the Roman Catholic Apostolic religion; see art. 4 of the CONST. OF ARGENTINA (1853). See also section 3.2.3, *supra*, on state support in Argentina. There is even a hint of personal interests as the records subsequently state that, still according to the Argentine representative, it is "unfortunately a fact that there had been a great decline in belief in the modern world and that great numbers of people belonged to no religious group. Many social evils had their origin in the fact that men had lost

religion of the state.[13] Also other states that defended the position that official establishment of religion is not in itself contrary to the right to freedom of religion or belief exhibit positive forms of state–religion identification.[14]

There were states that claimed the exact opposite: compliance with the norm of freedom of religion or belief can only be fully guaranteed in a genuinely secular state. Not surprisingly, this position was predominantly defended by states with a history of secularism and strict separationism, including the then Communist states. The USSR, for instance, emphasized that it:

> …ensured freedom of conscience and of thought for all its citizens *by* separating the Church from the State, secularizing education and authorizing all form of worship as well as antireligious propaganda.[15]

Clearly, separationism is presented here as a prerequisite to compliance with freedom of religion or belief. At some point in the drafting debates the principles of secularism and separationism were even proposed to be included into the provisions on religious freedom.[16] It must be noted that some states were rather sympathetic towards this view.[17] Furthermore, in the discussions on the draft-article on freedom of religion or belief, religious states themselves occasionally expressed concerns about the formulations of the religious freedom principle that were on the table. This, by implication, shows that some states were all too aware of the fact that there could be a direct correlation between a codified norm of freedom of religion and the (un)tenability of their constitutional relations with religion. For instance, a contribution of a Saudi Arabian representative to a Third Committee meeting in which the 'right to change one's religion or belief' was discussed, is recorded as follows:

> Another interesting point was raised by the fact that under the constitutions of certain countries the Head of State had to be a follower of a certain religion.

---

all religious and ethical standards. However, the faith of those who still held to a belief had been strengthened and purified" (A/C.3/SR.1025, para. 28). The following paragraph (29) records the same representative referring to "man's right to revere his Maker".

[13] Third Committee, 1025th Meeting (1960), A/C.3/SR.1025, para. 37.

[14] *E.g.* E/CN.4/SR.712, pp. 10–11 (UK); also Ecuador manifested itself as sympathetic towards this view (E/CN.4/SR/825, p. 3) even though this state had actually already disestablished the Roman Catholic Church from the state; however, at the time of the recorded intervention (1965) the ties between church and state were not quite as loose as under the present 1998 Constitution.

[15] Commission on Human Rights, Fifth Session, 116th Meeting (1949), E/CN.4/SR.116, p. 14 (emphasis added); and again in: Commission on Human Rights, Eighth Session, 319th Meeting (1952), p. 8.

[16] E/CN.4/873/Annex II, p. 12 (USSR).

[17] *E.g.* E/3873, p. 77 (similar proposal to include a provision for separation by Ukrainian SSR); see also, *mutatis mutandis*: E/CN.4/SR116, pp. 9–11 (France); E/CN.4/SR.161, paras. 10 and 27 (USA); E/CN.4/SR.161, para. 26 (Yugoslavia; on the equality of all citizens before the law, regardless of one's religious affiliation); E/CN.4/SR.161, para. 40 (India; criticizing its own system of plural jurisdictions/religious laws).

> For such countries it would raise constitutional difficulties if the article stressed the right of everyone to change his religion. Difficulties might also arise in countries where the law stemmed from religion. He was thinking, for instance, of marriage and inheritance laws.[18]

Similarly, the Egyptian representative to a Commission on Human Rights meeting considered that the provision on freedom of religion:

> ...should be limited to the expression of the essential principle of freedom of thought and religion...If the Covenant went any further [i.e. by codifying the right to change one's religion], its ratification would encounter innumerable difficulties, owing to the large number and variety of religions, customs and laws. The Egyptian delegation would willingly support the text...on the condition however, that the words "to change his religion or belief" were deleted.[19]

Thus, the latter states, in the final analysis, actually did not—at the time—defend the view that any type of state–religion identification is reconcilable with the norm of freedom of religion or belief. The passages cited show an awareness or fear that if the freedom of religion provisions were to be codified in a certain fashion, this would have direct ramifications for their constitutional state–religion relationships. Also the final annotations on the whole drafting process of the Covenant, as prepared by the then Secretary-General of the UN, reveal this awareness:

> A provision in the covenant on the right to change one's religion...would create uncertainty and difficulty for those States whose constitutions or basic laws were religious in origin or in character.[20]

Unfortunately, this sense of "uncertainty and difficulty" on the part of some states resulted in dropping the right to change one's religion from the provisions on religious freedom (rather than in changing the challenged domestic principle).[21] However, considering the fact that the Human Rights Committee in the meantime has construed the right to freedom of religion or belief so as

---

[18] Third Committee, 1021st Meeting (1960), A/C.3/SR.1021, para. 11 (Mr. Baroody, Saudi Arabia).

[19] Commission on Human Rights, Fifth Session, 116th Meeting (1949), E/CN.4/SR116, p. 8; see also Commission on Human Rights, Sixth Session, 161st Meeting (1950), E/CN.4/SR.161, para. 28 (Egypt).

[20] UN Secretary-General, *Annotations on the Text of the Draft International Covenants on Human Rights*, A/2929 (1955), Ch. VI, para. 108.

[21] There were indeed states that argued that rather than using these types of difficulties as arguments to weaken the provisions on freedom of religion or belief, states should endeavour to bring their system in line with the to be adopted human rights norms; *e.g.* E/CN.4/SR.161, paras. 10 and 27 (USA); E/CN.4/SR116, pp. 9–11 (France); and E/CN.4/SR.161 (1950), para. 40 (India): India's representative "would rather witness the disappearance of the system of personal laws in her country than restrict a person's right to change his religion" (India has not abolished its system of sectarian personal status laws yet though).

to include a right to change one's religion,[22] we may conclude that the quoted "difficulty" remains alive: states that are "religious in origin or in character" may be fundamentally incompatible with norms of human rights law. In other words, the concerns that were highlighted (ironically, mostly by religious states themselves) half a century ago remain just as valid today.

It should be reiterated at this point, that the above discussion is only of limited legal relevance: even if one were to conclude (on the basis of a different—selective—reading of the *travaux*) that the drafters clearly did not intend to prohibit certain models of state–religion relationships, that in itself does not rule out the possibility of human rights monitoring bodies extrapolating principles from human rights law on the basis of which state–religion relationships may be assessed.

7.2.2 *Establishment, Religious Freedom and the Legal Doctrine*

Though a fair portion of the literature supports the view that the norm of freedom of religion or belief does not condemn establishment per se;[23] academic accounts arguing the opposite position can be increasingly discerned.[24] Perhaps it could be maintained that traditionally there was a clear-cut, or at least a strong, consensus holding that establishment of religion in itself does not prejudice the religious rights of people who do not adhere to the state religion—this position is undeniably being challenged at present.

Of course, critical discourse on forms of establishment of religion with a strong basis in political philosophy is nothing new. It must be observed that those philosophical movements, influenced by Enlightenment ideals, that criticized establishment of religion prior to the era of international human rights law made use of very similar tools or concepts (namely so-called 'natural rights', in many ways the predecessors of human rights). Hence, it does not come as a complete surprise that forms of positive identification of the state with religion would at some point come under attack from human rights advocates.

---

[22] Human Rights Committee, General Comment 22, para. 5: the right to 'have or adopt' a religion or belief "necessarily entails the freedom to choose a religion or belief, including the right to replace one's current religion or belief with another or to adopt atheistic views". The right to change one's religion, moreover, was already acknowledged by art. 18 of the Universal Declaration of Human Rights, G.A. res. 217A (III), U.N. Doc. A/810 at 71 (1948), of 10 December 1948 (hereinafter also: UDHR).

[23] See note 4, *supra*. The same is implied by certain recommendations adopted by some international organizations, notably the Council of Europe, *e.g.*: Parliamentary Assembly of the Council of Europe, *Recommendation 1804: "State, religion, secularity and human rights"* (2007), para. 5; and Parliamentary Assembly of the Council of Europe, *Recommendation 1396: "Religion and democracy"* (1999), para. 6.

[24] Ahdar & Leigh, *supra* note 4, p. 127, who themselves are of a very different view, even consider this position (establishment amounts *ipso facto* to a breach of religious liberty) to be the "prevailing view" presently.

W. Cole Durham's *Comparative Framework* was a pioneering work in so far as it substantiated the correlation between state–religion identification and religious freedom in a comprehensive manner.[25] In the present context, particularly his rejection of a form of "complete identification" (i.e. a complete coincidence of the state and religion) is relevant. Durham argues in this respect: "To the extent that extreme situation is reached or approached, there is clearly an absence of religious freedom."[26] After having assessed state practices that surround the different parts of the state–religion identification spectrum, Durham's concludes that:

> ...maximal religious liberty tends to be achieved when church-state identification is in the accommodation or non-hostile separation mode. Of course, substantial religious liberty can also exist in cooperationist or endorsed church regimes...However, there is always a sense in such regimes that smaller religious communities have a kind of second-class status, and to the extent that public funds are directly supporting programs of major churches, there is a sense that members of religious communities are being coerced to support religious programs with which they do not agree.[27]

De Jong, in the conclusion of his account on five decades of UN cooperation in the field of freedom of religion or belief, condemns forms of establishment of religion (partly) on the basis of the right to freedom of religion or belief. He contends that:

> ...a government may have such strong feelings itself on a religion or belief that it wishes to integrate it into the State system. However, throughout this [book] I have maintained that the freedom of thought, conscience and religion requires separation of State and Church. Even though the international community has never recognized this principle...What I object to... is a permanent link between the State as such and a particular religion or belief. The State should serve the interests of all of its citizens regardless of their religion or belief.[28]

Brugger elaborates on the difficulty of reconciling a strong identification of the state with a religion on the one hand, and the state's international human rights obligations on the other:

> ...human rights conventions, which protect all religious and philosophical beliefs, show that while such pacts do not have the authority to replace the internal constitutional order, they do have an effect on the structural relationship

---

[25] W. Cole Durham, *Perspectives on Religious Liberty: A Comparative Framework, in* Religious Human Rights in Global Perspective: Legal Perspectives 1 (J.D. van der Vyver & J. Witte, eds., The Hague/Boston/London: Martinus Nijhoff Publishers, 1996).

[26] *Ibid.*, p. 16.

[27] *Ibid.*, p. 24.

[28] Cornelis D. de Jong, The Freedom of Thought, Conscience and Religion or Belief in the United Nations (1946-1992) (Antwerp/Groningen/Oxford: Hart/Intersentia, 2000), pp. 739-740. It must be observed that De Jong primarily condemns establishment as a violation of the non-discrimination (see next sub-section).

> between the church and state...[T]hey rule out a complete identification of church and state... due to the fact that this model does not tolerate any form of non-religious being or disassociation from the preferred religion or church.[29]

He claims, moreover, that interferences with the freedom to have or adopt a religion or belief (the *forum internum*, that is, the 'inner belief' or passive aspect of freedom of religion or belief) cannot be ruled out:

> Structural non-neutrality, unequal treatment or identification with a particular religion often leads to illegitimate force and discrimination...When state authority is allied with a particular religion or church, external force leads to an internal pressure to manipulate one's conscience in fear of exclusion from the dominant social and political order. The same applies when the state places its authority and reputation in one church, and it is clear that the state primarily identifies itself with this institution.[30]

Thus, the very act of establishment of religion may have a proselytizing or even coercive effect that might not be compatible with the international norms on religious freedom as these norms include a provision that states: "No one shall be subject to coercion which would impair his freedom to have or to adopt a religion or belief of his choice."[31]

Another, principled account on the issue of maximizing freedom of religion and equality is the model presented by Shelton and Kiss.[32] Their 'model law on freedom of religion' draws on international guidelines and seeks to deal convincingly and critically with the major pitfalls that come to the fore when one looks at worldwide state practice. In their comments on the proposed law they explain:

> The Model Law proposes a system in which there is no official or established religion. Religious organisations and matters of religion are deregulated. Such a system promotes individual freedom of choice, basing religious affiliation on personal affinities rather than state-sanctioned inducements and coercion... Deregulation should also increase individual and local control over religion, with more power to the laity. The result may be a reinforcement of democratic principles, as religious organisations are forced to be responsive to the needs of the community they serve if they wish to maintain their resources.[33]

---

29 Winfried Brugger, *On the Relationship between Structural Norms and Constitutional Rights in Church-State-Relations, in* Religion in the Public Sphere: A Comparative Analysis of German, Israeli, American and International Law (Brugger & Karayanni, eds., Berlin: Springer, 2007), p. 49.

30 *Ibid.*, p. 52.

31 Art. 18, para. (2), of the ICCPR.

32 Dinah Shelton and Alexandre Kiss, *A Draft Model Law on Freedom of Religion, With Commentary, in* Religious Human Rights in Global Perspective: Legal Perspectives (J.D. van der Vyver & J. Witte, eds., The Hague/Boston/London: Martinus Nijhoff Publishers, 1996), pp. 578–584. See in particular article 1, par. d, and article 6 of their draft-law.

33 *Ibid.*, p. 581. Ultimately, Shelton and Kiss seem to argue in favour of state neutrality rather than strict separation between the state and religion: "the government may aid religious organisations. However, aid should be given to programs. It should be neutral, not based on who the recipient is, but on what the money is used for. Similarly, religious beliefs should be

This model law insists on the detachment of all links between states and official religions, which, by implication, is clearly a critique of more establishmentarian models. Again the message is: disestablishment is necessary for maximized freedom and equality.

These—and other[34]—accounts support the claim that the rights of people adhering to non-dominant and non-traditional religions and the rights of non-believers may in fact be *ipso facto* threatened by the existence and preservation of an official religion. Durham makes the important point that it should also be borne in mind that under regimes of strong identification of the state with religion "even the majority religion is likely to suffer because of extensive state involvement".[35]

7.2.3 *Establishment of Religion & Non-Discrimination*

It is a common mistake to assess forms of state–religion identification solely in light of the right to freedom of religion or belief (being the Covenant's only article expressly dealing with the issue of religious belief). Most establishmentarian accounts (defences of the establishment of religion) are in fact premised on this error.[36] The train of thought in those accounts is that establishment is not per se contrary to human rights law because establishment of religion does

---

accommodated when there is no meaningful threat to individual religious liberty... [However, state laws] should be less concerned with reinforcing the views of the dominant religion and more protective of those without the numbers and influence to ensure significant and effective protection through the political process for their religious liberty" (*ibid.*, p. 582).

[34] *E.g.* PIERRE LANARÈS, LA LIBERTÉ RELIGIEUSE DANS LES CONVENTIONS INTERNATIONALES ET DANS LE DROIT PUBLIC GÉNÉRAL (Roanne: Horvath, 1964), pp. 202–204; Myres S. McDougal, Harold D. Lasswell & Lung-chu Cheng, *The Right to Religious Freedom and World Public Order: The Emerging Norm of Non-Discrimination*, 74 MICHIGAN LAW REVIEW 865 (1976), p. 890; MYRES S. MCDOUGAL, HAROLD D. LASSWELL & LUNG-CHU CHEN, HUMAN RIGHTS AND WORLD PUBLIC ORDER: THE BASIC POLICIES OF AN INTERNATIONAL LAW OF HUMAN DIGNITY (New Haven: Yale University Press, 1980), pp. 655–656 and 680; Janos Toth, *Human Dignity and Freedom of Conscience*, WORLD JUSTICE 202 (1968), p. 216 (references De Jong); SEBASTIAN POULTER, ETHNICITY, LAW, AND HUMAN RIGHTS: THE ENGLISH EXPERIENCE (Oxford: Oxford University Press, 1998), p. 62; Peter Edge, *Religious Remnants in the Composition of the United Kingdom Parliament*, *in* LAW AND RELIGION: CURRENT LEGAL ISSUES (R. O'Dair & A. Lewis, eds., Oxford: Oxford University Press, 2001), pp. 454–455; Paul Weller, *Equity, Inclusivity and Participation in a Plural Society: Challenging the Establishment of the Church of England*, *in* LAW AND RELIGION IN CONTEMPORARY SOCIETY: COMMUNITIES, INDIVIDUALISM AND THE STATE (P. Edge & G. Harvey, eds., Aldershot: Ashgate, 2000), pp. 53-67 (references Ahdar & Leigh).

[35] Durham, *supra* note 25, p. 16.

[36] *E.g.* FRANCESCO RUFFINI, RELIGIOUS LIBERTY (transl. J. Parker Heyes; London: Williams & Norgate/New York: G.P. Putnam, 1912), p. 521: "true and complete religious liberty can exist also apart from Separation. When the State has assured full liberty of belief or disbelief to its own citizens, without this implying the least prejudice in the enjoyment of their rights as citizens; when the State has guaranteed to religious associations full liberty for the manifestation of their forms of worship, protecting them against any sort of attack, the State has done all that can be demanded of it in regard to religious liberty" (quoted by Ahdar & Leigh, *supra* note 4, p. 131). Be that as it may, the question remains whether the state has done all that can be demanded of it in regard to the principle of equality before the law. Ahdar & Leigh's account, *supra* note 4, is largely premised on this reasoning as well. In their Chapter 5, "Is Establishment Consistent with Religious Freedom",

not necessarily infringe upon the religious rights of those who do not adhere to the state religion. States with an established religion *and* an acceptable record in the field of religious rights would then substantiate this point. The error here involves the equation of the total set of human rights norms with the norm of religious freedom. An acceptable record of non-interference with the religious rights of minorities tells us little about potentially institutionalised or *de facto* practices of discrimination on the basis of religion. It is therefore postulated that the issue of establishment of religion should not be scrutinized solely in light of the right to freedom of religion or belief but also on the basis of other fundamental rights and norms. In that context, particularly an assessment of establishment of religion on the basis of the 'equality before the law' principle shows that the legal establishment of a religion is problematic if not indeed incompatible with human rights law. In Chapters 8–11 it will be outlined how forms of establishment of religion in practice translate into substantive infringements of the non-discrimination principle in many respects. Within the present context it is most relevant to point out that establishment of religion could be considered an *ipso facto* violation of the equality principle.

The non-discrimination principle or equality principle codified by the ICCPR reads:

> All persons are equal before the law and are entitled without any discrimination to the equal protection of the law. In this respect, the law shall prohibit any discrimination and guarantee to all persons equal and effective protection against discrimination on any ground such as…religion…or other status.[37]

Arguments against establishment of religion based on the equality principle have perhaps most persuasively been advanced by De Jong:

> A particularly sensitive issue is the existence of an established Church: it is often maintained that this does not affect a State's policies as such, for they can still be

they conclude that mild forms of establishment do not necessarily go at the expense of religious freedom: "The internal forum is untouched. Positive religious liberty remains similarly unimpaired. Regarding negative religious liberty, establishment *ipso facto*…does not produce any direct or indirect coercion or compulsion in religious matters" (p. 147). Whether internal and external religious freedoms are truly completely untouched by establishment may very much be doubted according to other authors, as we have seen above. But more importantly, perhaps, concluding that establishment does not affect religious liberties per se tells us little to nothing about the negative impact establishment may have on other fundamental rights. Admittedly, they do briefly address other possible objections, namely the fact that establishment may alienate dissimilar or non-believers, plus the argument that establishment may be at odds with the equality principle. They, however, rather uncritically dismiss these concerns. The gist of their arguments is that religious freedom and religious equality would be two different issues, and to insist on formal equality would be pedantic given the interest the majority of the population has in maintaining the traditional ties that exist between the state and the predominant religion. It will be clear that their account and the present account differ on the point as to how much weight much be given to equality or non-discrimination on grounds of religion or belief.

[37] Art. 26 of the ICCPR.

> entirely non-discriminatory. I disagree with this point of view: firstly, in practice it may be difficult for other religions or beliefs to obtain precisely the same rights as an established Church; secondly, *the very existence on an established Church has the effect of singling out one particular religion or belief as being official.* If one belongs to another religion or belief, there is *automatically* some distance between the believer and the State. This *in itself* can be regarded as discriminatory State behaviour...[38]

Other authors seem sympathetic to this view as well.[39]

Thus, it would appear that the answer to the question of whether this provision (article 26 of the ICCPR, the equality principle) forms a so-called accessory right or an independent substantive right is crucial to the debate. In other words, can article 26 of the ICCPR only be violated in conjunction with a substantive right enshrined in the Covenant or can we consider the equality principle to be an autonomous right? The drafting history,[40] literature and contemporary jurisprudence clearly indicate the latter. Though the non-discrimination principle codified by article 2 of the Covenant always has to be read in conjunction with the individual human rights outlined by the Covenant (and can thus indeed never be violated in itself),[41] article 26 of the Covenant is undoubtedly, in the words of Nowak, an "independent and autonomous

---

[38] De Jong, *supra* note 28, p. 740 (emphasis added).

[39] *E.g.* Kevin Boyle, *Indivisibility of Human Rights, Social Justice and Article 18 of the Universal Declaration, in* Innovation and Inspiration: Fifty Years of the Universal Declaration of Human Rights (Baehr, Flinterman, Senders, eds., Amsterdam: Royal Academy of Arts and Sciences, 1999), p. 146: "The proposition that religion...should be autonomous from the state can...be said to flow from the requirements of a democratic society which respects human rights including the requirement that each citizen should count equally with all other citizens"; Johan D. van der Vyver, *The Relationship of Freedom of Religion or Belief Norms to Other Human Rights, in* Facilitating Freedom of Religion or Belief: A Deskbook (Lindholm, Durham and Tahzib-Lie, eds., Leiden: Martinus Nijhoff Publishers, 2004), p. 106. Some scholars, alternatively, read the freedom of religion or belief and the non-discrimination principle in conjunction and argue that forms of establishment of religion violate the former *because* they amount to an act of discrimination. Marshall, for instance, states that "a state church or its equivalent...is always an instance of religious discrimination and, therefore, a limit on religious freedom"; Paul Marshall, *The Nature of Religious Freedom and Religious Persecution, in* Religious Freedom in the World. A Global Report on Freedom and Persecution (P. Marshall, ed., Nashville: Broadman & Holman Publishers, 2000), p. 15.

[40] *E.g.* A/C.3/SR.1100, paras. 8 and 19 and A/C.3/SR.1100, para. 2 (see Nowak, *supra* note 4, p. 605).

[41] Art. 2, para. (1), of the ICCPR explicitly states that: "Each State Party to the present Covenant undertakes to respect and to ensure to all individuals within its territory and subject to its jurisdiction *the rights recognized in the present Covenant*, without distinction of any kind, such as race, colour, sex, language, religion, political or other opinion, national or social origin, property, birth or other status" (emphasis added). Also art. 2, para. (2), of the Declaration on the Elimination of All Forms of Intolerance and of Discrimination Based on Religion or Belief, G.A. res. 36/55, 36 U.N. GAOR Supp. (No. 51) at 171, U.N. Doc. A/36/684 (1981), of 25 November 1981 [hereinafter: "UN Religious Tolerance Declaration (1981)"] is formulated as an accessory principle.

right".[42] Although it is true that the Human Rights Committee in its early jurisprudence only dealt with article 26 issues in conjunction with other rights protected by the Covenant, since the 'social security cases' against the Netherlands it is clear that states may be convicted for violating article 26 of the ICCPR in itself.[43] The Human Rights Committee fully settled the issue in its *General Comment on Non-Discrimination* of 1989:

> Article 26 not only entitles all persons to equality before the law as well as equal protection of the law but also prohibits any discrimination under the law...While article 2 limits the scope of the rights to be protected against discrimination to those provided for in the Covenant, article 26 does not specify such limitations. That is to say, article 26 provides that all persons are equal before the law and are entitled to equal protection of the law without discrimination, and that the law shall guarantee to all persons equal and effective protection against discrimination on any of the enumerated grounds. In the view of the Committee, article 26 does not merely duplicate the guarantee already provided for in article 2 but provides in itself an autonomous right. It prohibits discrimination in law or in fact in any field regulated and protected by public authorities. Article 26 is therefore concerned with the obligations imposed on States parties in regard to their legislation and the application thereof. Thus, when legislation is adopted by a State party, it must comply with the requirement of article 26 that its content should not be discriminatory. In other words, the application of the principle of non-discrimination contained in article 26 is not limited to those rights which are provided for in the Covenant.[44]

It may be concluded that the Committee has interpreted the right to equality before the law and equal protection of the law in such a manner that it forces the legislator to adopt laws devoid of any type of discrimination.[45] A discriminatory legal distinction is a distinction that is not based on criteria that can be considered "reasonable and objective".[46] Nowak convincingly argues in this context that:

> ...the Covenant...provides for an independent right to equality in Art. 26 in addition to the accessory prohibition of discrimination in Art. 2. This follows

---

[42] Nowak, *supra* note 4, p. 628.

[43] Human Rights Committee, *S.W.M. Broeks v. the Netherlands*, Communication No. 172/1984, U.N. Doc. Supp. No. 40 (A/42/40) at 139 (1987), of 9 April 1987; Human Rights Committee, *F.H. Zwaan-de Vries v. The Netherlands*, Communication No. 182/1984, U.N. Doc. CCPR/C/OP/2 at 209 (1990), of 9 April 1987; which line of jurisprudence has been continued in subsequent cases concerning article 26 of the ICCPR; *e.g.* Human Rights Committee, *A.P. Johannes Vos v. The Netherlands*, Communication No. 786/1997, U.N. Doc. CCPR/C/66/D/786/1997, of 29 July 1999; Human Rights Committee, *Mr. Michael Andreas Müller and Imke Engelhard v. Namibia*, Communication No. 919/2000, U.N. Doc. CCPR/C/74/D/919/2000 [2002], of 26 March 2002. See also Nowak, *supra* note 4, p. 608–609.

[44] Human Rights Committee, *General Comment 18: Non-discrimination* (Thirty-seventh session, 1989), Compilation of General Comments and General Recommendations Adopted by Human Rights Treaty Bodies, U.N. Doc. HRI/GEN/1/Rev.1 at 26 (1994) [hereinafter: General Comment 18], paras. 1 and 12.

[45] Cf. Nowak, *supra* note 4, pp. 628–629.

[46] Human Rights Committee, General Comment 18, para. 13.

> unambiguously from a grammatical, systematic interpretation of the two provisions…The Covenant contains no provision granting a right to sit on a park bench. But when a State party enacts a law forbidding Jews or blacks from sitting on public park benches, then this law violates Art. 26.[47]

Having established that the 'equality before the law' principle (article 26 of the ICCPR) is an autonomous right,[48] the following might be argued (analogously to Nowak's example): the Covenant certainly contains no right to have one's religion or belief legally declared the official religion of the nation—yet when the state does legally grant special recognition or status to the adherents of one religion it should grant the same legal recognition to other religions. A constitutional provision that designates a specific religion as the state religion has as a direct consequence that certain people belong to the state protected religion whilst others do not. The latter religions may or may not be recognized by means of additional agreements but even if that is indeed the case, this does not completely obviate the discriminatory nature of the establishment of one religion as the 'state' or 'official' one.

Interestingly, there has been some support for this argumentation by individual members of the Human Rights Committee. For instance, Tarnopolsky is recorded to have made the following remarks in 1980:

> Preferential treatment for one group, even if it did not violate article 18 of the Covenant, certainly violated art. 26. The fact that a provision was not directed against a group did not mean that it did not constitute a discriminatory measure against it. He wondered why all religions should not be treated on an equal footing…[49]

---

[47] Nowak, *supra* note 4, pp. 604–605.

[48] It may be noted at this point that the European Convention system lacks a proper autonomous equality principle. Thus, the dominant line of European Court of Human Rights' jurisprudence in which the European Court sanctions establishment of religion can best be explained in light of the fact that the European equivalent of the equality principle (article 14 of the European Convention on Human Rights) is an accessory right. See, most importantly: ECommHR., *Darby v. Sweden*, Appl. No. 11581/85,, 187 ECHR (Ser. A) (Annex), of 9 May 1989, para. 45: "A State Church system cannot in itself be considered to violate Article 9 [i.e. the right to thought, conscience and religion] of the [European] Convention. In fact, such a system exists in several Contracting States and existed there already when the Convention was drafted and when they became parties to it." The question whether a state church in itself forms a violation of the non-discrimination principle is not considered by the Commission because art. 14 of the ECHR is an accessory right. It is submitted, though, that the European Court could and indeed should revise its case law on establishment of religion on the basis of the more general prohibition of discrimination that is codified by Protocol 12. See art. 1 of the Protocol No. 12 to the Convention for the Protection of Human Rights and Fundamental Freedom, (ETS No. 177), of 4 November 2000.

[49] CCPR/C/SR.258 (1980), para. 51. See also, *e.g.*, CCPR/C/SR.236 (1980), para. 12 (Costa Rica), where a Member of the Committee is recorded as follows: "Article 75 of the Constitution made the Catholic religion the State religion and *thus* seemed to confer a privilege on the Catholic Church…that was perhaps not strictly in conformity with the Covenant" (emphasis added).

More importantly, there is increasing support for this type of argumentation in the work of the Special Rapporteurs on freedom of religion or belief. Special Rapporteur Asma Jahangir, in her 2007 Annual Report, argues:

> Formal or legal distinctions between different kinds of religious or faith-based communities carry the seed of discrimination insofar as such a distinction in their status implies a difference in rights or treatment. Consequently, the Special Rapporteur has voiced her concerns that the legalization of such a distinction between different categories of religion is liable to pave the way for future violations of the right to freedom of religion or for discrimination on the basis of religion or belief.[50]

Two different arguments against establishment of religion are discernible in this excerpt: (i) establishment of religion is likely to lead to some form of discrimination; (ii) the system of establishment *implies* differential treatment. The first concern, which is based on the acknowledgment that establishment of religion might foster discriminatory practices and thus impact on the state's scope for human rights compliance, precisely forms the object of research in the remainder of this study (Chapters 8–11). The second concern is of a more fundamental nature and comes down to an acknowledgment of the fact that, even if the state would in practice manage to minimize the discriminatory effects of the establishment of religion, the very act of establishing and maintaining an official religion sends out a discriminatory signal. In short, establishment of religion gives the appearance of preferences and perhaps prejudices on the part of the state. Rapporteur Odio Benito, in a pioneering report of 1987, similarly contended that:

> ...practices such as the establishment of a religion or belief by the State do in fact amount to certain preferences and privileges being given to the followers of that religion or belief, and are, therefore, discriminatory. While such practices may not per se constitute intolerance, they tend to lead to various authorities, organizations or groups to claim rights or to take action which may indeed amount to *further* and more accentuated discrimination against particular religions or beliefs.[51]

De Jong is of the same opinion as these two Special Rapporteurs as he concludes: "is not preferential treatment, other than affirmative action, *ipso facto* producing negative effects on other religious communities?"[52]

7.3 Official Anti-Religionism as Ipso Facto Human Rights Violation

A type of state–religion identification that in essence boils down to an anti-religious regime, a regime which officially rejects the concept of religion

---

[50] A/HRC/6/5 (2007), para. 26 (entitled: "State religion").

[51] Elizabeth Odio Benito, *Study on the Current Dimensions of the Problems of Intolerance and Discrimination on Grounds of Religion or Belief* (U.N. Doc. E/CN.4/Sub.2/1987/26, 1987), para. 88 (emphasis added).

[52] De Jong, *supra* note 28, p. 341.

altogether, can be considered, in itself, at odds with principles of human rights law, in particular the right to freedom of religion or belief and the equality principle.[53] History has seen some regimes which attempted to ban all religious activity (communist Albania, for instance). At present, perhaps save the DPRK,[54] there is no regime that approximates such an extreme form of disassociation with religion. Having said that, there are certainly states, both secular as well as religious, that outlaw specific religions (which will be discussed in the following Chapters).

It is submitted that a state that establishes itself as an 'atheistic state' breaches the non-discrimination principle for similar reasons that were advanced with respect to religious states: it legally divides people into those who adhere to the state belief (or rather *weltanschauung*) and those who do not. It must be observed that post-1989 communist state ideologies translate into different policies on the treatment of religions in comparison to pre-1989 state communism.[55] Whereas previously communist ideology generally translated into militant state atheism and the oppression of most if not all forms of religious activity, presently state socialism leads to state control over religion. Having said that, from a human rights perspective the latter form of state practice must be deemed objectionable as well. Though the framework of international human rights law permits states to place restrictions on the exercise of religion or belief (if those restrictions meet certain strict legal thresholds),[56] a system that seeks *a priori* control over manifestations of religion cannot be reconciled with the right to freedom of religion or belief. Besides the fact that a system of stringent state control over religion inevitably collides with religious freedoms, these systems reflect the existence of certain prejudices and biases about religion on the part of the state—which is in itself objectionable.

7.4 Conclusion

In this Chapter it has been contended that although human rights law on the face of it appears indifferent to the issue of state–religion identification, legal principles can in fact be extrapolated from human rights law that have a

---

[53] Cf. Durham's (*supra* note 25) rejection of forms of "negative identification"; and Brugger, *supra* note 63, p. 49: "[human rights conventions] require foremost a friendly posture of the state toward religion and thus contradict the combative stance."

[54] See also Human Rights Committee's Concluding Observations: A/56/40 vol. I (2001) 98 at para. 86(22): "in the light of the available information that religious practice is repressed or strongly discouraged, serious concern is expressed that the State party's practice in this respect does not meet the requirements of article 18 of the Covenant". DPRK has been discussed in some detail in Chapter 6 (section 6.3), *supra*.

[55] See Chapter 6 (section 6.2), *supra*.

[56] See art. 18, para (3), of the ICCPR.

profound bearing on the question of (il)legitimacy of the different forms of relationships between the state and religion. Particularly, a preliminary legal assessment of establishment of religion on the basis of the autonomous 'equality before the law' principle shows conclusively that legal establishment of religion is incompatible with human rights law. At the same time it was attempted to invalidate the main establishmentarian arguments in favour of the treatment of one religion as the official one.

To some authors the act of establishing a religion comes down to seeking to establish the superiority of the religion in question over other religions and non-religious beliefs.[57] At the very least it can be conceded that a state that constitutionally promotes a religion to the level of 'state religion' officially endorses this religion. Thus, it attaches a seal of quality to the religion in question.[58] A related argument is based on the analogy with ethnicity. Few people would find difficulty in accepting that a state that makes arbitrary legal distinctions on the basis of ethnicity would be acting contrary to human rights law; even if the state at the same time declares to ensure the rights and freedoms of ethnic minorities. Imagine, for instance,[59] a constitutional provision that would be along the following lines:

(i) We the people, establish State *x* as a White State; (ii) the rights of non-whites will be equally respected.

Admittedly, the analogy fails in so far as religions, unlike ethnicity, can (in theory) be changed. However, the fact that people could join the religion that is being favoured by converting into the religion in question is hardly an appropriate defence of establishment. Quite the contrary, in the above we have seen that some scholars argue that the very risk that people would feel compelled to join the religion that is protected and favoured by the state is precisely what is objectionable. Thus, constitutionally pinpointing the character of the state and its nation by referring to a single religion must be considered a deliberate act of exclusion.[60] It must be borne in mind that Constitutions outline the most fundamental characteristics of the state and as such reflect a shared ethos of a nation. In that context, it would be preferable if a Constitution would hint at achievements (independence, democracy, fundamental rights,

[57] *E.g.* Rajaji Ramanadha Babu Gogineni and Lars Gule, *Humanism and Freedom from Religion, in* FACILITATING FREEDOM OF RELIGION OR BELIEF: A DESKBOOK (Lindholm, Durham and Tahzib-Lie, eds., Leiden: Martinus Nijhoff Publishers, 2004), p. 708.

[58] Cf. Willy Fautre, *Western Europe: Trends in Religious Liberty, in* RELIGIOUS FREEDOM IN THE WORLD. A GLOBAL REPORT ON FREEDOM AND PERSECUTION (Marshall, ed., Nashville: Broadman & Holman Publishers, 2000), p. 15.

[59] The example could be amended by replacing ethnicity by gender, sexual orientation, social status, etc.

[60] An argument based on: Ruth Gavison, *Jewish and Democratic? A Rejoinder to the "Ethnic Democracy" Debate*, 4.1 ISRAEL STUDIES 58 (1999): "...I doubt the wisdom of defining Israel as

etc.), feats, characteristics, etc., that unite rather than divide a people. As religious belief is as a rule not among the uniting factors in society it is, arguably, best left out of the Constitution altogether (apart from a codification of the right to freedom of religion or belief, naturally).[61] Much of the criticism regarding establishmentarianism formulated in this Chapter is clearly aimed above all at all forms of clear-cut establishment of religion; however, it could easily be extended to all those forms of state support that boil down to the state endorsing certain religious, metaphysical phenomena: those metaphysical notions, needless to say, are virtually never shared or identified with by the entire population.[62]

Establishmentarian accounts can, lastly, be criticized in so far as they diffuse the highly misleading and rather hazardous assumption that forms of establishment of religion can be readily made permissible, simply by upholding the religious rights of minorities. The relevant, ultimate ramifications of the application of human rights law, as argued throughout this study, are: (i) the right to freedom of religion or belief empowers people—not states—to freely choose and practice a religion or belief; (ii) no one should be treated differently because of one's religion or belief; more specifically, if the state grants certain forms of support or privileges to some religious believers it should (unless there are 'reasonable and objective' criteria that justify otherwise) make those privileges available to others as well. The remainder of Part II of this study is intended to substantiate the claim that most, if not all, of the states that are officially entangled with a single religion fail to fully comply with these principles. The existing regimes of positive state identification with a religion are largely characterized by forms of institutionalised discrimination and *de facto* practices of discrimination on grounds of religion or belief (or lack thereof). This claim will be substantiated by carrying out a range of thematic case studies on, among other issues, Religious Laws and the State (see the following Chapter), State Entanglement with Religion & the Equal Religious Rights of Others, Free

---

a Jewish and democratic state...in the Basic Laws in a quasi-constitutional process that did not include a serious consultation and agreement with the Arab citizens of Israel".

[61] As Martin contends most convincingly: "the priority of faith...cannot be translated in civic and constitutional terms. Such priorities are laid on human beings by religious commitment in a manner which cannot be articulated as constitutive of the state or as a matter of policy in the public realm". David Martin, On Secularization: Towards a Revised General Theory (Aldershot: Ashgate, 2005), p. 89 (in relation to the debate on European constitutionalism and the question whether references to religion are legitimate).

[62] See Part I, particularly Chapter 3, *supra*, on state support to and state acknowledgement of religious phenomena. It is contended here that not only clear-cut forms of establishment have an excluding effect. Every time a Constitution mentions "We the People, proclaim" (etc.) in the same breath with "In the Name of God" (or any other expression of faith) an entire section of the population is ignored. In this context it is important to bear in mind that "democracy does not equal the rule of the majority but also takes into account the legitimate rights of minorities. And these are precisely what are at stake here" (De Jong, *supra* note 28, p. 340).

Speech & Religion, Religion & Employment, Religion & Civil Association (see Chapter 9), Religion & Education (see Chapter 10), and Religion & Politics (see Chapter 11). At the same time it must be observed that in some secular or separationist states, the ideals of state secularism and separationism have come to be considered ends in themselves. It will be explained that this has given rise to situations where the principles of secularism and separationism are construed so as to impose special (unacceptable) limits on the exercise of religions.

CHAPTER EIGHT

RELIGIOUS LAWS & THE STATE

8.1 Introduction

The remainder of the second part of this study is intended to substantiate the claim that certain forms of state practice that surround and characterize states that are officially entangled with religion run counter to different norms of international human rights law. It will equally be highlighted that different types of human rights abuses can be discerned in states which are premised on or which act in accordance with rather objectionable interpretations of the principles of secularism and separationism. Starting with the former issue, this Chapter deals with what arguably characterizes the most strict type of 'religious states': state enforcement of religious laws and principles. This topic merits separate discussion in so far as it has raised many human rights concerns that are of a different quality and degree than the ones assessed in the Chapters to come. In other words, in the Chapters to come we will see how religious incentives in more indirect ways may lead to discriminatory forms of state practice, whilst here we deal with problems that emerge because states directly apply principles that are said to have derived from religious laws.

Content-based assessment of the various sets of 'religious laws' from a human rights perspective is, unlike many of the topics addressed in the following Chapters, fairly well-explored territory. Hence, as far as content-based assessment of religious laws is concerned this account will largely limit itself to conveying the state of play by means of outlining the main findings of the academic authorities in this field.

This Chapter is also intended, however, to add some new elements to this debate. The human rights discipline traditionally has focused on the content of principles and norms that are (ostensibly) derived from religious laws so as to point out the difficulty of reconciling these principles with norms of human rights law. In the latter part of this Chapter it is argued that, moreover, a series of more fundamental (or 'systemic') human rights problems surround and characterize those systems of domestic political organization that are premised on state enforcement of religious laws. From the outset it must be pointed out that these fundamental concerns do not by any means imply a rejection of the notion of religious laws as such (the content-based concerns do raise substantive questions concerning religious laws yet always about specific notions that are said to derive from religious laws). These systemic objections rather amount to a dismissal of state intervention, in terms of a pro-active role as enforcer and guardian, with the issue of observance of religious laws.[1] These fundamental concerns are based on the notions of: (i) freedom *from* religion; (ii) equality before the law; and (iii) transparency, legal certainty and checks and balances.

8.2 State Interference with Enforcement of Religious Laws: Substantive Concerns

In must be observed, first of all, that in most, if not all, states 'religious laws' are being observed in so far as a country's population generally includes religious communities or individual believers who endeavour to abide by (some of) the religious tenets and rules that follow from their religions. Some states stand out, though, in that they take control over, or otherwise interfere with, the issue of religious observance. In Chapter 2 varying degrees of this phenomenon were distinguished: from the extreme situation in Saudi Arabia which declares the Quran to be its true Constitution and which largely enforces pre-modern Shari'a law without major alteration to the different segments of public and private life, to states in which religious law has a bearing on, besides family law matters, a limited amount of public policy issues (notably criminal law),[2] to states in which only aspects of family law, inheritance or other so-called 'personal status' matters are directly governed by religious laws.[3] It must be observed that the latter group form the majority at present, although processes of Islamization that can be discerned in different countries of the Muslim world may bring about changes in that respect in the future.

In this section the 'traditional' human rights concerns with religious laws will be outlined. The concise overview in this section shows that the fact that human rights violations stem from certain principles or doctrines that are said to be derived from religious laws (e.g. Shari'a law, Halakhah law, Hindu law) is fairly well established both by religious and legal scholars working in the human rights discipline.[4] These scholars have demonstrated that problems primarily emerge in the fields of: (i) gender equality; (ii) the right to change or

---

[1] An-Na'im in his recent book on the role of Shari'a in predominantly Muslim states argues something similar (though partly based on different arguments as used here); which would appear to be a departure from, or at least an important supplement to, his earlier work. See Abdullahi Ahmed An-Na'im, Islam and the Secular State: Negotiating the Future of Shari'a (Cambridge, US/London: Harvard University Press, 2008).

[2] *E.g.* Iran, Pakistan, the Sudan, Libya, and some northern states of Nigeria. See Vincent O. Nmehielle, *Sharia Law in the Northern States of Nigeria: To Implement or Not to Implement, the Constitutionality is the Question*, 26 Human Rights Quarterly 730 (2004), pp. 732–733, on recent developments surrounding the introduction of Shari'a criminal law in the northern states of Nigeria.

[3] See Chapter 2, section 2.4, *supra*.

[4] With respect to Shari'a, most importantly: Abdullahi Ahmed An-Na'im, Toward an Islamic Reformation: Civil Liberties, Human Rights, and International Law

abandon a religion (i.e. the issue of the position and treatment of converts and apostates); and (iii) the rights of religious minorities and non-believers.

8.2.1 *Religious Laws & Gender Inequality*

Some interpretations of rules and principles that derive from religious laws are difficult to reconcile with modern ideas of human rights. It goes without saying that this is something different altogether from claiming that a particular religion and human rights are incompatible. It is important, therefore, to consistently distinguish between a religion on the one hand, and the different, often constantly evolving religious legal traditions that surround the different religions on the other.[5] It is mostly religious family law or religious personal status law that have an important bearing on the issue at stake. Karayanni has argued in this context that:

> ...within the religious laws of the different religious communities there exist a number of norms that are discriminatory in nature, especially in terms of gender. In fact many religious norms still applicable by the different religious communities discriminate explicitly against women and work to preserve the internal patriarchal hierarchy.[6]

Also the Human Rights Committee acknowledges the existing problems as it considers that the "[i]nequality in the enjoyment of rights by women throughout the world is deeply embedded in tradition...including religious attitudes."[7] It is the objective of this section to identify some of the existing religious legal

---

(Syracuse: Syracuse University Press, 1990); ANN ELIZABETH MAYER, ISLAM AND HUMAN RIGHTS: TRADITION AND POLITICS (Boulder/Oxford: Westview Press, 1999) (the latter two accounts explore different possibilities of reinterpreting and reforming pre-modern conceptions of Shari'a law); Donna E. Arzt, *The Application of International Human Rights in Islamic States*, 12(2) HUMAN RIGHTS QUARTERLY (1990); and KAMRAN HASHEMI, RELIGIOUS LEGAL TRADITIONS, INTERNATIONAL HUMAN RIGHTS LAW AND MUSLIM STATES (Martinus Nijhoff Publishers, 2008)(although Hashemi offers a more optimistic account on the compatibility of Islamic principles and international human rights standards, also in his account various necessary re-interpretations and reforms are proposed); as to Halakhah, most importantly the work of Frances Raday, *e.g.*: Frances Raday, *Israel – The Incorporation of Religious Patriarchy in a Modern State*, 4 INTERNATIONAL REVIEW OF COMPARATIVE PUBLIC POLICY 209 (1992); as to Hindu, Christian and Parsi law on personal status (in India), see *e.g.* Kirti Singh, *Obstacles to Women's Rights in India, in* HUMAN RIGHTS OF WOMEN: NATIONAL AND INTERNATIONAL PERSPECTIVES (Cook, ed., Philadelphia: University of Pennsylvania Press, 1994). For additional references, see the remainder of this section.

[5] Cf. Hashemi (*ibid.*) who distinguishes between Islam and 'Islamic legal traditions'.

[6] Michael Karayanni, *The "Other" Religion and State Conflict in Israel: On the Nature of Religious Accommodation for the Palestinian-Arab Minority, in* RELIGION IN THE PUBLIC SPHERE: A COMPARATIVE ANALYSIS OF GERMAN, ISRAELI, AMERICAN AND INTERNATIONAL LAW (Brugger & Karayanni, eds., Berlin: Springer, 2007), p. 340, on the laws of the different religious communities in Israel.

[7] Human Rights Committee, *General Comment 28: Equality of Rights between Men and Women* (article 3), U.N. Doc. CCPR/C/21/Rev.1/Add.10 (2000) [hereinafter: General Comment 28], para. 5.

traditions that are discriminatory against women. The focus will be predominantly on *Shari'a* (Islamic) law and *Halakhah* (Jewish) law.[8]

(i) *Shari'a & Gender Inequality*

Some states, including Bahrain, Egypt, Iran, Saudi Arabia, Yemen, constitutionally put the position of women directly in the perspective of the need for compliance with Islamic law.[9] Mayer argues specifically with respect to the Egyptian constitutional provision on the status of women:[10]

> In a famous formulation fraught with ambiguity and equivocation, it provides that the State has responsibility for maintaining a balance between a woman's duties toward the family and activity in society, as well as for her equality with men in the fields of political, social, cultural and economic life, without detriment to the laws of the shari'a. Of course, the significance of all this hinges on the meaning attributed to the final phrase. If it is given much weight and if the laws

[8] It must be observed that in those states in which other sets of religious laws are applied, i.e. states that sanction a situation wherein different religious courts have a monopoly over family matters and issues of personal status, similar patterns of structural gender inequality can be discerned. In India, for instance, all different religious communities are, as far as family and personal status matters are concerned, governed by the different sets of religious personal laws. See, *e.g.*, Indian Christian Marriage Act of 1872, the Parsi Marriage and Divorce Act of 1936, the Hindu Marriage Act of 1955, the Hindu Succession Act of 1956, the Hindu Adoption and Maintenance Act of 1956, the Hindu Minority and Guardianship Act of 1956 and the Muslim Personal Law Application Act of 1937. Singh, *supra* note 4, p. 379, concludes that "[t]he main characteristic of all the personal laws is that they are anti-women, anti-liberal, and anti-human". See also Ursula King, *Hinduism and Women: Uses and Abuses of Religious Freedom, in* FACILITATING FREEDOM OF RELIGION OR BELIEF: A DESKBOOK 523 (Lindholm, Durham and Tahzib-Lie, eds., Leiden: Martinus Nijhoff Publishers, 2004), particularly pp. 526–529; and Anika Rahman, *Religious Rights Versus Women's Rights in India: A Test Case for International Human Rights Law*, 28 COLUMBIA JOURNAL OF TRANSNATIONAL LAW 473 (1990). There is increasing political pressure to adopt national, uniform laws on the issue of personal status. Another example is Israel: although the focus here will be on the application of Jewish law in the framework of the Rabbinical courts of Israel, it should be borne in mind that other sets of religious laws are applied by the other religious courts (i.e. Christian, Shari'a and Druze courts). Interpretation and applications of Canon law principles by Christian Courts (as per the King's Order in Council 1922–1947, which stems from the British Mandate) regarding the position of women have been equally criticized on the basis of equality concerns (*e.g.* Raday, *supra* note 4, pp. 209, 210, 213 and 222). Only Druze law stands out as somewhat more liberal and egalitarian. See RUTH HALPERIN-KADDARI, WOMEN IN ISRAEL: A STATE OF THEIR OWN (Philadelphia: University of Pennsylvania Press, 2003), p. 261. Having said that, also with respect to the latter set of religious family law, according to the latter author, there remains enough reason for concern (*e.g.* inequality in custody matters).

[9] Art. 5, para. (b), of the CONST. OF BAHRAIN (2002); art. 11 of the CONST. OF EGYPT (1971); art. 21 of the CONST. OF IRAN (1979) (see also art. 20: the principle of equality between men and women must be construed in a way that is in accordance with Islamic criteria); art. 8 of the BASIC LAW OF SAUDI ARABIA (1992); and art. 31 of the CONST. OF YEMEN (1990).

[10] Which reads in full: "The State shall guarantee the proper coordination between the duties of women towards the family and her work in the society, considering her equal with man in the fields of political, social, cultural and economic life without violation of the rules of Islamic jurisprudence" (art. 11 of the CONST. OF EGYPT of 1971).

of the shari'a are taken to comprise the classical rules of personal status, the "equality" referred to is illusory.[11]

It may indeed be argued that some interpretations and applications of Shari'a principles on the position of women are difficult to reconcile with codified standards of international human rights law.[12] Particularly relevant here are the rights and principles enshrined in the UN *Convention on the Elimination of All Forms of Discrimination against Women*.[13] Mayer contends with respect to pre-modern interpretations of Shari'a law that:

> The premodern jurist treated woman as needing male tutelage and control, imposing many disabilities on women, putting them in a distinctly subordinate role vis-à-vis men within the family, and largely relegating them to secluded domesticity. Jurists condoned child marriages, which in practice meant that women were married off at early ages and against their wills by male marriage guardians. Women were required to be monogamous, whereas men could have up to four wives at a time. Wives owed obedience to their husbands, who were entitled to keep them at home and to beat them and withhold maintenance for disobedience. Husbands could terminate marriages at their discretion simply by uttering a divorce formula, whereas wives according to many jurists needed to overcome difficult hurdles to obtain a divorce over their husbands' objections. Men enjoyed great power as the guardians of minors, and after a divorce, men got custody of children once they passed the stage of infancy. In the scheme of succession, women got one-half the share of males who inherited in a similar capacity.[14]

Arzt similarly contends that:

> Probably the most celebrated inequality under traditional Islamic law is the unequal treatment of women, who are considered the wards of men. Women are legally disqualified from holding general political or judicial office, and within

---

[11] Ann Elizabeth Mayer, *Law and Religion in the Muslim Middle East*, 35 American Journal of Comparative Law (1987), p. 142.

[12] *E.g.* An-Na'im, *supra* note 4, pp. 181–182; Asma Mohamed Abdel Halim, *Challenges to the Application of International Women's Human Rights in the Sudan, in* Human Rights of Women: National and International Perspectives 397 (Cook, ed., Philadelphia: University of Pennsylvania Press, 1994), specifically on the status of women under Islamic law as applied in the Sudan; Sara Hossain, *Equality in the Home: Women's Rights and Personal Laws in South Asia, in* Human Rights of Women: National and International Perspectives 465 (Cook, ed., Philadelphia: University of Pennsylvania Press, 1994); Courtney W. Howland, *Safeguarding Women's Political Freedoms under the International Covenant on Civil and Political Rights in the Face of Religious Fundamentalism, in* Religious Fundamentalisms and the Human Rights of Women 93 (Howland, ed., New York: Pargrave, 1999).

[13] Convention on the Elimination of All Forms of Discrimination against Women, G.A. Res. 34/180, 34 U.N. GAOR Supp. (No. 46) at 193, U.N. Doc. A/34/46, of 18 December 1979 (entered into force: 3 September 1981) [hereinafter: CEDAW]. Iran, Nauru, Palau, Somalia, Sudan and Tonga are the only states that are not party to this Convention. The United States of America has signed CEDAW (17 July 1980) though fails in ratifying it. It must be observed that some religious states that have ratified CEDAW have at the same time entered reservations on the issue of gender equality (this issue will be discussed in more detail in section 8.4, *infra*).

[14] Mayer, *supra* note 4, p. 99. See for a similar assessment: An-Na'im, *supra* note 4, p. 176.

> the family they lack the capacity to initiate a marriage contract or obtain a unilateral divorce. By law their inheritance of property is usually about half the share of a male with the same degree of relationship to the deceased. Husbands have the right to chastise their wives for "disobedience", including by "light beating". Muslim women can leave the home to seek employment not to fulfil personal ambitions but only when they lack all other means of support. Moreover a woman's testimony in court is worth only one-half of a man's testimony.[15]

Since the late nineteenth century official interpretations of Shari'a law are characterized by gradual reforms in virtually all Islamic states (perhaps the least so in Saudi Arabia).[16] It must be observed, however, that the state's (alleged)[17] endeavour to implement and abide by the norms of Shari'a law still gives rise to many instances of inequality.

Far from being exhaustive, the following overview is intended to give some insight into the ways in which women's rights are restricted in this process of implementing Shari'a law:

Inequality in Marriage Options and During Marriage

The prevalent prohibition of marriages between Muslim women and non-Muslim men violates the rights of women to freely choose a spouse (this norm is enforced in, for instance, Algeria, Bahrain, Kuwait, Morocco, Pakistan, United Arab Emirates and Yemen).[18] The same holds true, naturally, if a woman is forced to convert to Islam in order to be able to marry a Muslim man (e.g. in Saudi Arabia). The latter practice is, in addition, in violation of

---

[15] Arzt, *supra* note 4, p. 208.

[16] Cf. Mayer, *supra* note 4, p. 99; Arzt, *supra* note 4, pp. 222–223.

[17] Strict adherence to religious rules and doctrine does not necessarily stem from religious zealotry; political opportunism, i.e. incentives to preserve the (patriarchal) status quo, is an important factor in this context as well. See Ann E. Mayer, *Religious Reservations to the Convention on the Elimination of All Forms of Discrimination against Woman: What Do They Really Mean?, in* Religious Fundamentalisms and the Human Rights of Women 105 (Howland, ed., New York: Pargrave, 1999); Ann E. Mayer, *The Internalization of Religious Positions on Human Rights: How Religious Particularisms are Uniting in a Campaign against Women's International Human Rights, in* Global Justice and the Bulwarks of Localism: Human Rights in Context 223 (Eisgruber and Sajó, eds., Leiden: Martinus Nijhoff Publishers, 2005); Mayer, *supra* note 4, p. 117. The fact that the notion of Shari'a law results in different forms of state practice in different Islamic states shows that there is no monolithic conception of Islamic law. This is further substantiated by the fact that within one state, over time, changes in the official interpretation can be discerned. See for a detailed overview: Nisrine Abiad, Sharia, Muslim States and International Human Rights Treaty Obligations: A Comparative Study (London: British Institute of International and Comparative Law, 2008), particularly Ch. 2, pp. 59–99.

[18] Art. 16, para. (1)(a), of CEDAW. The Human Rights Committee has condemned this practice as well, *e.g.*: A/60/40 vol. I (2004) 35 at para. 84(27) (Morocco). See also Human Rights Committee, General Comment 28, para. 24, which makes clear that "laws or practices that prevent the marriage of a woman of a particular religion with a man who professes no religion or a different religion" are contrary to art. 3 of the ICCPR. Occasionally, the marriage may be performed in case the man converts to Islam. Such instances of forced conversions are in violation of the right to freedom of religion (art. 18 of the ICCPR).

her equal right to freedom of religion and the prohibition of coercion in religious affairs.[19] The UN Committee on the Elimination of Discrimination against Women (CEDAW Committee) which monitors compliance with the CEDAW Convention has stated in this context that "[a] woman's right to choose a spouse and enter freely into marriage is central to her life and to her dignity and equality as a human being."[20]

The practice of polygamous marriages (sanctioned in, for instance, Algeria, Syria, United Arab Emirates and Yemen) runs counter to women's equal rights as well.[21] The CEDAW Committee considers in this respect:

> Polygamous marriage contravenes a woman's right to equality with men, and can have such serious emotional and financial consequences for her and her dependents that such marriages ought to be discouraged and prohibited. The Committee notes with concern that some States parties, whose constitutions guarantee equal rights, permit polygamous marriage in accordance with personal or customary law.[22]

Human rights law also makes explicit the fact that men and women have the "same rights and responsibilities *during* marriage".[23] The CEDAW Committee observes that:

> The form and concept of the family can vary from State to State, and even between regions within a State. Whatever form it takes, and whatever the legal system, religion, custom or tradition within the country, the treatment of women in the family both at law and in private must accord with the principles of equality and justice for all people...[24]

Looking at state practice, An-Na'im concludes in this context that:

> ...Shari'a family law...violates the human rights of Muslim women in even the most "secularized" Islamic societies. This branch of Shari'a is enforced as the

[19] See also Bahia G. Tahzib-Lie, *Women's Equal Right to Freedom of Religion or Belief: An Important but Neglected Subject, in* Religious Fundamentalisms and the Human Rights of Women 117 (Howland, ed., New York: Pargrave, 1999), on women's equal right to freedom of religion.

[20] Committee on the Elimination of Discrimination against Women, *General Recommendation 21: Equality in Marriage and Family Relations* (Thirteenth session, 1992), U.N. Doc. A/49/38 at 1 (1994) [hereinafter: General Recommendation 21], para. 16. The practice of forced marriage is also contrary to human rights law according to the CEDAW Committee (same para.).

[21] Art. 5 in conjunction with art. 15 and 16 of CEDAW. The practice of polygamy also constitutes a violation of art. 3 of the ICCPR (see Human Rights Committee, General Comment 28, para. 24). See also An-Na'im, *supra* note 4, p. 176.

[22] Committee on the Elimination of Discrimination against Women, General Recommendation 21, para. 14. See also Cornelis D. de Jong, The Freedom of Thought, Conscience and Religion or Belief in the United Nations (1946-1992) (Antwerp/Groningen/Oxford: Hart/Intersentia, 2000), p. 527, referring to polygamy as one of "the main difficulties of Islamic countries with the international obligations concerning marriage".

[23] Art. 16, para (1)(c), of CEDAW (emphasis added).

[24] Committee on the Elimination of Discrimination against Women, General Recommendation 21, para. entitled "Article 16", section 13.

> official law of the great majority of predominantly Muslim countries today, and even in some non-Muslim countries, like India…where Muslims are a minority. Moreover, the underlying assumptions and norms of this branch of Shari'a have a negative impact on the human rights of women in broader socio-political terms. The basic problem can be outlined as follows. Shari'a family law is fundamentally premised on the notion of male guardianship over women (*qawama*), and is consequently characterized by many features of inequality between men and women in marriage, divorce, and related matters.[25]

Equal rights during marriage means, among other things, that spouses should have equal rights and responsibilities in family matters and all matters arising from their relationship, from the running of the household, to the choice of residence, to the administration of assets and not least, the upbringing of children. In the latter regard, it must be observed that Shari'a interpretations that render the religion of the child automatically as Islamic by virtue of the child having a Muslim father—and thus regardless of the religion of the mother—violate women's equal right as a parent in deciding upon matters relating to their children (e.g. in Algeria, Saudi Arabia and Qatar).[26]

Inequality at the Dissolution of Marriage

Under human rights law all forms of discriminatory treatment in relation to the grounds and procedures for separation or divorce, child custody, maintenance or alimony, visiting rights or the loss or recovery of parental authority are prohibited.[27] Existing interpretations of Islamic personal status laws on divorce and child custody tend to put women at a disadvantage and thus violate the principle of equal rights at and after the dissolution of a marriage.[28] An-Na'im argues that these disadvantages become manifest in the following ways:

> A Muslim man may divorce his wife, or any of his wives, by unilateral repudiation, *talaq*, without having to give any reasons or justify his action to any person or authority. In contrast, a Muslim woman can obtain divorce only by consent of the husband or by judicial decree for limited specific grounds such as the husband's inability or unwillingness to provide for his wife.[29]

Equality in regard to the dissolution of marriage implies that the grounds for divorce and annulment should be precisely the same for men and women. The same holds true for all decisions with regard to property distribution, alimony and the custody of children.

---

[25] Abdullahi Ahmed An-Na'im, *State Responsibility to Change Religious and Customary Laws, in* Human Rights of Women: National and International Perspectives (Cook, ed., Philadelphia: University of Pennsylvania Press, 1994), p. 181.

[26] Art. 16, para 1 (d), of CEDAW.

[27] Art. 16 of CEDAW.

[28] Most notably, the interpretations that prevail in the legal orders of Bahrain, Syria, Qatar and the United Arab Emirates.

[29] An-Na'im, *supra* note 4, p. 90.

Inequality in Inheritance

Interpretations of religious laws that favour male heirs in adjudicating their inheritance claims or regulations that restrict women's inheritance claims, which are as a rule legally curtailed by half, violate women's equal economical rights (e.g. in Algeria, Egypt, Iran, Maldives, Oman and Syria).[30] Such regulations can be particularly discriminatory vis-à-vis non-Muslim women.

Inequality of the Value of Testimony

Interpretations of Islamic law which hold that the testimony of a woman is not equal to that of a man violate women's right to equal treatment in all stages of judicial procedures.[31] Commonly the testimony of a woman is worth half that of men; in other words, the testimonies of two women are required to equal that of one man, either as a general rule or with regard to specific legal subject matters only (e.g. in Kuwait, Maldives, Mauritania, Saudi Arabia and Qatar). An-Na'im remarks in this context:

> ...Shari'a law of evidence discriminates among witnesses on grounds of gender and religion. The testimony of women...is inadmissible in the more serious criminal cases of *hudud* and *qisas*...In civil matters, the testimony of Muslim women is accepted, but it takes two women to make a single witness. None of these restrictions applies to the testimony of a Muslim male, who is always a fully competent (*adl*) witness under Shari'a unless disqualified by his specific personal conduct.[32]

This practice is bound, at the same time, to be contrary to the 'right to equal recognition as a person before the law'.[33]

Modesty Rules

Interpretations of Islamic law that prescribe so-called 'modesty rules' for women, in terms of obligatory garments, limited access to public places (on account of men being present in these places), or limited freedom to carry out outdoor activities, etc., naturally, violate the equality principle on numerous counts.

---

[30] Art. 2 in conjunction with art. 5 of CEDAW (see also CEDAW Committee, General Recommendation 21, paras. 34–35); this practice also constitutes a violation of art. 3 of the ICCPR (see Human Rights Committee, General Comment 28, para. 24). See also An-Na'im, *supra* note 4, p. 91 and p. 176.

[31] Art. 15, para. (2), of CEDAW. These practices are also contrary to art. 14 (right to equality before courts and tribunals and to a fair trial; in conjunction with equality norms as enshrined in artt. 2, 3 and 26) of the ICCPR. See Human Rights Committee, *General Comment No. 32, Article 14: Right to equality before courts and tribunals and to a fair trial*, U.N. Doc. CCPR/C/GC/32 (2007) [hereinafter: General Comment 32], para. X. This is also confirmed in the jurisprudence of the Human Rights Committee; *e.g.* Human Rights Committee, *Graciela Ato del Avellanal v. Peru*, Communication No. 202/1986, Views of 28 October 1988, paras. 10.1–10.2.

[32] An-Na'im, *supra* note 4, p. 90.

[33] Art. 16 (taken in conjunction with art. 3) of the ICCPR. See also Human Rights Committee, General Comment 28, para. 19.

It goes without saying that if blanket clothing requirements are applied, the right to freedom of religion or belief will inevitably be violated (e.g. in Iran and Saudi Arabia).[34] Interpretations of Islamic principles which prevent women from freely travelling without such requirements as a male chaperon or the consent of a third party (husband or male relative) to the issuance of a passport or other travel documents run counter to the freedom of movement (e.g. in Iran or Saudi Arabia).[35] The Human Rights Committee has explicitly condemned discriminatory restrictions on the freedom of movement based on gender inequality.[36]

(ii) *Halakhah & Gender Inequality*

Existing interpretations of Jewish *Halakhah* law similarly seek to preserve the patriarchal nature of the state and run counter to the principle of gender equality in many respects.[37] Shetreet argues in this context:

> The world according to *halacha* is divided into two spheres: the public, which is the man's place, and the private, which is the domain of women. According to Maimonides, women may not be appointed to public office. Such *halachic* imperatives are, it is said, dictated by woman's fragile nature, as well as by the imperative of strict female modesty. Further *halachic* rulings involve the relationship between wife and husband, which is one of domination-subordination.[38]

It must be observed that existing official interpretations and applications of Halakhah law, similar to the development of Islamic law in that respect, have been subjected to reform processes in more recent times. Having said that, the application of this body of law still generates a wide range of human rights abuses. Israel's Women's Equal Rights Act has not done away with the Rabbinical Courts' monopoly in applying Jewish law to family matters and issues of personal status, thereby in effect sanctioning discrimination against women based on interpretations of religious precepts.[39]

---

[34] Art. 638 (part of the Chapter on "Offences against Public Moral") of the Islamic Penal Code of Iran of 1991 (amended 1996) provides: "women who appear in public without a proper *hijab* should be imprisoned from ten days to two months or pay a fine of 50,000 to 500,000 Ryal." The enforcement of rules on religious attire may also be at odds with the right to freedom of religion or belief of those who actually adhere to the religion where these rules (are said to) derive from. This type of (systemic) concern will be elaborated on in more detail in section 8.3, *infra*.

[35] Art. 12 of the ICCPR.

[36] Human Rights Committee, *General Comment 27: Freedom of movement* (Art.12), U.N. Doc CCPR/C/21/Rev.1/Add.9 (1999), para. 18. See also Human Rights Committee, General Comment 28, para. 16.

[37] Cf. Raday, *supra* note 4, p. 209.

[38] Shimon Shetreet, *The Model of State and Church Relations and Its Impact on the Protection of Conscience and Religion: A Comparative Analysis and a Case Study of Israel, in* RELIGION IN THE PUBLIC SPHERE: A COMPARATIVE ANALYSIS OF GERMAN, ISRAELI, AMERICAN AND INTERNATIONAL LAW (Brugger & Karayanni, eds., Berlin: Springer, 2007), p. 144.

[39] Women's Equal Rights Act of 1951, no. 5711 (1951). See also Nitza Berkovitch, *Women and the Women's Equal Rights Law in Israel*, 198 MIDDLE EAST REPORT (1996), p. 19.

Raday argues that "the establishment of patriarchy is most clearly expressed in the ultimate power of the male not to release his wife from the bonds of marriage."[40] Raday gives a good insight into the exact ramifications in terms of gender inequality:

> If the husband does not agree to give his wife a *get* (divorce writ), then there is no jurisdiction, religious or secular, that can free her from the marriage. The rabbinical courts may recommend that the husband divorce his wife or may even order him to do so, but if he refuses to comply, she remains married to him... [T]he refusal of the husband to divorce his wife results in the wife's legal inability to remarry and to set up any kind of new, informal family life as a practical matter. If she has a sexual relationship with another man, then she risks being considered a rebellious wife and, consequently, losing her rights to spousal maintenance payments or child custody. Moreover, if at any future time her husband dies or releases her from marriage, she will be prohibited from marrying her lover...If the wife refuses her consent, the husband may nonetheless be able to acquire a rabbinical license to remarry. Moreover, if he sets up a new family without that license, he will not suffer the penalties that are imposed upon an undivorced wife. This asymmetry derives from the fact that originally, polygamy was allowed under Jewish law...If a woman is widowed before the couple had children, the widow must obtain a *haliza* (a release) from her deceased husband's brother before she is free to remarry.[41]

The application of Jewish law in courts does not only affect the status of women but potentially also that of their children. Karayanni argues in this regard:

> ...probably the more severe outcome [of the application of Jewish law] concerns the status of children of the Jewish woman...if she, for example, chooses to unilaterally release her husband from the marriage and conceives a child with another man. This child is considered "illegitimate" (*mamzer*) and will carry severe restrictions on his or her capacity to marry. However, no such restrictions are necessarily borne by the similarly "illegitimate" children of a married man.[42]

Discriminatory grounds for divorce, discriminatory grounds for marriage and remarriage, inequality in regard to the dissolution of marriage, discriminatory penalties for adultery, are all at odds with the principle of gender equality.[43] It is important to reiterate the position of the CEDAW Committee in this respect:

> ...many countries in their legal systems provide for the rights and responsibilities of married partners by relying on the application of common law principles,

---

[40] Frances Raday, *Religion, Multiculturalism and Equality: The Israeli Case*, 25 Israeli Yearbook on Human Rights (1995), p. 193.

[41] Frances Raday, *Religion and Patriarchal Politics: the Israeli Experience*, *in* Religious Fundamentalisms and the Human Rights of Women 105 (Howland, ed., New York: Pargrave, 1999), p. 159–160. See also Shetreet, *supra* note 38, pp. 144–145, touching largely upon the same issues; and Karayanni, *supra* note 6, p. 341.

[42] Karayanni, *supra* note 6, p. 341.

[43] CEDAW Committee, General Recommendation 21, on art. 16 of CEDAW. See also Human Rights Committee, General Comment 28, paras. 25–26. Also cf. Human Rights Committee: A/53/40 vol. I (1998) 45 at para. 325 (Israel).

> religious or customary law, rather than by complying with the principles contained in the [CEDAW] Convention. These variations in law and practice relating to marriage have wide-ranging consequences for women, invariably restricting their rights to equal status and responsibility within marriage.[44]

As an aside, not solely the application of Islamic or Jewish religious laws raises concerns in the field of marriage or its dissolution. In Malta, the Catholic ecclesiastical authorities are granted a monopoly over "the marriage bond", which means in practice that divorce is not possible.[45]

Some interpretations of Jewish legal principles limit women's equal right to freedom of religion or belief. Raday argues in this context that:

> The exclusion of Orthodox Jewish women from wearing a *tallit* [i.e. Jewish prayer shawl], reading from a Torah scroll and praying aloud in a group are obvious ways of excluding women from both ritual and worship.[46]

Thus, we see how the application of interpretations of religious laws may translate into discriminatory implementation (or partial non-implementation) of other fundamental rights, notably the right to freedom of religion or belief.[47]

(iii) *Cultural Traditions & Violations of Women's Rights*

Some cultural traditions can be discerned which seriously affect women's rights and which cannot be said to be accompanied by a prevalent religious legal tradition. For instance, it may be that the type of cultural practice actually predates the religion in question. It may be that the dominant view within the legal-religious doctrine is that the tradition in question has never been officially internalized by the religion in question whilst, at the same time, in some regions the tradition is perpetuated on the basis of alleged compliance with religious precepts. One might think in this regard of female genital mutilation (FGM),[48]

---

[44] Committee on the Elimination of Discrimination against Women, General Recommendation 21, para. 17.

[45] Concordat between the Republic of Malta and the Holy See on the Recognition of Civil Effects of Canonical Marriage and on the Judgments of Ecclesiastical Authorities and Tribunals Concerning the Marriage Bond of 3 February 1993. See art. 4, para. (2), on the duty to "enlighten future marriage partners as to the specific nature of canonical matrimony and consequently about ecclesiastical jurisdiction over the marital bond".

[46] Frances Raday, *Claiming Equal Religious Personhood: Women of the Wall's Constitutional Saga, in* Religion in the Public Sphere: A Comparative Analysis of German, Israeli, American and International Law (Brugger & Karayanni, eds., Berlin: Springer, 2007), p. 260.

[47] See also Tahzib's account, *supra* note 19, on the often neglected issue of women's equal right to freedom of religion.

[48] FGM predates Islam; *e.g.* Rosemarie Skaine, Female Genital Mutilation: Legal, Cultural and Medical Issues (Jefferson, N.C.: McFarland, 2005).

honour killings,[49] dowry deaths[50] and *satī* (widow-burning).[51] All of these practices are more often than not condemned rather than supported on the basis of interpretations of ancient legal-religious sources. It will be clear that all states in which such traditions are perpetuated, for whichever reason, are under an obligation to take measures to counter these practices.[52]

In conclusion, under international human rights law states parties are obliged to ensure that religious or cultural attitudes are not used to justify violations of women's rights.[53]

8.2.2 *Apostasy*

Under a strict, pre-modern interpretation of Islamic law, Muslims who abandon Islam are to be severely punished. Mayer explains in this regard that:

> ...apostates were to be given an opportunity to repent and return to Islam, but if they refused, they were to be executed if they were male and imprisoned until they changed their minds if they were female. Premodern *shari'a* rules also

---

[49] Human Rights Watch considers that honour crimes "are not specific to any religion, nor are they limited to any one region of the world." Human Rights Watch, *Integration of the Human Rights of Women and the Gender Perspective: Violence Against Women and "Honor" Crimes (Item 12)*, Human Rights Watch Oral Intervention at the 57th Session of the UN Commission on Human Rights, 6 April 2001.

[50] Something largely specific to the Indian subcontinent. Dowry issues result in several thousands of deaths each year (according to Government estimations). Art. 304B of the Indian Penal Code of 1860 (inserted by Law amending the Penal Code of 1986) provides that a death shall be deemed a "dowry death" and that the husband (or relatives) shall be deemed to have caused the death of the woman in question whenever the death of a woman is "caused by any burns or bodily injury or occurs otherwise than under normal circumstances within seven years of her marriage and it is shown that soon before her death she was subjected to cruelty or harassment by her husband or any relative of her husband for, or in connection with, any demand for dowry." See also the Dowry Prohibition Act of 1961, law 28/1961. The preamble of the latter law links this phenomenon to ancient marriage rites in the Vedic period. See also Bhavani Sitaraman, *Law as Ideology: Women, Courts and 'Dowry Deaths' in India*, 27(3) International Journal of the Sociology of Law 287 (1999).

[51] Largely specific to the Indian subcontinent. It may be said that "[t]he origins of the custom are mysterious; there is no reference to it in the Vedas [the ancient texts that form the foundation of the Hindu tradition], except for a hint in the rituals for the antyeshti (funeral) rite which describes how a widow might lie beside her husband on the unlit pyre" (Oxford Dictionary of World Religions, p. 861). Some of the ancient Hindu Law Books indeed seem to sanction this tradition; *e.g.* Brihaspati Smriti, XXV–1/14: "Now the duties of a woman (are as follows):... After the death of her husband, to preserve her chastity, or to ascend the pile after him"; The Institutes of Vishnu (Sacred Books of the East, Vol. 7; transl. Julius Jolly; Oxford: Clarendon Press, 1880, pp. 110–111). *Satī* is defined by art. 2, para. (c) of the Commission of Sati (Prevention) Act of 1987, law 3/1988, as "the burning or burying alive of: (i) any widow along with the body of her deceased husband or any other relative or with any article, object or thing associated with the husband or such relative; or (ii) any woman along with the body of any of her relatives, irrespective of whether such burning or burying is claimed to be voluntary on the part of the widow or the women or other-wise".

[52] Cf. Human Rights Committee, General Comment 28, para. 10–11.

[53] Art. 2, para. (f), of CEDAW; artt. 2–3 of the ICCPR; and art. 4 of the UN Religious Tolerance Declaration (1981). See also Human Rights Committee, General Comment 28, para. 5.

> provided that apostasy constituted civil death, meaning, among other things, that the apostate's marriage would be dissolved and the apostate would become incapable of inheriting. Naturally, the *shari'a* imposed no penalties on converts to Islam from other faiths.[54]

Mayer, An-Na'im and others have shown that other, less stringent readings are possible by pointing out that the fact that there is actually no Quranic verse stipulating such severe punishments for apostasy and that the *Sunna*, Muhammad's sayings and the examples he set, are rather ambiguous on the issue.[55] Having said that, it could be argued that current state practice is still largely inspired by pre-modern legal discourse. Mayer contends in this regard:

> Muslim attitudes are still influenced by the *shari'a* rule prohibiting conversion from Islam, and the transformation of Islam into state ideologies has encouraged the equation of abandoning Islam with treason.[56]

Though in modern times the Islamic rule on apostasy has in many parts of the Muslim world been the subject of reform, it will be clear that all existing Shari'a-inspired prohibitions of apostasy run counter to the fundamental right to freedom of religion or belief.

The freedom to 'have or adopt' a religion or belief (which includes the freedom to change one's religion)[57] is a so-called absolute right under international

---

[54] Mayer, *supra* note 4, p. 149; see also An-Na'im, *supra* note 4, pp. 107–114; and Arzt, *supra* note 4, p. 209.

[55] Abdullahi Ahmed An-Na'im, *The Islamic Law of Apostasy and its Modern Applicability: A Case form the Sudan*, 16 Religion (1986), p. 211; An-Na'im, *supra* note 4, p. 109; Mayer, *supra* note 4, pp. 157–158. See also Shaikh Abdur Rahman, Punishment of Apostasy in Islam (Lahore: Institute of Islamic Culture, 1988), pp. 54–55; and Nazila Ghanea, *Apostasy and Freedom to Change Religion or Belief, in* Facilitating Freedom of Religion or Belief: A Deskbook (Lindholm, Durham and Tahzib-Lie, eds., Leiden: Martinus Nijhoff Publishers, 2004), pp. 681–683. The Quran speaks in reprimanding terms of the act of apostasy on several (around 200) occasions (*e.g.* The Holy Qur'an, transl. Abdullah Yusuf Ali, 5:36: "As to those who reject Faith, if they had everything on earth, and twice repeated, to give as ransom for the penalty of the Day of Judgment, it would never be accepted of them, theirs would be a grievous penalty"; see also 2:6; 2:24; 2:26; 2:28; 2:39; 2:85; 2:90; 2:91; 2:98; 2:121; 2:126; 2:161; 2:171; 2:212; 4:89; 5:57, etc.). However, it is never referred to as a *hadd* offence, i.e. as an offence for which there is only one fixed (severe) sentence. On the contrary, it is described as an act that deserves severe punishment in the afterlife. In short, as far as the Quran is concerned, it is Allah who will deal with apostates, not the Muslim community. As far as the *Sunna* are concerned, on the other hand, it appears that whenever apostates were ordered to be killed, the perpetrators were never put to death *merely* for the crime of apostasy, but always at the same time, and perhaps *particularly*, for other crimes that warranted the death penalty, *e.g.* murder or crimes against the state (Mayer, *supra* note 4, pp. 157–158; An-Na'im, 1986, *ibid.*, pp. 211–212).

[56] Mayer, *supra* note 4, p. 149.

[57] Art. 18 of the ICCPR does not explicitly mention a right to change one's religion or belief; however, the Human Rights Committee has clarified that the right to 'have or adopt' a religion or belief "necessarily entails the freedom to choose a religion or belief, including the right to replace one's current religion or belief with another or to adopt atheistic views" (Human Rights Committee, General Comment 22, para. 5). The right to change was already acknowledged by art. 18 of the Universal Declaration of Human Rights. See also the discussion in Chapter 7, text around note 22, *supra*.

human rights law: no interferences whatsoever are permitted with respect to this internal aspect of the right to freedom of religion or belief.[58] It is thus evident that those states (e.g. Afghanistan, Iran, Jordan, Kuwait, Pakistan, Qatar, Saudi Arabia, northern Sudan and Yemen)[59] that retain this prohibition as a matter of religious-criminal law or as a matter of policy, violate the right to freedom of religion or belief. This holds true even if the prohibition in practice does not necessarily result in convictions, considering the deterring effect and coercive force these bans have as such. Also, states that in practice generally refuse to recognize conversions away from Islam (e.g. Egypt) act contrary to the right to freedom of religion or belief. The same, naturally, holds true for states that deprive apostates of their citizenship (Maldives).

Also 'Muslim dissidents' and non-Muslims may suffer from anti-apostasy measures. The best example of the former is given by the treatment of Ahmadis in Pakistan who were constitutionally stigmatized as apostates ("non-Muslims") in 1974.[60] These constitutional amendments were a decade later followed by Penal Code revisions which paved the way towards what might be called an official anti-Ahmadi campaign. One of the provisions of these anti-Ahmadi laws reads:

> Any person of the Quadiani group or the Lahori group (who call themselves 'Ahmadis' or by any other name), who, directly or indirectly, poses himself as

[58] This *forum internum*, or 'inner belief freedom', mentioned in para. 1 of art. 18 of the ICCPR, is not subject to the grounds for limitation mentioned in para. 3 of the same article (in other words, only the freedom to manifest a religion or belief, the *forum externum*, can under circumstances be limited). See Human Rights Committee, General Comment 22, para. 3. Not even in time of public emergency is it possible for the state to derogate from the ramifications of the right to freedom of religion or belief; see art. 4, para. (2), of the ICCPR.

[59] While other (parts of) states are at present considering to extend the application of Shari'a law to criminal matters, notably northern Nigeria (see Nmehielle, *supra* note 2, pp. 732–733), which may have repercussions on the issue of apostasy.

[60] 'Ahmadis' is used as a collective name for two minority communities that consider themselves Muslims: the Ahmadiyya Muslim Community and the Lahore Ahmadiyya Movement for the Propagation of Islam. Ahmadis are followers of Mirzā Ghulām Ahmad Qādiyāni (1835–1908). Many core Islamic beliefs and rituals are shared by Ahmadis; however, certain aspects of Ahmadiyya beliefs are considered controversial if not heretical by mainstream Sunni and Shi'a Muslims. These doctrinal issues concern predominantly positions on the life and role of Jesus, the Prophethood of Muhammad and the status of the religious founder and reformer, Ahmad. The Ahmadiyya Muslim Community renders prophet status to Ahmad and in so doing questions the Finality of the Prophethood of Muhammad, something which 'orthodox Muslims' consider contrary to Quranic doctrine, particularly: The Holy Qur'an, 33:40, which states: "Muhammad is…the Seal of the Prophets" (trans. Abdullah Yusuf Ali). The Constitution (Third Amendment) Order, President's Order 24/1985, No. F.17(3)/85 Pub., of 1985 (effective from 19 March 1985), states: "In the Constitution and all enactments and other legal instruments, unless there is anything repugnant in the Subject or context: (a) "Muslim" means a person who believes in the unity and oneness of Almighty Allah, in the absolute and unqualified finality of the Prophet-hood of MUHAMMAD (PBUH), the last of the Prophets, and does not believe in, or recognize as a prophet or religious reformer, any person who claimed or claims to be a prophet, in any sense of the word or of any description whatsoever, after MUHAMMAD (PBUH); and (b) "non-Muslim" means a person who is not a Muslim and include a person

> Muslim, or calls, or refers to, his faith as Islam, or preaches or propagates his faith, or invites others to accept his faith, by words, either spoken or written, or by visible representations, or in any manner whatsoever outrages the religious feelings of Muslims, shall be punished with imprisonment of either description for a term which may extend to three years and shall also be liable to fine.[61]

The treatment of Bahá'ís as Muslim apostates or the treatment of the Bahá'í faith as an illegal offshoot of Islam, primarily in Iran (but also in, for instance, Afghanistan and Egypt), shows strikingly that Islamic law on apostasy does not solely affect the religious rights of Muslims.[62]

The prohibition of apostasy, moreover, may have far-reaching civil law implications. An-Na'im points out the following:

> The legal effects of all the acts of an apostate are suspended pending his repentance or death. His rights to dispose of his property, for example, is immediately held to be in abeyance (*mawqof*) until he either repents or is executed, or dies if he had escaped punishments. If he repents and returns to Islam, on the one hand, all his property rights are restored, including the rights to dispose of it in usual ways. If he dies an apostate, on the other hand, his estate falls to the Public Treasury. An apostate also lacks the capacity to himself inherit from others. A Marriage is immediately dissolved (*faskh*) upon the apostasy of either spouse.[63]

Furthermore, as Mayer has contended, the prohibition of apostasy or conversion may in practice form an obstacle for women trying to escape from being subject to the applicable principles of Islamic law which have so important a bearing on their status (see previous sub-section).[64]

In conclusion, it may be reiterated that all states that follow an interpretation of religious law that comes down to a condemnation of the acts of apostasy or conversion act contrary to the right to freedom of religion or belief, which includes the right to replace one's current religion or belief with another or to recant one's religion or belief.[65]

8.2.3 *Inferior Status of Religious Minorities*

Pre-modern interpretations of Shari'a rendered those non-Muslims who were 'People of the Book' (*Ahl al-Kitab*), meaning believers in the revealed Scriptures

---

belonging to the Christian, Hindu, Sikh, Buddhist or Parsi community, a person of the Qadiani group or the Lahori group (who call themselves "Ahmadis" or by any other name), or a Bahai, and a person belonging to any of the Scheduled Casts."

[61] Art. 298-C of the Penal Code, introduced by Ordinance No. F.17 (1) 84-Pub, Anti-Islamic Activities of Quadiani Group, Lahori Group and Ahmadis (Prohibition and Punishment) Ordinance, XX/1984 of 26 April 1984. The same Ordinance added an article on the "Misuse of epithets" to the Penal Code (art. 298-B) which specifically targets Ahmadis as well.

[62] See Nazila Ghanea, Human Rights, the UN & the Bahá'ís in Iran (The Hague: Kluwer Law International, 2002).

[63] An-Na'im, *supra* note 55, p. 212; see also Mayer, *supra* note 4, pp. 151–153.

[64] Mayer, *supra* note 4, pp. 151–152.

[65] Human Rights Committee, General Comment 22, para. 5.

(mainly Christians and Jews),[66] a protected status as *Dhimmi*;[67] other types of religious believers were dismissed as infidels and were not to enjoy any civil and political rights.[68] The *dhimma* status as a notion of Islamic law is considered an elaboration on certain Quranic verses, for instance:

> Fight those who believe not in Allah nor the Last Day nor hold that forbidden which hath been forbidden by Allah and His Prophet, nor acknowledge the religion of Truth, (even if they are) of the People of the Book, until they pay the *jizyah* with willing submission, and feel themselves subdued.[69]

The latter part of the quotation came to mean that, in exchange for admitting one's inferior status as Dhimmi by paying a poll tax (*jizya*), People of the Book were to be tolerated. This also implied that the use of force against those who did not wish to acknowledge Muslim superiority was permitted. An-Na'im remarks in this context:

> Since non-Muslims were given the choice between embracing Islam, becoming *dhimmis* and paying *jizya* if they qualified for that status, or fighting the Muslims, it cannot be said that there was no compulsion in religion.[70]

Notwithstanding the fact that Dhimmis were tolerated, pre-modern interpretations of Islamic law rendered Dhimmis second-class citizens. Both An-Na'im and Arzt underscore the fact that Dhimmis were not allowed to hold political or judicial office or to exercise authority over Muslims in any other way.[71] Dhimmis, however, were distinctly better off than 'unbelievers' as the latter were not to be tolerated at all: they were offered a choice between accepting Islam or death.[72]

Again, it should be acknowledged that interpretations of Shari'a have evolved. For one thing, religious minorities in predominantly Muslim states are no longer forced to pay a special tax to buy their protection and, in so doing, admit their inferiority. Having said that, adherents of religious

[66] The *dhimma* status was at a later stage extended to Zoroastrians as well as to other non-Muslims; An-Na'im, *supra* note 4, p. 89.

[67] An-Na'im, *supra* note 4, p. 89; Mayer, *supra* note 4, p. 135.

[68] An-Na'im, *supra* note 4, p. 88.

[69] The Holy Qur'an (transl. Abdullah Yusuf Ali), 9:29.

[70] An-Na'im, *supra* note 4, p. 149; which is intended as a reference to the Quran, 2:256, stating "Let there be no compulsion in religion" (The Holy Qur'an, transl. Abdullah Yusuf Ali).

[71] Abdullahi A. An-Na'im, *Religious Minorities under Islamic Law and the limits of Cultural Relativism*, 9:1 Human Rights Quarterly 1 (1987), p. 11; Arzt, *supra* note 4, pp. 208–209.

[72] Mayer, *supra* note 4, p. 135; see also An-Na'im, *supra* note 71, pp. 10-11; Arzt, *supra* note 4, p. 209. The difference in treatment between People of the Book and unbelievers is also reflected by the Quran. See The Holy Qur'an (transl. Abdullah Yusuf Ali), 9:5: "But when the forbidden months are past, then fight and slay the Pagans wherever ye find them, and seize them, beleaguer them, and lie in wait for them in every stratagem (of war); but if they repent, and establish regular prayers and practise regular charity, then open the way for them: for Allah is Oft-forgiving, Most Merciful".

minorities remain at a disadvantage in many respects and some forms of institutionalised discrimination on the basis of religion or belief as well as many *de facto* discriminatory practices can be discerned. Discrimination of religious minorities is largely similar to the patterns of inequality suffered by women under certain Islamic legal traditions (see previous sub-section). Inequality of religious minorities presently becomes manifest in the following ways: discriminatory obstacles to inter-religious marriages,[73] inequality in inheritance,[74] inequality of the value of testimony,[75] and inequality with respect to holding public office. As to the latter point, in Chapter 11 of this study it will be demonstrated that the *dhimma* notion is still largely intact in Islamic states in so far as it remains the case that most senior political and judicial offices in these states can only be held by Muslims.

Iran is arguably the state that most faithfully reflects a pre-modern interpretation of the position and status of non-Muslims.[76] The Constitution of Iran proclaims that:

> Zoroastrian, Jewish, and Christian Iranians are the *only* recognized religious minorities, who, within the limits of the law, are free to perform their religious rites and ceremonies, and to act according to their own canon in matters of personal affairs and religious education.[77]

Persons that are not considered People of the Book (here meant to include Zoroastrians) are devoid of constitutional protection. This situation has particularly negatively impacted on the rights of Iranian Bahá'ís.[78]

---

[73] I.e. non-Muslim people are often not free to choose their spouse: it is often impossible for a non-Muslim man to have a Muslim wife (as that would mean, given the dominance of patriarchal societal structures, that a non-Muslim would exercise authority over a Muslim; the other way around would often not raise legal obstacles; hence, the fact that this is as much of an issue of gender discrimination as an issue of religious discrimination). See Kamran Hashemi, *The Right of Minorities to Identity and the Challenge of Non-discrimination: A Study on the Effects of Traditional Muslims'* Dhimmah *on Current State Practices*, 13 International Journal on Minority and Group Rights (2006), p. 22; see also Abdullahi A. An-Na'im (ed.), Inter-Religious Marriages among Muslims: Negotiating Religious and Social Identity in Family and Community (Delhi: Global Media Publications, 2005).

[74] *E.g.* Iran and Qatar. See CERD Committee's Concluding Observations: A/57/18 (2002) 38 at para. 197 (Qatar). See art. 881 (*Bis*) of the Civil Code of Iran (transl. Taleghany et al.): "An infidel does not inherit from a Muslim; and if there be a Muslim among the heirs of an infidel deceased, the infidel heirs do not inherit, even if they belong to a class and degree closer to the deceased than the Muslim heir".

[75] *E.g.* Judges in Saudi Arabia are authorized to discount or value less the testimony of non-Sunni persons.

[76] An-Na'im, *supra* note 71, pp. 12–13.

[77] Art. 13 of the Const. of Iran (1979) (emphasis added).

[78] See Ghanea, *supra* note 62; Mayer, *supra* note 4, pp. 143–144; An-Na'im, *supra* note 71, p. 13; Martin Douglas, The Persecution of the Bahá'ís of Iran, 1844-1984 (Ottawa: Association for Bahá'í Studies, 1984). See also Human Rights Committee, A/48/40 vol. I (1993) 44 at para. 263 (Iran).

8.3 Systemic Human Rights Concerns Regarding State Intervention in the Observance of Religious Laws

The human rights discipline traditionally has focused on the content of principles and norms that are—said to be—derived from religious laws so as to point out the difficulty of reconciling these principles with norms of human rights law. In the previous section many of these conflicting norms have been identified. It is not difficult to establish that under human rights law, states are obliged to rescind or alter domestic laws, policies or practices that reflect these conflicting principles which are based on interpretations of religious laws. Firstly, with respect to gender equality, the CEDAW Convention explicitly stipulates that State Parties must:

> ...condemn discrimination against women in all its forms, agree to pursue by all appropriate means and without delay a policy of eliminating discrimination against women and, to this end, undertake:...To take all appropriate measures, including legislation, to modify or abolish existing laws, regulations, customs and practices which constitute discrimination against women...[79]

All state parties to the ICCPR are similarly obliged to take all necessary steps to enable all persons, regardless of religious affiliation or sex, to enjoy the rights of this Covenant, which may imply overcoming similar obstacles.[80] The Human Rights Committee has clarified that all measures that affect members of minority religions in terms of, for instance, ineligibility for government service or economic disadvantages are incompatible with the ICCPR and must consequently be abolished or altered.[81] Thus it may be concluded that:

> ...every state has the responsibility to remove any inconsistency between international human rights law binding on it, on the one hand, and religious and customary laws operating within the territory of that state, on the other.[82]

In the remainder of this Chapter it is argued that, in addition to the above indicated substantive objections that can be made to the application of *specific principles* that are prevalent in some religious legal traditions, a series of more fundamental objections can be made that concern the very *system* of those forms of political organization that are premised on state enforcement of religious laws. These systemic objections amount to a dismissal of state

[79] Art. 2, para. (f), of CEDAW. Art. 5, para. (a), specifically requires that: "States Parties shall take all appropriate measures:...To modify the social and cultural patterns of conduct of men and women, with a view to achieving the elimination of prejudices and customary and all other practices which are based on the idea of the inferiority or the superiority of either of the sexes or on stereotyped roles for men and women".

[80] Art. 2 of the ICCPR. See Human Rights Committee, General Comment 28, para. 3.

[81] Human Rights Committee, General Comment No. 22, para. 9. The same follows from art. 4 of the UN Religious Tolerance Declaration (1981).

[82] An-Na'im, *supra* note 25, p. 167.

intervention, in terms of a pro-active role as enforcer and guardian, with the issue of observance of religious laws. These fundamental concerns are based on the notions of: (i) freedom *from* religion; (ii) equality before the law; and (iii) transparency, legal certainty and checks and balances.

8.3.1 *Freedom from Religion*

Part I of this study outlined how some religious states constitutionally reserve an important position and role for the religious laws that derive from the dominant religion within the political organization of the state. This structure generally branches off into different measures and safeguards which aim to ensure that religious laws are mainstreamed with the legislative, executive and judicial activities of the different state bodies.[83] This section is intended to demonstrate that religious pluralism and tolerance on the one hand, and a state that takes too active an interest in fostering the observance of the religious laws of a single religion on the other, are mutually exclusive notions.[84]

Limitations on the right to freedom of religion or belief and forms of discrimination based on religion or belief are inevitable in any state that considers itself the enforcer and guardian of the religious laws of the state or predominant religion. The right to freedom of religion or belief includes positive freedoms: the freedom to have or adopt a religion or belief and the freedom to manifest one's religion or belief. As the right to freedom of religion or belief also covers a right not to profess any religion or belief and as, moreover, no one may be subject to coercion which would impair one's right to freely choose a religion or belief,[85] it must be concluded that a so-called negative freedom is also enclosed. Freedom of religion or belief as a negative freedom may be referred to as the right to be free *from* religion. Freedom from religion guards against any unwanted religious interference on the part of the state. Such protection, naturally, is of particular importance to non-believers. Also religious minorities may benefit from this right; whilst the same holds true for people that actually (nominally) belong to the predominant religion. In short, both non-believers and members of religious minorities, as well as adherents

[83] See Chapter 2, section 2.4.1, *supra*, for the different measures which are adopted to ensure a strong religion–law nexus.

[84] *E.g.* CCPR/C/SR.365 (1982), 7 at para. 20 (member Ermacora), arguing that religious pluralism is a precondition for human rights compliance; and CCPR/C/SR.364 (1982), 12 at para. 61 (Iran): "how [could] a constitutional Law based on the principles of the Koran…be compatible in every respect with the Covenant. How could a legal system based on the precepts of a single religion protect all the human rights enshrined in the Covenant?" (member Vallejo); E/CN.4/1984/SR.43 (1984), 6 at para. 17 (Sudan).

[85] Human Rights Committee, general Comment 22, para. 2: "Article 18 protects…the right not to profess any religion or belief"; art. 18, para. (2), of the ICCPR: "No one shall be subject to coercion which would impair his freedom to have or to adopt a religion or belief of his choice". See Human Rights Committee, General Comment 22, para. 5, for an elaboration on the prohibition of coercion.

of the state-sanctioned religion, suffer human rights abuses under regimes that actively interfere with the issue of observance of religious laws.

It can hardly be disputed that whenever the state subjects those citizens that do not belong to the state religion to the religious laws of the latter religion, the religious rights and freedoms of this group are transgressed. We have already come across some cases in which principles that are said to derive from the laws of the dominant religion are applied to the entire population, regardless of religious affiliation (for instance, religious 'modesty rules' and religious dress rules in some of the stricter Islamic societies). At this point it may be added that occasionally religious dietary rules (prohibitions) or burial prescriptions are extended to the entire population. Religious family law or personal status laws commonly apply only to the religious members in question. However, some exceptions are perceivable. For instance, Shari'a law in most Islamic states is also applied to cases in which just one of the parties is Muslim.[86] Some states apply Shari'a law, under certain circumstances, where neither party is Muslim (for instance, Egypt and Morocco).[87]

Another good example is provided by the treatment of secular Jews in Israel in so far as it may be argued that they are to some extent subjected to Jewish Halakhah law.[88] Perhaps most importantly in this regard is the fact that civil marriage does not exist in Israel, only religious marriages are recognized.[89] As Rabbis have a monopoly on marriage, secularists are forced to abide by the Halachic rules on marriage if they do want to get married, which amounts to a violation of their freedom from religion and their right to family life.[90] Moreover, although Israel formally permits civil burial,[91] in practice the rabbinical administration has a monopoly on burials due to a lack of places for non-religious burial. This amounts to a violation of the government's positive duty to protect the rights of secular Jews, and forms in effect an encroachment upon their freedom from religion.[92]

---

[86] Mayer, *supra* note 4, p. 152; and Mayer, *supra* note 11, p. 143. The previously discussed ban on inter-religious marriage under Islamic law naturally has a bearing on the position of non-Muslims as well.

[87] Mayer, *supra* note 11, p. 145.

[88] See Barak Medina, *Does the Establishment of Religion Justify Regulating Religious Activities? – The Israeli Experience, in* RELIGION IN THE PUBLIC SPHERE: A COMPARATIVE ANALYSIS OF GERMAN, ISRAELI, AMERICAN AND INTERNATIONAL LAW (Brugger & Karayanni, eds., Berlin: Springer, 2007), particularly p. 319 and p. 322.

[89] As per the Rabbinical Courts Jurisdiction (Marriage and Divorce) Law of 1953. *Funk-Schlesinger v. Minister of Interior*, [1963] HJC 143/62, however, opened up the possibility of recognizing civil marriages conducted abroad. In *Segev v. Rabbinical Court*, [1967] HJC 130/66, a 'private marriage' between persons who otherwise, because of Halachic restrictions, were unable to marry was sanctioned. See Shetreet, *supra* note 38, p. 153.

[90] Art. 23 of the ICCPR; see Human Rights Committee, General Comment 19, para. 4. See also Committee on the Elimination of Discrimination against Women, General Recommendation 21, para. 39.

[91] Right for Alternative Civil Burial Act of 1996, 5756/1996.

[92] Shetreet, *supra* note 38, p. 154. See also Human Rights Committee, A/53/40 vol. I (1998) 45 at para. 325 (Israel).

The fact that regimes that actively interfere with the issue of observance of religious laws may violate the rights of the adherents of the state religion is often overlooked or trivialized. The fact that the state in this case takes an active interest in the religion one belongs to does not generate advantages only. Under international human rights law one is free to have or adopt a religion or belief and to freely determine what this religion means in terms of religious obligations. In other words, under human rights law it is ultimately the individual that may identify for him or herself which religious laws derive from the religious doctrine in question.[93] State intervention with the issue of observance of religious laws ultimately comes down to state enforcement of state-sanctioned interpretations of these laws. In that respect, state enforcement of religious laws and principles is bound to be accompanied by the enforcement of at least some rules that encroach on people's personal convictions about what to believe and how to practise that belief. Moreover, under human rights law a person who, nominally, considers him or herself to belong to a certain religion, is in fact free to neglect a religious duty that derives from the religious laws or doctrine of a religion.[94] Thus, the fact that a person, who neglects some of the obligations that are considered eminent by orthodox followers of the same religion, may not be considered a true believer by the religious community or by the religious establishment is irrelevant from a human rights perspective. A person may consider him or herself a Christian (nominally) and not regularly attend church services. A person may in theory consider him or herself a Muslim and yet not wish to fully abide by the 'five pillars of Islam' or each and every principle deriving from Shari'a law.[95] Human rights law empowers each individual to personally establish what one's belief means in terms of one's duties, obligations, sacraments and rituals. This would certainly rule out the adoption by the state of measures that may be deemed coercive. State intervention with the issue of observance of religious laws and duties comes down to precisely that: a degree of religious coercion.

A related systemic concern with the institutionalized enforcement of religious laws stems from the fact that women are typically excluded from the

---

[93] Cf. An-Na'im, *supra* note 1.

[94] Unless a religious duty or principle happens to coincide with a duty enshrined in (secular) state laws of course; for instance, refraining from certain harmful acts which are criminalized by the state's penal code.

[95] The observance of religious duties cannot be considered to take place in a spirit of voluntariness if penal law prohibitions are in place that threaten to punish any neglect of one's religious duties. See, *e.g.* artt. 14–16 of the Syariah Criminal Offences Act (Federal Territories) of Malaysia of 1997, Act 559 (applicable to the Federal Territories of Kuala Lumpur and Labuan), which respectively penalize (i) the failure to perform the Friday prayers in a mosque for three consecutive weeks; (ii) the selling to any Muslim of any food, drink, cigarettes or openly eating, drinking or smoking during the hours in which Ramadan is to be observed; and (iii) anyone that refuses or willfully fails to pay the *zakat* (alms). Similar prohibitions can be found in the Penal Codes of, *e.g.*, Iran, Pakistan and Saudi Arabia.

decision-making and adjudicating process (this can be distinguished from concerns surrounding the patriarchal *content* of the religious laws discussed in the previous section). As Raday has argued, women are largely "excluded from all the various religious forums that authoritatively interpret the religious-legal norms that govern their existence".[96] Women are put at a disadvantage by eligibility rules on holding judicial posts in religious courts and tribunals, which, in turn, affects the scope for revision of any of the attitudes and practices that negatively affect their status and position.[97] The CEDAW Committee has commented that:

> …in certain cases the law excludes women from…serving as judges in religious or traditional tribunals vested with jurisdiction on behalf of the State…These provisions discriminate against women, deny to society the advantages of their involvement and skills in these areas of the life of their communities and contravene the principles of the Convention.[98]

In conclusion, states that consider themselves the guardian and enforcer of religious laws ignore the negative freedoms that are intrinsic to the right to freedom of religion or belief, freedoms which are to be enjoyed by both nonbelievers and members of religious minorities as well adherents of the dominant religion.

8.3.2 *Equality before the Law & Equal Protection of the Law*

A second systemic concern with state intervention with religious observance in terms of actively enforcing religious laws or authorizing religious courts to interpret and enforce religious laws is that this generally results in a system of so-called legal pluralism. A state that effectively sanctions parallel jurisdictions is difficult to reconcile with the human rights norm that demands that all persons, regardless of religious affiliation, are equal before the law and are entitled without any discrimination to the equal protection of the law.[99]

---

[96] Raday, *supra* note 41, p. 158, with respect to the Israeli situation particularly. This concern can be extended to other religious states. See also Committee on the Elimination of Discrimination against Women, *General Recommendation 23, Political and Public Life* (Sixteenth session, 1997), U.N. Doc. A/52/38/Rev.1 at 61 (1997) [hereinafter: General Recommendation 23], paras. 10 and 31; and Human Rights Committee, general Comment 28, para. 29.

[97] Israeli women cannot become judges in the Rabbinical Courts and may not be ordained as Rabbis. See Chief Rabbinate of Israel Law of 1980; Rabbinical Courts Jurisdiction (Marriage and Divorce) Law of 1953. See Shetreet, *supra* note 38, p. 145; and CEDAW Committee's Concluding Observations: A/52/38/Rev.1 part II (1997) 87 at para. 157 (Israel), condemning this practice. The same holds true for most of the Islamic states. See An-Na'im, *supra* note 4, Chapter 2. See Chapter 11, section 11.2.1, *infra*, on discriminatory eligibly criteria for public and judicial offices.

[98] Committee on the Elimination of Discrimination against Women, General Recommendation 23, para. 31.

[99] Art. 26 of the ICCPR.

The previous section on freedom from religion illustrated that it is exceptionally problematic, from a human rights perspective, to subject citizens that do not belong to the state religion to the religious laws of this state-protected religion. It is now added that it is, at the same time, very problematic in terms of the state's human rights obligations, to effectively sanction a system of parallel jurisdictions in which different religion-based family laws or personal status laws are applied to different people depending on their religious affiliation (besides Israel and India, one can think of those Islamic states that reflect remnants of a system based on *dhimma* or based on the Ottoman *millet* system).[100]

Thus, the ultimate ramification of the state's obligation to consider everyone equal before the law and entitled without any discrimination to the equal protection of the law is that the state is under a duty to enact uniform state laws, most importantly, in the present context, a uniform civil code on matters of family law that equally applies to all members of different religious groups. One can find support for this position in the work of UN treaty monitoring bodies.[101]

---

[100] I.e. those Islamic societies in which religious minorities, notably Jews and Christians, are tolerated and permitted to live in accordance with their own religious precepts and to adjudicate cases in accordance with their own religious laws. See Chapter 2, section 2.2.3, *supra*, on *millet*; and section 8.2.3, *supra*, on *dhimma*. See art. 13 of the Const. of Iran (1979). NB: in India increasing political pressure can be discerned calling for the enactment of uniform laws.

[101] *E.g.*, most explicitly, Committee on the Elimination of Discrimination against Women: A/60/38 part II (2005) 109 at paras. 99–100 (Lebanon): "The Committee is concerned that no unified personal status law exists in the country and that each Lebanese citizen is subject to the laws and courts pertaining to his or her religious community in regard to the regulation of personal status…The Committee urges the State party to *adopt a unified personal status code* which is in line with the Convention and would be applicable to all women in Lebanon, irrespective of their religious affiliation" (emphasis added); and A/55/38 part I (2000) 7 at paras. 60–61 (India): "The Committee notes that steps have not been taken to reform the personal laws of different religious and ethnic groups, in consultation with them, so as to conform with the Convention. The Committee is concerned that the Government's policy of non-intervention perpetuates sexual stereotypes…The Committee also calls upon the Government to follow the directive principles in the Constitution and Supreme Court decisions and *enact a uniform civil code* that different ethnic and religious groups may adopt" (emphasis added); see also Human Rights Committee, General Comment 32, para. III, stating that the state is under an obligation to "protect the rights under the Covenant of any persons affected by the operation of customary and religious courts". It must be observed that apart from the latter comment, the Human Rights Committee has largely restricted itself to forms of criticism regarding the content of religious laws and the state's role in implementing these laws, *e.g.*: A/59/40 (Vol. I) (2004), para. 76(16) (Gambia); A/58/40 (Vol. I) (2003), para. 77 (5) (Egypt); A/53/40 vol. I (1998), 45 at para. 325 (Israel); A/48/40 Part I (1993), para. 245 (Iran); A/48/40 Part I (1993), paras. 193, 245 and 669 (Egypt). See furthermore: CEDAW Committee, *e.g.*: A/52/38/Rev.1 part II (1997), 87 at para. 157 (Israel); CRC Committee, *e.g.*: CRC/C/121 (2002) 131 at paras. 560–561 and 576 (Israel); CRC, CRC/C/97 (2000) 8 at para. 27 (Iran); and CERD Committee, *e.g.*: CERD, A/60/18 (2005) 54 at para. 295 (Nigeria). Interestingly, within the European context, the European Court of Human Rights has taken a firm stance against a system of parallel jurisdictions that "would introduce into all legal relationships a distinction between individuals grounded on religion". See ECtHR, *Refah Partisi (the Welfare Party) and Others v. Turkey*, (Grand Chamber Judgement), Application Nos. 41340/98, 41342/98, 41343/98 and 41344/98, Judgement of 13 February 2003, para. 119 (Grand Chamber citing and endorsing the conclusions reached by the Chamber).

It is worth reiterating at this point that none of these systemic concerns imply a rejection of the notion of religious laws as such. Individuals are in principle free to observe religious laws (in so far as doing so does not negatively affect the rights and freedoms of others).[102] These systemic objections rather amount to a dismissal of *state* intervention with the issue of observance of religious laws. The fact that someone considers him or herself an adherent of a certain religion does not amount to consent on his or her part to be subjected to the entire set of religious laws and principles that have traditionally accompanied the religion in question. This holds true regardless of the fact of whether one is only a nominal member (i.e. someone who is 'born into the religion' and considers him or herself religious on that basis), a more active member, or someone who deliberately converted into the religion in question. Furthermore, the act of marriage should not be construed as a waiver of women's equal rights, particularly considering the fact that civil marriage is often not an alternative in religious states.[103] In short, states may not rely on norms of human rights law, primarily the right to freedom of religion or belief as enjoyed by persons or religious groups, to justify instances of discrimination against certain groups, notably religious minorities and women.[104]

Finally, it must be pointed out that even in situations where the state has adopted, alongside measures that allow the different religious communities to enforce their own religious family laws, national uniform regulations on the same issue which the different religious communities are free to adopt (one could think of the 'uniform civil law' discourse that has emerged in India in recent decades), there is still some cause for concern. The fact remains that individuals within these communities may face obstacles in opting for the national regulation (thus ignoring the religious laws) on account of pressure from within the religious communities. People who opt to be subjected to the national regulations in so doing make public the fact that they prefer secular laws over abiding by the religious precepts identified by his or her religious

[102] The content-based concerns raised in the previous sections imply that interpretations of religious laws that would negatively affect the rights and freedoms of women or religious minorities may not be freely observed. This is fully in line with international human rights law: the freedom to manifest one's religion or belief may be limited if such is necessary to protect the fundamental rights and freedoms of others (art. 18, para. 3, of the ICCPR). Arguably, the state is not merely entitled to apply restrictions in this field but actually obliged. See, *e.g.*, artt. 2–3 of the ICCPR; art. 2, para. (f), of CEDAW; and art. 4 of the UN Religious Tolerance Declaration (1981).

[103] Cf. Raday, *supra* note 4, pp. 214–215, commenting on the situation in Israel. See also, *mutatis mutandis*, Human Rights Committee, General Comment 28, para. 21, explaining that freedom of religion or belief may not be relied upon to justify discrimination against women.

[104] Cf. Human Rights Committee, General Comment 28, para. 31; and Human Rights Committee, *Sandra Lovelace v. Canada*, Communication No. R.6/24 of 29 December 1977, U.N. Doc. Supp. No. 40 (A/36/40) at 166 (1981), para. 16: "Article 27 [of the ICCPR: minority rights] must be construed and applied in the light of the…the provisions against discrimination, such as articles 2, 3 and 26 [of the ICCPR], as the case may be."

community. In short, equality rights and particularly arguments based on equal access to the law would suggest that the introduction of a uniform civil code must always supersede altogether the system of sectarian parallel jurisdictions.

8.3.3 *Transparency, Legal Certainty and Checks & Balances*

The maxim that everyone ought to know the law is a legal fiction. Having said that, uniform codes of law are immeasurably more transparent than any set of religious laws, which as a rule lack a universally accepted version, which ever since their initial conception have stirred controversy amongst religio-legal scholars over their exact interpretation (hence the distinct religio-legal schools of thought),[105] and which consequently bestow upon (religious) courts a significant level of discretion.[106] In short, national uniform codes of law foster transparency and legal certainty and are, moreover, infinitely more democratic.[107] At least within a framework of competitive politics, typically, representatives of different sections of the populations are involved and consulted in the process of codifying state laws. Of course, in practice there may still be a risk, particularly in states with an overwhelming religious majority, that lawmakers or judges yield to religious principles deriving from the dominant religion (e.g. Tunisia).[108] This risk in itself does not affect the value of adopting uniform state laws (moreover, below it will be demonstrated that human rights law identifies a range of measures that may minimize this risk).[109] The codification and application of uniform laws, naturally, fosters a system based on 'checks and balances', meaning a system based on the ideal that different state bodies keep each other in check in terms of the limitations to their powers. Particularly in states with a judicial system that is characterized by the possibility of a Constitutional or Supreme Court examining adopted laws in light of constitutional principles (including

---

[105] See for instance the different schools of thought mentioned in Chapter 2, note 146, *supra*.

[106] See Human Rights Committee, *e.g.*: A/48/40 vol. I (1993) 44 at para. 253 (Iran); CCPR/C/SR.366(1982), 4 at para. 15. It could be argued, moreover, that those states that instruct (religious) courts to apply religious laws also to criminal matters violate basic safeguards (*e.g. nullum crimen sine lege*, see art. 15 of the ICCPR, etc.) surrounding the application of norms of criminal law on account of the lack of transparency and predictability of (unwritten) norms of religious criminal law.

[107] See also the views of UN treaty monitoring bodies, *supra* note 101.

[108] Cf. Mayer, *supra* note 11, pp. 143–144. Tunisia has adopted a national code (Tunisian Code of Personal Status 1956) on family law and personal status matters which applies to all citizens, which as such is rather unique within the Muslim world and which in practice means that Tunisia has countered some of the traditional practices of inequality vis-à-vis women and religious minorities. However, the Code may still be criticized as it in many respects draws exclusively on, and is in practice often interpreted in light of, Sharia principles.

[109] See Chapter 11 on such principles as the equal right to vote, the prohibition of predetermining a religion–law nexus, the prohibition of reserving political seats for the dominant religion, and the prohibition of posing religious qualifications for holding public office. It will be clear, at the same time, that compliance with these principles presupposes at least a degree of commitment to the equality principle on the part of the state.

fundamental rights) or even directly in light of norms of international human rights law,[110] the codification and application of uniform laws is bound to foster human rights compliance in many ways.

8.4 Religious Reservations to Norms of International Human Rights Law

Thus far it has been explained how strictly religious states apply sets of religious laws to certain areas of domestic public policy. Some religious states have 'internationalized' this approach in that the state's commitment to religious laws also determines the state's policy towards the implementation of norms of international law. As to the field of international human rights law specifically, this is characterized by reservations that are entered to rights and principles enshrined in international human rights covenants.[111] An important caveat in this context is that strict adherence to religious rules and doctrine does not necessarily stem from religious zealotry: political opportunism—incentives to preserve the (patriarchal) status quo—is an important factor in this context as well, if not the most important factor. The work of Ann Elizabeth Mayer has clarified that there is no monolithic conception of Islamic law and, second, that this body of law, as formulated by pre-modern (male) jurists, is often protected and exploited by contemporary (male) state officials in a rather opportunistic fashion.[112] If there was such a thing as a monolithic conception of Islam and Islamic law then one would assume that these norms would neatly translate into a uniform attitude towards norms and principles of international law. The fact that some Islamic states have entered reservations to human rights treaties and others have not and the fact that, looking at the precise nature of religious reservations, many differences among states can be discerned, manifests that entering these reservations is above all a matter of politics.

Having said that, the fact remains that in those states that identify strongly with a single religion there is an evident risk that religious norms are construed (by the powers that be) so as to create possibilities of derogating from the norms of international human rights law. These 'religious reservations' can be concrete and thereby leave room for compliance with other provisions.[113]

---

110 The latter largely depends on whether the state has adopted a so-called monist or dualist approach to norms enshrined in international law.

111 See sec. II of the Vienna Convention on the Law of Treaties, on the issue of reservations.

112 For references to Mayer's work, and to the recent, detailed study by Abiad, see *supra*, note 17.

113 *E.g.* Kuwait's reservation to art. 21 (adoption) of the Convention on the Rights of the Child, G.A. res. 44/25, annex, 44 U.N. GAOR Supp. (No. 49) at 167, U.N. Doc. A/44/49, of 20 November 1989 (entered into force: 2 September 1990) [hereinafter: CRC]: "The State of Kuwait, as it adheres to the provisions of the Islamic Shariah as the main source of legislation, strictly bans abandoning the Islamic religion and does not therefore approve adoption."

Religious reservations, however, are sometimes of such general or vague nature that the entire treaty is undermined as the question of compliance with human rights law becomes a matter of political discretion.[114] The latter type of sweeping reservations is objectionable and generally can and should be dismissed as incompatible with the object and purpose of the human rights treaty in question.[115] Religious reservations to a treaty's principal state obligations are, naturally, always contrary to object and purpose of the treaty.[116] This explains the large number of official objections expressed by other states with regard to these sweeping religious reservations as well as the many concerns raised by the treaty monitoring bodies in question.[117]

Religious reservations can be subdivided into the following categories:

- Religious reservations to (the full implications of) the right to freedom of religion or belief (Bahrain, Iraq, Jordan, Maldives, Mauritania, Oman, Syria, United Arab Emirates);[118]
- Religious reservations to equality rights (Bahrain, Bangladesh, Egypt, Iraq, Israel, Kuwait, Libya, Malaysia, Maldives, Morocco and Qatar);[119]

---

[114] See also Mayer, *supra* note 17, p. 91 (on Shari'a reservations specifically).

[115] Cf. art. 19, para. (c), of the Vienna Convention on the Law of Treaties.

[116] *E.g.* Bahrain's reservations to art. 2 and 16 of CEDAW; Bangladesh's reservation to art. 2 of CEDAW; Egypt's reservations to artt. 2 and 16 of CEDAW; Iraq's reservations to artt. 2 and 16 of CEDAW; Morocco's reservations to artt. 2 and 16 of CEDAW; and Maldives' reservation to art. 16 of CEDAW.

[117] To give just one example, Austria has objected to Maldives' reservation entered to CEDAW upon acceding and rightly considered that the "reservation made by the Maldives is incompatible with the object and purpose of the Convention and is therefore inadmissible under article 19 (c) of the Vienna Convention on the Law of Treaties...Austria therefore states that this reservation cannot alter or modify in any respect the obligations arising from the Convention for any State Party thereto." The berated reservation holds that "[t]he Government of the Republic of Maldives reserves its right to apply article 16 of [CEDAW] concerning the equality of men and women in all matters relating to marriage and family relations without prejudice to the provisions of the Islamic Sharia, which govern all marital and family relations of the 100 percent Muslim population of the Maldives." Dozens of official protests, similar to the quoted one, can be discerned in relation to religious reservations to the different UN human rights covenants. The Human Rights Committee is of the opinion – contested by some states – that it falls to the Committee to determine whether a specific reservation is compatible with the object and purpose of the Covenant. In that role, it will also look into objections to a reservation made by States. See Human Rights Committee, *General Comment No. 24: Issues relating to reservations made upon ratification or accession to the Covenant or the Optional Protocols thereto, or in relation to declarations under article 41 of the Covenant*, CCPR/C/21/Rev.1/Add.6, of 4 November 1994, particularly paras. 17–18. In fact, in their Concluding Observations, the different UN treaty monitoring bodies have indeed repeatedly pointed out that certain religious reservations are incompatible with the object and purpose of the Covenant in question, *e.g.*: A/60/38 part II (2005) 129 at paras. 245–246 (Israel's reservations to CEDAW); CRC/C/97 (2000) 31 at paras. 158–159 (Jordan's reservations to CRC); CRC/C/111 (2001) 36 at paras. 156–157 (Oman's reservations to CRC); CRC/C/118 (2002) 90 at paras. 371–372 (UAE's reservations to CRC); CRC/C/132 (2003) 116 at paras. 533–534 (Syria's reservations to CRC); CRC/C/133 (2003) 93 at paras. 442–443 (Bangladesh's reservations to CRC).

[118] See Bahrain's and Mauritania's reservations to art. 18 of the ICCPR; see Iraq's, Jordan's, Maldives', Oman's, Syria's and UAE's reservations to art. 14 of CRC (children's right to freedom of religion or belief).

[119] See Bahrain's reservation to art. 3 of the ICCPR (equal protection of Covenant rights) and Bahrain's reservations to art. 2 (state duties to ensure equality between men and women) and 16

- Religious reservations which make leeway for derogation from the Covenant in case of incompatibility between Covenant rights (notably the equal right to marry and found a family) and religious family or personal status laws (Bahrain, Israel, Kuwait, Mauritania and Qatar);[120]
- Generic Shari'a/Islamic principles reservations (Brunei Darussalam: CEDAW and CRC;[121] Iran: CRC;[122] Mauritania: CEDAW and CRC;[123] Oman: CRC;[124] Qatar: CRC and CAT;[125] Saudi Arabia: CERD and CRC[126]).

(equality of men and women in all matters relating to marriage and family relations) of CEDAW; Bangladesh's reservation to art. 2 of CEDAW; Egypt's reservations to artt. 2 and 16 of CEDAW; Israel's first reservation to art. 7, para. (b), of CEDAW (equality between men and women to hold public office and perform all public functions at all levels of government; Israel entered this reservation so as to sanction the practice of barring women from functioning as judges on religious courts); Iraq's reservations to art. 2, paras. (f) and (g), art. 9 (women's equal rights to acquire, change or retain their nationality and women's equal rights with respect to the nationality of their children), and art. 16 of CEDAW; Kuwait's reservation to art. 16, para. (f), of CEDAW (equal rights with regard to guardianship, wardship, trusteeship and adoption of children); Libya's reservation to art. 2 and artt. 16, paras. (c) and (d), of CEDAW; Malaysia's reservations to art. 5, 7 and 16 (partially withdrawn in 1998) of CEDAW; Maldives' reservations to art. 7, para. (a) (equal rights as regards eligibility for election to all publicly elected bodies; which reservation is entered to ensure that the President of Maldives will be male) and art. 16 of CEDAW; Morocco's reservations to artt. 2 and 16 of CEDAW; Qatar's reservations to artt. 2, 9, 15 and 16 of CEDAW.

[120] Which in practice largely boils down to a reservation to the equality principle proper (see previous item). See Bahrain's, Israel's, Kuwait's and Mauritania's reservations to art. 23 of the ICCPR. See also Israel's second reservation to CEDAW, regarding article 16; and Qatar's reservation to art. 15 of CEDAW.

[121] Brunei's reservation to CEDAW reads: "The Government of Brunei Darussalam expresses its reservations regarding those provisions of the said Convention that may be contrary to the Constitution of Brunei Darussalam and to the beliefs and principles of Islam, the official religion of Brunei Darussalam..."; its reservation to CRC reads: "[The Government of Brunei Darussalam] expresses its reservations on the provisions of the said Convention which may be contrary to the Constitution of Brunei Darussalam and to the beliefs and principles of Islam, the State, religion...".

[122] Iran's reservation to CRC reads: "The Government of the Islamic Republic of Iran reserves the right not to apply any provisions or articles of the Convention that are incompatible with Islamic Laws and the international legislation in effect."

[123] Mauritania's reservation to CEDAW reads: "have approved and do approve it in each and every one of its parts which are not contrary to Islamic Sharia and are in accordance with our Constitution..."; its reservation to CRC reads: "In signing this important Convention, the Islamic Republic of Mauritania is making reservations to articles or provisions which may be contrary to the beliefs and values of Islam, the religion of the Mauritania People and State."

[124] Oman's second reservation to CRC reads: "A reservation is entered to all the provisions of the Convention that do not accord with Islamic law or the legislation in force in the Sultanate".

[125] Convention against Torture and Other Cruel, Inhuman or Degrading Treatment or Punishment, G.A. Res. 39/46, annex, 39 U.N. GAOR Supp. (No. 51) at 197, U.N. Doc. A/39/51 (1984), of 10 December 1984 (entry into force: 26 June 1987) [also referred to as CAT]. Qatar's reservation reads: "Any interpretation of the provisions of the Convention that is incompatible with the precepts of Islamic law and the Islamic religion...". Qatar's reservation to CRC reads: "[The State of Qatar] enters a general reservation...concerning provisions incompatible with Islamic Law."

[126] Saudi Arabia's reservation to the International Convention on the Elimination of All Forms of Racial Discrimination, G.A. res. 2106 (XX), Annex, 20 U.N. GAOR Supp. (No. 14) at 47, U.N. Doc. A/6014 (1966), 660 U.N.T.S. 195, of 21 December 1965 (entered into force: 4 January 1969) [hereinafter: CERD] reads: "[The Government of Saudi Arabia declares that it will] implement the provisions [of the above Convention], providing these do not conflict with

Finally, it should be observed that more indirect or covert religious reservations can be discerned as well. For instance, Maldives has entered a reservation to the ICCPR that reads: "[t]he application of the principles set out in Article 18 [the right to freedom of religion or belief] of the Covenant shall be without prejudice to the Constitution of the Republic of Maldives." It is only when we acknowledge the fact that this Constitution, firstly, states that the Maldives shall be a "state based on Islam" and that "the official religion shall be Islam", and, secondly, does not actually contain a right to freedom of religion or belief, that we can appreciate the nature and extent of this reservation.[127]

8.5 Conclusion

The human rights discipline has been much concerned with certain interpretations of religious laws that in practice negatively affect primarily the rights of women and religious minorities. These problems and the processes in which they manifest themselves have been concisely charted in the first part of this Chapter. The latter part of the Chapter attempted to add some new elements to this debate. It is contended that, on top of the substantive concerns, a series of more fundamental human rights issues surround and characterize the very systems of domestic political organization that are premised on state enforcement of religious laws. These systemic objections amount to a dismissal of state intervention with the issue of observance of religious laws. These fundamental concerns are based on the notions of: (i) freedom *from* religion; (ii) equality before the law; and (iii) transparency, legal certainty and checks & balances.

It must be emphasized that none of the systemic concerns are intended to prejudice processes of reforming religious laws, from within the religious communities, in accordance with reinterpretations by legal-religious scholars and on the basis of content-based criticisms. The two discourses can be further developed simultaneously and doing so will in fact have a mutually reinforcing effect: reforming prevalent interpretations of religious laws so as to bring them more in line with equality rights of women and religious minorities benefits from gradually disentangling religious laws from state authority as the centre of gravity for enforcement, and vice versa.

---

the precepts of the Islamic Shariah"; its reservation to CRC reads: "[The Government of Saudi Arabia enters] reservations with respect to all such articles as are in conflict with the provisions of Islamic law."

[127] See also Pakistan's reservation to the International Covenant on Economic, Social and Cultural Rights, G.A. res. 2200A (XXI), 21 U.N.GAOR Supp. (No. 16) at 49, U.N. Doc. A/6316 (1966), 993 U.N.T.S. 3, of 16 December 1966 (entered into force: 3 January 1976) [hereinafter: ICESCR].

In this Chapter an active role for the state as enforcer of religious laws has been firmly dismissed. However, nothing in this Chapter is intended to argue in favour of banning religion altogether from the public realm. It will be discussed in Chapter 11 that as far as human rights law is concerned, it is not necessary or desirable and, more importantly, not permitted for the state to pro-actively eradicate religion from the political discourse. In that respect, it will at the same time be shown that certain pitfalls need to be avoided and that crucial constitutional safeguards must be in place to prevent the adoption of laws which discriminate on the ground of religion or belief.

CHAPTER NINE

STATE ENTANGLEMENT WITH RELIGION & THE EQUAL RELIGIOUS RIGHTS OF OTHERS, FREEDOM OF EXPRESSION, FREEDOM OF ASSOCIATION AND EQUAL EMPLOYMENT OPPORTUNITIES

9.1 Introduction

The issue of state interference with the observance of religious laws merited separate discussion as human rights violations surrounding this issue clearly have a special origin and often can be said to be of a distinct nature. We have seen that those forms of state practice that are characterized by a direct commitment to upholding religious laws are as a rule particularly at odds with international standards on the rights and freedoms of women and religious minorities (including non-believers). The objective of this Chapter is to further substantiate the claim (which was made in the conclusion of Chapter 7) that most, if not all, of the states that are officially entangled with a single religion—including the states that do, but also including many states that do not, actively interfere with the observance of religious laws—fail to fully comply with the principle that no one should be treated differently because of one's religion or belief. It will be demonstrated, firstly, that the large majority of existing regimes of positive state identification with a religion are not devoid of forms of institutionalised discrimination or *de facto* practices of discrimination on the ground of religion or belief (or lack thereof). This claim will be substantiated by carrying out a range of thematic case studies on, among other issues, Establishment of Religion & the 'Equal Religious Rights of Others', Religion & Freedom of Expression, Religion & Freedom of Association and Religion & Equal Employment Opportunities.

Secondly, it will be equally highlighted that in some secular or separationist states the ideals of state secularism and separationism have come to be considered ends in themselves. That is to say, these principles are not merely used instrumentally so as to enhance other values such as democracy or human rights protection but have become important yardsticks for public policy as such. This has given rise to situations where the principles of secularism and separationism are construed so as to impose special—and occasionally unacceptable—limits on the activities of religions (principally in the field of organizational freedom of religious organizations) or special limits on the manifestation of certain beliefs (principally in the field of the freedom to manifest a religion itself, the field of conscientious objections, and the field of 'Politics and Religion'). The issues of 'Religion & Education' and 'Religion & Politics' will be discussed in separate Chapters (10–11), partly because the human rights questions that emerge in these fields are of a different nature and partly because the key to preventing and redressing most of the, thus far, indicated human rights issues are to be found in these two fields.

9.2 Establishment of Religion & the Equal Religious Rights of Members of Other Religions

The relevant, ultimate ramifications of human rights law, as argued throughout this study, are: (i) the right to freedom of religion or belief empowers people (not states) to freely choose and practice a religion or belief; and (ii) no one should be treated differently because of one's religion or belief.[1] The latter implies that if the state grants certain forms of support or privileges to some religious believers it should, unless there are 'reasonable and objective' criteria that justify otherwise, make those privileges available to others as well. If we take these two notions, freedom of religion and non-discrimination on the basis of religion, in conjunction, we may speak of 'equal religious rights'. In this section it is demonstrated that the practice of many states that are officially entangled with religion is characterized by encroachments upon people's equal religious rights. In other words, regimes of positive state identification with religion are surrounded by practices that directly restrict people's right to freedom of religion or belief; or by practices that amount to a form of exclusive support to one religion (putting non-dominant or non-traditional religions at a disadvantage), or by both.

9.2.1 *Establishment of Religion & Limited Domestic Conceptions of the Right to Freedom of Religion and Belief*

The international standards on the right to freedom of religion or belief as enshrined in the UN *International Covenant on Civil and Political Rights* are as follows:

> 1. Everyone shall have the right to freedom of thought, conscience and religion. This right shall include freedom to have or to adopt a religion or belief of his choice, and freedom, either individually or in community with others and in public or private, to manifest his religion or belief in worship, observance, practice and teaching.
> 2. No one shall be subject to coercion which would impair his freedom to have or to adopt a religion or belief of his choice.

[1] Artt. 18 and 26 of the ICCPR.

3. Freedom to manifest one's religion or beliefs may be subject only to such limitations as are prescribed by law and are necessary to protect public safety, order, health, or morals or the fundamental rights and freedoms of others…[2]

The first freedom, the freedom to "have or to adopt" a religion or belief or to not have or adopt a religion, must be afforded unconditionally. Theistic, non-theistic, atheistic, traditional and newly established religions or beliefs equally qualify for the protection offered by the right to freedom of religion or belief.[3] The manifestation of one's religion or belief is not an absolute freedom. However, restrictions must be prescribed by law and must be necessary to protect public safety, order, health, morals or the fundamental rights and freedoms of others, which is an exhaustive list of grounds for limitation.[4] All state parties to the ICCPR must ensure that the right to freedom of religion or belief is appropriately enshrined in domestic legislation and also otherwise appropriately 'internalized'.[5] Presently, the focus will be on the legal transposition and internalization of the freedom of religion or belief clause itself. In the context of internalizing the right to freedom of religion or belief, a range of different shortcomings come to the fore. We can distinguish between:

(i) The complete absence of a domestic right;
(ii) Freedom of religion is not recognized as a *universal* right;
(iii) Codification of too limited a notion of 'freedom of worship;'
(iv) Domestic clauses compare unfavourably to international standards in that they omit one of the fundamental freedoms this right encompasses (i.e. the *forum internum* or the *forum externum*);
(v) The failure to recognize a right to conscientious objection;
(vi) 'Religion' as such functions as a ground for limitation;
(vii) The freedom of religion clause does not lead to the annulment of (discriminatory) bans on proselytism;

---

[2] Art. 18, paras. (1)–(3), of the ICCPR. See also article 18 of the Universal Declaration of Human Rights (1948).

[3] Human Rights Committee, General Comment 22, para. 2, in which paragraph the Committee furthermore considers that the "terms 'belief' and 'religion' are to be broadly construed". This means first of all that, for art. 18 to be applicable, it is irrelevant whether the religion in question is of a theistic or secular nature. It is also irrelevant whether a religion is traditional or newly established or whether it has many adherents or just a few. Having said that, not every conceivable belief constitutes a "belief" in the sense of article 18. The Human Rights Committee deemed that a belief that consists primarily or exclusively in the worship and distribution of marijuana cannot be brought within the scope of article 18. See Human Rights Committee, *M.A.B., W.A.T. and J.-A.Y.T. v. Canada*, Communication No. 570/1993, U.N.Doc. CCPR/C/50/D/570/1993, decision of 8 April 1994.

[4] Human Rights Committee, General Comment 22, para. 8.

[5] See art. 2, para. (2), of the ICCPR. See also Human Rights Committee, *General Comment 31: Nature of the General Legal Obligation on States Parties to the Covenant*, U.N. Doc. CCPR/C/21/Rev.1/Add.13 (2004), para. 7. Over 160 (and over 85 per cent of the total of UN Member States) states are party to the ICCPR.

(viii) The freedom of religion clause does not, in practice, lead to the annulment of measures that give rise to a legal duty to reveal one's religious affiliation;
(ix) Certain illegitimate (secular) restrictions on this right can be discerned at the more secular end of the state–religion identification spectrum.

(i) *Freedom of Religion or Belief Not Constitutionally Protected*

Some states have not domestically codified a right to freedom of religion or belief: Algeria, Comoros, Maldives, Mauritania, Saudi Arabia, Somalia, Vatican City and Yemen.[6] Algeria has adopted an ordinance in 2006 which affirms a limited right to freedom of religion for Muslims and which largely restricts this right for non-Muslims.[7] The lack of recognition of a right to freedom of religion or belief by the Maldives means in practice that all citizens are automatically considered Muslim and barred from exercising other religions. Under the recently adopted Constitution, non-Muslims cannot obtain citizenship status. Converting away from Islam may thus result in the loss of citizenship.[8]

(ii) *Freedom of Religion or Belief as a Non-Universal Right*

Incompatible domestic freedom of religion or belief clauses should, naturally, be distinguished from the complete absence of a domestic right to freedom of religion or belief. In that respect, it should be observed, first of all, that incompatible domestic freedom of religion of belief clauses can be discerned across the board. That is to say, domestic freedom of religion or belief provisions that notably deviate from the international standards are clearly visible under the religious extreme of the state–religion identification spectrum, whilst such deviations can also be discerned under the intermediate and more secular parts of the spectrum. Having said that, different types and different degrees of deviation can be discerned. States with a positive identification with religion tend to reflect substantive shortcomings that predominantly consist of the denial of one of the two fundamental religious freedoms guaranteed by international human rights law (the *forum internum* or the *forum externum*). Secular states and other non-religious states on the other hand do, as a rule, recognize both freedoms: the freedom to have or adopt a religion or belief (often explicitly including the right to change) as well as the freedom to manifest a religion

[6] Comoros, Saudi Arabia and the Vatican City are not party to the ICCPR.
[7] Ordinance 06-03 of 20 March 2006.
[8] Art. 9 of the Const. of Maldives (2008): "a non-Muslim may not become a citizen of the Maldives." The Human Rights Committee furthermore identifies Kuwait as a state where conversion may result in the loss of nationality: A/55/40 vol. I (2000) 65 at paras. 483–484 (Kuwait). Saudi Arabia's citizens, too, are *de jure* automatically considered Muslims.

or belief. These states, however, tend to permit (secular) grounds for limitation that are not enumerated in international human rights law.[9]

Clearly, a distressing shortcoming of a domestic freedom of religion or belief clause occurs if the right is not considered universally applicable to everyone. International human rights law as a rule provides guarantees to every person present in a country.[10] In previous chapters we have already seen some examples of states that constitutionally grant freedom of religion or belief to some yet not all religious groups present in the country. Iran, for instance, only tolerates—aside from the Islamic branches or schools of thought that deviate from the state-sanctioned orthodoxy (i.e. the Twelver Shi'a branch)[11]—Zoroastrian, Jewish and Christian communities.[12] It is clear, by implication, that Bahá'ís and non-believers are deprived of religious rights or the right not to believe respectively. The persecution of Bahá'ís in other countries, particularly Brunei Darussalam, Egypt, Iraq and Afghanistan, reflects a similar non-universal conception of the right to freedom of religion or belief.[13] Similarly, Pakistan's official persecution of the Ahmadis shows that freedom of religion or belief is applied selectively by this state.[14] Some states deny citizenship status to adherents of specific religions, including: Eritrea (Jehovah's Witnesses) and Burma (Rohingya Muslims).[15]

(iii) *'Freedom of Worship'*

'Freedom of worship' is too narrow an interpretation of the right to freedom of religion or belief for two reasons: (i) 'freedom of worship' does not sufficiently recognize the right to adopt a secular belief or life stance; and (ii) worship is merely one possible way in which one may give expression to one's faith. The freedom to manifest one's religion or belief under international human rights law covers a broad range of acts, namely: worship, observance, practice and teaching.[16] The Human Rights Committee has elaborated on these four categories as follows:

---

[9] See discussion in sub-section (ix), *infra*.

[10] Certain civil/political rights apply only to citizens.

[11] Art. 12 of the Const. of Iran (1979) provides: "Other Islamic schools [than the Twelver school] are to be accorded full respect, and their followers are free to act in accordance with their own jurisprudence in performing their religious rites."

[12] Art. 13 of the Const. of Iran (1979). See Chapter 8, section 8.2.3, *supra*, on the fact that the status of these minorities does by no means equate to the status of Muslims.

[13] The Bahá'í faith and Wahhabism are outlawed in Iraq as per Law No. 105 of 1970 and Revolutionary Command Council Resolution 201/2001 (which mandates the death penalty) respectively.

[14] See Chapter 8, section 8.2.2, *supra*.

[15] Egypt, until recently, could have been added to this list as Bahá'ís used to be barred from obtaining ID cards. Recent developments show that some welcome and long overdue reforms are being implemented. See sub-section (viii), *infra*.

[16] Art. 18, para. (1), of the ICCPR.

> The concept of worship extends to ritual and ceremonial acts giving direct expression to belief, as well as various practices integral to such acts, including the building of places of worship, the use of ritual formulae and objects, the display of symbols, and the observance of holidays and days of rest. The observance and practice of religion or belief may include not only ceremonial acts but also such customs as the observance of dietary regulations, the wearing of distinctive clothing or headcoverings, participation in rituals associated with certain stages of life, and the use of a particular language customarily spoken by a group. In addition, the practice and teaching of religion or belief includes acts integral to the conduct by religious groups of their basic affairs, such as the freedom to choose their religious leaders, priests and teachers, the freedom to establish seminaries or religious schools and the freedom to prepare and distribute religious texts or publications.[17]

In sum, under international human rights law everyone has the right to have or to adopt a religion *or belief* and to manifest this religion in worship as well as *observance, practice and teaching.* A constitutional clause codifying a right to worship falls short of the international standards. States that constitutionally delimit the right to freedom of religion or belief to a 'freedom of worship' include: Bahrain ("inviolability of worship");[18] Costa Rica ("free exercise of… forms of worship that are not opposed to universal morality or good customs"),[19] Indonesia ("freedom of worship"),[20] Jordan ("free exercise of all forms of worship and religious rites"),[21] Malta ("free exercise of…religious worship")[22] and Morocco ("freedom of worship for all").[23] The freedom of worship of God (Denmark)[24] is arguably even narrower as it does not only exclude secular beliefs but also those religious believers that do not belong to a theistic religion.[25]

---

[17] Human Rights Committee, General Comment 22, para. 4.

[18] Art. 22 of the Const. of Bahrain (2002).

[19] Art. 75 of the Const. of Costa Rica (1949); which has been criticized by the Human Rights Committee: U.N. Doc. A/35/40 (1980), para. 347.

[20] Art. 29, para. (2), of the Const. of Indonesia (1945).

[21] Art. 14 of the Const. of Jordan (1952).

[22] Art. 40, para. (1), of the Const. of Malta (1964).

[23] Art. 6 of the Const. of Morocco (1972). Laos, finally, has not – despite having ratified the ICCPR recently (September 2009) – yet codified a proper freedom to manifest provision (see art. 30 of the Const. of Laos of 1991) either. Leaving out the *forum externum* appears not to be an unintentional omission, considering the fact that state practice shows that Laos actively limits the free exercise of particularly non-Buddhist beliefs. A Decree on Religious Activity envisages a system of state control over religious activity in Laos: public manifestations of religion or belief need official approval. Buddhism, however, is exempted from this rule. See Prime Ministerial Decree No. 92 of 5 July 2002 on the Administration and Protection of Religious Activities in Lao PDR.

[24] Art. 67 of the Const. of Denmark (1953): "The citizens shall be entitled to form congregations for the worship of God in a manner consistent with their convictions, provided that nothing at variance with good morals or public order shall be taught or done."

[25] The scope of this right has been questioned by the Human Rights Committee: U.N. Doc. A/43/40 (1988), para. 181 (Denmark). To appreciate the difference between 'freedom of worship of God' and the broader 'freedom of worship' it is important to point out that 'worship' can be defined as "[t]he offering of devotion, praise, and adoration to that which is deemed worthy of such offering" (Oxford Dictionary of World Religions, p. 1045). In other words, not

(iv) *Freedom to Manifest Only: No 'Freedom to Have or Adopt'*

Religious states, naturally, take an active interest in the preservation and further spread of the predominant religion. Compliance with the right to freedom of religion or belief is only partially beneficial to that objective. This acknowledgment appears to have the following ramifications in practice. People that are born into the predominant religion, naturally, ought to be completely free to exercise this religion. The co-existence of small religious minorities is not necessarily to be firmly opposed by the state. The conversion of adherents of the other, non-dominant religions *into* the dominant religion is encouraged or is at least not officially discouraged. On the other hand, conversions *away* from the predominant religion are certainly not in the interest of a religious state and are, therefore, to be discouraged. This also means that proselytism of religious minorities by members of the dominant religion is to be allowed, yet, vice versa strongly discouraged or prohibited (see below).

It is for these reasons that freedom of religion or belief in some religious states has come to mean, officially or *de facto*, that everyone is free to exercise the religion one is 'born into'. This clearly is a very narrow interpretation of the right to freedom of religion or belief. Governments must allow conversions away from the dominant religion.[26] A good example of a constitutional formulation of the freedom of religion or belief principle that solely reflects the *forum externum* can be found in Oman's Constitution:

> The freedom to practise religious rites in accordance with recognised customs is guaranteed provided that it does not disrupt public order or conflict with accepted standards of behaviour.[27]

Similar domestic formulations of the freedom of religion or belief clause that one-sidedly emphasize everyone's freedom to exercise a religion (and omit the freedom to have/adopt a religion and hence the freedom to convert), may be observed in: Iraq,[28] Kuwait,[29] Norway,[30] Qatar[31] and the United Arab

---

only a Deity, but also other notions may be worshipped, such as religious founders/leaders in non-theistic religious traditions, or ancestors, spirits, animals, artefacts, etc., which can be observed in some religio-cultural traditions.

[26] The fact that domestic freedom of religion or belief clauses should include or at least permit the freedom to change one's religion has been consistently emphasized by the Human Rights Committee, *e.g.*: A/48/40 vol. I (1993) 44, para. 263 (Iran)(by implication); A/49/40 vol. I (1994) 41 at para. 235 (Jordan); A/55/40 vol. I (2000) 24 at para. 117 (Morocco); A/55/40 vol. I (2000) 65 at para. 483 (Kuwait)(by implication); A/57/40 vol. I (2002) 72 at para. 83(20) (Yemen); A/60/40 vol. I (2004) 35 at para. 84(21) (Morocco); A/60/40 vol. I (2005) 65 at para. 91(18) (Yemen). See also CERD Committee: A/49/18 (1994) 68, para. 473 (Sudan).

[27] Art. 28 of the Basic Law of the Sultanate of Oman (1996). Oman is not a party to the ICCPR.

[28] Art. 41 of the Const. of Iraq (2005).

[29] Art. 35 of the Const. of Kuwait (1962).

[30] Art. 2, para. (1), of the Const. of Norway (1814): "All inhabitants of the Realm shall have the right to free exercise of their religion".

[31] Art. 50 of the Const. of Qatar (2003). Qatar is not a party to the ICCPR.

Emirates.[32] Particularly the Governments of Kuwait and Qatar, in practice, inhibit conversions away from Islam. The absence of the *forum internum* in the Norwegian Constitution is perhaps less surprising when one considers that Norway explicitly demands that the "inhabitants professing [the Evangelical-Lutheran state religion] are bound to bring up their children in the same."[33]

(v) *Failure to Recognize the Right to Conscientious Objections*

The Human Rights Committee was initially reluctant to accept that a right to conscientious objection to military service flows from the right to freedom of thought, conscience and religion.[34] However, particularly due to political pressure from within the former UN Commission on Human Rights this right received recognition within the UN human rights system in the late 1980s.[35] The Human Rights Committee eventually made a U-turn and recognized this right in 1993:

> Many individuals have claimed the right to refuse to perform military service (conscientious objection) on the basis that such right derives from their freedoms under article 18 [freedom of religion or belief]. In response to such claims, a growing number of States have in their laws exempted from compulsory military

---

[32] Art. 32 of the CONST. OF THE UNITED ARAB EMIRATES (1971). UAE is not a party to the ICCPR.

[33] Art. 2, para (2), of the CONST. OF NORWAY (1814). This provision, it goes without saying, in itself runs counter to fundamental norms of human rights law. See Human Rights Committee, CCPR/C/NOR/CO/5 (2006), para. 15 (Norway). See also Chapter 10, section 10.2.1, *infra*.

[34] *E.g.* Human Rights Committee, *L. T. K. v. Finland*, Communication No. 185/1984, U.N. Doc. CCPR/C/OP/2 at 61 (1990), para. 5.2; and Human Rights Committee *Aapo Järvinen v. Finland*, Communication No. 295/1988, U.N. Doc. CCPR/C/39/D/295/1988 (1990), para. 6.2. Art. 8, para. (3)(c)(ii), of the ICCPR speaks of "countries where conscientious objection is recognized" (in the context of exempting alternative service from the scope of the provisions on forced and compulsory labour), which the Human rights Committee initially took to mean (by implication) that the Covenant does not preclude the institution of compulsory military service. This reasoning was also employed in: Human Rights Committee, *J. P. K. v. The Netherlands*, Communication No. 401/1990, U.N. Doc. CCPR/C/43/D/401/1990 (1991), para. 6.5; *C.B.D. v. The Netherlands*, Communication No. 394/1990, U.N. Doc. CCPR/C/45/D/394/1990 (1992), para. 6.3; Human Rights Committee, *M. J. G. v. The Netherlands*, Communication No. 267/1987, U.N. Doc. CCPR/C/OP/2 at 74 (1990), para. 3.2; and Human Rights Committee, *T. W. M. B. v. The Netherlands*, Communication No. 403/1990, U.N. Doc. CCPR/C/43/D/403/1990 (1991), para. 6.5. See BAHIYYIH G. TAHZIB, FREEDOM OF RELIGION OR BELIEF: ENSURING EFFECTIVE INTERNATIONAL LEGAL PROTECTION (The Hague/Boston/London: Martinus Nijhoff Publishers, 1996), pp. 280–281, for a more detailed description.

[35] Most importantly in that regard: Commission on Human Rights Resolution 1989/53. Also the then UN Secretary Generals repeatedly brought the matter to the attention of the international community even before the matter was resolved by the Human Rights Committee. The same applies to the then UN Special Rapporteur on the Elimination of All Forms of Intolerance and Discrimination based on Religion or Belief: in his analysis of state practice then Rapporteur d'Almeida Ribeiro did not shy away from criticizing governments that did not recognize the right to conscientious objection (*e.g.* E/CN.4/1987/35; E/CN.4/1989/44; and E/CN.4/1992/52). For a comprehensive political history, see CORNELIS D. DE JONG, THE FREEDOM OF THOUGHT, CONSCIENCE AND RELIGION OR BELIEF IN THE UNITED NATIONS (1946–1992) (Antwerp/Groningen/Oxford: Hart/Intersentia, 2000), Chapter 4.

> service citizens who genuinely hold religious or other beliefs that forbid the performance of military service and replaced it with alternative national service. The Covenant does not explicitly refer to a right to conscientious objection, but the Committee believes that such a right can be derived from article 18, inasmuch as the obligation to use lethal force may seriously conflict with the freedom of conscience and the right to manifest one's religion or belief.[36]

Devising a conscientious objections scheme that is equitable and fair proves not to be a straightforward matter. The following human rights considerations should be taken into account. It is clear, first of all, that the state may not restrict the right to conscientious objection to military service to certain religions. States should treat all religions and beliefs (including secular ones) equally and the state itself is not in a position to decide on the question which are pacifist faiths and which not or enter into doctrinal debates as to the question whether or not military service is truly incompatible with specific religions or beliefs (which does not mean that the state may not inquire into the details of the objection or seek to ascertain whether certain beliefs are truly held by an objector).[37] Secondly, it is crucial that whenever the state requires conscientious objectors to fulfil alternative service,[38] the length of this service may not be significantly longer than military service. States may be inclined to double or treble the period of alternative service so as to test the sincerity of the convictions held by the objector. It must be observed that this approach would apportion a punitive element to the alternative service which runs counter to the norm that conscientious objectors may not be discriminated against because of their failure to fulfil military service.[39] Thirdly, conscientious

---

[36] Human Rights Committee: General Comment 22, para. 11.

[37] Cf. Human Rights Committee, *G.M. Brinkhof v. The Netherlands,* Communication No. 402/1990, U.N. Doc. CCPR/C/48/D/402/-1990 [1993], Views of 27 July 1993, para. 9.3; see also Human Rights Committee, General Comment 22, para. 11 ("When this right is recognized by law or practice, there shall be no differentiation among conscientious objectors on the basis of the nature of their particular beliefs"); and Commission on Human Rights Resolution 1998/77, para. 3.

[38] The question as to whether conscientious objections may simply be granted as such or that all objectors must be required to carry out alternative service is a different issue. It must be observed that arguments based on the non-discrimination principle have been advanced that would in fact favour providing alternative service as an obligatory alternative to conscientious objectors. *E.g.* E/CN.4/1992/52 (Report of the Special Rapporteur on Religious Intolerance, 1992), para. 185.

[39] Cf. Human Rights Committee, *Frédéric Foin v. France,* Communication No. 666/1995, U.N. Doc. CCPR/C/67/D/666/1995 (9 November 1999), Views of 9 November 1999; Human Rights Committee, *Richard Maille v. France,* Communication No. 689/1996, U.N. Doc. CCPR/C/69/D/689/1996 (2000), Views of 31 July 2000; and Human Rights Committee, *Vernier and Nicolas v. France,* Communications Nos. 690–691/1996, Views adopted on 10 July 2000. See also Commission on Human Rights Resolution 1998/77, para. 6; and, in more general terms: Human Rights Committee, General Comment 22, para. 11 ("there shall be no discrimination against conscientious objectors because they have failed to perform military service"). Interestingly, in earlier jurisprudence the Committee had considered the extended length of alternative service to be neither unreasonable nor punitive, see Human Rights Committee, *Aapo Järvinen v. Finland,* a case of 1988 (*supra* note 34), para. 6.6.

objections must not only be available prior to being conscripted into the army but must also be open to those who are already performing military service, as one may develop a conscientious objection whilst serving.[40] Finally, a range of general principles of fair procedure must be observed. For instance, conscientious objectors should be given full information about their rights.[41] Furthermore, decisions regarding their status should be made by impartial tribunals, independent from military authorities or there should at least always be a right to appeal to a non-military judicial body.[42]

Turning to actual state practice, it appears that many states fail to take account of one or more of the above principles. Interestingly, failures in adequately transposing and implementing the right to conscientious objection can be discerned across the board: both religious as well as secular states reflect different shortcomings in this respect. The most common human rights law violations in this context appear to be:[43]

Right to Conscientious Objection Not Guaranteed

In some states the core right to conscientious objection is not (sufficiently) guaranteed. Such states include: Azerbaijan,[44] Belarus,[45] Colombia,[46] Eritrea,[47]

---

[40] Preamble of the Commission on Human Rights Resolution 1998/77. It may be added at this point that the right to conscientious objection is, naturally, far less of an issue in states with professional armies; however, one could certainly make an argument in favour of regulations that would allow professional soldiers to be discharged of their functions if they develop conscientious objections after having joined the army on a voluntary basis. Germany, Netherlands and the United Kingdom are among the countries that have adopted such regulations (resp.: Government Decree of 21 October 2003 on professional soldiers & conscientious objections; art. 3 of the Law on Conscientious Objection 1962; and Instruction No. 6 on Retirement or Discharge on the Grounds of Conscience).

[41] E/CN.4/1992/52 (Report of the Special Rapporteur on Religious Intolerance: Angelo Vidal d'Almeida Ribeiro), para. 185.

[42] *Idem.*

[43] The following overview is partly based on the findings of: Marc Stolwijk, The Right to Conscientious Objection in Europe: A Review of the Current Situation (QCEA, 2005).

[44] Though the right to conscientious objection is *de jure* recognized (art. 76 of the Const. of Azerbaijan of 1995 and art. 2 of the Law on the Armed Forces of 1992), in practice no adequate legal framework is in place under which one can actually claim this right and the principle of alternative service is politically opposed. See concerns raised by the Special Rapporteur on freedom of religion or belief (hereinafter also: Special Rapporteur on FoRB): A/HRC/4/21/Add.2 (2006), paras. 62–66; and Human Rights Committee: A/57/40 vol. I (2002), 47 at para. 77(21).

[45] Both the Law on Universal Military Duty and Military Service of 1992 as well as the Constitution envisage civil service; however, an appropriate law on conscientious objection and civil service has never been adopted. See A/53/40 vol. I (1998), 26 at para. 152, for concerns about Belarus' state practice formulated by the Human Rights Committee.

[46] A/59/40 vol. I (2004), 35 at para. 67(17).

[47] Amnesty International, *Annual Report 2008*, p. 125. Convicted objectors are mostly Jehovah's Witnesses. Eritrean state practice has been condemned by the Special Rapporteur on FoRB: A/HRC/7/10/Add.1 (2008), para. 95.

Israel (men),[48] Kuwait,[49] Mexico,[50] Morocco,[51] Republic of Korea,[52] Singapore,[53] Syria,[54] Tajikistan,[55] Turkey,[56] Turkmenistan,[57] and Venezuela.[58]

Conscientious Objection Applied in a Discriminatory Manner

Some states determine that only religious people or, even more specifically, only members of specific religions may object to military service. In Kyrgyzstan and Ukraine, for instance, conscientious objections are open to members of registered religious organizations whose teachings prohibit the use of arms (which in practice is generally construed so as to mean Jehovah's Witnesses).[59] In Romania, similarly, only "members of religious groups that do not allow the discharge of military service under arms" can be granted exemptions from obligatory military service.[60] This is interpreted so as to include Adventists, Baptists, Jehovah's Witnesses, Pentecostals, and Seventh Day Adventists. In Finland, Jehovah's Witnesses are automatically exempt from military service upon proof of membership.[61]

---

[48] Artt. 39–40 of the Defence Service Law, Law No. 5746–1986, provide for a partial conscientious objection exemption scheme for women. In 1995, Israel established a Conscientious Objection Committee which is empowered to grant exemptions also to men. However, the legal status of this body, consisting of army representatives, is unclear and its procedures are not transparent. See Amnesty International, *Israel – The Price of Principles: Imprisonment of Conscientious Objectors*, 1999; and the Human Rights Committee: A/58/40 vol. I (2003), 64 at para. 85(24).

[49] A/55/40 vol. I (2000) 65 at paras. 494–495.

[50] CCPR/C/123/Add.2 (2000), paras. 60–63; and A/54/40 vol. I (1999), 61 at para. 332 (Mexico).

[51] A/60/40 vol. I (2004), 35 at para. 84(22).

[52] Convicted objectors are mostly Jehovah's Witnesses. In 2007, the Government announced that it will revise its laws (possibly providing for alternative civil service) in the near future. South Korean state practice has been condemned by the Special Rapporteur on FoRB: E/CN.4/2000/65, para. 87 and E/CN.4/2006/5/Add.1, para. 305.

[53] Objectors risk 3 years' imprisonment: art. 4 of the Enlistment Act, Law No. 25 of 1970 (amended in 2001). Convicted objectors are mostly Jehovah's Witnesses.

[54] A/60/40 vol. I (2005), 78 at para. 94(11).

[55] A/60/40 vol. I (2005), 70 at para. 92(20).

[56] Section 1 of the Military Service Act, Law No. 1111, of 17 July 1927: "every man of Turkish nationality shall be obliged to perform military service" (see also art. 72 of the CONST. OF TURKEY of 1982). The European Court of Human Rights convicted Turkey in 2006 for repeatedly imprisoning someone for objecting to military service (as this amounted to inhuman or degrading treatment or punishment): ECtHR, *Ülke v. Turkey*, Application No. 39437/98, Judgement of 24 January 2006. Turkish state practice has also been condemned by the Special Rapporteur on FoRB: A/55/280/Add.1(2000), paras. 45 and 139; and E/CN.4/2006/5/Add.1, para. 364.

[57] Amnesty International, *Annual Report 2008*, p. 306. State practice has also been condemned by the Special Rapporteur on FoRB: A/HRC/7/10/Add.1 (2008), para. 251.

[58] A/56/40 vol. I (2001), 49 at para. 77(26).

[59] A/55/40 vol. I (2000), 57 at paras. 410 (Kyrgyz Republic). See art. 2 of the Law on Alternative Civilian Service [Ukraine] 1999; as condemned by the Human Rights Committee in: A/57/40 vol. I (2002), 32 at para. 74(20)[Ukraine].

[60] Art. 6.3 of the Government Decree No. 618/1997 in conjunction with art. 4 of the 1996 Law on the Preparation of the Population for Defence, Law No. 46/1996.

[61] Act on the Exemption of Jehovah's Witnesses from Military Service of 1987; this state practice is considered discriminatory by the Human Rights Committee: A/53/40 vol. I (1998), 40 at para. 271; and A/60/40 vol. I (2004), 22 at para. 81(14).

Discriminatory Nature or Length of the Alternative Service

In many states that do provide alternative service the nature or length of alternative service is discriminatory. This is the case in: Armenia,[62] Austria,[63] Bosnia and Herzegovina,[64] Bulgaria,[65] Cyprus,[66] Estonia,[67] Finland,[68] Georgia,[69] Greece,[70] Kyrgyzstan,[71] Latvia,[72] Lithuania,[73] Poland,[74] Romania,[75] Russia,[76] Serbia,[77] Slovakia,[78] Switzerland,[79] and Ukraine.[80]

---

[62] The length of alternative service is 42 months (whereas military service is 24 months): Law on Alternative Service of 2003 (entry into force: 1 July 2004). See also the concerns raised by the Special Rapporteur on FoRB: E/CN.4/2006/5/Add.1, para. 11.

[63] The length of alternative service is 12 months (whereas military service is 8 months): Law on Civilian Service of 1986 (amended through 1996).

[64] Alternative service is one and a half times as long as military service (6 and 4 months respectively): Defence Law of 2004.

[65] Alternative service is one and a half times as long as military service (13.5 and 9 months respectively): Law for Replacement of Military Obligations with Alternative Service of 1998.

[66] Up to 34 months ("unarmed military service outside the armed forces"; whilst military service is 25 months); section 5 of the National Guard Law, No 20/1964; see for condemnations of this practice by the Human Rights Committee: A/49/40 vol. I (1994), 53 at paras. 321 and 330; and A/53/40 vol. I (1998), 33 at para. 197.

[67] Alternative service is twice as long as military service (16 instead of 8 months); Defence Forces Service Act of 2000; as condemned by the Human Rights Committee: A/58/40 vol. I (2003,) 41 at para. 79(15).

[68] Non-Military Service Act of 1991 (amended 2008): alternative service is 362 days, 215 days longer than regular military service (Amnesty International, *Annual Report 2008*, p. 132). See also concerns in: *Report of the Working Group on the Universal Periodic Review* [Finland], A/HRC/8/24 (2008), para. 36.

[69] Alternative service is twice as long as military service (36 instead of 18 months); art. 6 of the Law on Alternative Service of 1997; as condemned by the Human Rights Committee: A/57/40 vol. I (2002) 53 at paras. 78(18).

[70] Alternative service is twice as long as military service Law (Law No. 2510/1997); as condemned by the Human Rights Committee: A/60/40 vol. I (2005), 60 at para. 90(15).

[71] Alternative service is twice as long as military service: A/55/40 vol. I (2000) 57 at paras. 410–411.

[72] Alternative service is twice as long as military service; as condemned by the Human Rights Committee: A/59/40 vol. I (2003) 25 at para. 65(15).

[73] Alternative service is 18 months, i.e. one and a half times the length of regular military service; article 23.2 of the Law on National Conscription, Law No. 1593/1996 (amended 2002); a practice condemned by the Human Rights Committee in: A/53/40 vol. I (1998) 30 at para. 176 and A/59/40 vol. I (2004), 52 at para. 71(17).

[74] Alternative service is 18 months (whereas military service is 10 months): Law on Alternative Service of 2004; as condemned by the Human Rights Committee: A/60/40 vol. I (2004), 40 at para. 85(15).

[75] Alternative service is 12 months (whereas military service is 8 months): Law on the Preparation of the Population for Defence, Law No. 46/1996 and Government Decree 618/1997 on substitute service; as condemned by the Human Rights Committee in: A/54/40 vol. I (1999) 68 at para. 376.

[76] Alternative service is 42 months whereas regular military service is 24 months: article 5.1 of the Law on Alternative Civilian Service; criticized by the Human Rights Committee in: A/50/40 vol. I (1995), 65 at paras. 382 and 400; and A/59/40 vol. I (2003), 20 at para. 64(17).

[77] Alternative service is 9 months whereas military service is 6 months; Decree on Military Service (amended 2005).

[78] Alternative service is one and a half times the length of military service (9 and 6 months resp.): Civilian Service Act, Law No. 207/1995.

[79] Alternative service is 390 days, i.e. one and a half times the length of regular military service; Federal Law on the Armed Forces and Military Administration of 1995.

[80] Alternative service is 27 month (whereas military service is 18 months); Law on Alternative Civilian Service of 1999.

Conscientious Objection only Prior to Joining the Army
In some states individuals cannot claim the status of conscientious objector once they have entered the armed forces (e.g. in Armenia, Austria, Bosnia and Herzegovina, Bulgaria, Cyprus, Estonia, Georgia, Greece, Lithuania, Poland, Romania, Russia, Serbia, Slovakia, and Ukraine).[81] This state practice must be dismissed as one may, of course, develop a conscientious objection whilst serving.

(vi) *'Religion' as Ground for Limitation*

Some states that positively identify with a religion have codified grounds for limitation, for instance, "established customs", "accepted standards of behaviour", or "decency", that are not recognized by international law.[82] These illegitimate grounds may be (ab)used to enforce the state-sanctioned conception of religious morality at the expense of a universal right to freely manifest one's religion or belief. The most explicit example of religion itself being recognized as a ground for limiting the right to freedom of religion is given by the Constitution of Panama, which lists "Christian morality" as a ground for limitation.[83] In other words, the state may inhibit manifestations of religion or belief that would run counter to the state's interpretation of Christian morality.

It must be observed that 'religion' as such is certainly not a legitimate ground for limiting religious manifestations. Though the concept of 'morals' is listed under the recognized grounds for limiting the freedom to manifest a religion or belief,[84] the Human Rights Committee has observed in that respect that:

> ...the concept of morals derives from many social, philosophical and religious traditions; consequently, limitations on the freedom to manifest a religion or belief for the purpose of protecting morals must be based on principles *not deriving exclusively from a single tradition.*[85]

---

[81] As to Greece, see explicitly: Law No. 2510/1997. Condemned by the Special Rapporteur: E/CN.4/2006/5/Add.1, para. 138.

[82] Art. 22 of the Const. of Bahrain (2002): "customs" as a ground for limitation; art. 41 of the Const. of Bangladesh (1972): codifies a generic ground for limitation: "subject to law"; art. 13, para. (2) of the Const. of Greece (2001): "good usages" as ground for limitation; art. 14 of the Const. of Jordan (1952): "customs" as a ground for limitation; art. 35 of the Const. of Kuwait (1962): "established customs" as a ground for limitation; art. 2 of the Constitutional Proclamation of Libya (1969): "established customs" as a ground for limitation; art. 40, para. (3), of the Const. of Malta (1964): "decency" as ground for limitation; art. 28 of the Basic Law of the Sultanate of Oman (1996): "accepted standards of behaviour" as ground for limitation (Oman is not a party to the ICCPR); art. 20 of the Const. of Pakistan (1973); generic ground for limitation: "subject to law" (Pakistan has not yet ratified the ICCPR).

[83] Art. 35, first sentence, of the Const. of Panama (1972). Criticized by the Human Rights Committee: U.N. Doc. A/39/40 (1984), para. 416.

[84] Art. 18, para. (3), of the ICCPR.

[85] Human Rights Committee, General Comment 22, para. 8 (emphasis added).

In other words, manifestations of religion or belief cannot be limited solely with a view towards protecting the predominant religion or the set of morals deriving from it.[86]

(vii) *Proselytism Bans*

Besides the above mentioned failures in adequately transposing the freedom of religion or belief into domestic laws, we can discern different instances where the same norm is not sufficiently internalized into the domestic legal order. That is to say, in spite of the constitutional freedom of religion clause, legislation that negatively affects the legal status of the right to freedom of religion or belief remains in place. Perhaps the best example is a discriminatory prohibition of proselytism. The issue of discriminatory prohibitions of proselytism is related to the topic discussed in the previous sub-section: if religious minorities are prohibited from proselytizing adherents of the official religion, protection of the predominant religion *de facto* functions as a ground for limiting the freedom to manifest one's religion (at least as far as members of these minorities are concerned).

Before addressing the discriminatory nature of most proselytism prohibitions, it may be worth reflecting briefly on the issue of proselytism as such. One may think that a proselytism ban could in theory be a measure taken in the interest of citizens, namely to protect privacy rights, to ensure religious harmony, to ban unsolicited interference with one's private thoughts and convictions, in sum, to actually protect people's religious and other freedoms. However, it should be acknowledged that the right to freedom of expression together with the freedom to manifest a religion or belief (which encompasses "teaching of religion") protects proselytizing activities to the extent that these activities do not amount to coercive practices.[87] In the latter respect, it must at the same time be reiterated that the freedom to manifest one's religion is not an absolute freedom. In the present context, particularly the need to ensure

[86] Something the Human Rights Committee has repeatedly pointed out, *e.g.*: U.N. Doc. A/39/40 (1984), para. 416 (Panama); U.N. Doc. A/38/40 (1983), para. 194 (Austria); U.N. Doc. A/37/40 (1982), para. 180 (Jordan); U.N. Doc. A/35/40 (1980), para. 253 (Colombia).

[87] Cf. OSCE/ODIHR, *Guidelines for Review of Legislation Pertaining to Religion or Belief* (prepared by ODIHR's Advisory Panel of Experts on Freedom of Religion or Belief in consultation with the Council of Europe's Venice Commission, June–July 2004), p. 20. See also Oslo Coalition on Freedom on Religion or Belief, *Missionary Activities and Human Rights: Proposing a Code of Conduct regarding Missionary Activities* (Oslo: Oslo Coalition, March 2008); this Code of Conduct recognizes a right to propagate one's religion (ethically) and at the same time identifies a state duty to "ensure that an individual is not subject to coercion or manipulation impairing his right to have or to adopt a religion or belief of his choice" (para. 3.4.1). See also, *e.g.*: De Jong, *supra* note 35, p. 128; Natan Lerner, *Proselytism, Change of Religion, and International Human Rights*, 12 Emory International Law Review 477 (1998); Natan Lerner, Religion, Secular Beliefs and Human Rights: 25 Years After the 1981 Declaration (Leiden/Boston: Martinus Nijhoff Publishers, 2006, Chapter 7 ("Proselytism and Change of Religion").

compliance with the rights and freedoms of others as legitimate ground for limitation is of the utmost importance.[88] In other words, both believers and non-believers have in principle a right to express and disseminate their thoughts and beliefs and to try to convince others of the truth or falsehood of religious or non-religious ideas and beliefs. However, this does not mean that the state must tolerate practices of coercion, forcible conversion, improper pressure, brainwashing or manipulation.[89]

It is submitted that proselytizing activity does not per se affect the rights and freedoms of others. Proselytizing activity may, under circumstances, be at the expense of the rights and freedoms of others, namely when the proselytizer adopts coercive means and shows no respect for the person's right to maintain his or her religion or belief, or when the proselytizer targets inappropriate groups (one might think of captive audiences, subordinates,[90] intellectually disabled persons or children[91]). Thus, it might be concluded that the right to freely manifest a religion or belief in a liberal democratic society must be balanced with the need to ensure the rights and freedoms of others.[92]

In view of this, it may be argued that generic constitutional prohibitions or blanket criminal law prohibitions of proselytism (sweeping bans that do not take into account the distinction between legitimately propagating one's faith and coercive practice), must be considered contrary to the right to freedom of religion or belief and the right to freedom of expression. This appears to be the case in: Armenia,[93] Cambodia,[94] Greece (Constitution),[95] Indonesia,[96] Nepal[97] and Uzbekistan.[98] More specific prohibitions of 'proselytism as coercion' are, as such, less problematic from a human rights perspective. In this context

[88] Cf. Arcot Krishnaswami, *Study of Discrimination in the Matter of Religious Rights and Practices* (U.N. Doc. E/CN.4/Sub.2/200/Rev.1, 1960), para. III.A.(xi).

[89] In the European context the problems have been 'resolved' by distinguishing between proper proselytism, which is protected by human rights law, and "improper proselytism", which is not. Cf. the 'Greek proselytism cases' starting with: ECtHR, *Kokkinakis v. Greece*, Appl. No. 14307/88, of 25 May 1993, particularly para. 48.

[90] In the European context: cf. *Larissis and Others v. Greece*, (140/1996/759/958–960) [1998] ECHR, Judgement of 24 February 1998.

[91] Cf. Oslo Coalition's *Code of Conduct regarding Missionary Activities (supra* note 87).

[92] Art. 18, para. (3), of the ICCPR.

[93] Art. 8 of the Law on the Freedom of Conscience and Religious Organizations of 17 June 1991 (amended 1997 and 2001; hereinafter: "1991 Armenian Law").

[94] Decree of 26 June 2007 on proselytism, Ministry of Cults and Religions, prolonging the 2003 ban.

[95] Art. 13, para. (2), of the Const. of Greece (2001): "Proselytism is prohibited."

[96] As per the Guidelines for the Propagation of Religion of 1978.

[97] Art. 23. para. (1), of the Interim Const. of Nepal (2007).

[98] Art. 5 of the Law on Freedom of Conscience and Religious Organizations of 1 May 1998 (hereinafter: "1998 Uzbek Law").

one may think of: Greece (Statute),[99] Cyprus,[100] several states of India,[101] Kyrgyzstan,[102] and Moldova.[103] Having said that, the latter prohibitions always carry with them the risk that they are construed as a means to restrict the freedom to manifest certain religions (e.g. Sri Lanka).[104] Further to this it is useful to emphasize the views of the Human Rights Committee: "Limitations may be applied only for those purposes for which they were prescribed and must be directly related and proportionate to the specific need on which they are predicated".[105]

Particularly relevant is the fact that bans on proselytism more often than not are rather one-sided measures (*de jure* or *de facto*). Typically, adherents of the majority religion are free to proselytize non-believers and adherents of religious minorities; however, the latter groups may not attempt to convert people away from the predominant religion. These measures are, naturally, designed to protect the state-promoted religion. This practice runs counter to human rights law for two reasons: (i) the protection of the state religion is not recognized as a legitimate ground for limiting the right to freedom of religion or belief of others;[106] and (ii) grounds for limitation may not be used in a discriminatory fashion.[107]

---

[99] Section 4 of Law No. 1363/1938 (as mended by section 2 of Law No. 1672/1939): "By 'proselytism' is meant, in particular, any direct or indirect attempt to intrude on the religious beliefs of a person of a different religious persuasion, with the aim of undermining those beliefs, either by any kind of inducement or promise of an inducement or moral support or material assistance, or by fraudulent means or by taking advantage of his inexperience, trust, need, low intellect or naïvety".

[100] Art. 18, para. (5), of the CONST. OF CYPRUS (1960): "The use of physical or moral compulsion for the purpose of making a person change or preventing him from changing his religion is prohibited."

[101] Himachal Pradesh, Arunachal Pradesh, Orissa, Madhya Pradesh, Chhattisgarh, and Gujarat have State Bills on Religious Freedom which seek to specifically outlaw forced conversions, or forms of proselytism that use fraudulent means or which come down to offering financial or material benefits in exchange for conversion.

[102] The Law on Religion of the Kyrgyz Republic of 12 January 2009 (hereinafter: "2009 Kyrgyz Law") prohibits "aggressive action aimed at proselytism".

[103] Art. 1[b] of the Law of the Republic of Moldova on Denominations, No. 979-XII, of 24 March 1992 (amended in 1998 and 2002; hereinafter: "1992 Moldovan Law") forbids "excessive proselytism", which is defined as "any attempt to pressure one's religious convictions by force or abuse of authority".

[104] See Sri Lanka's draft-Bill on the Prohibition of Forcible Conversions of 2004 (partly considered unconstitutional by the Supreme Court, currently being reconsidered by a Parliamentary Committee). The Bill, on the face of it (see title), appears to be intended to outlaw coercive practices. However, in actual fact it proposes a range of measures which amount to restrictions on the manifestation of religious beliefs proper. For one thing, it intends to make it compulsory for everyone to notify the authorities of a religious conversion within a limited amount of time.

[105] Human Rights Committee, General Comment 22, para. 8.

[106] Human Rights Committee, General Comment 22, para. 8: "The Committee observes that paragraph 3 of article 18 is to be strictly interpreted: restrictions are not allowed on grounds not specified there".

[107] *Idem.* ("Restrictions may not be imposed for discriminatory purposes or applied in a discriminatory manner").

Discriminatory proselytism bans come in two main versions: (i) bans that target concrete religious minorities so as to specifically forbid these groups from proselytizing; and (ii) more general bans that do not allow proselytizing activity aimed at members of the state religion.[108] Although it will be clear that there is often a considerable overlap, the following analytical distinction can be made: the former type of ban seems particularly concerned with safeguarding the state-sanctioned religious orthodoxy against the influences of what are considered deviant 'sects', whereas the latter type of prohibition is more concerned with simply maintaining maximum adherence to the state-protected religion.[109] A good example of the former is given by the proselytism ban that specifically targets the Ahmadis in Pakistan. The 'anti-Ahmadi laws', introduced in Pakistan in 1984, specifically forbid Ahmadis to proselytize:

> Any person of the Quadiani group or the Lahori group (who call themselves 'Ahmadis' or by any other name), who...preaches or propagates his faith, or invites others to accept his faith...shall be punished with imprisonment of either description for a term which may extend to three years and shall also be liable to fine.[110]

Another example is the governmental decree that forbids Jehovah's Witnesses in Gabon to proselytize.[111]

Examples of the second type of ban (proselytizing members of the majority religion) can mostly be found in Islamic states and other states that strongly identify with Islam.[112] States that (*de jure* or *de facto*) forbid proselytizing activity vis-à-vis Muslims include: Algeria, Brunei Darussalam, Comoros, Iran, Jordan, Kuwait, Libya, Maldives, Malaysia, Morocco, Qatar, Saudi Arabia, Somalia (regional bans), United Arab Emirates and Yemen.[113] Nearly all these

---

[108] See also Tad Stahnke, *Proselytism and the Freedom to Change Religion in International Human Rights Law*, 1 Brigham Young University Law Review (1999), pp. 265–266.

[109] Cf. Paul M. Taylor, *The Questionable Grounds of Objections to Proselytism and Certain Other Forms of Religious Expression*, 3 Brigham Young University Law Review (2006), p. 811.

[110] Art. 298C of the Penal Code as introduced by Ordinance No. F.17 (1) 84-Pub of 26 April 1984.

[111] Jehovah's Witnesses Decree of 1970. It must be noted that this regulation is not being implemented at present.

[112] It may be reiterated that this ban may in practice be further supported by apostasy prohibitions in those Islamic states that consider conversion away from Islam a (capital) offence under Islamic law. See Chapter 8, section 8.2.2, *supra*.

[113] Algeria: artt. 10–11 of Ordinance 06-03 (jail sentences and fines are prescribed for different types, i.e. organized or in a private capacity, of proselytism); Brunei: more specifically, proselytizing activity by all religions or denominations other than the state-protected Shafi'i branch of Islam is prohibited; Comoros: the Penal law of 1982 defines the proselytizer as someone who "divulges, promotes, or teaches Muslims a religion other than Islam"; Maldives: conversion away from Islam may, moreover, result in the loss of citizenship; Malaysia: art. 11, para. (4), of the Const. of Malaysia (1957) and, with respect to Federal Territories of Kuala Lumpur and Labuan, art. 5 of the Syariah Criminal Offences Act (Federal Territories) of 1997, Act 559; Morocco: art. 220 of the Moroccan Penal Code defines the proselytizer as someone who

states encourage or do not discourage (and occasionally actually facilitate) Islamic proselytism initiatives vis-à-vis non-Muslims. It must be acknowledged, finally, that not only predominantly Muslim states adopt one-sided proselytism bans. Proselytism by any religion other than the national church (the Armenian Apostolic Church) is forbidden in Armenia.[114] Proselytism bans in Burma, Bhutan and Laos in practice have come to mean that non-Buddhist (i.e., chiefly, Evangelical Protestant) missionary activity is forbidden.[115]

(viii) *Legal Measures Encroaching on the Privacy of Religious Beliefs*

The right to freedom of religion or belief implies that "no one can be compelled to reveal his thoughts or adherence to a religion or belief".[116] The rationale of this norm is given by the fact that the knowledge of people's religious affiliation may foster practices of discrimination. Some states have codified a right to freedom of religion or belief as such, yet fail to internalize this important ramification. Brunei Darussalam, for instance, recognizes that religions may be practised;[117] however the government requires that those who wish to abandon their religion or to convert ask prior official permission. This policy may deter people from (openly) embracing another religion or (openly) abandoning a religion.

Another relevant example is Egypt. Although the Egyptian Constitution provides that the state shall guarantee the freedom of belief,[118] the Government until very recently required all Egyptians of the age of 16 years or older to obtain an ID card which reflects, amongst other personal details, one's religious affiliation.[119] As the Egyptian Government officially recognizes only the

"employs means of seduction with the intention of turning a Muslim away from the Muslim faith"; Qatar: Qatari Penal Code of 2004, Act No. 11/2004, provides for different prison sentences for different types of proselytism of Muslims (i.e. organized proselytism or individual initiatives); Somalia: proselytism by non-Muslims is prohibited in Puntland and Somaliland; UAE: as per the Federal Penal Code of 1987, Law No. 3/1987 (and the Penal Codes of the constituent states). Finally, in some other states that identify with Islam (*e.g.* in Bangladesh, Djibouti, Egypt, Syria, Tunisia) proselytizing Muslims is not strictly speaking forbidden but officially or *de facto* discouraged (*e.g.* it may result in the non-renewal of visas, withdrawal of residence permits, etc). Anti-proselytism policies in Egypt are based on art. 98, para. (f)(religious strife and blasphemy), of the Egyptian Penal Code (as amended by Law 147/2006).

[114] Art. 8 and 17 of the 1991 Armenian Law (*supra* note 93).

[115] Bhutan's Governmental policy is based on art. 9 of the National Security Act of 1992 (which strictly speaking provides for governmental action against inciting religious hatred); Laos' policy is based on art. 9 of the Const. of Laos (1991) in conjunction with Prime Minister's Decree 92 on Religious Practice. Furthermore, the "anti-conversion laws" currently being considered in Sri Lanka (see *supra*, note 104) particularly aim at preventing Buddhists from being proselytized.

[116] Human Rights Committee, General Comment 22, para. 3.

[117] Art. 3, para. (1), of the Const. of Brunei Darussalam (1959).

[118] Art. 46 of the Const. of Egypt (1971).

[119] As per art. 48 of Civil Status Law, 143/1994 and Law 181/1955 on Personal Cards. These regulations are currently in the process of being reformed (see note 122, *infra*).

Abrahamic religions (Judaism, Christianity and Islam), members of other religions, notably the Bahá'ís, found themselves forced to either repudiate their beliefs or live without a national ID card (the latter, naturally, may form serious obstacles with respect to obtaining birth or death certificates, inheritance, pensions or even medical care).[120] Thus, it is clear that the issue of privacy of one's religious thoughts cuts right across the fields of freedom of religion or belief and the right not to be discriminated against on the basis of religion or belief.[121] A decision by Cairo's Administrative Court in favour of recognition of Bahá'ís and their right to obtain an ID card forced the Minister of Interior of Egypt to issue a new Decree on religious affiliation on government documents changing the Civil Status Law of 1994 and allowing for people not belonging to any of the Abrahamic religions to not have religious affiliation included in official documents.[122] Better still, of course, would have been to abolish the entire system of including religious affiliation in official documents as presently everyone (employers, civil servants, etc.) can still see—given the dash in the box for 'religious affiliation'—if someone is not a Muslim or a member of the Abrahamic religions. In sum, this recent development must be applauded as it is a first step towards recognition of Bahá'ís as citizens with civil rights; however, the new system is clearly not sufficient to prevent *de facto* discrimination against Bahá'ís.

The practice of requiring state officials to take a 'religious oath' upon entering public office is a related matter.[123] If the religious aspects of the oaths of office are obligatory, interferences with non-believers' equality rights and religious freedoms (*from* religion) are inevitable. Something that might easily be overlooked in this context is the fact that offering a choice between a religious oath and a secular affirmation does not fully solve this problem in so far as it still forces people to reveal their (lack of) faith.

It must be added at this point that numerous other forms of state practice amount to limitations of the right to freedom of religion or belief. The issue of discriminatory proselytism bans and legal duties to reveal one's religious affiliation were singled out in this section because these measures directly (negatively) affect the very legal status of the right to freedom of religion or belief. The remainder of this Chapter and the remainder of Part II of this study

[120] Human Rights Watch, *Egypt: Prohibited Identities – State Interference with Religious Freedom* (HRW/EIPR, Volume 19, No. 7(E), 2007), pp. 2–3.

[121] It must be noted that religious affiliation is mentioned on ID cards in other states as well (*e.g.* Jordan). Human rights monitoring bodies have spoken out against the inclusion of religious affiliation into identity documents on several occasions; see, *e.g.*, Committee on the Rights of the Child's Concluding observations: CRC/C/140 (2004) 81 at paras. 408–409 (Burma); and CRC/C/114 (2002) 25 at paras. 136 (Greece)(regarding school graduation certificates).

[122] Cairo's Administrative Court decision of 29 January 2008. Interior Minster's Decree on religious affiliation on government documents of 19 March 2009 (entry into effect: 14 April 2009).

[123] This issue will be discussed in much more detail in Chapter 11, section 11.2.1(v), *infra*.

demonstrate, moreover, that the right to freedom of religion or belief is often not sufficiently mainstreamed into different specific state policies, notably the areas of politics, employment and education.

(ix) *Illegitimate Secular Limits on Freedom on Religion or Belief*

To conclude this section on discernible failures in adequately transposing and internalizing the norm of freedom of religion or belief into domestic laws, the main failures at the more secular end of the state–religion identification spectrum must be identified. Here shortcomings are of a very different nature. Both the *forum internum* and the *forum externum* are as a rule sufficiently recognized.[124] However, some of the more secular states list (secular) grounds for limitation that are not enumerated in international law. This practice does not so much affect the legal right to freedom of religion or belief as such, yet potentially (negatively) affects the practical implementation of the second type of freedom: the freedom to manifest a religion or belief. In other words, the present shortcoming consists of the fact that interferences with the free exercise of beliefs could occur on the basis of certain grounds for limitation that according to international human rights law do not in fact justify these limitations.

The legitimate grounds for limiting the *forum externum* are: "public safety", "order", "health", "morals" and "the fundamental rights and freedoms of others".[125] This is an exhaustive list of grounds for limitation.[126] In view of this, it is not acceptable to limit manifestations of religions or beliefs in the interest of: "defence" (Botswana, Jamaica, Lesotho, Mauritius, Seychelles, Sierra Leone, Swaziland, Zambia and Zimbabwe),[127] (national) "security" (Bulgaria, Côte d'Ivoire, Lithuania and Poland),[128] "education" (Ethiopia),[129] "social tranquillity"

---

[124] There are exceptions, *e.g.*, Sweden, which recently disestablished its state church, constitutionally protects (see art. 1 of Ch. 2 of the Instrument of Government of 1974; which is one of the four parts of the Constitution of Sweden) the "freedom of worship" (i.e. a limited interpretation of the *forum externum*; plus: the *forum internum* is omitted); secular Kazakhstan constitutionally protects (see art. 19 of the Constitution of the Republic of Kazakhstan of 1995) the right to "determine and indicate or not to indicate" a religious affiliation (i.e. *forum externum* is omitted).

[125] Art. 18, para. (3), of the ICCPR.

[126] Human Rights Committee, General Comment No. 22, para. 8.

[127] Art. 11, para. (5)(a), of the Const. of Botswana (1966); art. 13, para. (5), of the Const. of Lesotho (1993); art. 11, para. (5), of the Const. of Mauritius (1968); art. 21, para. (2)(a), of the Const. of Seychelles (1993); art. 24, para. (5)(a), of the Const. of Sierra Leone (1991); art. 24, para. (4)(a), of the Const. of Swaziland (2005); art. 19, para. (5), of the Const. of Zambia (1991); art. 19, para. (5), of the Const. of Zimbabwe (1979); and art. 21, para. (6)(a), of the Const. of Jamaica (1962).

[128] Art. 37, para. (2), of the Const. of Bulgaria (1991); art. 9 of the Const. of Côte D'Ivoire (2000); art. 26 of the Const. of Lithuania (1992); and art. 53, para. (5), of the Const. of Poland (1997). Codification of this ground for limitation is all the more remarkable since the Human Rights Committee (General Comment No. 22, para. 8) explicitly refers to this ground as an illegitimate ground for limitation.

[129] Art. 27, para. (5), of the Const. of Ethiopia (1995).

(Niger),[130] "national unity" (Niger),[131] or "to prevent a public nuisance" (Fiji).[132] Generic grounds for limitation that provide too much discretionary power to the authorities such as (respect of) "the law" (Burkina Faso, Côte d'Ivoire, France, Mali, Paraguay, Rwanda and Togo) are not allowed either.[133]

Finally, listing respect for the secular nature of the state (Benin and Turkey)[134] as a ground for limiting the right to freedom of religion or belief would only be justifiable if it could be established that actively undermining the secular nature of the state automatically fosters violations of the fundamental rights and freedoms of others (as the protection of the latter *is* a recognized ground for limitation).[135] It will be clear that there is a fundamental difference between actually attempting to overthrow, or merely verbally challenging the secular nature of the state. In that respect it must be observed that if this type of ground for limitation, based on strict notions of secularism, is not accompanied by firm constitutional safeguards of the rights of religious people to freely express their religious opinions, there is a risk that these notions could in practice be abused by the secular regime to act against what it considers 'undesirable' religious activity.

9.2.2 *Establishment of Religion & Unequal Treatment of Other Religions*

So far it has been argued that forms of establishment of religion are surrounded by a range of different shortcomings regarding the legal transposition and internalization of the freedom of religion or belief clause into domestic laws and policies. In this section it will be demonstrated that the 'equal religious rights of others' are further encroached upon by numerous establishmentarian states in so far as these states grant exclusive or discriminatory support to the dominant religion, thus putting non-dominant or non-traditional religions at a disadvantage. The most important ramification of the non-discrimination

---

130 Art. 23 of the Const. of Niger (1999).

131 *Idem.*

132 Art. 35, para. (4)(b), of the Const. of the Fiji Islands (1998).

133 Art. 7 of the Const. of Burkina Faso (1991); art. 9 of the Const. of Côte d'Ivoire (2000); art. 4 of the Const. of Mali (1992); art. 33 of the Const. of Rwanda (2003); art. 25 of the Const. of Togo (1992); article 10 of the 1789 French Declaration of Human Rights; and art. 24, para. (1), of the Const. of Paraguay (1992).

134 Art. 23 of the Const. of Benin (1990): "The exercise of a creed and the expression of beliefs shall take place with respect for the secularity of the state"; and art. 24, para. (5), of the Const. of Turkey (1982)(by implication). Chad, it might be added within this context, considers the protection of "the secularity of the state" a legitimate limit on the right to freedom of *expression* (art. 5 of the Const. of Chad of 1996).

135 *E.g.*, within the European context, cf. ECtHR, *Refah Partisi (the Welfare Party) and Others v. Turkey*, (Grand Chamber Judgement), Application Nos. 41340/98, 41342/98, 41343/98 and 41344/98, Judgement of 13 February 2003, para. 93: "the principle of secularism is certainly one of the fundamental principles of the State which are in harmony with the rule of law and respect for human rights and democracy. An attitude which fails to respect that principle will not necessarily be accepted as being covered by the freedom to manifest one's religion and will not enjoy the protection of [the right to freedom of religion or belief]".

principle is that no one should be treated differently because of one's religion or belief. In this respect, different types of shortcomings can be discerned: (i) discrimination on the basis of religion or belief, including discrimination on the basis of gender for religious reasons, is not (explicitly) prohibited; and (ii) *de jure* or *de facto* discriminatory practices are perceivable in as far as the state privileges certain religions over others.

(i) *Discrimination on the Basis of Religion Not Prohibited*

Naturally, not many states would admit to discriminating on the basis of religion or belief—some such exceptions can be discerned though. Iran's constitutional norms on religious freedom and on religious minorities, for instance, explicitly divide the population into four different groups, each with a different status: (Twelver) Shi'a Muslims (adherents of the official religion), other Muslims (*de jure* recognized and respected), People of the Book (*de jure* tolerated) and non-Muslim who do not adhere to one of the Abrahamic religions (not granted rights or freedoms).[136] Given the fact that people in Iran are categorized into these different classes by virtue of their religion, it hardly comes as a surprise that Iran has not codified a provision that prohibits religious discrimination.[137] Other domestic non-discrimination clauses that omit 'religion' as a prohibited ground for unequal treatment may be observed in Algeria[138] and Mauritania.[139] States that omit 'gender' or 'sex' amongst the prohibited grounds include: Egypt,[140] Iran,[141] Jordan,[142] Kuwait[143] and Malaysia.[144] This is presumably done for religious reasons as well. In this regard, one might speak of 'discrimination on the basis of gender for religious reasons'. It should be pointed out, finally, that some states have not constitutionally codified a non-discrimination provision at all (Brunei and Saudi Arabia).

(ii) *Different Treatment of Different Religions*

The different religions and beliefs that are present in the country should be treated equally by the state.[145] The rationale behind this rule clearly is that if a

---

[136] See art. 12–14 of the Const. of Iran (1979).

[137] Art. 19 of the Const. of Iran (1979): "All people of Iran, whatever the ethnic group or tribe to which they belong, enjoy equal rights; colour, race, language, and the like, do not bestow any privilege". The phrase "and the like" could in theory be construed so as to include religion; however, this is certainly not Iran's interpretation.

[138] Art. 29 of the Const. of Algeria (1976).

[139] Art. 1 of the Const. of Mauritania (1991).

[140] Art. 40 of Const. of Egypt (1971).

[141] Art. 19 of the Const. of Iran (1979).

[142] Art. 6 of the Const. of Jordan (1952).

[143] Art. 29 of the Const. of Kuwait (1962).

[144] Art. 8, para. (2), of the Const. of Malaysia (1957).

[145] Cf. Human Rights Committee, General Comment 22, para. 2; also confirmed in: Human Rights Committee, *G.M. Brinkhof v. The Netherlands*, Communication No. 402/1990, U.N. Doc. CCPR/C/48/D/402/1990 [1993], Views of 27 July 1993; and Human Rights Committee,

state were to treat different religions differently, for instance by means of exclusively or disproportionally supporting the state or predominant religion, other religions and beliefs would be put at a disadvantage. This, naturally, may have a negative impact on the position of individual believers belonging to those non-dominant or non-traditional religions or beliefs. Although traditional relationships between the state and religion might explain discriminatory forms of support *historically*, it is submitted that in the era of fundamental equal rights these relationships in themselves do not provide 'objective and reasonable' criteria for making distinctions between different religions.

In what remains of this section, a variety of forms of discriminatory state support and discriminatory privileges will be discussed: financial benefits, church tax systems and other historical prerogatives that are perpetuated by the state.

Financial Benefits

Financial benefits can take the form of direct financial support, state remuneration of the clergy, but also for instance tax exemptions. The state may not discriminate between religions when it comes to granting financial support to religion.[146] It must be observed that there is no clear-cut right for organized religions to be funded by the state;[147] however, it follows from the equality

A. H. Waldman v. Canada, Communication No. 694/1996, Views of 3 November 1999. The Human Rights Committee, moreover, has reiterated the same point repeatedly in its Concluding Observations, *e.g.*: A/59/40 vol. I (2004) 52 at para. 71(16) (Lithuania); A/59/40 vol. I (2004) 61 at para. 73 (13) (Liechtenstein); A/60/40 vol. I (2004) 22 at para. 81 (14) (Finland); A/58/40 vol. I (2003) 45 at para. 80(7) (Luxembourg); A/56/40 vol. I (2001) 38 at para. 74 (16) (Argentina); A/56/40 vol. I (2001) 83 at para. 83 (22) (Czech Republic); A/53/40 vol. I (1998) 40 at para. 271 (Finland); A/53/40 vol. I (1998) 30 at para. 175 (Lithuania); A/49/40 vol. I (1994) 41 at para. 235 (Jordan); A/48/40 vol. I (1993) at para. 232 (Iran); and A/48/40 vol. I (1993) at para. 445 (Haiti).

[146] Cf. Human Rights Committee; *e.g.*: A/56/40 vol. I (2001) 38 at para. 74 (Argentina): "The preferential treatment, including financial subsidies, accorded to the Catholic Church over other religious denominations constitutes religious discrimination under article 26 of the Covenant"; A/58/40 vol. I (2003) 45 at para. 80 (Luxembourg): "The Committee notes…that the State party grants financial assistance to the Christian and Jewish communities only…The State party should guarantee non-discriminatory treatment of communities of religion and belief in respect of financial assistance and, to this end, ensure that all criteria in this regard are revised to guarantee that they are in keeping with the Covenant"; A/53/40 vol. I (1998) 45 at para. 324 (Israel): "Preference given to the Jewish religion in the allocation of funding for religious bodies, to the detriment of Muslims, Christians, Druze and other religious groups, is of concern. Regulations and criteria for funding should be published and applied to all religious groups on an equal basis"; see furthermore: A/48/40 vol. I (1993) 30 at para. 134 (Luxembourg); A/48/40 (1993), para. 117 (Luxembourg); A/43/40 (1988), para. 71 (Trinidad and Tobago); A/43/40, para. 181 (Denmark); A/41/40 (1986), para. 145 (Sweden); A/41/40 (1986), para. 212 (Finland); A/36/40 (1981), para. 57 (Venezuela); A/34/40 (1979), para. 159 (Romania); A/33/40 (1978), para. 79 (Sweden); see also CCPR/C/SR.52 (1978), para. 8 (Sweden); CCPR/C/SR.258 (1980), para. 41 (Italy); CCPR/C/SR.638 (1985), para. 11 (Sweden); CCPR/C/SR.767 (1987), para. 6 (Trinidad and Tobago); and CCPR/C/SR.781 (1987), para. 33 (Denmark).

[147] Cf. De Jong, *supra* note 35, p. 289.

principle that if the state were to decide to provide funding to religion it must adopt an equitable approach and not discriminate against certain religions or beliefs, notably non-traditional or non-dominant ones.[148] In view of this, it must be concluded that nearly all states with an established or a state-supported religion/church grant the state-protected religious denomination financial privileges that run counter to the equality principle.[149] In that regard, one may think particularly of most states with an established or state-supported Roman Catholic Church, and most predominantly Muslim states; discriminatory financial support schemes flow, furthermore, from the ties between the state and religion in: Bhutan, Cyprus, Denmark, Greece, Iceland, Israel, and Norway.[150]

Discrimination in this area can only be avoided by either granting no financial benefits whatsoever or by ensuring that: (i) decisions as to the allocation of financial benefits are based on objective criteria;[151] (ii) benefit schemes are equally applicable to non-religious faith organizations; and (iii) the principle of proportionality is observed as far as possible.[152]

As to the first issue, a criterion that would determine that support is only granted to cover activities of a certain nature (such as humanitarian aid,

[148] See also OSCE/ODIHR, *Guidelines* (*supra* note 87), p. 16 and pp. 20–21.

[149] A clear exception in this context is the United Kingdom which does not provide direct financial support to its established church.

[150] As for some of this states, this follows logically from the level of integration between the state and (one) religion at the exclusion of others (most predominantly Muslim states; see also Chapter 2). As for states with an established or supported Catholic Church: as per Concordats between these state and the Holy See and further agreements between the state and these Churches (see also Chapters 2 and 3). In some of these states benefits have been partially extended on the basis of additional agreements with other religions. Luxembourg, which has not formally established the Roman Catholic Church, may be added to the list. Art. 106 of the Const. of Luxembourg (1868) provides that: "The salaries and pensions of ministers of religion shall be borne by the State and regulated by the law". Pursuant agreements between the state of Luxembourg and religious organizations, the financial support to the Roman Catholic Church has been extended to Greek Orthodox, Russian Orthodox, Romanian Orthodox, Serbian Orthodox, Anglican and some Protestant denominations as well as to Jewish congregations; other religious minorities, however, notably Muslim organizations, do not yet receive similar funding. As for Bhutan: the state provides direct financial support to the Central Monk Body, i.e. the national organization of Buddhist monks, and also contributes towards the building of temples and monasteries. Cyprus: the state-supported Greek Orthodox Church of Cyprus benefits from tax exemption schemes. Denmark: the state provides exclusive funding to the Evangelical-Lutheran State Church; moreover, the state levies church taxes at the municipal level on behalf of this Church solely (see next sub-section). Greece: the state provides direct financial support to the Greek Orthodox Church, pays the salaries of priests and provides financial support towards costs of religious training of priests and of religious buildings; some of the benefits are extended to Muslim communities but not to other religious communities, notably the Jewish community. Iceland: the state provides financial support to the Evangelical Lutheran Church, *i.e.* on top of the church tax scheme from which all recognized religions benefit (see next sub-section). Israel: some benefits are extended to other religions but overall Judaism is financially privileged. Norway: the state provides direct financial funding to the Evangelical-Lutheran Church of Norway.

[151] Cf. De Jong, *supra* note 35, p. 293; and OSCE/ODIHR, *Guidelines (supra* note 87), p. 16.

[152] Cf. De Jong, *supra* note 35, p. 290.

education, medical services, or activities of cultural significance such as the publication of books, exhibitions, etc.)[153] could be considered objective. The rejection of a claim for support on the basis of the non-recognized status of the religion in question would not be objective as states may not discriminate between religions in the process of registration of religions in the first place. Below it will be outlined that religious association laws are often used in practice to confirm or cover up historical financial prerogatives of the dominant and traditional religion of the state.[154] If a state's predominant religion or church is automatically granted financial support yet other religious groups are to go through arduous procedures to reach that same level of legal recognition, the policy of allocation of financial benefits can hardly be considered to be 'based on objective criteria'. The same holds true, *a fortiori*, if religious association laws lay out illegitimate registration criteria that non-dominant or non-traditional religious communities can never meet.

With respect to the second point, it must be acknowledged that if funding is only made available to religious organizations, secular faith organizations (e.g. Humanist organizations) are put at a disadvantage. In that respect, Belgian state practice stands out positively as both religious leaders of recognized religions as well as non-religious leaders ("representatives of organisations recognized by the law as providing moral assistance according to a non-religious philosophical concept") are granted remuneration and pensions.[155]

As to the third issue (proportionality): state support, if granted, should as far as possible reflect actual adherence (religions and churches have an interest in claiming high numbers for a variety of reasons, these figures are therefore not necessarily the most reliable).[156] One major complicating factor in this context is the issue of compensation for religious properties which have been transmitted to or which at some point in history have been appropriated by the state. The procedures for this type of compensation should be proportional, that is, closely reflecting the actual value of the properties concerned. It has been observed that in reality these measures may be (ab)used by the state to support the dominant religion rather incommensurately.[157]

It was noted above that the financial aid in principle may be made conditional upon certain objective criteria (for instance, the aid is only granted if it will be employed to fund certain types of activities). Having said that, the fact

---

[153] *E.g.* art. 2, para (3), of the CONST. OF THE MARSHALL ISLANDS (1979).

[154] See section 9.4, *infra*.

[155] Art. 181, para. (2), of the CONST. OF BELGIUM (1994). The recognized religions are at present: Anglicanism, Islam, Judaism, Orthodox Christianity, Protestantism, Roman Catholicism and Secular Humanism.

[156] A further complication is given by the often large discrepancy between nominal adherence and the number of religious members that actually make use of the facilities and services provided.

[157] De Jong, *supra* note 35, p. 290.

that the state renders financial support to religion does not in itself authorize the state to interfere with the internal affairs of those religious organizations that accept state funding. It must be emphasized that religious organizations enjoy the following freedoms:

- the freedom to worship or assemble in connection with a religion or belief, and to establish and maintain places for these purposes;
- the freedom to establish and maintain appropriate charitable or humanitarian institutions;
- the freedom to make, acquire and use to an adequate extent the necessary articles and materials related to the rites or customs of a religion or belief;
- the freedom to write, issue and disseminate relevant publications in these areas;
- the freedom to teach a religion or belief in places suitable for these purposes;
- the freedom to solicit and receive voluntary financial and other contributions from individuals and institutions;
- the freedom to train, appoint, elect or designate by succession appropriate leaders called for by the requirements and standards of any religion or belief;
- the freedom to establish and maintain communications with individuals and communities in matters of religion and belief at the national and international levels.[158]

It is submitted that a religious organization that accepts state funding by no means waives any of these freedoms. It has been observed that an established religion in practice might, paradoxically, be less free as regards certain internal institutional affairs than non-recognized religions.[159] The Church of England, for instance, is supported as the established Church of England: to date this church is not completely free in its institutional affairs as the Monarch (in practice the Government) formally appoints its bishops.[160] Also, wherever the official scriptures or articles of faith enjoy constitutional confirmation, amendments of such religious doctrines typically require governmental consent (as is the case in England and Greece).[161]

---

[158] This list draws on some of the freedoms that are enumerated in art. 6 of the UN Religious Tolerance Declaration (1981); some of these points are also mentioned in: Human Rights Committee, General Comment 22, para. 4.

[159] Roland Minnerath, *The Right to Autonomy in Religious Affairs, in* Facilitating Freedom of Religion or Belief: A Deskbook (Lindholm, Durham and Tahzib-Lie, eds., Leiden: Martinus Nijhoff Publishers, 2004), p. 315.

[160] *Ibid.*, p. 315; state interference with the appointment of Catholic bishops in Catholic states was abolished by the Vatican II (the Second Vatican Council took place in the 1960s).

[161] *Ibid.*, pp. 314–315. See art. 3, para. (3), of the Const. of Greece (2001): "The text of the Holy Scripture shall be maintained unaltered".

'Religion Tax'

As for the issue of 'religion tax', it will be clear that if a state were to collect 'religion tax' or 'church tax' from people that do not actually adhere to the state or predominant religion in question, the state acts contrary to the non-coercion principle and the freedom from religion principle.[162] It could be argued that even in cases where 'opt-out clauses' are provided for, the system remains highly problematic in terms of human rights compliance as no one should ever be forced to reveal one's belief or lack thereof.[163]

A second concern, much related to the issue discussed in the previous sub-paragraph, is that a church tax system in practice often exclusively or disproportionally benefits the state or predominant religion. This certainly holds true for state–religion relationships in Denmark,[164] Finland,[165] and Switzerland[166] and to a lesser extent to Austria,[167] Germany,[168] Iceland,[169] and San Marino[170] (in the latter states we can see how this system is of benefit to some of the larger or more traditional religions, but not to all religious groups or organizations). It is submitted that these practices encroach on people's equal religious rights.[171] Religious organizations that do not profit from these schemes may themselves be in a position to ask for financial contributions from their members; however, that does distract from the fact that they are put at a disadvantage by the above described form of state interference. It has

162 Cf. Human Rights Committee; on the need for opt-out clauses, *e.g.*: A/44/40 (1989), para. 592 (Italy); A/38/40 (1983), para. 113 (Iceland); A/36/40 (1981), para. 124 (Italy); A/34/40 (1979), para. 412 (Finland); A/33/40 (1978), para. 240 (Norway); see also CCPR/C/SR.392, para. 20 (Iceland); CCPR/C/SR.896, para. 27 (Bolivia); CCPR/C/SR.258, para. 30 (Italy).

163 Human Rights Committee, General Comment 22, para. 3.

164 The state levies a so-called 'church tax' at the municipal level on behalf of the state church (the Evangelical-Lutheran Church) solely.

165 The two national churches, the Evangelical Lutheran Church and the Orthodox Church, benefit from the church tax that is levied by the state.

166 The (24) cantons that have established or that officially support one of the three traditional religions (Roman Catholicism, Old Catholicism or Protestantism) provide financial support to that denomination; some cantons have extended the church tax scheme to the two other traditional religions as well as to Jewish congregations.

167 The (at present 13) officially recognized 'religious societies' benefit from, among other things, a state-directed tithing scheme and tax exemptions.

168 The state collects on behalf of those religious organizations that have acquired a corporation-under-public-law status a church tax from the members of those religious organizations (registered religious organizations are also granted tax exemptions as non-profit organizations). See art. 137, para. (5) in conjunction with para. (6), of the Weimar Constitution (1919) incorporated, pursuant art. 140, into the Basic Law for the Federal Republic of Germany (1949). Many Christian denominations and the Jewish community are recognized as such a public law corporation, yet as yet no Muslim organization has acquired the required legal status.

169 The church tax levied by the state is given (proportionally) to the officially recognized religions (the state has refused to acknowledge some denominations, *e.g.* the Community of Christ in Reykjavik; other religions have never applied for recognition, notably Jewish congregations).

170 The Roman Catholic Church receives funding from tax revenues, which scheme is extended solely to the Waldesian Church, the Bahá'ís and Jehovah's Witnesses.

171 See also OSCE/ODIHR, *Guidelines (supra* note 87), p. 21.

been suggested that a state that renders such a 'service' should be compensated by the religious organization(s) that benefit from it for the costs incurred.[172] This would indeed neutralize the financial privilege to some extent (Germany is a good example here).[173] It is submitted that such a system still reflects a discriminatory attitude on the part of the state in so far as it signals the state's willingness to commit itself to such a sophisticated practical link with the dominant religion(s) but not with minority ones.

Historical Prerogatives of Predominant Religions

Wherever religion has in practice taken up state functions or functions with important implications for the public good or public services, be it in the field of civil registration services,[174] marriage, health services, education, etc., the state must ensure that any such arrangement does not develop into practices that discriminate against minority religions or the rights of the non-religious. If the state were to grant the predominant religion a monopoly in any of these fields, violations of the rights and freedoms of the latter groups are inevitable.

As for the institution of marriage, the fact that this traditionally has been (or has become)[175] a religious institution does mot mean that presently, in the era of human rights law, the state has no obligations in this field. In Chapter 8 it was argued that the state in fact is under a human rights obligation to ensure that civil marriage is always open as an alternative to religious marriage. If the state fails in this respect the rights and freedoms of the non-religious are inevitably infringed upon.

The same applies to the area of education. As this issue will be separately discussed in Chapter 10, it will presently suffice to make the following remarks. Though the possibility of religious education as such has a sound basis in human rights law, the state may not contract out all primary education to religious organizations or accept a situation wherein primary school education remains monopolized by religion. The state has a positive duty to provide for non-denominational education.[176]

Another relevant issue is the traditional relationship between politics and religion. Establishmentarian states traditionally granted state religions political prerogatives by means of reserving a number of seats in representative bodies for representatives of the state religion, or by adopting eligibility criteria

---

[172] De Jong, *supra* note 35, p. 344.

[173] The German system requires that those organizations that avail themselves of this service pay a fee to the state.

[174] On this particular issue, see De Jong, *supra* note 35, p. 288.

[175] The institution of marriage predates recorded history (and, consequently, modern religion). See, *e.g.*, Edward A. Westermarck, The History of Human Marriage (London: Macmilan and Co., Ltd, 1903); Franz C. Muller-Lyer, The Evolution of Modern Marriage (New York: Alfred Knopf, 1930).

[176] See Chapter 10, section 10.2, *infra*.

concerning some (senior) political offices that require the office holder to possess the right religious qualifications. The issue of religious requirements for holding public office, which have remained largely intact in states with an official religion, will be discussed in detail in a separate Chapter.[177]

Religious Holidays & Days of Rest

The freedom to "observe days of rest and to celebrate holidays and ceremonies in accordance with the precepts of one's religion or belief" is recognized by the 1981 UN Religious Tolerance Declaration.[178] On account of the traditional ties between the state and the traditional, predominant religion, the official national holidays and the weekly day of rest normally largely correspond with (some of) the religious holidays and the day of rest observed by the traditional religion in question. By contrast, holidays or days of rest observed by minority religions are generally devoid of such official or *de facto* recognition. It will be clear that the issue touches both on questions of religious freedom as well as on questions of non-discrimination and is perhaps best discussed as an issue of 'equal religious freedom'.

The issue at hand is not as straightforward as many other issues of equality/non-discrimination. For example, as to the issue of prerogatives of the traditional religion in the field of politics it is relatively uncomplicated to establish the rule that states are not to reserve political seats for representatives of the latter religion as that runs counter to principles of a fair democracy and the equal rights of minorities. As there are only so many days that can be observed as holidays or days of rest without doing damage to the economy, adopting a fair and equitable approach is not free from problems. Having said that, religious pluralism should by no means be construed so as to mean that an equitable approach is out of the question or that anything goes: it will be contended that there are most definitely ways of internalizing a degree of flexibility into the state's approach from which members of the different religions may benefit.

It must be postulated, first of all, that the norm that states must respect people's freedom to "observe days of rest and to celebrate holidays and ceremonies in accordance with the precepts of one's religion or belief" does not require the state to officially declare all religious days of rest and holidays of the different religions as official days of rest and holidays. It has been recognized fairly early on in the history of the UN that such an approach is simply not practicable.[179] To this it may be added that the other extreme, designating a series of

---

[177] See Chapter 11, section 11.2.1(iv), *infra*.

[178] Art. 6, para. (h), of the UN Religious Tolerance Declaration (1981); moreover, the *forum externum* includes the observance of holidays and days of rest according to: Human Rights Committee, General Comment 22, para. 4. 'Holidays' is of course a contraction of the Old English 'holy days'.

[179] Krishnaswami, *supra* note 88, p. 35.

national holidays and opting for a day of rest in a way that is not beneficial to any of the religions so as to 'equally disadvantage all', may also not be practicable or desirable.[180] In order to address the issue at hand, it is necessary to distinguish between the right to observe a weekly day of rest and the right to observe occasional religious holidays.

As to the first issue, many states with a population that traditionally adhered to a particular religion have designated or accepted as the weekly day of rest the one that is mandatorily observed by this group.[181] In many of these states, meanwhile, processes of secularization and immigration have eroded the religious homogeneity of the population (which is not to say that in all those states adherents of non-traditional religions or non-believers are necessarily actively challenging the present situation). Some have argued that maintaining the status quo in these societies would not amount to a human rights violation.[182] It is submitted here that the legitimacy of the arrangement more specifically depends on the precise ramifications for: (a) religious minorities and their mandatory days of rest; and (b) non-religious people who do not necessarily have an interest in a fixed weekly day of rest. In that respect, it must be observed that, strictly speaking, the official designation of a fixed legal day of rest might amount to distinctive treatment on the basis of religion or belief if this construction particularly benefits one particular group of believers (the majority religion, normally). An act of differentiation, however, may be legitimized if so-called 'objective and reasonable' criteria and reasons can be advanced.[183] Similarly, to the extent that differentiation in this field amounts to an interference with the *forum externum* of religious minorities and non-believers, these measures may be justified in so far as overriding reasons of public interest can be advanced. Considering the recognized grounds for limitation in this area, one may, for instance, construe standardization of working days for economic reasons as

---

[180] Particularly as far as the weekly day of rest is concerned, it may be argued that the more devout adherents of the predominant religion are likely to cease work on their religious day of rest either way; which would mean that the week becomes split up into two small working weeks in between the 'neutral day of rest' and the traditional, religious one. Cf. Ruth Gavison, *Days of Worship and Days of Rest: A View from Israel, in* Religion in the Public Sphere: A Comparative Analysis of German, Israeli, American and International Law (Brugger & Karayanni, eds., Berlin: Springer, 2007), p. 402.

[181] If there is no clear-cut predominant religion but rather, for instance, two or three more or less equally large religious communities it would be logical to either allow each individual to choose for his or herself or to design a system of rotation (the fact that something along those lines is not likely to be introduced is not as much because it would be absolutely impracticable but rather because of a lack of political and societal will to make any amendments in this regard). See also De Jong, *supra* note 35, p. 317–318.

[182] *E.g.* Krishnaswami, *supra* note 88, p. 35–36; Gavison, *supra* note 180, p. 393, considers that "international human rights law does not prohibit the choice of a day of rest of public offices on the religious day of rest and worship of the majority religion".

[183] Human Rights Committee, General Comment 18, para. 13.

an 'order' argument. However, a strong counter-argument here is that standardization of working days may certainly contribute to 'public convenience', yet it cannot be considered an absolute prerequisite to maintaining public 'order'—hence, state interference is not strictly necessary in a democratic society. It would, moreover, appear that it is not strictly necessary for a state to fix a weekly day of rest in order to comply with international labour standards,[184] considering the fact that the labour law norm which calls for 'regular days of rest' can be guaranteed by adopting more flexible arrangements. Finally, also 'morals' of a non-religious nature (e.g. curtailing 'excessive consumerism', guaranteeing a fixed period of 'public peace and quiet'), arguably, do not warrant rigorous state interference in this field. In other words, the question emerges whether there is actually a plausible and legitimate (secular) reason for state interference with the observance of days of rest. De Jong has argued in this regard:

> Many companies in western countries are in favour of flexible working hours, including on the traditional weekly days of rest. Discussion on shopping hours and days continues and there too the trend is towards flexibility. Against this background, it should be possible to limit state intervention to a minimum, whereby only the number of holidays would be fixed, leaving it to the individuals concerned to determine how these should be allotted.

State interference with the observance of days of rest, in terms of explicitly designating a fixed day of rest which coincides with the day of rest observed by the majority religion, particularly raises questions regarding the rights and freedoms of non-religious people. The Constitution of Tonga is illustrative in that regard as it explicitly declares that:

> The Sabbath Day shall be kept holy in Tonga and no person shall practise his trade or profession or conduct any commercial undertaking on the Sabbath Day except according to law; and any agreement made or witnessed on that day shall be null and void and of no legal effect.[185]

The fact that people ignoring the Sabbath rule are subject to a fine (some exemptions are granted to tourism-oriented enterprises) forms a limit on the equal religious freedoms of non-religious people (in this context, freedom *from* religion). The Supreme Court of Canada struck down Canada's Lord's

---

[184] *E.g.* art. 6 of the ILO Convention concerning Weekly Rest in Commerce and Offices, C106 (entry into force: 4 March 1959); and art. 2 of the Convention concerning the Application of the Weekly Rest in Industrial Undertakings of 1921, C14 (entry into force: 19 June 1923).

[185] Art. 6 of the CONST. OF TONGA (1875), which article reflects traces of the Vava'u Code of 1839, which in turn, was greatly inspired by Methodist missionary convictions. The only other Constitution that legally protects the Sunday as the weekly day of rest is the German one: "Sundays and holidays recognized by the Land shall remain under legal protection as days of rest from work and for the promotion of spiritual purposes."

Day Act precisely on account of it being at odds with the right to freedom of religion or belief enshrined in the *Canadian Charter of Rights and Freedoms*:

> The Lord's Day Act to the extent that it binds all to a sectarian Christian ideal, works a form of coercion inimical to the spirit of the Charter. The Act gives the appearance of discrimination against non-Christian Canadians. Religious values rooted in Christian morality are translated into a positive law binding on believers and non-believers alike. Non-Christians are prohibited for religious reasons from carrying out otherwise lawful, moral and normal activities. Any law, purely religious in purpose, which denies non-Christians the right to work on Sunday denies them the right to practise their religion and infringes their religious freedom. The protection of one religion and the concomitant non-protection of others imports a disparate impact destructive of the religious freedom of society. The power to compel, on religious grounds, the universal observance of the day of rest preferred by one religion is not consistent with the preservation and enhancement of the multi-cultural heritage of Canadians...[186]

The above concerns and arguments point at non-interference with the observance of a religious day of rest as recommended policy. This state policy seems a necessary yet not quite sufficient strategy. In a state that refrains from explicitly designating a fixed day of rest, the regulation of regular days of rest will largely be conferred to the level of individual employers. It is submitted that the state has a positive duty to mainstream religious tolerance into the policy area of employment and more specifically to encourage employers (in practice by liaising with the employers' federations) to adopt flexible policies in the field of work schedules. In this respect, it must be observed that some positive developments along these lines can be discerned. Norway, for instance, provides in its labour laws for the following option:

> The employer and the employee may enter into a written agreement concerning work on Sundays and public holidays...allowing the employee corresponding time off on the days that are equivalent to Sundays and public holidays according to the employee's religion.[187]

Bulgarian equality legislation serves as a useful example as well. It urges employers to take account of the religious needs of their employees, whilst realistically recognizing the economical and logistical issues employers are faced with. It provides that:

> In the cases when it would not lead to a disproportionate burden on the employer in organising and carrying out the production, and in the cases when there exist ways to compensate the objectively possible unfavourable consequences for the general production result, the employer shall provide working conditions, in

---

[186] *R. v. Big M Drug Mart Ltd.*, [1985] 1 S.C.R. 295, Judgement of 25 April 1985. See Lord's Day Act, R.S.C. 1970, c. L-13, s. 4; and the Canadian Charter of Rights and Freedoms, Schedule B to the Canada Act 1982, c. 11 (which came into force on 17 April 1982).

[187] Art. 10, para. (5), of the Working Environment Act of 1977 (as amended through 2007).

> view of the working time and the days off, complying with the requirements of the religion or belief, professed by a worker or employee.[188]

The New Zealand Human Rights Act attempts to introduce a similar policy, albeit in more general terms:

> Where a religious or ethical belief requires its adherents to follow a particular practice, an employer must accommodate the practice so long as any adjustment of the employer's activities required to accommodate the practice does not unreasonably disrupt the employer's activities.[189]

In sum, rather than considering religious pluralism an insurmountable problem in this regard, it may be considered the key to solving the issue, for it is increasing religious pluralism—together with the fact that many states are moving towards '24/7 economies'—which enables accommodation of the various preferences as to working and not working on specific days.

The second main issue in this field is the observance of the occasional religious holidays. Again, in a pluralist society it is impracticable to officially recognize the holy days of all religious communities. Having said that, also in this field flexibility is not out of the question. The state could in theory recognize a mixture of the main holidays of the main religions. However, yet again a system based on minimal state interference in combination with an encouragement of employers to, as far as possible, accommodate the individual's preferences would seem the recommendable and most realistic road.[190] Krishnaswami has indicated as a general benchmark in this field that:

> ...public authorities must take care to mete out approximately equal treatment to all faiths. As a general rule the prescriptions of each religion or belief relating to

[188] Art. 13, para. (2), of the Law on the Protection Against Discrimination, 199/2003 (entered into force: 1 January 2004).

[189] Art. 28, para. (3), of the Human Rights Act 1993 [New Zealand], Act No. 82 (amended 3 December 2007); this provision appears to particularly aim at accommodating religious practices at work, such as daily prayers, but could be seized to adopt flexible arrangements regarding weekly days of rest. It may at this point be added that there are states with a longer experience with the issue at hand. See, *e.g.*, art. 7 of the Hours of Work and Rest Law of Israel, Law No. 5711-1951, of 1951: "The weekly rest shall include: (1) in the case of a Jew, the Sabbath day; (2) in the case of a person other than a Jew the Sabbath day or Sunday or Friday, whichever is ordinarily observed by him as his weekly day of rest". This clause is further protected by the non-discrimination provision (art. 9C, para. (a), of this Act) which holds that employers may not discriminate on the basis of religion or the fact that specific days of rest come with that religion. It must be observed, at the same time, that the designation of the Sabbath as a compulsory day of rest may be objectionable for secular Jews. Rather than forcing Jews to take the Sabbath off it could have accommodated Jews to take that day off should they desire so.

[190] Some forms of best practice could also be highlighted in this context, *e.g.*: Argentina: although the state (*de facto*) observes a number of Christian holidays as national holidays (Good Friday, Immaculate Conception and Christmas), it provides at the same time for the possibility of paid holidays and absence from school for Jews and Muslims during their most important holy days. See the Declaration of Non-working Days for Jewish Inhabitants Act, Act No. 24571, of 1995 (as supplemented by Pay of Workers on Jewish and Muslim Holidays Act, Act No.

> holidays...should be taken into account, subject to the overriding consideration of the interest of society as a whole.[191]

In conclusion, the state's human rights obligations in this field revolve around ensuring that it is possible for every person to observe the holy days of one's religion.

9.3 Religion & Freedom of Expression

Blasphemy is a serious wrongdoing in all monotheistic world religions.[192] Blasphemy prohibitions in states with a population that predominantly adheres

---

25151, of 1999). The original Act provided for paid holidays for the Jewish holy days of New Year (Rosh Hashanah), the Days of Atonement (Yom Kippur) and Passover (Pesach); an Act of April 2006 extends paid leave for those who wish to observe Jewish holy days from 3 to 7 days. See furthermore: Declaration of Non-working Days for Muslim Inhabitants Act, Act No. 24757, of 1996 (as supplemented by: Pay of Workers on Jewish and Muslim Holidays Act, Act No. 25151, of 1999), which provides that the Muslim New Year (Hegira), the day after the end of Ramadan (Eid al-Fitr) and the day of the Holy Day of Sacrifice (Eid al-Adha) are holidays for Muslims. See also the report by then Special Rapporteur on FoRB, Mr. Abdelfattah Amor, E/CN.4/2002/73/Add.1, paras. 29–32 and para. 125.

[191] Krishnaswami, *supra* note 88, p. 35–36.

[192] *E.g.* the Tanakh or Hebrew Bible prescribes the death penalty by means of stoning: Holy Bible (English Standard Version), Leviticus 24:10–23: "Now an Israelite woman's son, whose father was an Egyptian, went out among the people of Israel. And the Israelite woman's son and a man of Israel fought in the camp, and the Israelite woman's son blasphemed the Name, and cursed. Then they brought him to Moses. His mother's name was Shelomith, the daughter of Dibri, of the tribe of Dan. And they put him in custody, till the will of the Lord should be clear to them. Then the Lord spoke to Moses, saying, 'Bring out of the camp the one who cursed, and let all who heard him lay their hands on his head, and let all the congregation stone him. And speak to the people of Israel, saying, Whoever curses his God shall bear his sin. Whoever blasphemes the name of the Lord shall surely be put to death. All the congregation shall stone him. The sojourner as well as the native, when he blasphemes the Name, shall be put to death...' So Moses spoke to the people of Israel, and they brought out of the camp the one who had cursed and stoned him with stones. Thus the people of Israel did as the Lord commanded Moses." The New Testament of the Christian Bible speaks of earthly punishments as well as possible repercussions in the afterlife, yet solely with regard to blasphemy against the Holy Spirit: Holy Bible (English Standard Version), Matthew 12: 30–32: "Whoever is not with me is against me, and whoever does not gather with me scatters. Therefore I tell you, every sin and blasphemy will be forgiven people, but the blasphemy against the Spirit will not be forgiven. And whoever speaks a word against the Son of Man will be forgiven, but whoever speaks against the Holy Spirit will not be forgiven, either in this age or in the age to come." See also Mark 3:28–29: "Truly, I say to you, all sins will be forgiven the children of man, and whatever blasphemies they utter, but whoever blasphemes against the Holy Spirit never has forgiveness, but is guilty of an eternal sin". The Quran speaks of earthly punishments as well as possible repercussions in the afterlife: The Holy Qur'an (transl. Abdullah Yusuf Ali), 9:74: "They swear by Allah that they said nothing (evil), but indeed they uttered blasphemy, and they did it after accepting Islam; and they meditated a plot which they were unable to carry out: this revenge of theirs was (their) only return for the bounty with which Allah and His Messenger had enriched them! If they repent, it will be best for them; but if they turn back (to their evil ways), Allah will punish them with a grievous penalty in this life and in the Hereafter: They shall have none on earth to protect or help them." Other Quranic references to blasphemy (including references that render Christian or Jewish doctrine blasphemous deviations from true doctrine) include: 2:88; 4:155; 5:17; 5:64; 5:68; 5:73; 6:19; 9:74; 11:9; 14:28; and 39:8.

to a specific religion have traditionally been brought into being and enforced so as to protect that dominant religion specifically.[193] There is a notable difference between the blasphemy prohibition in states that officially identify with Islam and blasphemy bans in states that are predominantly Christian. In the latter states, where the prohibitions historically developed into provisions of statutory law (Penal Codes, typically) or where, springing from ancient cannon law, blasphemy became centuries ago a common law offence, the ban (ultimately)[194] came to be used to solely counter intentionally insulting speech or publications vis-à-vis God, key doctrinal figures (Jesus Christ, chiefly), or the established religion as such. Thus criminalized are such forms of public speech or publication that are meant to shock or harm the feelings of the dominant religious community. In other words, merely having misgivings about certain doctrinal aspects of a religion or the mere denial of God does, as a rule,[195] not qualify as blasphemy or blasphemous libel in these jurisdictions. In contrast, in the Islamic legal context there has always been (and there still is, as we will presently see) a considerable overlap between the crimes of apostasy and blasphemy. Intentionally insulting Allah, Muhammad, or indeed the religion of Islam itself constitutes a punishable offence—yet, on top of that abandoning Islam as such is, as a rule, considered an act of blasphemy since such an act of disbelief, in the final analysis, amounts to an insult to the Muslim community as a whole and, more importantly, to God.

In more recent times,[196] both domestic as well as international legal initiatives can be perceived surrounding the issue of 'defamation of religion(s)'.

---

[193] This section is largely based on: Jeroen Temperman, *Blasphemy, Defamation of Religions & Human Rights Law*, 26(4) Netherlands Quarterly of Human Rights (2008), pp. 517–545.

[194] Needless to say that in past times 'the Church' did not shy away from cracking down on atheists and apostates for merely denying God's existence or on specific forms of scientific research for potentially undermining Church doctrine.

[195] There are exceptions, *e.g.*: sec. 36 of Ch. 272 of the Criminal Code of Massachusetts: "Whoever wilfully blasphemes the holy name of God by *denying*, cursing or contumeliously reproaching God, his creation, government or final judging of the world, or by cursing or contumeliously reproaching Jesus Christ or the Holy Ghost, or by cursing or contumeliously reproaching or exposing to contempt and ridicule, the holy word of God contained in the holy scriptures shall be punished by imprisonment in jail for not more than one year or by a fine of not more than three hundred dollars, and may also be bound to good behavior" (emphasis added). This provision is clearly at odds with the Supreme Court's non-establishment doctrine based on the First Amendment (1789) to the federal Const. of the USA (1787).

[196] The 'Counter-Defamation Discourse' as a competing paradigm (competing with conventional individualistic approaches to human rights law, that is), both domestically as well as within international forums, was significantly re-vitalised by the 'Danish cartoon row' in 2006 (it was, however, already emerging long before that particular affair: one can think of the 'Rushdie affair' in the late 80s). This controversy revolved around cartoons that, *inter alia*, mockingly depicted Muhammad in the Danish newspaper *Jyllands-Posten*. The cartoons were published in September 2005 (and were republished in many countries since) though the reaction in terms of protests in the Muslim world took place somewhat later, most visibly in February and March 2006.

The question that emerges is how the issues of blasphemy and defamation of religion relate to international human rights law. In this section, firstly domestic approaches to dealing with blasphemy and defamation of religion are identified and analysed. Subsequently, these forms of state practice are further scrutinized in light of international human rights law, particularly the right to freedom of expression. It will be contended that the so-called 'Counter-Defamation Discourse' that is emerging may have negative ramifications for fundamental rights and must be dismissed.

9.3.1 *Domestic Counter-Blasphemy and Counter-Defamation Measures*

Blasphemy prohibitions have developed over time and in radically different contexts. This sub-section is intended to chart contemporary blasphemy and religious defamation prohibitions.

Firstly, many predominantly Christian states have traditionally taken measures to counter blasphemy. Some of those states (though certainly not all, as will become apparent) have in more recent times abolished or simply 'neglected' the relevant legal provisions. A distinction is visible between generic blasphemy prohibitions and discriminatory bans that seek to protect just one religion (Christianity) against blasphemous acts or, even more specifically, solely one specific Christian Church or denomination (the latter would be the case, as a rule, in states which had constitutionally established a specific Christian denomination as the state church).

Blasphemy and blasphemous libel, notoriously, were common law offences in England and Wales for many centuries; these offences were officially abolished as recently as May 2008.[197] Though a proper definition is lacking, on the basis of the jurisprudence pertaining to this offence it has been proposed that blasphemy was committed:

> ...by anyone who makes public words, pictures or conduct whereby the doctrines, beliefs, institutions, or sacred objects and rituals of the Church of England by law established are denied or scurrilously vilified or there is objectively contumelious, violent or ribald conduct or abuse directed towards the sacred subject in question, likely to shock and outrage the feelings of the general body of Church of England believers in the community.[198]

A House of Lords' Select Committee on Religious Offences paved the way towards abolishment of this offence as it considered the legal concept both

[197] See art. 79 of the Criminal Justice and Immigration Act 2008 (c. 4) (the abolishment entered into effect on 8 July 2008). Some months earlier, on 5 March 2008, the House of Lords had voted in favour of the amendment to the Criminal Justice Bill as proposed by the Government. Scotland has its own regulations on blasphemy, an offence not penalized since the 1840s. Northern Ireland does not have blasphemy laws anymore.

[198] Select Committee on Religious Offences in England and Wales, *Religious Offences in England and Wales: First Report*, Session 2002–2003 (published in HL Paper 95–I, 2003), Appendix 3: Blasphemy, para. 6.

obsolete as well as, in the final analysis, contrary to fundamental human rights norms. With respect to its archaic nature the Committee considered the following:

> The legal notion of blasphemy dates back many centuries. Faith was seen to be the root of society's political and moral behaviour. Therefore, to challenge that faith or to offend against it was to seriously threaten the very fabric of political and moral society and had to be punished severely. Clearly, that is no longer the case. Some might regret that, but it does not alter the fact that the law is now concerned with the preservation of the peace of the realm, and the concern is not so much with views of the deity as with the satisfactory state of society.[199]

With respect to UK's human rights obligations, the Committee considered that the ban's limited scope (it offered protection against blasphemous acts merely to the Church of England) runs counter to the non-discrimination principle,[200] and moreover, the ban would infringe upon the right to freedom of expression.[201] Some Commonwealth jurisdictions inherited the offence of blasphemy, be it as a common law offence (e.g. Australia)[202] or as a prohibition codified by a Penal Code (e.g. Canada and New Zealand).[203]

Other predominantly Christian states may serve as an example. The Constitution of Ireland provides that "[t]he State acknowledges that the homage of public worship is due to Almighty God. It shall hold His Name in reverence, and shall respect and honour religion."[204] It is hardly surprising, therefore, that the Constitution renders blasphemy a punishable offence[205] (something that has been subsequently codified and further outlined by statutory law).[206] It must be noted that also in Ireland an ongoing debate is apparent concerning

---

[199] *Ibid.*, para. 2.

[200] *Ibid.*, para. 11: "It is doubtful that an objective and rational justification could be provided for the difference in treatment of different religions and their beliefs, so there is a significant risk of the law of blasphemy violating [the non-discrimination principle]".

[201] *Ibid.*, para. 10–13; which, interestingly, implies that the Committee disapproved of the European Court of Human Rights' judgements in which the Court actually sanctioned the blasphemy ban, *e.g.*: ECtHR, Application No. 17419/90, *Wingrove v. the United Kingdom*, Judgement of 25 November 1996. The Select Committee on Religious Offences went as far as expressing an expectation that the European Court will revise its stance on blasphemy laws in future cases (*ibid.*, para. 12).

[202] Some Australian states have codified the offence explicitly in their state Criminal Codes. *E.g.* sec. 574 of the Crimes Act of New South Wales of 1900, which formulates it negatively, stating that "[n]o person shall be liable to prosecution in respect of any publication by him or her orally, or otherwise, of words or matter charged as blasphemous, where the same is by way of argument, or statement, and not for the purpose of scoffing or reviling, nor of violating public decency, nor in any manner tending to a breach of the peace" (in other words, if the publication is in fact for one of the latter reasons, one may be liable for prosecution).

[203] Art. 296 of the Canadian Criminal Code, R.S., 1985, c. C-46; and art. 123 of the New Zealand Crimes Act of 1961.

[204] Art. 44, para. (1), of the CONST. OF IRELAND (1937).

[205] Art. 40, para. (6)(i), of the CONST. OF IRELAND (1937).

[206] See art. 13, para. (1), of the Defamation Act of 1961, which was replaced in 2009 by a new Defamation Bill, which upholds the crime of blasphemy (sec. 36).

the tenability of this offence. The Irish Law Reform Commission is "of the view that there is no place for the offence of blasphemous libel in a society which respects freedom of speech" and has consequently advised its abolishment.[207] This makes it all the more remarkable that in 2009 a new Defamation Act was adopted which retains the crime of blasphemy.[208]

The Greek constitutional blasphemy prohibition is *de jure* non-discriminatory.[209] However, this constitutional provision was transfigured into discriminatory blasphemy prohibitions by the Greek Penal Code[210] which are used in practice to protect the Greek Orthodox Church specifically against blasphemous publications.[211] The Scandinavian states with Lutheran state churches all have incorporated generic blasphemy prohibitions into their Penal Codes.[212]

In many Islamic states the blasphemy prohibition can by no means be considered a dead letter—state practice shows that they are very much alive. The Constitution of Pakistan, for instance, provides that "[e]very citizen shall have the right to freedom of speech and expression". This freedom, however, is "subject to any reasonable restrictions imposed by law in the interest of the glory of Islam".[213] This ground for limiting the fundamental freedom of expression uncompromisingly paved the way for codification of a broad range of criminal

---

[207] Law Reform Commission, *Consultation Paper on the Crime of Libel*, August 1991, para. 231; *Corway v Independent Newspapers (Ireland) Ltd*, 4 IR 484 [1999], moreover, made future prosecution highly unfeasible under the previous (1961) Defamation Act.

[208] Art. 36 of the Blasphemy Act 2009, Bill No. 43/2006, which entered into force in July 2009, states: "(1) A person who publishes or utters blasphemous matter shall be guilty of an offence and shall be liable upon conviction on indictment to a fine not exceeding €25,000. (2) For the purposes of this section, a person publishes or utters blasphemous matter if: (a) he or she publishes or utters matter that is grossly abusive or insulting in relation to matters held sacred by any religion, thereby causing outrage among a substantial number of the adherents of that religion, and (b) he or she intends, by the publication or utterance of the matter concerned, to cause such outrage."

[209] Art. 14, para. (3), Const. of Greece (2001) provides: "The seizure of newspapers and other publications before or after circulation is prohibited. Seizure by order of the public prosecutor shall be allowed exceptionally after circulation and in case of: an offence against the Christian *or any other known religion*" (emphasis added).

[210] Artt. 198 and 199 of the Greek Penal Code, attaching a penalty to blasphemy vis-à-vis God (punishable with imprisonment of up to two years; art. 198), divinity (punishable with imprisonment of up to three months; art. 198) or *Greek Orthodox religion* as such (punishable with imprisonment of up to two years; art. 199).

[211] A recent notorious case is the 2005 trial against Gerhard Haderer. In 2005, Gerhard Haderer's book *The Life of Jesus* was banned on account of its being considered blasphemous (a case instigated by the Greek Orthodox Church). Haderer was given a six-month suspended prison sentence. In appeal, however, both the ban and the prison sentence were revoked.

[212] Sec. 10 of Chapter 17 ("Offences Against Public Order") of the Penal Code of Finland, Act 39/1889, a provision updated as recently as 1998 and still enforced occasionally (*e.g.* in 2005); art. 142 of the Norwegian Penal Code criminalizes "contempt for any religious creed" (not enforced for decades), something in line with the Constitution as art. 100 of the Const. of Norway (1814) explicitly limits the freedom of expression in the interest of countering "contempt for religion"; and art. 140 of the Danish Penal Code penalizes anyone who "mocks or scorns" religious doctrines or acts of worship (not enforced since the 1930s).

[213] Art. 19 of the Const. of Pakistan (1973).

law provisions dealing with "Offences Relating to Religion",[214] including different blasphemy prohibitions. Defiling of the Quran,[215] Muhammad[216] or other Islamic holy personages[217] is punishable with life imprisonment, death or imprisonment respectively. The Pakistani situation perfectly illustrates how anti-blasphemy laws may be enacted or used to crackdown on specific religious minorities that deviate from the state-sanctioned religious orthodoxy. The Ahmadis were constitutionally stigmatised as apostates ("non-Muslims") in 1974.[218] As their religious beliefs, rituals and particularly their doctrinal opinions (e.g. on Jesus, the role and status of religious founder and reformer Ahmad, the finality of Prophet-hood) are not in keeping with the official Islamic orthodoxy as sanctioned and protected by the regime, Ahmadi religious beliefs are, when expressed publicly, per definition 'blasphemous' and punishable under Pakistani criminal law. The 'anti-Ahmadi laws' of 1984 criminalized a range of specific deviations from what the state considers 'pure doctrine' and are basically designed to make it impossible for Ahmadis to openly practice and propagate their faith.[219] One such anti-Ahmadi clause stipulates that an Ahmadi who "in any manner whatsoever outrages the religious feelings of Muslims" shall be punished with imprisonment or a fine.[220] This prohibition, it goes without saying, lacks any objective criteria and is susceptible to grave abuses.

The Iranian Constitution does not provide for an individual right to freedom of expression. It codifies a limited interpretation of 'freedom of the press'. This freedom is only granted in as far as the exercise of this freedom is in accordance with "fundamental principles of Islam".[221] The dissemination of thoughts by means of the Radio and Television is to be guaranteed "in keeping

---

[214] See Chapter XV of the Pakistan Penal Code of 6 October 1860, XLV/1860.

[215] Art. 295-B of the Pakistan Penal Code; inserted by Amendment Ordinance I of 1982.

[216] Art. 295-C of the Pakistan Penal Code; inserted by the Criminal Law Amendment Act, 111 of 1986, S. 2.

[217] Art. 298-A of the Pakistan Penal Code (inserted by the Second Amendment Ordinance, XLIV of 1980).

[218] See section 8.2.2, particularly the text around note 60 (Chapter 8), *supra*.

[219] Art. 298-B of the Pakistan Penal Code; inserted by Anti-Islamic Activities of Quadiani Group, Lahori Group and Ahmadis (Prohibition and Punishment) Ordinance, XX of 1984: "Any person of the Quadiani group or the Lahori group (who call themselves 'Ahmadis' or by any other name) who by words, either spoken or written, or by visible representation: (a) refers to or addresses, any person, other than a Caliph or companion of the Holy Prophet Muhammad (peace be upon him), as 'Ameer-ul-Mumineen', 'Khalifatul-Mumineen', 'Khalifa-tul-Muslimeen', 'Sahaabi' or 'Razi Allah Anho'; (b) refers to, or addresses, any person, other than a wife of the Holy Prophet Muhammad (peace be upon him), as 'Ummul-Mumineen'; (c) refers to, or addresses, any person, other than a member of the family 'Ahle-bait' of the Holy Prophet Muhammad (peace be upon him), as 'Ahle-baft';...shall be punished with imprisonment of either description for a term which may extend to three years, and shall also be liable to a fine."

[220] Art. 298-C of the Pakistan Penal Code; inserted by the Anti-Islamic Activities of Quadiani Group, Lahori Group and Ahmadis (Prohibition and Punishment) Ordinance, XX of 1984.

[221] Art. 24 of the Const. of Iran (1979).

with the Islamic criteria and the best interests of the country".[222] The Penal Code provides that:

> Anyone who insults the Islamic sanctities or any of the imams...should be executed if his insult equals to speaking disparagingly of Prophet Muhammad. Otherwise, [he/she] should be imprisoned from one to five years.[223]

In Iran blasphemy prohibitions are implemented at the expense of the rights and freedoms of religious minorities, notably the Bahá'ís. Moreover, the restrictions on freedom of expression are in practice also abused to crackdown on supporters of political reform[224] (which includes Muslims, especially the women's rights movement).

Other states with constitutional provisions that seek to curtail the right to freedom of expression in the interest of respect for Islam include: Bahrain (respect for "Islamic doctrine"),[225] Morocco (respect for "the religion of Islam"),[226] and the Maldives (respect for "the basic tenets of Islam").[227] Bahrain and the Maldives have statutory laws in place to protect the state religion and to counter blasphemy.[228] Other states that forbid blasphemous acts against Islam or otherwise *de jure* or *de facto* curtail the exercise of free speech in the interest of respect for Islam include: Afghanistan (recently the blasphemy prohibition has come to be used to target the Bahá'í minority specifically),[229] Algeria,[230] Jordan,[231] Kuwait,[232] Malaysia,[233] Oman,[234]

---

222 Art. 175 of the Const. of Iran (1979).

223 Art. 513 (part of the Chapter "Insulting the Religious Sanctities or State Officials") of the Islamic Penal Code of Iran of 1991.

224 See, *e.g.*, *Report Submitted by the Special Rapporteur on the Right to Freedom of Opinion and Expression: Mission to the Islamic Republic of Iran* (4 to 10 November 2003), E/CN.4/2004/62/Add.2, 12 January 2004.

225 Art. 23 of the Const. of Bahrain (2002)

226 Art. 39 of the Const. of Morocco (1996).

227 Art. 25 of the Const. of Maldives (1998).

228 The Press Law of 2002 (47/2002) in conjunction with the 1976 Bahraini Penal Code is used to penalize the act of criticising the state's official religion in Bahrain; the Maldives Penal Code, Act Number 1/8127/1/1381H, makes mention of "offences relating to the religion of Islam".

229 Blasphemy is *de facto* punishable with death (by hanging) unless the blasphemer recants his/her actions within three days (the Chapter of the Penal Code of 1976 dealing with "Crimes against Religions", however, does not condemn blasphemy explicitly). In 2007 the General Directorate of Fatwas and Accounts under the Supreme Court issued a ruling on the status of the Bahá'í faith to the effect that it is considered distinct from Islam and a form of blasphemy.

230 Art. 11 of the Ordinance 06–03 makes the publication or distribution of documents which are intended to "shake the faith" of Muslims punishable.

231 Insulting God or the Prophet is punishable with a prison sentence under Jordanian penal law.

232 Art. 111 of the Penal Code of 1960, 16/1960 (in conjunction with Kuwait's Printing and Publications Law) makes denigration of a religion or a religious school of thought a punishable offence. Article 19 of the Law of Publications and Release of 6 March 2006 delimits blasphemy to Islamic doctrine.

233 Though artt. 295–298A (i.e. Chapter XV – "Offences Relating to Religion") of the Federal Malaysian Penal Code, Act No. 574 of 7 August 1997, provide sentences for different acts of defiling religions (i.e. in a non-discriminatory fashion), the constituent states have adopted legislation to specifically protect Islam against blasphemous acts.

234 Art. 209 of the Penal Code of Oman (adopted by royal decree 7/1974).

Saudi Arabia,[235] and Yemen.[236] 'Neutral' blasphemy prohibitions (bans that do not explicitly single out a specific religion) may in practice be enforced one-sidedly so as to solely protect Islam. One may think of Bangladesh, which *de jure* forbids insulting the "religious feelings" of people.[237] Other examples are Egypt, which *de jure* bans defamation of the "heavenly religions"[238] and Qatar, which *de jure* bans defamation of "a divinely revealed religion that is protected under the Islamic sharia," referring to the Abrahamic religions.[239]

Other states with a positive form of state–religion identification that forbid blasphemy include: officially 'monotheistic' Indonesia (which has codified a non-discriminatory ban that is *de facto* predominantly used in cases dealing with insults of Islam),[240] and Israel (which has codified a non-discriminatory prohibition of insulting religions, which has occasionally resulted in convictions of people who have insulted religions other than Judaism).[241]

Perhaps surprisingly, some secular or non-religious states prohibit blasphemy as well.[242] In those states the ban normally stems from the time when the state still identified positively with a specific religion. It must be observed that completely non-discriminatory bans, i.e. prohibitions that seek to equally protect both religious faiths as well as *non*-religious beliefs against defamation, can also be discerned (Germany is a good example).[243]

9.3.2 *The Interplay between Freedom of Expression and Freedom of Religion under International Human Rights law*

From the above comparative legal survey it can be concluded that 'the protection of religion' in some states, most visibly so in states that identify strongly with a single religion, functions as a ground for limiting the right to freedom

---

[235] Blasphemy is punishable with the death penalty (beheading) or a prison sentence. Apostasy cases are more often than not treated as blasphemy cases as the act of denouncing Islam is considered *ipso facto* blasphemous.

[236] Art. 103 of Press and Publications Law of 22 December 1990, No. 25/1990.

[237] Art. 295A of the Bangladeshi Penal Code of 1860: though it attaches a penalty to the malicious intention of hurting religious feelings of people in a general fashion, in practice the clause is predominantly used to penalize acts that insult Islam. Occasionally the prohibition has been employed to target Ahmadi publications specifically. It must be observed that since the early 1990s, the Bangladeshi High Court has brought several initiatives to a standstill which were intended to designate Ahmadis as non-Muslims and to codify Pakistani-style anti-Ahmadhi laws.

[238] Article 98(f) of the Egyptian Penal Code (as amended by Law 147/2006).

[239] The Criminal Code of Qatar, Act 11/2004.

[240] Article 156 of the Indonesian Criminal Code.

[241] *E.g.* in December 2006; an Israeli citizen was sentenced to nine months' imprisonment for throwing a pig's head – with the words 'Prophet Mohammed' written on it as well as a crescent moon (a symbol of Islam) drawn on it – into the courtyard of Hassan Bek mosque, Tel Aviv.

[242] *E.g.* Austria (art. 188 of the Austrian Penal Code); India (artt. 295A and 298 of the Penal Code of India); Italy (artt. 402–406 of the Italian Penal Code); and Turkey (art. 175 of the Penal Code of Turkey).

[243] See article 166 of the German Penal Code; it penalizes both insulting religions as well as insults aimed at secular beliefs (*Weltanschauung*).

of expression. In this study it has repeatedly been argued that 'religion' as such, however, is not a legitimate ground for limiting fundamental rights under international human rights law.[244] In view of this, it is submitted that international human rights law does not recognize a right to have one's religion or belief at all times exempted from criticism, ridicule or insult or a right, in other words, to respect for one's religious feelings. Put differently, the right to freedom of religion or belief does not by implication place a duty on all people to at all times have respect for everyone's religion or belief. Notwithstanding these considerations, it must be observed that freedom of expression, unlike the specific freedom to hold opinions,[245] is not an absolute right. The ICCPR explicitly considers that the freedom of expression (which is elaborated upon by the ICCPR as the "freedom to seek, receive and impart information and ideas of all kinds, regardless of frontiers, either orally, in writing or in print, in the form of art, or through any other media of his choice")[246] carries with it "special duties and responsibilities".[247] The only grounds for limitation provided in this respect, however, are "the rights or reputations of others" and "national security", "public order", "public health" and "morals".[248] In other words, the 'protection of religion' is no legitimate ground for limiting the freedom of expression (elsewhere the Human Rights Committee has explained that "morals", as a ground for limitation, ought not to be equated with the normative framework of the predominant religion of the state).[249] The 'rights of others to freedom of religion or belief' in theory fits in as a ground for limitation of the right to freedom of expression. However, it submitted in that regard that: (i) this ground should not be equated with a right to respect for one's religious feelings; and (ii) forms of criticism, ridicule or insult of religion do not necessarily or automatically constitute a limit or threat to people's freedom of religion or belief. Criticism (or ridicule) of a religion or belief does not necessarily affect a person's freedom to have or adopt a religion or belief or to freely exercise the religion or belief in question. It is submitted that the onus is on the state to establish that in a particular case fully granting the freedom of expression actually impedes or jeopardizes the freedom of religion or belief of others. The sole reference to the likelihood of a group of religious believers being insulted by a particular publication, exhibition, film, play, etc., certainly

---

[244] See especially section 9.2.1(vi), *supra*.

[245] Art. 19, para. (1), of the ICCPR. See Human Rights Committee, *General Comment 10: Article 19: Freedom of expression (Art. 19)* (1983), U.N. Doc. HRI/GEN/1/Rev.1 at 11 (1994) [hereinafter General Comment 10].

[246] Art. 19, para. (2), of the ICCPR; Human Rights Committee, General Comment 10, para. 2.

[247] Art. 19, para. (3), of the ICCPR.

[248] Art. 19, para. (3), of the ICCPR; Human Rights Committee, General Comment 10, para. 4.

[249] Human Rights Committee, General Comment 22, para. 8 (within the context of "morals" as a legitimate ground for limiting the right to freedom of religion or belief).

does not establish that. This is not to say that a public speech or publication, etc., can never be at the expense of someone's right to freedom of religion or belief. There are limits to expressing disrespect: advocacy of religious hatred that constitutes incitement to discrimination, hostility or violence is strictly forbidden under international human rights law.[250]

The Human Rights Committee has furthermore provided that "when a State party imposes certain restrictions on the exercise of freedom of expression, these may not put in jeopardy the right itself."[251] It is submitted that constitutional or penal law restrictions on the right to freedom of expressions in the interest of protecting religion do jeopardise the right itself as they are, as a rule, left open for discretionary use and indeed abuse.[252] Counter-blasphemy/defamation laws authorise the powers that be to decide, first of all, what constitutes a religion, and second, what qualifies as an insult to that religion. It is also submitted that blasphemy/defamation prohibitions that are designed to protect just one religion (the state or predominant religion) are *a fortiori* objectionable as restrictions on fundamental rights may not be based on a discriminatory criterion or applied in a discriminatory manner.[253]

There is much to be praised in the way the Human Rights Committee has dealt with the issue at stake.[254] The issue before the Committee in *Malcolm Ross v. Canada*[255] was whether Canada had breached the applicant's right to freedom of expression by sanctioning his removal from his teaching job, following (mostly off-duty)[256] statements in which he had denigrated Judaism and urged other people to hold Jews in contempt. The objectionable comments were published in books and pamphlets with such titles as "Web of Deceit", "The Real Holocaust", "Spectre of Power" and "Christianity vs.

---

[250] Art. 20, para. (2), of the ICCPR. See also Human Rights Committee, *General Comment 11: Article 20: Prohibition of propaganda for war and inciting national, racial or religious hatred* (Nineteenth session, 1983), Compilation of General Comments and General Recommendations Adopted by Human Rights Treaty Bodies, U.N. Doc. HRI/GEN/1/Rev.1 at 12 (1994).

[251] Human Rights Committee, General Comment 10, para. 4.

[252] Similar concerns are expressed in the Human Rights Committee's Concluding Observations, *e.g.*: A/48/40 (1993), paras. 587 and 607 (Ireland); A/55/40 vol. I (2000), para. 310 (UK).

[253] Human Rights Committee, General Comment 22, para. 8. See also Human Rights Committee's Concluding Observations, *e.g.*: A/46/40 (1991), para. 568 (UK); A/55/40 vol. I (2000), para. 310 (UK).

[254] Particularly when compared to the case law on similar issues of the European Court of Human Rights. See Temperman, *supra* note 193, pp. 533–544, for a criticism of the approach taken by the European Court of Human Rights with regard to blasphemy and religious defamation cases.

[255] Human Rights Committee, Communication No. 736/1997, *Malcolm Ross v. Canada*, U.N. Doc. CCPR/C/70/D/736/1997 (2000), Views of 18 October 2000.

[256] The domestic procedure also shows some evidence of expressions of religious hatred whilst in function, namely the "repeated and continual harassment in the form of derogatory name calling of Jewish students, carving of swastikas into desks of Jewish children, drawing of swastikas on blackboards and general intimidation of Jewish students" (*ibid.*, para. 4.3, based on statements made by students before the Board of Inquiry).

Judeo-Christianity".[257] During the procedures before the domestic tribunals, the Canadian Human Rights Board of Inquiry had considered:

> It would be an impossible task to list every prejudicial view or discriminatory comment contained in his writings as they are innumerable and permeate his writings. These comments denigrate the faith and beliefs of Jews and call upon true Christians to not merely question the validity of Jewish beliefs and teachings but to hold those of the Jewish faith and ancestry in contempt as undermining freedom, democracy and Christian beliefs and values. Malcolm Ross identifies Judaism as the enemy and calls on all Christians to join the battle.[258]

The Committee reasoned that the teacher's right could reasonably be restricted on the basis of 'the rights and reputations of others', more specifically the right of others 'to be protected from religious hatred'.[259] To that effect, the Committee first of all emphasized that the rights or reputations of others for the protection of which restrictions may be permitted under the right to freedom of expression may relate to other persons or to a community as a whole (i.e. a community of believers, which is not the same as a religion).[260] In other words, restrictions are in principle permitted on statements which are of a nature as to raise or strengthen hostile feelings vis-à-vis adherents of a certain religion, in order to uphold the latter's right to be protected from religious hatred.[261] In its reasoning, following the findings of both the Canadian Board of Inquiry and the Canadian Supreme Court, the Committee emphasized that the author's statements not merely denigrated Judaism, but actually "called upon true Christians…*to hold those of the Jewish faith and ancestry in contempt*".[262] In view of this, the Committee found little difficulty in concluding that "the restrictions imposed on him were for the purpose of protecting the 'rights or reputations' of persons of Jewish faith."[263]

The Committee, however, was not simply satisfied with this acknowledgment that the limitation of the freedom of expression in this case can *in abstracto* be justified by reference to this ground for limitation: it actually inquired into the necessity of the interference with the right to freedom of expression. In this particular case, this aspect of the assessment was fairly straightforward as the Canadian Supreme Court had already established that

---

[257] *Ibid.*, para. 4.2.

[258] *Idem.*

[259] *Ibid.*, para. 11.5; in the same paragraph the Human Rights Committee elaborates on 'the right [of others] to have an education in the public school system free from bias, prejudice and intolerance'. The right of others 'to be protected from religious hatred' is based on article 19, para. (3), in conjunction with art. 20, para. (2), of the ICCPR.

[260] Such was already established in: Human Rights Committee, General Comment 10, para. 4; and subsequently confirmed in Human Rights Committee, Communication No. 550/1993, *Robert Faurisson v. France*, U.N. Doc. CCPR/C/58/D/550/1993(1996), Views of 8 November 1996.

[261] Particularly since such restrictions derive support from the principles reflected in article 20, para 2, of the ICCPR. See *Malcolm Ross v. Canada, supra* note 255, para. 11.5.

[262] *Ibid.*, para. 11.5 (emphasis added).

[263] *Idem.*

there was a correlation between the expressions of the author and the "poisoned school environment" experienced by Jewish children in the School district.[264] The Committee had no reason to cast doubt on that consideration.[265] In this context it is also important to acknowledge, as the Committee noted, that the influence exerted by school teachers may justify restraints in order to ensure that legitimacy is not given by the school system to the expression of views which are discriminatory.[266]

9.3.3 *The Emerging Counter-Defamation Discourse*

The Human Rights Committee rightly insists on this crucial distinction between merely insulting speech and speech that may qualify as advocacy of religious hatred that constitutes incitement to discrimination, hostility or violence. Within the United Nations, developments are apparent that challenge this approach. These developments could very well be at the detriment of important fundamental rights, notably the right to freedom of expression but also the right to freedom of religion or belief as such. In the latter respect, it must be observed that the recognition of too general a limitation on the right to freedom of expression (such as the notion that 'the religious feelings of citizens' must be respected) could in practice seriously inhibit the free exercise of a religion by non-dominant religious groups as the very exercise of one's religion in a certain fashion might be considered heretical in the eyes of another person. The persecution of Ahmadis in Pakistan (and elsewhere) and of Bahá'ís in Iran (and elsewhere) are striking examples.

Within the UN human rights framework there is a movement discernable which carries with it the risk that the above described 'givens' of international human rights law become blurred—this movement may be referred to as the 'Counter-Defamation Discourse'. From 1999–2005 the UN Commission on Human Rights adopted the so-called "Combating Defamation of Religions" resolutions,[267] a trend continued since 2007 by its successor, the Human Rights Council.[268] A similar development can be perceived within the UN General

---

[264] *Ibid.*, para. 4.6–4.7 (following earlier observations made by the Board of Inquiry; *ibid.*, para. 4.6).

[265] *Ibid.*, para. 11.6.

[266] *Ibid.*, para. 11.6.

[267] Commission on Human Rights Resolutions: 1999/82 of 30 April 1999 (the first defamation Resolution was entitled "Defamation of Religions"; though an earlier draft spoke of "Defamation of Islam"); 2000/84 of 26 April 2000 ("Defamation of religions"); 2001/4 of 18 April 2001 ("Combating defamation of religions as a means to promote human rights, social harmony and religious and cultural diversity"); 2002/9 of 15 April 2002 ("Combating defamation of religions"); 2003/4 of 14 April 2003 ("Combating defamation of religions"); 2004/6 of 13 April 2004 ("Combating defamation of religions"); and 2005/3 of 12 April 2005 ("Combating defamation of religions").

[268] Human Rights Council: Human Rights Council Resolution 4/9 of 30 March 2007 ("Combating defamation of religions"); Human Rights Council Resolution 7/19 of 27 March

Assembly since 2005.[269] In general terms, these Resolutions are annually proposed by (a member state on behalf of) the Organization of the Islamic Conference[270] and are, as a rule, not unanimously adopted (the opposition can be considered rather significant),[271] with the states voting against typically consisting of a list of European states, plus Canada and the USA and some of the Pacific states.[272]

Whilst some UN member states have expressed concern about the Resolutions' one-sided focus on defamation of Islam,[273] it would appear that

---

2008 ("Combating defamation of religions"); and Human Rights Council Resolution 10/22 of 26 March 2009 ("Combating defamation of religions").

[269] GA: Resolution 60/150 ("Combating defamation of religions") of 16 December 2005, A/RES/60/150; Resolution 61/164 ("Combating defamation of religions") of 19 December 2006, A/RES/61/164; Resolution 62/154 ("Combating defamation of religions") of 18 December 2007, A/RES/62/154; and Resolution 63/171 ("Combating defamation of religions") of 18 December 2008.

[270] OIC: an inter-governmental organization consisting of 57 states established to safeguard Islamic interests.

[271] Especially considering the fact that many resolutions in these bodies are adopted without a vote (i.e. by consensus). See the following overview for the exact voting patterns: (i) Commission on Human Rights: whilst the original Resolution 1999/82 of 30 April 1999 and subsequent Resolution 2000/84 of 26 April 2000 were adopted without a vote, Resolution 2001/4 of 18 April 2001 was put to the vote: 28 states voted in favour, 15 against, whilst 9 states abstained; henceforth the Defamation Resolutions were always put to the vote: Resolution 2002/9 of 15 April 2002 was carried by 30/15/8; Resolution 2003/4 of 14 April 2003 by 32/14/7; Resolution 2004/6 of 13 April 2004 by 29/16/7; and Resolution 2005/3 of 12 April 2005 by 31/16/5; (ii) Human Rights Council: Resolution 4/9 of 30 March 2007 was carried by 24/14/9; Human Rights Council Resolution 7/19 of 27 March 2008 by 21/10/14; and Human Rights Council Resolution 10/22 of 26 March 2009 by 23/11/13; (iii) General Assembly: Resolution 60/150 of 16 December 2005 was carried by 101/53/20; Resolution 61/164 of 19 December 2006 by 111/54/18; Resolution 62/154 of 18 December 2007 by 108/51/25; and Resolution 63/171 of 18 December 2008 by 86/53/42.

[272] Naturally, depending on the composition of those bodies at the time of voting: within the UN GA, the European opposition is joined by the US, Canada, Australia and New Zealand (and, typically, some of the smaller pacific states); within the UN Human Rights Council, the European opposition is presently joined by Canada.

[273] Though the Resolutions are entitled Combating Defamation of Religions, the preamble and actual content of those Resolutions reflect a rather one-sided emphasis on Islam. See, for example, the following excerpts from a GA Combating Defamation of Religions Resolution (Res. 62/154 of 18 December 2007): "the negative projection of Islam in the media and the introduction and enforcement of laws that specifically discriminate against and target Muslims, particularly Muslim minorities following the events of 11 September 2001" (preamble); "Islam is frequently and wrongly associated with human rights violations and terrorism" (para. 5); "the ethnic and religious profiling of Muslim minorities in the aftermath of the tragic events of 11 September 2001" (para. 6); "acts of violence, xenophobia or related intolerance and discrimination against Islam or any other religion" (para. 8); and "incitement to religious hatred, against Islam and Muslims in particular" (para. 9). A recent Human Rights Council Defamation Resolution (Human Rights Council Resolution 7/19 of 27 March 2008, 'Combating defamation of religions') contains no less than 11 references to "Islam" or "Muslim(s)". Several UN member States have expressed concern about the limited scope of such formulations: for example Guatemala (in relation to Resolution 60/150 of 16 December 2005, as recorded in the official records, UN Doc. A/60/PV.64); and India (during Third Committee deliberations Concerning the most recent UN GA Combating Defamation of Religions Resolution, Res. 62/154, as recorded in UNGA/SHC/3909). In the debates in the Human Rights Council on the 2008 Defamation Resolution similar concerns were raised by EU Member States and again by India.

the major problem with these Resolutions is their overall tenor: the protection of religions as a concern of the international community. 'Combating defamation of religion' is, strictly speaking, not a human rights issue as human rights law is not interested in religions. Human rights law is not concerned with their doctrines, their survival or their reputation—human rights law is concerned with people and their rights and freedoms. One might argue that defamation of religions is indirectly relevant to the human rights discourse to the extent that it can be maintained that such defamation "could lead to social disharmony and violations of human rights".[274] There is a crucial difference, however, between the illegal act of advocacy of religious hatred that constitutes incitement to discrimination, hostility or violence, or simply causing offence, be it in the form of criticism, ridicule or insult of religion, by denying religious doctrinal views, or indeed by blaspheming. Any human rights-based approach tackling the issue of religious intolerance should take this crucial distinction into account. States certainly should take actions against speech/publications advocating religious hatred.[275] The latter observation, however, by no means implies that religions per se should be protected by international law or that all forms of criticism, ridicule or insult aimed at religion should be firmly countered, for that would amount to seriously excavating the fundamental right to freedom of expression. The Counter-Defamation Discourse, regrettably, manifests itself as a move towards the latter alternative:

> ...everyone has the right to hold opinions without interference and the right to freedom of expression...the exercise of these rights carries with it special duties and responsibilities and may therefore be subject to limitations as are provided for by law and are necessary for respect of the rights or reputations of others, protection of national security or of public order, public health or morals and *respect for religions and beliefs*...[276]

The latter ground for limiting the right to freedom of expression—"respect for religions and beliefs"—is, it is worth reiterating, *not* recognized by international human rights law.[277]

---

[274] In the words of a GA Resolution: Resolution 62/154 ("Combating defamation of religions") of 18 December 2007, preamble.

[275] Art. 20, para. (2), of the ICCPR states: "Any advocacy of national, racial or religious hatred that constitutes incitement to discrimination, hostility or violence shall be prohibited by law." See also art. 4 of CERD.

[276] GA Resolution 62/154 ("Combating defamation of religions") of 18 December 2007, para. 10 (emphasis added). See also GA Resolution 61/164 ("Combating defamation of religions") of 19 December 2006, para. 9; and Human Rights Council Resolution 4/9 of 30 March 2007 ("Combating defamation of religions"), para. 10.

[277] It may be added at this point that the European Court of Human Rights has issued a series of judgements based on the questionable notion of 'respect for the religious feelings of citizens' as a special limit on the right to freedom of expression. See, *e.g.*: ECommHR, *Gay News Ltd. and Lemon v. the United Kingdom*, Application No. 8710/797, Judgement of May 1982; ECtHR, *Otto Preminger-Institute v. Austria*, Application No. 13470/87, Judgement of 20 September 1994; ECtHR, *Wingrove v. the United Kingdom*, Application No. 17419/90, Judgement of 25 November 1996;

Realizing that boldly making up, out of thin air, new grounds for limitation is not the best way to sell these Resolutions, later editions seem to have toned down this particular point somewhat. That (strategically inspired) step forward, however, does not seriously alter the overall gist of these resolutions: exercising certain fundamental freedoms, notably freedom of expression, may collide with the need for respect of religions—this clash, so the argument in those Resolutions goes, needs to be resolved in favour of the latter. In this manner, the Resolutions in question attempt to make 'combating defamation of religions' a concern of the international community: there is a clash of interests and, given the importance of religions to many people's lives, this clash need to be resolved in favour of religions.

A recent Human Rights Council Resolution on defamation makes explicit something that in previous Defamation Resolutions was merely implied: the Human Rights Council emphasizes "that respect of religions and their protection from contempt is an essential element conducive for the exercise by all of the right to freedom of thought, conscience and religion".[278] Legally speaking, this is not the case, or at least not in these absolute terms. Universal respect of religions is no prerequisite for full enjoyment of the right to freedom of religion or belief. Again it is the lack of differentiation that is objectionable. Disrespect and contempt clearly come in different dimensions: most forms of unpopular speech/publications are protected by freedom of expression and do in actual fact not affect people's freedom of religion or belief in any way whatsoever (people taking offence not being indicative of a human rights violation). Some extreme forms of expression indeed transcend the latter instances and are illegal under international law: this is where we enter the realm of advocacy of religious hatred that constitutes incitement to discrimination, hostility or violence. Failing to distinguish between those different dimensions opens up the door to (justifications of) legislation of anti-blasphemy/defamation laws that might very well limit free speech altogether. Legislating respect for religion is certainly not what is needed from a human rights perspective. It is submitted that harmful abuses of the right to freedom of expression can be effectively countered on the basis of the norms and prohibitions which are already codified in international human rights law.

In conclusion, the Counter-Defamation Discourse is not the appropriate way of dealing with contemporary issues of religious intolerance. The

---

ECtHR, *Murphy v. Ireland*, Application No. 44179/98, Judgement of 3 December 2003. Subsequent blasphemy/defamation cases (*e.g.* ECtHR, *I.A. v. Turkey*, Application No. 42571/98, Judgement of 13 September 2005; and ECtHR, *Klein v. Slovakia*, Application No. 72208/01, Judgement of 31 October 2006) can be criticized for different reasons, although it could be argued that they may signal a step in the right direction. See Temperman, *supra* note 193, pp. 533–544.

[278] Human Rights Council Resolution 7/19 of 27 March 2008 ("Combating defamation of religions"), para. 10.

Counter-Defamation Discourse is utterly unacceptable because it: (i) seeks to shift the emphasis from protection of the rights of individuals to protection of religions per se; (ii) introduces grounds for limitation of human rights, particularly of the right to freedom of expression, that are not—and should not become—recognized by international human rights law (e.g. 'respect for religions', 'respect for people's religious feelings'); and (iii) seeks to reformulate the right to freedom of religion or belief so as to include a right to have one's religious feelings respected (something that goes hand in hand with (i) and (ii) clearly). It goes without saying that the striking difference with the approach taken by the Human Rights Committee can be explained by referring to the fact that the 'treaty-based bodies' are composed of independent human rights experts whereas the political bodies such as the GA, the former Commission on Human Rights and the newly established Human Rights Council, can be subject to agendas that are not necessarily in the best interest of international human rights law.

There is no abstract 'clash' between freedom of expression and freedom of religion or belief. The portrayal of the two as being perpetually at odds, as inevitably 'clashing' whenever being implemented, is a flawed and hazardous one.[279] Limiting the right to freedom of expression in the interest of the right to freedom of religion or belief in many cases would come down to seriously stretching the scope of the latter right. Proceeding along those lines would not only be to the detriment of the fundamental right of freedom of expression; too broad a right to freedom of religion or belief as a right to respect for one's religion also jeopardises the right to freedom of religion or belief itself. Clearly, in conceiving of the prohibition of advocacy of religious hatred as a limit on freedom of expression (as far as speech/publications pertaining to religions is concerned) rather than mere 'respect for religions', a rather high threshold for limitation of the right to freedom of expression is suggested.[280] In this section it was endeavoured to show that there are very good legal reasons to do so. Most importantly, in any attempt to counter acts of religious intolerance it is

---

[279] Cf. *Report of the Special Rapporteur on freedom of religion or belief, Asma Jahangir, and the Special Rapporteur on contemporary forms of racism, racial discrimination, xenophobia and related intolerance, Doudou Diène, further to Human Rights Council decision 1/107 on incitement to racial and religious hatred and the promotion of tolerance*, A/HRC/2/3, 20 September 2006 (the Chapter "Defamation of Religion and the Right to Freedom of Religion or Belief", paras. 22–50, was prepared by the Special Rapporteur on FoRB), para. 38.

[280] It goes without saying that for the prohibition of advocacy of religious hatred that incites violence or discrimination to be applicable, the violence or threats of violence must be aimed at the religious groups (usually minorities or otherwise vulnerable groups) that are also attacked in the speech or publication in question. Violence or threats of violence aimed at the person behind the publication or speech are not relevant within the context of art. 20, para. (2), ICCPR. Arguing otherwise would come down to supporting 'abuse of right'-scenarios whereby one could actually trigger this clause *by becoming violent*; i.e. one could force the authorities to interfere with someone's freedom of expression by behaving in a violent fashion: it seems clear from the wording of the hate speech prohibition that that scenario is excluded.

pivotal that we do not throw the baby out with the bath water. Virtually all speech/publications that criticize or insult religions, naturally, will be deemed offensive by someone just as propagating religious opinions or views might be offensive to an atheist; however, not all forms of unpopular speech constitute illegal speech.

In sum, the right to respect for one's religious feelings does not exist in international human rights law. In the words of Asma Jahangir, the Special Rapporteur on freedom of religion or belief: "the right to freedom of religion or belief, as enshrined in relevant international legal standards, does not include the right to have a religion or belief that is free from criticism or ridicule."[281] The 'rights of others to freedom of religion or belief' is in theory a legitimate ground for limitation, but whenever this ground is put forward as a possible limitation of the right to freedom of expression, the onus is on the state to establish that in a particular case fully granting the freedom of expression impedes or threatens to impede the freedom of religion or belief of others. Criticism (or ridicule) aimed at religion does not automatically affect a person's right to freedom of religion or belief. It is thus clear that, in the context of speech and publications about religions, the threshold for restricting the right to freedom of expression is a high one: the protection of the state-sanctioned orthodoxy does not suffice as a justification and neither does a perceived need to ensure respect for the religious feelings of citizens.

9.4 Religion & Freedom of Association

The issue of freedom of association is inextricably linked with the freedoms enjoyed by organized religious groups.[282] In this section it will be argued that states may not discriminate between religions in the process of official registration of religions. It will be outlined that religious association laws are often used in practice to confirm or cover up historical financial prerogatives of the predominant traditional religion of the state (in states that maintain *de jure* or *de facto* ties with this religion), or to restrain the activities of religious groups (in secular states with strict interpretations of state secularism or separationism). Thus it may be that financial support schemes are based on *prima facie* neutral criteria ("all recognized/registered religions and beliefs receive funding") but the rules for registration, in turn, are actually not. If a state's predominant religion or church is automatically granted financial support, but other religious groups have to go through arduous procedures to reach that

---

[281] A/HRC/2/3, *supra* note 279, para. 36.

[282] Art. 22 of the ICCPR codifies everyone's right to freedom of association. See art. 6 of the UN Religious Tolerance Declaration (1981) for some of the ramifications in the field of (organized) religion.

same level of legal recognition, the policy of allocation of financial benefits can hardly be considered 'based on objective criteria'. The same holds true, *a fortiori*, if religious association laws lay out illegitimate registration criteria which non-dominant or non-traditional religious communities can simply never meet.

Thus, two different issues which may both lead to discrimination against certain religions can be distinguished from each other: (i) basic recognition as a legal entity by the state (and the basic rights that come with this status); and (ii) eligibility criteria for state funding (this mechanism is often interwoven with the issue of the status of religious groups).[283]

As to the first issue, status as a legal entity and the basic rights and protections connected with that status are generally indispensable for any religious organization nowadays. As Durham argues:

> ...legal entity status is vital because, as a practical matter, a religious organization of any appreciable magnitude cannot operate effectively and efficiently without such status. A contemporary religious community needs to interact with the secular legal order in countless ways in order to carry out its affairs.[284]

The right to establish and maintain charitable or humanitarian institutions based on religious precepts is recognized.[285] It is submitted that the right to establish and maintain religious organizations (of a more general nature) is also implied by reading the freedom to manifest a religion in conjunction with the right to freedom of association.[286] Clearly the most objectionable policy in this context is proactively outlawing a certain religion or denomination on account of the religion in question being considered 'heretical' (one can, for instance, think of the treatment of Ahmadis or Bahá'ís in some Islamic states as discussed earlier) or 'dangerous' or otherwise undesirable. In the latter respect, it may be noted that these groups and minorities are in practice typically countered by so-called 'anti-sect policies' (one can think in that regard of the Falun Gong and certain Christian movements in China;[287] or bans on Jehovah's Witnesses in, for instance, Eritrea[288] and Singapore[289]). Short of banning and actively persecuting a religion or belief, but objectionable in many

---

[283] W. Cole Durham, *Facilitating Freedom of Religion or Belief through Religious Association Laws, in* Facilitating Freedom of Religion or Belief: A Deskbook (Lindholm, Durham and Tahzib-Lie, eds., Leiden: Martinus Nijhoff Publishers, 2004), p. 330, differentiates between the recognition of "base level legal entity status" and multi-tier systems with possibly more benefits for "upper tier" structures. Durham's work gives greater recognition to the major problems occurring in the field of religious association and his account is in many ways pioneering.

[284] *Ibid.*, p. 322.

[285] Art. 6, para. (b), of the UN Religious Tolerance Declaration (1981).

[286] Artt. 18 and 22 of the ICCPR.

[287] Official anti-Falun Gong measures were introduced in 1999.

[288] Since 1992; Pentecostals are also liable to be arrested.

[289] Jehovah's Witnesses are banned since 1972; the Unification Church is also illegal.

ways, are those measures that pose unreasonable registration requirements (for basic legal recognition by the state) that certain religions or beliefs simply cannot meet. It has been observed that registration systems as such can, in principle, be reconciled with human rights law.[290] However, the precise requirements for registration must be strictly in accordance with the international standards on freedom of association in conjunction with freedom of religion or belief. *In abstracto* it can be contended that states may enact laws governing the registration and functioning of religious organizations so as to facilitate and accommodate religious activity. However, states could in practice enact or enforce these laws so as to control religious groups and limit the freedom to manifest a religion or belief. The trend of enacting and enforcing religious association laws with a view towards gaining a degree of state control over religious affairs is particularly visible in former communist states.[291]

As to the second issue, state practice shows that state funding may be dependent on mere legal recognition as a religious or ideological organization, or funding may be dependent on being recognized as a special category of religious organization (and may thus further hang on rules determining and qualifying eligibility). It has been argued before that there is no clear-cut right for organized religions to be funded by the state;[292] however, it follows from the equality principle that if the state were to decide to provide funding to religion it must adopt an equitable approach and not discriminate against certain religions or beliefs.

In sum, on the basis of state policies towards recognition of religious groups and more specifically on the basis of the terms and criteria enshrined in so-called 'religious association laws'[293] it might happen that: (i) a religious community is denied legal entity status altogether; or (ii) a religious community might be granted this basic legal status but finds itself disadvantaged nonetheless when compared to churches or religious organizations that are granted a (higher) status making them eligible for additional benefits. The following overview of state practice is intended to chart the main problems in this field.

---

[290] De Jong, *supra* note 35, p. 320 *et seq*., rightly argues that the establishment of religious organizations, being a manifestation of religion, is not an absolute right and thus may be subjected to the recognized grounds of limitation. See Durham, *supra* note 283, pp. 358–365 for a comprehensive analysis of religious association laws in light of the applicable limitation clauses.

[291] See also Giovanni Barberini, *Religious Freedom in the Process of Democratization of Central and Eastern European States, in* LAW AND RELIGION IN POST-COMMUNIST EUROPE 7 (Ferrari & Durham, eds., Leuven: Peeters, 2003), pp. 15–19, singling out Russia, Lithuania and Bulgaria as the most restrictive states in this regard.

[292] Cf. De Jong, *supra* note 35, p. 289. See also section 9.2.2, *supra*.

[293] The general term for laws and regulations in the field of registration of religious organizations, defined by Durham, *supra* note 283, pp. 325–326 as "the entire range of laws governing entities that religious groups or communities can use in structuring their legal affairs."

9.4.1 *Numerical Requirements*

As regards the base-level recognition of legal entity status, it is submitted that unreasonable numerical requirements are not legitimate. The Human Rights Committee has considered that the right to freedom of religion or belief:

> …is not limited in its application to traditional religions or to religions and beliefs with institutional characteristics or practices analogous to those of traditional religions. The Committee therefore views with concern any tendency to discriminate against any religion or belief for any reason, including the fact that they are newly established, or represent religious minorities that may be the subject of hostility on the part of a predominant religious community.[294]

Thus, the key question is what is reasonable and what is unreasonable in this context. One plausible argument posits: why should numerical requirements for religious organizations be any different from regular civil non-profit associations covered by domestic association laws?[295] Thus, if a domestic law on civil associations allows, say, a minimum of two persons to establish a non-profit association, it might be considered unreasonable if religious organizations must meet higher minimum membership criteria.

---

[294] Human Rights Committee, General Comment 22, para. 2. Examples of cases in which the Human Rights Committee found this principle breached in the specific context of religious associations include: Human Rights Committee, *Sister Immaculate Joseph and 80 Teaching Sisters of the Holy Cross of the Third Order of Saint Francis in Menzingen of Sri Lanka v. Sri Lanka*, Communication No. 1249/2004, U.N. Doc. CCPR/C/85/D/1249/2004 (2005), Views of 21 October 2005 (the refusal to acknowledge/register this order amounted to a violation of art. 18 in conjunction with art. 26 of the ICCPR); Human Rights Committee, *Sergei Malakhovsky and Alexander Pikul v. Belarus*, Communication No. 1207/2003, U.N. Doc. CCPR/C/84/D/1207/2003 [2005], Views of 26 July 2005. It is worth noting that at the European level, the European Court of Human Rights has provided a comprehensive set of benchmarks on the issue of recognition/registration/religious autonomy in its case law. Dealing with different aspects of recognition/registration (see, *e.g.*: ECtHR, *Metropolitan Church of Bessarabia and Others v. Moldova*, Application no. 45701/99, Judgement of 13 December 2001; ECtHR, *Hasan and Chaush v. Bulgaria*, Application no. 30985/96, Judgement of 26 October 2000; ECtHR, *Moscow Branch of the Salvation Army v. Russia*, Application No. 72881/01, Judgement of 5 October 2006; ECtHR, *Church of Scientology Moscow v. Russia*, Application No. 18147/02, Judgement of 5 April 2007; ECtHR, *Biserica Adevărat Ortodoxă din Moldova and Others v. Moldova*, Application No. 952/03, Judgement of 27 February 2007; ECtHR, *Svyato-Mykhaylivska Parafiya v. Ukraine*, Application No. 77703/01, Judgement of 14 June 2007), the Court reasons, *inter alia*, that basic legal-entity status is indispensible for religious organizations and that the state (as 'neutral and impartial organizer of the different religions') may, consequently, not raise such legal obstacles as to prevent certain religious groups from acquiring legal recognition. In some cases (*e.g.* ECtHR, *Religionsgemeinschaft der Zeugen Jehovas and Others v. Austria*, Application No. 40825/98, Judgement of 31 July 2008,) the Court went further than that, arguing that those multi-tier systems that distinguish between different religious groups (on the basis of their traditional ties to the country or numerically, etc.) so as to grant them different privileges are also at odds with the state duty to remain neutral and impartial in exercising its regulatory power in the sphere of religious freedom and in its relations with different religions, denominations and beliefs. See also, *e.g.*: ECtHR, *Verein der Freunde der Christengemeinschaft and Others v. Austria*, Application No. 76581/01, Judgement of 26 February 2009.

[295] Cf. Durham, *supra* note 283, pp. 388–389.

For sure, numerical requirements that prevent more recently emerging (and therefore likely to be relatively smaller) religious communities from being officially recognized and to enjoy the benefits that might be connected with gaining legal personality must be deemed discriminatory. Newly established religions are to be treated on a par with traditional religions. A minimum membership criterion of 20,000 persons, as is the case in Slovakia, is clearly unreasonable.[296] This registration criterion has been dismissed as being "among the most restrictive of any democratic state in the entire world".[297] Other states that pose numerical requirements for acquiring base-level legal entity status include: Armenia (200 members);[298] Austria (300 members);[299] Belarus (20 members);[300] Bosnia and Herzegovina (300 members);[301] Croatia (500 members);[302] Czech Republic (300 members);[303] Estonia (12 members);[304] Hungary (100 members);[305] Kazakhstan (10 members);[306] Kyrgyzstan (200 members);[307] Latvia (10 members);[308] Lithuania (15 members);[309] Macedonia

---

[296] Sec. 11 of the Law on the Freedom of Religious Belief and on the Status of Churches and Religious Societies, Law No. 308/1991 (1991), as amended by Law No. 192/1992 (effective 1 June 1992), and by Law No. 394/2000 Coll. (2000) (effective since 1 January 2001).

[297] Peter Mulík, *Church and State in Slovakia, in* LAW AND RELIGION IN POST-COMMUNIST EUROPE (Ferrari & Durham, eds., Leuven: Peeters, 2003), p. 320. These regulations have also been criticized by the Human Rights Committee: A/52/40 vol. I (1997) 58 at para. 382 (Slovakia).

[298] Art. 5, para. (e), of the Armenian Law (*supra* note 93). Armenian religious association laws have been criticized by the Human Rights Committee: A/54/40 vol. I (1999) 29 at para. 115 (Armenia); and by the CERD Committee: A/57/18 (2002) 50 at para. 282 (Armenia).

[299] Sec. 3, para. (2), of the Law on the Status of Religious Confessional Communities, BGBl. 19/1998, of 1998 (hereinafter: "1998 Austrian Law").

[300] Art. 14 of the Law of the Republic of Belarus on Religious Freedom and Religious Organizations, Law No. 137–3, of 31 October 2002 (hereinafter: "2002 Belarusian Law").

[301] See Law on Religious Freedom [BiH] of 2004 (hereinafter: 2004 BiH law).

[302] Art. 21, para. (1), of the Law on Legal Position of Religious Communities of 4 July 2002 (hereinafter: "2002 Croatian Law").

[303] Sec. 10, para. (2)(c), of title III of the Law on Churches and Religious Societies, No. 3/2002, of 27 November 2001 (hereinafter: "2001 Czech Law").

[304] Art. 13, para. (1), of the Churches and Congregations Act of 12 February 2002 (hereinafter: "2002 Estonian Law").

[305] Art. 9, para. (1)(a), of the Law on Freedom of Conscience and Religion and the Churches, Act IV of 1990 (hereinafter: "1990 Hungarian Law"). Hungarian religious association laws have been criticized by the Human Rights Committee: A/57/40 vol. I (2002) 60 at para. 80(14).

[306] Art. 9 of the Law on Freedom of Religion and Religious Associations [of Kazakhstan] of 5 May 1992 (amended 2005) (hereinafter: "1992 Kazakh Law").

[307] See the 2009 Kyrgyz Law (*supra* note 102); previously (dictated by a 1991 Law in conjunction with a 1997 Presidential Decree on religious associations) the requirement was only 10 members.

[308] Art. 7, para. (1), of the Law on Religious Organizations [of Latvia] of 7 September 1995 (amended by Laws of 17 June 1996; 27 February 1997; 19 February 1998 and 19 July 2000; hereinafter: "1995 Latvian Law").

[309] Art. 11 of the Law on Religious Communities and Associations, Law No. 89–1985, of 1995 (amended by Law No. VIII-394 of 2 July 1997 and by Law No. VIII-1677 of 11 May 2000; hereinafter: "1995 Lithuanian Law"); Lithuanian religious association laws have been criticized by the Human Rights Committee: A/53/40 vol. I (1998) 30 at para. 175 (Lithuania); and A/59/40 vol. I (2004) 52 at paras. 71(16) (Lithuania).

(50 members);[310] Moldova (10 members);[311] Poland (100 members);[312] Romania (300 members);[313] Russia (10 members);[314] Serbia (approximately 75 members),[315] Tajikistan (10 members);[316] Turkmenistan (5 members);[317] Ukraine (10 members);[318] and Uzbekistan (100 members).[319]

Some states pose numerical requirements for acquiring a special status that entitles the religious group in question to more (financial and other) privileges than those with mere legal entity status. These states include: Austria (approximately 16,500 members, in order to qualify as a "state recognized religion");[320] Czech Republic (10,000 members, in order to qualify as a religious society with "special powers");[321] Romania (approximately 23,000 members, in order

---

[310] Art. 10 of the Law on Religious Communities and Religious Groups, No. 35, of 1997. However, this clause was declared unconstitutional by the Macedonian Constitutional Court in 1998; see Constitutional Court of the Republic of Macedonia Judgement of 24 December 1998. Although the different religious communities and groups have *de jure* equal legal status, in practice the state maintains the closest ties with the two largest religions, the Macedonian Orthodox Church and the Islamic community. Cf. Stefan Kostovski, *Church and State in Macedonia, in* Law and Religion in Post-Communist Europe (Ferrari & Durham, eds., Leuven: Peeters, 2003), p. 214.

[311] Art. V, para. (2), of Decree no. 758, of 13 October 1994, pursuant art. 24 of the Law of the Republic of Moldova on Denominations, No. 979-XII, of 24 March 1992 (amended in 1998 and 2002; hereinafter: "1992 Moldovan Law"); criticized by the Human Rights Committee: A/57/40 vol. I (2002) 76 at para. 84 (13).

[312] Art. 31 of the Law Regarding the Guarantees of Freedom of Religion and Belief [of Poland] of 1989 (hereinafter: "1989 Polish Law").

[313] Law of 27 December 2006 (hereinafter: "2006 Romanian Law").

[314] Art. 9, para. (1), of the Law on the Freedom of Conscience and Religious Associations, No. 125-FZ, of 1997 (amended by Law No. 45-FZ of 26 March 2000 and by Law No. 112-FZ of 25 July 2002; hereinafter: "1997 Russian Law"); this criterion applies to "religious organisations", not to "religious groups". The latter do not have legal entity status, though, and face many other restrictions: compare art. 7 ("Religious Groups") and art. 8 ("Religious Organisations") and see artt. 15–24 (rights of religious organizations; not enjoyed by religious groups) of the 1997 Russian Law.

[315] Law on Churches and Religious Communities on 27 April 2006 (hereinafter: "2006 Serbian Law"), which speaks of 0.001 per cent of the population. This criterion does not apply to the seven religions which are recognized by the law as "traditional religions" (viz., Serbian Orthodox Church, Roman Catholic Church, Slovak Evangelical Church, Reformed Christian Church, Evangelical Christian Church and the Islamic and Jewish community) and which are automatically registered.

[316] Art. 14 of the Law of the Republic of Tajikistan on Religion and Religious Organizations of 1994 (amended 1997 and 1999) (hereinafter: "1994 Tajik Law").

[317] The requirement used to be 500 members under the 1993 Law on Religion; a 2004 decree issued by President Niyazov brought that number back to 5 (see also art. 15 of the Law of Turkmenistan on Public Associations of 21 October 2003; hereinafter: "2003 Turkmen Law").

[318] Art. 14 of the Law on the Freedom of Conscience and Religious Organizations of 1991 (amended 1992 and 1996) (hereinafter: "1991 Ukrainian Law).

[319] Art. 8 of the 1998 Uzbek Law (*supra* note 98).

[320] Sec. 11, para. (2), of the 1998 Austrian law (*supra* note 299) requires an adherence of "2 persons per thousand Austrians". This has been deemed discriminatory by the Human Rights Committee: A/54/40 vol. I (1999) 42 at para. 192 (Austria).

[321] Art. 11, para. (4), of the 2001 Czech Law (*supra* note 303); the state can make an exception if it deems that the religious societies in question represent "significant world denominations with long-standing tradition" (art. 27, para. 7).

to qualify as "state recognized denomination")[322] and Turkmenistan (50 members, in order to qualify as "religious organisation").[323]

9.4.2 *Presence Requirements*

Registration criteria that require the religion in question to exist in a state for a certain number of years are equally illegitimate. The Human Rights Committee has clarified that traditional and newly founded religions should be treated equally.[324] Minimum duration requirements can nonetheless be found in religious association laws of several states. Occasionally this rule is posed as a requirement for base-level legal entity recognition (for instance: Croatia: 5 years;[325] Mexico: 5 years;[326] and Peru: 10 years[327]). Generally, however, minimum duration requirements must be met in order to be granted a special, more privileged or protected status. This is the case in: Austria (20 years, to qualify as upper-tier "state recognized religion");[328] Belarus (20 years, to qualify as "religious association");[329] Czech Republic (10 years, to qualify as religious society with so-called "special powers");[330] Lithuania (25 years, to qualify

---

[322] The 2006 Romanian Law (*supra* note 313) requires an adherence of 0.1 percent of the population.

[323] See the 2003 Turkmen Law (*supra* note 317) in conjunction with the 2004 Presidential Decree on Religion.

[324] See also Durham, *supra* note 283, pp. 388–390, analysing 'minimum duration requirements'.

[325] Art. 21, para. (1), of the 2002 Croatian Law (*supra* note 302).

[326] Art. 7, para (II), of the Law of Religious Associations and Public Worship (1992) (hereinafter: "1992 Mexican Law").

[327] Art. 3 of Ministerial Resolution No. 377-2003-JUS of 13 October 2003. See Guillermo García-Montúfar, Moisés Arata Solís & Scott E. Isaacson, *Advances in Religious Liberty in Peru*, 2 Brigham Young University Law Review 385 (2004), pp. 413–415 for a criticism of this requirement.

[328] Sec. 11, para. (1), of the 1998 Austrian law (*supra* note 299); in order to qualify as a "state recognized religion" (which enjoys more privileges than "confessional communities") the religion in question, moreover, must have been registered as (lower-status) "confessional community" for at least ten years (out of these 20 years). See Christopher J. Miner, *Losing my Religion: Austria's New Religion Law in Light of International and European Standards of Religious Freedom*, 2 Brigham Young University Law Review 607 (1998), for a criticism of these requirements.

[329] To be more precise, a religious association must consist of at least ten religious communities, one of which must be present in the country for at least 20 years; art. 15 of the 2002 Belarusian Law (*supra* note 300). This provision has been criticized by Ruth Wedgwood in her concurring opinion annexed to: Human Rights Committee, *Sergei Malakhovsky and Alexander Pikul v. Belarus*, Communication No. 1207/2003, U.N. Doc. CCPR/C/84/D/1207/2003 [2005], of 26 July 2005.

[330] Art. 11, para. (1), in conjunction with art. 7 of the 2001 Czech Law (*supra* note 303). Newly established religions that have just recently been recognized have to wait 10 years before they can exercise the "special powers" of art. 7 (which in fact include some basic manifestations of religion such as the founding of denominational schools). See Jiří Rajmund Tretera, *Church and State in the Czech Republic, in* Law and Religion in Post-Communist Europe (Ferrari & Durham, eds., Leuven: Peeters, 2003), p. 89, for further criticism. See also the concerns raised by the Human Rights Committee: A/56/40 vol. I (2001) 83 at para. 83(22).

as recognized religion);[331] Romania (12 years, to qualify as "state recognized denomination");[332] Russia (15 years, to qualify as "religious organisation");[333] Portugal (30 years, to qualify as a religious community that is "settled in the country").[334] Spain's religious association law specifies that those religious beliefs with "notorious influence in Spanish society", which leans towards a combination of a numerical and a duration requirement, can enter into special cooperation agreements with the state.[335]

The first type, minimum duration requirements for obtaining base-level legal entity status, seriously affects the core freedoms of religious manifestation and association. The second type (upper-tier requirements) amounts to discrimination between religions. Those multi-tier schemes posing particularly high minimum duration requirements for the recognition as upper-tier religious community status are designed so as to safeguard the historical prerogatives of traditional religions (in most of the Eastern European examples above that would be the national Orthodox Church).

9.4.3 *Other Illegitimate Registration Requirements*

Furthermore, registration requirements may be considered illegitimate if they are excessively burdensome or leave too wide a margin of discretion to the authorities.[336] As to the former point, the requirement that official registration needs to be obtained at both the national as well as the local level would appear to be excessively burdensome (as is the case in, for instance, Kazakhstan and Russia).[337] Similarly, the demand that religious organizations must annually

---

[331] Art. 6 of the 1995 Lithuanian Law (*supra* note 309). "Recognized religion" is not the highest status: the highest status with the most privileges is granted to the "traditional religious communities" which have been directly indicated by the state as per the 1995 Law (see art. 5). If a request for recognition as "recognized religion" is denied, it may only be resubmitted after 10 years (art. 6).

[332] See the 2006 Romanian Law (*supra* note 313); the Romanian registration system has been dismissed as "the most burdensome registration system in all of Europe". See Institute on Religion and Public Policy, *Religious Freedom in Romania* (Submission for Romania to the United Nations Universal Periodic Review; IRPP: Washington DC, 2008), executive summary.

[333] Artt. 8, 9, 11 and 27 of the 1997 Russian Law (*supra* note 314). Religious groups that do not meet this requirement can obtain base-level legal entity status; however, such groups are not allowed to exercise many of the rights religious organizations enjoy: see art. 27, para (3) of the law. Lev Simkin, *Chuch and State in Russia, in* LAW AND RELIGION IN POST-COMMUNIST EUROPE 261 (Ferrari & Durham, eds., Leuven: Peeters, 2003), p. 266 argues that the principal motive behind the 1997 Law was the protection of the Russian Orthodox Church.

[334] Or: "established abroad more than 60 years ago"; see art. 37 of the Law on Religious Freedom, No. 16/2001, of 21 June 2001 (hereinafter: "2001 Portuguese Law"). These communities, among other things, can enter into special agreements with the Government (art. 45) and enjoy fiscal benefits (artt. 32 and art. 65).

[335] Art. 7, para. (1), of the General Act on Religious Liberty of 1980 (hereinafter: "1980 Spanish Law").

[336] Cf. Durham, *supra* note 283, pp. 392–399.

[337] Under the 1992 Kazakh Law (*supra* note 306) and under the 1997 Russian Law (*supra* note 314) respectively.

provide the registration authorities with data on their religious activities and must notify the same authorities (failure of which may result in the suspension or dissolution of the organization) about their wish to continue their activities seems excessively burdensome as well (Russia).[338]

A good example of excessive discretion on the part of the authorities is given by the Chinese registration procedures which require an "Opinion" (undefined) from the local government to be included in the application that is sent to the national Religious Affairs Bureau.[339] The fact that far-reaching discretion on the part of the state is problematic from a human rights perspective is further illustrated by the *Sister Immaculate Joseph* case.[340] The Teaching Sisters of the Holy Cross of the Third Order of Saint Francis in Menzingen of Sri Lanka (the 'Order') had applied for an 'incorporated status' under Sri Lankan Law. This status, which has been granted to many other religious societies, would better enable them to realize the objects of their Order, including for example teaching and the construction of places of worship. The application was rejected by the Sri Lankan authorities, ostensibly because (i) this status would enable the Order to coercively or otherwise improperly propagate their religion; and (ii) such might ultimately impair the state-supported religion (Buddhism). The Human Rights Committee concluded that no evidence for this was advanced.[341] It would have done well to additionally underscore the fact that particularly the second concern (the need to protect the dominant religion) is, at any rate, *not* a legitimate ground for limiting the fundamental right to freedom of religion or belief.

So-called 'one (national) church per religion' rules also foster abuse and discrimination. In Latvia, for instance, congregations of the same denomination may establish only one national religious association in the country.[342] This clause has effectively prevented both the Confessional Lutheran Church as well as the Autonomous True Orthodox Church in Latvia from being recognized as a church at the national level.[343]

Even if no presence/duration requirements are posed, the criteria for registration as a religious organization may still be of such a nature that discrimination against newly established religions is inevitable. Armenian registration

---

[338] Art. 10, para. (9) and subsequent final provisions, of the 1997 Russian Law (*supra* note 314).

[339] Art. 3 of the Registration Procedures for Venues of Religious Activity of 1994; see Durham, *supra* note 283, p. 393.

[340] Human Rights Committee, *Sister Immaculate Joseph and 80 Teaching Sisters of the Holy Cross of the Third Order of Saint Francis in Menzingen of Sri Lanka v. Sri Lanka* (*supra* note 294).

[341] *Ibid.*, para. 7.4.

[342] Art. 7, para. (3), of the 1995 Latvian Law (*supra* note 308).

[343] For a criticism of this type of rule, see Ringold Balodis, *Church and State in Latvia, in* LAW AND RELIGION IN POST-COMMUNIST EUROPE 141 (Ferrari & Durham, eds., Leuven: Peeters, 2003), pp. 153–155.

law, for instance, demands that a religious association "is based on any historically canonized Holy Scriptures".[344] States are not in a position to determine what constitutes a religion worthy of recognition and what not. Belarusian religious association law, too, seems to require special proof of the merits of newly emerging religions:

> A religious community confessing a faith previously unknown in the Republic of Belarus must include in its application information about its teachings and worship practices, including information about the history and origin of the religion practiced by the community, forms and methods of its activities, attitudes toward marriage and family, education, fulfillment of state responsibilities, receipt of medical treatment by followers of the given religion, and other meaningful information in response to inquiries of the State Governance Body on Religious Affairs.[345]

Still the most objectionable and glaring type of restriction one can discern in the present context is an outright ban on the unregistered exercise of religion (which is the case in Belarus,[346] China,[347] Kazakhstan,[348] Turkmenistan,[349] and Uzbekistan[350]). Under an optional registration system, a religious group may of course decide not to apply for legal entity status (which may result in the impossibility of carrying out certain civil law actions and transactions). Registration schemes may not, however, be made mandatory under international human rights law. No one needs advance permission to practise a religion or belief, be it alone or together with others. Registration, in short, may never become a precondition for exercising core religious freedoms.[351]

---

[344] Art. 5, para. (b), of the 1991 Armenian Law (*supra* note 93). It is furthermore provided that its doctrine must form "part of the international contemporary religious-ecclesiastical communities" (para. c).

[345] Art. 17 of the 2002 Belarusian Law (*supra* note 300); the timeframe for reviewing the application is, moreover, in the case of new religions extended to 6 months (normally 1 month).

[346] Artt. 14 and 16 of the 2002 Belarusian Law (*supra* note 300) make state registration for all religious groups and organizations mandatory. The lack of registered status does not only imply that a religious organization cannot carry out the economic rights as listed in art. 38 of the law; it also has no right "to conduct religious…activities".

[347] China solely protects "normal religious activities" (art. 3 of the Religious Affairs Regulations of 30 November 2004; entry into effect: 1 March 2005); unregistered religious activity is illegal. Art. 12 of the same regulations provides: "Group religious activities of religious citizens should… be carried out at registered places of religious activity…"

[348] The 1992 Kazakh Law (*supra* note 306), as amended in 2005 and as applied by the authorities, effectively renders unregistered religious activity illegal.

[349] Unregistered religious activity is illegal and punishable under Turkmen law. Recent (2004) presidential decrees have somewhat eased Turkmen laws on religious practice. See also the concerns raised by the CERD Committee: A/57/18 (2002) 49 at para. 265 (Turkmenistan); and A/60/18 (2005) 61 at para. 323 (Turkmenistan).

[350] The 1998 Uzbek Law (*supra* note 98), particularly artt. 8–14, makes registration compulsory and effectively criminalizes unregistered religious activity. Art. 8 provides "[r]eligious organizations…can carry out their activities after their registration". Uzbek state practice has been criticized by the Human Rights Committee: A/56/40 vol. I (2001) 59 at para. 79(24) (Uzbekistan); and A/60/40 vol. I (2005) 56 at para. 89 (22) (Uzbekistan).

[351] Cf. OSCE/ODIHR, *Guidelines* (*supra* note 87), p. 17.

In conclusion, it may be reiterated that registration systems as such can be reconciled with human rights law (on the basis of the fact that the manifestation of a religion is not an absolute freedom nor is the right to freedom of association).[352] Equitable policies of recognition and registration of religions and religious organizations could in fact facilitate religious freedoms. This is precisely why human rights monitoring bodies have equally criticized states that insist on the uniformity or homogeneity of the nation and refuse to acknowledge the fact that (certain) religious minorities are present or fail to acknowledge that the question of minority rights might be an issue at all.[353] Having said that, it follows from the above comparative legal analysis that a number of states, unfortunately, design and implement religious association laws not with a view towards facilitating religious freedom but rather so as to tightly control the practice of religion or to actively discriminate against minority religions or against what these governments consider dangerous 'sects'.[354] In short, the precise requirements for registration must strictly accord with the international standards on freedom of association and freedom of religion or belief.

9.5 Religion & Employment

This section examines the question whether and under which circumstances religion or belief may be a legitimate ground for making distinctions in the field of employment hiring policies. The relevance and timeliness of this question is given by the fact that employment is one of the areas of life where religious believers are most likely to face discrimination or harassment.[355] Religious discrimination in employment hiring policies may manifest itself, generally speaking, in two, potentially overlapping, ways: (i) a religion might be posed as a specific precondition for obtaining a certain position; or (ii) people adhering to certain religions are refused precisely because of their religious affiliation. The first measure may be taken by employers because they consider that the nature of the job requires a specific religious affiliation or, alternatively, may simply be on account of a preference on the part of the

[352] See the third paragraph of art. 18 and the second paragraph of art. 22 of the ICCPR respectively on the legitimate (if based on positive law) grounds for interferences with these freedoms.

[353] C.f., *e.g.*, Human Rights Committee: A/59/40 vol. I (2004) 56 at paras. 72 (26) (Belgium): "The Committee is concerned that not a single mosque has yet been granted official recognition in Belgium". See also Human Rights Committee's Concluding Observations in: A/48/40 vol. I (1993) 139 at para. 709 (Egypt); A/49/40 vol. I (1994) 41 at para. 235 (Jordan); A/49/40 vol. I (1994) 47 at para. 281 (Italy); A/50/40 vol. I (1995) 57 at para. 322 (Ukraine); ICCPR, A/50/40 vol. I (1995) 65 at para. 401 (Russia); and A/53/40 vol. I (1998) 13 at para. 66 (Senegal).

[354] For an example of a case in which the Human Rights Committee dismisses too tight a state control over religious practice, see *Sergei Malakhovsky and Alexander Pikul v. Belarus* (*supra* note 329).

[355] Vickers, Religious Freedom, Religious Discrimination and the Workplace (Oxford and Portland: Hart Publishing, 2008), p. 6, referring to a UK governmental study.

employer for people of a certain religion. The latter policy (refusing people because they adhere to certain religions) would, naturally, normally be an informal one and gives evidence of prejudices on the part of the employer vis-à-vis persons of a specific religion.

The issue at stake can also be considered particularly pressing as the topic of religious rights in the workplace forms a relatively grey area within the human rights discipline.[356] This has to do with the following: human rights law, typically, concerns the relationship between the state and individuals. States are identified as the principal duty bearers and individuals as the rights holders.[357] This situation begs the following questions:

(i) does the state have a duty to guarantee freedom of religion or belief at work (which, if answered in the affirmative, would imply a duty of imposing certain norms and principles on employers)?;
(ii) to what extent does the norm of non-discrimination apply to the workplace (particularly considering the 'religious ethos' of some organizations and employers)?; and more specifically:
(iii) should the latter two principles—freedom of religion or belief and the right to be free from religious discrimination—'clash' in practice, which norm prevails?

As to the first and second questions, a distinction made between people on any of the grounds mentioned in the equality clauses enshrined in international human rights law (colour, sex, political beliefs, religion or belief, etc.) amounts to discrimination, unless the differentiation is based on 'reasonable and objective criteria'.[358] Although the principal duty bearer of the non-discrimination principle is of course the state, it is not hard to establish that states are under a positive obligation to do everything in their power to ensure that employers do not discriminate on the basis of religion or belief (or lack thereof) in their hiring policies by means of issuing appropriate laws, regulations and policies in the field of employment.[359]

---

[356] Vickers (*ibid.*) has carried out pioneering work in this field.

[357] Recent discussions and developments in international (human rights) law complicate these mechanisms somewhat, *e.g.*: given the phenomenon of 'horizontal application' of human rights law or the emergence of positive state duties, a broader range of acts (including non-state acts) is covered by human rights law; ongoing attempts can be perceived, academically and politically, to hold multi-national companies accountable for violations of international human rights law; with the emergence of international criminal law, individuals may be held accountable for gross human rights violations; certain so-called group rights may be applicable to a given case alongside individual rights; etc. These developments, arguably, find their rationale in attempts to maximize compliance with individual rights.

[358] See Chapter 7, text around note 46, *supra*.

[359] Art. 6 (the right to work) in conjunction with art. 2 (necessary state action & non-discrimination clause) of the ICESCR. See also art. 4 of the UN Religious Tolerance Declaration (1981). Relevant applicable norms are of course also formulated within the framework of the ILO.

As to the third question, the issue is whether certain people, groups or organizations may (or even must) be exempted from state laws, notably the non-discrimination principle, because of reasons of religion or reasons of conscience. Some seemingly opposing concerns within this debate can be identified: on the one hand, there is of course the freedom of each individual to act in accordance with the dictates of his or her conscience (*forum externum*) and the related yet far more abstract notion of the 'autonomy of a religious community' and its interest in preserving its 'religious identity'.[360] On the other hand, a range of state duties and public interests can be underscored, including the state's duty to guarantee everyone's individual (equality) rights and to guard against infringements of other human rights norms, notably the right to work; alongside, more generally, the state's interest in ensuring that state laws are obeyed as well as the state's and the public's interest in a high level of access to employment.

Some states have endeavoured to accommodate religious organizations and religious people by exempting them from generally applicable (equality) laws and regulations that would otherwise, potentially, cause conscientious problems for these organizations or persons. It will be argued in this section that some of these exemption policies can be applauded in so far as they foster religious freedom (without harming the rights and freedoms of others). It will be contended at the same time that some exemption schemes overstep the mark and in fact act to the detriment of fundamental equality rights (arguably without even truly maximizing anyone's religious freedom).

Religious exemption rules and policies can mainly be discerned in the fields of: (i) employment; (ii) membership criteria of and access to services rendered by religious organizations;[361] and (iii) the educational system (the latter issue is dealt with separately in Chapter 10). In what follows, the focus will be on the first field. The question that needs to be addressed is whether religious organizations or employers are allowed to make distinctions on the grounds

---

[360] The latter is, arguably, covered (to some extent) by human rights law if one takes a collective interpretation of the *forum externum* in conjunction with the freedom of association.

[361] *E.g.* in the UK, religious organizations as well as charities may restrict membership of the organization on grounds of religion or belief. See artt. 57 and 60 of the Equality Act of 2006, Law c.3/2006. This does not apply to those organizations, though formally of a religious nature, whose sole or main purpose is commercial. Membership restrictions on grounds of religion or belief in this context may be considered 'objective and reasonable' or at least tolerable. More questionable are membership restrictions on the grounds of sex or sexual preferences for (alleged) religious reasons. CEDAW has repeatedly argued in the past that the reluctance of the Netherlands to take actions against the SGP, an orthodox Protestant political party founded in 1918 which until very recently restricted party membership to men allegedly on account of biblical motives, was in violation of the Covenant. See CEDAW Committee's Concluding Observations: A/56/38 part II (2001) 63 at para. 219; and CEDAW/C/NLD/4, pp. 47–48. See also Kent Greenawalt, *Freedom of Association and Religious Association, in* FREEDOM OF

of religion or belief in their hiring policies. Although discrimination in this context is often 'multi-dimensional',[362] it is, analytically, possible to distinguish between: (i) distinctive treatment on the grounds of religion or belief; and (ii) distinctive treatment on other grounds (e.g. gender or sexual orientation) because of (alleged) religious reasons.

9.5.1 *Distinctive Treatment on Grounds of Religion or Belief*

Employment practices show that in this context two types of defences against potential charges of discrimination are advanced: (i) so-called 'genuine occupational requirements'; and (ii) the preservation of an 'institutional religious ethos'. The remainder of this section concerns itself with states' reactions (in terms of rejection or accommodation) to these defences. It will be contended that only the former defence can be supported from a human rights perspective.

(i) *Genuine Occupational Requirements*

It stands to reason that if being of a certain religion is absolutely essential to appropriately carrying out the tasks and responsibilities of a certain job that religious affiliation may be made a precondition for obtaining that job. In this context we may speak of so-called 'genuine occupational requirements'. An occupational requirement is only 'genuine' if there is an evident link between the nature of the work and the religious affiliation in question. A simple preference on the part of the employer for someone of a certain religion would clearly not suffice, nor would a prejudice on the part of the employer against certain religions. Thus it will be clear that a genuine occupational requirement can only apply to a limited amount of positions. Actual ecclesiastical positions, naturally, fall within this category (the right of religious groups to freely

---

Association (Princeton, N.J.: Princeton University Press, 1998), pp. 114–116, on similar issues. A related question is whether religious organizations may limit their services to people adhering to the same religion. UK law serves as a useful example as it explicitly allows religious organizations and charities to restrict their services to people adhering to the religion in question (see art. 57, para. (3), and art. 58 of the Equality Act of 2006, Law c.3/2006). The OSCE/ODIHR *Guidelines (supra* note 87), pp. 15–16, convincingly argue that the legitimacy of restrictions in this field depends on whether there are solely religious or also *public* services (and tax money) at stake: "Although differential treatment may be permissible, it is appropriate to draw attention to the competing values of religious autonomy for institutions and the right of citizens to be free from discrimination on the grounds of religion, especially when the employers receive public financing or tax deductions for their activities". More questionable, again, would be service restrictions on the grounds of sex or sexual preferences for (alleged) religious reasons. One can think of Catholic adoption agencies that refuse to place children with homosexual couples.

[362] Cf. Vickers, *supra* note 355.

appointment their religious leaders is also directly protected by the norms on freedom of religion).[363] In the latter respect, it may be considered that the distinctive treatment on the ground of religion is actually perfectly 'objective and reasonable' and would thus not amount to discrimination.[364] Any type of job that is not of a clear-cut clerical nature would not automatically justify posing religion as an occupational requirement. The 'easy cases' when it comes to positions that do certainly not merit a religious occupational requirement involve such positions as cleaning personnel, janitors, secretarial personnel, catering staff,[365] etc. The requirements posed for all those positions in between these two extremes, naturally, are the most difficult to judge. This is further complicated by the fact that the state is not in a position to make close assessments as to whether belonging to a religion is truly essential in the discharge of certain functions and positions within these organizations, as too intrusive an examination to that effect may encroach upon these organizations' religious autonomy. Having said that, states are obliged, without going quite as far as that, to do everything within their capabilities to prevent any form of abuse and needless interferences with people's equality rights. In particular, states have a responsibility in ensuring that (hereinafter referred to as 'the human rights test'):

(i) employers always make genuine occupational requirements explicit in the recruitment process for reasons of transparency and fairness;
(ii) religious occupational requirement are only applied if such is proportionate in the given circumstances (that is to say, granting the exemption may not disrupt overriding interests of access to employment);
(iii) legal venues are open to individuals to challenge occupational requirements that are *manifestly* illegitimate (be it before a Court, or before specialized institutions such as an Equal Rights Commission or an Equal Opportunities Ombudsman); and:
(iv) the burden of proof, in the latter cases, is always on the employer to justify the religious occupational requirement.

A good example of state practice in this area is the fairly recently adopted British legislation[366] (largely intended to implement an EU Council Directive

[363] See art. 6, para. (g), of the UN Religious Tolerance Declaration (1981).

[364] The relevance being that if that is indeed the case, we may not, strictly speaking, refer to these cases as instances that can legitimately be exempted from the ramifications of the equality principle, but rather as instances that do not amount to unequal treatment in the first place.

[365] As far as the latter position is concerned, it is not unimaginable that knowledge of certain religious dietary needs, such familiarity with *halal* or *kosher* food, can be posed as a requirement for certain positions within certain institutions.

[366] The Regulations do not apply to Northern Ireland which since long has its own, similar, regulations in place (Fair Employment and Treatment Order of 1998).

on the same issue)[367] which exempts employers from the general prohibitions on religious discrimination if:

(a) being of a particular religion or belief is a genuine and determining occupational requirement;
(b) it is proportionate to apply that requirement in the particular case; and
(c) either:

(i) the person to whom that requirement is applied does not meet it, or
(ii) the employer is not satisfied, and in all the circumstances it is reasonable for him not to be satisfied, that that person meets it…[368]

This genuine occupational requirement exemption can be applied both to employers that have an ethos based on religion or belief (religious organizations, charities, etc.) and to those that have not (e.g. a non-denominational private hospital that wishes to hire the services of a chaplain). Similar genuine occupational requirement schemes can be found in the laws of:[369] Austria,[370] Belgium,[371] Bulgaria,[372] Canada,[373] Cyprus,[374] Czech Republic,[375] Denmark,[376] Finland,[377] Germany,[378] Greece,[379] Hungary,[380] Ireland,[381] Italy,[382] Latvia,[383]

---

[367] Art. 4, para. (1), of Council Directive 2000/78/EC ("Employment Framework Directive") of 27 November 2000.

[368] Art. 7, para (2), of the Employment Equality (Religion or Belief) Regulations, No. 1660/2003, of 26 June 2003.

[369] The following overview is largely indebted to the country reports on measures to combat discrimination drafted by the EU Legal Expert Network (2007).

[370] Art. 20, para. (1), of the Federal Equal Treatment, State Law 66/2004, which deals mainly with private employment. And art. 13b, para. (1), of the Act Amending the Federal Equal Treatment Act, State Law 65/2004, which deals mainly with federal public employment (both Acts use the phrase "*eine wesentliche und entscheidende berufliche Voraussetzung*").

[371] Art. 8 of the Law Combating Certain Forms of Discrimination, BS 30 V 07, of 10 May 2007.

[372] Art. 7, para. (2), of the Law on the Protection against Discrimination, 199/2003 (entered into force: 1 January 2004).

[373] Art. 15, para. (1)(generic occupational requirement exception), of the Canadian Human Rights Act, R.S., 1985, c. H-6.

[374] Section 5(2) of the Law on Equality of Treatment in Occupation and Employment, No.58 1/2004.

[375] Art. 16, para. (3), of the Labour Code, No. 46/2004; and art. 4, para. (3) of the Law on Employment, No. 435/2004.

[376] Art. 6 of the Act on Equal Treatment in Employment and Occupation, No. 459/1996 (amended 2004).

[377] Art. 7, para. (1), of the Non-Discrimination Act, No. 21/2004.

[378] Art. 8 of the Law on the Transposition of European Anti-Discrimination Directives, BGBl. I, 1897, of 14 August 2006 (amended Dec. 2006).

[379] Artt. 5 and 9 of the Law on the Implementation of the Principle of Equal Treatment, No. 3304/2005, of 27 January 2005.

[380] Art. 22, para. (1)(a), of the Law on Equal Treatment and Promotion of Equal Opportunities, No. CXXV/2003, of 28 December 2003.

[381] Art. 37, para. (2), of the Employment Equality Act, No. 21/1998.

[382] Art. 3, para. (3), of Decree No. 216 of 9 July 2003.

[383] Para. (9) of art. 29 read in conjunction with para. (2) of the same article of the Labour Law of 2002 (amended through 2006).

Luxembourg,[384] Malta,[385] New Zealand,[386] Norway,[387] Poland,[388] Portugal,[389] Slovakia[390] and the United States of America.[391]

It cannot be overemphasized that these exemption schemes essentially provide for a defence to charges of direct discrimination. Needless to say, therefore, such schemes should be drafted and construed very narrowly and monitored by the judiciary or equality rights bodies (whilst having regard for the religious autonomy of religious ethos organizations). The Belgian exemption scheme stands out positively, as it provides for such safeguards.[392] In the same respect, Poland's and Hungary's occupational requirement exceptions are examples of exemption schemes that would not pass the above human rights test as they are framed in far too general and unconditional a manner.[393]

Religious occupational requirements posed by public institutions are not per se objectionable but must clearly be subjected to additional (judicial) scrutiny. For instance, a state-run hospital might find itself in need of the service of a chaplain and justifiably treat religious affiliation as an occupational requirement within the context of the advertising and hiring procedures surrounding this position. On the other hand, exemptions regarding forms of distinctive treatment in the fields of recruitment for the armed forces or state security services would normally not be legitimate. New Zealand, for instance, sanctions religious discrimination when it comes to recruitment for positions dealing with national security.[394]

(ii) *Religious Ethos Exception*

Far more problematic from a human rights perspective are so-called 'religious ethos exemptions'. States that have adopted religious ethos exemption schemes grant certain types of employers a far more flexible, if not, unconditional

---

[384] Article 18 of the Law [transposing EU Directive 2000/78 into domestic law] of 28 November 2006 (this law effectively inserts a new article, art. L-252-1 (1), into the Labour Code).

[385] Sec. 4 of the Equal Treatment in Employment Regulations, No. 461/2004.

[386] Art. 28, para. (2)(b)(i), of the Human Rights Act 1993, Act No. 82 (amended through 3 December 2007).

[387] Art. 13(3), para. (1), of the Working Environment Act of 1977 (amended through 2007).

[388] Art. 18(3b), para. (2), of the Labour Code of 26 June 1974 (amended through 2003).

[389] Article 23, para. (2), of the Labour Code, Law No. 99/2003 (amended by Law 35/2004).

[390] Art. 8 of the Act on Equal Treatment in Certain Areas and Protection against Discrimination, Law No. 365/2004.

[391] Title VII of the Civil Rights Act of 1964, Pub. L. 88-352, 78 Stat. 241, in the American juridical doctrine and jurisprudence commonly described as a 'bona fide occupational requirement'.

[392] See art. 8. para. (3), of the Law Combating Certain Forms of Discrimination, BS 30 V 07, of 10 May 2007.

[393] Particularly objectionable is the fact that the necessity principle (i.e. the fact that religious affiliation must be considered a *determining* factor for posing an occupational requirement) is omitted or at least not underscored sufficiently.

[394] Art. 25 of the Human Rights Act 1993, Act No. 82 (amended through 3 December 2007). The British equality regulations include a similar exemption for the purpose of "safeguarding national security". See art. 24 of the Employment Equality (Religion or Belief) Regulations Statutory, No. 1660, of 2003.

permission to discriminate on the basis of religion in their hiring policies. These exemptions are not granted because being of certain religion is inextricably linked up with the position at hand (and thus absolutely necessary in order to fulfil the tasks and responsibilities that come with the position) but rather with a view towards accommodating those organizations that wish to maintain their 'religious identity'. The earlier mentioned British legislation[395] provides for such an exemption (something that is sanctioned if not encouraged by the mentioned EU Council Directive).[396] The religious ethos clause in question is largely similar to the above quoted genuine occupational requirement provision with the crucial difference in phrasing being that the word "determining" (before "occupational requirement") is omitted.[397] This, as Vickers argues, would suggest:

> ...a less rigorous approach in deciding whether the particular job requires a particular characteristic than that required by [the general genuine occupational requirement clause], where the emphasis is clearly on the nature of the job itself. In relation to religious employers it may be possible to argue that a workplace is, for example, Muslim or Hindu, because its staff are all from the same religion, and it operates according to a religious ethos. Such a religious employer would be able to require that all staff share that religion, even categories of staff...for whom religion is not a determining requirement. This type of employer currently exists, for example, Christian medical practices, which run their workplaces according to Christian principles...Under [the] wider religious ethos exception it appears that such discrimination will continue to be allowed.[398]

Similar types of religious ethos exemption schemes can be found in the laws of: Austria,[399] Belgium,[400] Bulgaria,[401] Cyprus,[402] Denmark,[403] Germany,[404]

---

[395] Art. 7, para (3), of the Employment Equality Regulations (*ibid.*).

[396] Art. 4, para. (2), of Council Directive 2000/78/EC of 27 November 2000.

[397] Compare para (2) and para (3) of art. 7 of the Employment Equality Regulations (*supra* note 368); the latter clause, moreover, stipulates that when the different tests (proportionality test, etc.; see paras. a–c) are applied, regard must be had "to that ethos and to the nature of the employment or the context in which it is carried out". The latter further suggests that a fair degree of discretion and flexibility in applying these exemptions is intended.

[398] Lucy Vickers, *Freedom of Religion and the Workplace: The Draft Employment Equality (Religion or Belief) Regulations 2003*, 32(1) Industrial Law Journal 23 (2003), pp. 27–28.

[399] Art. 20, para. (2), of the Federal Equal Treatment, State Law 66/2004, which deals mainly with private employment; and art. 13b, para. (2), of the Act Amending the Federal Equal Treatment Act, State Law 65/2004, which deals mainly with federal public employment (both Acts use the phrase: "*eine wesentliche, rechtmäßige und gerechtfertigte berufliche Anforderung angesichts des Ethos der Organisation*"; in other words, the word "*entscheidende*" (decisive), as used in the provisions on genuine occupational requirements, has been omitted).

[400] Art. 13 of the Law Combating Certain Forms of Discrimination, BS 30 V 07, of 10 May 2007.

[401] Art. 13, para. (3), of the Law on the Protection Against Discrimination, 199/2003 (entered into force: 1 January 2004).

[402] Article 7 of the Law on Equality of Treatment in Occupation and Employment, No.58 1/2004.

[403] Art. 6 of the Act on Equal Treatment in Employment and Occupation, No. 459/1996 (amended 2004).

[404] Art. 9 of the Law on the Transposition of European Anti-Discrimination Directives, BGBl. I, 1897, of 14 August 2006 (amended December 2006).

Greece,[405] Hungary,[406] Ireland,[407] Italy,[408] Latvia,[409] Luxembourg,[410] Malta,[411] Malaysia,[412] Netherlands,[413] Poland,[414] Singapore,[415] Slovakia,[416] and Spain.[417]

It is submitted that the religious ethos exemption strikes the wrong balance between the (collective) freedom to manifest a religion or belief and the right not to be discriminated against on grounds of religion or belief. Firstly, preservation of a 'religious ethos' may in itself be regarded as too abstract and subjective a notion to justify derogations from the equality principle. Secondly, it is not at all self-evident that preserving a particular ethos generally requires that all or most positions within a particular organization (even those that are not inextricably linked up with the religious affiliation in question) be occupied by people that share the organization's religion. In other words, though it is clear that religious ethos exemption schemes may foster discrimination on the basis of religion, it is not at all clear whether these schemes actually maximize the religious freedom of employees of religious ethos organizations. In short, the phenomenon of the religious ethos exemption scheme opens up the door to tolerating instances of religious discrimination far too wide.

Ireland's religious ethos exemption scheme goes even further as it only requires the differential treatment to be 'reasonable' (i.e. not genuine or determining). Ireland's religious exemption scheme has been criticized by the Human Rights Committee because the state allows organizations that provide important public services (e.g. medical institutions which are under the direction or control of a body established for religious purposes) to avail of it.[418] The Belgian, Bulgarian and Dutch religious ethos exemption schemes stand out positively in so far as the threshold for granting the exemption is not significantly lowered in comparison to their genuine occupational requirement schemes. It is thus clear that the latter states have refused to copy

---

[405] Art. 9, para. (2), of the Law on the Implementation of the Principle of Equal Treatment on Anti-Discrimination, No. 3304/2005, of 27 January 2005.

[406] Art. 22, para. (1)(b), of the Law on Equal Treatment and Promotion of Equal Opportunities, No. CXXV/2003, of 28 December 2003.

[407] Art. 37, para. (1), of the Employment Equality Act, No. 21/1998.

[408] Art. 3, para. (5), of Decree No. 216 of 9 July 2003.

[409] Labour Law of 2002 (amended in 2006).

[410] Article 18 of the Law [transposing EU Directive 2000/78 into domestic law] of 28 November 2006.

[411] Sec. 4 of the Equal Treatment in Employment Regulations, No. 461/2004.

[412] Art. 8, para. (5)(b), of the CONST. OF MALAYSIA (1957).

[413] Art. 5, para. (2), of the General Equal Treatment Act of 1994 (amended 2004) (which is not, strictly speaking, formulated as religious ethos exemption as such, but it certainly resembles one).

[414] Art. 18(3b), para. (4), of the Labour Code of 26 June 1974 (amended through 2003).

[415] Art. 12, para. (3)(b), of the CONST. OF SINGAPORE (1963).

[416] Art. 8, para. (2), of the Act on Equal Treatment in Certain Areas and Protection against Discrimination, Law No. 365/2004.

[417] Art. 34, para. (2) of Law No. 62/2003 of 30 December 2003 on fiscal, administrative and social measures.

[418] A/55/40 vol. I (2000) 61 at para. 443.

verbatim the broader religious ethos exemption as provided by the mentioned EU Employment Framework Directive.[419]

9.5.2 *Discrimination on Other Grounds for Religious Reasons*

Distinctive treatment on other grounds because of (alleged) religious reasons can also be discerned within employment hiring policies. It has been argued that making distinctions in the field of employment matters on religious grounds could under certain circumstances be considered tolerable. It was underscored, at the same time, that this is only the case if this is done so as to ensure that those jobs that can, reasonably speaking, only be fulfilled by people of a certain religion will be indeed occupied by the appropriate persons. A related question is whether employers may, for (alleged) religious reasons, discriminate on grounds other than religion, for instance on the grounds of gender or sexual orientation.

It is submitted that states should *not* provide for exemptions in this field largely for the same reasons as why religious ethos exemption schemes should be dismissed: if no evident link between the nature of the work and the occupational requirement can be discerned, exemption schemes will foster human rights abuses. Homosexuals are refused by religious ethos employers not because this characteristic would make them genuinely unsuited for the job but because of a prejudice on the part of the organization against this characteristic itself. The same applies to the position of women within these organizations: if religious ethos employers refuse to accept women for (senior) positions this is (generally) the case because this idea (an active role for women within the organization) is in itself opposed. Even if the religious ethos employer were to be genuinely convinced that women are incapable of discharging the relevant tasks, the question remains if the state should pro-actively and explicitly accommodate these employers by devising a religious ethos exemption scheme. Thus, it must be emphasized that this dismissal of the religious ethos exemption (here including exemptions regarding distinctive treatment on grounds other than religion) is by no means proposed in the naïve understanding that doing so will eliminate practices of religious discrimination, discrimination against women and discrimination against homosexuals in the workspace. This dismissal is merely premised on the acknowledgement that in the era of fundamental equality rights, states ought not to actively encourage religious discrimination or homophobic or misogynous/patriarchal practices.[420]

---

[419] See, *e.g.*, Olivier De Schutter, *Country Report Belgium: Report on Measures to Combat Discrimination (Directives 2000/43/EC and 2000/78/EC)* (EU Legal Experts Network, 2007), p. 64, for a description of the legislative history regarding this provision in Belgium.

[420] Human Rights Committee, General Comment 28, para. 5, again serves as a useful legal opinion in that respect: "States parties should ensure that…religious or cultural attitudes are not used to justify violations of women's right to equality before the law and to equal enjoyment of all Covenant rights."

Turning to relevant state practice, the religious ethos exception provided by Slovakia's Equality Law is a good example of an exemption scheme that actually sanctions distinctive treatment on the basis of sex or sexual orientation by organizations and other legal entities whose activities are based on religion or belief, in matters related to employment.[421] Ireland's religious ethos exemption scheme is not limited to distinctions based on religion or belief either.[422] Norwegian law explicitly sanctions discrimination on the basis of sexual orientation by and within religious communities in the working environment:

> Discrimination on the basis of homosexual [forms] of cohabitation in connection with appointment in posts associated with religious communities, where special requirements based on the nature of the post or the purpose of the activities of the employer are specified in the advertisement of the vacant post, shall not be in contravention of the prohibition against discrimination on the basis of sexual orientation.[423]

The British regulations similarly provide for a religious ethos exemption scheme to facilitate derogations from the general rule of non-discrimination on the basis of sexual orientation in employment matters within organized religion.[424] New Zealand has adopted an exemption scheme which sanctions different treatment based on sex "where the position is for the purposes of an organized religion and is limited to one sex so as to comply with the doctrines or rules or established customs of the religion."[425] Belgian and Dutch exemption schemes stand out positively as regulations that explicitly forbid distinctive treatment on any other ground than religion or belief.[426]

9.6 Conclusion

This Chapter endeavoured to demonstrate that the different modes of state–religion identification are surrounded and characterized by policies and forms of state practice with far-reaching ramifications for compliance with human

---

[421] Art. 8, para. (2), of the Act on Equal Treatment in Certain Areas and Protection against Discrimination, No. 365/2004. This is also contrary to the EU Council Directive (*supra* note 367) as the latter makes clear that the difference in treatment "should not justify discrimination on another ground [than religion or belief]" (art. 4, para. 2).

[422] Compare sections (a) and (b) of para. (1) of art. 37 of the Employment Equality Act, No. 21/1998.

[423] Art. 13(3), para. (3), of the Working Environment Act of 1977 (as amended through 2007).

[424] A requirement related to sexual orientation can be applied so as to comply with "the doctrines of the religion" or so as to avoid conflict "with the strongly held religious convictions of a significant number of the religion's followers". See art. 7, para. (3), of the Employment Equality (Sexual Orientation) Regulations, No. 1661/2003.

[425] Art. 28 of the Human Rights Act, Act No. 82/1993 (amended through 3 December 2007).

[426] Belgium: art. 13, second sentence, of the Law Combating Certain Forms of Discrimination, BS 30 V 07, of 10 May 2007; the Netherlands: art. 5, para. (2), of the General Equal Treatment Act of 1994 (amended 2004).

rights law. Different human rights norms are affected in this context, ranging from people's equal religious rights, to the right to freedom of expression, to the right to freedom of association and the right to work. With regard to the more religious parts of the state–religion identification spectrum it was observed that these systems, in actual practice, are not devoid of forms of institutionalised discrimination and *de facto* instances of discrimination on grounds of religion or belief (or lack thereof). This claim was substantiated by carrying out a range of thematic case studies on, among other issues, Establishment of Religion & the 'Equal Religious Rights of Others', Religion & Freedom of Expression, Religion & Freedom of Association and Religion & Equal Employment Opportunities. With regard to the more secular parts of the state–religion identification it was outlined, at the same time, that in some secular or separationist states the ideals of state secularism and separationism have come to be considered 'ends in themselves'. This has given rise to situations where the principles of secularism and separationism are construed so as to impose special (illegitimate) limits on the activities of religions, principally in the field of organizational freedom of religious organizations, or special limits on the manifestation of certain beliefs, principally in the field of the freedom to manifest a religion itself (*forum externum*) and more specifically the field of conscientious objections.

The remaining questions are how the parameter of state–religion identification may affect the educational system of a state and how it may affect compliance with fundamental political rights. These issues will be discussed in Chapters 10 and 11 respectively.

CHAPTER TEN

RELIGION & EDUCATION

10.1 Introduction

It is hard to ignore the tension that exists between the liberty of parents or legal guardians "to ensure the religious and moral education of their children in conformity with their own convictions"[1] on the one hand, and children's autonomous right to freedom of religion or belief on the other.[2] The recognition of parental rights in this context can be considered rather unique in so far as it provides a third party with rights vis-à-vis the individual. In other words, it provides a third party with a right to interfere with someone's (the child's) freedom or at least to temporarily exercise it on the latter's behalf. With the entry into force of the *Convention on the Rights of the Child*, the paradigm has arguably shifted from prior and decisive parental rights to an autonomous children's right to freedom of religion or belief (with parental rights being accessory).[3] The Children's Rights Convention has sought to constructively deal with the tension at stake: it recognizes children's right to freedom of religion or belief whilst urging state parties at the same time:

> ...to respect the rights and duties of the parents and, when applicable, legal guardians, to provide direction to the child in the exercise of his or her right [to freedom of religion or belief] *in a manner consistent with the evolving capacities of the child.*[4]

---

[1] Art. 18, para. (4), of the ICCPR. This provision was ultimately added after extensive debates in the drafting committees. Originally proposed by Greece (A/C.3/L.875) and therefore often referred to as the "Greek Amendment" in the *travaux préparatoires*. For opposition, see, *e.g.*, A/C.3/SR.1025 (1960), para. 57 (USSR). See also art. 26, para. (3), of the UDHR; art. 14, para. (2), of Convention on the Rights of the Child, G.A. res. 44/25, annex, 44 U.N. GAOR Supp. (No. 49) at 167, U.N. Doc. A/44/49, of 20 November 1989 (entered into force: 2 September 1990) [hereinafter: CRC]; art. 13, para. (3), of ICESCR; and art. 5, paras. (1) and (2), of the UN Religious Tolerance Declaration (1981).

[2] Art. 14, para. (1), of CRC states: "States Parties shall respect the right of the child to freedom of thought, conscience and religion." For a recent, comprehensive study of children's right to freedom of religion or belief as a right recognized by international law, see Sylvie Langlaude, The Right of the Child to Religious Freedom in International Law (Leiden: Martinus Nijhoff Publishers, 2007).

[3] Cf. Eva Brems, Article 14: The Rights to Freedom of Thought, Conscience and Religion (A Commentary on the United Nations Convention on the Rights of the Child) (Leiden/Boston: Martinus Nijhoff Publishers, 2006), p. 25. In this context it is worth emphasizing that the children's right to freedom of religion of belief as incorporated into CRC is of a later date and the CRC could be considered the *lex specialis* in this context.

[4] Art. 14, para. (2), of CRC (emphasis added); for a study on this parameter and its legal relevance, see G. Lansdown, The Evolving Capacities of the Child (Florence: UNICEF Innocenti Research Centre, 2005).

It would indeed appear to be essential to take account of the evolving capacities of the child if we want the 'best interest of the child' to be our guiding principle.[5] Parental guidance, in the words of Brems, "has to recede as the child's capacities evolve".[6] Taking that conception as the point of departure, this Chapter examines the state's role in guaranteeing children's rights (to education, freedom of religion or belief and equality), as well as parental rights, in the context of its obligation to provide education. As soon as it is clear what an educational system that takes sufficient account of these rights looks like, it will be possible to further scrutinize the position and role of teachers within such a system.

10.2 Access to Appropriate Education

The state has to respect the child's right to education which implies, *inter alia*, making available free primary education to all.[7] The following overview is intended to outline the relevant religious freedoms and equality norms and the various human rights violations that are discernable in this context.

10.2.1 *Prohibition of Compulsory Religious Upbringing*

A child's upbringing and its education obviously touch upon each other in many ways. In that respect, it may be noted as a preliminary observation that a legal requirement that would force parents to raise their children as a member of a particular religion would constitute an infringement of both parental and children's rights. Such a coercive measure, naturally, would annihilate parents' liberty to decide (in a manner consistent with the evolving capacities of the child) on the religious and moral education of their children in conformity with their own convictions. It would be wrong, in this context, to solely associate this position with the more stringent Islamic states[8] as the Norwegian Constitution provides:

> The Evangelical-Lutheran religion shall remain the official religion of the State. *The inhabitants professing it are bound to bring up their children in the same.*[9]

---

[5] See art. 3 and 18, para. (1), of CRC on the 'best interests of the child' notion. See also art. 5 of the UN Religious Tolerance Declaration (1981).

[6] Brems, *supra* note 3, p. 26.

[7] Art. 13 of ICESCR.

[8] *E.g.* art. 9 of the Basic Law of Saudi Arabia (1992) stipulates: "The family is the kernel of Saudi society, and its members shall be brought up on the basis of the Islamic faith, and loyalty and obedience to God, His Messenger, and to [its] guardians…"; art. 21 of the Const. of Qatar (2003) states: "The family is the basis of the society. A Qatari family is founded on religion…".

[9] Art. 2, para. (2), of the Const. of Norway (1814) (emphasis added).

There is clearly no place for such a coercive norm in a liberal democracy as it makes (*de jure*, at least) a travesty of religious freedom.[10] Most religious people will want to teach their children the essence of their beliefs, but it is certainly not for the state to command that they in fact do so. Moreover, it is certainly not unimaginable that liberal (nominal) church members would wish for their children to make up their own mind when the time is right. Under human rights law they are most definitely entitled to make that decision. In the latter respect, Slovenian constitutional provisions stand out positively in so far they have due regard for the child's evolving capacities and best interests:

> Parents have the right to provide their children with a religious and moral upbringing in accordance with their beliefs. The religious and moral guidance given to children must be appropriate to their age and maturity, and be consistent with their free conscience and religious and other beliefs or convictions.[11]

10.2.2 *Prohibition of Compulsory Religious Education*

Compulsory religious education is contrary to international human rights law.[12] In the view of the Human Rights Committee solely "public school instruction in subjects such as the general history of religions and ethics [which] is given in a *neutral and objective way*" is compatible with the norms on freedom of religion or belief.[13] Consequently, "public education that includes instruction in a particular religion or belief is inconsistent with article 18.4 [of the ICCPR: parental liberties]".[14] Having said that, the Human Rights Committee does sanction religious instruction in public schools if adequate provision is made for opt-out clauses, thus accommodating the wishes of parents or legal guardians who do not want their child to attend religion classes.[15]

---

[10] The Human Rights Committee has repeatedly condemned Norway's state practice: A/55/40 vol. I (2000) 22 at para. 78; and A/49/40 vol. I (1994) 21 at para. 93.

[11] Art. 41, para. (3), of the CONST. OF SLOVENIA (1991).

[12] *E.g.* CRC/C/150 (2005) 149 at paras. 694 and 695 (Costa Rica): "the Committee is concerned at the fact that classes on Catholicism are part of the curriculum, which is discriminatory for non-Catholic children…The Committee recommends that the State party devise a curriculum that will ensure that the child's freedom of religion can be fully realized in the educational system without any discrimination"; and CRC/C/62 (1997) 25 at paras. 150 and 171 (Myanmar); see also ICESCR Committee, E/1994/23 (1993) 32 at para. 126 (Iran).

[13] Human Rights Committee, General Comment No. 22, para. 6 (emphasis added; particularly referring to art. 18, para. (4), of the ICCPR).

[14] *Ibid.*

[15] *Ibid.* The Committee on Economic, Social and Cultural Rights is roughly of the same view as it has postulated that "public school instruction in subjects such as the general history of religions and ethics *if it is given in an unbiased and objective way*, respectful of the freedoms of opinion, conscience and expression" is permitted and "public education that includes instruction in a particular religion or belief" is in principle inconsistent with human rights law "unless provision is made for non-discriminatory exemptions or alternatives that would accommodate the wishes of parents and guardians". See Committee on Economic, Social and Cultural Rights,

The state thus can be said to fulfil its human rights obligations if it either designs an educational system (a public school curriculum) which is sufficiently neutral or non-religious in itself or, in case it does allow religious education in public schools, if it grants adequate opt-out rights. The Human Rights Committee applied these principles to the case of *Leirvåg v. Norway*.[16] The case revolved around a new mandatory religious subject that the Norwegian government had introduced (in August 1997) in the Norwegian school system entitled "Christian Knowledge and Religious and Ethical Education" (CKREE), replacing the previous Christianity subject and the life stance subject.[17] This was challenged by humanist parents who felt that the subject was not neutral enough and that the available opt-out clauses were insufficient. The Human Rights Committee concluded that the teaching of CKREE cannot be said to meet the requirement of being delivered in a neutral and objective way. It reached this conclusion, firstly, in light of the fact that the object clause of the Education Act in question prescribed that the object of primary and lower secondary education shall be "in agreement and cooperation with the home, to help to give pupils a Christian and moral upbringing".[18] And, secondly, because of the fact that some of the *travaux préparatoires* of the Act made it clear that the subject gives priority to tenets of Christianity over other religions and philosophies of life.[19] In line with the Human Rights Committee's reading of the international norms on freedom of religion or belief in this context, this new course could still be saved if it could be concluded that Norway had sufficiently guaranteed exemption rights that would accommodate the wishes of parents or guardians. However, the Human Rights Committee noted that only a partial exemption scheme was in place and that the way in which this scheme was implemented in practice left the rights of the applicants unprotected.[20] In this context the Human Rights Committee considered that:

> …the present system of partial exemption imposes a considerable burden on persons in the position of the authors, insofar as it requires them to acquaint themselves with those aspects of the subject which are clearly of a religious nature, as well as with other aspects, with a view to determining which of the other aspects they may feel a need to seek – and justify – exemption from. Nor would it be implausible to expect that such persons would be deterred from exercising that right, insofar as a regime of partial exemption could create problems

---

General Comment No. 13: The Right to Education (Art. 13), E/C.12/1999/10, of 8 December 1999 (emphasis added), basing its considerations on art. 13 of ICESCR. It will be contended *infra*, however, that such opt-out clauses in practice often prove to be highly problematic.

[16] Human Rights Committee, *Leirvåg v. Norway*, Communication No. 1155/2003, Views of 3 November 2004.

[17] It must be noted that the Committee on the Rights of the Child had raised objections with regard to the previous situation: CRC/C/15/Add.23 (1994), para. 9.

[18] *Leirvåg v. Norway, supra* note 16, para. 14.3.

[19] *Idem*.

[20] *Ibid*., para. 14.4.

> for children which are different from those that may be present in a total exemption scheme. Indeed as the experience of the authors demonstrates, the system of exemptions does not currently protect the liberty of parents to ensure that the religious and moral education of their children is in conformity with their own convictions. In this respect, the Committee notes that the CKREE subject combines education on religious knowledge with practising a particular religious belief, e.g. learning by heart of prayers, singing religious hymns or attendance at religious services...While it is true that in these cases parents may claim exemption from these activities by ticking a box on a form, the CKREE scheme does not ensure that education of religious knowledge and religious practice are separated in a way that makes the exemption scheme practicable.[21]

The Committee furthermore highlighted the problem of 'loyalty conflicts' that can be experienced by children in this context.[22] The latter point reveals a more fundamental concern about religious education in the curriculum of public schools: though opt-out clauses may remedy the compulsion element, such safeguards cannot prevent possible ostracization of those children that avail of these exemption schemes (something that has also been observed by the Committee on the Rights of the Child with respect to Italy).[23] The Human Rights Committee also explicitly objected to the requirement to give reasons for exempting children from lessons focusing on imparting religious knowledge, as this practice creates even further obstacles for parents who seek to ensure that their children are not exposed to religious ideas.[24] The Committee on the Rights of the Child has expanded the state duties in the present context as it has determined that the state is under an obligation to ensure that parents are actually aware of the fact that religious instruction is not compulsory.[25]

It follows from the above considerations that any constitutional provision along the lines of 'the teaching of religion *x* shall be compulsory for pupils' is fundamentally contrary to parental and children's rights.[26] Saudi Arabia, for instance, has constitutionally stipulated that education must aim at "instilling the Islamic faith in the younger generation".[27] Maldives' educational system is framed so as to "inculcate obedience to Islam" and "instil love for Islam".[28] The combined focus of protecting youth "against perversions" and providing

---

[21] *Ibid.*, para. 14.6.

[22] *Ibid.*, para. 14.7.

[23] CRC/C/15/Add.198 (2003), para. 29 (Italy): "children, especially in elementary schools, may suffer from marginalization if they abstain from religious instruction, which is mainly covering Catholic religion."

[24] *Leirvåg v. Norway, supra* note 16, para. 14.7.

[25] CRC/C/15/Add.198 (2003), paras. 29–30 (Italy).

[26] *E.g.* art. 24, para. (10), of the TRANSITIONAL FEDERAL CHARTER OF THE SOMALI REPUBLIC (2004) provides: "Teaching of Islam shall be compulsory for pupils in both Public and Private Schools".

[27] Art. 13 of the BASIC LAW OF SAUDI ARABIA (1992).

[28] Art. 36, para. (c), of the CONST. OF MALDIVES (2008).

them with religious knowledge as the main objective of state education (as in Yemen) will also fail the above human right test.[29] Compulsory state education that is aimed at the development of the "religious consciousness" (Greece)[30] of pupils or state education that is organized to endow "members of the younger generation...with religious...learning" (Liechtenstein)[31] may similarly be deemed contrary to the religious rights of parents and the religious and educational rights of children. The Constitution of Malta provides that "[r]eligious teaching of the Roman Catholic Apostolic Faith shall be provided in all State schools as part of compulsory education".[32] This is in keeping with Malta's policy of delegating the teaching of "which principles are right and which are wrong" to authorities of the Roman Catholic Apostolic Church.[33] The Slovak Republic, though officially secular, has included a (Christian) religious subject in the public school curriculum.[34] Turkey, an otherwise strictly secular state, has made religious instruction (with a profound emphasis on Sunni Islam) a compulsory part of the curricula of primary and secondary schools.[35] It can be argued, at the same time, that state-run compulsory instruction—or indoctrination—in secular ideologies such as the North Korean *Juche* ideology is similarly at odds with the prohibition of coercion.[36]

10.2.3 *Access to Non-Denominational Education*

State duties in the area of education consist of obligations to refrain from interferences but also, importantly, of obligations to proactively guarantee availability and access. Thus, the state must respect the right of parents not to avail of the schools established by the public authorities and their right to opt for private educational institutions (i.e. denominational schools) so as to ensure the religious and moral education of their children in conformity with

---

[29] Art. 53 of the CONST. OF YEMEN (1990).

[30] Art. 16, para. (2), of the CONST. OF GREECE (2001).

[31] Art. 15 of the CONST. OF LIECHTENSTEIN (1921).

[32] Art. 2, para. (3), of the CONST. OF MALTA (1964).

[33] Art. 2, para. (2), of the CONST. OF MALTA (1964).

[34] As per the Concordat between the Slovak Republic and the Holy See about Catholic Upbringing and Education of March 2004. Art. II(4) provides: "The Catholic religion is taught as one of the compulsory eligible subject matters in primary schools and in secondary schools..." Officially, an ethics subject may be taught as an alternative; it should be acknowledged, however, that the Catholic ecclesiastical authorities, as per the Concordat, seem to be very influential in the field of education.

[35] Art. 24 of the CONST. OF TURKEY (1982).

[36] DPRK's constitutional provision on public education stipulates that: "the State shall put the principles of socialist education into practice and raise the new generation to be steadfast revolutionaries who will fight for society and the people, to be people of a new communist type who are knowledgeable, morally sound and physically healthy" (art. 43 of the CONST. OF DPRK OF 1972). See also art. 39 of the CONST. OF CUBA (1976) which requires that state education is based on the "ideology of Marx".

their own convictions.[37] Furthermore, public school education, it goes without saying, should be open to all children regardless of their parents' religious affiliation.[38] The standards on the right to education further imply that the state is under a positive obligation to ensure that sufficient public schools with appropriate curricula are available at all times. This means that a predominantly religious society cannot completely contract out the issue of education to private religious institutions. In this respect, the Human Rights Committee very recently reproached Ireland, observing that:

> ...the vast majority of Ireland's primary schools are privately run denominational schools that have adopted a religious integrated curriculum thus depriving many parents and children who so wish to have access to secular primary education... The State party should increase its efforts to ensure that non-denominational primary education is widely available in all regions of the State party, in view of the increasingly diverse and multi-ethnic composition of the population of the State party.[39]

If the state fails in its positive duty to provide for non-denominational education, be it by actively contracting out this issue to religious organizations or by maintaining historical church prerogatives (effectively allowing primary school education to be monopolized by religion), various educational and religious rights are inevitably infringed.[40] Ireland's Equality Act makes the situation for children of non-religious parents worse as it allows denominational schools (which are nearly all Catholic) to refuse admission of pupils who do not adhere to the denomination concerned, on the grounds of the preservation of the 'religious ethos' of the school.[41] Such a system fosters serious human rights violations: (i) given the lack of secular state-run schools and the possibility that children of non-religious parents are turned away by denominational schools, no appropriate form of education might be available at all to children of non-religious parents; (ii) secular parents who prefer religious education over no education at all might feel compelled to obtain the necessary religious affiliation (e.g. by means of conversion or baptism of their children) so as to be able to enrol their children.[42]

---

[37] As long as these schools conform to such minimum educational standards laid down by the state. *E.g.* art. 13, paras. (3) and (4), of ICESCR; art. 5, para. (1)(b), of the UNESCO Convention against Discrimination in Education of 14 December 1960; also implied by art. 5, para. (2) of the UN Religious Tolerance Declaration (1981).

[38] See also Carolyn Evans, *Religious Education in Public Schools: An International Human Rights Perspective*, 8(3) Human Rights Law Review 449 (2008), p. 451.

[39] CCPR/C/IRL/CO/3 (2008), para. 2.

[40] See Alison Mawhinney, *Submission to the Human Rights Committee with Respect to the Third Periodic Report of Ireland* [NGO Information], March 2008; this shadow report is a response to CCPR/C/IRL/3, paras. 409–411.

[41] Art. 7, para. (3)(c), of the Equal Status Act, No. 8/2000, of 2000.

[42] Both problems are reported in the mentioned shadow report, *supra* note 40, pp. 2 and 4; similar concerns have been raised by CERD Committee: A/60/18 (2005), 30 at para. 142.

The state is also under an obligation to ensure that public schools are not only public schools on paper and that, if teaching in religion takes place, non-discriminatory exemptions (opt-out clauses) and/or alternative non-religious classes (e.g. ethics classes) are offered. The Committee on the Rights of the Child criticized Polish state practice in this respect, observing that:

> ...despite regulations guaranteeing that parents can choose for their children to attend ethics classes instead of religion classes in public schools, in practice few schools offer ethics courses to allow for such a choice and students require parental consent to attend ethics courses.[43]

The state is arguably also under an obligation to ensure that public schools uphold their public (non-denominational) character so that all who wish to attend may do so without obstacles or scruples. For instance, as Russo points out in relation to Republika Šrpska, if religious symbols are present in public schools all over the state, children of non-believers or of persons belonging to minority religions may not have access to adequate state education.[44] Very recently, the European Court of Human Rights (in a Chamber judgement) considered in relation to the Italian public educational system that the display of Catholic symbols in classrooms amounts to an illegitimate restriction of the right of parents to educate their children in conformity with their convictions and of the right of children to believe or not to believe.[45] This essentially means that, under the European Convention system, states must observe confessional neutrality in the context of public education (moreover, the judgement seems to indicate that the same arguments may apply to all premises used by public authorities).

Some treaty monitoring bodies have criticized the *laissez-faire* attitude towards education for other, perhaps even more fundamental reasons. It has been observed that whenever the state fails in its positive duty to provide for sufficient non-denominational schools, or if it is satisfied with a situation wherein the different religions organize education in accordance with their tenets, it may be actively contributing to religious segregation. The Committee on Economic, Social and Cultural Rights, for instance, assessing the educational system in Northern Ireland, observed that it:

> ...is heavily segregated, with most Protestants attending Protestant schools and most Catholics attending Catholic schools and only approximately 2 per cent of the school population attending integrated schools. The current government

---

[43] CRC/C/15/Add.194 (2002), para. 32.

[44] Charles J. Russo, *Religion and Education in Bosnia: Integration Not Segregation?*, 3 Brigham Young University Law Review (2000), p. 945, on the fact that Christian Orthodox religious symbols are present in most public schools.

[45] ECtHR, *Lautsi v. Italy*, Application No. 30814/06, Judgement of 3 November 2009, determining a violation of art. 2 of Protocol No. 1 (right to education) examined jointly with Article 9 (freedom of thought, conscience and religion) of the European Convention. See Protocol No.1 to the ECHR, ETS No. 009, of 20 March 1952 (entry into force: 18 May 1954).

> policy, which appears to consist of a willingness to consider the conversion of existing Protestant or Catholic schools into integrated schools if it is the wish of the majority in a given school, is ineffective and likely to preserve the status quo.[46]

It is thus clear that a far more pro-active policy on making appropriate education accessible to all is called for.

Granting religious ethos exemptions to denominational schools in states that provide sufficient secular public education does not need to be too problematic (albeit perhaps fundamentally objectionable). Be that as it may, the above example of Ireland shows that the opposite situation needs to be firmly criticized: if the state fails in its obligation to provide sufficient non-denominational public education it is clear that the policy of granting religious ethos exemptions aggravates the lack of access to education. Besides Ireland, the UK[47] and New Zealand[48] expressly sanction religious discrimination by denominational schools in their enrolment policies.

10.2.4 *Further Access Issues: State Schools & Secular Dress Codes*

The question of dress codes has become a contentious issue that can in practice affect access to education. Banning the wearing of religious symbols or clothing in state schools may affect access to those for whom wearing such items is religiously compulsory.[49] Wearing clothes or displaying symbols is indisputably covered by freedom of religion or belief.[50] It must be reiterated, however, that the freedom to manifest a religion is not absolute. The question thus is whether in the educational context interests can be advanced that warrant interference with this freedom.

Unlike the European Court of Human Rights, which has sanctioned such bans in the interest of preserving secularism and the rights and freedoms of others,[51] the UN treaty monitoring bodies have not yet fully come to terms

---

[46] E/1998/22 (1997) 56 at para. 301 (UK); reiterated in 2002: E/2003/22 (2002) 39 at paras. 226 and 245 (UK).

[47] Art. 59 of the Equality Act of 2006, Law c.3/2006.

[48] Art. 58 of the [New Zealand] Human Rights Act of 1993.

[49] The issue of religious attire clearly cuts across a broad range of fundamental rights, freedoms and principles as well as state interests that all need to be considered in this debate (*e.g.* the right to freedom of religion or belief in both its positive and negative forms, elimination of religious discrimination, elimination of racial discrimination, elimination of gender discrimination, access to employment, access to education, children's rights, teachers' rights, etc.). For a comprehensive account, see DOMINIC MCGOLDRICK, HUMAN RIGHTS AND RELIGION: THE ISLAMIC HEADSCARF DEBATE IN EUROPE (Portland: Hart Publishing, 2006), particularly Chapter 9 (for a human rights approach).

[50] Art. 6, para. (c), of the UN Religious Tolerance Declaration (1981); Human Rights Committee, General Comment No. 22, para. 4.

[51] ECtHR, *Leyla Şahin v. Turkey*, Application No. 44774/98, Judgement of 10 November 2005, para. 116. However, as dissenting Judge Tulkens rightly pointed out, it cannot, *in abstracto*, be taken for granted that wearing a headscarf, in the capacity of a student, in university

with this type of prohibition.[52] It could be argued though that the major concerns the latter bodies have identified so far lean towards a disapproval of such state practice. The Human Rights Committee, in *Hudoyberganova v. Uzbekistan*,[53] concluded that the suspension of a female Muslim student by a language institute for wearing a headscarf constituted a violation of her right to freedom of religion or belief.[54] However, it must be borne in mind that the Committee came to this decision mainly because Uzbekistan had not advanced any particular ground for limiting this student's religious rights.[55] This would suggest that the outcome of similar cases before the Committee could be different in the future if the state could convincingly argue that recognized grounds for limitations are at stake and if the state would substantiate the necessity of upholding those grounds at the expense of the freedom to manifest a religion. Committee member Wedgwood (who deemed the facts of the case, as presented by the different parties, too obscure to rule on it) considered that:

> ...a state may be allowed to restrict forms of dress that directly interfere with effective pedagogy, and the covering of a student's face would present a different set of facts.[56]

---

buildings per se contravenes the principle of secularism or is aimed at calling the principle of secularism into question (see Dissenting Opinion Judge Tulkens, para. 7). The *Şahin* line of reasoning was confirmed by the European Court in: *Dogru v. France*, Application No. 27058/05, Judgement of 4 December 2008. More recently (and arguably in an attempt to prevent a further accumulation of similar cases against France), the European Court, based on these earlier judgements, has started to declare all such cases against France that revolve around the expulsion of pupils from schools for wearing conspicuous symbols of religious affiliation, inadmissible (*e.g.*, *Aktas v. France*, Application No. 43563/08, Judgement of 17 July 2009; *Bayrak v. France*, Application No. 14308/08, Judgement of 17 July 2009; *Gamaleddyn v. France*, Application No. 18527/08, Judgement of 17 July 2009; *Ghazal v. France*, Application No. 29134/08, Judgement of 17 July 2009; *J. Singh v. France*, Application No. 25463/08, Judgement of 17 July 2009; *R. Singh v. France*, Application No. 27561/08, Judgement of 17 July 2009).

[52] In addition to the cases dealt with and observations made by the treaty bodies in the following overview, attention may be drawn to a headscarf case before the CEDAW Committee: *Rahime Kayhan v. Turkey*, Communication No. 8/2005, Decision of 27 January 2006, which was declared inadmissible for failure to exhaust domestic remedies.

[53] Human Rights Committee, *Raihon Hudoyberganova v. Uzbekistan*, Communication No. 931/2000, U.N. Doc. CCPR/C/82/D/931/2000 (2004), Views of 05 November 2004.

[54] The duty for Muslim women to wear a headscarf is said to follow from the Qur'an, *e.g.* sura 24:31 (THE HOLY QUR'AN, transl. Abdullah Yusuf Ali): "And say to the believing women that they should lower their gaze and guard their modesty; that they should not display their beauty and ornaments except what (must ordinarily) appear thereof; that they should draw their veils over their bosoms and not display their beauty except to their husbands, their fathers, their husband's fathers, their sons, their husbands' sons, their brothers or their brothers' sons, or their sisters' sons, or their women, or the slaves whom their right hands possess, or male servants free of physical needs, or small children who have no sense of the shame of sex; and that they should not strike their feet in order to draw attention to their hidden ornaments. And O ye Believers! Turn ye all together towards Allah, that ye may attain Bliss."

[55] *Raihon Hudoyberganova v. Uzbekistan*, *supra* note 53, para. 6.2.

[56] *Ibid.*, Individual opinion by Committee member Ms. Ruth Wedgwood.

The pedagogy argument (including the issue of identification of students during examinations) particularly pertains to religious attire that covers the face (such as the *niqāb*) or the face and parts of the body (such as the *burqa*).

The recently adopted French Law on Secularity and Conspicuous Religious Symbols in Public Schools has been scrutinized by various treaty bodies and though no outright condemnation can be discerned, the concerns that have been raised lean towards a disapproval of this state practice.[57] The Committee on the Rights of the Child, for instance, noted that:

> …the [French] Constitution provides for freedom of religion and…the law of 1905 on the separation of church and State prohibits discrimination on the basis of faith. The Committee equally recognizes the importance the State party accords to secular public schools. However, in the light of articles 14 and 29 of the Convention [CRC], the Committee is concerned by the alleged rise in discrimination, including that based on religion. The Committee is also concerned that the new legislation…on wearing religious symbols and clothing in public schools may be counterproductive, by neglecting the principle of the best interests of the child and the right of the child to access to education, and not achieve the expected results.[58]

The CRC Committee, short of condemning the law in absolute terms, clearly challenges the necessity of this interference with religious rights.[59] As France is under a clear human rights obligation to guarantee that children are not excluded from the school system or marginalized, the Committee suggests that France should "consider alternative means" (e.g. mediation) of ensuring the secular character of public schools.[60] It further argues that the "dress code of schools may be better addressed within the public schools themselves, encouraging participation of children."[61] Also the Committee on the Elimination of Racial Discrimination is concerned that the ban might have a discriminatory impact and may affect the universality of the right to education in France.[62] The Special Rapporteur on freedom of religion or belief, during her fact-finding mission in France, confirmed the negative human rights implications of the ban on religious symbols and clothing in public schools. She observed that "[a]lthough the scope of the new law applies equally to all

---

[57] *Loi en application du principe de laïcité, le port de signes ou de tenues manifestant une appartenance religieuse dans les écoles, collèges et lycées publics*, Law No. 2004-228, of 15 March 2004.

[58] CRC/C/140 (2004) 124 at para. 604; see also CRC/C/15/Add.240 (2004).

[59] Similarly, CRC/C/118 (2002) 68 at paras. 285 and 286 (Tunisia): "The Committee is concerned about information brought to its attention which indicates that the exercise of the right to freedom of religion may not always be fully guaranteed, particularly with regard to regulations prohibiting the wearing of a headscarf by girls in schools…The Committee recommends that the State party take all necessary measures to ensure the full implementation of the right to freedom of thought, conscience and religion."

[60] CRC/C/140 (2004), para. 605.

[61] *Idem.*

[62] A/60/18 (2005) 26 at para. 112.

religious symbols, its application disproportionately affects young Muslim women wearing the headscarf".[63] Many other negative developments were observed which are worth quoting in some detail:

> ...47 children have been expelled from schools, including three Sikh pupils who had refused to remove their under-turban. French tribunals have usually upheld these expulsions...It is however difficult to assess the number of pupils who have chosen not to abandon their religious signs. In addition to dismissals, some have removed themselves from the school system by abstaining from registering with a school...A large number of...women told the Special Rapporteur about the difficulties they had endured because they had freely chosen to wear the headscarf. Many had been intimidated or humiliated for expressing their personal opinion on the question. Even in cases where young girls were obliged to wear headscarves by their families, the law is said to have provoked particularly painful situations within the families. Some girls who did not wear the headscarf before the law have decided to wear it when they leave the school as a form of protest. Some informed the Special Rapporteur that they felt torn between loyalty to their religious community and their commitment to women's rights...The adoption of the law is also said to have radicalized a fraction of the Muslim youth...Another religious minority that has been seriously affected by the adoption of the law is the Sikh community. Their members reported to the Special Rapporteur that displaying religious symbols was an essential part of their faith. They described the painful experiences they endured when their children had to cut their hair, as a result of the rigid application of the law by some educational institutions...The law also appears to have sent the wrong message to a certain portion of the population which has come to believe that the wearing of religious symbols per se, and in particular headscarves, is generally unlawful. As a result of the new law, a portion of the population has come to associate the headscarf solely with gender inequality and oppression. The Special Rapporteur was informed about instances where women were refused access to shops or were insulted in the street because they wore the headscarf. For the same reasons, some women were dismissed from their employment, while others found it difficult to find employment.[64]

Short of condemning the ban in absolute terms, the concerns raised by the Special Rapporteur reveal that she has serious misgivings about the state practice concerned.

An issue that seems to be under-emphasized in both in the European Court's approach as well as in the considerations of the UN treaty monitoring bodies is the distinction between teacher vs. pupil.[65] Krishnaswami, in his seminal study published in 1960, already argued that though the preservation of the non-denominational character of a school is a legitimate concern, "it is desirable that persons whose faith prescribes such apparel should not be

---

[63] E/CN.4/2006/5/Add.4, para. 63.

[64] *Ibid.*, paras. 61–67. This study concerns 2005 data.

[65] Judge Tulkens in her Dissenting Opinion to the case of *Leyla Şahin v. Turkey (supra* note 51) notes the legal relevance of this distinction (para. 7 *et seq.*).

unreasonably prevented from wearing it."[66] It can certainly be acknowledged that the preservation of the non-denominational character of public schools is a legitimate state interest as it touches upon the state obligation to protect "the rights and freedoms of others" (a legitimate ground for limiting manifestations of religion). The key question thus is which acts do and which acts do not affect the neutral character of public schools. Do religious manifestations by pupils necessarily have a bearing on the non-denominational character of public schools and do religious manifestations by pupils necessarily affect the fundamental rights and freedoms of others?

Though certainly entering the 'public realm', public school pupils do not represent the state in any way whatsoever as they simply make use, in a private capacity, of a service that is provided by the state (to that it can be added that freedom of religion or belief is in principle protected "in public or private"[67]). As to public school teachers who have voluntarily taken up posts in a neutral environment, one could advance arguments based on the teacher's position as role-model and deduce from this position a need to maintain a sense of neutrality. It would be hard to establish such a duty of impartiality for pupils. The argument that tolerating the wearing by pupils of religious clothing in the class room might negatively affect the right to freedom of religion or belief of others is, *in abstracto*, too vague or theoretical a risk to function as a ground for limitation. Certainly, the freedom to manifest a religion or belief is subject to the protection of the rights and freedoms of others. However, as Judge Tulkens notes in her dissenting opinion in *Leyla Şahin v. Turkey* (in which the European Court sanctioned a ban on headscarves in Turkish university buildings), the application of this ground for limitation can only be deemed necessary in a democratic society if it can be established, *in concreto*, that a person, by means of wearing a religious symbol or piece of clothing, undermined or was liable to undermine the convictions of others (for instance, if it can be established that a headscarf is worn as a means to exert pressure or to proselytise young children, etc.).[68] Similarly, if public order arguments are advanced to legitimize interferences with the right to display religious symbols or wear distinctive clothes, it must, on a case-by-case basis, be established that the latter religious manifestations actually undermine or jeopardize public order.

Finally, it should be pointed out that the UN Special Rapporteur on freedom of religion or belief has developed general criteria in order to evaluate, from a human rights perspective, restrictions and prohibitions on wearing religious symbols (consisting of "aggravating indicators" that identify legislative and

---

[66] Arcot Krishnaswami, *Study of Discrimination in the Matter of Religious Rights and Practices* (U.N. Doc. E/CN.4/Sub.2/200/Rev.1, 1960), p. 33.

[67] Art. 18, para. (1), of the ICCPR.

[68] Dissenting Opinion Judge Tulkens appended to the case of *Leyla Şahin v. Turkey* (*supra* note 51), para. 8.

administrative actions which typically are incompatible with international human rights law and "neutral indicators" that identify policies that in themselves do not contravene these standards).[69] These indicators provide a well-balanced set of legal benchmarks.

10.2.5 *The Problem with Opt-Out Provisions*

It was indicated before that the Human Rights Committee has argued that religious instruction in public schools could be sanctioned if adequate provision is made for non-discriminatory exemptions or alternatives that would accommodate the wishes of parents or legal guardians. However, the Committee has at the same time indicated in its case law that the actual application of exemption schemes proves highly problematic. Many human rights related problems surrounding the issue of opt-out clauses can be discerned.

First of all, opt-out clauses are, naturally, not adequate remedies if the subject of religion is too closely integrated into the curriculum. For instance, in its reply to the issues raised by the Human Rights Committee, Ireland pointed out that an exemption scheme is in place for the withdrawal of pupils from religious instruction.[70] However, since all schools that receive state funding ('national schools') are obliged to teach an 'integrated curriculum' whereby religion is integrated with other subjects so as to ensure that a religious spirit informs the whole work of the school,[71] it is clear that the provision of opt-out clauses in Ireland is purely symbolic. As Mawhinney argues, a "child cannot be opted out of unscheduled and potentially continuous religious teaching which is woven into the very fabric of daily education."[72] It is clear that if the state fails to provide sufficient exemption schemes in this context, serious human rights violations are inevitable: people are forced to sacrifice either their religious freedoms or the right to education.

Furthermore, as no one may be forced to reveal one's religion or belief,[73] opt-out schemes may not require parents or children to outline their precise objections to attending the religion classes that are part of the curriculum. The Human Rights Committee reprimanded Greece for precisely this reason, as Greek public school students can opt-out of compulsory instructional classes in the Christian Orthodox religion only after declaring their religion.[74] Requirements that fall short of disclosure of one's religious affiliation may

---

[69] E/CN.4/2006/5, paras. 36–60 (Ch. III: "Religious Symbols"), particularly para. 55.

[70] CCPR/C/IRL/Q/3/Add.1 (2008), paras. 136–137.

[71] Cf. Alison Mawhinney, *Freedom of Religion in the Irish Primary School System: a Failure to Protect Human Rights*, 27(3) Legal Studies 379 (2009). See the [Irish] Education Act, Law No. 51/1998, of 1998, in particular art. 9, para. (d), which stipulates that schools must "promote the…spiritual…development of students".

[72] Mawhinney, *supra* note 40, p. 3.

[73] Human Rights Committee, General Comment No. 22, para. 3.

[74] A/60/40 vol. I (2005) 60 at para. 90(14).

nonetheless be problematic from a human rights perspective. For instance, a condition to give reasonable grounds for obtaining the exemption carries with it the risk that parents might feel compelled to disclose intimate aspects of their own religious and philosophical convictions.[75]

Exemption schemes must be non-discriminatory. People of all religions and religious denominations must be in a position to avail of the existing opt-out provisions. If a subject that is a compulsory part of the curriculum of a public school is intended to instruct pupils solely or predominantly in the tenets of the dominant religion, children of parents belonging (nominally) to that religion must be in a position to be exempted from this subject. What counts, after all, is not one's religious affiliation, but whether religious instruction is desired or objected to.[76]

A contentious issue arises when parents and child disagree about the desired form of education. For instance, the parents want the child to take religious classes but the child does not or, vice versa, the parents want the child to be exempted from religion classes but the child actually wants to be enrolled. The Committee on the Rights of the Child has expressed its concern that in Poland "students require parental consent to attend ethics courses".[77] As the CRC Committee explicitly reiterated the notion of "the child's evolving capacities" in the same context,[78] it could be deduced that from a certain age on the child's autonomous right to freedom of religion or belief prevails in case of a conflict with the parents' wishes. The same could be argued with respect to disagreements over the larger educational enrolment choice between denominational and non-denominational education. The CRC Committee has not determined the precise age from when the child is empowered to make such decisions. From the fact that the CRC Committee requires, under the state reporting procedure,[79] information on the legal age for choosing a religion or attending religious school teaching in conjunction with the Committee's emphasis on the evolving capacities of the child, one could deduce that autonomous children's rights must be granted to children some years before maturity.[80] In view

[75] Both the Human Rights Committee as well as the European Court of Human Rights have considered the Norwegian exemption scheme for this reason contrary to religious rights. See Human Rights Committee, *Leirvåg v. Norway, supra* note 16, para. 14.7; and European Court of Human Rights, *Folgerø and Others v. Norway*, Application No. 15472/02, Judgement of 29 June 2007, particularly para. 98.

[76] This argument is based on a case before the European Court of Human Rights: *Hasan and Eylem Zengin v. Turkey*, Application No. 1448/04, Judgement of 9 October 2007. Turkish educational law provided for the possibility of exemption only to two categories of pupils of Turkish nationality, namely those whose parents belong to Christianity or the Jewish faith; children of Muslim parents, consequently, could not opt-out these classes.

[77] CRC/C/15/Add.194 (2002), para. 32.

[78] *Ibid.*, para. 33.

[79] Committee on the Rights of the Child, *General Guidelines for Periodic Reports* (CRC/C/58, 1996), para. 24.

[80] Cf. Brems, *supra* note 3, p. 30; she notes that some states have adopted legal provisions in that respect. *E.g.*, Germany has stipulated that children can make these choices autonomously

of this, setting the age of acquiring fully autonomous rights at the age of 20 years (e.g. Nauru)[81] surely amounts to an interference with religious rights. If we take the Children's Rights Convention's notion of the "evolving capacities of the child" seriously, we must conclude that parental rights and powers diminish as the child gets older. Indeed, as Brems argues, it is the state's duty:

> ...to guard the limits of parental direction in matters of religion and conscience, and if necessary to *offer protection to children against infringement of their freedom of thought, conscience and religion by their parents*.[82]

In conclusion, considering the range of serious human rights related problems that emerge within the context of applying opt-out provisions one may very well wonder whether opt-out provisions in practice can actually ever *fully* protect the religious rights of parents and children and the educational rights of children. It is submitted that exemption schemes must meet the following minimum conditions: (i) religious instruction must be limited to a specific subject (and not inextricably interwoven with the educational system); (ii) exemptions must be open to everyone; and (iii) people, both parents and children, must be informed about the availability of these schemes. Carolyn Evans argues, moreover, that exemption schemes "work best when they can be for a whole subject and when a meaningful alternative class is available to substitute for the one that is being missed."[83] Even if all these conditions are met, the fact remains that opt-out clauses in the reality of every day school life may have a negative (stigmatizing) impact on those children that are exempted from certain classes.[84] If the latter concern holds true and cannot be remedied, we may have to reconsider the tenability of religious instruction in public schools. The issue of potential marginalization, in other words, provides a firm case against doctrinal religious instruction in public

---

from age 14: Religious Education Act, RGBl S. 939, of 15 July 1921; while the Swiss Civil Code sets this age at 16 years.

[81] Art. 11, para. (3), of the CONST. OF NAURU (1968). Antigua and Barbuda, Belize, Dominica, Fiji, Grenada, Saint Kitts and Nevis, Saint Lucia, Saint Vincent and the Grenadines and Singapore set the age rather high as well (thus not taking seriously the evolving capacities of the child), namely at 18 years. See art. 11 of the CONST. OF ANTIGUA AND BARBUDA (1981); art. 11 of the CONST. OF BELIZE (1981); art. 9 of the CONST. OF DOMINICA (1978); art. 35 of the CONST. OF THE FIJI ISLANDS (1998); art. 9 of the CONST. OF GRENADA (1973); art. 11 of the CONST. OF SAINT KITTS AND NEVIS (1983); art. 9 of the CONST. OF SAINT LUCIA (1978); art. 9 of the CONST. OF SAINT VINCENT AND THE GRENADINES (1979); art. 16 of the CONST. OF SINGAPORE (1963).

[82] Brems, *supra* note 3, p. 29.

[83] C. Evans, *supra* note 38, p. 469.

[84] Cf. Alison Mawhinney, *The Opt-Out Clause: Imperfect Protection for the Right to Freedom of Religion in Schools*, 2(2) EDUCATIONAL LAW JOURNAL 102 (2006); pp. 109–113. Russo, *supra* note 44, p. 945, argues something similar in relation to Bosnia and Herzegovina: "In theory, religious education classes in public schools in BiH are optional. The reality is that in some cantons and municipalities, children who do not choose to attend these classes are subject to pressure and discrimination from peers and teachers."

schools per se, something that does not prejudice the possibility of neutral education *about* religions (see the conclusion to this Chapter).

10.2.6 *No State Duty to Provide Religious Education*

The right to freedom of religion or belief and the right to education taken in conjunction do not constitute a state duty to provide religious education.[85] Quite the contrary, as we have seen before, the state is forbidden to pursue policies that do not respect parents' religious and philosophical convictions or the child's right to freedom of religion or belief. Any type of compulsory religious education in public schools would inevitably interfere with some children's right to freedom of religion or belief and with parental rights in this context.[86] In view of these considerations and the conclusions reached in the previous sub-section, it is submitted that under human rights law the state may stipulate that all state-administered educational activity will be strictly "non-denominational" (e.g. Portugal),[87] "non-religious" (e.g. Mali),[88] "neutral" (e.g. Gabon),[89] "secular" (e.g. Azerbaijan, Belarus, Burkina Faso, France, Mexico, Moldova, Nicaragua, New Zealand),[90] or of an otherwise non-religious nature (e.g. Cape Verde, India, Japan, Mozambique and the USA).[91] It must be observed that a non-denominational public school criterion does not, strictly speaking, rule out a neutral subject *about* religion. Some Constitutions or laws speak of a 'separation between religion and education' (e.g. Tajikistan,

---

[85] Cf. Brems, *supra* note 3, p. 26. Also the *travaux préparatoires* pertaining to art. 14 CRC reveal that states did not wish to commit to such a duty.

[86] Cf. Brems, *ibid*, p. 26–27.

[87] Art. 43, paras. (2) and (3), of the Const. of Portugal (1976); see also art. 4 of the Law on Religious Freedom, No. 16/2001, of 21 June 2001. In practice, however, and as per the 2004 Concordat with the Holy See, public schools may teach a course on Catholicism. See particularly the clauses (art. 19) of the Concordat between Portugal and the Holy See of 18 May 2004 on the role of Catholicism in the public school curriculum and the dominance if not monopoly of the Catholic ecclesiastical authorities in the field of teaching of religious subjects.

[88] Art. 18 of the Const. of Mali (1992).

[89] Art. 1, para. (19), of the Const. of Gabon (1991).

[90] Art. 18, para. (3), of the Const. of Azerbaijan (1995); art. 9 of the Law of the Republic of Belarus on Religious Freedom and Religious Organizations, Law No. 137-3, of 31 October 2002; art. 27 of the Const. of Burkina Faso (1991); [French] Law Concerning the Separation of the Churches and the State of 1905 (see also the preamble to the former (1946) Constitution, which contained the principle of secular education as its 11th principle: "secular education … is a duty of the State"); art. 3 of the Const. of Mexico (1917); art. 35, para. (8), of the Const. of Moldova (1994); art. 124 of the Const. of Nicaragua (1986); New Zealand Education Act of 1964.

[91] Art. 49, paras. (4) and (5) Const. of Cape Verde (1992): "The State shall not program education and culture in conformity with any philosophical, aesthetical, political, ideological or religious directives…Public education shall not be religious"; art. 28, para. (1), of the Const. of India (1950): "No religious instruction shall be provided in any educational institution wholly maintained out of State funds"; art. 20 of the Const. of Japan (1946): "The State and its organs shall refrain from religious education"; art. 113 of the Const. of Mozambique (1990): "Public education shall not pertain to any religion"; USA: as per Supreme Court jurisprudence on the First Amendment.

Turkmenistan, Ukraine and Uzbekistan).[92] This, presumably, does rule out any subject on religion, including neutral ones.[93]

The state, however, may not prohibit educational activity outside these state schools and must allow religion-oriented education as an alternative so as to guarantee that parents are in a position to ensure the religious and moral education of their children in conformity with their own convictions. In other words, an absolute ban on religious education (i.e. in both public as well as private educational institutions) would constitute a human rights violation (e.g. Ethiopia).[94] It is precisely because there is under human rights law in principle no room for religious instruction in public schools and consequently no state duty to provide religious instruction, that the right to give and receive denominational education elsewhere (outside the realm of the state educational system) must be ensured. Many states constitutionally guarantee that right.[95] Education given in such (private) institutions must, however, conform to minimum standards laid down by the State.[96]

---

[92] Art. 6 of the Law of the Republic of Tajikistan on Religion and Religious Organizations of 1994 (amended 1997 and 1999); art. 11 of the Const. of Turkmenistan (1992); art. 35 of the Const. of Ukraine (1996); art. of the [Uzbek] Law on Freedom of Conscience and Religious Organizations of 1 May 1998.

[93] In the conclusion of this Chapter a state duty to include a neutral subject on religions into the curriculum is developed. These forms of state practice would clearly run counter to such a duty.

[94] Art. 90, para. (2), of the Const. of Ethiopia (1995): "Education shall be provided in a manner that is free from any religious influence"; which provision in practice is interpreted to mean that religion courses may not be taught in public or in private educational institutions.

[95] *E.g.* art 11, para. (2), of the Const. of Botswana (1966); art. 27 of the Const. of Burkina Faso (1991); art. 23 of the Fundamental Law of Equatorial Guinea (1991); art. 78, para. (2), of the Const. of Kenya (1969); art. 13, para. (2), of the Const. of Lesotho (1993); art. 22 of Const. of Senegal (2001); art. 30 of the Const. of Togo (1992); art. 19, para. (3), of the Const. of Zimbabwe (1979); art. 35, para. (3), and art. 39, para. (2), of the Const. of the Fiji Islands (1998); art. 22, para. (3), of the Const. of the Bahamas (1973); art. 11, para. (3), of the Const. of Belize (1981); art. 93 of the [Canadian] Constitution Act (1867) and art. 29 of the [Canadian] Constitution Act (1982) (Schedule to the Canada Act); art. 9, para. (3), of the Const. of Dominica (1978); art. 21, para. (4), of the Const. of Jamaica (1962); art. 9, para. (3), of the Const. of Saint Lucia (1978); art. 9, para. (3), of the Const. of Saint Vincent and the Grenadines (1979); art. 19, para. (3), of the Const. of Barbados (1996); art. 14 of the Const. of Mauritius (1968); art. 21, para. (7), of the Const. of Seychelles (1993); art. 24, para. (3), of the Const. of Sierra Leone (1991); sec. XXVIII(iii) of the Const. of Uganda (1995); art. 19, para. (3), of the Const. of Zambia (1991); art. 45, para. (4), of the Const. of East Timor (2002); art. 11, paras. (2) and (3), of the Const. of Kiribati (1979); art. 2, para. (3), of the Const. of the Marshall Islands (1979); art. 12, para. (2), of the Const. of Samoa (1960); art. 16, para. (2), of the Const. of Singapore (1963); art. 11, para. (2), of the Const. of Solomon Islands (1978); art. 22, para. (3), of the Const. of Tuvalu (1986); art. 28 of the Const. of Šrpska (1992); art. 41 of the Const. of Croatia (1990); art. 23 of the Const. of the Netherlands (1983); art. 53, para. (3), of the Const. of Poland (1997); art. 43 of the Const. of Serbia (2006); art. 15, para. (3), of the Const. of Switzerland (1999); art. 68 of the Const. of Colombia (1991); art. 9, para. (3), of the Const. of Grenada (1973); art. 11, para. (3), of the Const. of Saint Kitts and Nevis (1983); and art. 1, para. (19), of the Const. of Gabon (1991).

[96] See art. 13, paras. (3) and (4), of the ICESCR.

The state is under no obligation to fund these special (private) denominational schools: if sufficient public education is made available and if the state allows parents to send their children to alternative schools, the state has discharged its duties flowing from the international standards on the right to education.[97] The argument that funding public education, but not religious education, amounts to discrimination between secularists and religious people can be dismissed: public education, ideal-typically, is offered to everyone and is not designed for the purposes of educating children of secular parents solely or designed so as to instil secular principles into youths. This is not to say that the topics covered—e.g. biology, history or sexual education classes—or the teaching methods employed—e.g. mixed gymnastics classes—could not be objectionable to religious parents. The latter does not render the exclusive funding of public education discriminatory. True, religion as a subject might not be covered in public schools or religion might be taught in a neutral fashion ('teaching about religions'); however, public education cannot be said on that account to be designed to actively promote secularism as an ideology.

Having said that, under human rights law the state is in principle free to fund denominational schools.[98] If it does so, it must make this funding available without discrimination. In *Waldman v. Canada* the Human Rights Committee considered that Canada's differential treatment of Roman Catholic religious schools (which are publicly funded as a distinct part of the public education system; something that is constitutionally protected) and other types of religious schools (which are private by legal necessity; in the present case it concerned a private Jewish school) was at odds with the non-discrimination principle.[99]

---

[97] Human Rights Committee, *Arieh Hollis Waldman v. Canada*, Communication No. 694/1996, U.N. Doc. CCPR/C/67/D/694/1996, Views of 5 November 1999, para. 10.6: "the Committee observes that the Covenant does not oblige States parties to fund schools which are established on a religious basis".

[98] Some states constitutionally guarantee a right for private, denominational schools to receive funding. *E.g.* art. 14 of the CONST. OF BENIN (1990) "private schools may benefit from state subsidies under conditions determined by law"; art. 20, para. (3), of the CONST. OF ZIMBABWE (1979); art. 35, para. (3), and art. 39, para. (2), of the CONST. OF THE FIJI ISLANDS (1998); art. 22, para. (3), of the CONST. OF THE BAHAMAS (1973); art. 9, para. (3), of the CONST. OF DOMINICA (1978); art. 73 of the CONST. OF GUATEMALA (1985); art. 21, para. (4), of the CONST. OF JAMAICA (1962); art. 9, para. (3), of the CONST. OF SAINT LUCIA (1978); art. 9, para. (3), of the CONST. OF SAINT VINCENT AND THE GRENADINES (1979); art. 19, para. (3), of the CONST. OF BARBADOS (1996); art. 24 of the CONST. OF BELGIUM (1994); art. 23, para. (7), of the CONST. OF THE NETHERLANDS (1983); art. 24, para. (3), of the CONST. OF SWAZILAND (2005); art. 35, para. (3), of the CONST. OF THE FIJI ISLANDS (1998); art. 2, para. (3), of the CONST. OF THE MARSHALL ISLANDS (1979); art. 213 of the CONST. OF BRAZIL (1988).

[99] *Arieh Hollis Waldman v. Canada, supra* note 97, para. 10.6. Interestingly, a similar case was declared inadmissible by the Human Rights Committee a day earlier as the applicants did not seek publicly funded religious schools for their children, but on the contrary, sought the removal of the public funding to Roman Catholic schools. The Committee reasoned that if this were to happen, the applicants' personal situation in respect of funding for religious education would not be improved. As the applicants, in the eyes of the Human Rights

10.2.7 *Neutral and Objective Public School Education About Religions*

Religious instruction in the public educational system is not compatible with human rights law unless sufficient provision is made for non-discriminatory exemptions or alternatives that would accommodate the wishes of parents. In line with these benchmarks, the Human Rights Committee has considered that compulsory public school instruction in subjects such as the general history of religions and ethics, if given in a neutral and objective way, is permissible and does not, as such, affect the liberty of parents to ensure the religious and moral education of their children in conformity with their own convictions (the state may offer exemption rights also in the context of neutral education about religions, though such is, strictly speaking, not necessary). This was first established in *Hartikainen v. Finland* (1981).[100]

The question that emerges is: what does neutral and objective public school education about religions entail? It is at least clear what would not qualify as neutral and objective education about religions:[101] (i) any form of religious instruction in which religious claims are made and presented as truths and/or which aims at making the pupils (better) members of the religion involved; or (ii) any form of anti-religious education, i.e. education that renders all religious belief superstition, or active propagation of atheism.[102] It would appear that the most important criterion in this context is that the manner in which the subject is taught reflects a profound commitment to the freedom of religion or belief of all pupils. It is clear in that respect that much care should be taken that religious claims are indeed presented as religious claims and not as absolute truths. Consistently instructing pupils in a specific religion would

---

Committee, had consequently not sufficiently substantiated how the public funding given to the Roman Catholic schools at present causes them any disadvantage or affects them adversely, the Committee deemed they could not claim to be victims of a human rights violation; see Human Rights Committee, *Grant Tadman et al v. Canada*, Communication No. 816/1998, U.N. Doc. CCPR/C/67/D/816/1998, Views of 4 November 1999. Thus, it would appear that the nature of the complaint was decisive in generating so different an outcome compared to the (otherwise very similar) *Waldman v. Canada* case.

[100] Human Rights Committee, *Erkki Hartikainen v. Finland*, Communication No. 40/1978, U.N. Doc. CCPR/C/OP/1 at 74 (1984), Views of 9 April 1981; the gist of this decision was later incorporated into: Human Rights Committee, General Comment No. 22. This case dealt specifically with an *alternative subject* on the history of religions and ethics that was offered and made compulsory to those children whose parents or legal guardians objected to religious instruction (i.e. those children that availed of the available exemption scheme). It may be added at this point that the Human Rights Committee in the meantime has explained that also a *regular subject* on the history of religions and ethics (provided that it is taught in a neutral and objective way) is permitted as part of the curriculum of public schools. See Human Rights Committee, General Comment No. 22, para. 6.

[101] Cf. C. Evans, *supra* note 38, p. 463. Evans' model (*ibid.*, p 461) consists of 6 approaches to dealing with religion in the educational framework; she categorises these objectionable forms as "religious or ideological instruction".

[102] *E.g.* art. 39 of the Const. of Cuba (1976) requires that state education is based on the "ideology of Marx".

clearly be at odds with the requirements of neutrality and objectivity; however, giving more attention to certain religions (for instance, the three largest present in a country) than to others is not necessarily a sign that the norms of neutrality or objectivity are transgressed as long as the focus on any specific religion is not disproportionate. Care should also be taken to include sufficient emphasis on non-religious beliefs (humanism, agnosticism, atheism, etc.). Inaccurate and prejudicial materials need to be avoided at all costs and negative stereotypes about certain religions which are based on such inaccurate information should certainly not be reinforced.[103] As one authoritative study sums it up:

> Preparation of curricula, textbooks and educational materials for teaching about religions and beliefs should take into account religious and non-religious views in a way that is inclusive, fair, and respectful…Curricula should be developed in accordance with recognized professional standards in order to ensure a balanced approach to study about religions and beliefs. Development and implementation of curricula should also include open and fair procedures that give all interested parties appropriate opportunities to offer comments and advice… Curricula focusing on teaching about religions and beliefs should give attention to key historical and contemporary developments pertaining to religion and belief, and reflect global and local issues. They should be sensitive to different local manifestations of religious and secular plurality found in schools and the communities they serve. Such sensitivities will help address the concerns of students, parents and other stakeholders in education.[104]

It is submitted that compliance with those benchmarks would indeed be a first decisive step towards ensuring the neutral and objective nature of a religion subject taught at public schools.

10.3 Teachers, Education & Human Rights Law

We have seen how parental guidance rights and children's autonomous right to freedom of religion or belief have a major impact on how the educational system of a state must be framed. It is not surprising therefore that human rights law will also have a bearing on the providers of education. Focusing on fundamental rights of teachers but also on their professional duties, this section will scrutinize the concrete ramifications of human rights law on the position of teachers.

10.3.1 *Employing Teachers*

As to the issue of hiring policies regarding teachers, it is necessary to distinguish between public schools and denominational (private) schools.

---

[103] Seventh key guiding principle of the OSCE Office for Democratic Institutions and Human Rights (ODIHR), *Toledo Guiding Principles on Teaching About Religions and Beliefs in Public Schools* (Warsaw: OSCE/ODIRH, 2007) [hereinafter also: "Toledo Guidelines"], p. 17.

[104] *Ibid.*, 7th–10th key guiding principles, p. 17.

(i) *Public Schools: No Religious Discrimination*

It will be clear that religious affiliation (or the lack of it) may not be posed as an occupational requirement for public school teachers or staff.[105] No one may be disqualified by reason of his or her religious opinions or his or her observing of or omitting to observe religious duties or practices from being a teacher or any other type of employee at a public school.[106] It is submitted, furthermore, that religious affiliation cannot be posed as an occupational requirement for teaching a neutral subject *about* religions (rather than 'religious instruction') at public schools. It would appear, after all, that for this type of position it is essential to possess "knowledge, attitude and skills to teach religions and beliefs in a fair and balanced way".[107] As the most important skills and qualities that need to be considered in this regard relate to professional expertise and specifically to a commitment to the right to freedom of religion or belief of pupils, an individual's personal set of beliefs of lack thereof cannot be sufficient reason to hire or exclude that person from the teaching position.[108]

As has been outlined already, religious instruction within public schools is compatible with human rights law if sufficient provision is made for non-discriminatory exemptions or alternatives that would accommodate the wishes of parents. A very limited religious occupational requirement provision could thus be acceptable solely covering these positions.[109] This does not mean, however, that the state has no obligations in this regard or that all arrangements as to hiring appropriate persons to teach the religion subjects suffice. The Human Rights Committee has, for instance, condemned Costa Rican legislation[110] which confers on the National Episcopal Conference the power to select the providers of such religious instruction, something that effectively means that non-Catholics are barred from teaching religion in the

---

[105] See *infra* for one exception in this regard.

[106] Some states have specific legal provisions in place to guarantee this; *e.g.* art. 59, para. (2), of the UK School Standards and Framework Act 1998 (c. 31).

[107] *Toledo Guidelines, supra* note 103, p. 16 (6th key guiding principle).

[108] *Ibid.*, p. 59 (Section D: "Who Should Teach about Religions and Beliefs?").

[109] Notwithstanding the arguments of a more fundamental nature that were made regarding religious subjects taught at public schools and the related concern that opt-out mechanisms often appear not to be sufficient to remedy all human rights issues that emerge in this context (see section 10.2.5, *supra*). If we were to conclude, on the basis of those concerns, that religious instruction at public schools is no longer tenable, the present discussion on the possibility of allowing for a genuine occupational requirement scheme regarding the position of religion teachers, naturally, loses its significance.

[110] *Ley de Carrera Docente* [Teacher's Career Law], Law No. 4565, of 4 May 1970. The Portuguese system, based on the 2004 Concordat with the Holy See, could be criticized for the same reasons. See particularly the clauses (art. 19) of the Concordat between Portugal and the Holy See of 18 May 2004 on the role of Catholicism in the public school curriculum and the dominance if not monopoly of the Catholic ecclesiastical authorities in the field of teaching of religious subjects.

public school curricula.[111] In other words, even if in a specific public school class there would be a higher demand to receive instruction in Protestantism, this class is unlikely to get a Protestant teacher to teach the religion subject as religious education teachers in public schools must be certified by the Catholic Bishops' Conference.

(ii) *Denominational Schools: Genuine Occupational Requirement Exemptions*

It stands to reason that denominational schools may pose religion as an occupational requirement in their policy regarding the hiring of teachers insofar as religious instruction forms an essential aspect of the position and religious affiliation, therefore, constitutes a genuine and determining occupational requirement.[112] In order to facilitate this, general religious occupational requirements exemption schemes may be declared applicable to functions within denominational schools. Some states have concrete legal exemptions in place regarding teaching positions (e.g. Greece, Malta, Netherlands, New Zealand and the UK).[113] It is clear that the state in this context is to strike a balance between the non-discrimination principle (equal rights of candidate employees), on the one hand, and the need to facilitate and foster the liberty of individuals and private legal entities to establish and direct educational institutions outside the state educational system on the other. As long as an appropriate public school system is in place (creating teaching positions for people of all religious or non-religious affiliations), these exemption schemes do not need to be too problematic from a human rights perspective.

It is submitted that exemptions from the non-discrimination principle may not extend to positions for which religious affiliation is not a genuine and determining requirement (cleaning personal, canteen personnel, receptionists, etc). Requiring religious affiliation as a condition for obtaining non-teaching positions would amount to discrimination on the ground of religion or belief as there are no reasonable and objective criteria discernible that

---

[111] A/49/40 vol. I (1994), paras. 158 and 162 (interestingly, the Human Rights Committee seems to deviate here from *Delgado Páez v. Colombia*, see subsequent footnote, para. 5.7, in which it had sanctioned Colombia's state practice to allow the Church authorities to select religion teachers).

[112] See Human Rights Committee, *William Eduardo Delgado Páez v. Colombia*, Communication No. 195/1985, U.N. Doc. CCPR/C/39/D/195/1985, Views of 12 July 1990, para. 5.7.

[113] Artt. 58 and 60 of the UK School Standards and Framework Act 1998 (c. 31); art. 16 of Greek Law 1771/1988; art. 5, para. (2)(c), of the [Dutch] General Law on Equal Treatment of 2 March 1994; art. 28 of the Human Rights Act of New Zealand, Act No. 82/1993 (amended through 3 December 2007) (in conjunction with sec. 65 of the Private Schools Conditional Integration Act 1975); art. 45 of the Const. of Malta (1964). See Chapter 9, section 9.5.1, *supra*, for a discussion on religious occupational requirements in general and on concrete state practice in this regard.

would merit making distinctions in this context. Moreover, in the event that religion is not integrated into the overall curriculum and religious subjects and non-religious subjects are taught separately, it will be difficult, under human rights law, to justify a religious occupational requirement for teachers of other subjects than the religion subject—even in the context of a denominational school. It is reiterated that the interest of upholding a 'religious ethos' does not justify forms of discrimination on any ground under human rights law ('religious ethos exemption' schemes have been criticized in Chapter 9).[114]

10.3.2 *Position and Role of Teachers*

As to the issue of the position and role of teachers, it is again necessary to distinguish between public schools and denominational (private) schools.

(i) *Public School Teachers & Religion*

Though under human rights law religious instruction in public schools can be sanctioned if appropriate opt-out provisions are in place, it is clear at the same time that public school teachers themselves cannot be required to give religious instruction.[115] Teachers at a public school may not receive any less remuneration or be deprived of, or disqualified from, any promotion or other advantage by reason of the fact that he or she does or does not give religious education or by reason of his or her religious opinions or of his or her observing of or omitting to observe religious duties or practices.[116] That being said, it is submitted that in the interest of the child's right to freedom of religion or belief appropriate steps may be taken against public school teachers who are hired to *neutrally* teach about religion but are found to contravene the norms of neutrality and objectivity (be it because too confessional an approach is taken or because the person reveals anti-religious sentiments). As instruction in a particular religion or belief within public schools is in principle inconsistent with the ICCPR, such neutrality requirements can easily be extended to all teaching positions: public school teachers may not abuse their position so as to instil religious or atheist views in pupils. This is not to say, however, that religion may never be made the subject of discussion in classes other than the religion subject (e.g. in history classes, etc.). It is submitted that the right to freedom of religion of belief and parental guidance rights do not embody any

---

[114] See Chapter 9, section 9.5.1, *supra*.

[115] Some states have laws in place to guarantee this; *e.g.* art. 59, para. (3), of the UK School Standards and Framework Act 1998 (c. 31): "No teacher at the school shall be required to give religious education"; art. 7 of the Basic Law for the Federal Republic of Germany (1949): "No teacher may be obliged against his will to give religious instruction".

[116] Some states have laws in place to guarantee this; *e.g.* art. 59, para. (4), of the UK School Standards and Framework Act 1998 (c. 31).

right to be kept ignorant about religion or secular philosophies in the course of one's public school education.[117]

(ii) *Public Schools & Religious Dress*

A very topical and contentious debate revolves around the question of to what extent public school teachers may convey religious messages or propagate their religious affiliation in non-verbal ways in front of pupils, i.e. by means of displaying religious symbols or wearing religious clothing. The interests that are to be balanced in this context are the right to freedom of religion or belief of the teacher and the right to freedom of religion or belief of pupils, including the right to be free from religious coercion. In that regard it may be reiterated that the freedom to manifest a religion or belief covers both private as well as public acts of religious observance and that the freedom to manifest a religion is not absolute. Unlike the regional European Court of Human Rights (see below), the international (UN) human rights bodies have not yet resolved this issue in a resolute manner. In general, following the UN Special Rapporteur's recommendations on the matter, it can be said that:

> ...contentious situations should be evaluated on a case-by-case basis, e.g. by weighing the right of a teacher to manifest his or her religion against the need to protect pupils by preserving religious harmony according to the circumstances of a given case.[118]

The Committee on the Rights of the Child has declared itself (somewhat) against religious dress prohibitions aimed at public school teachers. Scrutinizing Germany's state practice, the CRC Committee expressed its concern at draft-laws:

> ...aiming at banning schoolteachers from wearing headscarves in public schools, as *this does not contribute to the child's understanding of the right to freedom of religion and to the development of an attitude of tolerance*...The Committee recommends that the State party take educational and other measures aimed at children, parents and others to develop a culture of understanding and tolerance, particularly in the area of freedom of religion, conscience and thought by, inter alia, avoiding measures which single out a particular religious group.[119]

The CRC Committee makes a fair point here, particularly considering the fact that the Children's Rights Convention explicitly states that the state parties agree that the education of the child be directed to the development of respect for human rights and fundamental freedoms.[120] Fostering such respect for

---

[117] This argument is based on considerations expressed by the European Court of Human Rights in the *Folgerø and Others v. Norway* case, *supra* note 75, para. 89.

[118] E/CN.4/2006/5, para. 51.

[119] CRC/C/137 (2004) 51 at paras. 281 and 282 (emphasis added).

[120] Art. 29, para. (1)(b), of CRC.

fundamental rights including respect for everyone's right to freedom of religion or belief requires a level of religious tolerance; something to which a child's education should also contribute.[121] Banning public expressions of religions may not be most conducive to that cause.

On the other hand, a meaningful distinction can be made between pupils and teachers in this context. The former do not represent the state in any why whatsoever while public school teachers carry out a public service and thus can be considered to represent the state.[122] Particularly in the public domain the state needs to guard against infringements of the freedom from religion principle, to prevent all forms of religious coercion and above all to avoid all forms of religious indoctrination. The latter point seems to have been a relevant factor in the eyes of the European Court of Human Rights in *Dahlab v. Switzerland*. The case revolved around a Swiss primary school teacher who was (pursuant to the Swiss Public Education Act which contains norms on the non-denominational nature of the Swiss educational system) instructed by the educational authorities to stop wearing a headscarf whilst discharging of her professional duties. The European Court reasoned that:

> ...it is very difficult to assess the impact that a powerful external symbol such as the wearing of a headscarf may have on the freedom of conscience and religion of very young children. The applicant's pupils were aged between four and eight, an age at which children wonder about many things and are also more easily influenced than older pupils. In those circumstances, it cannot be denied outright that the *wearing of a headscarf might have some kind of proselytising effect*, seeing that it appears to be imposed on women by a precept which is laid down in the Koran and which, as the Federal Court noted, is hard to square with the principle of gender equality. It therefore appears difficult to reconcile the wearing of an Islamic headscarf with the message of tolerance, respect for others and, above all, equality and non-discrimination that all teachers in a democratic society must convey to their pupils. Accordingly, weighing the right of a teacher to manifest her religion against the need to protect pupils by preserving religious harmony, the Court considers that, in the circumstances of the case and having regard, above all, to the tender age of the children for whom the applicant was responsible *as a representative of the State*, the Geneva authorities did not exceed their margin of appreciation and that the measure they took was therefore not unreasonable.[123]

It appears that for the European Court two factors are decisive: the impressionable nature of children as well as the fact that primary school teachers are state representatives and in that capacity need to abide by the state's

---

[121] Art. 29, paras. (1)(d), of CRC.

[122] The latter holds true, *de facto*, regardless of the question of how the position of teachers is precisely dealt with at the municipal level, i.e. whether they are considered civil servants or not.

[123] ECtHR, *Dahlab v. Switzerland*, Application No. 42393/98, ECtHR Judgement of 15 February 2001 (emphasis added).

self-addressed rules on neutrality. *In abstracto* this would appear to be a sound reasoning. Protection of the rights of others is a recognized ground for limiting the freedom to manifest a religion. However, the European Court's reasoning contained little in the way of substantiation of how, in this case, the rights of others (the pupils) were undermined. It actually follows from the facts of the case that during the period of this teacher's employment the school had not received a single complaint from parents. In that respect it is hard to see how the argument that the wearing of a headscarf "might have some kind of proselytising effect" could in itself amount to a pressing social need to interfere with someone's freedom of religion or belief.[124] In this particular case the interference could only be based on the argument that primary school teachers are state representatives and that state neutrality needs to be upheld. If the preservation of notions of state neutrality (or secularism) is indeed among the decisive factors for the European Court of Human Rights (being an 'public order' issue and, more indirectly, a matter of protecting 'the rights and freedoms of others'), then it must be noted that the European Court failed to make an appropriate distinction between teachers and pupils in cases that concern the wearing of religious clothing or the display of religious symbols in public schools.[125]

In conclusion, states are well-advised to follow the recommendation of the UN Special Rapporteur on freedom of religion or belief to evaluate contentious situations on a case-by-case basis by weighing the right of a teacher to manifest his or her religion against the need to protect the fundamental rights and freedoms of pupils.[126] The key question in this debate seems to be: what contributes most to the child's right to freedom of religion or belief and to the development of an attitude of tolerance. States certainly have an interest in upholding the neutrality of the state and thus must be in a position to take appropriate action if in a concrete case it is established that a teacher's manifestation of a religion or belief in the classroom actually harms or jeopardizes the fundamental rights of pupils. The possibility of such state interferences need to be provided by laws on religious symbolism in the public realm that are sufficiently neutral and not needlessly rigid. The message which pupils are likely to get from blanket bans (i.e. regulations in which there is no room for taking account of the particulars of the case) or from specific bans on Islamic headscarves, is one of intolerance against religions or one of intolerance against Muslims specifically.[127]

---

[124] See also Dissenting Opinion Judge Tulkens (in *Leyla Şahin v. Turkey, supra* note 51), para. 5.

[125] Compare *Dahlab v. Switzerland (supra* note 123) and *Leyla Şahin v. Turkey (supra* note 51).

[126] E/CN.4/2006/5, para. 51.

[127] Cf. Paul M. Taylor, Freedom of Religion: UN and European Human Rights Law and Practice (Cambridge: Cambridge University Press, 2005), p. 172 (on the Dahlab case specifically).

(iii) *Denominational School Teachers*

Needless to say that the position and role of teachers in denominational schools is fundamentally different: they are generally expected if not required to instruct pupils in the tenets of the religious denomination in question. The only question that remains to be answered is to what extent teachers in religious schools are free in how they give effect to the denominational character of the school. May a school take steps against a teacher who deviates from religious orthodoxy or from the school's specific religious standpoints or religious mission statement? This issue was put before the Human Rights Committee in *Delgado Páez v. Colombia.* William Eduardo Delgado Páez was appointed and functioned as a teacher of religion and ethics at a secondary school in Leticia, Colombia. However, being an advocate of 'liberation theology', his views on how these religion classes should be run differed from the views of the local ecclesiastical and educational authorities. At some point he was informed that he could no longer teach religion classes and ultimately the incident and subsequent discontent resulted in Mr. Delgado's resignation.[128] The Human Rights Committee concluded that the requirements posed by the ecclesiastical and educational authorities to teach the Catholic religion in its traditional form did not violate Mr. Delgado's right to freedom of expression or freedom of religion or belief.[129] From this case the rule may be deduced that anyone who voluntarily becomes an employee of a denominational school may, to a reasonable extent, be required to abide by this organization's ethos.[130]

10.4 Conclusion: An Emerging State Duty to Provide Neutral Education about Religions?

This Chapter focused on children's, parental and teachers' rights (and duties), in the light of the state's overall obligation to provide for appropriate education. It has been emphasized that any form of compulsory religious education is contrary to international human rights law. A religious subject may be

[128] *Delgado Páez v. Colombia, supra* note 112; see paras. 2.1–2.10 for the particulars of the case.

[129] *Ibid.* paras. 5.7–5.9. The Committee did ultimately establish a violation of art. 25, para. (c), of the ICCPR as it considered that the constant harassment and the threats against his person (in respect of which the state party had failed to provide protection) made the author's continuation in public service teaching impossible (para. 5.9) (something that clearly was specific to this case).

[130] Some states have laws in place to guarantee this. *E.g.* art. 60, para. (5)(b), of the UK School Standards and Framework Act 1998 (c. 31), which deals with schools with a religious character and provides that "regard may be had, in connection with the termination of the employment of any teacher at the school, to any conduct on his part which is incompatible with the precepts, or with the upholding of the tenets, of the religion or religious denomination so specified".

taught in public schools if adequate opt-out clauses are provided for. Case law and state practice, however, show that the application of exemptions in this field often proves highly problematic. The inoperable nature of the opt-out clauses in the reality of every day school life and the potentially stigmatizing impact on the child are obstacles that cannot be easily dismissed or remedied.

The state is under no duty to provide religious instruction. In this Chapter we have seen that human rights law provides convincing arguments to keep religious instruction out of the public school curriculum. Teaching *about* religions in a neutral and objective way in public schools, on the other hand, is perfectly compatible with international human rights law. Compulsory public school instruction in subjects such as the general history of religions and ethics, if given in a neutral and objective way, is permissible and does as such not affect the liberty of parents to ensure the religious and moral education of their children in conformity with their own convictions. The question that emerges is whether, from a human rights perspective, a case could be made for a state *duty* to include neutral education about religions into the public school curriculum? Voices to that effect can increasingly be heard.

Carolyn Evans argues that "'plural religious education' is the approach to religion in public schools that best complies with international human rights standards."[131] She describes this type of education as follows:

> ...students learn about the basic practices, beliefs, rituals etc of a variety of religions. They are presented with information about these religious traditions but are not taught that any of them are (un)true. The instruction may also extent to philosophies and beliefs of a non-religious nature.[132]

Evans' account is focused on the question of how children can be given the tools to understand the role of religion in society and in the world in a way that they are protected from religious indoctrination. She concludes that neutral education about religions compares favourably to all types of religious instruction but also to forms of strict educational secularism in which there is no place for religion at all in the class room.[133] The *Toledo Guiding Principles on Teaching About Religions and Beliefs in Public Schools*, a study recently issued by the OSCE Office for Democratic Institutions and Human Rights (ODIHR), can be seen as a strong plea for the inclusion of neutral subjects about religions and beliefs into the curriculum of public schools in a way that respects children's rights.[134] In what follows some of the arguments in support of this idea will be outlined.

First of all, one could wonder with some justification whether strict educational secularism is feasible as such a curriculum, in the words of Evans,

---

[131] C. Evans, *supra* note 38, p. 449.
[132] *Ibid.* p. 461.
[133] *Idem.*
[134] *Toledo Guidelines, supra* note 103.

"would be unable to properly examine causes of many European wars, to explore the meaning of great works of art, music and literature, or engage with current debates…"[135] In other words, as religions and beliefs will inevitably be touched upon in the curriculum, public school officials would be well-advised to reflect on this issue and develop an informed approach to dealing with the issue of religion in a way that would enable the school to do justice to children's and parental rights. The message pupils could get from obstinately avoiding religious issues at all costs could be that religion and religious persons are to be avoided at all costs.

Second, international human rights law contains explicit requirements related to the content of children's education.[136] States parties to the Children's Rights Convention have agreed that the education of the child shall be directed to the "development of respect for human rights and fundamental freedoms" and to the "preparation of the child for responsible life in a free society, in the spirit of understanding, peace, tolerance, equality of sexes, and friendship among all peoples, ethnic, national and religious groups and persons of indigenous origin".[137] The state duty to promote religious tolerance also flows from the UN Religious Tolerance Declaration (1981). The latter document argues that "it is essential to promote understanding, tolerance and respect in matters relating to freedom of religion and belief" and, more concretely, that children shall be "brought up in a spirit of understanding, tolerance, friendship among peoples, peace and universal brotherhood, respect for freedom of religion or belief of others".[138] One could argue that these state duties include a positive obligation for the state to design an educational system in which pupils are taught the idea of religious tolerance and respect for freedom of religion or belief of others.[139] It could also be contended that these notions—religious tolerance and respect for freedom of religion or belief of others—require a basic level of understanding of religious beliefs. If children do not receive any neutral education on the issue of religious beliefs they are likely to base their knowledge solely or chiefly on insights conveyed by close relatives or the media. These portrayals of, and insights on, (certain) religions may not always be accurate or conducive to tolerance. Thus, neutral education about religions and beliefs based on sound scholarship and taught in an inclusive, fair and respectful manner could offer a welcome if not necessary counterbalance.

---

[135] C. Evans, *supra* note 38, p. 461, fn 39. The *Toledo Guidelines, supra* note 103, p. 19, make a similar point: "Much history, literature and culture is unintelligible without knowledge of religions and beliefs. Therefore study about religions and beliefs is an essential part of a well-rounded education. Learning about religions and beliefs forms part of one's own stock of education, broadens one's horizon and deepens one's insight into the complexities of both past and present."

[136] See also C. Evans, *supra* note 38, p. 454–455.

[137] Art. 29, paras. (1)(b) and (d), of CRC.

[138] Preamble and art. 5, para. (3), of the UN Religious Tolerance Declaration (1981).

[139] Cf. the *Toledo Guidelines, supra* note 103, p. 19.

As we are dealing with public school education on the subject of religion that is given in a neutral and objective way, this subject may be made compulsory to all pupils[140]—and in light of the above considerations it perhaps ought to be made compulsory. Inevitably there will be parents who do not want their children to receive such pluralist religious education, even if—or possibly because—it is taught in a neutral fashion. Here the question is to what extent these parents should be accommodated by making provision for opt-out clauses: which norm is to prevail if the child's right to education is to be balanced with parental rights? It is submitted that precisely because the paramount value of religious tolerance is at stake, and because of the existence of clear state duties to promote that value, that children's educational rights should triumph in this balancing act. As children have a right to education that is directed to preparing them for a responsible life in a free and tolerant society in which human rights are respected, it could be argued that "[t]oo significant a system of exclusions may end up denying the child an education that fulfils…the aims of developing respect for civilisations other than his or her own and for human rights more generally."[141]

Finally, states that aim at incorporating a neutral subject about religions and beliefs into the curriculum of public schools are well-advised to follow the guidelines issued by the OSCE/ODIHR on this subject as in these benchmarks a commitment to religious freedom and other human rights is thoroughly integrated into curriculum building endeavours.[142]

---

140 Human Rights Committee, General Comment No. 22, para. 6.
141 C. Evans, *supra* note 38, p.455.
142 *Toledo Guidelines, supra* note 103.

CHAPTER ELEVEN

RELIGION & POLITICS

11.1 Introduction

The second part of this study has illustrated that certain modes of state–religion identification are surrounded by forms of state practice that have a negative bearing on the domestic interpretation and actual implementation of human rights law. It cannot be denied that in many cases the mode of religion–state identification impacts on the scope for human rights compliance. In that respect, both with regard to states that identify strongly with a religion and as well as with respect to states that act upon questionable interpretations of the principles of secularism and separationism, it has been demonstrated that various human rights norms are denied or curtailed on account of the state's religious or excessively secular commitments. In some cases we have seen how religion or state secularism itself may function as a ground for limiting fundamental rights. The state's commitment to uphold certain religious principles may foster inadequate interpretations of norms of international human rights law or inspire questionable balancing acts in which human rights principles are sacrificed in favour of religious incentives and duties. In some strictly secular states something similar can be perceived: secularism becomes an end in itself. Rather than enhancing values such as democracy or human rights protection (being the historical underlying rationale of these principles) the principles of secularism and separationism are construed so as to impose special limits on the free manifestation of religion. As we have seen, most of these forms of adverse state practice, though often based on or derived from 'higher ideals', actually have a foundation in domestic laws. Thus, it would appear that the key to dealing with the *problematique* at hand lies within the very system of political organization of the state. It is postulated that if the political organization of the state were to avoid a range of pitfalls and to internalize a set of safeguards specifically dealing with the issue of religion–state identification, many of the discussed human rights abuses could be prevented or remedied. It must be acknowledged from the outset that some of the most basic safeguards proposed in this Chapter signify the difference between a liberal democracy and a religious totalitarian state. In other words, some of the safeguards proposed in this Chapter presuppose a degree of democratic goodwill (the existing system of political organization must constitute at the least a 'formal democracy').[1]

11.2 Ensuring Equal Inclusion through the Political Constellation of the State

It is postulated that the way the political constellation of a state is framed must ensure that all religions are treated equally.[2] The state's identification with a particular religion may upset the fairness and genuineness of a democracy in many ways; in fact, in extreme cases, it may altogether disqualify a state from being considered a genuine democracy. It is pivotal that the state ensures that no religion is *a priori* privileged or that some religions or beliefs are *a priori* excluded or disadvantaged. By means of reflecting on existing state practice, it will be possible to identify which pitfalls need to be avoided and to propose a range of safeguards that need to be internalized by the state.

11.2.1 *No Political Privileges for Religions or Beliefs*

Privileging religions within the political discourse, other than for reasons of affirmative action, effectively undermines the principle of democratic governance. Under international human rights law, every citizen has the right and the opportunity, without distinction on the basis of religion or belief, to take part in the conduct of public affairs, directly or through freely chosen representatives. All citizens also enjoy the right to vote at genuine periodic elections by universal and equal suffrage.[3] Violations of fundamental equality and fundamental political rights occur whenever the right to vote or the right to run for public office is made conditional upon belonging to a certain religion. It will be outlined that a wide range of infringements of people's democratic rights are discernible in those political systems in which religion plays too decisive a role.

(i) *Equal Right to Vote*

One of the most glaring violations of civil and political rights occurs if the right to vote is solely granted to persons belonging to a certain religion. The previous Constitution of Maldives provided that only Muslims were qualified

---

[1] This implies that some of the measures proposed do, unfortunately, not provide a remedy against adverse state practice that has no foundation in democratically adopted laws. Totalitarian states are not interested in preventing or remedying human rights abuses. The issue of 'democratizing non-democratic states' falls outside the scope of this study.

[2] This follows from artt. 25–26 of the ICCPR.

[3] Art. 25 of the ICCPR; art. 21 of the UDHR.

to vote.[4] This situation is essentially unchanged as under the present constitution only Muslims are considered citizens.[5] Also, those states that deny certain religious minorities citizenship status, naturally, effectively disenfranchise these people. In that regard one may think of the treatment of Jehovah's Witnesses in Eritrea, or the denial of political rights to the Bahá'ís in some Islamic states.

(ii) *Prohibition of Predetermining a Religion–Law Nexus*

Under human rights law the will of the people forms the basis of the government's authority; this will is to be expressed in periodic and genuine elections which shall be by universal and equal suffrage.[6] The outcome of this process may be any decision that is compatible with human rights norms. It is submitted that a state may not *a priori* narrow the outer limits of what the will of the people may constitute to the commands and prescriptions of the dominant religion. Such a measure, firstly, does not take the will of the people seriously. The majority of a population, even when it (nominally) adheres to a certain religion, could be willing to take a decision that is contrary to a rule that is said to derive from the religion in question. Under human rights law a population is fully entitled to make that decision. Put differently, the fact or assumption that a democratically made decision is incompatible with religious norms is immaterial under human rights law. Secondly, such a measure makes a complete travesty of the rights of religious minorities and the non-religious.

If the political organization of a state is based on the premise that all laws adopted should have a sound basis in the dominant religion's doctrine and should be compatible with the tenets of the dominant religion, natural democratic deliberation processes are out of the question: concrete legislative decisions will not be made because they are supported by the majority of the people, but because they are the only decisions permitted. The argument that the religious demography of a state (i.e. a predominant adherence to one religion) would in itself render democratic legitimacy to this type of constitutional arrangement, completely overlooks the rights of religious minorities and the non-religious.

Religious rights of the *majority*, the adherents of the state-protected religion, are in fact at stake as well, considering the fact that under international human rights law everyone is free to interpret a religious doctrine and to

[4] Art. 134 of the Constitution of the Republic of Maldives (1998) (replaced).

[5] Art. 26 of the CONST. OF MALDIVES (2008) provides that every citizen has the right to vote. The provision no longer explicitly states that only Muslims can vote; however, non-Muslims cannot obtain citizenship status (art. 9) and are consequently not allowed to vote.

[6] Art. 25 of the ICCPR; art. 21 of the UDHR. See Thomas M. Franck, *The Emerging Right to Democratic Governance*, 86(1) AMERICAN JOURNAL OF INTERNATIONAL LAW 46 (1992), on the 'right to democratic governance'.

personally identify the religious commands one wants to live in accordance with. The state's interpretation of a religious doctrine, in terms of its commands and prohibitions derived from it, may not be the same as the individual believer's interpretation. Thus, state laws based on religious doctrine and one's own religious conscience may very well be dissimilar. An-Na'im makes the point that there is no such thing as objectively applying or objectively enforcing religious laws as they are always interpreted through human agency.[7] Consequently, some degree of religious coercion with respect to the adherents of the dominant religion is inevitable.[8] Religious believers are, in many ways, in a better position to exercise their faith if they can voluntarily comply with religious norms and if religious precepts are not enforced through state agency.[9]

In light of these considerations, it must be concluded that the rigid manner in which particularly Afghanistan, Iran, Iraq, Maldives, Pakistan and Saudi Arabia constitutionally ensure that legislation shall not be contrary to Islam or Shari'a constitutes a serious violation of democratic rights, something that cannot be expected to be remedied by the judiciary as the judiciary in these jurisdictions is, typically, explicitly (that is, constitutionally) instructed to scrutinize legislation for compatibility with religion.[10] Some states (e.g. Iran and Pakistan) have taken further measures to ensure compatibility between legislation and Islam by establishing special Guardian Councils and by commissioning these bodies to scrutinize laws and policies on the basis of Islamic principles.[11] Naturally, in states with such a tight nexus between the laws and one religion, religious coercion and violations of the freedom from religion principle are inevitable. Also, precisely because in these regimes there is such a strong correlation between Islam and the legislative, executive and judicial branches, most public offices will automatically only be open to adherents of Islam, resulting in forms of unequal treatment in the area of political rights,

---

[7] Cf. ABDULLAHI AHMED AN-NA'IM, ISLAM AND THE SECULAR STATE: NEGOTIATING THE FUTURE OF SHARI'A (Cambridge, US/London: Harvard University Press, 2008), pp. 10–11 and pp. 282–283.

[8] For an account on the violation of religious rights of those who adhere to the state religion, see Jeroen Temperman, *The Neutral State: Optional or Necessary? – A Triangular Analysis of State-Religion Identification, Democratisation & Human Rights Compliance*, 1(3) RELIGION AND HUMAN RIGHTS: AN INTERNATIONAL JOURNAL 269 (2006), pp. 284–286.

[9] Cf. An-Na'im, *supra* note 7, pp. 1–9. An-Na'im, in his pioneering account, also outlines that the view that a genuine 'Islamic state' must enforce Shari'a law is a dangerous illusion (*ibid.*, p. 2 and pp. 45–83).

[10] See *supra*, Part I, Chapter 2.4.1(i), for a detailed description. For a comprehensive study on the place accorded to Islam and/or Islamic law in the legal order of predominantly Muslim states, see also NISRINE ABIAD, SHARIA, MUSLIM STATES AND INTERNATIONAL HUMAN RIGHTS TREATY OBLIGATIONS: A COMPARATIVE STUDY (London: British Institute of International and Comparative Law, 2008).

[11] Art. 91 of the CONST. OF IRAN (1979); and art. 228–230 of the CONST. OF PAKISTAN (1973).

which, in turn, means that for the affected minorities there is often little scope for reform. Reform-minded Muslims face the additional obstacle that calling for reform may be construed as an 'anti-Islamic activity' by the regime, which could result in serious repercussions.[12]

The same largely holds true for states that require that all adopted laws have a sound basis in Islam.[13] Constitutional requirements that demand that the dominant religion (and/or its religious laws) functions as the main or principal source of legislation (e.g. Bahrain, Egypt, Oman, Somalia and UAE) allow for relatively more leeway than constitutional requirements that demand that the dominant religion (and/or its religious laws) functions as the *sole* source of legislation (e.g. Mauritania and Yemen), but it will be clear that either requirement ruins free and open democratic deliberation processes and constitutes a violation of the equality principle. If a state's constitution simply identifies a religion as a possible source for legislation (e.g. Kuwait, Qatar and Syria) the democratic process is not necessarily significantly affected,[14] since legislative action that is not strictly based on the normative framework provided by the official religion remains a possibility. There is some evidence, however, that the distinction is rather symbolic and that no legal ramifications are to be attached to it. Mayer argues the following in this context:

> Although fundamentalists attach great importance to wording stipulating that shari'a be "the" source, it does not appear that the adoption of one or the other wording is actually correlated in practice with the presence of a greater or lesser proportion of shari'a-based rules in a given legal system…For example, Egypt, by a 1980 referendum, changed its Constitution to make shari'a "the main source" of legislation, rather than "a main source" of legislation, as it had previously been, a change in wording that appears to have been designed as a symbolic gesture…to placate Islamic fundamentalist critics of the Sadat government.[15]

This constitutional arrangement (singling out one specific religion) still amounts, regardless of the exact legal implications of this nuance in terminology in practice, to a violation of the equality principle as it grants legal privileges to one religion.

It must be emphasized that it is by no means argued here that there is categorically no room for religious ideals or incentives at any stage of the democratic decision making process. It is rather submitted that a state may never predetermine that all legislative action should have a sound basis in the religious tenets of one particular religion. A democracy that genuinely respects

---

[12] *E.g.* Special Rapporteur on the Right to Freedom of Opinion and Expression, 2E/CN.4/2004/62/Add.2 (2004) (Iran); Human Rights Committee, A/48/40 vol. I (1993) 44 at para. 262 (Iran).

[13] See *supra*, Part I, Chapter 2.4.1(ii), for a detailed description.

[14] See *supra*, Part I, Chapter 2.4.1(iii), for a detailed description.

[15] Ann Elizabeth Mayer, *Law and Religion in the Muslim Middle East*, 35 American Journal of Comparative Law (1987), p. 138.

both the will of the people as well as fundamental minority rights, and a state based on the premise that it is the state's sacred duty to ensure that all legislative decisions made should be in the service of the dominant religion, are mutually exclusive. It is therefore submitted that human rights law effectively prohibits the state from predetermining a religion–law nexus.

(iii) *Prohibition of Reserving Political Seats for the Dominant Religion*

Occasionally, a case can be made for sanctioning distinctions on grounds that are normally considered unacceptable (race, religion, gender, etc.) on the basis of affirmative action considerations: if a certain minority has historically been affected by discriminatory laws and policies or societal circumstances and if the repercussions of these adverse practices are still evident, appropriate steps may be taken to bring the enjoyment of rights and freedoms of that particular minority on a par with the rest.[16] Be that as it may, it is clear that the perpetuation of special prerogatives of the *majority* at the expense of the rights of minorities is never acceptable (as this policy comes down to making distinctions on unacceptable grounds whilst there are no 'objective and reasonable' reasons for doing so).

A constitutional requirement that more than half the number of the members of the Government shall profess the official religion of the state, as practised by Norway,[17] is clearly at odds with the notion of equal political rights. In the UK, the Church of England is guaranteed 26 (of the 731) seats in the House of Lords, the upper house of the UK Parliament. This measure stems from historical Church prerogatives (the Lords Spiritual actually formed the majority of the House in the 16th century). Although it is clear that this particular measure will not dramatically upset the democratic process, this measure indisputably amounts to a form of unequal treatment of religions. It is submitted that, from an equal rights perspective, any predetermining of a religious quorum for a political state body, however fractional, makes a democracy 'partly unjust'. The same holds true for forms of more indirect involvement of dominant religions in the allocation of seats in political bodies of the state. Belize may function as an example here: though it does not expressly reserve seats in the Senate for representatives of the dominant religion, a minimum of one Senator (out of the 12) is to be appointed by the Governor General in accordance with the advice of an association of Christian churches.[18] These

---

[16] For a historical account of this notion, see Terry H. Anderson, The Pursuit of Fairness: A History of Affirmative Action (Oxford: Oxford University Press, 2004); for a comprehensive empirical study, see Thomas Sowell, Affirmative Action Around the World: An Empirical Study (New Haven, CT: Yale University Press, 2004).

[17] Art. 12, para. (2), of the Const. of Norway (1814).

[18] See art. 61, para. (4), sec. (c), of the Const. of Belize (1981).

arrangements would be less problematic, from a human rights perspective, if minority religions would be included in these advisory or co-optation procedures.[19]

Human rights law rejects the reservation of political seats for the dominant religion. On the basis of the non-discrimination principle one could argue for the following remedies to these forms of unequal treatment: (i) extending the same political privileges to other religions and beliefs; or (ii) abolishing them altogether. It is submitted that arrangements that allow for direct political representation of the different religious groups,[20] even if a more inclusive approach is taken, inevitably raise obstacles to the natural democratic process and to equality rights. Any effort to justly divide up all or a percentage of the seats of a representative body over various religions raises the following human rights questions: (i) how to identify the religions to be included in this scheme?; (ii) how to ensure the equal rights of the non-religious?; (iii) how to ensure proportionality—assuming that is a just criterion—in light of the fact that many societies may be subject to constant demographical changes? State recognition of religions for the purpose of being included in direct political representation schemes is inevitably arbitrary: the state cannot possibly recognize all of the potentially numerous religions that are present within the country; yet solely recognizing the "major religious faiths" (e.g. Malawi and Mauritius)[21] constitutes unequal treatment on the basis of religion. Non-religious beliefs in many countries are bound to be neglected as they are not normally as strongly organized as religions tend to be. The case of Lebanon[22] further strikingly shows that although *prima facie* direct political representation of religions groups would appear to be the measure *par excellence* to accommodate differing religious interests, fully guaranteeing equality rights in these systems is hardly feasible.[23] It is submitted that direct religious representation may under limited circumstances serve a legitimate purpose in post-conflict societies; however, sectarianism should always be treated as a temporary solution only.

---

[19] See section 4.2.2, *supra*, for some examples of the latter (St. Lucia and Timor-Leste).

[20] See section 4.2.1, *supra*, for a detailed description.

[21] Art. 68 of the Const. of Malawi (1994); art. 31, para. (2) in conjunction with First Schedule of the Const. of Mauritius (1968).

[22] The Constitution of Lebanon uniquely provides for a complete confessional distribution of seats for the Parliament, the Senate as well as other public offices and positions (*e.g.* senior public service positions, members of the judiciary, but also members of the military and security institutions and so-called public and mixed agencies). The system of equal representation between Muslims and Christian—both religions occupy 64 out of the 128 seats in Parliament—does not come down to proportional representation as there are more Muslims than Christians in Lebanon (plus: no seats are allocated to minorities which are both non-Muslim *and* non-Christian). See artt. 22, 24, 95 of the Lebanese Const. (1926) the Taif Agreement of 22 October 1989 and the National Pact of 1943. For concern about the Lebanese system, see also Human Rights Committee's Concluding Observations: A/52/40 vol. I (1997) 53 at para. 353 (Lebanon).

[23] See *supra*, Part I, Chapter 4, section 4.2.1, for a detailed description of the Lebanese system of equal religious representation.

(iv) *Prohibition of Posing Religious Qualifications for Holding Public Office*

The fundamental democratic right to take part in the conduct of public affairs in conjunction with fundamental equality rights implies that every person, regardless of religious affiliation, should be in a position to run for public offices. The Human Rights Committee has clarified that restricting eligibility for government service to members of the predominant religion violates the rights of members of minority religions and of non-believers.[24] The interest of a state in preserving and promoting a state religion does not justify any form of unequal treatment in this area. Constitutional provisions that pose religious qualifications for holding certain public offices are thus in violation of international human rights law.[25] Unfortunately, many religious states perpetuate religious discrimination in this area.

Executive

In some states the highest executive offices are reserved for members of the dominant religion. In Mauritania, Pakistan, Somalia, Syria, Tunisia and Yemen only Muslims are eligible to become President.[26] This clearly corresponds with the concept of *dhimma* which holds, as outlined before,[27] that though People of the Book must be tolerated, they should not hold positions in which they exercise power over Muslims.

The President as well as the Vice-President of Maldives must be a follower of the Sunni branch of Islam specifically.[28] In Lebanon, as per political pacts on the sectarian distribution of the top three offices (the ruling troika), the office of President is reserved for Maronite Christians,[29] while the office of Prime Minister is reserved for Sunni Muslims and the Speaker of Parliament must be a Shi'a Muslim. Maldives goes beyond reserving only the highest

---

[24] Human Rights Committee, General Comment 22, para. 9.

[25] Cf. Human Rights Committee's Concluding Observations, *e.g.*: A/48/40 vol. I (1993) 44 at para. 269 (Iran): "Measures restricting eligibility for government service to members of the predominant religion…are incompatible with the prohibition of discrimination based on religion or belief and the guarantee of equal protection under article 26 of the Covenant"; and A/52/40 vol. I (1997) 53 at para. 353 (Lebanon): "The Committee notes with concern that every Lebanese citizen must belong to one of the religious denominations officially recognized by the Government, and that this is a requirement in order to be eligible to run for public office. This practice does not comply with the requirements of article 25 of the Covenant."

[26] Art. 23 of the Const. of Mauritania (1991); art. 41 of the Const. of Pakistan (1973); art. 40 of the Transitional Federal Charter of the Somali Republic (2004); art. 3 of the Const. of Syria (1973); artt. 38 and 40 of the Const. of Tunisia (1959); and art. 106 of the Const. of Yemen (1990).

[27] See Chapter 8, section 8.2.3, *supra*.

[28] Artt. 109 and 132 of the Const. of Maldives (2008).

[29] The issue of precise religious affiliation is a very contentious one in Lebanon; no official census has been carried out since 1932. If one compares Christians as such to Muslims as such (i.e. without making further distinctions as to specific denomination or branch), Muslims outnumber Christians. If one were to compare Christians to both Sunni Muslims and Shi'a Muslims, the former group may be considered the largest.

political offices to the dominant religion: all members of the Cabinet of Maldives must be Sunni Muslims.[30]

In some of the more strictly religious states most of the highest public offices can only be taken up by religious people for the simple fact that these positions coincide with religious positions. Put differently, religious leaders in these states *ex officio* exercise public authority (one may think of the secular powers religious leaders and/or clergy have in for instance Iran, Brunei Darussalam, Oman, Malaysia, Bhutan and the Vatican City).[31] Naturally, these arrangements will have a similar discriminatory effect as provisions that pose religious qualifications for public office. Another dimension to the debate is given by religious dynasties or hereditary monarchies that traditionally identify with and promote one religion,[32] especially insofar as the position of Head of State (and relatives) in some of these states is invested with far-reaching executive powers.[33]

Legislature

In some states, membership of the representative legislative bodies is restricted to members of the dominant religion. For instance, only Sunni Muslims can become members of the People's *Majlis* of the Maldives.[34] If one is "of good character" and "not commonly known as one who violates Islamic Injunctions" and if one moreover "has adequate knowledge of Islamic teachings and practices" and of "obligatory duties prescribed by Islam" then one is eligible to become a member of the Pakistani *Majlis-e-Shoora* (the bicameral Parliament composed of the National Assembly and the Senate).[35] In order to be eligible

---

[30] Art. 130 of the Const. of Maldives (2008).

[31] See Part I, section 2.4.2, *supra*.

[32] *E.g.* the Al Khalifa Dynasty of Bahrain, the House of Hashim of Jordan, the Alaouite Dynasty of Morocco, the Al Bu Sa'id Dynasty of Oman, the House of Thani of Qatar, the House of Saud of Saudi Arabia. Art. 9 of the Const. of Qatar (2003) explicitly states: "The Heir Apparent must be a Muslim…".

[33] See examples mentioned in previous footnote. There are other states that are officially ruled by a Monarch as Head of State who is simultaneously guardian of the dominant religion (*e.g.* England, Norway and Thailand); however, in these cases we cannot speak of a 'ruling family/elite' as their executive powers are limited and their roles nowadays mostly ceremonial. Although these arrangements thus do not necessarily undermine any democratic principles, some human rights concerns are nonetheless discernable: mainly freedom of religion or belief issues (i.e. as regards the Monarch him or herself) and non-discrimination issues (the Monarch's role as protector and promoter of one specific religion over others). See art. 4 of the Const. of Norway (1814): "The King shall at all times profess the Evangelical-Lutheran religion, and uphold and protect the same"; art. 9 of the Const. of Thailand (2007): "The King is a Buddhist and Upholder of religions"; while the Monarch of England is the "Supreme Governor of the Church of England".

[34] The main legislative body; not a proper Parliament as a number of its members are not elected but appointed by the President. See art. 73 of the Const. of Maldives (2008).

[35] Art. 62, paras. (d) and (e), of the Const. of Pakistan (1973). It has to be acknowledged, though, that 10 seats in the National Assembly (Lower House) are reserved for Non-Muslims

for becoming a member of the House of Representatives of Yemen on must "fulfil his religious duties".[36] This would mean in theory that a non-Muslim (who fulfils his/her religious duties) is eligible;[37] however, as the legislature has to take account of the constitutional principle that Shari'a is the source for all legislation, a role for non-Muslims in the legislative discourse remains very ambiguous. Moreover, the provision is in clear violation of the rights of non-believers.

Judiciary

Only Sunni Muslims can become judges in Maldives. In order to be eligible to become Judge of the Supreme Court, one must, moreover, be educated in Shari'a law.[38] It may be added at this point that state practice of religious states shows that qualification criteria for the judiciary based on religious principles occasionally discriminates on grounds other than religion, namely gender.[39]

(v) *Prohibition of Religious Oaths of Office*

The requirement that one has to swear a religious oath (i.e. an oath containing the words "I swear before God..." and/or "So help me God!") prior to taking public office discriminates against non-religious persons (and against adherents of beliefs that cannot accept the religious nature of the oath).[40] Compulsory religious oath schemes are comparable to posing religious qualifications insofar as these provisions seek to exclude non-religious people or people from dissimilar faiths from holding public office. One could of course feign endorsement of the religious nature of the oath with a view towards entering the public office in question, though this possibility does not distract from the fact that these schemes are in violation of the prohibition of religious coercion, freedom from religion and equality principles.

At an analytical level, it is useful to distinguish between compulsory religious oath schemes and optional religious oath schemes. By 'compulsory

---

(art. 51); the requirements based on Islamic principles do not apply to them. There are no such special provisions made with regard to the Senate (Upper House).

[36] Art. 63 of the CONST. OF YEMEN (1990).

[37] Note the striking difference in formulation between art. 63 (House of Representatives) and art. 106 (President) of the CONST. OF YEMEN (1990): "religious duties" vs. "Islamic duties" respectively.

[38] Art. 149 of the CONST. OF MALDIVES (2008).

[39] See, *e.g.*, CEDAW Committee's Concluding Observations: A/52/38/Rev.1 part II (1997) 87 at para. 157 (Israel): "Regret is expressed over the fact that women cannot become religious judges...". The same holds true, needless to say, for Shari'a Court judges in Islamic states.

[40] Cf. Human Rights Committee in its Concluding Observations, *e.g.*: A/55/40 vol. I (2000) 61 at para. 450 (Ireland): "The government should reform constitutional provisions requiring judges to make a declaration with religious references"; A/48/40 vol. I (1993) 119 at para. 607 (Ireland): "The Constitutional requirement that the President and judges must take a religious oath excludes some people from holding those offices"; and A/35/40 (1980), para. 347 (Costa Rica).

religious oaths' is meant that the legislation in question does not provide explicitly for a secular alternative. Thus, failure to take the religious oath would normally mean an absolute obstacle to entering the public office in question. By 'optional religious oath' is meant that the legislation in question contains religious oaths for certain public offices but explicitly provides for a secular alternative (i.e. a solemn affirmation) and/or explicitly allows omission of the religious aspects of the standard oath.[41]

Compulsory religious oaths can be found in the laws of: Bahrain (Deputies and Members of the Consultative Council); Colombia (President); Egypt (President and MPs); Georgia (President); Greece (President); Haiti (President and Judges); Iran (President and Members of the *Majlis*); Ireland (President, Members of the Council of State and Judges); Jordan (Prime Minister, Senators and Deputies); Lebanon (President); Lesotho (Regent); Kuwait (Members of the National Assembly); Liechtenstein (Members of Government and MPs); Maldives (*inter alia*: President, Members of Cabinet, Members of the People's *Majlis* and Judges); Nauru (Members of Cabinet, MPs and Judges); Norway (Regent); Oman (Prime Minister, Ministers and Deputies); Qatar (Prime Minister, Ministers and Members of the Advisory Council); Romania (President, Prime Minister and Ministers); Rwanda (*inter alia*: President, Prime Minister, Ministers, Senators and Supreme Court Judges); Samoa (Prime Minister, Ministers, MPs and Judges); Somalia (President and Prime Minister); Sudan (President and Ministers); Syria (President, Ministers, Members of the National Assembly and Supreme Court Judges); Timor-Leste (President); Tonga (Ministers, MPs and Judges); Tunisia (President); United Arab Emirates (President, Ministers and Members of the Federal National Council); and Yemen (President, Members of Government and MPs).[42]

---

[41] If the option of a solemn affirmation is provided, such is usually, in the constitutional or statutory provision in question, placed between parenthesis or brackets directly after the religious parts of the oath, *e.g.*: "I swear before God [or solemnly affirm] that ...". Alternatively, the religious aspects of the oath are sometimes put between parenthesis or brackets, indicating that they may be omitted, *e.g.*: "(So help me God!)".

[42] Art. 78 of the Const. of Bahrain (2002); art. 192 of the Const. of Colombia (1991); artt. 79 and 90 of the Const. of Egypt (1971); art. 71 of the Const. of Georgia (1995); art. 33 of the Const. of Greece (2001)(the President does not swear to God but "in the name of the Holy, Consubstantial, and Indivisible Trinity"); artt. 135-1 and 187 of the Const. of Haiti (1987); artt. 67 (*Majlis*; Muslims swear "In the Name of God, the Compassionate, the Merciful. In the presence of the Glorious Koran, I swear by God, the Exalted and Almighty..."; the second paragraph accommodates members belonging to minority religions as they are permitted to "swear by their own sacred books while taking this oath") and 121 (President) of the Const. of Iran (1979); artt. 31, 34 and 42 of the Const. of Ireland (1937); artt. 43 and 80 of the Const. of Jordan (1952); art. 91 of the Const. of Kuwait (1962) (art. 60 for oath of the Emir); art. 50 of the Lebanese Const. (1926); Schedule 1 to the Const. of Lesotho (1993); artt. 54 and 108 of the Const. of Liechtenstein (1921); Schedule 1 to the Const. of Maldives (2008); First Schedule to the Const. of Nauru (1968); art. 44 of the Const. of Norway (1814) (art. 9 on the oath taken by the Monarch); art. 50 of the Basic Statute of Oman (1996) (art. 7 on the oath of the Sultan); artt. 92 and 119 of the Const. of Qatar (2003) (artt. 10 and 74 for

States that have adopted *optional religious oaths* schemes for the inauguration of public offices include: Austria (President; Members of Government and Governors); Barbados (Judges); Belize (Governor-General, Ministers, Members of National Assembly and Judges of the Supreme and Appeal Courts); Botswana (*inter alia*: President, Cabinet Members and Judges); Fiji (President, Prime Minister, Ministers and Judges); Finland (Judges); Germany (President); Ghana (*inter alia*: President, Cabinet Members and MPs); Greece (MPs); Grenada (Governor-General, Ministers and MPs); Indonesia (President); India (President); Jamaica (Governor-General, Prime Minister, Ministers and Parliamentary Secretaries); Lesotho (MPs, Ministers and Judges); Lithuania (MPs); Kiribati (President, Prime Minster, Ministers and MPs); Malawi (President); Mauritius (President, Prime Minister, Ministers and Judges); Namibia (President); Netherlands (Ministers and MPs); New Zealand (*inter alia*: Judges); Nigeria (*inter alia*: President, Ministers, MPs and Judges); Panama (President); Philippines (President); Saint Kitts and Nevis (Governor-General, Ministers and MPs); Sierra Leone (President, Ministers, MPs and Judges); Solomon Islands (Governor-General and Members of Cabinet); Suriname (President, Ministers and MPs); South Africa (President, Ministers, MPs and Judges); Swaziland (Prime Minster, Ministers, MPs and Judges); Tuvalu (Governor-General and Members of Cabinet); United Kingdom (Members of Government, MPs and Judges); and Zimbabwe (MPs, Members of Cabinet and Judges).[43]

---

the oaths of the Heir Apparent and the Emir); artt. 82 and 104 of the CONST. OF ROMANIA (1991); artt. 61 and 104 of the CONST. OF RWANDA (2003); Third Schedule to the CONST. OF SAMOA (1960); artt. 42 and 49 of the TRANSITIONAL FEDERAL CHARTER OF THE SOMALI REPUBLIC (2004); artt. 56 and 71 of the INTERIM CONST. OF THE SUDAN (2005); art. 77 of the CONST. OF EAST TIMOR (2002); artt. 7, 63, 90, 96 and 116 of the CONST. OF SYRIA (1973); artt. 83 and 95 of the CONST. OF TONGA (1875); art. 42 of the CONST. OF TUNISIA (1959); artt. 52, 57 and 73 of the CONST. OF UAE (1971); and art. 159 of the CONST. OF YEMEN (1990).

[43] Art. 62, para. (2), art. 72 and art. 101, para. (4), of the CONST. OF AUSTRIA (1920); Schedule 1 to the CONST. OF BARBADOS (1996)(the option of a secular, solemn affirmation is not explicitly codified but would appear to be available in light of art. 19, para. 5, of the Constitution); Schedule 3 and artt. 32, 46, 71, 99 and 103 of the CONST. OF BELIZE (1981); Botswana: Act on Promissory Oaths, Law 36 of 1966 (amended through Act 39 of 1968; Act 41 of 1972; Act 20 of 1977; S.I. 66 of 1988; Act 14 of 2005; Act 18, 2006); Schedule to the CONST. OF THE FIJI ISLANDS (1998); art. 7 of the Code of Judicial Procedure of Finland (amended through 2002); art. 56 of the BASIC LAW FOR THE FEDERAL REPUBLIC OF GERMANY (1949); Second Schedule to the CONST. OF GHANA (1992); art. 59 of the CONST. OF GREECE (2001) (MPs in principle "swear in the name of the Holy Consubstantial and Indivisible Trinity" though it is added that Members of Parliament who are of a different religion or creed shall take the same oath according to the form of their own religion or creed; this provision does not explicitly accommodate non-believers); artt. 20, 40 and 65 of the CONST. OF GRENADA (1973); art. 9 of the CONST. OF INDONESIA (1945); Schedule 1 to the CONST. OF KIRIBATI (1979); art. 60 of the CONST. OF INDIA (1950); First Schedule to the CONST. OF JAMAICA (1962); Schedule 3 to the CONST. OF LESOTHO (1993); art. 5 of the Law on the Enforcement of the Constitution of Lithuania (1992); art. 81 of the CONST. OF MALAWI (1994); Third Schedule of the CONST. OF MAURITIUS (1968); art. 30 of the CONST. OF NAMIBIA (1990); [New Zealand] Oaths and Declarations Act of 1957, Law No. 88/1957; [Dutch] Law on the Swearing-in of Ministers, Assistant Secretaries and Members

No one should be compelled by the state to take a religious oath.[44] It is submitted that in the context of inaugurations of public offices the state can ensure this only by formulating and implementing one uniform, non-religious oath (i.e. a solemn affirmation or declaration). One may think that a state that insists on offering the possibility of taking a religious oath could sufficiently secure the rights of non-believers by making the religious oath scheme purely optional, that is, by always offering a secular alternative (see the above overview). However, it must be acknowledged that in that situation it remains problematic from a human rights perspective that a non-believer is forced to reveal that he or she is not religious (and thus not a member of what would normally be the dominant religion).[45] The Human Rights Committee has clarified that the right to freedom of religion or belief implies that "no one can be compelled to reveal his thoughts or adherence to a religion or belief".[46] In light of this norm, it is submitted that optional religious oath schemes in which taking a religious oath is the rule and secular affirmations the tolerated exception, are incompatible with human rights law. Such a scheme, after all, reflects the existence of a presumption that persons occupying public offices normally are religious. Arguably, an optional religious oath scheme in which secular affirmations are identified as the rule and religious additions to that affirmation the tolerated exception is permissible. One may think of Polish constitutional provisions on oaths which dictate secular affirmations to which each time the following sentence is added: "The oath may also be taken with the additional sentence 'So help me God'".[47] Austrian constitutional law is comparable as it

---

of Parliament of 27 February 1992; Seventh Schedule to the Const. of Nigeria (1999); art. 176 of the Const. of Panama (1972); article 7, sec. 5, of the Const. of the Philippines (1987); Schedule 4 and artt. 24, 39 and 60 of the Const. of Saint Kitts and Nevis (1983); Second Schedule to the Const. of Sierra Leone (1991); Schedule 1 to the Const. of Solomon Islands (1978); artt. 65, 93, 114 and 125 of the Const. of Suriname (1987); Schedule 2 to the Const. of South Africa (1996); Second Schedule to the Const. of Swaziland (2005); Schedule 4 to the Const. of Tuvalu (1986); UK: Promissory Oaths Act 1868 (c.72), Parliamentary Oaths Act 1866 (c.19), Oaths Act 1978 (c.19), Constitutional Reform Act 2005 (c. 4), sec. 20 of the Government of Wales Act 1998 (c. 38), and Scotland Act 1998 (c. 46); and Schedule 1 of the Const. of Zimbabwe (1979).

[44] Cf. Arcot Krishnaswami, *Study of Discrimination in the Matter of Religious Rights and Practices* (U.N. Doc. E/CN.4/Sub.2/200/Rev.1, 1960), pp. 42–43. Krishnaswami argues that such holds true for all contexts (*e.g.* also as witness in a Court, etc.) and regardless of whether a refusal is punishable or not. Human Rights Committee, General Comment 22, para. 3; see also Human Rights Committee in its Concluding Observations (*supra* note 40).

[45] Such was recently for the European Court of Human Rights precisely the reason to deem also *optional* religious oaths incompatible with the European Convention: ECtHR, *Alexandridis v. Greece*, Application No. 19516/06, Judgement of 21 February 2008; the way the Greek oath of office scheme was designed meant that Mr. Alexandridis was forced to reveal that he is not a member of the Greek-Orthodox Church.

[46] Human Rights Committee, General Comment 22, para. 3.

[47] Artt. 104 (Deputies), 130 (President) and 151 (Prime Minister and Ministers) of the Const. of Poland (1997).

codifies a set of secular oaths, to which it is added each time that "[t]he addition of a religious assertion is admissible".[48]

Some states (including some that provide for optional religious oaths schemes) have explicitly codified that no person shall be compelled to take an oath contrary to his or her religion or belief or to take an oath in a manner contrary to his or her religion or belief (e.g. Antigua and Barbuda, Bahamas, Barbados, Belize, Dominica, Fiji Islands, Grenada, Guyana, Kenya, Kiribati, Mauritius, Seychelles, Sierra Leone, Solomon Islands, Saint Kitts and Nevis, Saint Lucia, Saint Vincent and the Grenadines, Tuvalu, Zambia and Zimbabwe).[49] This constitutional safeguard is conducive to freedom of religion or belief, the equality principle as well as to fundamental political rights.

11.2.2 *Avoiding Rigid Measures: No Total Elimination of Religion From the Public Arena*

In light of the observations so far made about human rights violations that stem from too active an interest on the part of the state in religion, one could be tempted to conclude that the best safeguard against adverse forms of state practice is to ban religion altogether from the public realm. Human rights law, however, decides against that approach: eliminating religion from the public realm and from the political discourse in particular is too rigid a measure and cannot be deemed necessary in a democratic state. In a genuine liberal democracy constitutional safeguards are in place so as to ensure that laws and regulations that are ultimately adopted through competitive polices will be designedly non-discriminatory and so as to ensure that, should laws be discriminatory in effect, effective remedy procedures are in place to avoid further discriminatory practices.

(i) *A Case Against Bans on Religious Political Parties*

A prohibition of religious political parties is codified by some states that take a strict interpretation of principles of state secularism and/or separationism.

---

[48] Art. 62, para. (2)(Federal President), art. 72 (Members of the Federal Government) and art. 101, para. (4)(Governors), of the Const. of Austria (1920).

[49] Art. 11 of the Const. of Antigua and Barbuda (1981); art. 22, para. (4), of the Const. of the Bahamas (1973); art. 19, para. (5), of the Const. of Barbados (1996); art. 11, para. (4), of the Const. of Belize (1981); art. 9, para. (4), of the Const. of Dominica (1978); art. 35, para. (6), of the Const. of the Fiji Islands (1998); art. 9, para. (4), of the Const. of Grenada (1973); art. 145, para. (4), of the Const. of Guyana (1980); art. 78, para. (4), of the Const. of Kenya (1969); art. 11, para. (5), of the Const. of Kiribati (1979); art. 11, para. (4), of the Const. of Mauritius (1968); art. 21, para. (4), of the Const. of Seychelles (1993); art. 24, para. (4), of the Const. of Sierra Leone (1991); art. 11, para. (5), of the Const. of Solomon Islands (1978); art. 11, para. (4), of the Const. of Saint Kitts and Nevis (1983); art. 9, para. (4), of the Const. of Saint Lucia (1978); art. 9, para. (4), of the Const. of Saint Vincent and the Grenadines (1979); art. 23, para. (5), of the Const. of Tuvalu (1986); art. 19, para. (4), of the Const. of Zambia (1991); and art. 19, para. (4), of the Const. of Zimbabwe (1979).

These states include: Belarus, Bulgaria, Burkina Faso, Cape Verde, Republic of the Congo, Guinea, Guinea-Bissau, Kyrgyz Republic, Liberia, Mexico, Moldova, Mozambique, Niger, Nigeria, Portugal, Rwanda, Senegal, Tanzania, Togo, Turkmenistan and Uzbekistan.[50] One can clearly discern a considerable amount of former Soviet states or states that were under French (secular) administration in past times. There are some non-secular states that have adopted a similar ban: Algeria, Djibouti, Egypt, Equatorial Guinea, Ethiopia, the Gambia, Ghana, Sierra Leone and Tunisia.[51] It must be pointed out that bans on religious political parties are not necessarily adopted to serve the objective of secularism: in some of these states the ban would appear to stem from past politicized religious strife or a desire to outlaw a specific (extremist) organization as a political entity.

States may not demand that all political parties are founded on the tenets of one specific religion or that their agendas and activities are at all times perfectly in keeping with the state-sanctioned view on religion.[52] It is submitted, however, that the other extreme, an absolute ban on religious political parties, does not follow from and is actually at odds with human rights law.[53] One

---

[50] Art. 8 of the Law of the Republic of Belarus on Religious Freedom and Religious Organizations, Law No. 137–3, of 31 October 2002 (hereinafter: "2002 Belarusian Law") in conjunction with art. 5 of the CONST. OF BELARUS (1996); art. 11 of the CONST. OF BULGARIA (1991); art. 13 of the CONST. OF BURKINA FASO (1991); art. 125 of the CONST. OF CAPE VERDE (1992); art. 52 of the NEW CONST. OF THE REPUBLIC OF THE CONGO (2002); art. 3 of the FUNDAMENTAL LAW OF GUINEA (1990); art. 4 of the CONST. OF GUINEA-BISSAU (1991); art. 8 of the CONST. OF THE KYRGYZ REPUBLIC (1993); art. 79 of the CONST. OF LIBERIA (1986); art. 130 of the CONST. OF MEXICO (1917); art. 20 of the Law of the Republic of Moldova on Denominations, No. 979-XII, of 24 March 1992 (amended in 1998 and 2002; hereinafter: "1992 Moldovan Law"); art. 76 of the CONST. OF MOZAMBIQUE (1990); art. 9 of the CONST. OF NIGER (1999); art. 222 of the CONST. OF NIGERIA (1999); art. 51 of the CONST. OF PORTUGAL (1976); art. 54 of the CONST. OF RWANDA (2003); art. 4 of the CONST. OF SENEGAL (2001); art. 20 of the CONST. OF TANZANIA (1977); art. 7 of the CONST. OF TOGO (1992); art. 28 of the CONST. OF TURKMENISTAN (1992); art. 57 of the CONST. OF UZBEKISTAN (1992).

[51] Art. 42, para. (3), of the CONST. OF ALGERIA (1976); art. 6 of the CONST. OF DJIBOUTI (1992); art. 5, third sentence (inserted in 2007, after having been approved by the people in public referendum), of the CONST. OF EGYPT (1971); art. 9 of the FUNDAMENTAL LAW OF EQUATORIAL GUINEA (1991); art. 60 of the CONST. OF THE GAMBIA (1996); art. 55 of the CONST. OF GHANA (1992); and art. 35 of the CONST. OF SIERRA LEONE (1991). As regards some of these states, French and other colonial influences, again, cannot be ignored.

[52] Cf. Human Rights Committee, *e.g.* A/48/40 vol. I (1993) 44 at para. 262 (Iran).

[53] Cf. Committee on the Elimination of Racial Discrimination's Concluding Observations, *e.g.*: A/52/18 (1997) 39 at para. 285 (Bulgaria): "Although the right to associate and to found political parties is stated as a general principle in the Constitution, it is noted with concern that the State party prohibits the foundation and registration of political parties formed on…religious bases."; and cf. Human Rights Committee's Concluding Observations, *e.g.*: A/53/40 vol. I (1998) 52 at para. 365 (Algeria): "The State party's restriction on the right to form political parties effectively prohibits political activists' rights to associate with one another or to vote for representatives of their choice, in view of the wide range of proscribed categories (religious…). Since it took effect, this law has been invoked to ban or prevent the legalization of more than 30 parties. Current legislation should be amended so as to bring it into conformity with the conditions required by the Covenant with respect to restrictions on the freedom of association." At the European level, the fact that the European Convention does not bar religious political

argument is that political parties enjoy a collective form of freedom of expression.[54] A second argument is that a law that would allow political parties to identify with secular ideologies such as 'socialism', 'liberalism', 'nationalism', etc., but not with a religious label is at odds with the non-discrimination principle and the rights to freedom of association, expression and religion or belief. This type of differentiation can hardly be considered reasonable or objective. Thirdly, the fact that a political party largely draws on a specific religious tradition in itself does not mean that such a party is incapable of proposing laws that are neutral in scope and that do not seek to exclusively or primarily advantage members of the religion in question. Such is arguably different with regard to unstable states, especially conflict or post-conflict societies, in which religious strife is the order of the day or is looming. As regards (post)conflict societies, this measure could be defended as a means to prevent religious differences from becoming overtly politicized. All restrictions, if they can be considered reasonable in this context, must be treated as temporary solutions only. It must also be pointed out that none of this is intended to claim that states can or should not take action against those parties or entities that blatantly disregard human rights law or that seek to undermine democracy; the argument simply holds that fundamental political and equality rights and the freedoms of association, expression and religion or belief in particular, prevent liberal democracies from codifying an *a priori*, absolute ban on religious political parties.

Different types or degrees of bans on religious political parties can be perceived, ranging from absolute prohibitions of such parties, to bans of political organizations which by name associate with a religion to non-absolute types of ban.

Absolute Prohibitions

A good example of the former is given by the Constitution of Bulgaria as it states in plain terms: "There shall be no political parties on…religious lines".[55] Similar uncompromising restrictions can be found in the (constitutional) laws of: Belarus, Burkina Faso, Cape Verde, Republic of the Congo, Guinea, Kyrgyz

---

parties per se has been postulated by the European Court of Human Rights in, *e.g.*, ECtHR, *Refah Partisi (the Welfare Party) and Others v. Turkey*, (Grand Chamber Judgement), Application Nos. 41340/98, 41342/98, 41343/98 and 41344/98, Judgement of 13 February 2003, para. 100 ("a political party animated by the moral values imposed by a religion cannot be regarded as intrinsically inimical to the fundamental principles of democracy").

[54] This argument is based on considerations made by the European Court of Human Rights; *e.g.*: *United Communist Party of Turkey and Others v. Turkey*, Application No. 19392/92, 26 EHHR 121 [1998], Judgement of 30 January 1998, paras. 42–43; *Freedom and Democracy Party (ÖZDEP) v. Turkey*, Application No. 23885/94, 31 EHRR 674 [2001], Judgement of 8 December 1999, para. 37; *Refah Partisi and Others v. Turkey, ibid.*, paras. 87–89.

[55] Art. 11 of the CONST. OF BULGARIA (1991).

Republic, Moldova, Niger, Rwanda, Senegal, Tanzania, Togo, Turkmenistan and Uzbekistan.[56]

Prohibition of Religious Affiliation by Name, Emblem or Motto

Some states forbid political parties from identifying by name (and/or emblems, motto etc.) with a religion. The Constitution of Guinea-Bissau, for instance, provides that "[t]he names of political parties may not be identified with…the name of [any]…church, religion, cult, or religious doctrine".[57] Similar constructions can be found in the Constitutions of: Liberia, Mexico, Mozambique, Nepal and Sierra Leone.[58]

On the face of it, such bans could be equated with absolute bans as described above. However, a subtle difference should be acknowledged as this construction arguably allows for a margin, albeit it very minimal, in which a nexus between political parties and religiosity can be realized, though the fact remains that the political party cannot formally be named after its religious inspiration. In short, such a ban seems less rigid than a clear-cut prohibition

[56] Art. 8 of the 2002 Belarusian Law (*supra* note 50) in conjunction with art. 5 of the CONST. OF BELARUS (1996); art. 13 of the CONST. OF BURKINA FASO (1991); art. 125, para. (2), of the CONST. OF CAPE VERDE (1992); art. 52 of the NEW CONST. OF THE REPUBLIC OF THE CONGO (2002); art. 3, para. (3), of the FUNDAMENTAL LAW OF GUINEA (1990); art. 8, para. (4), of the CONST. OF THE KYRGYZ REPUBLIC (1993); art. 20 of the 1992 Moldovan Law (*supra* note 50); art. 9 of the CONST. OF NIGER (1999); art. 54 of the CONST. OF RWANDA (2003); art. 4 of the CONST. OF SENEGAL (2001); art. 20 of the CONST. OF TANZANIA (1977); art. 7 of the CONST. OF TOGO (1992); art. 28 of the CONST. OF TURKMENISTAN (1992); and art. 57 of the CONST. OF UZBEKISTAN (1992). In some states political affiliation with religion is *de facto* taboo (*e.g.* Ethiopia and France). Occasionally, constitutional or statutory laws contain provisions that further expand or elaborate on the ban on religious political organizations. A Belarusian law elaborates on the constitutional ban on religious political parties by stipulating that "[r]eligious organizations can neither participate in activities of political parties and other public associations pursuing political ends, nor render financial or other support to them" (art. 8 of the 2002 Belarusian Law, *supra* note 50). The Constitution of Kyrgyzstan further elaborates that "[n]o religious organizations shall pursue political goals and objectives" (art. 8, para. (4), of the CONST. OF THE KYRGYZ REPUBLIC of 1993), which should be distinguished from the standard prohibition provided in the same article. The difference concerns a prohibition of forming religious political organizations vs. a ban forbidding existing religious organizations from adopting a political agenda in the future. A good example of a law that only provides for the latter is Ukrainian law on religious associations as it provides that: "Religious organizations shall not perform governmental functions...Religious organizations shall not participate in the operation of political parties, they shall not provide political parties with financial assistance, shall not nominate candidates to government bodies, shall not campaign for nor finance election campaigns of candidates to such government bodies. The clergy shall enjoy the right to participate in political life on an equal basis with all citizens" (art. 5 of the Law on the Freedom of Conscience and Religious Organizations of 1991, amended 1992 and 1996).

[57] Art. 4, para. (5), of the CONST. OF GUINEA-BISSAU (1991).

[58] Art. 79, para. (d), of the CONST. OF LIBERIA (1986); art. 130 [3] of the CONST. OF MEXICO (1917); art. 76 of the CONST. OF MOZAMBIQUE (1990); art. 142, para. (4), of the INTERIM CONST. OF NEPAL (2007), drawing on art. 113 if the Constitution of the Kingdom of Nepal (1990) (abrogated); and art. 35, para. (5) (b), of the CONST. OF SIERRA LEONE (1991), the same article, in para. (5)(c), codifies an absolute ban.

of religious political parties. Either way, these constructions are at odds with the non-discrimination principle in conjunction with the rights to freedom of association, expression and religion or belief.

Non-Absolute Bans

Some states require political parties to respect the secularity of the state at all times (e.g. Benin, Mali and Turkey).[59] Such a provision would appear not to rule out the existence of religious political parties altogether, though it certainly would impact on their programmes and activities. The requirement to respect the secularity of the state forbids political parties from proposing new laws and regulations that would be contrary to the secular nature of the state, or to propose amendments to the Constitution that would have the same effect. This requirement, however, does not rule out political parties being affiliated with a religion per se. A religious political party can in theory adopt a party programme that perfectly respects the principle of secularism.

It is submitted here that such a constitutional demand that political parties respect the secular nature of the state are not—in itself[60]—contrary to human rights law. It has been argued in this study (Chapters 7–8) that establishing a state as a religious state or legally privileging a specific religion is at odds with human rights law: constitutional safeguards against such forms of religious establishment, provided they do not outlaw religious political parties altogether, are acceptable and may even be applauded in those states where the non-confessional status of the state is under siege by establishmentarian forces. To the extent that such requirements amount to an interference with the rights to freedom of association and expression, it would appear that these interferences can be deemed necessary in specific circumstances in a democratic state so as to uphold order and particularly the rights and freedoms of others. It will be clear at the same time that for this mechanism to be legitimate, such

[59] Art. 5 of the Const. of Benin (1990); art. 28 of the Const. of Mali (1992); and art. 68 of the Const. of Turkey (1982). This obligation is in Turkey further underlined by making it compulsory for Turkish Members of Parliament, upon assuming office, to take the following oath: "I swear upon my honour and integrity…to remain loyal to the…democratic and secular Republic, and to Atatürk's principles and reforms…" (art. 81 of the Const. of Turkey of 1982). It may be added at this point that the President of Turkey has to take a similar oath by which he swears to abide by the principles of the secular Republic of Turkey (art. 103 of the Const. of Turkey of 1982). The Turkish Constitution contains other principles safeguarding the secularity of the state, *e.g.*: the Department of Religious Affairs shall exercise its duties "in accordance with the principles of secularism" (art. 136 of the Const. of Turkey of 1982); and so-called reform laws that have been adopted with a view towards safeguarding the secular nature of the state cannot be rendered unconstitutional (art. 174 of the Const. of Turkey of 1982). For a description on these and other express political implications of secularism/separationism, see Part I, section 5.5.1, *supra*.

[60] Clearly, such clauses may not in practice be abused by the ruling coalition to crackdown on rival political forces; they must be administered by the judiciary or be open to judicial review.

limitations need to be enshrined by law and the onus is on the state to establish in any particular case that the application of these limitations is absolutely necessary in a democratic society. Consequently, firm constitutional safeguards need to be in place, not in the least the possibility of judicial review.

Some secular states, short of demanding that political parties are bound to respect the secularity of the state, raise concerns in their Constitutions about possible political affiliation with religion. The Constitution of Burundi, for instance, states: "In their organization and functioning the political parties must respond to the democratic principles...They may not foment violence, exclusion, and hatred in any of their forms...in particular those based on... religious...affiliation".[61] The Constitution of Gabon provides: "Political associations, parties or formations, syndicates, societies, establishments for social interests as well as religious communities of which the activities are contrary to law, or to the good relations of ethnic groups or ensembles, may be prohibited according to the terms of the law", which is immediately followed by: "Any act of...religious discrimination...shall be punished by law".[62] The Constitution of Madagascar bans political parties which propagate religious segregation.[63] The Russian Constitution similarly prohibits public associations "whose aims and actions are directed at...the incitement of...religious strife".[64] Also in Serbia political parties are expressly forbidden to incite religious hatred.[65] It may be argued that such clauses are permissible and may even be encouraged, particularly given the state's duty to actively prohibit the advocacy of religious hatred that constitutes incitement to discrimination, hostility or violence.[66]

Membership of Political Parties

It has been argued that posing religious qualifications for holding public office is contrary to human rights law, as human rights law provides that every citizen shall have the right and the opportunity, regardless of one's religious affiliation, to take part in the conduct of public affairs. Some states seek to further ensure that religious affiliation plays no role in the political discourse by forbidding political parties from posing religious criteria for party membership (Burundi, Ghana, Liberia, Nepal, Nigeria, Sierra Leone and Uganda).[67]

---

[61] Art. 78 of the Post-Transition Const. of Burundi (2005).

[62] Art. 1, para. (13), of the Const. of Gabon (1991).

[63] Article 14 of the Const. of Madagascar (1992).

[64] Art. 13, para. (5), of the Const. of Russia (1993).

[65] Art. 5 of the Const. of Serbia (2006). Also in Šrpska, part of Bosnia Herzegovina, political parties "inciting...religious hatred and intolerance shall be prohibited"; art. 31 of the Const. of Šrpska (1992).

[66] Art. 20, para. (2), of the ICCPR. See also art. 4 of CERD.

[67] Art. 78 of the Const. of Burundi (2005); art. 55, para. (4), of the Const. of Ghana (1992); art. 79, para. (b), of the Const. of Liberia (1986); art. 142, para. (4), of the Interim Const. of Nepal (2007); art. 222, para. (b), of the Const. of Nigeria (1999); art. 35, para. (5)

A prohibition of posing religious criteria for party membership as such does not affect the legality of founding a religious political party and must, therefore, be distinguished from a clear-cut ban on religious political parties. This measure simply requires that all political parties, including religious political parties, accept people from all religions as members. This distinction is relevant as it is not utterly unimaginable that an adherent to a dissimilar religion or a secularist would wish, indeed despite its religious nature, to join a certain religious political party because he or she subscribes to its overall political agenda. The rules at stake make possible precisely that: party membership regardless of religious affiliation. The prohibition at hand, however, does not self-evidently follow from human rights law. Though the state itself is obliged to take a fully egalitarian approach regarding public offices within the executive, legislative branch and judiciary, it is debatable to what extent this obligation extends to the issue of membership of political parties (often not being state bodies but privately founded organizations). Equality rules and the right to public participation on the one hand need to be balanced against the interest of party autonomy (freedom of association) on the other. Providing a fair degree of party autonomy (as a result of this balancing act) is in principle allowed and, to some extent, to be recommended. The Human Rights Committee is of the view that the state cannot dictate how religious organizations, including political alignments, are to choose their members. In *Paul Arenz et al v. Germany*, the Human Rights Committee considered that the policy of giving priority to the principle of party autonomy over a person's wish to be a member in a political party that does not accept him or her due to membership in another organization of ideological nature, falls within the margin of appreciation of the state and ultimately deemed the case inadmissible.[68] In sum, the right to take part in the conduct of public affairs does not seem to include an absolute right to join a political party of one's choice, the underlying rationale being that a residual right is always available: the freedom to found one's own political party.

On the other hand, given the close link between the right of every citizen to take part in the conduct of public affairs and the possibility of joining a political party, it cannot be denied that there is a positive state duty discernible in this context and that some minimum state regulation or supervision is called for.[69] It is submitted that restrictions of the freedom of association

---

(a), of the Const. of Sierra Leone (1991); and art. 71, para. (b), of the Const. of Uganda (1995). Sierra Leone, Ghana and Liberia have also codified an absolute ban on religious political parties.

[68] Human Rights Committee, *Paul Arenz et al v. Germany*, Communication No. 1138/2002, U.N. Doc. CCPR/C/80/D/1138/2002 (2004), Views of 24 March 2004.

[69] Cf. Human Rights Committee, *Paul Arenz et al v. Germany*, para. 8.5.

within the political context are legitimate to the extent that they are necessary to protect the citizens' equal right to take part in the conduct of public affairs. If religious organizations are granted a full license to discriminate on any ground they see fit, the state is likely to fail in its duty to protect fundamental equality rights. In the latter respect, it is submitted that religious political parties may not discriminate on grounds other than religion (e.g. gender). For that reason, the Committee on the Elimination of Discrimination against Women has repeatedly argued in the past that the reluctance of the Netherlands to take actions against the SGP, an orthodox Protestant political party founded in 1918 which until very recently restricted party membership to men allegedly on account of biblical motives, was in violation of fundamental women's rights.[70] Arguably, interferences with freedom of association in this context are also justifiable insofar as they prevent the political framework from degenerating into a purely sectarian political discourse (i.e. 'public order' and 'protection of rights and freedoms of others' arguments).

(ii) *Incompatibility Rules*

Incompatibility rules should be distinguished from 'no religious test' clauses. The latter are designed to ensure that religion shall play no role when it comes to appointing people for political offices while incompatibility rules deem certain active religious members ineligible for public offices. *Prima facie*, the latter rules appear to be the exact opposite of provisions posing religious qualifications for public offices; however, these eligibility rules do not require one to be secular or irreligious, but rather demand that one is not too active or prominent within a religion. They are typically designed to specifically bar clergy from public offices.

Ministers of religion or members of the clergy are barred from some specific or from all pubic offices or representative bodies in for instance: Antigua and Barbuda (House of Representatives); Argentina (Congress); Bolivia (all public offices); Burma (*Pyithu Hluttaw*, People's Assembly); Cyprus (a variety of public offices); Dominica (House of Assembly); El Salvador (Legislative Assembly); Guatemala (Judiciary); Honduras (all public offices); Israel (the Knesset); Kyrgyzstan (all public offices); Mexico (Presidency, Chamber of Deputies and most other public offices); Panama (most public offices); Paraguay (Presidency and Congress); Saint Kitts and Nevis (Parliament); Saint Lucia (Parliament); Saint Vincent and the Grenadines (House of Assembly);

---

[70] See, *e.g.*, CEDAW Committee's Concluding Observations: A/56/38 part II (2001) 63 at para. 219 (Netherlands); and CEDAW/C/NLD/4, pp. 47–48.

and Tajikistan (Legislative bodies).[71] In Tonga, Ministers of Religion cannot serve on juries.[72]

It would be hard to establish that such rules flow from human rights law. It has been argued (Chapters 7–8) that the state may not establish a certain religion as official and that it must ensure that state offices do not merge with religious offices; this, however, does not imply that states have to eliminate religion from the political discourse altogether and it does not mean, more specifically, that states must proactively disqualify anyone that holds a (senior) position within a religious community from holding public office. Incompatibility rules make, for reasons of determining eligibility for holding public office, distinctions on the ground of religion or belief that cannot be considered reasonable or objective. This is *a fortiori* the case if incompatibility rules are inherently discriminatory, that is, if the eligibility criteria permit membership of some religions or secular organizations but not of others.[73] Barring religious officials from running for public office is not strictly necessary in a democratic state: in a democratic state safeguards are in place—see *infra*—to ensure that state officials and representatives, once appointed or elected, do not adopt or implement discriminatory policies and, moreover, judicial remedies are available to quash inadvertent discriminatory consequences of state policies and laws. Also, incompatibility rules may force people

[71] Art. 39 of the Const. of Antigua and Barbuda (1981); art. 73 of the Const. of Argentina (1853); art. 238, para. (5), of the Political Const. of Bolivia (2009); art. IV, para. (33), of the Const. of Myanmar (2008); art. 101 of the Const. of Cyprus (1960); art. 32 of the Const. of Dominica (1978); art. 82 of the Const. of El Salvador (1983) (Ministers of religions are also forbidden from joining political parties); art. 207 of the Const. of Guatemala (1985); art. 77 of the Const. of Honduras (1982); Israel: art. 7 of the Basic Law: The Knesset (1958); art. 8 of the Const. of the Kyrgyz Republic (1993) (which forbids in absolute terms any "interference by members of religious organizations and cults with the functioning of state bodies"); artt. 55, para. VI (Chamber of Deputies), 82 (Presidency) and 130 (all other public offices) of the Const. of Mexico (1917); art. 42 of the Const. of Panama (1972) (which stipulates that Ministers of religious faiths and members of religious orders may hold public posts only when it concerns positions related to social welfare, public education, or scientific research); artt. 197 and 235 of the Const. of Paraguay (1992); art. 28 of the Const. of Saint Kitts and Nevis (1983); art. 26 (Senate) and 32 (House of Assembly) of the Const. of Saint Lucia (1978); art. 26 of the Const. of Saint Vincent and the Grenadines (1979); and art. 5 of the Law of the Republic of Tajikistan on Religion and Religious Organizations of 1994 (amended 1997 and 1999).

[72] Art. 28 of the Const. of Tonga (1875). Portugal has opted for a different (and clearly preferable) policy in this respect. Instead of excluding religious officials, it applies an exemption policy in this area: Portuguese Ministers of religion can get an exemption from jury service. See art. 18 of the Portuguese Law on Religious Freedom, No. 16/2001, of 21 June 2001.

[73] Cf. Human Rights Committee's Concluding Observations, *e.g.*: A/59/40 vol. I (2004) 39 at paras. 68(19) (Germany): "The Committee reiterates its concern that adherence to certain religious organizations or beliefs constitutes one of the main grounds for disqualifying individuals from obtaining employment in the public service"; and A/52/40 vol. I (1997) 32 at para. 186 (Germany): "It is of concern that membership in certain religious sects as such may, in some Länder of the State party, disqualify individuals from obtaining employment in the public service...". These observations would appear to be particularly concerned with the treatment of Scientology in some Länder.

(with political aspirations) to renounce their religion for the sake of becoming eligible for public office.[74] Needless to say, none of this is intended to argue that states may not require appointed public officials to abide by certain rules which could interfere with the free manifestation of religion whilst in office.

(iii) *Disfranchisement of Religious Officials*

As under international human rights law every citizen has the right to vote, depriving clergymen or other religious officials of the right to vote (e.g. Burma, Mexico and Thailand)[75] is manifestly incompatible with human rights law.

(iv) *Ban on Political Gatherings at Houses of Worship*

Another rigid measure to ensure strict separation between religion and politics is the prohibition of political meetings being held in religious buildings (this measure must be distinguished from a clear-cut prohibition of religious political parties). This prohibition can be found in the laws of, for instance, Belarus, France and Mexico.[76] The most elaborate version is codified by Belarus; it reads:

> Use of state symbolism, holding of meetings, rallies, electoral campaigns and other events of political nature, appearances in public and statements insulting representatives of state authorities, officials and individuals, are not allowed in places of public worship.[77]

Human rights law recognizes the right of peaceful assembly.[78] This right may be restricted, if and to the extent that such is necessary, in the interests of national security or public order. The onus is on the state to establish that a gathering jeopardizes national security or public order. It is submitted that an absolute, blanket ban on all forms of political gatherings at houses of worship cannot be reconciled with human rights law.

11.3 Conclusion: Recommended Safeguards

We have seen how in those political systems in which religion plays too decisive a role, the modus of state–religion identification may uncompromisingly

---

[74] See, most explicitly, the Bolivian constitutional incompatibility rule: art. 238, para. (5), of the Political Const. of Bolivia (2009): if ministers of religion renounce at least three month prior to the day of election, they become eligible for public office.

[75] Art. IX, para. (2)(a), of the Const. of Myanmar (2008); art. 130 of the Const. of Mexico (1917); art. 94 of the Const. of Thailand (2007) (Buddhist priests, novices, monks or clergymen are disfranchised on election days).

[76] Art. 8 of the 2002 Belarusian Law (*supra* note 50); art. 26 of the Law concerning the Separation of the Churches and the State [of France] (1905); and art. 130 of the Const. of Mexico (1917).

[77] Art. 8 of the 2002 Belarusian Law (*supra* note 50).

[78] Art. 21 of the ICCPR.

translate into a range of practices that are in violation of fundamental political and equality rights. All measures that aim at ensuring that the laws or policies that are to be adopted have a sound basis in the doctrine of the dominant religion undermine natural democratic deliberation processes. The same holds true for states that constitutionally reserve a percentage of seats within state bodies for members of the dominant religion. The most serious human rights abuses flow from measures that make the right to vote or the right to run for public office conditional upon belonging to a certain religion (the state or predominant religion). States have a duty to ensure that no civil disabilities are imposed, neither *de jure* nor *de facto*, on non-believers or members of minority religions. One way to ensure this at all governmental levels would be by constitutionally prohibiting all forms of religious tests for public office.[79] As Wood argues, "[f]or centuries, some form of religious belief, as least in a Supreme Being, or some formal religious affiliation, had been a well-established requisite for holding public office throughout the world."[80] Some states have codified an express[81] prohibition of religious tests for public office and in many states such discriminatory practices in the field of political rights have *de facto* come to an end. However, as we have seen in the above overview of global state practice, 'religious tests', both it in the form of explicit religious qualifications or in the form of compulsory religious oaths, are unfortunately yet to become universally abolished.

---

[79] The United States Constitution guarantees this principle as follows: "The Senators and Representatives…and the members of the several state legislatures, and all executive and judicial officers, both of the United States and of the several states, shall be bound by oath or affirmation, to support this Constitution; but no religious test shall ever be required as a qualification to any office or public trust under the United States." Art. VI, para. (3), of the CONST. OF USA (1787); see also U.S. Supreme Court's ruling in the case of *Torcaso v. Watkins*, 367 U.S. 488 (1961), Judgement of 19 June 1961.

[80] James E. Wood, Jr., *"No Religious Test Shall Ever Be Required": Reflections on the Bicentennial of the U.S. Constitution*, 29 JOURNAL OF CHURCH AND STATE 199 (1987), p. 201, in relation to the introduction of the prohibition of religious tests in the USA in the late 18th century. It was in light of the religious wars and religious persecution elsewhere in the world and the prevalent forms of religious discrimination (*e.g.* the English Test Acts: Test Act of 1672: 'An Act for Preventing Dangers Which May Happen from Popish Recusants', 25 Car. II. c. 2; and Test Act of 1678: 'An Act for the More Effectuall Preserving the Kings Person and Government by Disableing Papists from Sitting in Either House of Parlyament', 30 Car. II. st. 2) in combination with the religious diversity experienced in the original American states, that the (then) revolutionary idea took hold that in determining qualifications for public office there should not be any role for religion. See Wood, *ibid.*, pp. 199–206.

[81] See, *e.g.*, Art. 116 of the CONST. OF AUSTRALIA (1900): "no religious test shall be required as a qualification for any office or public trust"; art. 14 of the CONST. OF LIBERIA (1986): "no religious tests shall be required for any civil or military office or for the exercise of any civil right"; art. 3, sec. 5, of the CONST. OF THE PHILIPPINES (1987): "No religious test shall be required for the exercise of civil or political rights…"; art. 21, para. (5), of the CONST. OF SEYCHELLES (1993): "A person shall not be required to profess any religion as a qualification for public office". The same principle is implemented by France, as developed by the Council of State in its jurisprudence on the French *laïcité* principle.

Human rights law dictates that a state may not require that all laws and policies are based on one religion or one set of religious laws. However, human rights law is not categorically opposed to proposals for new laws being inspired by religious incentives as long as laws are not expressly proposed to favour one religion or to disfavour another. As An-Na'im argues, religious values may inspire legislative action as long as actual proposals for laws are not done in the name of any specific religion and as long as legislative proposals remain within the spirit of "civic reason".[82] The policy or law in question needs to be drafted in such a fashion that the rationale and its objectives are based on the type of reasoning that citizens, regardless of religious affiliation, can access and accept or reject.[83] Human rights law forbids the state to identify one set of religious laws for the legislature to abide by in the exercise of its functions; however, human rights law does not prevent democratically elected representatives from voting in favour or against new laws and policies on the basis of their religious and moral conscience. An-Na'im rightly suggests that laws on this matter may not even be able to prevent this:

> ...the objective of religious neutrality should not be sought through efforts to control religion or relegate it to the purely private domain, because this is neither possible nor desirable. Believers will always assert their religious convictions politically, and it is better to acknowledge and regulate this reality than to deny it and force such political expression of religious beliefs to go underground.[84]

That being said, it must be acknowledged that human rights law is concerned with both the *democratic quality* of the political order of a state (see also Chapter 7–8) and with the *final outcomes* of the political process (see also Chapters 8–10). As regards the former issue (democracy), human rights law insists that everyone, regardless of religious affiliation, has a right to vote and to take part in the conduct of public affairs. As regards the latter point, any outcome of a democratic deliberation process must be compatible with norms of international human rights law. That means that the legislature is not in a position to adopt laws that would directly and unreasonably favour adherents of the dominant religion or discriminate against members of minority religions or non-believers (direct discrimination). Also laws that are found to discriminate against certain groups in more indirect ways must be quashed or amended. In a democratic *Rechtsstaat* premised on checks and balances there is a of course an important role here for the judiciary to keep the legislature on the right track.[85]

---

[82] An-Na'im, *supra* note 7, pp. 85–101.

[83] *Idem.*

[84] *Ibid.*, p. 85 (see also p. 3).

[85] A good illustration is the (in)famous 'Lemon test' established by the US Supreme Court in: *Lemon v. Kurtzman*, 403 U.S. 602 [1971]. Though domestically increasingly under attack by conservative judges, from an international human rights perspective there is a lot to be said

Pragmatically the best way to ensure all this would be to simply keep religion out of the political discourse; however, from a human rights perspective we must conclude that this is not quite what is called for. Such an uncompromising measure would inevitably infringe upon certain fundamental rights: the rights to freedom of association, freedom of expression and freedom of religion or belief. In this Chapter it has been repeatedly argued that the drastic measure of the complete elimination of religion from the public realm (by banning religious political parties, by adopting strict incompatibility rules, etc.) cannot be considered necessary in a well-functioning democracy,[86] as in such a state less intrusive safeguards are available to ensure that religious incentives do not lead to discriminatory laws or policies. Most important, in this context, are the above mentioned powers of the judiciary to scrutinize the compatibility of laws with the equality principle, minority rights and other norms of human rights law.

Having said that, it will be clear that if we do allow a role for religion within the political arena constitutional safeguards must be in place to prevent human rights abuses. Many pitfalls were identified in this Chapter, both in relation to systems that insist on too strong a nexus between the state apparatus and the dominant religion as well as in relation to regimes that too rigidly seek to eliminate religion form the political discourse. The following set of safeguards draws on those conclusions as well as the ones reached in previous Chapters (7–10).

11.3.1 *The Case for State Neutrality & Non-Establishmentarianism*

Human rights law provides that people should not be treated differently because of their religion. The Human Rights Committee has not condemned state entanglement with religion in absolute terms, though it has expressed the position that states may not adopt measures discriminating against members of minority religions or non-believers, such as measures restricting eligibility for government service to members of the predominant religion or giving economic privileges to them or imposing special restrictions on the practice of non-dominant faiths, as all such measures run counter to the equality principle.[87] The second Part of this study shows that this position may be too lenient

---

for it. The threefold test holds that a law or policy (i) may not have an express religious objective; (ii) may not have the primary effect of either advancing or inhibiting any particular religion; and (iii) may not result in an "excessive government entanglement" with religion.

[86] Again, the caveat should be made that such is arguably different with regard to unstable states, especially conflict or post-conflict societies, in which religious strife is the order of the day or is looming. As regards (post)conflict societies, such measures could be defended as a means to prevent religious differences from becoming overtly politicized. All restrictions, if they can be considered reasonable in this context, must be treated as temporary solutions only.

[87] Human Rights Committee, General Comment No. 22, para. 9.

and uncritical an approach, as many, if not all states that are officially entangled with a single religion, fail to fully comply with these and other fundamental equality principles.

States must at all times act on the premise of neutrality and must commit themselves not to do away with this notion in the future.[88] In this study it has been argued that a plausible case can be made for considering forms of establishment per se incompatible with the autonomous non-discrimination principle (Chapter 7). It also cannot be denied that forms of establishment do as a rule translate into substantive human rights abuses and discriminatory practices in a variety of fields (see Chapter 8-10). In light of this, it is submitted that official state neutrality generates the widest scope for compliance with international human rights law. In the terms of this study, this would mean that a state positions itself as a non-religious state, that is, an '*a-confessional* state' (not to be confused with anti-religious) in the simple meaning of a state that does not *a priori* favour or disfavour any particular religion or belief. In order to ensure that this spirit of neutrality remains the driving force as far as the state's relation to the different religions and beliefs is concerned, a constitutional non-establishment clause appears to be in order. The second part of this study affirms that not 'anything goes', as far as the state's relation to religion is concerned. In this area, a broad web of important, far-reaching and

---

[88] A duty of state neutrality is implicit in the Concluding Observations of the UN Treaty Bodies and other international human rights monitoring bodies: Human Rights Committee, *e.g.*: A/56/40 vol. I (2001) 49 at para. 77(25) (Venezuela); A/54/40 vol. I (1999) 44 at para. 220 (Chile); A/46/40 (1996), para. 402 (UK); A/50/40 vol. I (1995) 42 at para. 212 (Paraguay); A/49/40 vol. I (1994) 31 at para. 158 (Costa Rica); CCPR/C/SR.1128 (1992), para. 38 (Algeria); A/46/40 (1991), para. 341 (Sweden); A/41/40 (1986), para. 69 (Luxembourg); A/41/40 (1986), para. 146 (Sweden); A/36/40 (1981), para. 366 (Norway); A/36/40 (1981), para. 82 (Denmark); CCPR/C/SR.327 (1981), para. 63 (Morocco); CCPR/C/SR.301 (1981) (Norway), para. 36; CCPR/C/SR.236 (1980), para. 12 (Costa Rica); CCPR/C/SR.251 (1980), paras. 17, 20 and 57 (Denmark); CCPR/C/SR.222 (1980) (Colombia), para. 7; CCPR/C/SR.170 (1979), para. 6 (Finland); Committee on Economic, Social and Cultural Rights, *e.g.*: E/1999/22 (1998) 43 at para. 236 (Israel); Committee on the Elimination of Discrimination against Women, *e.g.*: A/53/38/Rev.1 part I (1998) 28 at para. 351 (Dominican Republic); Committee on the Elimination of Racial Discrimination, *e.g.*: A/57/18 (2002) 50 at para. 282 (Armenia). The European Court of Human Rights has explicitly recognized a duty of state neutrality for quite some time now and has developed a fairly extensive doctrine on this notion, *e.g.*: ECtHR, *Metropolitan Church of Bessarabia and Others v. Moldova*, Application no. 45701/99, 35 EHRR 306 [2002], Judgement of 13 December 2001, para. 116; ECtHR, *Refah Partisi (the Welfare Party) and Others v. Turkey, supra* note 53, paras. 91, 94 and 128; ECtHR, *Leyla Şahin v. Turkey*, Application No. 44774/98, Judgement of 10 November 2005, para. 117; ECtHR, *Dogru v. France*, Application No. 27058/05, Judgement of 4 December 2008, para. 62; ECtHR, *Religionsgemeinschaft der Zeugen Jehovas and Others v. Austria*, Application no. 40825/98, Judgement of 31 July 2008, para. 97; ECtHR, *Hasan and Eylem Zengin v. Turkey*, Application no. 1448/04, Judgement of 9 October 2007, para. 54; ECtHR, *Hasan and Chaush v. Bulgaria*, Application no. 30985/96, Judgement of 26 October 2000, para. 78; ECtHR, *97 Members of the Gldani Congregation of Jehovah's Witnesses & 4 Others v. Georgia*, Application no. 71156/01, Judgement of 3 May 2007, para. 131; ECtHR, *Svyato-Mykhaylivska Parafiya v. Ukraine*, Application no. 77703/01, Judgement of 14 June 2007, para. 113.

interwoven state duties is discernable: if we take the ultimate ramifications of human rights law seriously, state neutrality could be derived from these norms. In sum, it is submitted that a constitutional promise of governmental non-denominationalism, for both present and future reference, best equips states to fully implement and mainstream fundamental rights.

It is precisely because we have to allow a role for religion to be played within public life, rather than to try to eradicate or ban it, that safeguards need to be in place to protect the rights and freedoms of non-dominant groups and to protect the democratic quality of the state. State neutrality and non-establishmentarianism balance these concerns. The combined principles of state neutrality and non-establishmentarianism allow for a political discourse in which religion can play a role but these maxims, at the same time, regulate that role by identifying certain boundaries that may not be crossed.[89] The combined principles of non-establishmentarianism and state neutrality mean the following in terms of the political discourse and in terms of (il)legitimate legislative action. First of all, these principles by no means imply that the state ought to pro-actively eradicate religion from the political discourse. Policies may, in the words of De Jong, "be inspired by certain religions or beliefs, their outcome should be purely non-discriminatory".[90] Thus, the concept of a religious political party is not per se at odds with these principles. Having said that, in terms of the *final outcomes* of the process of competitive politics, these principles certainly rule out the possibility of adopting a law with the exclusive or primary objective to reflect (a specific notion based on) the religious laws, principles or doctrine of one religion. The principle of state neutrality, furthermore, rules out the adoption of laws that grant exclusive privileges to one religious group, or laws that negatively and unreasonably affect a particular religious or non-religious group. Laws and policies, in other words, may not create unreasonable distinctions between groups of people on grounds of religion or belief. The combined principles of state neutrality and non-establishmentarianism, finally, reject all legislative actions that would result in an excessive or strong governmental entanglement with religion for the simple reason that such entanglement, in practice, leads to the human rights abuses identified in Part II of this study. Thus, state neutrality is a self-imposed prohibition of direct discrimination on grounds of religion or belief, supplemented

[89] As an aside, in some states the principle of state neutrality is rendered additional support by laws that require the different state bodies and their agents to respect the non-denominational character of the state at all times in its outward appearance (in official ceremonies, state symbols and symbolism within governmental buildings, etc.). *E.g.* art. 4 of the 2001 Portuguese Law (*supra* note 72); and art. 28 French 1905 Law Regarding the Separation of the Churches and the State. These measures can in principle be applauded as long as they have no negative ramifications on the individual rights of persons functioning in a private capacity.

[90] Cornelis D. De Jong, The Freedom of Thought, Conscience and Religion or Belief in the United Nations (1946–1992) (Antwerp/Groningen/Oxford: Hart/Intersentia, 2000), p. 740.

with a lasting commitment to prevent indirect discrimination as well as a durable commitment to redress any instances of inadvertent indirect discrimination. Again, it will be clear that under such a system the judiciary has a vital role to play in keeping the legislature in check.

11.3.2 *Supplementary Safeguard: State Duty to Act Against Parties that Seek to Dismantle the Democratic Nature of the State*

Under international human rights law states are obliged to prohibit advocacy of religious hatred that constitutes incitement to discrimination, hostility or violence.[91] This prohibition (once properly internalized domestically) applies to private parties as well as political entities; thus, states have a duty to act against political parties that advocate views of religious hatred.[92] The state duty to act against political incitement of religious discrimination arguably extends to those organizations that use the political discourse with a view towards wiping out equality and depriving minorities of fundamental rights. At the European level it has been established that a state is entitled to interfere with the freedom of political association if necessary to protect its neutrality and to prevent measures being introduced that could jeopardise the democratic nature of the state and threaten the paramount principle of equality before the law (e.g. the introduction of parallel jurisdictions based on a system of sectarian laws).[93] The European Court has stated that the freedom of religion, expression and association "cannot deprive the authorities of a State in which an association, through its activities, jeopardises that State's institutions, of the right to protect those institutions."[94] The European Court considered that:

> ...a political party may promote a change in the law or the legal and constitutional structures of the State on two conditions: firstly, the means used to that

[91] Art. 20, para. (2), of the ICCPR. See also art. 4 of CERD.

[92] *E.g.* Human Rights Committee's Concluding Observations: A/59/40 vol. I (2004) 56 at para. 72(27)(Belgium): "The Committee...is concerned that political parties urging racial hatred can still benefit from the public financing system, and observes that a bill designed to put an end to that situation is still being considered by the Senate (art. 20)." This Concluding Observation, made by the Human Rights Committee, focuses on racial hatred but the state duties that are described equally apply to political entities that propagate religious hatred (see the scope of art. 20, para 2, of the ICCPR). For a similar observation made by the CERD Committee in the context of racial hatred, see *e.g.*: A/55/18 (2000) 50 at para. 281 (Czech Republic): "[the Committee] is of concern that some organizations, including political parties, promoting racial hatred and superiority are hidden behind legally registered civic associations whose members are promoting xenophobia and racism. Concern is also expressed at the ineffective implementation of existing legislation to prosecute those who incite racial hatred and support racist movements. In light of article 4 of the Convention, the State party should strengthen law enforcement to ensure that these organizations are dismantled and their members prosecuted".

[93] ECtHR, *Refah Partisi (the Welfare Party) and Others v. Turkey, supra* note 53. Caveat: it is the gist of the Court's reasoning that is endorsed here; the actual application of the identified rules to the particulars of the case by the Court itself may in fact be criticized.

[94] *Ibid.*, para. 96.

> end must be legal and democratic; secondly, the change proposed must itself be compatible with fundamental democratic principles. It necessarily follows that a political party whose leaders incite to violence or put forward a policy which fails to respect democracy or which is aimed at the destruction of democracy and the flouting of the rights and freedoms recognised in a democracy cannot lay claim to the [European] Convention's protection against penalties imposed on those grounds...[95]

The European Court noted that in a democratic system there is a risk that totalitarian movements, organized in the form of political parties, may prosper under the regime while wishing to destroy democracy and the universal enjoyment of fundamental rights.[96] The European Court's reasoning seems to be based on the understanding that under human rights law the state is perhaps not merely entitled but actually obliged to defend its democratic nature.

The state must indeed guard against the possibility of human rights law being abused to destroy the rights of others. It will be clear that the 'abuse of rights doctrine' and incitement prohibitions could serve a useful purpose in this context, whilst it is equally clear that the judiciary and international human rights monitoring bodies ought to play an important supervisory role in that regard. As important as it is for states to protect their democratic and neutral character against political movements that want to destroy these characteristics, it is just as crucial to ensure that the possibility of interfering with the freedom of association can never be abused by the ruling Government. None of the above should be interpreted as a justification for any type of blanket ban on religious political parties. Interferences with free political association can clearly only be applied in exceptional circumstances: an imminent danger to democracy itself or to the promotion of fundamental rights and freedoms (for all). This implies on the one hand that religious political parties cannot be banned on the basis of a generic prohibition without reference to actual party activities or to the party's programme; on the other hand, a state does not have to wait until a political party seizes power and begins to take more concrete steps to implement a policy that is incompatible with democracy or human rights law. That is to say, circumstances could be such that a Court could justifiably establish the existence of an imminent danger at an earlier stage on the basis of for instance a party's programme or public expressions made by party leaders. The final say as to whether such imminent danger is discernable must lie with the judiciary and not with the ruling regime.[97]

[95] *Ibid.*, para. 98.

[96] *Ibid.*, para. 99.

[97] Cf., *e.g.*, Alfred Stepan, *Religion, Democracy and the "Twin Tolerations"*, 11(4) Journal of Democracy 37 (2000), p. 40.

Part III

Conclusion: The Emerging Right To Religiously Neutral Governance

CHAPTER TWELVE

TOWARDS RELIGIOUSLY NEUTRAL GOVERNANCE

The Relevance of State–Religion Identification

This study addresses the question of how the different modes of state–religion identification affect the state's scope for compliance with human rights. To answer this question, a twofold approach was called for: firstly, the focus was on the spectrum of state–religion relationships based on a comprehensive comparative legal analysis; secondly, the forms of state practice that surround the different forms of state–religion relationships have been scrutinized from a human rights perspective. Thus the study has endeavoured to present a human rights-based assessment of the various modes of state–religion identification and of the various measures and forms of state practice that surround these different state–religion relationships. The comparative legal framework as proposed in Part I is intended to do justice to the large spectrum of state–religion identification and to take account of the many nuances that exist between different forms of state practice. The proposed comparative framework is also intended to foster future research in the field of state–religion identification and human rights law. Part II of this book builds on this comparative legal framework. This part is premised on the notion that international human rights monitoring bodies are established so as to provide guidance on how to implement the adopted standards. Though they may not be in a position to dictate in detail how states ought to organize their political system internally, their official interpretations and applications of internationally adopted fundamental norms could very well, in themselves, have a bearing on the legitimacy and, ultimately, the tenability of certain forms of political organization. The research of Part II is further premised on the notion that the issue of state–religion identification does not only bear upon matters of religious freedom. In order to obtain answers to the type of questions posed by this study, state–religion relationships should be analysed in light of a multitude of human rights norms. In order to offer such a wider analysis of the large variety of often interwoven human rights-related issues, this study presents a range of thematic case studies. These thematic case studies substantiate that the variety of human rights questions that emerge under the different parts of the state–religion identification spectrum often cut across geographical regions. This indicates that it is not the specific religion with which the state identifies that forms obstacles to full human rights implementation, but rather the precise *modus* of state identification with religion.

The Case Against Establishmentarianism

The preliminary legal question as to whether there are forms of state–religion identification that are per se unacceptable may be answered in the affirmative. Traditionally it is argued that establishment of religion is and cannot be per se in conflict with human rights law. Such would be the case since human rights law does not explicitly exclude establishment and since the drafters of the relevant human rights treaties never intended to outlaw forms of establishment of religion. Moreover, so the argument goes, establishment of religion does not per se prejudice the religious rights of people who do not adhere to the state religion. In this account, however, it is argued that there are forms of relationships between the state and religion, namely forms of establishment of religion and forms of state atheism, that amount to *ipso facto* violations of international human rights law. Whether or not the original drafters of international human rights treaties intended to outlaw forms of establishment of religion, and whether or not an express non-establishment clause can presently be found in international human rights conventions, is only of limited legal relevance. If both questions would be answered in the negative, it still may not be assumed that human rights monitoring bodies will not be able or will not be allowed to extrapolate principles from human rights law on the basis of which different relations between the state and religion may be scrutinized. It is only when we scrutinize certain acts in the light of the meaning of specific treaty provisions that we can decide on questions of legitimacy. It is a common mistake to assess forms of state–religion identification solely in light of the right to freedom of religion or belief, being the only article expressly dealing with issues of religious belief. Most establishmentarian accounts are premised on this error. The train of thought in those accounts is that establishment is not per se contrary to human rights law because establishment of religion does not necessarily infringe upon the religious rights of those who do not adhere to the state religion. States with an established religion and an acceptable record in the field of religious rights would then substantiate this point. The error here involves the equation of the total set of human rights norms with the norm of religious freedom. An acceptable record of non-interference with the religious rights of minorities tells us little about potentially institutionalised or *de facto* practices of discrimination on the basis of religion. In this study it is contended that an assessment of establishment of religion on the basis of the autonomous 'equality before the law' principle shows most conclusively that legal establishment of a religion is very problematic and would indeed appear to be incompatible with human rights law. In the era of human rights law, states are forbidden from making arbitrary distinctions based on ethnicity, gender, religion, etc. The position that this does not impact in any way whatsoever on issues of internal political organization, seems no longer tenable.

Towards a Better Understanding of Systemic Objections to State Implementation of Religious Laws

The issue of state enforcement of religious laws and religious principles is possibly what best characterizes the most stringent type of 'religious states'. Although the issue of 'religious laws' is fairly well-explored territory within the human rights discipline, this study has aimed to contribute new elements to the debate by identifying a series of what might be considered more fundamental or systemic human rights problems surrounding those systems of domestic political organization that are premised on state enforcement of religious laws. Content-based assessment of religious laws raises substantive questions concerning specific interpretations of religious laws. States are under an obligation to ignore or alter these interpretations of religious laws in so far as they negatively affect the rights and freedoms of people, notably religious minorities and women. The systemic objections raised by this study amount to a dismissal of *state* intervention with the observance of religious laws. These fundamental concerns are based on the notions of: (i) freedom *from* religion; (ii) equality before the law; and (iii) transparency, legal certainty and checks and balances.

As to the first notion, considering the fact that the right to freedom of religion or belief also covers a right not to profess any religion or belief and as, moreover, no one may be subject to coercion which would impair one's right to freely choose a religion or belief, it must be concluded that a so-called negative freedom is enclosed. Freedom of religion or belief as a negative freedom may be referred to as the right to be free *from* religion. Both non-believers and members of religious minorities as well adherents of the state-sanctioned religion suffer human rights abuses under regimes that actively interfere with the issue of observance of religious laws. As to the former group, it can hardly be disputed that whenever the state subjects those citizens that do not belong to the state religion to the religious laws of the latter religion, the religious rights and freedoms of these communities are transgressed upon. One might in this context think of so-called religious 'modesty rules', religious dress rules, Sabbath rules, dietary rules, burial prescriptions, but also aspects of religious personal status laws that are occasionally applied to persons that do not adhere to the religion in question. The fact that regimes that actively interfere with the issue of observance of religious laws may also violate the rights of the adherents of the state religion is often overlooked or trivialized. State intervention with the issue of observance of religious laws ultimately comes down to state enforcement of state-sanctioned interpretations of these laws. In that respect, state enforcement of religious rules and principles is bound to be characterized by the enforcement of at least some rules and obligations that encroach on people's personal convictions about what to believe and how to practise that belief. A related systemic concern with the institutionalised enforcement of religious laws stems from the fact that women are typically excluded from the decision-making and adjudicating process, meaning effectively that they are hardly ever in a position to stimulate reform of those rules that so negatively affect their status and position.

As for the second notion (equality before the law), it must be observed that state intervention with religious observance generally results in a system of so-called legal pluralism. A state that sanctions parallel jurisdictions is difficult to reconcile with the human rights norm that demands that all persons, regardless of religious affiliation, are equal before the law and are entitled without any discrimination to the equal protection of the law. The state's endorsement of a system of parallel jurisdictions in which different religion-based family laws and personal status laws are applied to different people depending on their religious affiliation is very problematic in terms of the state's human rights obligations. The ultimate ramification of the state's obligation to consider everyone equal before the law is that the state is under a duty to enact uniform state laws, most importantly in the present context, a uniform (secular) civil code on matters of family law that equally applies to all citizens.

As for the third and final argument, state intervention with the issue of religious observance may be criticized in so far as religious laws lack transparency. This leads to legal uncertainty. These sets of law generally lack a universally accepted version, have ever since their initial conception stirred controversy amongst religio-legal scholars over their exact interpretation and bestow upon (religious) courts a significant level of discretion. By contrast, uniform codes of law, adopted by a representative body in the process of competitive politics, foster transparency and legal certainty and are, moreover, infinitely more democratic. The codification and application of uniform laws also fosters a system based on 'checks and balances', meaning a system premised on the ideal that different state bodies keep each other in check in terms of the limitations to their powers.

These systemic concerns, naturally, do not come down to a rejection of the notion of religious laws as such. Individuals are in principle free to observe religious laws (in so far this does not negatively affect the rights and freedoms of others). These systemic objections rather amount to a dismissal of *state* intervention with the issue of observance of religious laws. The fact that someone considers him or herself an adherent of a certain religion does not amount to consent on his or her part to be subjected to the entire set of religious laws and principles that have traditionally accompanied the religion in question. Also, none of the systemic concerns is intended to prejudice processes of reforming religious laws from within the religious communities, in accordance with reinterpretations by legal-religious scholars and on the basis of content-based criticisms. The two discourses can perfectly be further developed simultaneously and doing so will in fact have a mutually reinforcing effect: reforming prevalent interpretations of religious laws so as to bring them more in line with equality rights of women and religious minorities benefits from gradually disentangling religious laws from state authority as the centre of gravity for enforcement, and vice versa.

Refuting the Myth of the 'Anything Goes' Position

The assumption that forms of establishment of religion can be readily made permissible, namely simply by means of tolerating the rights of religious minorities and non-believers, is highly misleading and rather hazardous. A critical analysis of global state practice shows that most, if not all, of the states that are officially entangled with a single religion fail to fully comply with the principle that no one should be treated differently because of one's religion or belief or lack thereof. In practice, what we see is that regimes of positive identification with a religion are not devoid of forms of institutionalised discrimination or *de facto* practices of discrimination on grounds of religion or belief. This has been substantiated in this study by carrying out a range of thematic case studies on Establishment of Religion & the Equal Religious Rights of Others, Religion & Freedom of Expression, Religion & Freedom of Association, Religion & Equal Employment Opportunities, Religion & Education, and Religion & Politics.

Forms of establishment of religion in many cases negatively affect the 'equal religious rights of others'. Regimes of positive state identification with a religion are surrounded by practices that directly restrict people's right to freedom of religion or belief, by practices that amount to a form of exclusive support to one religion putting non-dominant or non-traditional religions at a disadvantage, or by both. As to the former issue, for the effective implementation of the right to freedom of religion or belief it is crucial that the norm is appropriately enshrined in domestic legislation and also otherwise appropriately internalized by the state. The legal transposition and internalization of the freedom of religion or belief in establishmentarian states reveal many shortcomings. Amongst the wide range of different shortcomings that come to the fore are: (i) a complete absence of a domestic right; (ii) freedom of religion is not considered a universal right; (iii) domestic clauses compare unfavourably with international standards in that they omit one of the fundamental freedoms this right encompasses (i.e. the *forum internum* or the *forum externum*); or (iv) 'religion' itself functions as a ground for limitation. Other forms of state practice can be discerned that show that, although the freedom of religion or belief clause has been codified, legislation that negatively affects the legal status of the right to freedom of religion or belief remains in place. One might think in this context of discriminatory bans on proselytism or measures that give rise to a legal duty to reveal one's religious affiliation. It must be observed that illegitimate restrictions on this right can also be discerned in more secular states. The latter types of shortcomings are characterized by the codification of (secular) grounds for limitation that are not enumerated in international law, such as "national defence" or "national security". This could lead to illegitimate interferences with the free exercise of beliefs.

The 'equal religious rights of others' are further encroached upon by numerous establishmentarian states in so far as these states grant exclusive or discriminatory support to the dominant religion, thus putting non-dominant or non-traditional religions at a disadvantage. The non-discrimination principle has as its most important ramification in the present context that no one should be treated differently because of one's religion or belief. Although traditional relationships between the state and religion might explain some of these discriminatory forms of support historically, it is submitted that in the era of fundamental and universal equality rights these relationships in themselves do not provide 'objective and reasonable' criteria for making distinctions between different religions. A variety of forms of discriminatory state support and discriminatory privileges can be discerned: financial benefits, church tax systems and many other historical prerogatives.

The issue of free speech in relation to religions has been extensively explored in this study. From the comparative legal survey it follows that 'the protection of religion' in some states, most visibly in states that identify strongly with a single religion, functions as a ground for limiting fundamental rights, particularly the right to freedom of expression. 'Religion' as such, however, is not a legitimate ground for limiting fundamental rights under international human rights law. International human rights law does not recognize a right to have one's religion or belief at all times exempted from criticism, ridicule or insult or a right, in other words, to respect for one's religious feelings. Put differently, the right to freedom of religion or belief does not by implication place a duty on all people to at all times have respect for everyone's religion or belief. The 'rights of others to freedom of religion or belief' in theory fits in as a ground for limitation of the right to freedom of expression. However, it is submitted that this ground should not be equated with a right to respect for one's religious feelings as forms of criticism, ridicule or insult of religion do not necessarily or automatically constitute a limit or threat to people's freedom of religion or belief. Criticism or ridicule of religion does not necessarily affect a person's freedom to have or adopt a religion or belief or to freely exercise the religion or belief in question. It is submitted that the onus is on the state to establish that in a concrete case fully granting the freedom of expression actually impedes or jeopardizes the freedom of religion or belief of others. The sole reference to the likelihood of a group of religious believers being insulted by a particular publication, exhibition, film, play, etc., does not establish that. This is not to say that a public speech or publication, etc., can never be at the expense of someone's right to freedom of religion or belief. There are limits to expressing disrespect: advocacy of religious hatred that constitutes incitement to discrimination, hostility or violence is strictly forbidden under international human rights law. The recently emerging 'counter-defamation discourse' aims at prohibiting all forms of expression that insult religions. These developments could very well be at the detriment of important fundamental rights, notably the right to freedom of expression but also —something that is unfortunately often ignored in the debate— the right to freedom of religion or belief as such. In the latter respect, it must be observed that the recognition of too general a limitation on the right to freedom of expression (such as the notion that 'the religious feelings of citizens' must be respected) could in practice seriously inhibit the free exercise of a religion by non-dominant religious groups since the very exercise of one's religion in a certain fashion might be considered heretical in the eyes of another person. Thus, the counter-defamation discourse is not the appropriate way of dealing with contemporary issues of religious intolerance. This discourse is utterly unacceptable because it seeks to shift the emphasis from protection of the rights of individuals to protection of religions per se. It seeks to reformulate the right to freedom of religion or belief so as to include a right to have one's religious feelings respected. It introduces grounds for limitation of human rights, particularly of the right to freedom of expression, that are not and should not become recognized by international human rights law.

The issue of freedom of association, too, is inextricably linked up with the freedoms enjoyed by organized religious groups. This study demonstrates that religious association laws are often used in practice to confirm or cover up historical financial prerogatives of the dominant and traditional religion (in states that maintain *de jure* or *de facto* ties with this religion) or to restrain the activities of religious groups (in secular states with strict interpretations of state secularism or separationism). Thus, it may be that financial support schemes are based on *prima facie* neutral criteria but the rules for registration, in turn, are actually not. If a state's predominant religion or church is automatically granted financial support yet other religious groups must go through arduous procedures to reach that same level of legal recognition, the policy of allocation of financial benefits can hardly be considered to be 'based on objective criteria'. The same holds true, *a fortiori*, if religious association laws lay out illegitimate registration criteria that non-dominant or non-traditional religious communities can simply never meet. On the basis of state policies towards recognition of religious groups and more specifically on the basis of the terms and criteria enshrined in so-called 'religious association laws', some religious communities are denied legal entity status altogether whilst other religious communities are granted this basic legal status but find themselves disadvantaged nonetheless when compared to churches or religious organizations that are granted a (higher) status making them eligible for additional benefits.

This study furthermore endeavoured to answer the question whether, to what degree and under which circumstances religion or belief may be a legitimate ground for making distinctions in the field of employment hiring policies. May certain people, groups or organizations be exempted from state laws on equal treatment because of reasons of religion or reasons of the conscience? There are seemingly opposing concerns within this debate: on the one hand, there is the freedom of each individual to act in accordance with the dictates of his or her conscience and the related yet far more abstract notion of 'autonomy of a religious community' and its interest in preserving its 'religious identity'. On the other hand, a range of state duties and public interests can be identified, including the state's duty to guarantee everyone's individual equality rights and to guard against infringements of other human rights norms, primarily the right to work; alongside, more generally, the state's interest in ensuring that state laws are obeyed as well as the state's and the public's interest in a high level of access to employment. Some states have endeavoured to accommodate religious organizations and religious people by exempting them from generally applicable (equality) laws and regulations that would otherwise, potentially, cause conscientious problems for these organizations or persons. It is submitted that some of these exemption policies, namely so-called genuine occupational requirements schemes, can be applauded in so far as they foster religious freedom (without harming the rights and freedoms of others), whilst other exemption schemes (notably those revolving around so-called religious ethos exceptions) overstep the mark and are in fact at the detriment of fundamental equality rights, arguably without even truly maximizing anyone's religious freedom. The dismissal, in this study, of religious ethos exemptions to generally applicable equality laws is premised on the acknowledgement that in the era of fundamental equality rights, states ought not to actively encourage religious discrimination or homophobic or misogynous/patriarchal practices.

What must the state's role be with respect to guaranteeing the child's rights to education, freedom of religion or belief and equality, etc., as well as parental rights, in the overall context of its obligation to provide education? There is a tension between the liberty of parents or legal guardians to ensure the religious and moral education of their children in conformity with their own convictions on the one hand and children's autonomous right to freedom of religion or belief on the other. In resolving this tension it is pivotal to take account of the 'evolving capacities of the child' and the 'best interest of the child' as important guiding principles. The state has to respect children's right to education which implies making available appropriate primary education to all. In that respect, it is must be observed, first of all, that compulsory religious education is contrary to the rights and freedoms of both parents and child. Thus, generally speaking, the state would fulfil its human rights obligations if it either designs public school curricula which are sufficiently neutral or non-religious in themselves or, in case it does permit religious instruction in public schools, if it grants adequate opt-out rights. These opt-out procedures, however, prove to be highly problematic in practice. Though opt-out clauses certainly remedy the compulsion element, such safeguards do not necessarily prevent some degree of ostracization of children that avail of these exemption schemes. Opt-out clauses are also not adequate remedies if the subject of religion is too closely integrated into the curriculum. Furthermore, opt-out schemes force parents that do not desire religious instruction for their child to reveal their (lack of) belief and their objection to instruction in the dominant religion. The fact that opt-out schemes are largely only safeguards on paper provides a firm case against doctrinal religious instruction in public schools per se. The standards on the right to education also imply that the state is under a positive obligation to ensure that sufficient public schools (with appropriate curricula) are available at all times. The question of dress codes is an issue that may in practice affect access to education. Banning the display of religious symbols or the wearing of religious attire in state schools may affect the access rights of those for whom wearing such items is religiously compulsory. The state's duty to allow for sufficient public schools with appropriate curricula further means that a predominantly religious society cannot completely contract out the issue of education to private religious institutions. Compulsory public school instruction in subjects such as the general history of religions and ethics, if given in a neutral and objective way, is permissible and does not, as such, affect the liberty of parents to ensure the religious and moral education of their children in conformity with their own convictions. This neutral type of religious education must respect the freedom of religion or belief of all pupils. It is clear in this respect that much care should be taken that religious claims are indeed presented as religious claims and not as absolute truths. Inaccurate and prejudicial materials need to be avoided at all costs and negative stereotypes about certain religions which are based on such inaccurate information should certainly not be reinforced.

As to the position of teachers, it is necessary to distinguish between public and denominational schools. It stands to reason that denominational schools may pose religion as an occupational requirement in their policy regarding the hiring of teachers insofar as religious instruction forms an essential aspect of the position (and religious affiliation, therefore, forms a genuine and determining occupational requirement). Public schools, naturally, may not make distinctions on the basis of religion or belief in their hiring policies. As to the issue of religious attire or symbols worn and displayed by public school teachers, contentious situations are best evaluated on a case-by-case basis by weighing the right of a teacher to manifest his or her religion against the need to protect the fundamental rights and freedoms of pupils. The key question in this debate seems to be: what does contribute most to the child's right to freedom of religion or belief and to the development of an attitude of tolerance.

States certainly have an interest in upholding the neutrality of the state and thus must be in a position to take appropriate action if in a concrete case it is established that a teacher's manifestation of a religion in the classroom actually harms or jeopardizes the fundamental rights of pupils. Blanket bans that are needlessly rigid may convey a message of intolerance to children.

Neutral education about religions compares favourably both to all types of religious instruction as well as to forms of strict educational secularism in which there is no place for religion at all in the class room. As religions and beliefs will inevitably be touched upon in the curriculum, public school officials would be well-advised to reflect on this issue and develop an informed approach to dealing with the issue of religion in a way that would enable the school to do justice to the rights of both children and parents.

The key to dealing with the *problematique* at hand lies in the system of political organization of the state. In this area, a wide range of pitfalls is to be avoided and an equally wide range of safeguards specifically dealing with the issue of religion–state relationships to be internalized. All religions and beliefs should be treated equally in the political constellation of a state. State identification with a particular religion upsets the fairness and genuineness of a democracy in many ways. In fact, in extreme cases it may disqualify a state from being considered a genuine democracy. Thus, it is pivotal that the state ensures that no religion is *a priori* privileged or that some religions or beliefs are *a priori* excluded. Measures that aim at ensuring that all laws or policies that are to be adopted have a sound basis in the doctrine of the dominant religion undermine natural democratic deliberation processes. The most serious human rights abuses in this area follow from those measures that make the right to vote or the right to run for public office conditional upon belonging to a certain religion (the state or predominant religion). Also, states may not constitutionally reserve a percentage of seats within state bodies for members of the dominant religion. At the same time, human rights law should not be construed as supporting measures that seek the complete eradication of religion from the public realm. Drastic measures such as the prohibition of religious political parties or strict incompatibility rules are generally (one exception may be a post-conflict society) incompatible with fundamental political rights and equality rights. It will be clear that if we do allow a role for religion to be played within the political discourse we must make sure that constitutional safeguards are in place to prevent human rights abuses. In the latter respect, it has been submitted that the combined principles of state neutrality and non-establishmentarianism allow for a political discourse in which religion can play a role but these maxims, at the same time, regulate that role by identifying certain boundaries that may not be crossed.

In the era of international human rights law, the 'anything goes' position would appear, in the final analysis, to be a myth. A broad web of important, far-reaching and interwoven state duties is discernable: if we take the ultimate ramifications of human rights law seriously, state neutrality could be derived from these norms. State neutrality is defined in this study as the self-imposed prohibition of direct discrimination on grounds of religion or belief, supplemented with a lasting commitment to prevent indirect discrimination as well as a durable commitment to redress any instances of inadvertent indirect discrimination. It is concluded that such a constitutional promise of non-denominationalism, for both present and future reference, best equips states to fully implement and mainstream fundamental rights. States must respect everyone's right to religiously neutral governance.

BIBLIOGRAPHY

Abdal-Haqq, I., 'Islamic Law: An Overview of Its Origin and Elements', in: *Understanding Islamic Law: From Classic to Contemporary* (H.M. Ramadan, ed., Lanham: AltaMira Press, 2006).

Abdel Halim, A.M., 'Challenges to the Application of International Women's Human Rights in the Sudan', in: *Human Rights of Women: National and International Perspectives* (Cook, ed., Philadelphia: University of Pennsylvania Press, 1994).

Abiad, N., *Sharia, Muslim States and International Human Rights Treaty Obligations: A Comparative Study* (London: British Institute of International and Comparative Law, 2008).

Ahdar, R.J., 'Reflections on the Path of Religion-State Relations in New Zealand', 3 *Brigham Young University Law Review* (2006).

Ahdar, R., & Leigh, I., *Religious Freedom in the Liberal State* (Oxford: Oxford University Press, 2005).

Alstine, M.P. Van, 'Dynamic Treaty Interpretation', 146 *University of Pennsylvania Law* Review (1998).

Anderson, T.H., *The Pursuit of Fairness: A History of Affirmative Action* (Oxford: Oxford University Press, 2004).

An-Na'im, A.A., (ed.), *Inter-Religious Marriages among Muslims: Negotiating Religious and Social Identity in Family and Community* (Delhi: Global Media Publications, 2005).

An-Na'im, A.A., *Islam and the Secular State: Negotiating the Future of Shari'a* (Cambridge, US/ London: Harvard University Press, 2008).

An-Na'im, A.A., 'Religious Minorities under Islamic Law and the limits of Cultural Relativism', 9:1 *Human Rights Quarterly* (1987).

An-Na'im, A.A., 'State Responsibility to Change Religious and Customary Laws', in: *Human Rights of Women: National and International Perspectives* (Cook, ed., Philadelphia: University of Pennsylvania Press, 1994).

An-Na'im, A.A., 'The Islamic Law of Apostasy and its Modern Applicability: A Case form the Sudan', 16 *Religion* (1986).

An-Na'im, A.A., *Toward an Islamic Reformation: Civil Liberties, Human Rights, and International Law* (Syracuse: Syracuse University Press, 1990).

Araujo, R.J., 'International Law Clients: the Wisdom of Natural Law', 28 *Fordham Urban Law Journal* (2001).

Arzt, D.E., 'The Application of International Human Rights in Islamic States', 12:2 *Human Rights Quarterly* (1990).

Balodis, R., 'Church and State in Latvia', in: *Law and Religion in Post-Communist Europe*, 141 (Ferrari & Durham, eds., Leuven: Peeters, 2003).

Barberini, G., 'Religious Freedom in the Process of Democratization of Central and Eastern European States', in: *Law and Religion in Post-Communist Europe* (Ferrari & Durham, eds., Leuven: Peeters, 2003).

Barbier, M., *La Laïcité* (Paris: L'Harmattan, 1995).

Barro, R.J. & McClearly, R.M., 'Religion and Economic Growth across Countries', 68 *American Sociology Review* (2003).

Barro, R.J. & McClearly, R.M., 'Religion and Political Economy in an International Panel', 45.2 *Journal for the Scientific Study of Religion* (2006).

Barro, R.J. & McClearly, R.M., 'Which Countries Have State Religions?', 120 *Quarterly Journal of Economics* (2005).

Barron, J.A. & Dienes, C.T., *First Amendment Law* (St Paul, Minn.: West Group, 2000).

Baubérot, J., (ed.), *La Laïcité: Evolution et Enjeux* (Paris: La Documentation Française, 1996).

Baubérot, J., *Histoire de la Laïcité Française* (Paris: PUF, 2000).

Bergh, A.E., (ed.), *The Writings of Jefferson* (Washington, D. C.: The Thomas Jefferson Memorial Association of the United States, 1907).

Berkovitch, N., 'Women and the Women's Equal Rights Law in Israel', 198 *Middle East Report* (1996).

Bernhardt, R., 'Evolutive Treaty Interpretation, Especially of the European Convention on Human Rights', 42 *German Yearbook of International Law* (1999).

Blaustein, A.P. & Flanz, G.H., (eds.), *Constitutions of the Countries of the World: A Series of Updated Texts, Constitutional Chronologies and Annotated Bibliographies* (New York: Oceana Publications, Inc., 1971, plus subsequent supplements).

Bordeaux, M., 'The Former Soviet Union: Trends in Religious Liberty', in: *Religious Freedom in the World: A Global Report on Freedom and Persecution* (P. Marshall, ed., Nashville: Broadman & Holman Publishers, 2000).

Boussinescq, J., *La Laïcité Française* (Paris: Le Seuil, 1994).

Boyle, K. & Sheen, J., *Freedom of Religion and Belief: A World Report* (London: Routledge, 1997).

Boyle, K., 'Indivisibility of Human Rights, Social Justice and Article 18 of the Universal Declaration', in: *Innovation and Inspiration: Fifty Years of the Universal Declaration of Human Rights* (Baehr, Flinterman, Senders, eds., Amsterdam: Royal Academy of Arts and Sciences, 1999).

Brems, E., *Article 14: The Rights to Freedom of Thought, Conscience and Religion* (*A Commentary on the United Nations Convention on the Rights of the Child*) (Leiden/Boston: Martinus Nijhoff Publishers, 2006).

Brown, P., *The Rise of Western Christendom: Triumph and Diversity, AD 200–1000* (Cambridge, USA: Blackwell Publ., 1996).

Brugger, W., 'On the Relationship between Structural Norms and Constitutional Rights in Church-State-Relations', in: *Religion in the Public Sphere: A Comparative Analysis of German, Israeli, American and International Law* (Brugger & Karayanni, eds., Berlin: Springer, 2007).

Bryce, J., *The Holy Roman Empire* (Macmillian, 1919; originally published in 1862).

Burdick, M.A., *For God and the Fatherland: Religion and Politics in Argentina* (Albany: State University of New York Press, 1995).

Campbell, T., Goldsworthy, J., & Stone, A., (eds.), *Protecting Human Rights: Instruments and Institutions* (Oxford: Oxford University Press, 2003).

Cantor, J. & Baum, K., 'The Limits of Conscientious Objection – May Pharmacists Refuse to Fill Prescriptions for Emergency Contraception?', 351(19) *New England Journal of Medicine* (2004).

Carlson, E.R., 'China's New Regulations on Religion: A Small Step, Not a Great Leap, Forward', 3 *Brigham Young University Law Review* (2005).

Carozza, P.G., 'Subsidiarity as a Structural Principle of International Human Rights Law', 97:1 *American Journal of International Law* (2003).

Coleman-Norton, P.R., *Roman State & Christian Church: A Collection of Legal Documents to A.D. 535* (Vol. I)(London: S.P.C.K., 1966).

Costa-Lascoux, J., *Les Trois âges de la Laïcité* (Paris: Hachette, 1996).

Daudelin, J. & Hewitt, W.E., 'Churches and Politics in Latin America: Catholicism at the Crossroads', 16 *Third World Quarterly* (1995).

De Jong, C.D., *The Freedom of Thought, Conscience and Religion or Belief in the United Nations (1946–1992)* (Antwerp/Groningen/Oxford: Hart/Intersentia, 2000).

Douglas, M., *The Persecution of the Bahá'ís of Iran, 1844–1984* (Ottawa: Association for Bahá'í Studies, 1984).

Du Plessis, L.M., 'Religious Human Rights in South Africa', in: *Religious Human Rights in Global Perspective: Legal Perspectives* (J.D. van der Vyver & J. Witte. eds., The Hague/Boston/London: Martinus Nijhoff Publishers, 1996).

Du Toit, C.W., 'Religious Freedom and Human Rights in South Africa after 1996: Responses and Challenges', 3 *Brigham Young University Law Review* (2006).

Duggal, K.S., *Ranjit Singh: a Secular Sikh Sovereign*, (Dehli: Abhinav Publications, 1989).

Durand-Prinborgne, C., *La Laïcité* (Paris: Dalloz, 1996).

Durham, W.C., 'Facilitating Freedom of Religion or Belief through Religious Association Laws', in: *Facilitating Freedom of Religion or Belief: A Deskbook* (Lindholm, Durham and Tahzib-Lie, eds., Leiden: Martinus Nijhoff Publishers, 2004).

Durham, W.C., 'Perspectives on Religious Liberty: A Comparative Framework', in *Religious Human Rights in Global Perspective: Legal Perspectives* (J.D. van der Vyver & J. Witte, eds., The Hague/Boston/London: Martinus Nijhoff Publishers, 1996).

Edelman, M., 'A Portion of Animosity: The Politics of the Disestablishment of Religion in Israel', 5 *Israel Studies* (2000).
Edge, P., 'Religious Remnants in the Composition of the United Kingdom Parliament', in: *Law and Religion: Current Legal Issues* (R. O'Dair & A. Lewis, eds., Oxford: Oxford University Press, 2001).
Endress, G., *An Introduction to Islam* (Edinburgh: Edinburgh University Press, 1994).
Esler, Ph.F., (ed.), *The Early Christian World* (London/New York: Routledge, 2000).
Evans, C. & Thomas, C.A., 'Church-State Relations in the European Court of Human Rights', 3 *Brigham Young University Law Review* (2006).
Evans, C., *Freedom of Religion Under the European Convention on Human Rights* (Oxford: Oxford University Press, 2001).
Evans, C., 'Religious Education in Public Schools: An International Human Rights Perspective', 8(3) *Human Rights Law Review* (2008).
Evans, M.D., *Religious Liberty and International Law in Europe* (Cambridge: Cambridge University Press, 1997).
Fautre, W., 'Western Europe: Trends in Religious Liberty', in: *Religious Freedom in the World: A Global Report on Freedom and Persecution* (Marshall, ed., Nashville: Broadman & Holman Publishers, 2000).
Fox, J. & Sandler, S., *World Separation of Religion and State in the Twenty First Century*, (Montreal, 2004).
Franck, Th.M., 'The Emerging Right to Democratic Governance', 86(1) *Amerian Journal of International Law* (1992).
French, P., *North Korea: The Paranoid Peninsula. A Modern History* (London: Zed Books, 2005).
García-Montüfar, G., Arata Solís, M. & Isaacson, S.E., 'Advances in Religious Liberty in Peru', 2 *Brigham Young University Law Review* (2004).
Garvey, J.H. & Schauer, F., *The First Amendment: A Reader* (St Paul, Minn.: West Publishing Co., 2000).
Gavison, R., 'Days of Worship and Days of Rest: A View from Israel', in: *Religion in the Public Sphere: A Comparative Analysis of German, Israeli, American and International Law* (Brugger & Karayanni, eds., Berlin: Springer, 2007).
Gavison, R., 'Jewish and Democratic? A Rejoinder to the "Ethnic Democracy" Debate', 4.1 *Israel Studies* (1999).
Ghanea, N., 'Apostasy and Freedom to Change Religion or Belief', in: *Facilitating Freedom of Religion or Belief: A Deskbook* (Lindholm, Durham and Tahzib-Lie, eds., Leiden: Martinus Nijhoff Publishers, 2004).
Ghanea, N., *Human Rights, the UN & the Bahá'ís in Iran* (The Hague: Kluwer Law International, 2002).
Gogineni Babu, R.R., & Gule, L., 'Humanism and Freedom from Religion', in: *Facilitating Freedom of Religion or Belief: A Deskbook* (Lindholm, Durham and Tahzib-Lie, eds., Leiden: Martinus Nijhoff Publishers, 2004).
Greenawalt, K., 'Freedom of Association and Religious Association', in: *Freedom of Association* (Princeton, N.J.: Princeton University Press, 1998).
Gustafson, L., 'Kenya: the Struggle to Create a Democracy', 2 *Brigham Young University Law Review* (1995).
Gustafsson, G., 'Church–State Separation Swedish-Style', in: *Church and State in Contemporary Europe: The Chimera of Neutrality* (J.T.S. Madeley & Z. Enyedi, eds., London: Frank Cass Publ., 2003).
Haarscher, G., *La Laïcité* (Paris: PUF, 1996).
Halperin-Kaddari, R., *Women in Israel: A State of Their Own* (Philadelphia: University of Pennsylvania Press, 2003).
Hashemi, K., *Religious Legal Traditions, International Human Rights Law and Muslim States* (Martinus Nijhoff Publishers, 2008).
Hashemi, K., 'The Right of Minorities to Identity and the Challenge of Non-discrimination: A Study on the Effects of Traditional Muslims' Dhimmah on Current State Practices', 13 *International Journal on Minority and Group Rights* (2006).
Heilman, B.E. & Kaiser, P.J., 'Religion, Identity and Politics in Tanzania', 23 *Third World Quarterly* (2002).

Hight, Sir J. & Bamford, H.D., *The Constitutional History and Law of New Zealand* (Christchurch: Whitcombe & Tombs, 1914).
Hoare, J.E. & Pares, S., *North Korea in the 21st Century. An Interpretative Guide* (Kent: Global Oriental, 2005).
Hossain, S., 'Equality in the Home: Women's Rights and Personal Laws in South Asia', in: *Human Rights of Women: National and International Perspectives* (Cook, ed., Philadelphia: University of Pennsylvania Press, 1994).
Howland, C.W., 'Safeguarding Women's Political Freedoms under the International Covenant on Civil and Political Rights in the Face of Religious Fundamentalism', in: *Religious Fundamentalisms and the Human Rights of Women* (Howland, ed., New York: Pargrave, 1999).
Iordache, R.E., 'Church and State in Romania', in: *Law and Religion in Post-Communist Europe* (Ferrari & Durham, eds., Leuven: Peeters, 2003).
Isaacson, S.E., 'A Practical Comparison of the Laws of religion of Colombia and Chile', 1 *International Journal of Not-for-Profit Law* (2003).
Issacharoff, S., 'Constitutionalizing Democracy in Fractured Societies', 58 *Journal of International Affairs* (2004).
Jacobsohn, G.J., *The Wheel of Law: India's Secularism in Comparative Constitutional Context* (Princeton University Press, 2003).
Jolly, J., transl., *The Institutes of Vishnu* (Sacred Books of the East, Vol. 7; Oxford: the Clarendon Press, 1880).
Kahn, P., *La Laïcité* (Paris: Le Cavalier Bleu, 2005).
Karandrea, E., 'Church and State in Albania', in: *Law and Religion in Post-Communist Europe* (Ferrari & Durham, eds., Leuven: Peeters, 2003).
Karayanni, M., 'The "Other" Religion and State Conflict in Israel: On the Nature of Religious Accommodation for the Palestinian-Arab Minority', in: *Religion in the Public Sphere: A Comparative Analysis of German, Israeli, American and International Law* (Brugger & Karayanni, eds., Berlin: Springer, 2007).
Karsh, E., *Islamic Imperialism: a History* (New Haven/London: Yale University Press, 2006).
Khan, A., 'Commentary on the Constitution of Medina', in: *Understanding Islamic Law: From Classic to Contemporary* (H.M. Ramadan, ed., Lanham: AltaMira Press, 2006).
King, U., 'Hinduism and Women: Uses and Abuses of Religious Freedom', in: *Facilitating Freedom of Religion or Belief: A Deskbook* (Lindholm, Durham and Tahzib-Lie, eds., Leiden: Martinus Nijhoff Publishers, 2004).
Kiviorg, M., 'Church and State in Estonia', in: *Law and Religion in Post-Communist Europe* (Ferrari & Durham, eds., Leuven: Peeters, 2003).
Klabbers, J., 'International Legal Histories: The Declining Importance of Travaux Préparatoires in Treaty Interpretation?', 50(3) *Netherlands International Law Review* (2003).
Klostermaier, K.K., *A Concise Encyclopedia of Hinduism* (Oxford: Oneworld Publ., 1998).
Kostovski, S., 'Church and State in Macedonia', in *Law and Religion in Post-Communist Europe* (Ferrari & Durham, eds., Leuven: Peeters, 2003).
Kretzmer, D., 'Constitutional Law', in: *Introduction to the Law of Israel* (A. Shapira, ed., Amsterdam: Kluwer, 1995).
Kuznecoviene, J., 'Church and State in Lithuania', in: *Law and Religion in Post-Communist Europe* (Ferrari & Durham, eds., Leuven: Peeters, 2003).
Kyriazopoulos, K.N., 'The "Prevailing Religion" in Greece: Its Meaning and Implications', 43 *Journal of State and Church* (2001).
Lansdown, G., *The Evolving Capacities of the Child* (Florence: UNICEF Innocenti Research Centre, 2005).
Lanarès, P., *La Liberté Religieuse dans les Conventions Internationales et dans le Droit Public Général* (Roanne: Horvath, 1964).
Langlaude, S., *The Right of the Child to Religious Freedom in International Law* (Leiden: Martinus Nijhoff Publishers, 2007).
Leadbetter, B., 'From Constantine to Theodosius (and beyond)', in: *The Early Christian World* (Vol. I) (Ph.F. Esler, ed., London/New York: Routledge, 2000).
Lerner, N., 'Proselytism, Change of Religion, and International Human Rights', 12 *Emory International Law Review* (1998).
Lerner, N., *Religion, Secular Beliefs and Human Rights: 25 Years After the 1981 Declaration* (Leiden/Boston: Martinus Nijhoff Publishers, 2006).

Lively, D.E., Robert, D.E., & Weaver, R.L., (eds.), *First Amendment Anthology* (Cincinnati: Anderson Publishing Company, 1994).

Macdonald, D.S., (revised and edited by D.N. Clark), *The Koreans: Contemporary Politics and Society* (Oxford: Westview Press, 1996).

Mahmood, T., 'Religion, Law, and Judiciary in Modern India', 3 *Brigham Young University Law Review* (2006).

Major, J.S., *The Land and People of Mongolia* (New York: Lippincott, Williams & Wilkins, 1990).

Mango, A., *Atatürk* (London: John Murray Publ., 1999).

Maoz, A., 'Religious Human Rights in the State of Israel', in: *Religious Human Rights in Global Perspective: Legal Perspectives* (J.D. van der Vyver & J. Witte, eds., The Hague/Boston/London: Martinus Nijhoff Publishers, 1996).

Marshall, P., (ed.), *Religious Freedom in the World: A Global Report on Freedom and Persecution* (Nashville: Broadman & Holman, 2000).

Marshall, P., 'The Nature of Religious Freedom and Religious Persecution', in: *Religious Freedom in the World: A Global Report on Freedom and Persecution* (P. Marshall, ed., Nashville: Broadman & Holman Publishers, 2000).

Martin, D., *On Secularization: Towards a Revised General Theory* (Aldershot: Ashgate, 2005).

Martínez-Torrón, J., 'Religious Freedom and Democratic Change in Spain', 3 *Brigham Young University Law Review* (2006).

Mawhinney, A., 'Freedom of Religion in the Irish Primary School System: a Failure to Protect Human Rights', 27(3) *Legal Studies* (2009).

Mawhinney, A., 'The Opt-Out Clause: Imperfect Protection for the Right to Freedom of Religion in Schools', 2(2) *Educational Law Journal* 102 (2006).

Mayer, A.E., *Islam and Human Rights: Tradition and Politics* (Boulder/Oxford: Westview Press, 1999).

Mayer, A.E., 'Law and Religion in the Muslim Middle East', 35 *American Journal of Comparative Law* (1987).

Mayer, A.E., 'Religious Reservations to the Convention on the Elimination of All Forms of Discrimination against Woman: What Do They Really Mean?', in: *Religious Fundamentalisms and the Human Rights of Women* (Howland, ed., New York: Pargrave, 1999).

Mayer, A.E., 'The Internalization of Religious Positions on Human Rights: How Religious Particularisms are Uniting in a Campaign against Women's International Human Rights', in: *Global Justice and the Bulwarks of Localism: Human Rights in Context* (Eisgruber and Sajó, eds., Leiden: Martinus Nijhoff Publishers, 2005).

McDougal, M.S., Lasswell, H.D. & Cheng, L., 'The Right to Religious Freedom and World Public Order: The Emerging Norm of Non-Discrimination', 74 *Michigan Law Review* (1976).

McDougal, M.S., Lasswell, H.D., & Chen, L., *Human Rights and World Public Order: The Basic Policies of an International Law of Human Dignity* (New Haven: Yale University Press, 1980).

McGoldrick, D., *Human Rights and Religion: The Islamic Headscarf Debate in Europe* (Portland: Hart Publishing, 2006).

Medina, B., 'Does the Establishment of Religion Justify Regulating Religious Activities? – The Israeli Experience', in: *Religion in the Public Sphere: A Comparative Analysis of German, Israeli, American and International Law* (Brugger & Karayanni, eds., Berlin: Springer, 2007).

Meyerson, D., *Rights Limited: Freedom of Expression, Religion and the South African Constitution* (Cape Town: Juta & Co, 1997).

Miles, W.F.S., 'The Mauritius Enigma', 10(2) *Journal of Democracy* (1999).

Miner, C.J., 'Losing my Religion: Austria's New Religion Law in Light of International and European Standards of Religious Freedom', 2 *Brigham Young University Law Review* (1998).

Minnerath, R., 'The Right to Autonomy in Religious Affairs', in: *Facilitating Freedom of Religion or Belief: A Deskbook* (Lindholm, Durham and Tahzib-Lie, eds., Leiden: Martinus Nijhoff Publishers, 2004).

Morales Hoyos, V.A., 'Religious Liberty and Cultural and Ethnic Pluralism in the Colombian Constitution of 1991', 2 *Brigham Young University Law Review* (1999).

Mulík, P., 'Church and State in Slovakia', in *Law and Religion in Post-Communist Europe* (Ferrari & Durham, eds., Leuven: Peeters, 2003).

Muller-Lyer, F.C., *The Evolution of Modern Marriage* (New York: Alfred Knopf, 1930).

Mwaipopo, R.A., 'Gender and the Law in Tanzania: Aspects of the Position of Women on Land and Property', in: *Human Rights, Constitutionalism and the Judiciary: Tanzanian and Irish Perspectives* (W. Binchy & C. Finnegan, eds., Dublin: Clarus Press, 2006).

Neff, S.C., 'An Evolving International Legal Norm of Religious Freedom: Problems and Prospects', 7 *California Western International Law Journal* (1977).

Nmehielle, V.O., 'Sharia Law in the Northern States of Nigeria: To Implement or Not to Implement, the Constitutionality is the Question', 26 *Human Rights Quarterly* (2004).

Nowak, M., *U.N. Covenant on Civil and Political Rights: CCPR Commentary* (Kehl am Rhein: N.P. Engel Publ., 2005, 2nd rev. ed.).

Odahl, C.M., *Constantine and the Christian Empire* (London/New York: Routledge, 2004).

Oegema, G.S., *The History of the Shield of David: the Birth of a Symbol* (Frankfurt am Main/ New York: Peter Lang Publ., 1996).

Orlin, T.S., 'Religious Pluralism and Freedom of Religion: Its Protection in Light of Church/ State Relationships', in: *The Strength of Diversity: Human Rights and Pluralist Democracy* (A. Rosas and J. Helgesen, eds., Dordrecht: Martinus Nijhoff Publishers, 1992).

Ottolenghi, E., 'Religion and Democracy in Israel', in: *Religion and Democracy* (D. Marquand & R.L. Nettler, eds., Oxford: Blackwell Publishers, 2000).

Peteva, J., 'Church and State in Bulgaria', in: *Law and Religion in Post-Communist Europe* (Ferrari & Durham, eds., Leuven: Peeters, 2003).

Pietrzak, M., 'Church and State in Poland', in: *Law and Religion in Post-Communist Europe* (Ferrari & Durham, eds., Leuven: Peeters, 2003).

Plowden, Ph., & Kerrigan, K., *Advocacy and Human Rights: Using the Convention in Courts and Tribunals* (London: Cavendish Publ., 2004).

Poulter, S., *Ethnicity, Law, and Human Rights: The English Experience* (Oxford: Oxford University Press, 1998).

Raday, F., 'Claiming Equal Religious Personhood: Women of the Wall's Constitutional Saga', in: *Religion in the Public Sphere: A Comparative Analysis of German, Israeli, American and International Law* (Brugger & Karayanni, eds., Berlin: Springer, 2007).

Raday, F., 'Israel – The Incorporation of Religious Patriarchy in a Modern State', 4 *International Review of Comparative Public Policy* (1992).

Raday, F., 'Religion and Patriarchal Politics: the Israeli Experience', in: *Religious Fundamentalisms and the Human Rights of Women* (Howland, ed., New York: Pargrave, 1999).

Raday, F., 'Religion, Multiculturalism and Equality: The Israeli Case', 25 *Israeli Yearbook on Human Rights* (1995).

Rahman, A., 'Religious Rights Versus Women's Rights in India: A Test Case for International Human Rights Law', 28 *Columbia Journal of Transnational Law* (1990).

Rahman, S.A., *Punishment of Apostasy in Islam* (Lahore: Institute of Islamic Culture, 1988).

Redlich, N., Attanasio, J. & Goldstein, J.K., *Understanding Constitutional Law* (New York: Matthew Bender, 1999).

Rubinstein, E., 'The Declaration of Independence as a Basic Document of the State of Israel', 3 *Israel Studies* (1998).

Ruffini, F., *Religious Liberty* (transl. J. Parker Heyes; London: Williams & Norgate/New York: G.P. Putnam, 1912).

Russo, C.J., 'Religion and Education in Bosnia: Integration Not Segregation?', 3 *Brigham Young University Law Review* (2000).

Ryskamp, G.R., 'The Spanish Experience in Church-State Relations: A Comparative Study of the Interrelationship between Church-State Identification and Religious Liberty', 3 *Brigham Young University Law Review* (1980).

Sabar-Friedman, G., 'Church and State in Kenya, 1986–1992: The Churches' Involvement in the 'Game of Change'', 96 *African Affairs* (1997).

Sarkar, B.K., 'Hindu Political Philosophy', 33 *Political Science Quarterly* (1918).

Sarkar, B.K., 'Public Finance in Ancient India', 97 *Annals of the American Academy of Political and Social Science* (1921).

Schaff, P., *History of the Christian Church* (1882).

Schanda, B., 'Church and State in Hungary', in: *Law and Religion in Post-Communist Europe* (Ferrari & Durham, eds., Leuven: Peeters, 2003).

Scharffs, B.G., 'The Autonomy of Church and State', 4 *Brigham Young University Law Review* (2004).

Scolnicov, A., 'Religious Law, Religious Courts and Human Rights within Israeli Constitutional Structure', 4 *International Journal of Constitutional Law* (2006).

Shelton, D., & Kiss, A., 'A Draft Model Law on Freedom of Religion, With Commentary', in *Religious Human Rights in Global Perspective: Legal Perspectives* (J.D. van der Vyver & J. Witte, eds., The Hague/Boston/London: Martinus Nijhoff Publishers, 1996).

Shetreet, S., 'The Model of State and Church Relations and Its Impact on the Protection of Conscience and Religion: A Comparative Analysis and a Case Study of Israel', in: *Religion in the Public Sphere: A Comparative Analysis of German, Israeli, American and International Law* (Brugger & Karayanni, eds., Berlin: Springer, 2007).

Shiffrin, H., & Choper, J.H., *The First Amendment: Cases – Comments – Questions* (St Paul, Minn.: West Publishing Co., 2000).

Short, M.I., *Law and Religion in Marxist Cuba: A Human Rights Inquiry* (New Brunswick: Transaction Publishers, 1993).

Simkin, L., 'Chuch and State in Russia', in: *Law and Religion in Post-Communist Europe* (Ferrari & Durham, eds., Leuven: Peeters, 2003).

Simmons, M.B., 'Julian the Apostate', in: *The Early Christian World* (Vol. I) (Ph.F. Esler, ed., London/New York: Routledge, 2000).

Singh, K., 'Obstacles to Women's Rights in India', in: *Human Rights of Women: National and International Perspectives* (Cook, ed., Philadelphia: University of Pennsylvania Press, 1994).

Sitaraman, B., 'Law as Ideology: Women, Courts and 'Dowry Deaths' in India', 27(3) *International Journal of the Sociology of Law* (1999).

Skaine, R., *Female Genital Mutilation: Legal, Cultural and Medical Issues* (Jefferson, N.C.: McFarland, 2005).

Smart, J., 'The Place of Islamic Law with the Framework of the Sierra Leone Legal System', 18 *African Law Studies* (1980).

Smart, N. & Hecht, R.D., (eds.), *Sacred Texts of the World: A Universal Anthology* (London: Quercus, 2007).

Smart, N., *The World's Religions* (Victoria: Cambridge University Press, 1992).

Smith, W., *Flags through the Ages and Across the World* (New York: McGraw-Hill Book Co., 1975).

Sowell, Th., *Affirmative Action Around the World: An Empirical Study* (New Haven, CT: Yale University Press, 2004).

Stahnke, T., 'Proselytism and the Freedom tó Change Religion in International Human Rights Law', 1 *Brigham Young University Law Review* (1999).

Stan, L. & Turescu, L., 'The Romanian Orthodox Church and Post-communist Democratisation', 52 *Europe-Asia Studies* (2000).

Stepan, A., 'Religion, Democracy and the "Twin Tolerations"', 11(4) *Journal of Democracy* (2000).

Suh, D., *Kim Il Sung: The North Korean Leader* (New York: Columbia University Press, 1988).

Tae-hoon, C., 'Juche Ideology', 12 *East Asian Review* (1997).

Tahzib, B.G., *Freedom of Religion or Belief: Ensuring Effective International Legal Protection* (The Hague/Boston/London: Martinus Nijhoff Publishers, 1996).

Tahzib-Lie, B.G., 'Women's Equal Right to Freedom of Religion or Belief: An Important but Neglected Subject', in: *Religious Fundamentalisms and the Human Rights of Women* (Howland, ed., New York: Pargrave, 1999).

Taylor, P.M., *Freedom of Religion: UN and European Human Rights Law and Practice* (Cambridge: Cambridge University Press, 2005).

Taylor, P.M., 'The Questionable Grounds of Objections to Proselytism and Certain Other Forms of Religious Expression', 3 *Brigham Young University Law Review* (2006).

Taylor, S.J., 'Disestablished Establishment: High and Earthed Establishment in the Church in Wales', 18 *Journal of Contemporary Religion* (2003).

Temperman, J.D., 'Blasphemy, Defamation of Religions & Human Rights Law', 26(4) *Netherlands Quarterly of Human Rights* (2008).

Temperman, J.D., 'The Neutral State: Optional or Necessary? – A Triangular Analysis of State–Religion Identification, Democratisation & Human Rights Compliance', 1(3) *Religion and Human Rights – An International Journal* (2006).

Thurston, P.J., 'The Development of Religious Liberty in Chile, 1973–2000', 3 *Brigham Young University Law Review* (2000).

Tibi, B., 'Post-Bipolar Order in Crisis: The Challenge of Politicised Islam', in: *Islam: Critical Concepts in Sociology* (Bryan S. Turner, ed., London: Routledge, 2003).

Tibi, B., *The Challenge of Fundamentalism: Political Islam and the New World Disorder* (Berkeley: University of California Press, 1998).

Toth, J., 'Human Dignity and Freedom of Conscience', *World Justice* (1968).

Tretera, J.R., 'Church and State in the Czech Republic', in: *Law and Religion in Post-Communist Europe* (Ferrari & Durham, eds., Leuven: Peeters, 2003).

Tully, J.J., 'The Place of Islamic Law in Sierra Leone', 84 *The Muslim World* (1994).

Vashkevich, A., 'The Relationship of Church and State in Belarus: Legal Regulation and Practice', 2 *Brigham Young University Law Review* (2003).

Vickers, L., 'Freedom of Religion and the Workplace: The Draft Employment Equality (Religion or Belief) Regulations 2003', 32(1) *Industrial Law Journal* (2003).

Vickers, L., *Religious Freedom, Religious Discrimination and the Workspace* (Oxford and Portland: Hart Publishing, 2008).

Vyver, J.D. van der, 'Legal Dimensions of Religious Human Rights: Constitutional Texts', in: *Religious Human Rights in Global Perspective: Legal Perspectives* (J.D. van der Vyver & J. Witte, eds., The Hague/Boston/London: Martinus Nijhoff Publishers, 1996).

Vyver, J.D. van der, 'The Relationship of Freedom of Religion or Belief Norms to Other Human Rights', in: *Facilitating Freedom of Religion or Belief: A Deskbook* (Lindholm, Durham and Tahzib-Lie, eds., Leiden: Martinus Nijhoff Publishers, 2004).

Weller, P., 'Equity, Inclusivity and Participation in a Plural Society: Challenging the Establishment of the Church of England', in: *Law and Religion in Contemporary Society: Communities, Individualism and the State* (P. Edge & G. Harvey, eds., Aldershot: Ashgate, 2000).

Westermarck, E.A., *The History of Human Marriage* (London: Macmilan and Co., Ltd, 1903).

Wilson, B.R., *The Social Dimensions of Sectarianism and New Religious Movements in Contemporary Society*, (Oxford: Clarendon Press, 1990).

Wood (Jr.), J.E., '"No Religious Test Shall Ever Be Required": Reflections on the Bicentennial of the U.S. Constitution', 29 *Journal of Church and State* (1987).

INDEX

www.ingramcontent.com/pod-product-compliance
Lightning Source LLC
LaVergne TN
LVHW080846300926
849162LV00003B/346
* 9 7 8 9 0 0 4 1 8 1 4 8 9 *